Contents

Chapter 9   Multiculturalism as Canada-Building Governance   290

Chapter 10   This Adventure Called Canada-Building   323

Preface

Canada is a society of paradox. Paradoxes prevail in a Canada that is rapidly changing and increasingly diverse, yet seemingly gridlocked into preferences and perceptions from the past without a definitive blueprint for forging ahead. This assessment is particularly relevant when applied to the domain of race, ethnic, and aboriginal relations. To one side, Canada remains a remarkably open society with a commitment to justice, inclusiveness, and tolerance that is widely admired and occasionally copied (Adams, 2007; Reputation Institute, 2015). This commitment is no mean feat, of course, since few other countries must address such a dazzling array of deeply divided and multilayered diversities, including Aboriginal peoples, national-minorities, and immigrant and racialized groups. But rather than imploding from within as one might expect from such an ethnic tinderbox, Canada is reaping a host of society-building dividends because of its multicultural commitments. It may be a bit of a stretch to equate Canada's official Multiculturalism with one of history's revolutionary ideals for reorganizing society; namely, the American, French, and Russian revolutions (Sandercock, 2006). Nevertheless, Canada's success in integrating immigrants is virtually unparalleled by international standards, with its official policy of Multiculturalism attracting widespread kudos for facilitating successful newcomer outcomes (Kymlicka, 2010).

To the other side, however, racial politics and ethnic confrontations continue to perplex and provoke (Johnson & Enomoto, 2007). Canada's status as a rich and fertile ground for living together with differences notwithstanding, the challenges of a cooperative coexistence are proving more complex than many had imagined. Every enlightened move forward is matched by a corresponding slip backward, with the result that debates over diversity transcend the simplistic categories of "good" or "bad," "right" or "wrong," hovering uneasily between these oppositional poles. The prospect of an uncontested coexistence is compromised by the proliferation of increasingly politicized faith-based communities and ethno-religious identity politics. Aboriginal (or Indigenous) peoples confront socio-economic conditions that, frankly, embarrass Canada's lofty reputation as a beacon of enlightenment (Anaya, 2014). The so-called "visible" (or more accurately, "racialized") minorities continue to endure discriminatory treatment, despite assurances and accommodations to the contrary (McDougall, 2009; Satzewich, 2011). Even the widely praised hallmarks of Canada's diversity agenda—immigration and multiculturalism—have drawn criticism as "too much" or "not enough" (Graves, 2015; Grubel, 2009; Mansur, 2011). Not surprisingly, paradoxes flourish precisely because of a growing reality gap between government promises and the lived realities of migrants and minorities at odds with widespread perceptions of Canada as a global pacesetter in the art of positively managing diversity. The fact that Canada's proposed principles do not always match people's lived-experience is the catalyst that drives the dynamics of race, ethnic, and aboriginal relations—as the following contradictions demonstrate:

- That race once mattered is beyond dispute. That race continues to matter at a time when most Canadians think it shouldn't or couldn't is proving a point of contention and confusion (Wallis & Fleras, 2008).

- Racism is widely perceived as a major problem in Canada (Fleras, 2014a). To the dismay of many, its existence has proven much more pervasive and tenacious than predicted, especially with the emergence of new and virulent forms of multi-racisms that are increasingly difficult to detect or eradicate (Agnew, 2007; Bishop, 2005; Henry & Tator, 2010; Hier & Bolaria, 2007).

- References to ethnicity increasingly pivot around the dynamics of competition and conflict rather than cuddly attachments for display in festivals and food courts (Howard-Hassmann, 1999; Maybury-Lewis, 2003). Moreover, concerns mount as ethnic identities and differences become increasingly politicized and pose a governance challenge in proposing to render Canada safe from ethnicity, yet safe for ethnicity.

- No amount of multicultural gloss can mask the obvious: Racialized women and men continue to experience inequities in power, income, and privilege (Block, 2010; Galabuzi, 2006; Jedwab & Satzewich, 2015; Pendakur & Pendakur, 2010; Teelucksingh & Galabuzi, 2005). That a growing legion of foreign-trained professionals are driving taxis or delivering pizzas points to Canada's mishandling of its immigration "advantage" by transforming a potential "brain gain" into a "brain drain" (Fleras, 2014b).

- Multiple narratives inform the aboriginal experience in Canada (Long & Dickason, 2011). One situates Aboriginal peoples at the forefront of economic and political developments, including a right to confer with first ministers at constitutional talks (Belanger, 2008; Coates, 2015; Frideres, 2011). Another acknowledges how poverty and disempowerment of aboriginal communities remain Canada's foremost human rights stain (Anaya, 2014; Frideres & Gadacz, 2012). Still another points to a growing militancy among aboriginal activists impatient with the snail-like progress of repairing a still-broken relationship with Canada (Kino nda niimi Collective, 2014).

- Constitutional guarantees for gender equality are commendable, but minority women (including Aboriginal women, women of colour, and immigrant/refugee women) continue to experience concurrent patterns of exclusion and discrimination, especially when gender intersects with race, ethnicity, and class to amplify patterns of exploitation or exclusion (McMullin, 2010; Zawilski, 2010).

- Many regard Canada's immigration policy and programs as one of the world's more progressive models (Satzewich, 2015; Simmons, 2010). Canada is one of the few countries in the world that can claim to be both an immigration society and a society of immigrants. Yet the system is increasingly criticized as "broken" and in need of a major overhaul (Bissett, 2008; Hawthorne, 2008; Moens & Collacott, 2008). Yet reforms by the then Conservative government (from tightening up the temporary foreign worker program to creating a new Express Entry pipeline to replace the old points system) have drawn both criticism and praise (Fleras, 2014b). Of particular note are continuing concerns over devising a refugee determination process capable of fast-tracking those in need of Canada's protection while staunching the flow of those who manipulate the system for expedited entry.

- Canada may be one of the few countries in the world with a formal policy of Multiculturalism. Nevertheless, the domain of multiculturalism remains one of the more politically charged battlegrounds of our era (Ryan, 2010), as demonstrated by debates over the politics of reasonable accommodation when applied to religious differences and faith-based communities (Fleras, 2009a; Stein et al., 2007). Concern is also growing that, in a globalized age of transmigration and diaspora, the relevance of multiculturalism as a place-based governance model is in doubt since immigrant identities and belonging are increasingly disconnected from place and origins (Fleras, 2011b).

- Canada's commitment to institutional inclusiveness is widely proclaimed and actively pursued. But difficulties undercut this commitment to accommodate by way of workplaces that reflect, represent, and respond to difference, while providing services that are available, accessible, and appropriate. Particularly worrying are institutional structures and unconscious mindsets that remain unmistakably "pale male" in composition, process, and outcomes (Jiwani, 2006; Kobayashi, 2005).

- Canada's Difference Model is attracting attention as a principled blueprint for living together with differences. At the core of this governance model is the principle of differential accommodation, namely, accommodating different ways of accommodating diversities (Jenson & Papillon, 2001). But diversity has become much more complex because of transmigration, identity politics, and emergent multiversal realities, in effect pointing to the necessity of governance models that are inclusive of diversities-within-diversities (Fleras, 2015).

- Debates over differences continue to question and contest. How much and what kind of differences can be tolerated by society? Conversely, how much imposed unity can it bear? Properly managed, a commitment to accommodate diversity may enhance creativity and connections. Without an overarching vision, however, the clash of differences can torpedo a commitment to community, cohesion, and identity (see Putnam, 2007).

Canada is indeed a paradox insofar as it extols respect for diversity, yet works as one of the world's premier integration systems (Rao, 2010). The very dynamic that triggers Canada's strength and pride—its management of diversities—may dissolve into weaknesses; conversely, weaknesses, such as Canada's thin nationalism, may morph into strengths in a globalized world of coming and going. In theory, Canada's track record on race, ethnic, and aboriginal relations should be getting better (whatever that might mean); in reality, it is not (however difficult that might be to measure). Instead of answers, Canadians are swamped with more questions. In lieu of certainty and resolution, confusion prevails. Canadians express dismay over the proliferation of aboriginal protests and occupations, legal challenges to the status quo, and the mounting anger of a disenfranchised population. English-speaking Canadians are perplexed by Quebec's seemingly insatiable demands for special status, while the Québécois are equally puzzled by Anglo intransigence over letting go. No less confusing are the increasingly forceful demands of ethnic and racialized minorities who want recognition and respect without sacrificing equality. Finally, newcomers to Canada are experiencing significant difficulties in "making a go of it" despite Canada's *bona fides* as an immigrant society of immigration (Fleras, 2014b). However important these issues, nobody can claim to have all the answers. That shouldn't be a problem; after all, too much reliance on answers assumes a discoverable objective reality that unlocks its "truth" to the privileged observer. But in a mind-dependent world that rejects the existence of objective truth except as discourses within contexts of power, the asking of questions may be just as important as the reassurance of finding answers.

To be sure, Canadians have become increasingly adept at "talking the talk" about living together with differences. Canada's diversity landscape is peppered with sometimes sanctimonious bromides about "tolerance," "a post-racial world," or "celebrating differences" that rarely say what they mean or mean what they say. Yet many Canadians are less enthralled with the idea of "walking the walk"—of putting their principles into practice. Keywords from "inclusion" and "integration" to "racism" and "diversity" are stretched to mean everything yet nothing, without much concern for precision and clarity. Concepts and theories intended to enlighten and clarify are ideologically loaded to the point of ambiguity and misuse, while the persistence of outdated frameworks bears mute testimony to an intellectual inertia best described as a "paralysis by analysis." The prospects of navigating this conceptual minefield are daunting and people end up "talking past" each other.

This eighth edition of *Unequal Relations* hopes to avoid the perils of sloppy reasoning, mindless clichés, lazy oversimplifications, and common-sense assumptions at odds with a balanced analysis. Every effort has been made to ground these free-floating concepts in ways that inform rather than inflame, enlighten rather than confuse, and empower rather than disengage. The end result is a critically informed introduction that frames the politics of race, ethnic, and aboriginal relations as fundamentally unequal relations against the backdrop of a complex, diverse, and changing Canada. Three dimensions of this Canada-building dynamic are emphasized: *constructed dimensions*, *contested dimensions*, and *community dimensions*, as follows:

1. A focus on the *constructed dimensions* reveals how the contours of race, ethnic, and aboriginal relations neither originate in a social vacuum nor unfold outside a wider context. Nor is there anything natural or inevitable about the dynamics of intergroup relations in society. Rather, they constitute socially constructed relationships of inequality within contexts of power, privilege, and property relations. That makes it doubly important to deconstruct the processes by which these fundamentally unequal relations are created, expressed, and maintained, as well as challenged and transformed by way of minority protest, government policy, ideological shifts, and institutional reform.

2. A focus on the *contested dimensions* envisages Canada as a conflicted site of competitively different groups in competition for scarce resources. Attention is drawn to the competitive struggles of Canada's three major Diversities (Aboriginal peoples, French and English "charter" groups, and ethnic and racialized migrants and minorities) as they jockey to define priorities, secure interests, coax alliances, and impose agendas. The centrality of power is shown to be critical in driving the dynamics of diversity. Certain groups dominate, not because of genetic superiority but because the powerful can invariably define options and control outcomes. Subdominant groups are subordinate, not because of racial inferiority, but because they lack access to equal opportunity and institutionalized power.

3. A focus on the *community dimensions* addresses the challenges of constructing a national community of commitment, cohesion, and consensus from a diverse and divided Canada. A principled framework is proposed for living together with differences by advancing the notion of an inclusive Canada that is safe *for* differences, yet safe *from* differences.

The content and organization of *Unequal Relations* subscribes to the adage of "continuity in change." The first edition of the book was published 25 years ago with the aim of providing a critical introduction to the dynamics of race, ethnic, and aboriginal relations in Canada. Instead of looking at race, ethnicity, or aboriginality as exotic cultures within Canada's multicultural mosaic, the book was designed to synthesize existing theoretical knowledge with current information to deconstruct the politics of diversity in an increasingly diverse, complex, and changing Canada. Admittedly, much in Canada has changed in the interim. But the book's animating logic remains unchanged; that is, the importance of analyzing race, ethnic, and aboriginal relations as essentially unequal relations with respect to how patterns of power, privilege, and property (wealth and income) are played out. Clearly, then, race, ethnicity, and aboriginality are not just physical attributes or social categories; more accurately, they constitute distinctive ways of seeing (and of being seen) and understanding (and being understood) the world within a broader context of inequality and injustice. And as long as these predominantly inequitable relations continue to puzzle and provoke, the politics of race, ethnicity, and aboriginality will remain a lively dynamic and contested domain.

Much is retained in this edition, including the basic chapter outline (despite the convergence of several chapters), the content in terms of concepts and applications to Canadian society, and the framing of race, ethnic, and aboriginal relations as socially constructed and fundamentally unequal. The book remains faithful to its core mission. *Unequal Relations* is neither a description of minority groups nor a catalogue of Canadian ethnic lifestyles. It rarely provides a literary platform for minority "voices" or stories by minority authors, although there is much to gain from such an approach (see Fong Bates, 2005, 2010). To the extent that historical fact is employed, it is history that influences the present rather than a chronology of the past—about the "is" rather than the "was" (Walker, 2001b). Priority is assigned to a macro-sociological study of institutional dynamics, intergroup relations, and power politics rather than micro-models of individual behaviour, personal attitudes, or life experiences. References to diverse ethnocultural groups reflect a focus on relations—from accommodations to conflicts—within a context of inequality and exclusions, thereby drawing attention to the centrality of power to complement that of identity and recognition (Fleras, 2014a). A deconstruction of the logic behind the politics of government policy, institutional reform, and minority resistance is evident throughout, yet the text tries to avoid regurgitating both blatant government propaganda, institutional spin, and ethnic posturing without dismissing the rationale that propelled these dynamics in the first place. Lastly, the text encourages students to critically engage with the paradoxes of diversity politics and the politics of difference—not by examining the issues and debates in the abstract—but through the activism of "painting themselves into the picture" (James, 1998).

Of course, the eighth edition of this text is not without changes—as might be expected in a domain in which the mix of social change with conventional wisdom is rarely constant, often contested, and subject to changes. The usual amendments are in evidence, including revisions, updates, deletions, and additions where necessary. Additional tables and diagrams have been introduced. Diversity data from the 2011 National Household Survey are incorporated whenever possible. A number of Debate boxes and Insight boxes have replaced those of earlier editions in the anticipation of keeping the material fresh and relevant. The text introduces newer concepts and vocabulary such as "multiversal," "microaggression," "complex (or hyper-) diversities," "racialization," "racism 3.0," "governance," "infrastructural racism," "transmigrants and transnationalism," "differential accommoda-tion," and "postmulticulturalism"—not because they are fashionable, but because they pro-mote innovative ways of thinking about the politics and dynamics of race, ethnicity, and aboriginality.

The tone of this textbook is constructively yet unapologetically critical, if only to coun-teract those discourses that uncritically depict Canada as fair, humane, and tolerant (Cannon, 2012; Hedican, 2013). Settler societies such as Canada or Australia routinely rely on national mythologies (or narratives) to paper over ("whitewash") contradictions of ori-gins and history (Razack, 2002). These self-serving narratives offer explanations that not only justify the colonial project but also rationalize its most destructive aspects, including the displacement and dispossession of Aboriginal peoples by European settlers, the impor-tation of cheap migrant labour for nation-building, and the marginalization of racialized minorities within a white society. Canada is portrayed as an empty land (*terra nullius* doc-trine) that was peacefully settled in ways consistent with the rights of discovery, notions of Eurocentric progress, and the principles of Christian civilization. To the extent that these narratives focus on the innocence and heroism of Western settlement and white entitle-ment, they reflect a very one-sided view of what really happened (Schick, 2008). Yet most Canadians have been taught to think of Canada as a kind, gentle society of good and just people instead of a "telling it like is," namely, a colonization project of conquest, expul-sion, and exploitation (Cannon, 2012). Fewer still are equipped to grapple with the "myth-conceptions" of a Canada that conveniently cloak a white supremacist history behind the soothing balm of "happy face" multiculturalism (Razack, 2004; Thobani, 2007; see also Leonardo, 2004). Even fewer still are capable of seeing how the privileging of whiteness in defining who gets what reinforces the dis-privileging of Aboriginal peoples and the disem-powering of racialized minorities. A commitment to unsettling ("deconstructing") Canada as privileged "white space" makes it doubly important to deconstruct the politics of obfus-cation by seeing Canada from the perspectives of those dispossessed and marginalized. It also raises the disturbing possibility that a white Canada is just as capable as any other regime of racially oppressive acts when the situation suits (Hedican, 2013).

To be sure, analyzing these highly politicized topics is neither for the timid nor the politically correct. The interplay of challenge with change invariably inflames passions that puncture people's complacency over identity and self-esteem, core cultural values, the legitimacy of conventional authority, and taken-for-granted privileges. Nevertheless, a commitment to a critically informed analysis is crucial in adjusting to the realities of a post-modern world, namely, to expect the unexpected, to think the unthinkable, and to cope with the uncontrollable. Ours is the age of diversities and difference, not simply in the descriptive or celebratory sense, but because an increasingly politicized diversity is capa-ble of flexing its muscles in the competition for valued resources. The boundaries of "being Canadian" are challenged by the deep differences and radical ethnicities of a society in the throes of transformative change, with the result being that traditional images and conven-tional assumptions about Canada are no longer applicable (Fleras, 2015). Moreover, it's not enough to simply understand the issues associated with the politics of diversity and differ-ence, even when filtered through the prism (lens) of a diverse, changing, and unequal Canada. Emphasis must also focus on putting this knowledge into practice—either sup-porting or reinforcing a racialized status quo by doing nothing or, alternatively, by advanc-ing a just and inclusive Canada through critically informed activism. To their credit,

Canadians are slowly rising to the challenge of repairing the largely dysfunctional relationship that informs Canada's dystopian relation to Aboriginal peoples (Truth and Reconciliation Commission Report, 2015). Canada is also proving a pacesetter in balancing the concurrent demands and oppositional tensions of a multicultural governance that abides by the principles of inclusiveness. This *principled* approach to the constructive governance of race, ethnic, and aboriginal relations secures a rationale for living together with differences, respectfully and equitably. It also elevates Canada to the global forefront of countries that are attempting to manage the diversity dividend in ways necessary, fair, and just.

SUPPLEMENTS

The following instructor supplements are available for downloading from a password-protected section of Pearson Education Canada's online catalogue (www.pearsoned.ca/highered). Navigate to your book's catalogue page to view a list of those supplements that are available. See your local sales representative for details and access.

Test Item File

Available in Microsoft Word/Adobe Acrobat format, this test bank includes 25 multiple-choice questions, 15 fill-in-the-blank questions, and 1 essay question per chapter.

Learning Solutions Managers

Pearson's Learning Solutions Managers work with faculty and campus course designers to ensure that Pearson technology products, assessment tools, and online course materials are tailored to meet your specific needs. This highly qualified team is dedicated to helping schools take full advantage of a wide range of educational resources, by assisting in the integration of a variety of instructional materials and media formats. Your local Pearson Education sales representative can provide you with more details on this service program.

PART 1

Conceptualizing the Politics of Race, Ethnic, and Aboriginal Relations

It's been said that this "adventure" called Canada resembles an "enigma wrapped around a mystery inside a riddle." This confused entanglement of unknowables provides an intriguing twist to the turns in Canada's race, ethnic, and aboriginal relations. Put bluntly, Canada has no business even existing, given the implausibilities of its geography, history, and demographics. How can a deeply divided and multilayered Canada continue to survive and flourish under conditions that would otherwise topple other societies? And yet it now stands as one of the world's oldest federal systems (alongside Switzerland and the United States). Its lofty status as a society-building success has elicited playful inversions about Canada as "a solution in search of a problem" (as a Mexican ambassador once aptly put it). Translation: Canada remains one of the world's best places to live—a society so blessed with physical resources and human resourcefulness that it must "invent" problems that less-advantaged countries might dismiss or ignore. That Canadians continue to dwell on the negative at the expense of the positive, even though they have much to be thankful for, may say more about their being pampered than about having problems.

The prospect of "living together with differences" remains a perplexing and provocative challenge. The world we inhabit is rapidly changing, increasingly diverse, and sharply contested, with the result being that confusion and uncertainty often prove the rule rather than the exception. Just as scholars have had to rethink those social moorings that conventionally secured Canada, so too must Canadians grapple with a host of difference issues beyond their comprehension or control. Consider the following challenges:

1. Aboriginal peoples claim to be relatively autonomous political communities with collective and inherent rights to aboriginal models of self-determining autonomy over land, identity, and political voice (Maaka & Fleras, 2005). Is it possible to construct a national governance framework to accommodate these **postcolonial** claims for a renewed relationship involving the principles of partnership, power sharing, and peoplehood (Belanger, 2008)? Or is such an arrangement likely to create a "Swiss cheese" Canada—so full of holes that there is nothing to keep it together?

2. National minorities such as the Québécois are seeking to transform Canada's constitutional arrangements in hopes of constructing a new social compact based on the notion of Quebec as a nation rather than simply a province. The implications of this nationalism—in addition to that of the First Nations—underscore the challenges of forging unity from diversity.

3. Racialized minorities have become increasingly politicized in advancing a more inclusive Canada, one that is respectful of, reflective upon, and responsive to minority needs and demands. To the extent that doubts remain over the quality of institutional responses to the inclusiveness challenge, debates over reasonable accommodation are unlikely to subside (Fleras, 2014a).

4. New Canadians are experiencing a mixed reception. To one side, newcomers to Canada are embraced as integral in advancing its interests at local, national, and international levels. To the other side, both immigrants and asylum seekers may be perceived as troublesome constituents or "problem people"—an outlook seemingly at odds with Canada's much ballyhooed status as an immigration society (Graves, 2015).

5. A governance paradox is emerging. In a transnational world of transmigrants whose identities and affiliations span borders, does it still make sense to talk about integration or inclusion, multiculturalism or citizenship, as place-based governances when immigrants are increasingly uncoupled from a sense of singular belonging and unitary space (Fleras, 2014b)?

The prospect of coping with each of these dynamics—and doing so in a principled way—poses a challenge for Canadian society as we know it. But these challenges also represent a splendid opportunity for Canada-building along twenty-first-century lines. Part 1 of *Unequal Relations* addresses these challenges by providing a conceptual map for theorizing the politics of Canada's race, ethnic, and aboriginal relations. Chapter 1 begins by exploring the concept of intergroup dynamics as they apply to race, ethnicity, and aboriginality. Chapter 2 addresses the politics of race in contemporary society. Chapter 3 is concerned with unmasking the many faces of racism in Canada. Chapter 4 examines ethnicity as a powerful force—both beneficial and costly—in Canadian society, with particular emphasis on the politics of Quebecois nationalism. Chapter 5 looks at social inequality as it affects racialized minorities. Chapter 6 focuses on the increasingly contested domain of gendered inequality as it applies to minority and migrant women. Together, these six chapters provide an introduction to the complex, unequal, and changing domain of race, ethnic, and aboriginal relations.

CHAPTER 1

Race, Ethnic, and Aboriginal Relations: Patterns, Paradoxes, Perspectives

LEARNING OBJECTIVES

After reading this chapter, you will be able to:

1. Demonstrate how Canada's official multiculturalism can be differently interpreted, depending on the sociological model of society employed.

2. Understand why, when it comes to assessing Canada's track record on race, ethnic, and aboriginal relations, the expression, "the good, the bad, and the in-between" rings true.

3. Describe the differences that characterize the five governance models for managing race, ethnic, and aboriginal relations.

4. Appreciate the value of sociological models of society for analyzing race, ethnic, and aboriginal dynamics.

5. Discuss Canada's diversities in terms of Aboriginal peoples, newcomers to Canada, and racialized minorities.

DEBATE

Framing Canada's Multiculturalism

To define Canada as multicultural is typically considered an understatement. References to **multiculturalism** in Canada range from the descriptive to the prescriptive, with the politics of policy in-between. Canada's population is known to be multiculturally diverse, Canadians generally subscribe to the multicultural values of openness and tolerance, and both minority and political elites are known to play multicultural politics to advance vested interests (Lupul, 2005). Canada is also multicultural because of its commitment to an official Multiculturalism (note the use of an uppercase "*M*" to denote official government policy; otherwise it is lowercase). Entrenchment of Multiculturalism in the *Constitution Act* of 1982, followed by the passage of the world's first and only *Multiculturalism Act* in 1988, has further secured Canada's status as a trailblazer in multicultural governance (Fleras, 2009b).

(Continued)

Many support an official Multiculturalism as a principled approach for living together with **differences** (Dasko, 2005; Environics Institute, 2015; Soroka & Roberton, 2010). Those familiar with the policy—and surveys suggest that the *majority* of Canadians are *unfamiliar* with what Multiculturalism is doing—express pride in a homegrown initiative that many regard as Canada's foremost contribution to global harmony (Adams, 2007). Canada's official Multiculturalism is viewed as "quietly" revolutionary—comparable in stature to the animating ideals of the French, American, and Russian revolutions as a governance framework (Sandercock, 2006). Others are openly critical of its weaknesses or usefulness (Paquet, 2008). They pounce on Multiculturalism as a good idea gone bad or, alternatively, a bad idea unfolding precisely to plan (Abu-Laban & Gabriel, 2002; Bannerji, 2000; Gregg, 2006; Mansur, 2010). Still others are unsure how to respond. Multiculturalism is "okay" in principle, but not if it (1) imposes inconveniences or costs, (2) makes excessive and illiberal demands, (3) shears apart Canada's social fabric, or (4) challenges core constitutional values. Yet others still acknowledge its paradoxical nature. On the one hand, Multiculturalism rarely means what it says or says what it means, with the result that it can mean everything—or nothing—depending on intentions or context (Fleras, 2014a). On the other hand, Multiculturalism has a tendency to deny what it sets out to affirm—differences—while reinforcing what it hopes to eliminate—inequality—neither embracing differences for fear of disunity nor denying them because of political correctness (Kivisto & Ng, 2005).

Clearly, then, Canadians express a love–hate relationship with Multiculturalism. Those who embrace Multiculturalism as the solution to Canada's **diversity** challenges are themselves dismissive of those who dismiss it as a governance headache. Conversely, those who denounce Multiculturalism as an evil incarnate are no less contemptuous of those who worship at the altar of diversity. In light of its paradoxical status, questions abound over the role of Multiculturalism in contributing to Canada-building. Is Multiculturalism a good thing or a bad thing for Canada? Hoax or help? Progress or regress? Benefit or cost? Living together or drifting apart? To what extent does any reference to the "good" or the "bad" say more about the evaluator's agenda than anything about what is being evaluated or assessed (with the result that any assessment is contingent on whether Multiculturalism advances a particular vision of Canada as modern or postnational [see Chapter 10])? What is the role of an official Multiculturalism in creating and sustaining patterns of inequality (i.e., as a problem) as well as challenging and changing these inequalities of exclusion (i.e., as a solution)? How does applying sociological models of society to Canadian Multiculturalism provide an insightful response to this complex question? The Debate Revisited box at the end of this chapter will explore a principled basis for making any such assessment.

INTRODUCTION: THE GOOD, THE BAD, AND THE IN-BETWEEN

Canada is globally admired for its resources and resilience in securing a true north strong and free (Reputation Institute, 2015). Overseas observers are astonished by Canada's resourcefulness in weaving a remarkably cohesive unity from the strands of diversity (Adams, 2007). They are also intrigued by how Canada manages to keep a lid on those ethnic tensions that have splintered other societies into warring factions. Questions invariably arise: Why does the commitment to an official Multiculturalism persist in Canada, whereas it's experiencing a backlash in European countries and elsewhere? How does one account for the relatively smooth transformation of once-stodgy provincial capitals such as Toronto and Vancouver into cosmopolitan complexes? What is the secret behind Canada's ability to balance the often-competing demands of Aboriginal peoples with those of the Québécois and racialized minorities without experiencing paralyzing strife? To be sure, the potential for unravelling Canadian society is always present. But while other countries are groping for solutions to accommodate difference, Canada is embarking on a promising if unprecedented quest for cooperative coexistence along principled lines (Kymlicka, 2007). Or, to put a slightly different spin to it, Canada constitutes a multicultural role model in the art of living together with differences equitably and in dignity (Fleras, 2009a).

How does this assessment stand up to scrutiny? Any response must begin with a sense of perspective. First, compared to its historical past, Canada's engagement with race, ethnicity, and aboriginality is showing signs of maturity. There is no shortage of cringe-inducing episodes and patterns that historically have scarred Canada's record. Canada originated in the dispossession of Aboriginal peoples and their lands, leaving behind a legacy that continues to diminish and demean. Canada-building was predicated on policies, programs, and practices that routinely exploited racialized minorities, including the exploitation of the Chinese during construction of the more dangerous sections of the trans-Canada railway (Li, 2003); the internment and dispossession of Japanese-Canadians during World War II (Kogawa, 1994); the enslavement of blacks and their segregation from mainstream institutions until the 1950s (Backhouse, 1999; Walker, 1997); and the pervasive anti-Semitism of the 1920s and 1930s, which culminated in the rejection of Jewish emigrants from Nazi Germany (Penslar, 2005). The extent to which this exclusion went beyond the perversions of a few misguided bigots and pervaded both societal structures and government policies says a lot about the politics of power (Wallis & Fleras, 2008).

Times appear to have changed. Evidence of Canada's historical advancement can be gleaned from a list of global firsts in the diversity sweepstakes. Canada's *Citizenship Act* of 1947 ignored the distinction between **immigrants** and native-born persons as grounds for citizenship. The *Immigration Act* of 1967 was one of the first pieces of legislation to abolish all quotas or preferences on the basis of race or ethnicity, with the result that Canada's colour-blind immigration policies may well prove to be this country's proudest achievement (Ibbitson, 2005). Canada is the only country in the world to have received the United Nations-sponsored Nansen Medal (awarded in 1986) for its humanitarian response to the global refugee problem. And with the provision of Section 35 of the 1982 *Constitution Act*, Canada became the world's first and only country to constitutionally enshrine aboriginal and treaty rights. The launch of the Residential School Truth and Reconciliation Commission in 2008 made Canada one of the first countries to establish such an official commission of inquiry (the final report was published in mid-2015) (Henderson & Wakeham, 2013). Similarly, passage of the *Canadian Multiculturalism Act* in 1988 solidified Canada's status as the world's first country to institutionalize an official Multiculturalism as a principled framework for positively managing diversity. Its glowing reputation is further secured by Canada's consistent high placement in quality-of-life surveys, including its ranking for eight consecutive years (between 1993 and 2000) as the world's best place to live, according to a human development index.

Second, consider global comparisons. Compared to other societies that routinely violate **human rights**, with abuses ranging from ethnic cleansing and mass expulsion to forced exploitation and coercive assimilation, Canada possesses an enviable reputation as a paragon of virtue, tolerance, and compassion (Global Creativity Index Report, 2015). Escalating numbers of mixed union couples from different ethnic and racialized backgrounds, including a 33 percent spurt between 2001 and 2006, attest to this openness (Agrell, 2010; also Mahtani, 2014). Canada's commitment to the promotion of aboriginal and minority rights is second to none, with both constitutional and statutory guarantees in place at the federal and provincial levels, although there is some evidence of backsliding at present (Maaka & Fleras, 2008). Canada's lofty status is further solidified with endorsement of human rights protection, ranging from passage of the *Bill of Rights* in 1960 to the *Charter of Rights and Freedoms* in 1982. Paradoxically, however, it's precisely this exalted status that exposes Canada to criticism. Even the smallest of infractions tend to be amplified in Canada because of its exacting standards, whereas such indiscretions would receive barely a mention in many foreign countries (Levitt, 1997). Not surprisingly, Canadians appear perplexed and angry when international bodies chastise Canada for relatively "minor" human rights violations, including its use of the term "visible minorities" as a descriptive label for racialized minorities (Fleras, 2008), yet rogue societies are allowed to get away with "bloody murder" without much condemnation.

Third, while Canada glitters in comparison to its past and with others, it also falls short of established benchmarks. Canadians are adept at "talking the walk" with respect to the ideals of tolerance, openness, and inclusiveness; however, they are less inclined to "walk the talk" by putting these ideals into practice. Canada's ongoing mistreatment of Aboriginal peoples is routinely criticized by the UN and UN observers as this country's most egregious human rights violation (Anaya, 2014). Relations between racialized minorities and the rest of Canada tend to waver uneasily between grudging acceptance and thinly veiled rejection, with the spectre of public backlash ever present. Discrimination and racism are not simply relics from the past; to the contrary, they are so deeply ingrained and structurally embedded that any possibility of their removal from Canadian society is remote (Fleras, 2014a; Jiwani, 2006; Razack, 2004; Thobani, 2007). Anti-Semitism persists, albeit in different guises (Schoenfeld, 2004; Weinfeld, 2005); white supremacist groups are proliferating through digital technology; racialized minorities (and aboriginal men and women) continue to be disproportionately represented in the criminal justice system; and recently arrived new Canadians find themselves increasingly marginalized in terms of income earnings and poverty levels. The fact that highly skilled newcomers cannot secure appropriate employment prospects consistent with their credentials and experiences exposes a gap between the immigrant ideals and the realities of an immigration society (Bauder & Shields, 2015). Clearly, all is not well, and yet these inconvenient blemishes on Canada's reputation are routinely papered over with polite fictions of tolerance, fairness, and generosity that ultimately do a disservice to Canada and Canadians.

MISMANAGING RACE, ETHNIC, AND ABORIGINAL RELATIONS: POLITE FICTIONS *VERSUS* INCONVENIENT TRUTHS

Nearly 45 years of study devoted to the inequalities of race, ethnicity, and aboriginality have made it abundantly clear: The Canada that is often acclaimed as a beacon of enlightenment in managing diversity is not necessarily the same Canada experienced by the disenfranchised such as Aboriginal peoples, racialized minorities, and the newest Canadians (also Cannon, 2012). Consider the following disjunctures that fracture Canada's national image of itself: Race matters, even though it shouldn't; racism is not a relic from the past but insidious and ever-present; racialized men and women remain stratified along Canada's vertical mosaic; recent immigrants are doing more poorly than ever in the labour market, despite Canada's designation as an immigration society; Aboriginal peoples continue to live in conditions that would embarrass many third world countries; and our vaunted standard of living is crafted on the appropriation of aboriginal land and the exploitation of cheap migrant labour for Canada-building. This gap between normative ideals and lived experiences generates a profound distaste (and occasionally denial or anger) in those for whom these revelations border on incredulous or bewildering. "How can this be?" they ask, in a post-racial and pro-multicultural Canada with its abundant resources, resourcefulness of its people, array of generous social programs, and a principled commitment to the colour-blind principle of judging and rewarding individuals on the basis of merit rather than melanin (see also Johnson, 2015, for similar comments from the United States).

Most of us have been taught to think of Canada as a kinder, gentler society of good and just people who disapprove of racism and racially based exploitation. But contrary to what they have been led to believe, Canadians live in a Canada that is not always what it says it is or seems to be, despite Canada's *bona fides* as the world's premier multicultural society. The inequalities of exclusion that blight the lives and imperil the life chances of Aboriginal peoples, minorities, and migrants are real, difficult to dislodge, and pack a wallop (Alfred, 2011; Regan, 2011). Of course, most grudgingly acknowledge the existence of isolated pockets of inequality, albeit as little more than aberrations ("glitches") in otherwise egalitarian Canada (Henderson & Wakeham, 2013). They may be willing to concede the possibility of some unsavory episodes that mar the myth of a cooperative Canada-building venture by plucky settlers and honest politicians, although even this slight concession comes with strings attached. It is commonly believed that the advent of modern democracy and the enshrinement of human rights have addressed the legitimate grievances of Indigenous peoples and aggrieved minority groups. Accordingly, it's assumed that all Canadians are equal before the law, since everyone plays on the same "level playing field" regardless of race, ethnicity, or aboriginality. In other words, if indigenous and minority folk fail, it's their fault. This is hardly a surprising assessment: Both Americans and Canadians tend to equate poverty and inequality with moral failures rooted in individual psyches and personality flaws rather than to see them as reflective of structures or political economy (Royce, 2015). Pointing the finger of blame to personal incompetence plays into the spirit of then Prime Minister Harper's whitewash of Canada when claiming at a G-20 gathering in September 2009, "Canada has no history of colonialism." In Harper's defense, he may have conflated the concept of colonialism with territorial ownership of overseas ("salt water") colonies, rather than seeing it as a system of internal oppression for subjugating the peoples within. But this historical amnesia is rightly pilloried by Madelaine Drohan (2011:2) who skewers this myth conception:

> The skewed version of history in which Canada sprang fully formed as an international good guy, without any tawdry colonial past, is firmly embedded in the minds of many non-aboriginal Canadians today. They do not see themselves as the descendants or beneficiaries of European colonizers who used the same tactics to accumulate wealth and power in North America as they had successfully used in Africa, Asia, and Latin America. Nor would they recognize the remnants of that inequitable system that remain in place today.

In short, Canada was not a barren and unpopulated land mass that magically sprung into existence like mushrooms in the damp. Canada-building was forged in the crucible of colonial violence whose aftermath continues to reverberate throughout this "Indian" country. To the extent that these narratives focus on the innocence and heroism of western settlement at the expense of those victimized by this expansion, they reflect a very one-sided view of what really happened (Schick, 2008). To unlearn this version of Canadian history requires that the story be retold from a different perspective. That alone—a commitment to unsettling these notions of Canada as privileged "white space"—makes it doubly important to deconstruct the politics of power from the perspectives of those who were (and continue to be) dispossessed, marginalized, or exploited.

Those who persist in pursuing a narrative of "Canada the good" are in for a rude awakening. Settler societies such as Canada or Australia routinely rely on national mythologies (or narratives) to paper over ("whitewash") contradictions of origins and history (Razack, 2002). These self-serving narratives offer explanations that not only justify the colonial project but also rationalize its most destructive aspects in the hopes of whitewashing those profoundly awkward projects inconsistent with projected images of a morally progressive country. Imagine the shock of disillusionment to learn that Canada's squeaky clean image is manufactured and misleading rather than naturally occurring or honestly acquired. A profound sense of dismay settles in when discovering that Canada's constitutional commitment to "peace, order, and good government" is largely a polite fiction that glosses over some astonishingly ugly truths that invoke the worst of humanity's inhumanities, including genocide, slavery, ethnic cleansing, apartheid, forced internment, white supremacy, suppression of cultures, and a host of crimes against humanity. More specifically:

- Instead of "telling it like it is," Canada is portrayed as an empty land (*terra nullius* doctrine) that was peacefully discovered, explored, and domesticated in ways consistent with the rights of discovery, notions of Eurocentric progress, and the principles of Christian civilization. In reality, the settlement of Canadian society entailed a brutal colonization of Canada through conquest, expulsion, and exploitation of the inferiorized "other," that ruthlessly removed all barriers to expansion and settlement (Neu & Therrien, 2003; Cannon & Sunseri, 2011; Regan, 2011). In that Canada has never proved its legal jurisdiction over Aboriginal peoples' territory, it is relying on the racist doctrine of discovery to justify its legitimacy and authority (Editorial, International Working Group on Indigenous Affairs, 2015). Aboriginal peoples were imperiously pushed aside in the drive to domesticate Canada—a kind of Canadian-style ethnic cleansing that bullied or starved recalcitrant "natives" into submission (Carter, 1990; Daschuk, 2013; Woolford, 2013). Aboriginal children and adults during the 1940s and 1950s were unwittingly duped as guinea pigs for nutritional experiments (from halving milk rations for residential school children to withholding dental services; Moseby, 2013); aboriginal women endured forced sterilization under the guise of eugenics ("selective reproduction"; Stote, 2015); thousands of children from 1955 to 1985 were removed from their homes by child welfare authorities (without parental consent) and adopted out to non-aboriginal families or foster homes (the so-called Sixties Scoop; Alston-O'Connor, 2010); and aboriginal children were earmarked for residential schools that proved genocidal in consequence ("systemic") if not in intent (Fontaine & Farber, 2013; Truth and Reconciliation Commission Report, 2015). The legacy of colonialism and genocide bites deeply into the present: That Canada ranks eighth in the world according to a UN Development ranking, whereas Aboriginal peoples rank 63rd if they are disaggregated from Canada and treated as an independent entity—it is an indication of the skeletons that continue to rattle about in the Canadian closet.

- Canada's colour-coded bar was just as real and as fiercely defended as was Jim Crow segregation in the United States (minus the lynching). Slavery and the buying, selling, and owning of slaves (both blacks and Aboriginal peoples—albeit more as status symbols than as enslaved hands) was part of colonial Canada for two centuries (Cooper, 2006; Trudel, 2014). What dismay to discover that apartheid in Canada was openly condoned and enforced well into the 1950s before public opinion and anti-discrimination laws curbed flagrant expressions of racism and segregation. For example, black separate schools were not taken off the books in Ontario until 1964 (and Nova Scotia in 1983). To add insult to injury, it's quite possible that Canada's *Indian Act* and reserve system not only served as a template for South Africa's system of Bantustans ("separate homelands"), but also exemplify a made-in-Canada apartheid in progress—at least in form if not necessarily in function.

- Until recently, Canada self-defined itself as a staunchly "white man's" society (Thobani, 2007). Removal of this stigma from polite discourse notwithstanding, patterns of white privilege continue to prevail in what amounts to a white supremacist Canada (used in a way that differs from usual usage). The systemic whiteness of a white supremacist regime does not necessarily mean a belief in the superiority and domination of some races over inferior others, although most Canadians were openly and defiantly racist well into the 1960s before it became *déclassé* to be racist—at least in public if not in private. More accurately, a systemic white supremacism is located in those founding assumptions and foundational principles that underpin Canada's unwritten constitutional order, while justifying the routine exercise of "white privilege" (which could not possibly exist outside a white supremacist system). A systemic white supremacy also asserts the superiority of those cultural, social, moral, and psychological characteristics associated with whiteness in defining civilization, progress, and intelligence. Patterns of privilege and power are further sublimated in peoples' unconscious biases—in effect, conceding that subliminal prejudicial attitudes are more common in Canada than otherwise implied by references to Canadians as a polite, informed, and civil people.

- Appearances can be deceiving when matching progress with regress. The very things that make Canadians proud of "our home and *their* native land"—multiculturalism, inclusiveness, tolerance, or equal opportunity—are not what they seem to be. These ostensibly progressive initiatives obscure an openly white supremacist history behind the soothing balm of a happy face multiculturalism, incorporating patterns of racial stratification, relations of power, and hierarchies of inequality and exclusions (Jedwab & Satzewich, 2015; Razack, 2002). They also are perversely complicit in reproducing the inequalities of exclusion that inform a systemic white supremacism. Put bluntly, there is nothing neutral or value-free about Canada (i.e., "a level playing field"). More accurately, Canada is a socially constructed and ideologically infused convention whose guiding principles are racialized, gendered, and classed in ways that reward those on the "right" side of the ideological divide. Those who are socially located on the wrong side of the racialized track tend to see and experience Canada differently; namely, a Canada of two societies, *separate and unequal*.

- It's commonly assumed that existing inequalities and chronic exclusions reflect individual decisions or personal abilities (see Royce, 2015). The reality is often different, notwithstanding oft-recited references to Canada as a meritocratic society where one earns what they deserve. The persistence and pervasiveness of minority inequalities and migrant exclusions are institutionalized (i.e., structural and systemic) rather than a reflection of moral failure or personal flaws, and reflective of a neoliberal political economy that distorts the allocation of valued resources. Worse still, there is a hesitancy in seeing how the privileging of whiteness in defining who gets what contributes to the dis-privileging of Aboriginal peoples and the disempowering of racialized minorities. But instead of the situation improving as might be expected from a forward-looking Canada, the removal of discriminatory barriers and stigma of racism is not the unalloyed accomplishment of popular belief. Initiatives to improve the socioeconomic status and democratic citizenship of migrants, Aboriginal peoples, and minorities reflect the taint of expediency—a façade of legal compliance to stay one step ahead of the law—rather than a commitment to genuine equality. A stark truth prevails: Yes, Canada's migrants and minorities may possess the same formal rights because everyone is equal before the law (admittedly, what is legal is not necessarily what is fair or just). Yet, they must exercise these rights and achieve success in a profoundly *unlevel* playing field by going against the grain (i.e., "swimming upstream") of a system neither designed with them in mind nor constructed to advance their interests.

The cumulative impact of this exposé is unsettling, at best. The series of uncomfortable truths and inconvenient realities described herein may begin to unravel the rose-tinted perception that some may have about "what Canada is for." Reference to Canada as "the true north strong and free" may be little more than a comforting fiction that masks its grounded reality as racialized, patricentric, and supremacist society seemingly not adverse to denying, excluding, and exploiting those migrants, minorities, and Aboriginal peoples who fall outside the mold of a "real" Canadian. In looking to separate polite fictions from inconvenient truths, this eighth edition of *Unequal Relations* is informed by what might be called a critically informed approach to the study of race, ethnicity, and aboriginality. This text challenges the all-too-common tendency to analyze the Canadian project along the discursive lines of celebratory multiculturalisms or uncritical narratives of diversity and inclusion. Admittedly, no one should underplay Canada's largely unparalleled track record in advancing aboriginal and minority rights. Compared to the spate of human rights violations around the world, Canada sparkles as a paragon of virtue, although national ideals don't always match state practices. Nor should critics blithely dismiss the possibility that

Canada, despite its imperfections, may qualify as the world's least imperfect country in positively managing race, ethnic, and Aboriginal relations. But kudos aside, the gaps between the rhetoric of perfections ("comforting fictions") versus the reality of power ("inconvenient realities") are deflating, deserving of criticism, and worthy of outrage. What is glossed over in such a depoliticized discourse is a reluctance to interrogate the politics of white supremacy, settler colonialism, racist exclusions, and hetero-patriarchal normativity as a set of theories, imaginaries, and methods that must be subverted in the service of a fair and just society (Thobani, 2007).

My intent in drawing attention to this unflattering narrative of Canada and Canadians is not gratuitous provocation. It is my hope that, beneath the bleakness of this assessment of Canada, lies a deeper honesty that speaks truth to power. Nor do I intend to lambaste individual Canadians for the perils and predicaments described in this text; both corporate Canada and Canadian governments have vast resources at their disposal to coax Canadians into accepting a particular version of reality that blurs, omits, or distorts. To the contrary, the objective of this debunking exercise is much more pragmatic. It's my belief that there is nothing healthy or progressive in a refusal to talk about race, power, and inequalities if this reluctance is animated by a fear that such bluntness may expose uncomfortable realities. Because whether we are unaware or aware, if we approve or disapprove, the truth is already "de-myth-tified": Canada remains infrastructurally a racialized society whose commitment to managing race, ethnic, and aboriginal relations is compromised by the built-in biases of Euro-white constitutional order. The circulation of national myths and polite fictions not only paper over these unsupportable contradictions and inconvenient truths, but they also serve as tools of social control in deference to the status quo. The challenge is clearly before us: If Canadians want to create a more just, inclusive, and egalitarian society they must unflinchingly confront the colonial mentality of Canada's collective amnesia and moral indifference, disrupt those historical narratives as part of a massive truth-telling about Canada's relationship with the original inhabitants (Alfred, 2011), concede (however painfully) that they may be as racially oppressive as anyone else (Hedican, 2013:x), and paint themselves into the picture of activism by channeling the courage of their convictions into doing what is workable, necessary, and just.

This admittedly selective overview paints a discordant picture of Canadian race, Aboriginal, and ethnic relations. From a distance, Canada looks idyllic; up close the picture blurs, with little to boast about in the *mis*management of diversities and difference. That discord suggests the possibility of a *third* interpretation—that Canada is positioned somewhere in between the poles of good and bad: Neither a paragon of virtue nor the fountainhead of all evils, Canada's record of managing diversity probably falls somewhere in the middle. In comparison to the past or to other countries, Canada soars; when compared to the ideals that many Canadians espouse, Canada misses the mark. Initiatives for "managing" race, ethnicity, and aboriginality are at times enlightened, at other times callously expedient in securing national and vested interests, and hopelessly muddled at still other times, especially as Canadians strive to balance "national interests" with minority rights.

This chapter explores the politics, patterns, and paradoxes that inform Canada's race, ethnic, and aboriginal relations. A conceptual map is proposed for cutting through the analytical clutter that conceals as much as it reveals, confuses as much as it clarifies, and distorts as much as it enlightens. This chapter also analyzes the different governance models for managing race, ethnic, and aboriginal relations (namely, genocide, segregation, assimilation, integration, and pluralism); introduces sociological models of society (functionalism, conflict theories [Marxism and feminist theory], and symbolic interactionism) as explanatory frameworks for making sense of race, ethnic, and aboriginal dynamics; and demonstrates how these sociological models can cast light on Canada's official policy of Multiculturalism (see the Debate and Debate Revisited boxes). The theorizing of race, ethnic, and aboriginal relations along these lines provides a conceptual underpinning for the remaining chapters. First, however, the chapter begins with an overview of diversity in Canada based on 2011 National Household Survey data (Statistics Canada, 2013). The data below have been broken down into Diversity categories: Aboriginal peoples, immigrants, and racialized ("visible") minorities.

Diversity in Canada: A Snapshot and An Assessment

Canada is widely proclaimed as a multicultural society of diverse origins and identities. This claim has merit insofar as just over one in five Canadians is foreign-born (numbers are rounded), while just under one in five Canadians is "non-white" (i.e., racialized)—a figure that is likely to increase in light of Canada's robust immigration program. Canada's diversity is also manifest at the level of Aboriginal peoples whose growing population is reflected in and reinforced by their relative youthfulness (Aboriginal Affairs and Northern Development Canada [AANDC], 2013). The following figures provide a breakdown:

Ethnicity in General

- Over 200 ethnic origins (including Aboriginal) were reported by the total population in the 2011 National Household Survey. (In 1901, only 25 ethnic origins were reported.) Membership in 13 ethnic groups exceeded the 1 million mark, either alone or in combination with another ethnicity.
- Canadian was the most frequently reported ethnic origin in 2011, with

just over 10.6 million people, either alone or in combination with other ethnic origins, comprising 32 percent of the total responses, dropping from 39 percent in 2001. Following behind Canadian were English (6.5 million), French (5.1 million), Scottish (4.7 million), Irish (4.5 million), and German (3.2 million). Other ethnic categories that surpassed the 1 million mark included Italian, Chinese, First Nations or North American Indian, Ukrainian, East Asian, Dutch, and Polish (both single and multiple origins).

- Provincial and urban variations exist. For example, the top ethnic origins reported in Toronto are (in descending order) English, Canadian, Scottish, Chinese, and Irish.

Aboriginal Peoples

- The term "Aboriginal peoples" in the Constitution describes the descendants of the original occupants. Their constitutional status can be further subdivided into the categories of Status Indians (also First Nations or North American Indian), Métis, and Inuit. According to AANDC (2013) data, 1.4 million self-identified as Aboriginal, with First Nations accounting for 911 000 of the total (including 698 000 registered or status Indians and 213 000 non-registered or non-status Indians), 418 000 Métis, and 59 000 Inuit. First Nations (both registered and non-status) account for 65 percent of the aboriginal population; Metis account for about 30 percent, and Inuit account for just under 5 percent. Those who identify as Aboriginal peoples comprise 4.3 percent of Canada's population. The increase from 2.8 percent in 1996 is due in part to higher fertility rates and a greater willingness to adopt aboriginality as an identity marker. The proportion of Aboriginal peoples to non-aboriginals in Canada is second only to New Zealand, where the indigenous Maori tribes constitute just over 15 percent of the population.

- There is considerable provincial/territorial variation in Canada's aboriginal population. In numerical terms, Ontario has the largest number of aboriginal persons at just over 300 000, but they represent only 2.4 percent of the province's population, putting Ontario near the bottom of all provinces on a proportional basis. Ontario is followed by BC at 232 000, and Alberta at 221 000. As a percentage of the provincial population, 16.7 percent of Manitoba's population is aboriginal; next are Saskatchewan at 15.6 percent and Newfoundland and Labrador at 7.1 percent. Eighty-six percent of Nunavut's population is

aboriginal, followed by the North-West Territories at 52 percent and Yukon's 23 percent (AANDC, 2013).

- Status or registered Indians are entitled to reside on one of Canada's 2300 reserves. Seventy percent of reserves have fewer than 500 inhabitants. Two hundred and eighty-five reserves have fewer than 100 persons, while only 30 of 793 reserves delineated by Statistics Canada (from a total of 997) had populations of over 2000 (AANDC, 2013).

- Most Aboriginal peoples are living off-reserve and in cities. About 45 percent of all registered Indians live off-reserve, as do 75 percent of non-status Indians, 71 percent of Métis, and 46 percent of Inuit (AANDC, 2013). In 2011, Winnipeg boasted the largest urban aboriginal population at 78 415 (at 11%, Winnipeg has the highest percentage per total population of major cities in Canada), followed by Edmonton at 61 770 or 10 percent of its population.

Immigrants

- A total of 1 163 000 newcomers arrived between 2006 and 2011, boosting Canada's foreign-born population to 6 776 000. At 20.6 percent of the population, Canada possesses the highest proportion of foreign-born residents, just behind Australia (approx. 27%) and New Zealand (22%; Spoonley & Bedford, 2012), followed by Germany and the United States, each at about 13 percent. Of the 259 000 newcomers in 2013,

(Continued)

57.2 percent arrived through the economic class (including partners and dependents), 31.6 percent were admitted through the family reunification class, and the remaining 11.2 percent included the protected persons ("refugee") class and miscellaneous others.

- The largest share of immigrants between 2006 and 2011 was drawn from Asia and the Middle East (57%)—a slight drop from 60 percent between 2001 and 2006. European-born immigrants represented the second largest group, with nearly 14 percent of arrivals (before 1971, Europeans accounted for 79% of all newcomers). The share from Africa and the Caribbean/South/Central America has increased slightly to 12.5 percent and 12.3 percent, respectively. Of the Asian immigrants, 13 percent of arrivals were from the Philippines (13%), followed by China and India at about 10.5 percent each.

- Overall, 95 percent of Canada's foreign born live in four provinces, with the largest proportion in Ontario at 53 percent, followed by British Columbia at 18 percent, Quebec at 14.5 percent, and Alberta at 9.5 percent.

- Ninety-one percent of foreign born immigrants live in one of Canada's 33 Census Metropolitan Areas (CMA), with about 63 percent of both recent arrivals and the total immigration population settling in Montreal, Toronto, or Vancouver.

- Toronto remains the destination of choice for new immigrants. The foreign born accounted for about 46 percent of Toronto's population in 2011, with the result being that 37.5 percent of all foreign born in Canada live in Toronto. About 33 percent of immigrants between 2006 and 2011 settled in Toronto, compared to Montreal at 16 percent of the total and Vancouver at 13 percent.

- Mid-size cities are also experiencing significant growth. Calgary took in 6 percent of newcomers, while Edmonton and Winnipeg each received about 4 percent of the total.

Racialized (Visible) Minorities

Canada's Employment Equity Act defines visible (or racialized) minority as persons other than aboriginal and who are non-Caucasian in race and non-white in colour. The main visible minority categories include South/Southeast/West Asian, Chinese, black, Filipino, Latin American, Arab, Korean, and Japanese.

- Racialized minorities now comprise 6.3 million persons or 19.1 percent of Canada's /population, up from 16.2 percent in 2006. Sixty-five percent of all racialized minorities were born outside Canada, including 78 percent of those who arrived between 2006 and 2012.

- The largest racialized minority groups are South Asians (25% of the total), followed by Chinese (21%) and blacks (15%). Most South Asians reported ancestral backgrounds from the Indian subcontinent, followed by Pakistan and Sri Lanka.

- Ninety-five percent of racialized minorities lived in Ontario, Quebec, Alberta, and BC. Ontario is home to just over one-half (52%) of the national total.

- Ninety-six percent of racialized minorities live in cities (compared to 68.1% of the general population), including 2.6 million in Toronto and 1 million in Vancouver. Montreal, Toronto, and Vancouver alone are home to 75 percent of all racialized minorities in Canada. Intra-urban numbers are no less impressive: For example, racialized minorities account for 72 percent of the population in Markham Ontario, 70 percent of Richmond B.C.'s residents, and 66 percent of Brampton Ontario's population. By contrast, cities such as Moncton, Trois-Rivières, and Saguenay reported statistically insignificant levels of racialized minorities.

- Nearly 43 percent of Canada's racialized minority population live in Toronto; coincidentally, the same percentage (about 43%) of Toronto's population is racialized.

- Vancouver's visible minority population accounts for 42 percent of its total population; the figure for Montreal is 16.5 percent, with the vast majority living on the island rather than in the suburbs.

Clearly, these diversity figures look impressive; however, a sense of perspective is helpful. First, compared with those of other countries, Canada's diversity figures pale. Many societies are inherently diverse, that is, poly-ethnic or multinational in composition. Only a few countries do not have significant minorities or divisions based on race or ethnicity, with the exceptions including some East Asian countries in addition to several Muslim-based countries from which long-established minorities have fled (Glazer, 2010). As well, many countries are increasingly diverse, thanks to overall immigration and refugee flows and expansion of **transmigrant** links and **transnational** patterns of identity and belonging (Fleras, 2014b). For example, just over 35 percent of the population in the United States is non-white; namely, African American, Hispanic, Asian American, and Native American. The comparable figure for Canada is about 25 percent. Much of Canada's diversity is collapsed into four major regions: the 401 corridor from Windsor to Greater Toronto, Montreal, Calgary/Edmonton, and the Lower Mainland in British Columbia. With the exception of Aboriginal peoples, the rest of Canada is largely devoid of non-European diversity.

Second, Canadians are conflicted about the value of diversity. Some reject the principle of diversity and associated practices as inimical to Canada's interests and national identity. Others endorse the value and contribution of diversity, not only as a defining characteristic of Canada but also as a strength that improves our quality of life. Diversity is thus double edged: It's a source of economic strength, social creativity and problem solving, cultural vitality, and national pride. It's also a recipe for social conflict, racial tension, political instability, and urban problems—from service demands and spiraling housing prices to the erosion of civic networks and interpersonal trust (also known as "social capital") (Fleras, 2016; Putnam, 2007). In other words, diversity may make human existence interesting because of the benefits it brings; at the same time, it can make life more challenging by fraying the strands of social fabric, especially when diversity becomes demanding and politicized.

Third, the politics of diversity are more perplexing than implied by the mantra "celebrating differences" (Fleras, 2015a). Without a powerful sense of national identity or well-defined dominant culture, Canadians are reluctant to impose their values and norms on others, in effect posing difficulties regarding "where to draw the line" (Allemang, 2005). But how much diversity (and diversities-within-diversity) can Canada tolerate before it spins out of control without a hub to hold everything together? How much unity does Canada need to survive without stifling creativity and social change in the process? What kind of diversity is appropriate for Canada? Many Canadians endorse superficial expressions of diversity that do not entail costs or create inconveniences; however, anxiety levels mount over those deep differences that not only challenge the legitimacy of Canadian values, but also reflect an intolerance of others, in effect violating a core multicultural principle of agreeing to disagree (Glazer, 2010). Where are the limits of Canada's multicultural tolerance? How can we live together with our differences without those differences and competing rights getting in the way of equality, dignity, and solidarity? How does a multicultural Canada accommodate differences without compromising the common values and the rule of law that holds it together? What principles or criteria should be employed in deciding which cultural and religious practices are unacceptable to Canadian society? Who decides—and on what grounds—what differences count as well as what counts as differences (Johnson, 1994)? The answers to these questions are varied and problematic. Nevertheless, one thing is certain: The prospect of governing a **complexly diverse** world (Latham, 2008) of multiethnic, multireligious, multiracial, and multicultural Canada will prove increasingly difficult and demanding (Fleras, 2011b, 2015a; Harell & Stolle, 2010).

GOVERNANCE MODELS FOR MANAGING RACE, ETHNIC, AND ABORIGINAL RELATIONS

What exactly is meant by the expression "race, ethnic, and aboriginal relations"? What should be included in a study of race, ethnicity, and aboriginality (see Banton, 2005; Solomos & Bulmer, 2005)? Central to the study in this domain are the dynamics of intergroup relations over time and across space (Marger, 2001). These intergroup relations exist because individuals with a shared culture and similar ancestral backgrounds continue to identify (or are identified by others) with each other and engage in behaviour that promotes their interests at the expense of others (Kivisto & Ng, 2005). To be sure, pure racial, ethnic, and aboriginal groups do not exist. Nor is it accurate to say that "races" interact with each other, although relationships may involve perceptions of race. But because a significant racial, ethnic, and aboriginal component may inform the dynamics of intergroup relations, references to race or ethnicity may be invoked to (1) mobilize like-minded individuals into action, (2) justify patterns of action or inaction toward groups, and (3) provide a convenient label to simplify otherwise complex intergroup relations (Taras & Ganguly, 2002).

What produces the "relations" in race, ethnic, and aboriginal relations? A series of prolonged contact situations may account for various intergroup relations in ethnically mixed societies. First, a **dominant group** incorporates or annexes a foreign territory by force or "rights of (European) discovery." The British conquest of the French on the Plains of Abraham in 1759 is an example of this, one that continues to rankle and provoke. The colonization of Turtle Island (North America) by French, British, and Spanish settlers and opportunists has proven no less provocative. Second, colonization and frontier expansion result in the acquisition of land or resources through diplomatic channels. Territories may be acquired by purchase or through treaties such as those between Canada's Aboriginal peoples and the Crown. Forced migration is a third possibility that involves a foreign population being forcibly brought into the country for essentially exploitative purposes. The importation of Africans for slave labour into the United States—and into Canada, albeit on a more limited basis—is a classic example. Fourth, voluntary migration from overseas entails some degree of choice in making the move. It stands to reason that the interests and aspirations of "voluntary migrants" will differ from the interests of those who have been forcibly incorporated through annexation or colonization.

Sustained contact between and among groups invariably leads to a patterned network of intergroup relations. Ranging in scope from hostility to acceptance, with varying levels of accommodation in between, the exact trajectory of these intergroup dynamics will vary with the nature of the contact situation—its duration, timing, conflicts of interest, magnitude, and intensity. In most ethnoracially diverse countries, one group tends to be dominant because of military might or technological prowess. Both national governance and social institutions are organized around its agenda and priorities—and are enforced accordingly, either by consent or by coercion. By contrast, **subdominant minority group** members are disadvantaged in the competition for power or privilege and often have little option except to comply and obey—or else. Interaction based on these dominant–subdominant relationships gives rise to a limited number of patterned responses that can be collapsed into five governance models for "managing" diversities, namely *genocide, assimilation, segregation, integration,* and *pluralism.* In theory, each of these governance models reflects a set of assumptions about the status of difference in society, the preferred relationship between dominant and subdominant groups, prescriptions for managing diversities, and proposed outcomes for society-building. In reality, however, these governance models are neither uniformly consistent nor strictly separate from each other. Overlap is the rule rather than the exception only because reality itself is contextual rather than categorical. Moreover, these governance models are not always explicitly articulated as political preference, official governance, or codified into law, but in many cases they are, and that makes it doubly important to frame the management of race, ethnic, and aboriginal relations from a governance perspective.

Genocide

Genocide may be the most serious of punishable crimes under international law, and one of the few crimes for which UN military intervention supersedes the principle of state sovereignty. The concept of genocide encompasses a broad range of activities, according to the UN-based convention of 1948, including five classes of action: (1) the annihilation of group members with the intent of bringing about their disappearance as a people; (2) the creation of conditions such as destruction of community life that foster the dispersal of the group, in the process pushing remnants of the population to an edge from which recovery is difficult; (3) inflicting intense psychological abuse or physical discomfort culminating in the dissolution of the group; (4) the transfer of children from one group to another, thus bringing about the demise of the culture; and (5) the prevention of births through involuntary sterilization, birth control, or abortion (Stote, 2015).

Despite (or perhaps because of) its scope, genocide has proven difficult to define—a situation that *conveniently* impedes humanitarian assistance or UN-based intervention, even in contexts of extreme duress (Caplan, 2005). Generally speaking, most definitions include the notion of deliberate and systematic mass killings of a despised domestic minority who live in a territory controlled by often government-backed killers (Taras & Ganguly, 2002). A state that openly condones violence against its own citizens furnishes the key criterion that distinguishes genocide from related crimes against humanity (Rummel, 2005). Slaughter of this magnitude may be accomplished directly through military means, or indirectly through the spread of disease (Moseby, 2013), loss of livelihood and starvation (Daschuk, 2013), compulsory sterilization (Stote, 2015), or forced re-socialization (Miller, 2013; Truth and Reconciliation Commission Report, 2015). Others prefer a more expansive definition that includes the unintended yet fatal consequences of seemingly well-intentioned policy initiatives toward the minorities within (Fontaine & Farber, 2013). For example, the proselytizing work of missionaries in tribal areas is deemed as genocidal in consequence because of the destruction wreaked on many Indigenous people's communities.

Very few calamities meet UN criteria for genocide. Clear-cut examples of such catastrophes include the extermination of German Jews (and other "undesirables") under Nazi Germany, the Rwandan crisis in 1994 in which Tutsi (and moderate Hutu) were slaughtered by Hutu extremists, and the mass deportation and killings of Armenians by Turks between 1915 and 1917 (this charge is disputed by Turkey). Also widely viewed as genocidal were the **ethnic cleansing** campaigns by Serbs against Muslim populations in Bosnia, including the slaughter of 7000 Muslims in Srebenica in 1995. History is replete with genocidal-like purges of dehumanized minorities—whether deliberate or unintentional. In asserting colonial control over a land they saw as *terra nullius*, European settlers openly stalked and killed Australia's aboriginal populations. Likewise, Aboriginal peoples such as the Beothuk in Newfoundland lapsed into extinction because of disruptive contact with early European colonialists. The twentieth-century killing fields were no less punitive: Ukrainians suffered massive losses in famines engineered by Stalinist purges; the Khmer Rouge massacred up to 2 million Cambodians during the late 1970s; and the blatant mistreatment of indigenous populations by Brazilian settlers and miners in the Amazonian rainforest resulted in massive disruption to lives and livelihoods.

Violence is frequently endemic to genocides. As people are hacked, bludgeoned, raped, or shot to death, this butchery often comes across as random and uncontrollable. But appearances can be deceiving. This mass liquidation process is neither an isolated act nor an unintentional one perpetrated by poorly disciplined militia. The killing fields are neither an unfortunate byproduct of dormant tribal hatred nor a spontaneous spasm of uncontrolled primeval rage. To the contrary, genocide represents a calculated political decision to achieve political goals in a premeditated manner (Midlarsky, 2005). An orchestrated campaign of terror that sanctions the dehumanization and destruction of the "other" is activated to remove competitors or silence opponents. For example, the Darfuri conflict may be driven by a crude racist ideology of Arab supremacism for cleansing North African tribes. Competition for scarce resources is no less critical, as African farmers and nomadic Arab herders compete for what little land there is in the face of creeping desertification, followed by a fierce government crackdown on Darfuri insurgents who attacked a government outpost (Wrzesnewskyj, 2005). What may look like mindless aggression is often a ruthless strategy to defend a sacred ideal, to destroy a group perceived as a threat to the ruling regime, to diminish those who are hated or envied, to eliminate foreign elements from society, to consolidate elite advantage, or to secure economic gain (Rummel, 2005; see also Koenigsberg, 2004). In short, genocide does not necessarily erupt because of primitive urges, tribal hatred, or dormant hostilities. Outside of local outbursts that may spiral out of control, genocide involves the manipulation of racialized differences by cynical elites who will stop at nothing to retain power, achieve advantage, secure political support, conceal economic difficulties, and distract from internal squabbles (Ignatieff, 1995). The resurgence of genocide in recent years is as disconcerting as it is disturbing—disconcerting because many thought we had put that part of history behind us; disturbing because of the intensity and savagery that accompany the killings (Caplan, 2005, 2007).

Why have such crimes against humanity proven so common in recent years, despite seemingly severe sanctions and global outrage (Tatum, 2010)? How and why do neighbours who share social and cultural space suddenly "run amok" into murderous enemies? This lust for killing may compel a rethinking of human nature. That is: Are humans naturally good, but twisted by social circumstances beyond their control? Are genocides exceptions to the rule of natural goodness—even if many humans may be capable of unspeakable crimes against humanity under specific circumstances (Caplan, 2005)? Or, alternatively, are people naturally evil in the Hobbesian sense of living lives that are "nasty, brutish, and short," with the result that genocides reflect our hard-wiring as a flawed species? If this is the case, should we be asking ourselves if, in fact, the rules of law and reason are contrary to the human condition and secured only by an unremitting struggle that "goes against the grain" of doing what comes naturally (Ignatieff, 1994)? Perhaps John Maynard Keyes got it right when he claimed: "Civilisation is a thin and precarious crust, erected by the personality and will of the few, and only maintained by rules and conventions skillfully put across and guilefully preserved" (as cited in Skidelsky, 2004).

Assimilation

Generally speaking, **assimilation** has been referred to as a one-way process of absorption. The concept was borrowed from biology (absorption through digestion) and reflects a largely mistaken belief that social life could be better understood by drawing upon simplified analogies with the natural world (Jaret, 1995). But assimilation is rarely a simple and straightforward activity when applied to the human condition. It represents a complex and multidimensional process that unwinds at a varying pace, sometimes deliberately but often unconsciously, involves different intensities of absorption, ranges in scope from cultural to the social, and entails varying degrees of conformity (Zhou, 1997).

More specifically, assimilation involves a process whereby the dominant sector imposes its culture, authority, values, and institutions on subdominant sectors with a corresponding loss of their distinctiveness because of exposure to these conformity pressures. In the past, assimilation was endorsed as an official government policy in framing majority–minority relations. Under assimilation, all migrants and minorities were expected to adopt the cultural values and social practices of the ruling majority, if only to secure the grounds for centralized control and smooth governance. Yet, assimilationist policies were rarely intended to transform minorities in their entirety. The complete absorption of everybody was neither easily attained nor always desired; after all, few majorities possessed either the resources or the political will to enforce wholesale conformity. Endorsed instead was a commitment to dominant-conformity (or **anglo-conformity** in areas under British control). A dominant-conformity model required outward compliance with dominant values and practices rather than actual absorption into the mainstream, especially if the minority in question was deemed incapable of such a transition. To the extent that conformity, not uniformity, prevailed, select elements of a subdominant lifestyle could be tolerated as long as they (1) were restricted to the private or personal realm, (2) did not challenge prevailing patterns of authority, (3) conformed to majority notions of decency, and (4) did not violate moral principles or the law of the land.

Assimilation emerged as an "enlightened" social policy for its time, especially when compared with alternatives such as segregation, expulsion, or genocide. A commitment to assimilation secured a governance framework for managing Indigenous peoples in settler societies (Coulthard, 2014; Pearson, 2001). At times, this commitment was tacitly assumed as a guideline for government-Indigenous peoples' relations; at other times, it was explicitly articulated as official government policy. Through assimilation, the dominant element sought to (1) undermine the cultural basis of indigenous societies, (2) expose individuals to dominant norms as normal and acceptable, (3) convert the Indigenous people into patriotic, productive, and God-fearing citizens, and (4) facilitate their entry and transition into the mainstream. Dominant values, beliefs, and social patterns were valorized as inevitable or desirable; conversely, differences were demonized as inferior or irrelevant. Such Eurocentrism proved both paternalistic and patronizing. Those singled out for assimilation were often portrayed as children in need of discipline under the ever-vigilant eye of a judicious parent.

Recourse to assimilation no longer reigns as an explicit policy principle. There is little inclination to openly support an assimilationist agenda that once dismissed cultural differences as inferior, irrelevant, or a liability. Instead of a weakness to be denied or excluded, diversity is now touted as a strength to be nurtured, especially in padding the bottom line or as a gateway to global markets. Yet appearances can be deceiving: Although publicly scorned and officially rebuked as a model for managing diversity, assimilation as a process continues to play a prominent role in molding immigrants into the mainstream, reasserting core values, and excluding those who don't fit. Even in Canada, where diversity under an official Multiculturalism is respected, a degree of conformity is mandatory (for example, only French or English as languages of public communication) for any hope of success or advancement (Li, 2003). Moreover, as racialized minorities become increasingly involved in the mainstream, assimilation is proving the rule rather than the exception, given the often unintended consequences of choices made by individuals who are looking to settle down, fit in, and move up. Assimilation may unfold informally as well: Consider how the offspring of immigrants intermarry, live in demographically diverse neighbourhoods, are employed in all economic sectors (including "white-collar" jobs), and share comparable levels of education and income with other groups (Denton & Tolnay, 2002). Finally, assimilation can also be inferred as the logic underlying all government actions. The logical consequences of even seemingly progressive initiatives to assist racialized minorities (e.g., employment equity initiatives) may have the effect of assimilating them deeper into the system.

Segregation/Separation

The concept of **segregation** provides another governance model in the management of intergroup relations. Segregated societies are segmented into relatively autonomous dominant and subdominant groups who live apart because of perceived incompatibilities and power relations. The role of governments is critical in segregating within unequal contexts. In cases of *de jure* segregation, the government deliberately keeps the groups apart, thus stigmatizing and handicapping the vulnerable by confining them to inferior facilities. A *de facto* segregation results when the government tacitly condones a forced segregation by not actively intervening to dismantle the barriers that exclude and divide.

Segregation involves a forced and physical separation. Contact between the groups is kept to an absolute minimum, except in contexts of obvious benefit to the controlling sector. What little interaction exists is conducted primarily in the marketplace ("selective incorporation"), where the dominant group exercises monopolistic control over the economy and distribution of wealth. Compliance in unequal contexts is rarely secured by voluntary consensus of cultural values or social norms. In the absence of any morally legitimate basis to govern, the dominant group must rely on physical threats to compel obedience. Moreover, segregation can go beyond a physical separation of unequal groups. A social relationship involving unequal patterns of power and domination is also implicated (Jaret, 1995). The dominant group defines itself as superior because of technological prowess, military might, and moral superiority. "Others" are dismissed as inferior or irrelevant—or a threat—to the society-building process.

History is rife with governance models that segregate groups from one another. Few scenarios of segregation have been as highly profiled as that of apartheid in South Africa. A comprehensive set of segregation laws and practices were established that compartmentalized blacks and whites into separate groups at social, economic, and political levels. No less segregationist was the colour bar that existed in both the United States and Canada (Horton & Horton, 2004). Blacks were segregated from whites at institutional, occupational, interactional, and residential levels, in large part because of the power of the Ku Klux Klan, which terrorized the American South. To the dismay of many Canadians, many parts of Canada were no less segregated because of colour bars at schools, in public institutions, and in residential areas (Walker, 1997). Finally, the establishment of Canada's reserve system under the *Indian Act* of 1876 may also be interpreted as a version of segregation—at least in consequence if not intent—in light of the government's long-standing commitment to "no more Indians" as a solution to the so-called "Indian problem."

Segregation as a governance model is usually generated from the top down. It can, however, also be generated from below by groups who prefer **voluntary separation** from a society for lifestyle reasons or strategic purposes. Voluntary separation is not the same as segregation or apartheid, despite similarities in appearance and structure. Racialized minorities, Indigenous peoples, and religious groups may prefer to isolate themselves from the mainstream to preserve their independence and identity. For example, the Hutterites of western Canada and other communal religious sects have voluntarily divorced themselves from the outside world through expressions of religion, language, communal lifestyle, dress, and social interaction. Aboriginal peoples, too, are casting about for aboriginal models of self-determined autonomy as a basis for living *separately* together (Maaka & Fleras, 2005). Separatist ethnicities under a sovereign Québécois nationalism are also seeking to strategically "separate" from Canada without actually leaving it.

Integration

Integration represents a fourth model of governance for managing diversity-based intergroup relations. It emerged as a preferred governance model after World War II, owing to a growing disillusionment with alternative models for living together. Resentment over segregation was particularly notable because of international conventions that sought to protect human rights through the removal of discriminatory barriers. Of particular note was the mounting assertiveness by blacks and Aboriginal peoples, who bristled over second-class treatment in a Canada that had gone to war to protect overseas freedom but denied it to their own citizens. The concept of integration stood in opposition to that of segregation—defined as the forced separation of people who live apart from each other, socially and geographically. **Integration,** by contrast, involves a process whereby individuals interact with each other at all institutional levels (Jaret, 1995). A distinction between desegregation and integration is also useful. **Desegregation** entails dismantling physical or social barriers to formal equality; integration is seen as the positive dimension that incorporates disparate parts into a cooperative and functioning whole.

The concept of integration may have originated to describe social patterns, but references to integration now include a cultural dimension. Two variations underlie the integration-as-culture theme.

First, integration represents a two-way process of adjustment by which the dominant and subdominant sectors are brought together in a single comprehensive lifestyle, without either losing its distinctiveness. Whereas assimilation endorses a one-way process of absorption in which minority identities are folded into the mainstream, integration upholds a reciprocating system of synthesis that proposes full and equal participation without relinquishing cultural identity as the price of admission. The Council of the European Union (2004) adopted a set of principles that defined integration as a dynamic, two-way process of accommodation involving the host country that adapts to newcomer needs and immigrants who adopt to mainstream values.

A second variant involves a process by which the dominant and the subdominant groups merge together, like different colours of paint in a bucket. The result of this "blending" process is a new cultural entity, metaphorically captured by the concept of the **melting pot.** As an image that is often invoked to describe, and prescribe, American race and ethnic relations, all immigrants can be transformed into new Americans—a cultural alloy forged in the crucible of democracy, freedom, and civic responsibility (Glazer, 1997). To be sure, however popular and useful it may be, metaphors such as the "melting pot" are problematic shorthands because they grossly distort reality by oversimplifying complex issues (Kivisto & Ng, 2005). Immigrants to the United States are expected to create a new amalgam by melting into the American pot, yet this cauldron remains irrefutably "pale male" in composition and control. Any restructuring of American society is recast along the lines and priorities of the prevailing institutional framework, while the subdominant sector simply adds a "dash of spice" to an otherwise monocultural stew.

The concept of integration continues to attract growing attention (Alba & Foner, 2015; Craig, 2015; Wong & Tezli, 2013). An unprecedented movement of people across borders and continents puts pressure on societies to initiate interventions to facilitate their integration into the mainstream (George, 2006). The decline of multiculturalism as governance in many parts of the world has yielded a commitment to "civic integration" as a preferred governance model for managing diversity. And yet despite (or perhaps because of) its popularity, the concept of integration remains poorly defined or theorized. For some, integration falls somewhere in between multiculturalism and assimilation; for others, it's little more than a watered-down version of assimilation (Fekete, 2010). The outcomes of both integration and assimilation may be indistinguishable in practice, despite seemingly different starting points. Not surprisingly, while some associate integration with the attainment of equality and participation, others conjure up images of unwanted conformity, and still others wonder what all the fuss is about.

Pluralism

Many countries are seeking to come to terms with difference and diversity (Rex, 2004), yet the governments of these countries find themselves in a governance quandary. On the one hand, countries have historically sought the attainment of a culturally and linguistically homogeneous population, resulting in a deliberate rejection of difference (Guibernau, 2007). On the other, government policies that once diminished the value of difference for society-building now acknowledge the benefits of more inclusive models of race, ethnic, and Aboriginal relations. This acceptance of the legitimacy of diversity as a basis for governance within a national framework is called **pluralism**. Pluralism goes beyond a simple recognition of the existence of racial or ethnic minorities in society. It also acknowledges the possibility of constructing a unified society from (or despite) differences as a desired and valued component of progressive society. Not surprisingly, some degree of government intervention may be required to protect and promote minority needs, in part by reaffirming individual rights, rectifying past injustices, reducing social inequities by removing discriminatory barriers, providing positive actions through employment equity programs, and ensuring the protection of traditional language and culture.

Both culture-blind and culture-conscious variants of pluralism can be discerned. For some, a pluralistic society is one that ignores differences as a basis for rewards and recognition, thereby ensuring that everyone is equal before the law regardless of race or ethnicity. In that no minority group receives special treatment, neither positive nor negative, a society of many cultures is possible as long as people's cultural differences stay out of the public domain. For others, a pluralistic society is one that recognizes the centrality of differences to ensure that no one is excluded precisely because of their difference-based needs. Incorporating diversity as a basis for entitlements and recognition creates a culture-conscious model that embraces a dual ideal: People must be treated equally ("similarly") as a matter of course; they must also be treated as equals ("differently") as situations arise. In other words, a society of many cultures is possible if people's cultural differences are taken into account when necessary to ensure equity, participation, and inclusiveness.

A commitment to pluralism can be expressed in diverse ways—multiculturalism, biculturalism, binationalism, and multinationalism. Canada's pluralistic commitments are enshrined in the concept of an official Multiculturalism. Canada endorses the principles of ethnic and racialized diversity by creating a social climate in which everyone is different yet equal, no one is excluded from full and equal participation because of race or ethnicity, and institutional space is created for allowing all Canadians to interact without fear of ethnic entanglements. The United States has also experienced a multicultural turn in recent years (Glazer, 1997), including a critically insurgent style of multiculturalism that differs sharply from Canada's consensus-oriented and inclusive **multiculturalism** (Fleras, 2001; Goldberg, 1994a). **Biculturalism** resembles multiculturalism in many ways, but focuses on the relationship between two major groups or peoples who share an often uneasy partnership in relation to the other. For example, biculturalism (or, more accurately, binationalism) describes the relationship between the indigenous Maori peoples and the non-Maori

TABLE 1-1	Race, Ethnic, and Aboriginal Relations as Governance Models			
Governance Model	Assumptions about Diversity	Policy Objectives	Proposed Means	Anticipated Outcomes
Genocide	despised	annihilation	violence	racial purity
Assimilation	irrelevant	absorption	conformity	one people
Segregation	isolated	separation	force	colour bar
Integration	tolerant of	desegregation/ fusion/two-way	incorporation	formal equality
Pluralism	acceptance	living together with differences	inclusiveness	Multiculturalism, biculturalism, multinationalism

in New Zealand/Aotearoa (Fleras & Spoonley, 1999; Maaka & Fleras, 2008). Finally, **multinationalism** refers to the possibility of a society of multiple nations or many peoples who see themselves as political communities—autonomous (sovereign) in their own right, yet sharing in the sovereignty of society (Asch, 1997; Maaka & Fleras, 2005). Canada is increasingly described as a multinational coalition comprising Aboriginal peoples, the Québécois, and the English-speaking sectors including immigrants and their descendants.

To summarize, recurrent responses and patterned outcomes occur when competitively different groups come into sustained contact. A network of patterned relations is established, many of which become formalized into explicit governance models for managing race, ethnic, and aboriginal relations. Policy outcomes vary and may include those that deny differences (assimilation), reject minorities (segregation), and demonize out-groups (genocide); as well as those that espouse formal equality (integration) and positively engage diversity (pluralism). To be sure, some degree of overlap and duplication is inevitable in making the distinction; after all, social reality cannot possibly be squeezed into static and exclusive categories. Moreover, while definitions are critical for analysis and assessment, they do run the risk of simplifying, essentializing, or reifying what in reality is complex, shifting, and contextual. Table 1-1 highlights some of the key features of each governance model by comparing them in terms of their assumptions about diversity, policy/program objectives, means, and outcomes.

THEORIZING INTERGROUP RELATIONS: SOCIOLOGICAL MODELS OF SOCIETY AS EXPLANATORY FRAMEWORKS

Sociology as a discipline is often defined as the scientific study of social reality within society. "Society" can most profitably be defined as a complex, contested, evolving, and unequal network of relations in the broadest sense of the term, ranging from the interpersonal to the international, with intergroup dynamics occupying an intermediate position. For sociologists, the centrality of social reality is critical to a study of society. What is the nature of this social reality? Is it prone to stability, order, and cooperation, or is the natural state inclined toward conflict, control, and disorder? How is it constructed, expressed, and sustained, as well as challenged, resisted, and transformed? To assist in answering these questions, different sociological paradigms are proposed. Each of the models, including **functionalism**, **conflict theory** (including feminist and Marxist streams), and **symbolic interactionism** differs from the others not only in how it analyzes and assesses social reality but also in how it explains the dynamics of intergroup relationships within society, the status of diversity in society, and its role in advancing societal interests.

Functionalism Model

Functionalist models of society provide a once-popular approach to the study of race, ethnic, and aboriginal relations. For functionalists, society is viewed as a complex and integrated whole comprising interrelated parts that collectively contribute to its maintenance and survival. Society is compared to a living organism; like any life form, it consists of parts that mesh for effective functioning, resists disruptive changes, and reacts to any invasion by isolating or removing the disruption to ensure stability and the status quo. Under optimal conditions, all elements of a society operate smoothly to enhance its success, but tensions and conflicts associated with intrusive social change may unravel these relationships to a point of temporary disarray. Corrective measures are activated to remove potentially disruptive situations, thus restoring society to its natural state of equilibrium and order.

For functionalists, the combination of consensus, cooperation, and control are the keys to a successful society. To achieve this highly desirable state of unity and order, all members of society (but especially minorities) must internalize core beliefs and values. Not surprisingly, functionalists endorse assimilation (or integration) as the preferred model for race, ethnic, and Aboriginal relations. Failure to assimilate diversity is viewed as a potential threat to society. Assimilationist interventions include education and mass media as institutions of (re)socialization; initiatives such as official Multiculturalism for fostering consensus and shared values; and the introduction of employment equity programs calculated to improve the process of gainful employment. The anticipated result? A smoothly functioning society/nation that defuses any disruptive potential for living together differently.

Radical Conflict Models: Feminist and Marxist

Radical conflict models of society differ sharply from a functionalist perspective. Whereas functionalists espouse a normative theory of societal stability and consensus, radical models emphasize control, contradiction, confrontation, and change. This perspective portrays society as a complex and unstable site of unequal yet competing groups in perpetual competition over scarce and valued resources. Dominant groups will rely on peaceful or violent methods to preserve privilege, property, and power. Subdominant sectors are more likely to challenge the status quo through different strategies of resistance, ranging from outright confrontation to passive resistance.

For conflict theorists, then, the normal state of society resonates with contradiction, conflict, and change. Instead of consensus or stability, society is held together by force or the threat of force to impose control and deference to authority, and to solidify the prevailing distribution of power, privilege, and property (income and wealth). To be sure, a conflict model does not posit a *perpetual* state of conflict and confrontation. Conflict theorists are usually interested in what happens in the in-between spaces between clashes. Certain

hegemonic (control through consensus) techniques are employed to maintain and legitimize a fundamentally unequal order without resorting to coercive tactics. At times, the dominant group is powerful enough to defuse the potential for overt conflict. At other times, even opposing groups find it mutually advantageous to put aside their differences in pursuit of common interests. This "double-edgedness" suggests that conflict and cooperation are strategically different dimensions of a single struggle.

With their focus on inequality and power, radical conflict models have proven valuable in explaining the politics of difference. One major variant (that many define as a distinct paradigm of society) is **feminist theory**. Like radical conflict models in general, a feminist perspective acknowledges the centrality of inequality and domination. Society is perceived as a site of domination in which institutions and values are designed and organized to reflect, reinforce, and advance male interests and priorities with respect to power, privilege, and property (Pateman, 1988). But perhaps unlike other conflict models, a feminist perspective begins with the assumption that there is nothing natural or normal about patriarchal (male) domination. Rather, these patterns of domination, control, and inequality are socially constructed and culturally specific. And just as male-stream societies tend to construct demeaning and debilitating images of women, so too are minority women (including aboriginal women, immigrant and refugee women, and women of colour) defined and dismissed as irrelevant, inferior, or a threat. But, paradoxically, the social construction of this reality points to a solution: What has been socially constructed through human interaction can also be deconstructed through interventions, then reconstructed to create a society of gender equality.

Another variant of conflict theory incorporates **Marxist** perspectives. Marxist conflict theory positions the concept of **class** at the heart of all exploitation and conflict. Marxists argue that the fundamental contradiction in any complex society entails two social classes: the working (subdominant) and the ruling (dominant) class. The ruling class profits by owning the means of production; members of the working class survive by selling their labour to the ruling class. The ruling class will do anything to facilitate the flow of profits, for example, shaving the costs of labour by creating split labour markets (paying some workers more than others), in part by fomenting internal divisions that pit worker against worker rather than against the true source of the exploitation. Over time, Marxist thinking has moved away from strict economic determinism, without discarding the importance of class relations to group dynamics. That is, intergroup relations may be shaped by economic forces in addition to the centrality of ideas in shaping outcomes. In short, minority women and men are seen as active subjects in solving problems, defending interests, and mobilizing into action groups—albeit in contexts and within structures seemingly beyond their control—rather than as passive objects victimized by impenetrable forces.

Symbolic Interactionism Model

Both functionalist and conflict models define society as taken-for-granted. Society is portrayed as durable and real, existing above and beyond the individual, yet exerting vast leverage over people's behaviour. By contrast, **symbolic interactionist models** begin with the notion of society as an ongoing human accomplishment. Instead of something "out there" and determinative, the social realities that comprise society are perceived as socially constructed through meaningful interaction. According to this outlook, people do not live in a predetermined world of mechanistic outcomes. Rather, reality is constructed by applying provisional meanings to a variety of situations. Once a situation has been defined and redefined, jointly linked lines of action are developed. Society—as the sum total of these personal and group interactions at a given point in time and space—emerges from the interplay of these joint linkages. Not surprisingly, intergroup dynamics are couched in the framework of constant flux, dynamic tension, mutual adjustment, negotiated compromise, and ongoing movement.

A similar line of reasoning applies to race, ethnic, and aboriginal relations. Intergroup relations are not defined by system needs, class conflict, or gender wars. On the contrary, they assume diverse forms as social constructions within specific contexts. Race, ethnicity, and aboriginality are treated as "factors" in defining situations, and action is taken on the basis of these definitions to create jointly linked patterns of interaction. In attempting to control or change the world they live in, minorities activate group-specific identities for advancing collective action, especially when there is a competitive advantage to group affiliation. Patterned interaction is thus generated and sustained by opposing elements that compete for definitional control of the situation to attract constituencies and promote interests. From a minority point of view, the question revolves around the benefits of working either within the system or outside of it. From a majority perspective the question is no less perplexing: Should minorities be allowed entry into the mainstream, or is it better to exclude them from meaningful involvement? These interactional styles and outcomes are not mutually exclusive, but intersect to create diverse group dynamics.

One variant of symbolic interactionism is known as **collective definition** (Blumer & Duster, 1980). A collective definition approach emphasizes the process by which intra- and intergroup relations are formulated and reformulated because of opposing dynamics (dualisms) that prevail within and between all groups. Both the dominant and subdominant groups may be internally divided into competing factions or dualisms. At least two factions exist within the dominant sector: There are those who support the inclusion (assimilation or integration) of minorities, especially if there is something to be gained by doing so, and others who prefer the status quo (and the prevailing distribution of power, privilege, and property) that excludes minorities from full and equal participation. The subdominant sector is no less divided. Those factions who insist on assimilation into the dominant sector as a solution to their problems compete with those who endorse separation through the creation of parallel institutions and independent power bases.

Summary

Sociological models of society—functionalism, radical conflict theory, and symbolic interactionism—provide distinctly different ways of looking at social reality. These ideal-typical models differ from each other in defining (a) the nature of society, (b) the normal state of society, (c) the key question about society, (d) society's guiding metaphor, (e) what holds society together, and (f) an assessment of society (see Table 1-2).

In drawing attention to some aspects of social reality but away from others, advocates of each model selectively emphasize those aspects of reality that enhance their respective standpoints, while downplaying those that are inconsistent with the model. For functionalists, society is seen as basically good; as a result, anything that contributes to this cohesion and consensus is deemed as functional, whereas anything that disrupts it is dysfunctional and must be removed. The fact that society is fundamentally sound in functionalist models means that any improvement must focus on changing the individual. By contrast, both variants of a radical conflict model see society as fundamentally exploitative and/or dominating. For conflict theorists, anything that contributes to this control and inequality is negatively framed; conversely, anything that challenges these unequal relations is defined as progressive. Inasmuch as individuals are basically good while society is evil, the social and structural must be the locus of transformative change. For social interactionists, society is neither good nor bad. It represents a contested site involving meaningful interaction; therefore, nothing should be prejudged but should be analyzed and assessed on the basis of context. Table 1-2 provides a comparison of these sociological models.

Each of these sociological models of society can also be applied to the diversity and difference domain of race, ethnic, and aboriginal dynamics. For functionalists, diversity and difference pose a potential problem in need of solutions for the smooth functioning of society. For conflict theorists, diversity and difference may be manipulated by the ruling classes to advance interests or the status quo. However, the politicization of diversities can challenge and change the system toward more equitable outcomes. For symbolic interactionists, diversity and difference are neither good nor bad, but subject to negotiation and accommodation as the situation is defined. To be sure, no sociological model of society or its application to race, ethnic, and Aboriginal relations is inherently more correct than the other. After all, social reality is experienced at times as stable, ordered, and cooperative. At other times, it is experienced as exploitative, domineering, and wildly out of control because of rapid social changes. At still other times, it is experienced as open to negotiation and construction; that is, instead of viewing the world as something beyond one's control, people can define situations in ways that address their interests and act accordingly. In other words, social reality is experienced along the combined lines proposed by functionalism, radical conflict theorists, *and* social interactionism. One way

TABLE 1-2	Sociological Models of Society			
	Functionalism	Radical Conflict Theory (Marxist-based)	Radical Conflict Theory (feminist-based)	Symbolic Interactionism
The Nature of Society	Integrated whole of interrelated and functional parts	Site of class inequality	Site of male domination	Ongoing human accomplishment
The Normal State of Society	Stability, order, consensus, cooperation	Competition, conflict, control, change	Domination, conflict, control, change	Dynamic interactional process
The Key Question about Society	How is order achieved?	How does inequality persist?	How is domination maintained?	How is reality socially constructed?
Society's Guiding Metaphor	Organism analogy	Combat zone	Gender wars	Unscripted reality show
What Holds Society Together	Shared consensus	Hegemony + threat of force + power	Hegemony + threat of force + power	Negotiation, compromise, and self-interest
An assessment of society	Society is good.	Society is exploitative.	Society is dominating.	Society is just a blank slate.

of evaluating the analytical value of each sociological model of society is by analyzing Canada's official Multiculturalism along these paradigmatic lines (see the Debate Revisited box, below).

Canada's Official Multiculturalism as Problem or Solution? Perspectives Matter

Public and political reaction to Canada's Multiculturalism is sharply varied. For some, official Multiculturalism is perceived as a good governance in securing harmony and providing benefits; for others, Multiculturalism is thought to be bad because of its tendency to divide, control, or distract; for still others, it is good *or* bad depending on the criteria or both good *and* bad because of the context (Fleras, 2002). Who is right, and on what grounds? How can sociological models of society provide a principled response?

A functionalist model of society acknowledges the positive contribution of Multiculturalism in creating a cohesive and consensual Canada. For functionalists, Multiculturalism is by definition "functional," in large part because it fosters a social climate in which culturally different individuals can live together equitably without their differences getting in way of a cooperative coexistence. A radical conflict model of society disagrees with this positive spin. While functionalists point to the role of Multiculturalism in contributing to stability, cooperation, and order, conflict models emphasize its centrality in advancing the inequalities of exclusion. According to conflict theorists, an official Multiculturalism is little more than a case of "ruling elites controlling unruly ethnics." It represents a calculated ploy employed by both the Canadian state and the ruling elites to secure consent in preserving the prevailing distribution of power, privilege, and property. A commitment to Multiculturalism as an impression management device tends to foster a false consciousness (hegemony). The real sources of exploitation in society are camouflaged either by proposing cultural solutions to structural problems or by fostering "blame the victim" models that draw attention away from systemic barriers.

The controlling dimensions of multiculturalism are particularly evident when applied to women. Certain forms of multiculturalism, particularly those *laissez-faire* European models, tend to promote group rights over the individual rights of women. According to feminist conflict theory, women may be victimized in those multicultural contexts that promote cultural differences or religious beliefs at odds with women's opportunities and rights, in the process raising the question of whether those sexist standards within faith-based groups constitute a reasonable limit on a woman's equality rights (Okin, 1999; Stein, 2007; Whyte, 2007).

(Continued)

In short, both versions of radical conflict theory tar multiculturalism with the sin of fostering the "illusion of inclusion" by invoking polite fictions to gloss over inconvenient truths.

Symbolic interactionists differ from functionalists or conflict theorists in their treatment of an official Multiculturalism. Rather than assessing it on a scale of good or bad, Multiculturalism is framed as a negotiated site involving socially constructed and meaningful interactions. People define situations in terms of their perception of Multiculturalism and then respond on the basis of these definitions. Multiculturalism itself becomes a site in which different interests interact to impose their definition of the situation at the expense of others. Within the dominant sector, Multiculturalism may be endorsed by some as a basis for economic growth or cultural vitality. It may be rejected by others as a recipe for disaster that inadvertently reinforces ethnic divisions and intergroup conflicts. Conversely, the subdominant sector may support Multiculturalism as a window of opportunity in levelling the playing field or, alternatively, as little more than a hegemonic device for co-opting minorities into the mainstream. The interplay of these factions contributes to the ongoing and socially constructed dynamic that animates the politics of Canada's official Multiculturalism.

Each sociological model of society casts a different spin on official Multiculturalism. Multiculturalism is seen as "functional" in bolstering the collective and moral sentiments upon which order and stability are conveyed; in "conflict" terms, Multiculturalism reflects, reinforces, and advances an unequal status quo by promoting a kind of "assimilation in slow motion"; and for social interactionists, Multiculturalism is part of a broader process of collectively and socially constructing reality. To be sure, none of the models describing the effect of Multiculturalism in advancing a particular vision of society is inherently superior to the other. Each paradigm reflects a particular vision of a changing and diverse society as inherently good, intrinsically bad, or situationally in-between. Insofar as there is no consensus regarding the value or priority of one model over another, the interplay of these models provides a more complex and comprehensive view of what is going on. For example, there is little doubt that a commitment to an official Multiculturalism has created a more open and tolerant society, in part by making open expressions of racism a social taboo (functionalism). By the same token, an official Multiculturalism also provides a polite fiction that papers over inconvenient realities related to discrimination, inequality, and power relations (radical conflict theory) (Fleras, 2014a). And lastly, Multiculturalism is differently defined by diverse stakeholders (from politicians to minority spokespersons) in advancing their respective interests. Preference for one perspective over another is rarely a case of right or wrong. Rather, the secret lies in acknowledging the multidimensionality of Multiculturalism as simultaneously positive yet negative, empowering yet disempowering, constraining yet constructed—depending on specific criteria, context, and consequences.

Chapter Highlights

- Sociological interest in race, ethnic, and aboriginal relations as unequal relations focuses on the politics of intergroup dynamics within the contexts of power, privilege, and property. The emphasis is on how these relationships of inequality are constructed, expressed, and supported, as well as challenged and transformed, by way of government practices, institutional reform, ideological shifts, and minority resistance.
- Perspectives matter: Compared to the past, Canada has come a long way in managing diversity more equitably. In contrast to human rights violations in other countries, Canada is indeed a paragon of progress. Compared with the ideals that Canadians espouse, Canada still has a long way to go before closing the gap.
- Canada is an extremely diverse society. However, it's not nearly as diverse as some other countries; its diversity comes with benefits and costs, and debates over how much and what kind of diversity persist.
- Governance models for managing race, ethnic, and aboriginal relations include genocide, assimilation, segregation, integration, and pluralism. These governance models differ in terms of assumptions about diversity, stated objectives, preferred means, and anticipated outcomes.
- Sociological models of society provide an explanatory framework for analyzing racial, aboriginal, and ethnic relations. Functionalist models are concerned with demonstrating how diversities are managed to ensure stability and order. Radical conflict models envision society as a site of competition for scarce resources. Symbolic interactionist models emphasize the socially constructed nature of minority–majority relations.
- The framing of official Multiculturalism as a governance model—good, bad, good *or* bad, or good *and* bad—provides insights into a key sociological truism: How one interprets the status of diversity in society depends on which sociological model of society is employed.

Review Questions

1. What is meant by the concept of race, aboriginal, and ethnic relations?
2. Briefly compare and contrast the concepts of genocide, assimilation, integration, segregation/separation, and pluralism as governance models for managing race, aboriginal, and ethnic relations in terms of how diversity is defined in relationship to society.
3. Explain the role and status of diversity in society from the perspective of functionalist, conflict, and symbolic interactionist models of society.
4. Select any issue or incident involving racial, ethnic, or aboriginal relations; for example, immigration. Analyze the issue or incident sociologically by incorporating functionalist, radical conflict, and symbolic interactionist models of society.
5. Canada's record in managing racial, ethnic, and aboriginal relations can be summed up by the expression "the good, the bad, and the in-between." Indicate what is meant by this expression. Do you agree or disagree with this assessment? Why?

CHAPTER 2

The Politics of Race

LEARNING OBJECTIVES

After reading this chapter, you will be able to:

1. Distinguish between race as a biological fiction and race as a socially constructed process ("racialization").

2. Appreciate how race mattered in the past, race matters at present, and race will continue to matter.

3. Explain why phenomenon such as race do not need to be real to exert real consequences.

4. Describe how whiteness as racial privilege can only operate in a society constructed around the principles of a systemic white supremacy.

5. Discuss how the concept of the "racial rashomon effect" informs the debate over the frequency and nature of police racial profiling.

DEBATE

Police Racial Profiling: A Few Bad Apples or a Rotten Institutional Barrel?

Canada confronts a paradox in race relations. Some believe that racism is under control, while others think it is out of control. There are those who individualize the scope of racism ("a few bad apples"), preferring to frame it as random and aberrant actions that transgress the norms of a progressive Canadian society. Others prefer to emphasize its frequency, pervasiveness, and corrosive effects by framing it as institutionalized, deeply embedded within the fabric of a racialized society, resistant to change because of systemic barriers, and reflective of a system that is fundamentally rotten to the core, with the "bad apples" simply a manifestation of the creeping rot (Gosine, 2003). This perceptual divide is largely racialized (Newman, 2012). Minority discourses criticize Canada as a systemically racist society in need of transformation from the top down. For the mainstream, however, Canada is seen as fundamentally benevolent, with a few untutored lumps to spoil an otherwise healthy brew. A similar perceptual gulf prevails in the United States, where public attitudes toward the criminal justice system bifurcate

(Continued)

along racialized lines (Hurwitz & Peffley, 2010). Whites overwhelmingly see the system as colour-blind and fair (i.e., the "few bad apples" thesis), whereas blacks tend to perceive it as colour-coded and institutionally biased against them (i.e., the "whole rotten barrel" thesis) (Tator & Henry, 2006).

Nowhere is this polarization more evident than in the controversies swirling around the politics of police **racial profiling**. In the United States, cell phone video footage has caught law enforcement officers using excessive force while targeting a number of unarmed black men who were shot and killed for actions or evasions that normally don't require lethal force according to standard police training protocols (Taibbi, 2015; Wright, 2015). These high-profile killings quickly galvanized into a series of protest actions. The 2014 Pulitzer Prize winning paper, *the Guardian*, also reported that in the first half of 2015, 102 of the 464 individuals killed by police in the United States were unarmed, with blacks accounting for 32 percent of the victims and Latinos, just over 25 percent (Swaine, Laughland, & Lartey 2015).

In Canada, the issue of police racial profiling pivots around the debate over police stops (Cole, 2015; Rankin & Winsa, 2012). The police practice of stopping individuals not under arrest and entering their information into a massive database (a practice known as "carding") is not nearly as random as supporters contend, with Toronto blacks stopped at three times their rate in the population (blacks are also three times more likely to be carded by police in the Peel Region [Grewal, 2015]). A one-year study of police

stops in Kingston (Closs & McKenna, 2006; Wortley, 2005) arrived at a similar conclusion; namely, the significant over-representation of young black males stopped by police in proportion to their population. An internal report prepared for the Montreal police in 2009 (yet quietly shelved despite a database of 163 000 "contact reports") concluded that 40 percent of young black men in the communities of Montreal North and Saint Michel were stopped and asked for identification between 2006 and 2007, compared to approximately 5 percent of young white men in the same local population (Curran, 2010).

Let's put these findings into perspective: Statistical evidence suggests that police engage in some kind of differential policing that is tantamount to racial profiling (Tator & Henry, 2006). To the extent that disagreement exists over this charge, it tends to focus on the amount, scope, and rationale behind this practice (see Satzewich & Shaffir, 2009). For some, the fact that blacks are disproportionately stopped by the police is overwhelming proof of "anti-black racism" (James, Este, & Bernard, 2010). The police don't stop *what* they see (i.e., criminal behaviour), but stop *who* they see (i.e., racialized minorities). For others, the reports are dismissed as proving nothing or as methodologically flawed (Melchers, 2005). As far as the police are concerned, argues Mike McCormack, president of the Toronto Police Association (2015), only criminal behaviour is profiled, regardless of race or ethnicity, so that what critics claim is racial profiling constitutes instead a legitimate exercise in crime prevention (see Satzewich & Shaffir, 2009). For still others, the numbers do not speak for themselves. Yes, the data indicate disproportionality in stops, but statistics themselves cannot prove profiling, although the alarming amount of video footage coming to light would strongly suggest a pattern of racial bias in law enforcement (see also Swaine, Laughland, & Lartey 2015). Therein lies a troubling question: If the police don't racially profile, why does it appear *as if* they do, and what do they plan to do about righting this perceptual bias (Fleras 2014a)?

So what is going on? Who is right? Are appearances deceiving (Wortley, 2005; Wortley & Tanner, 2003)? Do the data point to an anti-black bias by police? Or is it the case that young black males are more likely to engage in unlawful or suspicious behaviour?

Are they more likely to attract police attention because of their visibility within public spaces? Do police engage in criminal profiling based on unlawful behaviour? How racialized are police actions for the purposes of control, (i.e., motivated by racialized stereotypes [Wortley, 2005])? Is a luxury car stopped because its driver is speeding, or because the driver fits a certain profile? If the police do profile, what is the nature of this profiling—random/isolated/individualized ("few bad apples") or institutionalized/routine/pervasive (the "whole rotten barrel")? Is it possible to explain in a principled way these divergent reactions to charges of police profiling? The Debate Revisited box at the end of this chapter will address these questions.

INTRODUCTION: "THE POWER OF A PERCEPTION"

Few will dispute the historical significance of **race** in shaping group outcomes and intergroup dynamics (Comack, 2011; Fleras, 2014a). References to race not only rationalized nineteenth-century European colonization, but also conferred a pseudo-scientific legitimacy that pigeonholed groups of people into mutually exclusive categories of unequal worth. The classification of colonized peoples into racialized "others" secured a simple yet self-serving explanation during the era of European exploration, capitalistic expansion, colonial settlements, and imperialist adventures. Race "mattered" for various reasons, but primarily as (1) a tool for justifying control and inequality, (2) an excuse for doing the inexcusable, (3) a framework for explaining the sweep of human differences, and (4) a rationalization for salving guilty consciences over un-Christian-like actions. The concept of race may have been little more than a fiction—a widely accepted **discourse** in defense of white domination—but its capacity to inflict injury was anything but fictitious.

That race mattered in the historical past is beyond doubt (Wallis & Fleras, 2008). In both the United States and Canada, an essentialized vision of race as natural and universal was widely assumed (Dalmage, 2004). Rather than simply an error of perception or exercise in rationalization, as Goldberg (2002) and others note (Thobani, 2007), the race concept justified the indefensible in enslaving or exploiting tribal peoples; it also facilitated the emergence of the modern nation-state, with whites as the dominant racial frame in control of a caste-like system. But many are dismayed that race continues to matter at a time when it shouldn't because, frankly, we should know better (Frederico & Luks, 2005; Tolley, 2015). Perceptions of race persist in exerting a pervasive influence at many different levels of lived reality—from where people live, to whom they hire, to what they can expect from life, to a construct for organizing social relations and decision making (Meer & Nayak, 2013). Race as a proxy for "inferior" or "disadvantaged" remains a tainted status or stigma of incompetence that is both deeply discrediting and shameful and that hinders and hurts. Race matters because it constitutes a lived experience for many, since a person's (or group's) perceived racial location in society influences their identity, experiences, opportunities, and outcomes. Insofar as social rewards are allocated on the basis of racial affiliation, race remains a key predictor of who gets what—of success or failure—not because minorities are racially inferior, but because people perceive others to be different and deficient, and rely on the power of those perceptions to deny or exclude. In other words, race isn't real in the naturally occurring sense of the world, but because people believe it's real, they act accordingly (as pointed out in the Debate at the start of this chapter) (Galabuzi, 2006; Hier & Bolaria, 2007). That race profiling remains a major problem in the policing of young black males (prompting references to the Summer of 2014 and the riots in Ferguson, Missouri as "the return of race to the national agenda" in the United States [Wallace-Wells, 2014]) reinforces a key theme of this chapter: race matters because it's a difference that makes a difference in increasing the probability of making (often bad) things happen.

The fact that race continues to matter for precisely the same reasons as it did in the past—to explain or to rationalize for purposes of control, exclusion, or exploitation those who are racially coded (that is, "racialized" or defined as different and inferior) (Dei, 2005, 2006)—should be cause for concern (Alexander, 2012). Moreover there is good reason to believe that race will matter in the future: First, racialized minorities will continue to foreground race as a component of identity, a source of discontent, and a platform for grievance resolution; second, societies will remain systemically racialized. Despite claims to postracial and race neutrality, societies continue to be designed, organized, and prioritized around whiteness as a dominant racial frame in defining what is normal, desirable, and acceptable. For example, Canadian society is neither as colour-blind nor as race-neutral as many claim. To the contrary, it is profoundly racialized in its founding assumptions, foundational principles, Eurocentric constitutional order, and governance structures that cumulatively advance dominant interests and agendas (see Doane, 2007; Goldberg, 2002; Mills, 1997; Omi & Winant, 1994). And as long as whiteness retains its privileged status in white superiority ("supremacist") societies that, paradoxically, claim to be colour-blind and race-neutral, race will continue to matter in privileging some while disempowering others (Cose, 1997; Morris & Cowlishaw, 1997).The institutionalization of a racialized and white supremacist Canada is conveyed by Constance Backhouse (1999:274) who chides the temptation to eliminate race from historical consideration in the mistaken hope of sugarcoating the past, the present and the future:

> . . . proponents of "race-neutrality" neglect to recognize that our society is not a race-neutral one. It is built upon centuries of racial division and discrimination. The legacy of such bigotry infects all of our institutions, relationships, and legal frameworks. To advocate "colour-blindness" as an ideal for the modern world is to adopt the false mythology of "racelessness" that has plagued the Canadian legal system . . . and serve[s] to condone the continuation of white supremacy across Canadian society.

Such persistence raises a perplexing question: Instead of being banished to the dustbins of history, as might be expected of this erroneous notion, the seemingly antiquated concept of race persists and provokes (Sarich & Miele, 2004; Wade, 2014). Why does a largely discredited concept from the past enjoy such enduring power in a pro-multicultural Canada that aspires to a post-racial status (Fleras, 2014a)? Divergent opinions are expressed by those who try to account for this persistence (Park, 2013). Some believe race is real and must be taken into account in explaining social reality. Others believe race should never enter public discourse because whatever heuristic explanatory value it possesses is offset by the damage inflicted through prejudice and stereotyping. In other words, critics purport that races do not exist, only perceptions of race categories that are elevated to objective status with material consequences. Still others see race as a biologically based ideological construction that is influential in shaping identities and predicting success (Harding, 2002). Although many reject the concept of race as scientifically valid, race matters not because it's biologically real, but because people perceive it to be real or act *as if* it were real, with often deadly consequences, in effect reaffirming W. I. Thomas's prescient notion that "phenomena do not have to be real to be real in their consequences."

Canadians appear to be deeply conflicted over the concept of race. In the merit-based and achievement-oriented society that Canada aspires to be, references to race are thought to be retrograde or offensive, especially when the value of a person is based on a stigma beyond one's control. A preoccupation with race compromises the so-called colour-blind principles of meritocracy ("individuals get what they deserve based on what they do rather than who they are") and liberal universalism, with its assertion that our commonalities as freewheeling individuals are more important for the purposes of recognition or reward than what divides us as members of racially distinct groups. And yet the paradoxes of race are all too real (Wallis & Fleras, 2008). Canadians explicitly reject the race concept, yet unconsciously employ race to make sense of the world. Race may be an accident of birth, but it profoundly molds a person's life or life chances. Race may be only skin deep, but it remains a marker of a person's worth and a predictor of success. Race should never justify differential treatment, either positive or negative, yet it is increasingly included as a tool for reversing discrimination (for example, reference to race as a proxy for disadvantage justifies race-based solutions, such as Employment Equity or affirmative action). Finally, reference to race is rejected in evaluating capacity and talents. Nevertheless, Canadians implicitly condone a race-based and unequal status quo that mocks Canada's Multiculturalism principles and inclusiveness commitments.

For many, the race concept has outlived its utility as social phenomenon; for others, it remains as relevant as ever as an explanatory framework; for still others, it serves as an indicator of identity, community, and history, even if utilizing racial categories may well intensify the injustice by reifying race (Goldberg & Solomos, 2002). Those who endorse the race concept tend to be dismissed as little more than "knuckle-dragging Neanderthals." Conversely, those who dismiss race as a fantasy are criticized for compromising a people's realities by trampling on their lived-experiences and desired identities. The dangers of delving into a topic that is both real yet surreal are captured below:

> [Race] . . . can be seen as nothing but a phantom invented to justify a myriad of power relationships but, on the other hand, is one of history's most instrumental agencies of social composition. How does one write about the most potent instrument of taxonomy ever imposed on humankind without giving added credence to the idea of race as a viable organizing tool? (Hall, 2000:120)

Not surprisingly, like sex in Victorian England, race is a taboo topic in contemporary polite society (Vucetic, 2014). Canadians appear reluctant to talk about race for fear it may provide more credibility than the term deserves, while reflecting poorly on anyone who dares use the *r* word in public. George Sefa Dei (2004) nails it succinctly when he alludes to race as the elephant in the room that everyone wants to ignore:

> Race has powerful material, political, and economic currency in our society. Rather than dismiss race, we ought to be honest about it and spend time reflecting on it through critical discussion, instead of sweeping it under the carpet and hope that this will settle everything. Racial categories such as "black," "white," and "brown," etc., no matter how imperfect, are not the problem in themselves. The reality is that these categories organize our society. Rather than deny them, we must challenge the interpretations attached to them.

Clearly, then, references to race must avoid dismissing it as purely an "illusion," without falling into the trap of **reifying** race as an objective category. Race may not be real in the naturally occurring sense of an objective world, but its perception and consequences are just as real as material reality. Under these circumstances, we would do well to remember that, when it comes to race, perception *is* reality—even when largely unfounded by empirical evidence.

In acknowledging how the politics of race represent one of the most bewildering dilemmas in contemporary society, this chapter raises key question that not only capture a sense of the complexities involved, but also secure chapter themes and content. Key questions provide coverage for this chapter's content: What propelled this compulsion to pigeonhole people into predetermined categories (Gallagher, 2007)? Is there any sociological justification for an ideological construct that links innate traits to a group's ranking in the social order (Rumbaut, 2011)? Why does race-based thinking persist in the present? Why and how does race continue to matter in justifying rules of entitlement and patterns of engagement despite claims of a post-racial Canada? Will race continue to matter in a so-called post-racial and race-neutral future? Should whiteness be racialized as a dominant racial frame and privileged racialized category? Is it fair to frame Canada as a white supremacist society whose superiority complex is systemic? While the questions are many, the possible answers are sharply contested, and this chapter addresses this paradox by exploring the race concept with respect to (1) meaning and content, (2) genesis and rationale, (3) impact and implications, and (4) validity and value. The chapter reveals those historical and social forces that advanced the race concept as a misguided yet powerful explanatory tool. It concludes by exploring why and how race will continue to matter in the future as long as Canada remains a racialized along a white supremacist axis (despite claims to race neutrality) that systemically privileges whiteness as the dominant racial frame. Emphasis throughout the chapter is on the deployment of race in defining "who gets what, and why" rather than on an analysis of race traits and typologies. In acknowledging that the issue is not about race *per se* but about people's belief in the existence of something called "race," a conceptual shift of significant import is suggested—from race as a biological *thing* to race as socially constructed *process* (i.e., "racialization") (Blank, Dabady, & Citro, 2004; Wallis & Fleras, 2008). Or, as nicely put by Rumbaut in his deconstruction of the conventional notions of race through a series of contrasts that cut to the core of this chapter:

> Race is a pigment of our imagination. It is a social status, not a biological one; a product of history, not of nature; a contextual variable, not a given. The concept of race is a historically contingent, relational, subjective phenomenon, yet it is typically misbegotten as a natural, fixed trait of phenotypic differences inherent in human bodies, independent of human will or intention. (Rumbaut, 2011:1)

RACE MATTERED: ON THE ORIGINS OF RACE THOUGHT

The concept of race in some form or another has been around for centuries (Vucetic, 2014). The concept itself originated with European expansion, conquest, and settlement, including the expansion of the cross-Atlantic slave trade, crude evolutionary theories, the appearance of human and biological sciences (with their focus on comparative anatomy), and international competition (Brace, 2005). European expansion in regions with culturally diverse populations spawned a global division of labour in which "races" were assigned particular economic functions based on their physical appearance, local resources, power to resist, geographical location, and cultural proximity to Europe (Walker, 1997). European imaginations were piqued by sustained contact with highly diverse populations whose appearances and cultures stimulated simultaneous amusement, fascination, and repulsion. This context of exploration and exploitation justified and engendered the race concept as an explanatory framework and a principle for humanity's inhumanity to those racialized as inferior. The race concept did not necessarily originate to justify European control or the domination of others (Coates, 2008), but was co-opted by white supremacists to advance their interests. Nor did "race thinking" give rise to racism, although racism often refers to the belief that some races are inferior to others (Vucetic, 2014); to the contrary, the reverse is more accurate. It's not human differences (race) that foster racisms, but racism that justifies the construction of race typologies to legitimize control, domination, and exploitation (Stanley, 2012).

Exploration and "Enlightenment"

Race thinking thrived in the intellectual climate of the Age of Enlightenment. Reference to race was consistent with Enlightenment philosophies that extolled the virtues of human progress and individual perfectibility (Anderson, 2007). Increasingly precise systems of classification were formulated and aligned hierarchically on the following assumptions: that each life form (1) occupied a distinctive and specific place within the natural order of things, (2) embodied a singular and defining essence that left no room for ambiguity, and (3) possessed a distinctive set of identifiable and fixed characteristics that distinguished it from others (Ewan & Ewan, 2006). The classification of diverse peoples into ranked race categories secured a "common-sense" framework for explaining human differences beyond simple references to climate or history. Far from being the product of irrationality or hate, the race concept bolstered an Enlightenment commitment to classifying the entirety of the world's plants, animals, and peoples into a single grand scheme (Goldberg, 1993).

There was no dearth of initiatives to study human diversity within a race-based framework. This preoccupation with classifying humans into categories of race reflected an Enlightenment-era quest for unitary schemes to explain the totality of human experience (Goldberg, 1993). Just as early anthropologists devised a host of unilinear evolutionary schemes to explain the coexistence of civilization with barbarism and savagery, so too did social theorists resort to race as an all-encompassing framework for understanding human differences and group inequalities (Biddiss, 1979). Within the race concept, the world was partitioned into a fixed and finite number of permanent categories, each with a distinctive assemblage of physical and cultural characteristics that were deemed to be predictive of value and behaviour, and ranked hierarchically in descending and ascending orders of superiority and inferiority. On the strength of measurements as proof of fundamental differences, a slew of classificatory schemes (or **racial typologies**) evolved from the eighteenth century onward, with the most common and widely known system of classification consisting of a threefold division of humanity into "Caucasoid" (white), "Negroid" (black), and "Mongoloid" (Asian or Oriental) (see Brace, 2005). Each of these categories was distinguished from the others by common physical features, cultural attributes, social patterns, psychological dispositions, and morality levels arranged hierarchically based on their cultural sophistication or biological proximity to European stock.

To be sure, references to race prevailed prior to European exploration and expansion. Embryonic forms of race thinking existed among the Chinese and Arabs in the late Middle Ages (Goldberg, 1993). Ancient peoples possessed an intense aversion to those who were different. But this antipathy toward others was anchored in superstition or ignorance rather than in comprehensive theories rooted in a quasi-scientific commitment to quantification and measurement (Jaret, 1995). Europeans, too, had long relied on other criteria for demonizing those beyond the pale of Christianity. For instance, the social order of the Middle Ages was divided into Christian and non-Christian sectors. Non-Christians were viewed as wild and untamed pagans who had crawled out from beneath the flat world to test Christian patience. Heathens were dispatched to the lower rungs of the ladder of creation—a stable and static hierarchy that relegated lesser beings to one end and Christians to the other.

The dichotomy between believers and non-believers should not be underestimated. The intensity and cruelty of the violence espoused by the Crusades, the Inquisition, and the Protestant Reformation—all in the name of God—verify this. Still, these earlier patterns of exclusion were no match for the ruthlessness unleashed under the banner of race. Disparaging non-Westerners as worthless and unsalvageable except as beasts of burden was one thing. It was quite another to construct elaborate classificatory schemes that invoked crypto-scientific explanations to legitimize worldwide exploitation and domination. With the publication of Robert Knox's *The Races of Man* in 1850, relations of inferiority/superiority were no longer aligned along the religious plane, but grounded in physical differences and hierarchies (Anderson, 2007). The European races self-anointed themselves as superior, while other so-called races were assigned an inferior status, with colour and character as badges of social inferiority. Of course, not all of Europe was awash with racists who relished every opportunity to disparage and exploit distant peoples (Biddiss, 1979). Concern and compassion surely existed. But Europeans were among the first to popularize the race concept as a quantifiable formula for explaining away human diversity in an expansionist era.

Justifying Colonial Exploitation

It's been suggested that Europeans manipulated the concept of race as one way of domesticating human diversity. The proliferation of racial doctrines or dogmas fed into mindsets and structures that condoned the negative treatment of those perceived as irrelevant or inferior. Under the sway of these dogmas, Europeans embarked on those civilizing crusades that cloaked the exploitation of inhabitants, with an attendant disregard for their human rights. The requirements of an expanding capitalist system were reflected in a demand for new foreign markets, investment opportunities, cheap labour, and accessible resources. In addition, European imperialist expansion intensified an obsession with accumulating foreign territories for nationalistic, decorative, or strategic reasons. Admittedly, the race concept did not necessarily originate to justify European control or domination of others; nevertheless, the imposition of these demeaning doctrines had a controlling effect on indigenous populations. When sanctioned by human and biological sciences, these classifications made group differences appear more rigid, entrenched, comprehensive, and scientifically valid (Stepan, 1982; Stocking, 1968). When harnessed to military prowess and technological advances, the effects proved fatal.

This predatory approach toward global relations concealed a paradox. First, how could the so-called civilized and Christian nations rationalize and justify the blatant exploitation of others? Second, how could colonialist exploitation be sustained without contradicting the image of Europeans as a sophisticated and enlightened people with a moral duty to civilize and convert? Answers to these uncomfortable questions inspired an ideology that condoned the mistreatment of others as natural or normal—even necessary. The contradiction between Christian ideals and exploitative practices was masked and mediated by the racist conviction that lower-ranked races would accrue benefits from servitude, exposure, and close supervision (Lerner, 1997). This ideology not only rationalized the sorting of populations along racial lines but also set the tone for asserting absolute European supremacy at the expense of those most vulnerable (Martin & Franklin, 1973). By dismissing overseas races as inferior or subhuman, Europeans could exploit "inferior stocks" with impunity and without remorse or guilt. And because racial differences were ingrained as fixed and immutable, Europeans were absolved of any wrongdoing or responsibility for "improving" the plight of the less fortunate in the name of progress. With consciences salved, they were free to do whatever was expedient to conquer or colonize.

Race reflects, reinforces, and advances the principle of white supremacy as a global system of domination (Keevak, 2011). According to Mills (1997), race is the quintessential racism project that requires a global theoretical framework to explain the displacement of indigenous peoples and exploited minorities. Or as Du Bois (1940) wrote, the history of the modern world is ". . . epitomized in one word—Empire; the domination of white Europe over Black Africa and Yellow Asia through political power built on the economic control of labour, income, and ideas" (p. 96). The apartheid regime in South Africa and the colour bar in the United States are the most egregious examples of race regimes on behalf of white interests; nevertheless, the settler states of Canada and Australia were no less racialized, sometimes openly, but often more subtly and systemically (Fleras & Spoonley, 1999). Race was more than something incidental to the functioning of the state, both then and now. More accurately, the modern state is a racist and racialized. Not only does it conceive of itself as racially configured in terms of identity and imagery, but it's also implicated in the reproduction of local conditions of racist exclusion by establishing and maintaining a system of racial domination that espouses colour-blind principles but tolerates colour-conscious discrimination. In that race underlies political systems of power and privilege, that alone should disabuse the reader of any notions of simple or simplistic solutions to the race problem (Vickers, 2002).

Doctrines of Racial Superiority

Race emerged as an eighteenth-century concept to label, describe, and classify large groups of people by reference to immutable traits such as the colour of their skin. Doctrines of racial superiority began to appear once racial types were assigned a fixed moral value—that is, prescribed by nature as superior or inferior, and backed by the unquestioned authority of science. These hierarchies were intrinsically racist in that they employed the authority of science to confirm the superiority of some groups over others (Stepan, 1982). The arbitrariness of the criteria or classification did not lessen its devastating impact. In justifying inequality between races, the doctrines endorsed the commodification of races as objects for exploitation or control, as targets of pity or contempt, and as victims of progress to be put down as gently as possible. The most egregious of these doctrines included *social Darwinism, eugenics*, and *scientific racism.*

Social Darwinism evolved into a widely acceptable doctrine of racial superiority toward the end of the nineteenth century. The doctrine borrowed a number of Darwin's biological propositions, then reworked them to further the aims of overseas exploitation. Foremost were the notions of a "struggle for survival" and "survival of the fittest" on a global scale. Social Darwinist philosophies provided a philosophical justification for Western **colonialism** by condoning the subjugation of colonized peoples on grounds consistent with the laws of nature (Stepan, 1982). The world was portrayed as a combat zone where populations were locked in mortal combat over scarce and valuable resources. Those who were better adapted in the competition prospered and progressed to the apex of the evolutionary ladder. Those with less adaptive attributes were banished to the bottom of evolutionary ladder. A race-based pecking order was established that awarded the spoils to the victor; for the vanquished, a life of servitude and suffering. These doctrines not only exonerated the colonialists of responsibility for colonizing the indigenes, but they also explained European superiority and justified out-group exploitation, while promulgating the virtues and inevitability of **capitalism** as the engine room of human progress and social enlightenment.

With **eugenics**, racist doctrines assumed even more sinister proportions. At the turn of the twentieth century, countries such as the United States, Britain, Russia, and Japan proposed the idea that the social, mental, and behavioural qualities of the human "race" could be improved by selective manipulation of its hereditary essence (Gillette, 2007). Fortified by the discovery of hereditary laws, the eugenics movement collectively advocated the improvement of human stock by purging undesirables through selective breeding procedures. Eugenics operated on the assumption that the genetically unfit were a threat to society. The so-called "defectives," such as racial minorities, the congenitally deformed, and the "retarded" would be sterilized in hopes of curbing the further "bastardization" of the human species (Banton, 1987). By contrast, racially superior stocks were encouraged to freely propagate to ensure the proliferation of the "fittest" (Stepan, 1982). Eugenicists in the United States were instrumental in restricting immigration from less "fit" countries in Eastern and Southern Europe. They promoted sterilization laws in 31 states that disproportionately targeted lower-income groups (Kevles, 1995). In Canada, the 1928 *Sexual Sterilization Act* in Alberta condoned the sterilization of nearly 3000 women, most of them poor or Aboriginal, before being repealed in 1972 (Caulfield & Robertson, 1996; Stote, 2015). Eugenics as an ideological movement under Nazi Germany culminated with the compulsory sterilization and mass destruction of millions of "undesirables." In time, however, eugenics collapsed as a doctrine, largely because of the declining legitimacy of race as an explanatory framework. Nevertheless, the idea of eugenics has persisted into the present, albeit in somewhat more muted forms, and without the backing of an explicit dogma.

Racial dogmas under the umbrella of **scientific racism** became especially marked in the United States. The existence of an indigenous Native population, a more mobile black population, and the ongoing influx of European immigrants transformed the United States into a fiercely contested site. The movement of black Americans from the south to the north further intensified competition in urban areas, where blacks competed with white immigrants for jobs and housing (van den Berghe, 1967). In light of such social turmoil, American whites capitalized on any scientific support that put racialized minorities in their place. The most popular of these was the intelligence quotient (IQ) test, which continues to fascinate some, but repel others.

Scientific racism was predicated on the premise that statistics could measure and evaluate the racial capacities between populations. The introduction of the IQ test proved invaluable in supporting a link between race and intelligence. The IQ test (or the Stanford-Binet test) was designed at Stanford University by French psychologist Alfred Binet to assist in locating deficiencies in French pupils' cognitive skills. American interests co-opted the test—which had never been intended to measure an individual's level of intelligence—and applied it indiscriminately. A notable application took place during the latter stages of World War I: Since blacks were more likely than whites to perform poorly on these Eurocentric tests, the IQ test quickly established itself as a means of racializing recruits. Those better-educated whites with high IQs became officers, while blacks and poor whites were consigned to "cannon fodder" status.

Repeated tests revealed that blacks, on average, scored about 15 percentage points less than whites on the IQ test. This gap was taken as proof that blacks were inherently intellectually inferior. With few exceptions, many believed that this biogenetic gap could never be bridged, even with environmental improvements and enrichment programs. But in their hurry to promote white intellectual supremacy, the advocates of the IQ test took some unwarranted liberties with the results. For example, while blacks scored consistently lower than whites as a group, the range of variation between black and white scores was comparable. The highest and the lowest scores within each category were approximately the same. Also relevant but widely ignored were variations in group averages. Whereas blacks on average scored about 15 percent lower than whites, 15 percent of the blacks scored higher than the average score for whites—implying by inference that some blacks were intellectually superior to many whites. Furthermore, both the social environment and the test's cultural bias were ignored as possible explanations for the obtained scores.

Debates persist about the relevance of race and scientific racism for explaining intellectual differences (Byrd & Hughey, 2015). For example, in a June 2005 issue of the journal *Psychology, Public Policy, and Law*, co-authors Philippe Rushton and Arthur Jensen asserted that genes explain 50 percent of the differences in IQ between different races, with Asians ranked higher than whites in intelligence, but whites higher than blacks. Two reasons may account for the tenacity of scientific racism. First, if intelligence is biologically innate and largely impervious to environmental modification, then the mainstream cannot be held responsible for the plight of those less fortunate. Historically, the results of these tests condoned the negative treatment of minorities, ranging from segregated facilities to inferior programs. These results can also be employed to preempt progressive change, as there is little hope for improvement, despite evidence that group averages can rise over time (Flynn, 1984). Second, IQ tests are an effective device for explaining away differences through their logical presentation of "facts" and simple causal explanations. They possess an aura of scientific validity that is substantiated by the quantification and measurement. The halo effect associated with science can also create the impression that race is a respectable intellectual position with a legitimate place in the national agenda.

TAKING RACE SERIOUSLY: RACE MATTERS

Its entrenchment in Western thought and practice notwithstanding, the legitimacy of race as scientific orthodoxy began to erode shortly after World War I (Walker, 1997). The race concept lost its clout as an explanatory framework, at least among the intellectual classes, thanks to the pioneering efforts of American anthropologists Franz Boas and Margaret Mead, who proposed social and cultural alternatives to explain human differences and behaviour; the American sociologist Robert Park, who framed race as a ruse devised by the ruling class to preserve their privilege; the Swedish sociologist/economist Gunnar Myrdahl, who suggested prolonged discrimination reinforced the perception of distinctive racial characteristics; and Sir Julian Huxley, who wrote in 1935 that references to race may have justified political ambitions, economic ends, social bitterness, and class prejudice, but that "human races don't biologically exist" (as cited in Pascal, 2006). The UNESCO Statement on Racism in 1950 asserted what was increasingly self-evident: Race was not a biological phenomenon but a social construct that inflicted staggering human costs. Without the backing of the United Nations, the race concept gradually lapsed into disrepute, at least in its most explicit form and within polite circles (Brattain, 2007). And yet a paradox prevails: Almost no one believes in race; nevertheless, race continues to be central yet submerged, unimportant yet all-consuming, a social fabrication yet a material reality, a familiar part of the social landscape yet conflicted in meanings and unrestrained by the demands of logic or proof (Pascale, 2007:23), and not a naturally occurring phenomenon but a socially constructed process.

Rethinking the Race Concept: From Race to Racialization

How valid is the race concept as an explanatory tool? Does it point to a naturally occurring biological reality consisting of distinct groups with fixed characteristics? Or does its value reside in explaining how differences between groups are socially constructed to secure control, exclusion, and exploitation? Most social scientists reject the validity of the race concept as germane to the understanding of human diversity (Brace, 2005; but see Sarich & Miele, 2004). Racial types and typologies have been discredited as pseudo-science and dangerous politics without any redeeming scientific value or empirical merit. Yet no matter how often discredited or dismissed as intellectually dead, race continues to bounce back as a politically charged marker of differences and discrimination. Often used unconsciously and without intentional malice, race remains a potent element in everyday life and social encounters, and its potential for conflict and misunderstanding should never be underestimated (Holdaway, 1996). Even a simple definition of race has proven elusive (Biddiss, 1979), given its status ". . . as a strange and flexible concept, with an endless capacity to confound" (Cose, 1997:1). Part of the problem reflects the multidimensionality of race as a concept in a constant state of flux, both fluid and malleable and sharply contested, in part because its meaning is socially constructed from an array of arbitrary characteristics that are deemed socially important (Gallagher, 2007; Keevak, 2011). Definitions tend to be highly politicized—dynamic and shifting as well as contradictory and ambiguous, but never far from the thrust and parry of privilege and power in how reality is defined, organized, and lived-in by both the dominant and subdominant sectors (James, 2005). In short, race constitutes a moving target that twists and bends across space and time—shifting its shape from race as a biological classification to race as a social myth; from race as objectively real to the reality of race as a social construction; from race as a thing ("noun") to race as a process ("verb"); from race as determinative to race as discourse; from race as a personal flaw to the embeddedness of race within society (Backhouse, 1999; Blank, Dabady, & Citro, 2004; Guess, 2006).

But the discourse over race has shifted in recent years (Fleras 2014a; Hier & Bolaria, 2007). Race was once defined as a thing—a fixed and tangible biological entity of distinct attributes that could be isolated and measured with seeming precision. At present, however, it is increasingly defined as a process (**"racialization"**) involving the imposition of racially linked meanings by the powerful on those less powerful (Markus & Moya, 2010). Racialization may be conceptualized as constructing (making) race; that is, a process of defining, categorizing, and evaluating people and their activities along racial lines (Stanley, 2012). A socially constructed activity is involved that (a) designates certain groups (or activities or spaces) as racially different by assigning biological significance to their perceived differences, (b) subjects them to differential treatment by virtue of a tainted association with negative stereotypes, and (c) disproportionately channels racialized minorities into certain domains such as poverty ("the racialization of poverty") because of prevailing preconceptions that restrict options and opportunities (Bleich, 2006; Coates, 2008; Galabuzi, 2006; Hyman, 2009; Stanley, 2012; Titley & Lentin, 2012). Two dimensions prevail: To one side, negative racial significance is conferred on patterns or activities on the basis of colour (for example "racializing crime"); to the other side, social characteristics are assigned to certain groups on the basis of perceived racial(ized) physical difference (for example, "criminalizing race").

The centrality of racialization as explanatory framework is widely accepted (Fleras, 2014a). With racialization, the concept of race is no longer framed as a description with deterministic values. It's framed instead as a socially constructed convention that is ideologically infused with preconceived notions within contexts of power (Helleiner, 2012). The significance of this shift from race to racialization cannot be underestimated. Shifting the focus from race as a thing (a biological entity) to race as a process or activity (social meanings assigned to groups of individuals) escapes a preoccupation with the physical attributes of racialized minority groups, their predictive power to determine thought and behaviour, their presumed inferiority, and the alignment of these groups into ascending and descending orders of importance or superiority (Guess, 2006). Emphasis instead focuses on the perceptions and motivations of those powerful enough to impose race (racialized) labels that control or restrict (Chan & Mirchandani, 2002). A commitment to race as racialization rejects theories of racism as a natural outcome of intergroup contact between races. Rather, racism in the broadest sense of dislike, domination, and disadvantage is seen as a precondition that legitimizes the expression of race thought and racial typologies (Stanley, 2012). Or, as Bonilla-Silva (1994)) points out, race thinking emerged as a category of difference and identity only when society became racialized in terms of what is acceptable and who is normal.

The implications of this racialization shift are critical in rethinking how race works (Fleras, 2014a). Put simply, there is no such thing as race relations in the sense of a "race" of people who stand in a relationship to another "race." What exists instead are relations that have been defined by reference to race, that is, "racialized." To the extent that the race concept has no empirical justification except in the perceptual sense, it is more accurate to speak of relationships that have been "racialized" (i.e., infused with racial overtones) than race relations *per se* (Bonilla-Silva, 1997). Race relations are not biologically based relations but relationships of inequality in which the "race" concept is imposed on racialized migrants and minorities to denote their status as inferior, irrelevant, or a threat. Furthermore, it is more accurate to say "racialized minorities," rather than "racial minorities," in part to avoid the impression of minorities as distinct categories of persons, in part to acknowledge how minorities are assigned these labels by those with the power to make them stick, and in part to reinforce the social constructedness of race concept as social control. In reflecting, reinforcing, and advancing relationships of power and politics, reference to race as racialization says more about those constructing and imposing the labels than about those who are racialized. In sum, reference to the racialization of race as a new theoretical lens provides insight into a discursive shift, namely, from race as pigmentation to race as a figment of peoples' imaginations (Rumbaut, 2011), from race as domination to race as hegemony (Winant, 2004), from race as a *noun* (a static thing) to race as a *verb* (a dynamic process), (Guinier & Torres, 2002).

Race Matters in Practice: Canada and the United States

Does race matter in Canada (Vickers, 2002)? Canadians and Americans are often perceived as poles apart when it comes to race relations. That race mattered in the United States is beyond dispute. Critics point to a country riddled with a historical legacy of slavery and segregation as well as lynching and the Ku Klux Klan. Race in the United States was animated by a belief in the innate differences between people as a basis for justifying unequal treatment. Even today, despite a chorus of claims of a post-racial America, the race subtext is unmistakable in public discourses about crime, poverty, and urban decay (Bonilla-Silva, 2013). Social problems are framed as black-or-white issues, with the result that everything from welfare to income is refracted through the prism of skin colour (Mitchell, 1998). Public debates take place in which welfare mothers, inner-city violence, urban decay, and hard drugs are essentially code words for "blackness" (Clark-Avery, 2007; White, 2007). Statistical evidence confirms how race matters when it comes to distinguishing the "haves" from the "have-nots." For example, public schools in the United States remain segregated, including Northeast public school districts, with 51 percent of black students attending schools in which students of colour comprise 90 percent of the student body. To be sure, race appears to be less important to Americans born after 1960; for example, in a 1999 Gallup poll that asked if Americans would vote for a black president, only 5 percent said no compared with 41 percent in 1967 (Newport, Moore, & Saad, 1999). In 1967, just six years after President Obama was born, 16 American states still banned interracial marriages (Frey, 2015). Nevertheless, the status for many black Americans continues to stagnate or even deteriorate in the aftermath of the civil rights revolution (Assante, 2003): The real median household income for blacks has declined, while an increasing number of black households and children hover below the federal poverty line.

To date, every socioeconomic indicator and demographic study reinforces how wealth, poverty, education, spatial segregation, and rates of incarceration continue to be correlated with race (Alexander, 2012; Richomme, 2012; Wise, 2009). For blacks, the stigma of being branded a felon for life cannot be underestimated. Without a job, it impacts access to entitlements and reintegration into the community, while enhancing the feasibility of re-offending and reincarceration (blacks comprise 7 percent of the US population, but over 40 percent of the prison population). Employers regularly exclude black ex-offenders from consideration for even entry-level, low-paying jobs, although a white male ex-offender just out of prison has the same chance of being considered for a job as a black male without a criminal record (Pager, 2007). Even the re-election of the first black president does not appear to have had an appreciable effect in dislodging race from national narratives or shifting prevailing patterns of power, privilege, and income/wealth, with some arguing the social and economic indices for many blacks has deteriorated (Early, 2014; Kitossa, 2011).

Compared with Americans, Canadians appear to reject the notion that race matters or that it should matter (Backhouse, 1999; James & Shadd, 1994:47). Canada is widely applauded for emphasizing achievement and merit rather than resorting to skin colour as the basis for recognition, reward, and relationships. Canadians like to exult in the myth that they have a deep aversion to judging others by the colour of their skin. Discussions about race tend to be muted, often employing circumlocutions such as "visible minorities" or "ethnicity" for fear of inflaming public passions (Fleras, 2008; Li, 2003). A quick reality check suggests otherwise. Canada's history is infused with a perception of Canada as a "white man's society"—a view reinforced by Robert Borden, who served as Prime Minister from 1911 to 1920, and who declared that the Conservative Party stood for "a white Canada" (as cited in Taylor, James, & Saul, 2007; see also Razack, 2002; Thobani, 2007). In keeping with the notion of Canada as a white nation, the ideals of racial purity played a pivotal role in defining who got in, and why (Agnew, 2007). Immigration programs capitalized on racial factors: immigrants with darker skins were less desirable than those with lighter skins, and considerable effort was expended to keep them out (Avery, 1995; Satzewich, 2007). Legislators and judges endlessly manipulated classifications of race into rigid definitions under Canadian law, erected racial hierarchies, justified racial discrimination, denied racial groups the right to vote, and segregated minorities according to race. For example, the paternalistic and archaic *Indian Act* of 1876, which remains in effect today, represents one of the few pieces of legislation in the world designed for a particular "race" of people. Perceptions of Aboriginal peoples as a so-called inferior race simplified the task of divesting the original occupants of their land and resources.

Race continues to affect contemporary Canada. Racialized minorities bear the brunt of negative treatment, ranging from local snubs to half-hearted service delivery. The so-called "race card" may be routinely invoked to instill public fears or to manipulate legal decisions that adversely affect minority women and men (Wallis & Fleras, 2008). Prevailing stereotypes and racial prejudices continue to influence people's level of involvement in society, while social rewards are allocated on the basis of racial affiliation. Foreign-born racialized minorities tend to earn less than whites, even when educational levels are held constant (Block & Galabuzi, 2011; Galabuzi, 2006; 2011; Pendakur, 2005), while minority women and men with professional degrees find it difficult to get jobs consistent with their credentials (Roscigno et al., 2007). Even the emergence of race-conscious state policies to ameliorate disadvantage such as the *Employment Equity Act* have endured criticism as tokenistic or divisive (see the Debate box at the beginning of Chapter 5). Those temporary foreign workers who happen to be racialized people of colour continue to be employed as cheap and disposable labour in often menial tasks and under conditions of precarity in a racialized division of labour (Galabuzi, 2006; Hennebry, 2010; Reitz & Banerjee, 2007). Clearly, race matters because minority experiences, identities, and opportunities continue to be racialized at the expense of their best interests (Fernando, 2006). As Kobayashi and Johnson (2007) put it:

> Canadian society is a landscape of negotiation, in which skin colour takes on multiple shades of meaning. As inhabitants of this landscape, we use culture, ethnicity and physical characteristics to assign places and positions to one another, to fix identities. We do so every day by a simple word or gesture, an exchange over a service counter, or a glance across the room, so that the racialized body is constantly marked and its meaning reinforced. Such assignments of place can deepen or reduce the racial divides created by the meanings we attribute to identity (p. 1).

In such a dynamic and political framework, the following insights into "race matters" are increasingly self-evident:

- Race matters not because it is real ("out there") or because people are inherently inferior, but because people perceive it to be real ("in here") and respond by acting in a manner consistent with this perception, often with discriminatory consequences for those who are negatively racialized (Wallis & Fleras, 2008). The meaning that people assign to reality (whether true or not) influences their actions in a way that reinforces (i.e., proves) the original meaning (i.e., it becomes a "self-fulfilling prophecy" [Rosado, 2013]).

- Race matters because where one is socially located in society in terms of race (as well as class, gender, and ethnicity and their interrelationships) remains a key factor in shaping how people think and act (and how others interact with them) and influences identities, experiences, opportunities, and outcomes.

- Race matters because settler societies such as Canada are racialized (Ikuenobe, 2013). That is, societies are known to make a distinction between "us" and "them," assign a devalued division of labour to the "other," and embed this devaluation of the other into the social/economic/political structure and ideology. These societies are designed, organized, and operate on values, agendas, and standards that privilege the dominant group as normal and superior while "others" are dismissed as irrelevant, inferior, or a threat. That the founding assumptions and foundational principles of contemporary constitutional orders continue to be racialized along colour-conscious lines points to a singular conclusion: Race will continue to privilege some, while disempowering others (Baber, 2010; Morris & Cowlishaw, 1997).

- Race matters as a lived experience because reference to race has a controlling effect on those who are racially devalued (or racialized). In a racialized society, minorities may *theoretically* possess equal rights and an equality of opportunity; in reality, they must exercise these rights without the benefit of institutionalized power and advantages of a head start in contexts neither designed with their realities in mind nor constructed to advance their interests. In other words, success is tantamount to "swimming upstream" because "making a go of it" entails a "going against the grain" of a systemically unlevel playing field.

- Race matters not because of biological ("racial") differences, but because an exclusive preoccupation with individual biological traits detracts from scrutinizing those opportunity structures that may account for inequalities. Nevertheless, recourse to race may be used to solve problems on the grounds that if race is the problem, it must be part of the solution.

- Race matters for racialized minorities because of its role as a positive indicator of identity, community, and history. Race-based distinctions that formerly stigmatized individuals as inferior or irrelevant now serve as a mark of distinction for racialized groups who are transforming the stigma of oppression into a mark of pride, identity, or resistance (Lerner, 1997). After all, to be without a racial identity in a racialized society, as Omi and Winant (1993:5) argue, runs the risk of having no identity at all.

- Race matters because whiteness matters, not in the sense of biological superiority, but because it is tacitly assumed to be normal and necessary in (1) defining who gets what (whites are thought to be more deserving of entitlements related to power and privilege), (2) establishing norms of right, acceptable, and desirable, and (3) providing a normative standard for judging and criticizing "others" (Feagin, 2006; Feagin & Cobas, 2008; Picca & Feagin, 2007). Ironically, those with the most power and privilege are least aware of their privileged status because their entitlements seem so normal—as the box that follows demonstrates.

Whiteness Matters: Is Canada a Code for White?

There is a paradox at play in contemporary race debates. Many believe that race shouldn't matter for two reasons: First, the concept lacks empirical validity or biological reality; second, skin colour (shorthand for race) should be irrelevant in an ostensibly merit-based and colour-blind society. And yet, in a white-dominated society, race matters. As Henry and Tator (1993) remind us, people's skin colour may be the single most important factor in determining their dignity, identity, self-esteem, and opportunities. Or, put in slightly more sociological terms, where one is socially located in society with respect to skin colour (or race) will profoundly influence a person's life (experiences), self-image (identity), and life chances (outcomes).

Most Canadians will admit that some racialized minorities are disadvantaged because of skin colour. Many may also concede that, because of colour-coded barriers, minority disadvantages may be more reflective of restricted opportunity structures than individual failure. But few Canadians are prepared to concede how "whiteness" as a dominant racial frame plays a critical role in privileging some at the expense of others (Wise, 2005). They are reluctant to acknowledge whiteness as a category of race, just as men are often excluded as a category of gender. As a result, whites will see "others" as "races," but view themselves as "raceless"—as a neutral and colourless norm that manages to be everything yet nothing, everywhere yet nowhere. Yet whites are "raced" just as men are "gendered," and failure to acknowledge this reality not only elevates whites above the fray of racial politics, but it also glosses over the possibility that, since all racism happens because of whiteness (as cited in the McGill Daily, 8 November 2012), it is not overt racism but whiteness within a white supremacist context that undermines the prospect of a cooperative coexistence (Kobayashi, 2009:72).

To be sure, reference to whiteness as privilege is not intended as an attack on whites. Nor is it employed in the literal sense to convey the biological superiority of whites as a distinct race. In keeping with the editors of *Race Traitor* magazine whose motto, "treason to whiteness is loyalty to humanity," advocates abolishing white privilege, the focus here is also critically self-reflective: first, challenging whites to think of their social location, experience, and identities as racialized (Byrne, 2010); second, analyzing whiteness as a structure, dynamic, and power relation that permeates every issue and institution in society (Garner, 2007; Kil, 2010); third, reflecting on how whiteness has operated openly or unconsciously as an unmarked and unearned marker of privilege (Henry & Tator, 2003); and fourth, acknowledging that a pattern of white privilege is improbable outside the context of a systemically white supremacist society (Leonardo, 2004; Fleras, 2014a).

Historically, Euro-North American societies have endorsed and continue to endorse a commitment to the principles and the practices of a white supremacism (hooks, 2013; Itwaru, 2009). Whiteness was perceived as next to godliness, that is, "The apex of white racial ideology was reached when it was assumed that white domination was a God-given right" (Richard Wright, 1945, as cited in Forum, 2009:1). Separate but interrelated logics bolstered white supremacy in the United States, including slavery, which anchors capitalism; genocide, which anchors colonialism; and orientalism, which anchors a call to war against unfriendlies in the Middle East (Smith, 2010). To be sure, Europeans did not automatically become white upon disembarking for North American shores. Groups such as the Irish or Italians or Jews had to learn and earn this status (Goldstein, 2006). Colonial Canada, too, was openly and defiantly insistent on its status as white space (Baldwin, Cameron, & Kobayashi, 2011:3–4), with whiteness and a white superiority complex as a normative category in the northern imaginary (Canada's Immigration Minister in 1908 declared, "the Conservative Party stands for a white Canada" [cited in Taylor et. al., 2007:158]). As Ian McKay (2008:350–351) writes:

Their Canada was in essence a White Settler society, and the nationalism of the majority of its people was a British nationalism. This Canada was . . . a grand experiment in "whiteness," an imagined community founded upon the British occupation of the northern section of North America. . . . To be a true Canadian was to be White, English speaking, and Protestant—with some allowance made for French Canadian

(Continued)

Catholics, provided they were deferential to the Empire. . . . Whiteness in Canada was an expression of confidence in British geo-political might and cultural pre-eminence . . . and visualized a future in which the backward and benighted peoples of the world would be redeemed and reordered through their exposure to their racial and cultural superiors.

But Canadians at present would be startled to learn they live in a white space (Gillborn, 2006). Most believe they simply live in a neutral space because whiteness is invisible to them regardless of the domain, from politics to policing, from education to entertainment. However compelling and reassuring, this belief is mistaken. The status of whiteness as the unmarked category upon which differences are constructed ensures its invisibility as an organizing principle in social relations and cultural expressions (Lipsitz, 1995). Every sphere of public life is deeply imbued ("racialized") with whiteness as code, imagery, and interaction to the point of normalization and taken-for-grantedness. Or, as University of Ottawa law professor, Rakhi Ruparelia (2012) writes, "Canada is a society of 'regular,' ethnicity free, white Canadians, and the rest of us—the ethnic 'Canadians'—are guests in our own home, tolerated (sort of), but at perpetual risk of overstaying our welcome."

For Gillborn (2006) this exercise in power and domination goes beyond the domain of white privilege, with its tendency to mask the structure and actions of domination that marginalize racialized others (also Peeples, 2006). Put candidly, the principle and practice of white privilege could not possibly exist outside the context of a white supremacist society. The exercise of white privilege and a white superiority complex is conditional on the existence of systemic white supremacy (i.e., in structural terms that promotes *whiteness* as ideologically superior not in the sense of white supremacist groups who advocate the biological superiority of *whites* but in the founding assumptions and foundational principles of a racialized constitutional order).

Three interlinked dimensions of whiteness can be discerned: (1) as structural advantage that generates a sense of entitlement, creates perks, and elevates social status, (2) as standpoint (social location) for interpreting reality (white gaze) in terms of what's important, normal, and acceptable, and (3) as a set of unmarked cultural practices that permeates the entirety of society (Frankenburg, 1993). More specifically, whiteness as:

- A passport to privileges as reflecting a legacy of domination that is taken for granted because it is seemingly non-racialized. The notion of whiteness is equivalent to owning property: Just as those who own property can access this wealth for greater enrichment, so too is whiteness a resource that enriches and empowers.

- A standpoint (or social location) from which whites understand the world, their position in it, and that of minorities who tend to be defined in deficit terms: Whiteness embodies a perspective, gaze, or state of mind (mindset) that upholds Eurocentric rules and cultural practices for success as normative and normalizing. It also constitutes a largely unmarked and unnamed location of structural advantage involving the design and organization of society (including the foundational principles of its constitutional order) for advancing white interests (Evans et al., 2009; also Frankenberg, 1993).

- A structure of domination: Whiteness is more than a series of practices or even privileges. Rather, it's embedded within the larger social structure and system of domination that rewards those racialized as whites and penalizes those defined as nonwhites. In the same way whiteness as race (i.e., racialization) is rendered invisible, so too are its privileges and benefits, which are taken for granted (McIntosh, 1988; Satzewich, 2007). Being white means one can purchase a home in any part of town without being "blacklisted" or "redlined" by the local real estate market. Being white allows one to go strolling around shopping malls without the embarrassment of being "blackballed" (e.g., followed, frisked, monitored, or fingerprinted). Being white ensures one a freedom of movement without being pulled over by the police for "driving while black" ("DWB") or "flying while Arab" ("FWA"). Being white simplifies identity construction since whiteness is naturalized as normal, whereas minority identities are a constructed and contested aspect of their existence because people must define who they are in relationship to the white other (see *Race Is a Four-Letter*

Word, National Film Board of Canada, 2006). Finally, being white allows one to take credit for success without raising suspicion. Conversely, blame for failure is attributed to a white individual alone, without implicating the entire community in the process.

In short, whiteness is a privilege that is largely unearned yet tacitly accepted as representing normality, dominance, and control. Stamped into one's skin by an accident of birth (Garner, 2007), whiteness is a kind of "passport" that opens doors and unlocks opportunities, in the same way identity cards in South Africa once defined privilege by the lightness or darkness of one's skin colour. Whiteness shapes people's lives by symbolizing (1) dominance rather than subordination, (2) normativity rather than marginality, and (3) privilege rather than disadvantage. Conversely, those without the privilege of whiteness are stigmatized as the "other" and demonized accordingly. Otherness (for example, blackness) represents the antithesis of whiteness in terms of privilege or entitlement—a highly visible stigma (or marked category) that denies, excludes, or exploits. Not surprisingly, there is a booming market for skin whiteners in parts of the world where whiteness is equated with beauty, success, and popularity.

Yet the privileging of whiteness is neither openly articulated nor logically deserved, but assumed and universalized as normal and natural, transcending scrutiny or criticism. Whiteness is the "natural" way of being human: that is, whites are unaware of their whiteness and privilege in the same way that

(Continued)

fish are unaware of their "wetness"—until it's too late. David Gillborn (2006) deftly explains how white standards and Eurocentric norms masquerade as colour-blind and normative principles:

> Most white people would probably be surprised by the idea of "White World"; they see only the "world," its whiteness is invisible to them because the racialized nature of politics, policing, education and every other sphere of public life is so deeply ingrained that it has become normalized—unremarked, and taken for granted. This is an exercise of power that goes beyond notions of *"white privilege"* . . .it is about *supremacy*. (p. 319)

Herein, then, lies the "genius" of white privilege. Whiteness is *everything yet nothing*: *everything*, because whiteness is the normative but unmarked standard by which reality is judged or interpreted without much awareness of the process; *nothing* because whiteness is perceived by whites to be inconsequential in privileging or disprivileging (Garner, 2007). Or, as James Baldwin once put it, "Being white means never having to think about it." And while whiteness (like power) may be invisible to those who benefit from it, to those who don't, it is painfully obvious and blatantly ubiquitous (Applebaum, 2010). Unlike whites who are rarely conscious of their whiteness, racialized people of colour have little choice except to confront their minorityness on a daily basis. Those in positions of disadvantage routinely experience the dynamics of being different, of having to defend these differences, and of being disadvantaged by them (Henry & Tator, 2003). No aspect of existence, no moment of the day, no contact, no

relationship, and no response is exempt from the stigma of otherness in a racialized society (Philip, 1996). For example, being white excuses a person from having to feel guilty about, be judged by, or make excuses for the misdeeds of individuals from the group. By contrast, transgressions by minority members often elicit mainstream criticism that blames the entire group for individual deviance, with a corresponding expectation of community responsibility for solving the problem. Or, as an Australian Aboriginal woman once put it, "If a whitefella does something wrong, he's wrong; if a blackfella does something wrong, we're all wrong" (as cited in Morris & Cowlishaw, 1997).

To be sure, not everyone views whiteness as an unmarked vehicle of privilege. White supremacist groups have cleverly transformed whiteness into victimhood—in much the same way as some men's movements have depicted males as victims of radical feminism and political correctness. Whiteness is valorized as the hallmark of an endangered or persecuted race, according to supremacists, one under threat and challenge by minorities because of quotas or "reverse discrimination" (see Ferber, 1998; hooks, 2013). For example, a study by researchers at Tufts University and Harvard concluded that whites now believe they are the primary victims of race-based discrimination since progress toward equality is thought to have transpired at their expense (New Black Woman, 2011; also hooks, 2013). A decline in perceived bias toward blacks is associated with increased bias toward whites, reflecting the ability of white supremacists to reframe news items to advance fears of a pending race war, with the result that anti-white bias is now seen as a bigger social problem than anti-black bias (Norton & Sommers, 2011). Besides, it is argued, racialized minorities have acquired unearned privileges at the expense of whites through affirmative action initiatives, with the result they have evened the score and cancelled out any racial injustice from the past (hooks, 2013).

Yet these challenges to "whiteness" need to be put into context. True, whites no longer possess the exclusive power and the uncontested privilege of the past. But moving over and making space is not the same as transforming patterns of institutional power or white privilege (see also the discussion of "subliminal racism" in Chapter 3). Moreover, as the noted anti-racist scholar Tim Wise (2008) points out, if privilege is associated strictly with money issues, not all whites are economically privileged or able to get everything they want or win every competition. However, if privilege is to include psychological benefits, then whites possess race privilege because they have the luxury of not worrying about their "race" as an additional impediment in looking for work or housing, whereas even rich black and brown folks are subject to the stresses of stereotyping and racial profiling in going about their business. In other words, the fact that some whites are poor, while some minorities are rich and possess power, doesn't alter the rule. That is, on balance, it pays to be white in a white-dominated society that subscribes to the principles of a white superiority complex.

Two final questions remain: First, are whites a race? Technically no,

because there is no such thing as race *per se*. But also yes, because in a world of perceptions where there is no position from nowhere, everybody is perceived to be racially located, whether they are aware of it or not. That alone makes it doubly important to racialize whiteness *as if* it were a "race" ("racialization")—not in the sense of biological superiority but as a social construct—if only to paint whites into the picture by recognizing whiteness as a manifestation of the human experience rather than assumed as a universal norm. Whiteness needs to be racialized in order to expose the dominant and hegemonic role that it plays in perpetrating exclusion and discrimination (Henry & Tator, 2003). After all, to exclude whiteness as an unmarked race category ("whiteness as the norm") that stands outside history or convention is to redouble its role in sustaining privilege by naturalizing it as normal, inevitable, and superior (Fleras & Spoonley, 1999; Guess, 2006).

The second question is no less provocative: Is whiteness synonymous with racism? That is, to what extent are the *systemically privileged* complicit in perpetuating social injustice? In that whiteness is tied to structures of domination and oppression, does being white make it synonymous with racism (see Applebaum, 2010)? No, not in the sense that being white automatically makes one a racist, despite the plethora of unearned privileges and advantages of whiteness. But yes, if those who wear these cloaks of entitlement insist in remaining oblivious to their advantages and the largely unearned privileges of whiteness in a systemic white society (Frankenburg, 1993;

(Continued)

Mackey, 1998). The racism in white-ness may also reflect the Eurocentric tendency to interpret reality from a white point of view ("white gaze") as natural and normal, while "othered" viewpoints are dismissed as irrelevant or inferior. Finally, whiteness may qual-ify as racism in that white privilege inheres within the founding assump-tions and foundational principles of Canada's constitutional governance in defining who gets what—without peo-ple's awareness of its presence or con-sequences. To be sure, whiteness may not set out to dominate and control; nevertheless, the interplay of Eurocen-tric rules and a white superiority com-plex may have a controlling effect in perpetuating a racialized status quo in defense of white privilege.

WILL RACE MATTER IN THE FUTURE?

The persistence and pervasiveness of race raises a central question: Will race continue to matter in a Canada organized along the lines of white superiority, yet ostensibly aspiring to the principles of a post-racial society (Wallis & Fleras, 2008)? Or do devel-opments in Canada (and the United States) portend the emergence of a colour-blind ideology and race-neutral ("post-racial") society that undercuts the legitimacy of race as an explanatory framework in predicting success or failure? Some would argue that we're nearly there (Foster, 2005). For many Americans, the election of Barack Obama is proof of an emerging post-racial society wherein race no longer matters in opportuni-ties and outcomes (Ikuenobe, 2013; Roberts, 2011; but see Alexander, 2012). Yet, while a staggering number of Americans believe that race had nothing to do with the non-indictment of white police officers who shot and killed unarmed black males, according to a December 2014 Pew Research Center poll, an almost similar number disagreed, resulting in a battle of narratives between the "it's not about race" version versus the "black lives matter" version that captures the paradoxicality of post-racial politics in the United States (Speri, 2014). Canadians, in turn, credit an official Multiculturalism for advancing Canada's status as a colour-blind society in defining "who gets what." Or, as Thobani, Razack, and Smith (2010:ix) point out, despite the inextricability of race and racism to nation-building, the dominant imagery of Canada remains one of an inclusive and multicultural society that has allegedly moved beyond the racialized origins and racist actions of the past.

The appeal of a colour-blind America where neither race nor racism matter has deep historical roots (Goldberg, 2007). Reference to the United States as post-racial was first mooted by the US Supreme Court in 1883 and on numerous occasions since then, such as the Civil rights movements of the 1950s and 1960s in addition to the multicultural movement of the 1990s (Alsultany, 2012). Martin Luther King Jr. once proclaimed a promised land where people would be judged by their actions, rather than their skin colour. A more updated version dismisses the salience of race in defining who gets what, in part by framing race in terms of cultural identity and life style choices (Giroux, 2008; see also Gallagher, 2009). Other high-profile supporters of racelessness as description or prescription include William Julius Wilson (1996) who contends that the combination of suburbanization and joblessness have elevated class rather than race as the key determinant in shaping the lives of Black Americans. Or consider Dinesh D'Souza, who, in his book *The End of Racism* (1995) argues that race/racism no longer is a major barrier to black success, given the illegalities of racial discrimination (also Gallagher, 2009). For D'Souza, merit, not racism, is pivotal in generating inequality or downward social mobility, thus putting the onus back on blacks for constructing a culture of success. The conclusion follows accordingly for devotees of a colour-blind ideology: With the onset of a colour-blind society, it's not society that needs to be less racist or to remove racist barriers. To the contrary, it is minorities who need to be more responsible, hardworking, and integrative, while those in the anti-racism industry need to scale back their rhetoric in deference to a new reality.

A commitment to the colour-blind and post-racial offers an optimistic take on the current state of race relations in Canada and the United States. According to the tenets of colour-blind ideology and the principle of liberal universalism, race no longer matters because, fundamentally, we are all the same under our skin and equal before the law. A combination of civil rights, human rights safeguards, and a multicultural orthodoxy not only discredits racial prejudice and discriminatory barriers, but also dislodges those structural and ideological barriers that block success. To be sure, a post-racial narrative acknowledges the continuing existence of race-based inequalities of exclusion ("outcomes"). The legacy and lingering effects of slavery, segregation, and racism are unlikely to quickly melt away. What differs under a colour-blind arrangement is the meritocratic ideal that race no longer matters in terms of access or opportunity. The re-election of a black president is proof of that. To the extent that inequalities or race persist, they are viewed as largely a relic from the past, restricted to isolated hate crimes and expressed by prejudicial individuals (Doane, 2007). Race-based disparities reflect the function of perceived cultural inferiorities and moral flaws rather than structural barriers or inaccessible opportunity structures (Byrd, 2011), so that racialized minorities have only themselves to blame for their poverty and disempowerment (Goldberg, 2007). In that a commitment to a colour-blind society renders race irrelevant in allocating resources, there is no justification for race-based equity programs; nor is there any rationale for taking race into policy-making considerations, even if the act of doing so is intended to ameliorate inequality or redress past injustices (Bonilla-Silva, 2013; Doane, 2006). To the contrary, race-based policies for the amelioration of racial inequality (e.g., employment equity or anti-racism) are deemed racist, unfair to whites, and a violation of core values pertaining to the meritocratic principles of a colour-blind society (Burnett, 2015). Those who challenge the principle of colour-blindness may be themselves accused of racism by virtue of hoisting group difference over shared similarities.

For others, however, neither Canada nor the United States are race-neutral or post-racial (Fleras, 2014a). It may be more accurate to say that both countries are being re-racialized because of social changes ("globalization") and ideological shifts (neoliberalism) that mask and reproduce inequalities behind the balm of post-racial and colour-blind (Thobani, Razack, & Smith, 2010; Winant, 2004). Race remains in effect because it is deeply entrenched in the founding assumptions and foundational principles of an unwritten constitutional order that define along racialized lines what is right, acceptable or desirable, and normal and necessary. A commitment to colour-blindness resembles the proverbial Trojan Horse in concealing the centrality of systemic racism, individualizing minority problems, securing social control through consent rather than coercion, and assuming a de-raced playing field where none exists (Bonilla-Silva, 2013; Feagin, 2006; Doane, 2006, 2007; Seshia, 2012). A powerful ideology has emerged that not only rationalizes and justifies racial inequalities in society, but that also absolves whites (or their proxies, namely, the state or government) of any responsibility for doing something about disparate outcomes and discriminatory practices, while justifying the dismantling of race-conscious public policies such as busing or affirmative action (Bonilla-Silva, 2015; Richomme, 2012). White supremacy—the systemic way in which a racialized order advantages whites and gives rise to white privilege at the expense of others (Strmic-Pawl, 2015)—is stronger still because it now operates under the guise of race as immaterial in generating inequitable outcomes (Bonilla-Silva, 2015). References to the racelessness in a post-racial, colour-blind society plays into the hands of a white superiority complex (Simpson, 2008). In other words, a commitment to a colour-blind playing field preserves the status quo by privileging meritocracy and equal opportunity, while allowing whites to deny race-based privilege without really addressing racial injustices (McCardle, 2008). Failure to confront structural racism not only simplifies claims to a race-blind society, but it also bolsters patterns of white privilege (Strmic-Pawl, 2015), as pointed out by Barlow (2012:18):

> Whites' capacity to deny the existence of racism, while continuing to benefit from racial privileges, was (and is) contingent on the development of structured racism. Once the patterns of racial privilege were built into the "normal" day-to-day operation of interlocking mass institutions, the defense of racism no longer required open claims of white superiority. It became increasingly feasible for whites to defend racial privileges by upholding standards of individual merit, community control, and other allegedly "race-neutral" claims.

In brief, there is no such thing as a race-neutral society. Human societies are socially created constructions that deliberately or inadvertently ("systemically") reflect, reinforce, and advance the realities, experiences, and interests of the dominant sector. The values, agendas, and priorities of those who created or control society are deeply ingrained within its governance, institutions, and foundational principles. The result is a racialized society; after all, the ideas and ideals pertaining to race (in terms of what is acceptable, normal, or desirable) are structurally aligned in ways that promote mainstream white interests over those of other racialized groups without people's awareness of the biases at play. Despite laws outlawing discrimination at individual and institutional levels, structural barriers and systemic biases remain that advance the interests of whites over those of non-whites, especially since the legal system cannot possibly eradicate deep-seated prejudices or subliminal biases that continue to influence people's identities, experiences, and outcomes. Clearly, then, a colour-blind society is a contradiction in terms, at least in the foundational sense, with the result being that race will continue to matter for the foreseeable future.

Appearances are deceiving. The most egregious dimensions of a racialized society are no longer tenable in light of Canada's conventions or commitments. But the combination of legal statutes and collective ideals that condemn race are no proof of a post-racial and colour-blind society. The seeming invisibility of race does not signal a retreat from racial intolerance or removal of race as an axis of social inequality but rather a shift from its extremes of the past to its everyday manifestations in a racialized social order (Simon-Kumar, 2015). Even moves to formally dismantle overt supports for racism cannot dislodge an entrenched structural whiteness and systemic white supremacism that hide behind a façade of formal fairness (Doane, 2006; Pitcher, 2009). In theory, formal equality before the law sounds good. In practice, migrants and minorities must exercise these rights in a context neither designed to reflect their realities nor constructed to advance their interests. Moreover, without special treatment to break the cycle of poverty and impoverishment, groups that are disadvantaged because of a late start will continue to fall further behind. Applying similar standards to unequal contexts by treating everyone alike tends to freeze the status quo, with its prevailing distribution of power and resources (Lentin, 2008). Or, as aptly put by Lyndon B. Johnson at the commencement address at Howard University on 4 June 1965 when acknowledging how the Civil Rights Movement dismantled legal barriers to individual achievement, but did nothing to remedy the generational impact of white privilege:

> You do not wipe away the scars of centuries by saying, "Now you are free to go where you want, do as you desire, and choose the leaders you please." You do not take a man who for years has been hobbled by chains, liberate him, bring him to the starting line of a race, saying, "You are free to compete with all the others," and still justly believe you have been completely fair . . .

In short, the embedded nature of race in constructing a future society cannot be ignored or underestimated (Goldberg, 2002; Vickers, 2002). In creating a Canada that *is safe for race and safe from race*, the challenge is twofold. First is the problem of acknowledging the continuing salience of race as a process of racialization in a racialized society that claims to be post-racial. The second challenge is to deconstruct the coded discourses by which people continue to attribute social significance to race in everyday life, despite laws and norms that discourage its use to differentiate, deny, or exclude (Li, 2007). In that structural bias and biased mindsets are unlikely to be dislodged in the foreseeable future, race will continue to matter whether we like it or not, approve or disapprove. Rethinking the race concept as a frame of reference is critical. Race is not a thing out there—a kind of naturally existing objective reality—but rather a socially constructed convention by which people are designated (racialized) as (racially) different and subject to discriminatory treatment ("racialization"). Moreover, race is not simply a psychological disorder or a mindset that reflects flawed assumptions about human nature. Rather, as a political project it is fundamental to the origins, character, and functioning of modern states, including its manifestations in justice and law enforcement, politics, legislation, and bureaucracy (a racialized society). References to race as a process of racialization that is located "in here" (within the framework of power and fabric of society) rather than race as a thing "out there" may well prove more difficult to dislodge.

DEBATE REVISITED

A Racialized Rashomon Effect

Reactions to charges of police racial profiling span the spectrum: Some say *no or hardly ever*; others say *yes and on a regular basis*; and still others say *maybe*, but a lot depends on one's perspective (Satzewich & Shaffir, 2009).

(Continued)

Police authorities at both local and provincial levels vehemently deny the existence of institutional (or systemic) racial profiling—either as principle or practice—although they are willing to concede the possibility of a few rogue officers who slipped through the screening/training process. For the police, then, only criminal behaviour is profiled, regardless of skin colour. This denial and the corresponding rationales tend to be rejected by academics (Henry & Tator, 2002; Tanovich, 2006; Tator & Henry, 2006), anti-racist organizations, and members of the black community (Brown, 2004; Smith, 2004). They generally support mounting evidence of police race profiling as consistent with what black male youth have long proclaimed: *Police tend to stop who they see rather than what they see* (Hurst, 2003).

Clearly, then, each racialized group assesses the situation differently. The differing perceptions of racism held by whites (racism as "individual prejudice") and racialized minorities (racism as "systemic bias" and "white advantage") make it difficult to communicate meaningfully (Bonilla-Silva, 2015). This perceptual gap was nicely captured by one senior police official who proclaimed, "You think we profile, we think we don't" (as cited in Hurst, 2003). Whites acknowledge the possibility of a "few bad apples" in an essentially colour-blind and fair police service, whereas minorities define policing as "rotten to the core" with the bad apples a sign of the decay (Tator & Henry, 2006).

Reference to the concept of the "Rashomon effect" may explain the disparity in police and black responses to the crisis. The acclaimed Japanese film director Akira Kurosawa explored this perspectival theme in his brilliantly conceived film *Rashomon*. This 1951 epic pivots around competing versions of a brutal incident involving a woman, her samurai husband, a bandit, and a peasant woodcutter as eyewitness, each differently interpreting the death of the husband (murder or suicide?) and the bandit's sexual tryst with the samurai's wife (rape or seduction?), resulting in wildly divergent accounts (Heider, 1988). In presenting this multi-perspectival viewpoint in which there are no innocent perspectives or value-free perceptions, Kurosawa tapped into the postmodernist credo that neither absolute truth nor objective reality exist, only discourses about truth or reality whose "truthfulness" or objectivity are situationally constructed. The process by which divergent viewers (participants) interpret the same incident in mutually exclusive ways based on their location in society has come to be known as the Rashomon effect.

According to the Rashomon effect, *where* one is socially located in society will influence how they see, understand, and relate to the world out there. For example, senior police officials who rarely encounter any discrimination because of their whiteness, power, and affluence tend to underestimate the magnitude and scope of racism. Their privileged status in terms of race and class diminishes the possibility of their being victimized along these grounds. They invariably believe the system is colour-blind and fair, thanks to the buffering effect of race and class, with the result that crime rate disparities are attributed to greater black criminality rather than discriminatory police behaviour (Hurwitz & Peffley, 2010; Satzewich & Shaffir, 2009). To the extent that racial profiling is thought to exist within the police service, it's defined by a prevailing police culture in motivational terms (i.e., racism as individualistic, intentional/deliberate, and randomly isolated). In other words, those unlikely to be victims tend to underestimate the scope and pervasiveness of racism by restricting its presence to a "few bad apples" who can be rehabilitated through sensitivity training.

By contrast, the racialized and less privileged see it differently insofar as they are differently located in society. (It could be argued that those with less power or on the margins of society may read situations more "accurately" because their survival depends on it [Bishop, 2005].) In light of their visibility, powerlessness, and poverty, blacks and other racialized minorities may emphasize the systemic extent and intensity of police profiling—largely because racial profiling is not something abstract or arbitrary but a reality that is always potentially present. Police racism is seen as part of the institutional structure of the "whole rotten barrel." In that discrimination pervades every nook of the criminal justice system in general and in policing specifically, whiteness/Eurocentricity remains the institutional norm, resulting in bias and second-class treatment of racialized minorities because of ingrained institutional policies and practices (Hurwitz & Peffley, 2010). Amassing arrests from random stops, strips, and searches amounts to little more than institutionalized harassment,

as police use their authority to "over-police" racialized minorities.

For the police, the Rashomon effect is double-edged. The existence of profiling within the service does not necessarily implicate police as racist in the conventional sense, since statistical data cannot prove motives. Nevertheless, they must acknowledge that their actions may be interpreted as profiling and racist by those with different lived experiences. But reference to a Rashomon effect does not exonerate police services of blame. Just because senior management rejects the practice of police profiling, there is no guarantee of rank-and-file compliance. Profiling exists because race is frequently a factor in making discretionary judgments, even if the motives behind the profiling may be largely unconscious (i.e., subliminal). The implications are far-reaching: If the problem of profiling is the result of a few rogue officers, energies must focus on behavioural modification through attitude change and consciousness-raising (Editorial, 2010a). If the problem is institutional, structural changes related to rules, priorities, and agendas are necessary. If the problem is job-related, the very concept of policing in a twenty-first century multicultural society may have to be rethought, in part by rejecting a "thin blue line" (us *versus* them) mindset with its militaristic overtones.

Regardless of right or wrong with respect to debates over how much or what kind, the impact of racial profiling cannot be lightly dismissed. Dangers lurk when profiling goes beyond personal prejudice and congeals into public policies that infringe on the civil rights of specific populations (Muharrar, 2005). Once a problem is racialized by profiling, it encourages a suspiciousness that typically stigmatizes an entire group for punitive treatment (reinforcing how the unlawful conduct of a small number of wrongdoers who call attention to themselves glosses over the vast majority who conduct themselves lawfully). Racialized profiling also results in selective police stops and searches that can prove to be an embarrassing inconvenience for some or a physically painful experience for others (Tator & Henry, 2006). A climate of distrust toward police is fostered, with the result that minority communities become unpoliceable, in part because of depolicing (police refusing to respond to situations involving racialized minorities), thus amplifying those very conditions that justify an even more invasive police presence. And when taken to the extreme, the politics of profiling can culminate in violence—a situation brought home by the social media capture of police brutality and killings of unarmed black males in the United States.

Chapter Highlights

- The politics of race are explored by looking at its value as an explanatory framework to account for human differences and disadvantages with respect to colonialist expansion and contemporary patterns of social control.
- The key theme of this chapter is this: Human differences exist, but race does not, at least in the naturally occurring sense of the word, although people act as if it does, in the process creating some very real impacts. Or as sociologist like to say, "phenomena do not have to be real to be real in their consequences."
- The term "racialized" or "racialization" is preferred over "race" when describing groups, relations, and activities. This shift toward racialized/racialization reinforces the social constructedness of race within contexts of power (race as verb/process) and away from race as a discreet biological category whose distinct attributes are thought to possess predictive powers (race as noun/thing).
- Race mattered in the past. The race concept implied belief in innate differences as unequal, determinative of behaviour, hierarchically ranked, and subject to control or exploitation.
- Race matters at present because of its value in predicting success or failure. Despite Canada's claims to a post-racial society, race matters not because of inherent properties but because peoples' attitudes toward race continue to matter. The framing and privileging of whiteness as a dominant racial frame reinforces how race matters (and will continue to matter) in solidifying Canada's status as a systemically white supremacist society.
- Race will continue to matter because (a) racialized minorities incorporate notions of race into their identities and challenges; (b) Canada remains a deeply racialized society in terms of the founding assumptions and foundational principles of its Eurocentric constitutional order; and (c) whiteness as a dominant racial frame is unlikely to be dislodged in the foreseeable future.

Review Questions

1. Race has little to do with genetics or biological reality, but everything to do with perceptions about genes and biology. That is, race is about ideology not biology, about society not physicality, about process not a thing. Explain the nature and significance of this shift in the race concept from a thing ("noun") to a process ("verb").

2. Why and how did racial doctrines emerge in nineteenth-century Europe? Are there any indications to suggest their continuation into the present?

3. What do we mean by the statement that there is no such thing as race relations, only relationships that have been "racialized"? What is the significance in moving beyond the race concept to a focus on racialization as an explanatory framework?

4. Race matters not because race is real, but because people believe it to be real and act according to this belief, with very real consequences. Explain what this means by references to the debate over police racial profiling.

5. Discuss what is meant by the concept of *whiteness as privilege* in a systemically white Canada.

CHAPTER 3

Racisms and Anti-racism

LEARNING OBJECTIVES

After reading this chapter, you will be able to:

1. Define the notion of racism as a complex, shifting, and multiple dynamic (i.e., a "verb") rather than a singular and static object (i.e., a "noun").

2. Explain why, when it comes to racism, Canada is arguably a racialized society that is racist in consequences.

3. Understand why defining racism is a tricky affair because of its many different dimensions, constituents, and sectors.

4. Compare how the origins and persistence of racism differ from its causes, consequences, and costs.

5. Describe how different types of anti-racism strategies reflect the different ways in which racism is defined.

DEBATE

Is Canada a Racist Society?

Is Canada a racist society? Some say "yes," others say "no," and still others say "maybe" or "it depends." If the answer is *no*, why do some believe it isn't? If *yes*, who says so, why, and on what grounds? If *maybe* or *it depends*, what criteria or context justify this response? Does a racist Canada reflect the interplay and cumulative sum of individual racisms? Or is it more accurate to say that Canada is the site of racisms and racists without necessarily implicating it as a racist society? Are racisms under control (decreasing) as many might predict in a Canada that claims to be post-racial? Or are they out

of control (increasing) as might be inferred if framing Canada as a racialized society? Answers to these questions are complex and problematic, particularly since Canadians remain conflicted and confused about the nature and scope of racisms in Canada (Fleras 2014a; Lamoin & Dawes, 2010). Yet some consensus is pivotal in the struggle to root out racism in a Canada that aspires to be otherwise.

A sense of perspective is critical for any progress to be made in this direction. For some, Canada is inherently racist in its design and outcomes, with a thin veneer of tolerance camouflaging a pervasive white superiority complex (Gilmour, 2015; Henry & Tator, 2009). A highly respected academic from Queen's University has claimed that "we live in a racist society" (as cited in the *Kingston Whig-Standard*, 2003), while the Supreme Court of Canada in 2005 acknowledged that racial prejudice against racialized minorities was an indisputable and notorious social fact (R. v. Spence, [2005] 3 S.C.R. 458, para 5). Others disagree with this dystopian view of Canada as foundationally racist (Satzewich, 2011). For them, Canada is a fundamentally sound society—the "least racist society in the world," according to Raymond Chan, the former Minister of State for Multiculturalism (Canadian Press, 2005). Notwithstanding the presence of a few bad apples to spoil an otherwise wholesome batch, Canada is perceived as largely colour-blind—a country where people are judged by what they do rather than who they are (Foster, 2005; Satzewich, 2011). For still others, perceptions of racism in Canada depend on how broadly or narrowly the term is defined and conceptualized (Satzewich, 2011); on the kind of measures employed to quantify its presence (Gilmour, 2015); and on where one is socially located in the wider scheme of things (see the Debate box in Chapter 2). Those in positions of privilege and authority are inclined to see racism as an individual and irrational aberration from the normal functioning of society. For minorities, however, racism is so hardwired into the very fabric of racialized society that it negates the possibility of a level, post-racial playing field (Bonilla-Silva, 2015; Das Gupta, 2009; Doane, 2006; Thobani, 2007).

Is Canada a racist society, or is it a society containing pockets of racism? Responses are trickier than one might anticipate. First, what is meant by the word "racist" when applied to Canadian society? Is racism about (a) race, ideology, culture, advantage, or structure; (b) the interpersonal, institutional, ideological, or infrastructural; or (c) prejudice, power, or discrimination? Second, how do we measure the concept of "a racist society" (Fleras & Spoonley, 1999)? Is a racist society defined by a minimum number of racial incidents per year based on national surveys or reported to authorities? Or should it be a measure of the institutionalized biases that unintentionally yet systemically perpetuate inequality? Can "institutional bias" be measured? How? Third, what kind of society qualifies as racist? A racist society is one where (a) state-endorsed racism is part of a broader governance project that defines belonging and entitlement along exclusionary lines; (b) racism openly flourishes and racists are free to roam with relative impunity; and (c) nothing is done to prevent racism or deal with its expression due to government indifference or complicity (Goldberg, 2002). Is a racist society one that claims to be post-racial yet is deeply racialized in terms of those founding assumptions and foundational principles that define what is normal, important, and acceptable? Clearly, then, the question, "Is Canada a racist society?" is more complex and the answer more elusive than it might appear at first glance, and the Debate Revisited box at the end of this chapter will explore this question more thoroughly and propose a plausible response.

INTRODUCTION: THE TOXICITY OF RACISM IN CANADA

From a distance, Canada strikes many as a paragon of racial tranquility (Fleras, 2014a). Racism may loom as the single most explosive and divisive force in other countries, including the United States, but surely not in Canada, where racism is publicly scorned and officially repudiated. In contrast to the United States, where racism continues to segregate or suppress, Canada's racism is perceived as relatively muted, isolated to fringe circles, a relic from the past, and generally under control (Satzewich, 2011). Laws are in place that criminalize racism; brazen racists and white supremacists are routinely charged for disseminating hate propaganda; race riots are virtually unheard of except in history books; and blatant forms of racial discrimination are vigorously challenged. Canada prides itself on being a society in which individuals are rewarded on the basis of merit, no group is singled out for negative treatment, and race is deemed to be irrelevant in determining a person's status or entitlements. Moreover, the popularity of terms such as "post-racial," "multiculturalism," "inclusiveness," and "equity" suggests that Canadians have learned to "talk the walk."

To their credit, Canadians are learning to "walk the talk," as well (United Nations, 2007). No longer are Aboriginal peoples excluded from Canada's political and constitutional affairs as was once the case (Ponting & Gibbins, 1980). As peoples with rights who also happen to be a growing resource power in Canada (Coates, 2015), they are clearly in ascendancy in reclaiming some degree of self-determining autonomy as the "nations within" (Fleras & Elliott, 1992; Maaka & Fleras, 2005). As proof, consider the "watershed" agreement in 2000 that finalized the Nisga'a settlement, thereby establishing a third tier of Aboriginal governance alongside the federal and provincial (see the Box in Chapter 7). Or the Supreme Court Tsilhqot'in Decision in June 2014 that for the first time in Canadian history secured aboriginal title and ownership to a specific parcel of land and resources beyond the domain of a reserve. Another positive indicator is the demographic revolution that has transformed once staunchly Anglo-centric cities such as Vancouver and Toronto into vibrant, cosmopolitan centres. Not surprisingly, Canada remains the destination of choice for migrants and minorities because of its much touted commitment to freedom, democracy, quality of life, and tolerance for diversities (Historica-Dominion Institute, 2010; Legatum Institute, 2015; MIPEX, 2015). Finally, nearly a half-century of an official Multiculturalism has catapulted Canada into the global spotlight as the go-to blueprint for democratic governance (Environics Institute, 2015). The fact that the United Nations Human Development Index had ranked Canada as the most livable country on the planet throughout much of the 1990s for eight consecutive years (by 2014, Canada had slipped to 8th on the list) must surely say something about its priorities and commitments.

But what sparkles from a distance loses lustre up close. Canadians could be smug about their enlightened status if racism were a mere blip on the historical screen but this, sadly, is far from the truth (Wallis, Sunseri, & Galabuzi, 2010). In line with its image as a defiantly white-man's country, Canada once possessed few qualms about defining itself as openly and proudly racist. Until the early 1950s, neither bigotry nor domination of racialized others were seen as racism in the sense of antipathy or inferiorization (according to the 2nd edition of the *Oxford English Dictionary*, the word "racism" did not appear in the English language until the mid-1930s). In that minorities were segregated or excluded, their treatment as second-class citizens was rationalized as a natural reflection of divine will or the iron-clad laws of evolutionary progress. Not only was racism deeply embedded in Canada's history, culture, law, and institutions (see Backhouse, 1999; Satzewich, 1998; Walker, 1997), but racism also furnished the ideological life support for capitalism at large, for society-building in general, and for the exploitation of racialized minorities in particular (Bishop, 2005; Bolaria & Li, 1988). Canada was founded on the colonization of its indigenous peoples, the dispossession of their land and resources, the exploitation of immigrant labour for Canada-building purposes, the preferential treatment of white European settlers (Thobani, 2007) and its preservation as white, British, and Protestant (Pitsula, 2013). Even that most quintessential of American racist institutions, slavery, flourished in Canada (Cooper, 2006; Trudel, 2014) as conveyed by this advertisement:

> TO BE SOLD, A BLACK WOMAN, named Peggy, aged about forty years; and a black boy her son, named JUPITER, aged about fifteen years, both of them the property of the subscriber. The woman is a tolerable Cook and washerwoman and perfectly understands making Soap and Candles. The Boy is tall and strong of his age, and has been employed in Country Business, but brought up principally as a House Servant—They are each of them Servants for life. . . . PETER RUSSELL. York, Feb. 10th 1806. (adapted from Bristow et al., 1993)

Other minorities suffered as well from a worldwide system of racial stratification in which peoples defined as white ruled and exploited those socially defined as nonwhite (Fleming & Morris, 2015):

- Migrants from Eastern European countries were vilified as an unwanted underclass to be kept out of Canada unless absolutely necessary.

- Paranoia and hate compelled authorities to intern thousands of minorities, including the displacement of 5000 Ukrainians (in addition to Germans and Austro-Hungarians) into concentration camps during World War I—at great personal cost to themselves and their families.

- An equally spiteful internment was inflicted on Japanese Canadians in British Columbia (Fukawa, 2009). Most were rounded up like Jews in Nazi Germany, their property confiscated and civil rights suspended, and were confined to labour-intensive camps. Restrictions on movement were not lifted until 1949.

- Contrary to public opinion, the Ku Klux Klan flourished in Canada, assuming a major profile during the 1920s and 1930s in central and western Canada (Backhouse, 1999; Pitsula, 2013). The "Kanadian Klan" aimed its invective at Catholics, French-Canadians, Asians, Jews, and blacks, who routinely encountered exclusion because of segregation at schools, in the housing market, and at public venues such as movie theatres, as demonstrated below.

The present may be equally racist, albeit more quietly and by consequence than loudly or by intent, more polite than openly blunt, often coded in polite language, camouflaged behind principled grounds, more pro-white rather than anti-minority, and more institution-alized than attitudinal (Chazan et al., 2011; Dovidio, Gaertner, & Kawakami, 2010; Stanley, 2012). People are generally puzzled by the persistence of racial discrimination and racial-ized inequality that persists despite a spate of human rights rulings, an official Multiculturalism, and numerous surveys pointing to a decline in the expression of racist attitudes (also Tinkler, 2012). Ambiguities prevail; for example, while the percentage of mixed race unions in Canada has nearly doubled from 1991 to 2011, from 2.6 percent to

Viola Desmond: Canada's Unsung Civil Rights Icon

Unlike in the United States, where there is at least an admission of the fact that racism exists and has a history, in this country one is faced with a stupefying innocence.

—Dionne Brand

On 14 April 2010, Nova Scotia apologized and granted a posthumous pardon to Viola Desmond, a black woman who was wrongfully convicted in 1946 for sitting in a whites-only section of a movie theatre. In the period after World War II, segregation of blacks from whites was still the norm in many parts of Nova Scotia (and elsewhere in Canada). But there were no Canadian laws enforcing segregation; rather, it was a matter of local custom resulting in uneven patterns of discrimination (Ayers, 2015). Despite mounting sensitivity about the inappropriateness of racism for a country that had just fought for freedom overseas, popular attitudes in the post-war era were unlikely to be translated into reforms without dramatic incidents, carefully planned logistics, and the inspiration of dynamic personalities. Viola Desmond provided this spark.

As a 32-year-old Halifax-born, African Canadian beautician, Desmond was driving from Halifax to Sydney when her 1940 Dodge broke down in New Glasgow. While awaiting the car repairs, she decided to see a movie at the Roseland Theatre. Desmond paid for what she thought was a general admittance ticket and sat downstairs—unaware of the theatre's rules that

blacks could sit only upstairs in the balcony seats. Once seated, she was asked to leave the "whites-only" house seats, but refused. Eventually the manager and a police officer forcibly removed her from the theatre and put her in jail overnight.

The next day, Desmond was charged and convicted of tax evasion. In her defense, Desmond argued that she had requested a ticket for the main floor, had paid for it, had no way of knowing that the balcony was the designated seating area for blacks because no one had posted signs to that effect, and had offered to pay for the difference when informed of the policy. All this was to no avail: According to the prosecution, Desmond had committed a crime. She didn't pay the full amount for front seats (40 cents including 3 cents tax) since the theatre would sell only a cheaper balcony ticket (30 cents including 2 cents tax) to a black woman. In other words, Desmond had evaded paying the proper amusement tax for a pricier ticket on the white segregated floor—*a difference of one cent.* Interestingly, the prosecution made no mention of race, although the unspoken truth was clear: Desmond was charged and eventually convicted of being a black person who dared step outside her defined place in society. She was fined $20 (about $250 in 2010 dollars) and $6 court costs (the alternative was 30 days in jail) for defrauding the government.

(Continued)

Desmond paid the fine in part because she had a family and a business to look after, including the first class of students in her beauty school who would have suffered had she spent time in jail (Ayers, 2015). But upon the advice of a doctor who examined her bruises and the injuries to her hip and knees, she decided to take legal action against the cinema and fight the case with the help of the newly created Nova Scotia Association for the Advancement of Coloured People (NSAACP). Although she lost the first appeal, Desmond won the second on a technicality, although few black Nova Scotians took comfort in this decision. As Walker (1997) notes, segregation was still legal according to the highest court of the province. Clearly, if transformative change toward equality was to be achieved, it had to begin with the law; after all, the problem of discrimination was systemic—rooted in society rather than a few overt racists. Under pressure from Labour, the church, and the NSAACP, the Nova Scotia government eventually dismantled and repealed its discriminatory laws by the mid-1950s (as did Ontario), thus making it illegal to discriminate on grounds of race in hiring or promotion or in serving customers at public institutions.

Desmond's conviction was never overturned by the higher courts, although she received a Royal Prerogative of Mercy Free Pardon in 2010 from the Nova Scotia government (Ayers, 2015). Nevertheless, her ordeal earned her the unofficial recognition as Canada's Rosa Parks. (According to Graham Reynolds, who holds the Viola Desmond Chair of Social Justice at Cape Breton University in Sydney [cited in Ayers, 2015], it should be the other way around, since Desmond's stand against segregation transpired nine years before Parks made history in the United States in 1955 for famously refusing to give up her seat at the front of the bus to a white man on a Montgomery, Alabama, bus.) Parks' arrest prompted a massive bus boycott that launched the civil rights movement, brought Martin Luther King Jr. into national prominence, and eventually led to a Supreme Court ruling outlawing segregation on public transport.

After the trial, Desmond closed her business and moved to Montréal, then to New York, where she died in 1965 at the age of 50. In an interesting twist of fate, Desmond's pardon was signed by Mayann Francis, Nova Scotia's first African Canadian and second female lieutenant-governor. Ironically, however, the timing of the 2010 pardon was marred by another incident in Nova Scotia, in which a biracial family was victimized by racialized violence: First a cross was burned on their lawn in winter, then their car was firebombed in mid-April. The conclusion seems inescapable: plus ça change, plus c'est la même chose (see Ayers, 2015; CBC News, 2010; Editorial, 2010b; Rooney, 2008; Walker, 2001a).

4.6 percent, according to Statistics Canada data (also Mahtani, 2014), 81 percent of British Columbians of Chinese and South Asian descent report they have experienced discrimination because of their ethnicity (McCue, 2014). Survey data support this conclusion.

According to the 2002 Ethnic Diversity Survey and Statistics Canada census data (Government of Canada, 2005), over a third of those interviewed had experienced discrimination because of their race or ethnicity, including 50 percent of black Canadians and 33 percent of South Asian and Chinese respondents. The Ethnic Diversity Survey also revealed that blacks in Canada were more likely to be targets of discrimination, with 32 percent indicating such experiences in the past five years, compared to 21 percent for South Asian Canadians and 18 percent for Chinese Canadians. More recent figures are no less striking. In 2013, there were 1167 police-reported hate crimes, or 3.3 per 100 000 of population (a decrease of 17% from 2012), with 51 percent of incidents motivated by hate toward a race or ethnicity (nearly half of which were directed at blacks) and 28 percent motivated by hatred toward a religious group (Allen, 2015; Statistics Canada, 2015). Thunder Bay (20.9) and Hamilton (17.4) had the highest rate per 100 000 of population, whereas Saint John, NB (0) and St. John's NL (0.5) had the lowest rates. According to the 2014 Annual Audit of Anti-Semitic incidents by B'nai B'rith, 1274 anti-Semitic incidents were reported in 2013—down slightly from 2011 (but a doubling in numbers since 2004), with decreases in harassment incidents offset by increases in vandalism and violence. Perhaps, then, no one should be surprised by a recent EKOS survey of 2950 adult Canadians in March of 2015 pointing to an erosion of openness to diversity (64% indicate an opposition to niqabs (full facial veiling) at citizenship ceremonies) and immigration, including 41 percent who believe Canada admits too many visible minority migrants (Graves, 2015; also Environics Institute, 2015).

In short, critics charge that racism is alive and well in Canada, with only its worst effects camouflaged by a Teflon veneer of tolerance and politeness (Henry & Tator, 2006). Yes, Canada may have been spared the stigma of institutionalized slavery or the ravages of American-style ghettos or race riots, yet such a fortuitous state of affairs may reflect exceptional good fortune and a powerful myth-making machine rather than enlightened policies or public goodwill. The Ontario Human Rights Commission (2005:1) pulled no punches in pointing out the reality behind the facade:

> Racialized persons experience disproportionate poverty, over-representation in the prison population, under-representation in the middle and upper layers of political, administrative, economic, and media institutions, and barriers to accessing employment, housing, and health care to name just a few. Courts have recognized that racism exists in Canada. It is all too easy for those who do not experience it to deny the reality of racism. This is counterproductive and damaging to our social fabric. Racial discrimination and racism must be acknowledged as a pervasive and continuing reality as a starting point.

Such an accusation may puzzle the reader; after all, at a cognitive level, many Canadians appear to have internalized the values of tolerance, equality, and justice, in addition to rejecting notions of racial inferiority. But while overt racism is strongly condemned, acts of blatant racism persist, in part because Canadians may react to racism with a surprisingly level of indifference (Kawakami, Dunn, Karmali, & Dovidio, 2009). Moreover, prejudicial racism persists at subconscious levels (Dovidio, Gluszek, John, et al., 2010), while institutions continue to deny and exclude because of rules and protocols that inadvertently exert a discriminatory impact (Teelucksingh, 2006). Rather than disappearing or becoming marginalized, racism assumes many different permutations to fit the tenor of the times, ranging from spontaneous individual outbursts to systemic institutional biases, to racialized foundational principles that inform Canada's **constitutional order** (Agnew, 2007; Fleras, 2014a; Lee & Lutz, 2005; Patriquin, 2007; Woodward, 2005). Even improvements can deceive: Although institutions have become more accommodative, says Hamlin Grange, president of the Toronto-based consultancy group DiversiPro, this commitment may reflect expediency ("staying one step ahead of the law") or appeasement ("cooling out" troublesome constituents). In that Canadians are more tolerant than in the past, this trend may say less about injustice or conviction but more about the art of impression management or political correctness.

Canada at present claims to be anti-racist and colour-blind, with a commitment to the principles of multiculturalism and inclusiveness. Such is the fear of being labelled racist, that Canadians may be reluctant to criticize migrants and minorities unless a higher principle can justify the criticism ("reverse discrimination," "jumping the queue," "equal opportunity"). In reality, racism continues to persist, albeit in constant motion and continually morphing into new and insidious forms so that it no longer means what it used to mean or what people think it should mean (Lee & Lutz, 2005). Racism discourses (i.e., distinctive ways of thinking and talking) have shifted, as well (see Hier & Walby, 2006). Once thought of as perpetrated by bad people with twisted attitudes inflicting abuse on those less fortunate, racism is increasingly framed in structural and systemic terms—from overt practices involving prejudice to a reframing of racism around power differences between racialized groups (Applebaum, 2010; Bonilla-Silva, 2015). Not surprisingly, racism is less likely to be defined as a naturally existing thing that can be isolated and contained, but more often as a floating signifier that can mean anything (from the institutional to the ideological to all points in between) depending on the context, criteria, and consequences. In other words, reference to racism as an easily identifiable "thing" out there no longer resonates with the same authority it once did. It has been displaced, as it were, by **discursive** frameworks that acknowledge racisms as a complex process and contradictory dynamic, within shifting contexts of power and inequality (Fleras, 2014a). Table 3-1 provides a brief summary of "racism talk" between then (racism framed as a thing or "noun") and now (reframing racism as a process or "verb").

Is Canada a racist society in which racism is out of control? Or is Canada the site of racism that is under control, thanks to an inclusive framework of applied human rights and an official Multiculturalism? Perhaps racisms in Canada should be assessed and depicted as lying somewhere in between the naiveté of the optimists and the cynical pessimism of the skeptics. Canada is home to a baffling blend of hardcore racists and resolute anti-racists, with most individuals aligned along the continuum between these extremes depending on the situation in which they find themselves. Accordingly, it makes no more sense to exaggerate the magnitude and scope of racisms in Canada than to underestimate its impact and implications. In acknowledging the many faces of racism ("multi-racisms") as a moving target difficult either to pin down or to put away (Frederickson, 2002), this chapter explores racisms in Canada as historically evolving, socially constructed, situationally defined, and deeply entrenched at interpersonal, institutional, ideological, and societal levels. The different dimensions of racism are defined in terms of (1) biology, (2) ideology, (3) culture, (4) structure, and (5) advantage. Reference to racism is dissected into its component elements; that is, prejudice (including ethnocentrism, xenophobia, and stereotyping), discrimination (including harassment), and institutional power. The different levels of racism are also compared, from the interpersonal (including hate racism, polite

TABLE 3-1	Conceptualizing Racisms: Evolving Trends, Shifting Discourses	
Then	**Now**	
Overt	Covert	
Deliberate intent	Unintended consequences	
Sender initiated	Receiver dependent	
Individual	Institutionalized	
Attitudinal	Systemic/Structural	
Pathology/problem	Business as usual	
Doing something	Doing nothing	
Focusing on differences	Ignoring differences	
Minority problem (inferior)	Majority problem (whiteness)	
Prejudice driven	Power driven	
Singular	Plural/Intersectional	
Direct, active, systematic	Indirect, passive, systemic	
Anti -minority	Pro-white	
Stationary object	Moving target/contextual	
Fixed definition	Perspectival (racial Rashomon)	
Thing (racism as noun)	Process (racism as verb)	

racism, and subliminal racism) and the institutional (including systematic and systemic racisms) to the ideological (including everyday and normative racism) and infrastructural (racism at the societal level). A fundamentally different way of thinking and talking about racism is introduced that reframes micro-aggressions as "Racism 3.0." The chapter also explores the origins of racisms, their persistence, contemporary causes of racisms, and the costs and consequences to minorities and society. Finally, various anti-racism strategies are described and corresponding solutions—individual, institutional, and inclusive—are proposed.

PROBLEMATIZING RACISMS IN CANADA

> Nowadays we seem to have a lot of racism but very few racists. How do you explain this para-dox? What is the nature of this racism that dares not to be identified as such? (Blaut, 1992:289)

Is there a lesson to be learned from media attention to the spate of police killings of unarmed black males in the United States, charges of police racial profiling in Toronto, and references to Winnipeg as Canada's most racist city? The profile of racism has expanded exponentially, despite claims that we live in a post-racial and pro-multicultural society, reinforcing its contested status as one of the defining issue of contemporary times (Fleras, 2014a). References to racism consist of those ideologies that explicitly extol racial superi-ority, those beliefs or practices involving coded comments about inferiority, and those indi-viduals and institutions without any clear racialized reference but whose actions may exert adverse consequences on marginalized minorities (Law, 2014; Titley & Lentin, 2012; Weiner, 2012). Such a range of references complicates any consensus over (1) defining racism, (2) determining its nature and magnitude, and (3) finding effective solutions. Insofar as references to racism can mean everything yet nothing—a kind of floating signifier full of sound and sizzle but stripped of substance—efforts to problematize the concept, types, and dynamics of racism in Canada can prove tricky. Consider the following points of debate and contention:

1. Are incidents of racism and racial discrimination increasing across Canada, or do numbers reflect a growing public awareness of racism with a corresponding willingness to report violations to the proper authorities?

2. How valid are all references to racism? Are people prone to exaggerate racism as a scapegoat to justify failure or as a smokescreen to foreclose debate by diverting attention from the issues at hand? Is any criticism directed at people of colour a form of racism by definition? Or is a reluctance to criticize minorities a kind of racism in its own right by implying minority actions are beyond reproach or immune to criticism? Is there a danger of overusing the word "racism"? Blaming racism for everything when race is irrelevant may be racist in its own right, in part because attention is deflected away from the root causes of minority problems. It also draws attention away from prejudice (stereotype and ethnocentrism) and discrimination as key factors.

3. To what extent is racism a case of individual ignorance or fear? Is there such a thing as a racist person or is it more accurate to say that individuals will think and act in ways definable as racist depending on the context or criteria? Or, should racism be interpreted as a socially constructed and complex system of practices and discourses that are historically defined, embedded within institutional structures, reflective of patterns of power, and woven into an ideological fabric?

4. Can racism as a form of domination be isolated and analyzed independently, or must it be seen as mutually constitutive of other forms of domination related to class, gender, ethnicity, or sexual preference in ways that intersect, interlock, and intensify to create a matrix of domination (Bonilla-Silva, 2015; Joseph et al., 2012; Fleming & Morris, 2015)?

5. Is racism about treating people differently or about treating them the same? For some, taking differences seriously is critical to challenging racism. For others, taking differences into account for any reason is fundamentally racist. For example, a post-civil rights commitment to colour-blindness, formal and legal equality, and equal opportunity is now seen as perpetuating new kinds of racism, since applying equal standards to unequal contexts tends to perpetuate patterns of racialized inequality.

6. Should racism be framed in universalistic terms that apply to all times and all places (see Mac an Ghaill, 1999), or do we live in a world of multi-racisms whose origins, expressions, and permutations vary according to time and place (Agnew, 2007; Law, 2014; McVeigh & Lentin, 2006; Sinha, 2006)?

7. Do whites who rarely experience racism because of their privileged status perceive it differently in terms of amount, scope, and types (individual prejudices) than racialized minorities do (institutional practices and systemic barriers) (Blodorn & O'Brien, 2011)? Do all racialized minorities experience racism in the same way, or is racism differently understood and experienced by blacks (as failures or deviants [see West, 2012]),

Muslims (as different or dangerous [Dunn, Klockerm, & Salabay, 2007]), Chinese (as rate-busting successes [Heer, 2012]), and Aboriginal peoples (as militant, unreasonable, or dysfunctional [Banting, Courchene, & Seidle, 2007])?

8. Is racism rational or irrational? Many regard racism as essentially irrational in that it discriminates against others on the basis of arbitrary characteristics; others frame it as a rational strategy employed by vested interests to secure advantage (Bonilla-Silva, 2015).

The problematizing of racism reinforces what many suspect: First, racism refuses to go away even though we would like it to. Instead, racism has proven notoriously resistant and adaptive—intellectually dead, as many have noted, but ready to leap into action during times of change, danger, or anxiety. In brief, racism is proving to be a "scavenger" ideology that parasitically pounces on the most unlikely of sources, bobbing and weaving to escape detection, and losing its precision if analyzed too closely (Frederickson, 2002). Second, racisms (in the plural) exist, to be sure, but ambiguities prevail in unpacking (deconstructing) the "what," "why," "who," "where," and "when." Certain actions are unmistakably racist; others are labelled racist for political or social reasons; yet others become defined as racist because of context, criterion, or consequences. Not surprisingly, racism has become so expansive in scope and application, with such an array of meanings from context to context, that it no longer conveys a meaning in the conventional sense of a single understood definition (Winant, 1998). Accordingly, racism can mean whatever people want it to mean, depending on the context, criteria, and consequences. And while such expansiveness may prove helpful at times, it can also confuse and provoke—no more so than in the contentious domain of racial micro-aggressions.

Micro-aggressions as Racism 3.0: Shifting the Racism Discourse

Two colleagues—one African American, the other Asian American—board a small plane (a "hopper" with a single row of seats on one side, a double row on the other) for a flight from Boston to New York (an actual incident from Sue et al., 2007). A white flight attendant tells them they can sit anywhere they want in the uncrowded plane; accordingly, they choose seats near the front and across the aisle from each other so they can freely converse. At the last minute, three white males in suits enter the plane and take the seats in front of them. Just before takeoff, the flight attendant asks the two colleagues if they would mind moving to the back of the plane to better balance its load. Both see the with resentment at the request to symbolically "sit at the back of the bus." They eventually express their outrage at the prospect of being treated as second class citizens; after all, they had boarded the plane prior to the entry of the white males. But the attendant reacts indignantly to these charges, claiming it was her responsibility to ensure flight safety by redistributing the plane's weight. She also claims to have their best interests in mind by providing them with more space and privacy (deAngelis, 2009). Repeated efforts to explain their perceptions and concerns simply generates more defensiveness and dismissals.

What's going on? Is this an example of the new face of racism or is it someone making a mountain out of a molehill (Mitra, 2014)? Were the colleagues overly sensitive to a legitimate request, thereby misinterpreting an action that lacked racist intent? (One of the colleagues acknowledged the probable sincerity of the attendant in her belief that she acted in good faith and without racial rancor [Sue et al., 2007]). Or did the attendant act out a hidden and unconscious (subliminal) animus towards blacks and/or Asians, albeit behind the pretext of concerns over safety and comfort? Was the offer to move them to the back informed by an implicit bias yet concealed behind coded language (Sue, 2011)? Is the attendant guilty of what is known as racial micro-aggression, namely, insults and slights directed at racialized minorities by seemingly well intentioned yet naïve individuals (Caplan & Ford, 2014)? Does reference to micro-aggression represent a new face of racism consistent with the post-racial sensitivities of the twenty-first century, or is its theoretical value compromised by the practical problems it poses in racializing all snubs or politicizing every criticism (Pettigrew, 2014)? Tanzina Vega (2014) captures a sense of both the potential and provocation of a new micro-racism that others dismiss as "micro-nonsense":

What is less clear is how much is truly aggressive and how much is pretty micro—whether the issues raised are a useful way of bringing to light often elusive slights in a world where overt prejudice is seldom tolerated, or a new form of divisive hypersensitivity, in which casual remarks are blown out of proportion.

Welcome to the new world of racialized bias that promises to scuttle how we see, think, and talk about racisms. Whereas both macro-racism 1.0 and mezzo-racism 2.0 conformed to the contours of a colour-conscious Canada, a so-called colour-blind and post-racial Canada creates a context for a micro-racism at odds with conventional theorizing. Micro-aggressions are those overt and subtle expressions of racism (from slurs to slights) that superficially look innocuous enough but implicitly embed an affront that's experienced as such by the micro-aggressed. These banalities consist of those commonplace interactions, both verbal and non-verbal, intentional or not, that racialized minorities experience as putdowns even if transgressors are oblivious to what's going on (Sue, 2010). These brief daily exchanges are imbued with coded negative messages—from confirming stereotypes to privileging the dominant group as the normative standard and others as aberrant; from essentializing all group members as undifferentiated to denying the pervasiveness of both discrimination at large or the transgressor's own bias. The list below provides examples of micro-aggressions that infiltrate everyday social life (from Sue et al., 2007):

(Continued)

Examples of Racialized Micro Aggressions

Expression by transgressor	Interpretation by the micro-aggressed
Where are you really from?	You are foreign/alien/not really Canadian
Those people. . . .	"Otherizing" the other as remote or alien
You speak good English	Who would have thought that someone of your race could be so articulate?
You are a credit to your race	Your group is usually less intelligent than you
When I look at you, I don't see race	Invalidating identity and people's lived-experiences
There is only one race, the human race	Denying the person as a racial/cultural being
Clutching a purse more tightly	You are a criminal
Following a customer of colour in a store	Acting on stereotypes
Being ignored at a counter	You are less valued/whites get preferential treatment
Taxi passes a racialized person for a white fare	You are dangerous, cannot be trusted
I'm not racist, I have black friends	Friendships do not exclude microaggressions
As a woman, I know what you are experiencing	I can't be a racist because I'm like you
Every can succeed if they work hard enough	Minorities are lazy or incompetent
It's post racial society	Race is irrelevant to success (you have only yourself to blame)
Asking minority person to settle down, be quiet	Do as you are told by knowing your place
Mistaking a racialized minority for service worker	Minorities occupy menial jobs
University buildings named after white males	You don't belong

Micro-aggressions encapsulate two dimensions: the unsuspecting but not entirely innocent sender (transgressor) and the aggrieved receiver (micro-aggressed). Those who perpetuate micro-aggressions may intend no malice since they are oblivious to their complicity in communicating putdowns

(McWhorter, 2014; Sue et al., 2007). They dismiss the seemingly banal interactions that animate everyday micro-aggressions by downplaying the repercussions of their careless words or thoughtless actions (Fleras, 2014a; Wesley & Shiels, 2007). Or, they go about their everyday lives without much attention to how their whiteness privileges and secures advantages for them at the expense of others. Yet these micro-aggressions instill a sense of bewilderment that fosters self-doubt and erodes self-esteem in the micro-aggressed, primarily because the coded subtexts and ambiguous contexts render them tricky to interpret or assess (Sue et al., 2007). Victims often struggle to determine if bigotry is at play or whether to trivialize the bullying by blaming themselves as hyper sensitive (Caplan & Ford, 2014; Sue, 2010). This passage from Caplan and Ford (2014:54) captures the confusion and uncertainties of racialized students at the receiving end of micro-aggressions:

> Much of the mistreatment comes in the form of microaggressions, so that people who are its targets spend a great deal of time in internal dialogue, asking themselves whether they imagined or misinterpreted what the other person said or did and, given the less than blatant form of the mistreatment, feeling apprehension and anguish about whether, if they try to name and object to what was done to them, they will only be told that they are overly sensitive or even that they are imagining it. They worry that speaking up to protest such treatment carries the risk of creating still more problems for themselves and other members of their respective group.

Admittedly, the "micro" in micro-aggression may imply an informality that diminishes its impact to the inconsequential. Moreover a single slur is unlikely to make a difference. But the cumulative weight of these numerous small slights (akin to "a tonne of feathers") establishes a context (or chilly climate) that renders minorities uncomfortable, marginal, or fearful—the symbolic equivalent of death by a thousand cuts (Derald Wing Sue in Fitzgerald, 2015). The totality of micro-incidents exerts an adverse effect in fostering personal strife, often more powerful than open bigotry by virtue of offloading the burden of proof to the micro-aggressed in figuring out what is going on (Essed, 1991; Sue, 2011). Clearly, then, references to the "micro" allude to its brevity and nuance rather than a denial of its power and consequences (Caplan & Ford, 2014).

To date, describing the concept of micro-aggression has proven the easy part. The theorizing of micro-aggression proves more formidable; for example, is micro-aggression simply an extension of polite racism or does it portend the making of new racism narrative? Do micro-aggressions fit into a racism 2.0 framework or is a new racism model pending that animates the debate over what counts as racism, what racism counts, who says so, and on what grounds? I would argue the concept of racism 3.0 secures a new discursive framework ("paradigm") that unapologetically situates racism within the lived-experiences of the micro-aggressed. In contrast to the outer-directedness of direct racism 1.0 and indirect racism 2.0,

(Continued)

racism 3.0 redirects the conceptual focus of racism from that of the "do-er" (sender-oriented) to the "done-to" (receiver-dependent), in the process proposing a new analytical model with far reaching theoretical and practical implications. Moving the frame of reference from intent to impact shines the spotlight on those demeaning snubs and subtle indignities (micro-aggressions) that racialized minorities experience on a daily basis. Unlike the egregious biases attending racism 1.0/2.0, the micro-aggressions of racism 3.0 are conveyed through the banalities of everyday language and the seemingly petty gestures of daily interaction. But in prioritizing the *lived-subjectivities* of racialized minorities as central to any analysis, the defining feature of racism 3.0 is neither the subtlety of the slur nor the seeming innocence of the transgressor. Its definitive aspect resides in assigning definitional priority to the victim's lived-experience in terms of how *they* see, assess, are affected by, and react to these covert micro-aggressions. In endorsing (and rephrasing) bell hooks' (1992) prescient notion of the need to unsettle dominant control of the minority gaze, the paradigmatic core of a racism 3.0 draws attention to racism from the perspective of the micro-aggressed (DeAngelis, 2009; Sue et al., 2007). Table 3-2 provides an ideal-typical comparison along select criteria, as per the left-hand column:

TABLE 3-2	Comparing Racism Discourses: 1.0, 2.0, 3.0		
	Racism 1.0	**Racism 2.0**	**Racism 3.0**
Framing Racism	Macro	Mezzo	Micro
Accounting for Racism	Ideological/ Supremacist	Structural/ Subliminal	Lived experience/ Human interactivity
Level of Expression	Overt/Egregious	Subtle/Systemic	Covert/Banal/Oblivious
Flow/Direction of Racism	Top down	Top down	Bottom up
Source of Racism	Sender oriented	Unintended effects	Receiver dependent
Focus of Analysis	Do-er	Doing	Done-to
Impact Level	Direct	Indirect consequences	Contextual
Source of Definition	External	External	Internal
Ontological Status	Objective/A thing *out there*	Objective/A thing *out there* or *in here*	Constructed reality/Inter-subjective experience

Reference to the concept of micro-aggression as racism 3.0 is not a claim to the discovery of a new kind of racism (Pierce, 1974). To the contrary, it's the linking of micro-aggression to a racism 3.0 that is transformative in realigning how sociologists may think and talk about racism. Both functionalist and conflict models of society tend to focus on racism as a thing *out there* that can be measured by uncovering those variables or factors that create or inhibit its existence. For some, racism is objectified as a deviant and/or irrational act by the deficient or the defiant, with an intention to hurt, exploit, or deny. For others, it's perpetuated within institutions and by institutional practices, without much thought to the systemic bias implicit in a "business as usual" mindset (Fleras, 2014a). By contrast, symbolic interactionism prefers to de-reify racism as a naturally occurring object amenable to analysis through official definition, formal measurement, and explanatory frameworks (also Harris, 2001). Racism is reframed instead as a set of inter-subjective meanings and lived experiences interpreted by individuals in the course of their daily lives and routine interactions (also Essed, 1991). For symbolic interactionists, nothing is inherently racist even though most people take for granted its objective existence. Rather, an activity becomes defined (interpreted or labelled) as racist and brought into existence through meaningful interaction and interpretive practices.

This discursive reframing of racism 3.0 as human accomplishment is consequential. It repudiates those frameworks that reify racism as a thing or object (a noun) based on what authorities or elites define as definitive (see also Henry, 2006; Hier & Walby, 2006). Rethinking racism as an inter-subjective dynamic also serves to remind that racism in the twenty-first century can no longer be reduced to a static and fixed thing out there, but requires a reassessment that elevates it to the level of a dynamic process within a specific context. A focus on consequences (not intent), the subliminal (not conscious), and the unintended (not deliberate) reinforces its status as banal—even boring—rather than egregious, predictable rather than exceptional, mundane rather than extraordinary, implicit rather than explicit, and fundamental rather than incidental (also Gopalkrishan & Habacan, 2007). The reframing of race from a noun (a thing) to that of verb (a process) may well reinforce the status of micro-aggressions as racism 3.0.

DEFINING RACISM

Definitions of racism have varied and multiplied over time and place. They cover such an impossibly broad range of (in)activities that racism can mean everything, yet ends up meaning nothing. Or, as Simon Holdaway (2003) writes, "Racism has been used in so many different ways that it has become a catch-all, sometimes referring to individual racists, sometimes to wholly reified institutions, and sometimes to whole societies, as if none of these phenomena have any relation to human action, other than one of straightforward determinism" (p. 50). Older theories associated racism with a specific set of beliefs and actions, with clearly defined victims and perpetrators. To be a racist in the past meant believing certain groups of people to be racially inferior and deserving of contempt, pity, or indifference. The situation is much different today, although, generally speaking, most definitions include some reference to the imagined attributes of race (Law, 2014). Racism can refer to situations in which racialized minorities (a) feel uncomfortable in the presence of whites (Paikin, 2010), (b) believe that progress is too slow in bringing about equality and inclusiveness, (c) acknowledge racism's presence as so subtle that only victims can recognize and experience it ("micro-aggressions" [Sue et al., 2007]), and (d) claim that any criticism toward them may reflect an unresolved bias.

References to racism are multidimensional and differently defined rather than singular or monolithic (Winant, 1998). While numerous definitions exist (reviewing even a small portion would be exhausting), most of them fall into one of five ideal-typical categories, namely, definitions of racism that focus on biology, ideology, culture, structure, and advantage. Phrased differently, definitions of racism have historically revolved around five major themes categorized accordingly: (1) dislike of others because of how they look (racism as biology); (2) disdain for others because of a particular world view (racism as ideology); (3) distrust of people for what they do (racism as culture); (4) exclusion of others that is institutionalized (racism as structure); and (5) a pattern of entitlement that benefits some and disadvantages others (racism as advantage). To be sure, many definitions incorporate several of these dimensions; after all, references to reality are contextual rather than categorical. Nevertheless, these distinctions may be analytically separated for conceptual purposes.

Racism as Biology Many definitions of racism are anchored in the root, "race," with its attendant notion that biology is destiny. References to *racism as biology* entail a belief in innate differences as socially significant in two ways. First, racism is defined as any belief that links thought and behaviour to biology (biological determinism). Qualities such as intelligence or morality are thought to be determined by genes or biology, according to this line of thinking, with the result that these hardwired racial differences are perceived as fixed and unalterable. Discriminatory treatment of others is then justified on the grounds of innate differences that are natural and fixed (Paikin, 2010). Second, racism can be defined as any treatment—either negative or positive—directed at others solely because of race (or skin colour). To deny or exclude others because of race is clearly racism; to provide preferential assistance to others because of race is no less racist. In both cases, individuals are singled out for different treatment on the basis of appearances rather than what they need or are entitled to.

Racism as Ideology Strictly speaking, the concept of race is concerned with cataloguing perceived differences into predetermined categories. Racism, by contrast, transforms these differences into a relatively coherent ideology that justifies the racial superiority of one group over another (Vucetic, 2014). According to definitions of racism as ideology, humanity can be partitioned into a set of fixed and discrete categories of population known as "race." Each of these racial categories embraces a distinctive and inherited assemblage of physical, cultural, and psychological characteristics that can be arranged in ascending or descending order of acceptance or desirability. From this emerges an ideology of intellectual or moral superiority—a hierarchy of superior and inferior races that unjustly diminishes others and justifies this denigration by reference to race. Reference to racism justified European imperialism and domination of others, although it was not until the late nineteenth century that arguments in support of racial inequality were pressed into an official state ideology of white superiority (Melle, 2009).

Many definitions continue to frame racisms as ideology (Hier & Bolaria, 2007). Both micro and macro variations prevail. In micro-level theories, racism is framed at the level of social psychology, with individuals and their attitudes as a primary focus. A pattern can be discerned: First, racism is defined as a set of ideas (beliefs) and ideals (norms, or values). Second, these beliefs induce individuals to formulate negative attitudes (prejudice). Third, these prejudicial attitudes generate the discriminatory actions that exclude or exploit.

Fourth, changing people's attitudes provides the key to eradicating racism. Definitions of racisms at the macro ideological level are conceptualized along collective lines. Racially formed categories secure an organizing principle of social organization that shapes both individual identities and societal dynamics. Take Marxist or socialist theories of racism (Bolaria & Li, 1988; Pitcher, 2012; West, 2009) as an example: Racism is critical in securing a modern capitalist economy, with racism as a hegemonic device that fragments the working class at the expense of its common interests. Those theories that posit class as a central explanatory framework tend to reduce racism to the level of a legitimating ideology (or a false consciousness) by the rich to divide, control, or distract the working classes (Bonilla-Silva, 2015).

Racism as Culture In recent years, the definitional focus of racism has shifted from biology-based racism to racisms rooted in cultural differences and incompatibilities (Byrd, 2011; Dunn et al., 2007; Seymour, 2010). Appeals to cultural inferiority and a dislike of others because of their differences are replacing a preoccupation with race (biology) as a basis for definition (Lamoin & Dawes, 2010). Racism is no longer defined as a discourse of dominance over racial inferiors, as was the case with colonialism. The objective then was to destroy "the others" as an impediment, exploit them for gain, or absorb them in the name of progress. With reference to race-as-biology no longer in vogue, the frame of emphasis has shifted toward the dangers that foreign cultural practices pose to national unity, identity, and citizenship (Fleras, 2004b). Dominant sectors are defined not as racially superior, but as culturally normal and superior. In turn, subdominant groups are dismissed as a culturally dangerous threat to a secular and liberal society, rather than as innately inferior. For example, while Islamophobia is widely acknowledged and pervasive, this fear of Muslims rarely invokes perceptions of racial inferiority but instead those of Islamist barbarity (Fekete, 2009). Muslims and Middle Eastern folk are racialized as an ethno-religious threat to security ("the terrorist within" [Sivanandan, 2009:viii]), as barriers to integration and belonging, and as people whose cultural differences clash with mainstream values and beliefs (Dunn et al., 2007; Gottschalk & Greenberg, 2008). In that cultural differences are vilified as dangerous, irrelevant, or inferior, the racialization of others through claims of cultural superiority has proven as exclusionary in advancing structures of inferiority and differentiation as have old-fashioned racial ideologies.

Racism as Structure Another set of definitions focuses on racism as structure. This broader definition goes beyond racism as a set of ideas or individual actions, despite the tendency for many to conflate racism with deviant acts that incite prejudice, hatred, or violence (Bonilla-Silva, 2015). Racism instead is defined as a key structural component of society that infiltrates its institutions and values, and permeates the mindsets of citizens (T. Coates, 2015). To be sure, structural definitions of racism do not reject the importance of ideological definitions. But in prioritizing racism as the controlling ideology of a racialized society (i.e., a society structured (or organized) along race lines) (Bonilla-Silva, 1997), racism is framed as the *source* of much ideology rather than as the result of it (Fleras, 2014a). The structural character of racism is situated within the bigger picture, namely, the reality that society is *founded on* the principle of advancing a racialized and Eurocentric society; *grounded in* the exploitation and oppression of Aboriginal peoples and racialized minorities; and *bounded* by the need to preserve the prevailing and racialized distribution of power and privilege (Feagin, 2006:47). Structural racism may explain why racisms continue to persist despite a raft of anti-racism interventions. Theorizing racism as structural situates it as foundational to a society's constitutional order, that is, the bedrock upon which notions of superiority are founded, constructed, defended. Removal of racism involves nothing less than the unsettling of power relations through the radical transformation of societal priorities, institutions, and values (Paradies, 2005).

Racism defined as structure is based on the idea that neither society nor institutions are neutral or value-free. To the contrary, their design, organization, assumptions, agendas, and operations reflect the founding assumptions and foundational principles of the dominant racial frame that privilege some, while disadvantaging others (Editorial, 2005b; Teelucksingh, 2006). A racialized bias with respect to what is desirable, normal, and acceptable is woven into the very fabric of society, in effect becoming so normalized that people tend to think of it as natural and self-explanatory (Kobayashi, 2001; Kumi, 2008). Societies racialized in power and privilege are self-perpetuating, resulting in the transmission of inequities from one generation to the next without much disruption to the racialized status quo. In short, defining racism as structure emphasizes the racialized arrangement of practices and beliefs that are sewn into the normative fabric of society, systemically embedded in institutions, practiced unobtrusively through communication, and experienced as part of the informal culture and ordinary interaction (Peter Li, in Eisenkraft, 2010). Moreover, once society is racialized through the construction of racialized categories, racism as structural assumes an ideological life of its own that cannot be reduced to other forms of oppression such as gender or class, or framed as a byproduct ("epiphenomena") (Dei, 2007).

Racism as Advantage Definitions of racism are often equated with disadvantages associated with outgroup membership (Powell, Branscombe, & Schmitt, 2005). Yet racism can also be validly framed in terms of in-group advantage or privilege, in effect reinforcing the idea that advantages experienced by one group occur at the expense and disadvantage of others. In the words of Wellman (1993:x), racism as advantage can be defined as those ". . .culturally sanctioned beliefs, which, regardless of intentions involved, defend the advantages whites have because of the subordinated position of racial minorities." As is the case with structural definitions, racism as advantage goes beyond individual prejudice, misperception, or hostility; rather it entails a defense of the racialized system from which advantage is derived on the basis of race. A privileged relationship exists in which whites benefit from a system of advantages (from cultural values to institutional practices) based on race privilege and a racialized status quo (Bonilla-Silva, 2015; Nell, 2012; Wellman, 1993). In other words, racism as a framework of dis/advantage is about perpetuating white superiority by infusing racial categories into all levels of society to promote and sustain white dominance while denying resources to racialized minorities (Lippard, 2011).

A Working Definition of Racism

One thing is clear from this overview of definitions of racism: A working definition of racism must go beyond a personal ideology based on race prejudice. It must focus on a system of dis/advantage founded on institutional power, anchored in values and beliefs, and predicated on a supremacist mindset. It must also incorporate actions that deny equality to minorities yet offer advantages to the mainstream; focus on institutional policies and practices that exclude or exploit others; and embrace a set of generalized beliefs and actions that imply the superiority of one group over others. Mindful of these preconditions and multiplicities, **racism** can be defined as *those ideas and ideals (ideology) that are embedded within individual attitudes, cultural values, institutional practices, and those structural arrangements that assert or imply the assumed superiority of one social group over another, together with the institutional power to put these perceptions into practice in ways that secure advantage for the mainstream but reinforce disadvantage for those racialized as different or inferior.*

This working definition draws attention to key attributes of racism, namely, its status as an ideology either articulated or implied, a racialized structure that benefits some at the expense of others, a corresponding set of practices that involves deliberate intent or reflects inadvertent consequences, and an impact that embraces both personal and institutional dimensions. More importantly, it demonstrates how racism transcends simple and surface level expressions of individual prejudice or irrational forms of bigotry that are divorced from the social structure (Feagin, 2006). Rather, it entails a complex system of exclusionary conditions and dynamics, including ideologies, discourses, discursive practices, institutions, and values within a particular social, cultural, and historical context that pervades, permeates, and interconnects all aspects of societal reality (Bonilla-Silva, 2015; Goldberg, 2002; Macedo & Gounari, 2006). Finally, the centrality of institutional power is duly acknowledged in this definition. In that racism is about power—and because those with power are rarely aware of it, yet disinclined to share it with others—any unmasking of racism is unlikely without a protracted struggle.

COMPONENTS OF RACISM

Racism does not reflect a monolithic reality. Rather, in a multicultural society, racism is a complex and multifaceted dynamic involving different components. Each of the components or building blocks of racism—namely, prejudice (including ethnocentrism, stereotypes, and xenophobia), discrimination (including harassment), and power—contributes to the totality of racism as an ideology and practice.

Prejudice

The concept of **prejudice** refers to negative, often unconscious, and preconceived notions about others. Prejudice arises because of a very normal tendency to prejudge persons or situations (Bakanic, 2009). It represents a precondition for processing information about the world; that is, it equips individuals with the cognitive tools to define situations and then act upon these definitions. Admittedly, there is nothing inherently racist about prejudice since everyone makes prejudgments when defining situations or making sense of our fast-paced world. Prejudice becomes a problem only when people put these prejudgments into practice to deny or exclude others.

In general, prejudice can be defined as any attitude, belief, or feeling toward members of a group that directly or indirectly implies negativity or hostility (Brown, 2010; Rosado, 2013). More specifically, prejudice consists of *prejudgments* that are irrational and unfounded on grounds of existing or compelling evidence. A preconceived set of attitudes is embraced that mistakenly encourages people to see and judge others without taking into account internal differences (Holdaway, 1996). According to psychologist Frances Aboud, prejudice provides a very simple way of seeing the world, and this craving for simplicity may be transformed into a preference for in-group members (as cited in Abel, 2001). Such ignorance may persist into adulthood; unlike ignorance, however, prejudice is inflexible and characterized by a refusal to modify beliefs when presented with contrary evidence. Attitudes and beliefs that pertain to racial prejudice often possess a deeply ingrained core that makes them resistant to wholesale change; after all, they serve a number of social and psychological functions that help people orient themselves to others and to the environment (John Dovidio, cited in APA, 2009).

At times, expressions of prejudice are conscious but politely worded to avoid open offence. At other times, individuals may not be aware of their prejudice except in those split-second moments when they find they have categorized people by racial groups or exposed a dormant dislike (Banaji & Greenwald, 2013). Tests, such as the Implicit Association Test, reveal how the vast majority of people of having hidden and unconscious prejudices that stand in sharp contrast to their explicitly egalitarian values (Banaji, 2003; Choudhury, 2015). Just as people don't always "speak their minds," so too do they rarely "know their minds," culminating in a disconnect between the conscious and the unconscious (Anderson, 2010). Individuals may be unwilling to admit (or self-report) prejudicial attitudes for fear of "blowing their cover" by answering in a socially undesirable way in a society that claims to be post-racial and pro-multicultural (Tinkler, 2012). This notion of prejudice as implicit (Bakanic, 2009; Caines, 2004)—a kind of "mental residue"—should not be discounted as trivial or inconsequential in predicting spontaneous behaviours (Hailey & Olson, 2013). Consider how the nature of law enforcement often requires police officers to make snap judgements based on subconscious and implicit prejudices about the dangers posed by suspects in criminal activity (also Mooney, 2014). In that people are a lot more prejudiced than they think they are—a survey of 2200 Canadians conducted by Leger Marketing for Ensemble and Association for Canadian Studies (2013) in the week of November 5, 2012, found that one in four Canadians report they have been victims of prejudice—no one should underestimate the potential of prejudice in perpetuating patterns of discriminatory inequality (Blank et al., 2004; Tinkler, 2012).

Prejudice is widely regarded as a psychological phenomenon with a corresponding set of rigid attitudes or authoritarian personality traits (Adorno et al., 1950; Allport, 1954 but see Reicher, 2007, for a reassessment). The creation of negative attitudes toward others is seen in part as a normal psychological process, wherein the world is divided into in-groups and higher status groups (that we favour) and out-groups (that we dislike) (Hailey & Olson, 2013). Others link these prejudgments with a visceral and deep-seated fear of those whose appearances or practices threaten the prevailing status quo. People who feel irrationally threatened by a particular group justify inflicting harm on "others" as acts of self-preservation. In that prejudice may involve a projection of fear or displacement of anxieties upon others, such beliefs may say more about the perpetrator than the victim (Curtis, 1997). Still others define prejudice as unmistakably social (or focus on its social dimensions to overcome the "prejudice problematic" that reduces racism to an individual attitude [Bonilla-Silva, 2015]). To them, it neither materializes out of unresolved psychological issues nor necessarily reflects a warped personality. Rather, prejudice arises from group interaction within unequal contexts involving an impulse to control others by disadvantaging them in the competition for scarce resources. In that prejudice is more the result of competition than its cause, a racialized system is perpetuated that privileges some and disprivileges others.

Ethnocentrism **Ethnocentrism** can be defined as a belief in the superiority of one culture over another. Like prejudice, ethnocentrism is a normal and universal process, reflecting patterns of socialization that focus on generating in-group loyalty. In some cases, a belief in cultural superiority is openly articulated, for example, by comparing other cultures or cultural practices with one's own standards of right, acceptable, or desirable. In other cases, ethnocentrism involves the universal tendency to interpret reality from one's cultural perspective as natural and normal—and assume that others are doing so as well or would be if they knew better—while dismissing other perspectives as inferior, irrelevant, or threatening. To be sure, there is nothing intrinsically wrong with endorsing one's cultural values as self-evident and preferable. Difficulties arise when these standards become a frame of reference for negatively evaluating others as backward, immoral, or irrational. Further problems appear when these ethnocentric judgments are manipulated to condone the mistreatment of others. In other words, ethnocentrism is two-edged: Favouritism toward one's group may forge in-group cohesion and morale; it can also foster out-group tension and hostility. And when those in positions of power put their ethnocentrism into practice, the results can get discriminatory.

Both prejudice and ethnocentrism often result in a proliferation of stereotypes about out-group members. **Stereotypes** are essentially generalizations about others, both unwarranted and unfounded on the basis of available evidence (Kashima, Fiedler, & Freytag, 2008). Stereotyping reinforces a universal tendency to reduce a complex phenomenon to simple (or simplistic) explanations that can be generalized to a whole category (Cohen, 2011; Dovidio, Hewstone, Glick, et al., 2010). It reflects an essentialized notion that all individuals within a certain category will act uniformly and predictably because of this membership (Essed, 1991). Racist stereotypes proliferate when people are judged based on stereotypes about their race or ethnicity: Germans are typed as industrious; Muslims as "bombers, billionaires, or belly dancers" (Shaheen, 2009); Aboriginal peoples are either warriors or on welfare; blacks are natural born athletes or criminals; and the Japanese are naturally gifted but emotionally distant. Those who are typecast often live up to these stereotypes (a kind of self-fulfilling prophecy), or down to them in the case of underperforming racialized minorities (Steele, 2006). Evidence also suggests that people tend to view out-groups as uniformly homogeneous and an undifferentiated mass rather than as individuals with personalities, skills, and talents.

As a strategy for simplifying the environment (Dovidio, Hewstone, Glick, et al., 2010), stereotypes in themselves are harmless. Problems arise when these preconceived mental images are used to justify the erection of discriminatory barriers or when they generate self-fulfilling practices. Employers who must make rapid-fire decisions may rely on subconscious stereotypes: Candidates with white-sounding names are much more likely to receive interviews (Jimenez, 2009; Oreopoulis, 2009). Experiments in the United States found that landlords responded positively to prospective Asian American tenants (perceived as quiet, passive, smart, hardworking, and punctual) but negatively to prospective black and Latino tenants (seen as lazy, prone to violence, and concentrated in low paying jobs [Feldman & Weseley, 2013]). Even model minority stereotypes underestimate the challenges associated with achieving these goals or with trying to be normal. For example, consider the stereotype of the "strong black woman" as a celebration of accomplishment under difficult circumstances. This very stereotype can also conceal patterns of suffering, anger, and desperation because of the burden and the painful consequences in living up to this image. Black women are subsequently ensnared in a double bind given the ease of reinforcing the very stereotypes people are trying to subvert. If they live up to the stereotype, their problems and fears are ignored so that they must fend for themselves. If they admit to weakness and vulnerability, they are criticized for not conforming to the powerful expectation (the stereotype) of self-reliance (Newman, 2012).

Like prejudice, stereotypes are social. Stereotypes do not necessarily represent an error in perception, at least no more so than prejudice is a case of erroneously processing information. More accurately, stereotyping is yet another instrument of social control. Consider how the dispossession of Aboriginal peoples' lands was facilitated through negative images of them as savages, cannibals, and brutes. A pervasive "anti-orientalism" in British Columbia fostered hatred against Asian populations, thereby simplifying the task of displacing 22 000 Japanese Canadians from the West Coast in 1942. In proving that the more things change, the more they stay the same, Asian-Canadians continue to be stereotyped as "too Asian" or in terms of "too many Asians" (Gilmour, Bhandar, & Heer, 2012; Heer, 2012). Hostility toward Islam continues to fester in the light of demeaning media stereotypes that portray Arab-Muslim Canadians as (1) members of a devalued and backward minority, (2) colonized peoples without democratic traditions, and (3) a ragtag collection of terrorists and religious fanatics (Goldberg, 2005; Hennebry & Momani, 2013; Karim, 2002; Shaheen, 2009).

All negative stereotypes are hurtful; nevertheless, not all negative portrayals have an equivalent impact. Context and consequence are critical in shaping different outcomes and responses. For example, members of a dominant group need not be unduly concerned with negative stereotyping about themselves. As a group, they have control over a wide range of representations that flatter or empower. Negative stereotypes might cause discomfort for "pale males"; nevertheless, men as a group possess both the political authority and economic clout to neutralize or deflect negative portrayals. In that power and privilege provide a protective buffer, even a constant barrage of negativity can be absorbed without harm or damage. But for minorities with specific vulnerabilities, stereotyping is a problem, given their lack of institutional power and resources (Elmasry, 1999). Each negative image or unflattering representation reinforces their peripheral status as not quite Canadian.

Xenophobia Xenophobia can be defined as an irrational fear of the other, with a corresponding dislike because of this fear. Nowhere is this more evident at present than in people's suspicions and hostility toward Muslims (Taras, 2012). An online poll of 1522 Canadians commissioned by the ACS and CRRF demonstrated that 52 percent of the respondents believe Muslims can't be trusted (70% in Quebec vs. 43% among English Canadians). Nearly as many believe discrimination against Muslims is mainly the fault of Muslims themselves, while the Internet is fingered as the main conduit for spreading anti-Muslim racism in Canada (Boswell, 2012). The consequences are unsettling: Xenophobia distorts the prism through which Muslims and Islam are viewed, culminating in a paranoia that leads to hatred, hostility, and discrimination (Lean, 2012).

Is Islamophobia a form of xenophobic racism (Satzewich, 2011; also Dunn, Klockerm, & Salabay, 2007)? Evidence would suggest yes. Since 9/11, Islamophobia has evolved into a triple threat in terms of politics, demographics, and the so-called "clash of civilizations" (Esposito, 2012). Islamophobia as cultural racism tends to essentialize, otherize, homogenize, and demonize by conflating all Muslims into a single nation of Islam (Afshar, 2013). Muslim women are portrayed as "backward, voiceless, deprived of basic rights, degraded by men, victims of violence, and uneducated" (Alsultany, 2012; Bangash, 2012; Razack, 2008; Taras, 2012). Framing Muslims and Middle Eastern people in this way provides a simple explanation and expediency that exonerates the West of any wrongdoing in the Middle East. Clearly, then, Islamophobia constitutes a form of prejudicial racism that reflects (a) discrimination against Muslims across a range of fields, (b) disadvantages that Muslim women and girls experience because of their religion and gender, (c) restrictions involving opposition to the building of mosques or wearing of full veiling for women in public domains, workplaces, or in service delivery, (d) biased media coverage, (e) hostility by political parties and extremist groups to gain votes and popularity (ENAR, 2012), and (f) conflating Islam and Muslims with extremism (Esposito, 2012). In short, they are seen as "guilty till proven innocent", while Islam is perceived as the cause rather than the context for terrorism.

Discrimination

The word "discrimination" can be employed in different ways. Non-evaluative meanings indicate a capacity to distinguish (e.g., a colour-blind person may not be able to discriminate [distinguish] between red and green). Evaluative meanings of discrimination can be used positively (a discriminating palate) or negatively (indicating narrow-mindedness). Section 15 of the *Canadian Charter of Rights and Freedoms* prohibits discrimination on the basis of race, ethnicity, or origins. Yet the Charter concedes the possibility of seemingly "discriminatory" measures, such as employment equity, to assist historically disadvantaged minorities. Distinctions are not discriminatory, in other words, if they have a demonstrably justified and legitimate goal of reversing discrimination by levelling the playing field (see the Chapter 5 Debate box on employment equity). Discrimination is also permissible if demonstrated to be a *bona fide* occupational requirement (for example, Canadian experience or fluency in one of the official languages). In brief, some forms of discrimination are acceptable—even essential—to the functioning of a complex and democratic society. But in situations where racism is framed as a form of social exclusion, discrimination is defined as the process for putting this exclusivity into practice (Saloojee, 2005).

Patterns of discrimination may be differently expressed—blatant or oblique, individualized or institutionalized, deliberate or unintended—with the result that the motivation behind an act is secondary to its effect on the victim (Rusk, 2005). The focus of discrimination itself has shifted: From a predominantly individual problem reflecting prejudicial attitudes and differential treatment, discrimination is increasingly perceived as largely systemic and embedded in a complex interplay of institutional relations and practices whose negative consequences reflect the differential effects of apparently neutral policies and similar treatment (George & Chaze, 2014; Henry & Tator, 2009). How discrimination as a concept has evolved over the course of Canadian social history is captured by Sheppard (2010):

a. Explicit discriminatory laws and policies prevailed into the late 1940s. Women—especially married women—were not treated as equal citizens under the law but were exposed to exclusions and discrimination. Those individuals with physical and mental disabilities endured explicit discrimination premised on eugenics, segregation, or institutionalization. Discrimination against gay men resulted in the criminalization of their sexual activity, while lesbianism was seen as otherworldly and deserving of penalty. Racist exclusions prevailed in immigration, employment, housing and voting laws, while racialized immigrants dealt with a Canada that could best be described as xenophobic, racist, and nativist.

b. A significant shift in thinking about discrimination and inequality emerged shortly after the end of WWII. The 1948 Universal Declaration of Human Rights incorporated equality (and anti-discrimination) as one of its foundational principles. Canadian law reform addressed the most overt government-sponsored forms of discrimination by eliminating most egregious forms of state bias. Inception of formal models of equality eventually resulted in the *Human Rights Act* of 1977, with its prohibitions against discrimination in specific contexts (including housing, employment, social services) and on the basis of unfounded prejudice and stereotypes related to race, religion, and sexual orientation.

c. By the late 1970s and early 1980s, Canadians had become increasingly aware of the systems-based nature of discrimination, both pervasive and institutionalized within normal patterns and practices of social exclusion (substantive conceptions of equality). As the promise of formal equality in a post-civic-rights era faded, the face of discrimination shifted from something random and discrete to an institutionalized and normatively (systemically) dynamic embedded in a complex interplay of organizational rules, relations, policies, and practices. The consequence of this shift proved transformative. Traditional and formal notions of equality as sameness were replaced by an awareness that institutions had to move over and accommodate needs-based differences. In other words, to paraphrase Colleen Sheppard (2010), the challenge was no longer about incorporating racialized minorities and women into a "palemale" world, but about modifying institutional worlds to make them more accommodative and responsive to those historically disadvantaged. Table 3-3 adapted from Sheppard (2010:18) captures the distinction between competing models of discrimination and inequality.

The interplay of these components—that is, differential treatment and differential effects because of race—produces a working definition of discrimination along the lines proposed by the United Nations (see Blank, Dabady, & Citro, 2004): **Discrimination** can be defined as any restrictive act, whether deliberate or not, that has the intent or the effect of adversely affecting ("denying" or "excluding") others on grounds other than merit or ability.

Is there a relationship between prejudice and discrimination? Often there is: Whereas prejudice refers to attitudes and beliefs, *discrimination* entails putting these prejudgments into practice. A vicious cycle can be discerned: Prejudice toward groups creates a

TABLE 3-3	Rethinking Discrimination: From Direct Impact Model to Adverse Effects Model	
Shift from	**Shift Towards**	
Discrimination as a largely individual problem reflecting random and discrete incidents	Discrimination is systemic; i.e., deeply and unintentionally embedded within normative values and institutional relations, practices, and policies	
Focus on prejudicial attitudes of perpetrators	Focus on the experiential effects on those victimized	
Discrimination as differential treatment	Discrimination as similar treatment in unequal contexts; i.e., the adverse effects stemming from the differential impact of seemingly neutral rules and rewards	
Doing something	Doing nothing when something needs to be done	
Discrimination framed in term of distinct and homogenous social groups	Discrimination reflects overlapping inequalities linked to intersecting identities rather than applied uniformly to whole groups	
Individual remedies and treatment	Institutional adjustment	

discriminatory effect resulting in marginalization and failure that then reinforces the original prejudice. And so the cycle continues, thus reinforcing the popular equation: Racism = Prejudice + Discrimination. But the distinction or relationship is neither clear-cut nor causal. Discrimination can exist without prejudice, especially when negative treatment of racialized minorities is institutionally embedded. Thus, institutions can operate on discriminatory grounds even if individuals themselves are free of prejudice (this is called systemic bias). Conversely, prejudice may flourish without its expression in discrimination. Individuals may be prejudiced, but compartmentalize these attitudes by refusing to act in a discriminatory manner for fear of losing face or facing retaliation. In brief, prejudice and discrimination are analytically distinct, if mutually related, concepts that can vary independently under certain conditions.

Harassment is commonly appraised as a type of discrimination. According to both the Ontario Human Rights Commission and the Canadian Human Rights Commission, harassment is an action (actions) that bother someone, threaten or intimidate them, entail unwelcome physical contact, or create unfair treatment because of race, ethnicity, gender, religion and so on—presumably for the purpose of demeaning, belittling, or humiliating others through actions that interfere with their rights, well-being, or performance. It includes persistent and unwelcome actions of a racially oriented nature (from racial jokes to degrading pictures to insults and name-calling) by those who ought reasonably to have known that their actions would cause offence or harm.

Both discrimination and harassment constitute an abuse of institutional power. Seemingly minor and isolated incidents may amount to harassment when viewed over time or within an institutionalized context. The creation of a chilly climate or "poisoned environment" because of harassment can also have an adverse effect on a person's work, study, involvement, or well-being. For some, harassment is ultimately defined from the perspective of the victim who determines what distinguishes offence from harassment, or consensual conduct from an abuse of power (see insert on micro-aggression in this chapter). Others disagree and insist on making a principled distinction between harassment and causing offence. They believe that the definition of "harassment" should be restricted to speech or behaviour that habitually targets a particular individual or group in a way that prevents full and equal participation. To include merely offending someone through random ethnic jokes or thoughtless remarks may have the perverse effect of expanding harassment to the point where it means everything yet nothing.

Institutionalized Power

Racism consists of a complex interplay of ideas and actions involving a mix of prejudice (stereotyping, xenophobia, and ethnocentrism) with that of discrimination (harassment). It also encompasses an ideology with a patterned set of responses that underscores the unequal treatment of minorities through political exclusion, economic exploitation, or social segregation. The key addition in this equation is the primacy of power (Dovidio, Gluszek, John, et al., 2010; Rosado, 2013). Without power, nothing happens—But not just any kind of power; rather, power that is institutionalized (i.e., backed by the authority of the state and bolstered by political arrangements and legal statutes). Those with access to institutional power possess the ability to transform human differences into prejudicial attitudes and discriminatory actions that advantages the mainstream at the expense of racialized minorities (Rosado, 2013).

Power is a complex and contentious concept that defies simple definition (Olsen, 2011). Many like to think of power as the capacity of A to get B to do something that B would otherwise not do. This predominantly Weberian approach characterizes power as something systematic that is: (1) possessed by individuals or actors, (2) intentionally and visibly exercised, (3) manifested in open competition or conflicts, and (4) directly observable through interaction (see Prus, 1999). But such a conceptualization is too narrow because it ignores the logic behind power that is systemic. A neo-Marxist orientation contends that power (a) is deeply embedded in the founding assumptions and foundational principles of a society's constitutional order yet manifest in the structure of social institutions and ideological values, (b) may exert unintended rather than deliberate effects that reflect the normal functioning of the system, (c) focuses on the minds of the subjects through dominant discourses (for example, media) that diverts attention from points of conflict yet sustains discriminatory social structures and unequal social relations (Brunon-Ernst, 2012; Henry & Tator, 2002), and (d) may assume a latent form rather than a visibly manifested one when setting rules, shaping the parameters of debate, and defining self-serving situations and options (Grabb, 2009). This systemic approach to power reinforces the cliché that power is most powerful when least visible and imprecise, or what Homi K. Bhabha (1998) calls the "tyranny of the transparent" (cited in Pinder, 2013:ix).

For Foucault, power is not something that can be measured in either/or terms. Nor should references to power be defined as (a) a "thing" that is possessed by a person or sovereign state; (b) concentrated exclusively in a status or office; (c) reflective of a zero-sum game of winners and losers; (d) coercive in nature; and (e) expressed in negative terms such as "excludes" or "oppresses" or "conceals." Rather, it should be employed in the Foucauldian sense as a dynamic (i.e., a "verb") involving a series of linkages, patterns of knowledge and speech, and network of relations that are dispersed throughout society (Dhamoon, 2009; Foucault, 1980). Following Foucault (1980), power is everywhere insofar as it's diffused (rather than concentrated), discursive (rather than coercive) and entrenched (rather than possessed) in discourses (accepted forms of knowledge and ways of knowing) and representations, arrangements, and allocations. Instead of wielding power in the conventional sense of control or oppression, people discipline others (and themselves) without any willful coercion on their part because of embedded values, beliefs, and norms both pervasive and powerful yet beyond awareness.

In short, racism is always about power relations (Bonilla-Silva, 2015; Mustachich, 2013). Power as a constituent of racism consists of virtually any type of exploitation or exclusion that institutionalizes in-group privileges at the expense of outgroup disadvantages (Al-Krenawi & Graham, 2003; Powell et al., 2005). It operates by privileging mainstream ideologies as common sense (Lee & Lutz, 2005), resulting in patterns of control under a system of ideas, laws, and practices that regulate the aspirations, actions, and livelihood of racialized minorities (Michael Brown, 2005). For example, the institutionalized power inherent within an old-white-boys' network effectively screens out minorities through discriminatory hiring and unintended promotional practices that deny or exclude. Not surprisingly, racism is less about people's attitudes, but more about the institutionalization of power to establish agendas, networks, and practices that reinforce the advantages of one group over another. bell hooks (1995) puts it into perspective by linking racism with power:

> Why is it so difficult for many white folks to understand that racism is oppressive not because white folks have prejudicial feelings about black people . . . but because it is a system that promotes domination and subjugation? (pp. 154–155)

Put bluntly, racism is about power, not pigmentation (Khayatt, 1994). Racism goes beyond individual prejudice, but focuses on those **institutional powers** that differentiate, categorize, and exclude. Racism is not about differences *per se* but about how those in positions of power racialize these differences to protect ruling-class privilege. Racism is not about treating others differently because they are different, but about their differential treatment within contexts of power that limit or oppress (Blauner, 1972). To be sure, those with the most power are frequently least aware of the privileges they possess (Scheurich & Young, 1997). This obliviousness is not surprising: When one group accumulates more power than other groups, the more powerful group constructs an environment that privileges its members at the expense of others. Moreover, the longer one group remains in power, the more their ways of thinking about what is acceptable and necessary become normalized and universalized as measures of merit and predictors of success.

SECTORS OF RACISM

That racism in one form or another exists in Canada is surely beyond debate at this point in our history. With the benefit of some prodding and sharp reminders, Canadians are increasingly facing up to our checkered past, with its bewildering mixture of tolerance and repression. Canada was founded on racist principles and with a tendency toward collective denial and historical amnesia (Henry & Tator, 2009; Lowman & Barker, 2015; Razack, 2004), and it continues to be racialized because of its foundational principles and fundamental values. Some forms of racism are now widely condemned and detested; other strands

TABLE 3-4	Sectors of Racism		
Interpersonal	Institutional	Ideological	Infrastructural
hate	systematic	Everyday	society
polite	systemic	Normative	
subliminal			

continue to be endemic to Canada, with few signs of disappearing. To complicate the issue further, the threat of social sanctions may have prompted a redefinition of racism in seemingly more innocuous ways. In other words, the battle against racism is not won; it's just gone underground.

Clearly, then, racism is not a uniform concept that reflects a singular experience or common reality. On the contrary, different types of racism can be discerned that vary in intent, levels of awareness, magnitude and scope, style or pattern of expression, and costs and consequences. These variations have led to the creation of a racism typology based on the following four sectors: (1) interpersonal racism (including hate, polite, and subliminal); (2) institutional racism (including systematic and systemic); (3) ideological racism (including normative [micro-aggressions] and everyday); and (4) infrastructural racism (society) (see Table 3-4). Unmasking each of these ideal types will expose the complex and multidimensional nature of racism as theory and practice. Envisaging racism as multifaceted also underscores the complexity of matching solutions to problems.

Interpersonal Racism

Interpersonal racism entails a pattern of dislike that occurs at the level of individual and group relations. This negativity is directed at the "other" because of who he is or what she stands for. Three types of interpersonal racism can be discerned: hate, polite, and subliminal.

Hate Racism The kind of racism that most commonly comes to mind is **hate racism**. It refers to the direct hatred of the racialized "other" that once prevailed in the past and continues to exist in the present among a handful of the deficient or defiant. Intrinsic to hate racism is its explicit and highly personalized character. Hate racism is expressed through sharply personal attacks on those who are perceived as culturally or biologically inferior. These personalized attacks often consist of derogatory slurs and minority name-calling—but physical abuse may also be involved as well as destruction of property through vandalism.

Even a cursory glance over Canada's past exposes the stain of hate racism (Walker, 1997; Wallis & Fleras, 2008). This may come as a shock to many readers. Certain myths are deeply entrenched in our collective memories, especially those that extol Canada's progressive status, the absence of American-style race riots and institutionalized slavery, and the entrenchment of multicultural and human rights principles. Close scrutiny suggests otherwise. Canada's treatment of racial, aboriginal, and ethnic minorities has left much to be desired (Backhouse, 1999; Lowman & Barker, 2015). Chinese, Japanese, Indo-Pakistanis, First Nations, Jews, Mid-east folk, and blacks have been and continue to be the object of dislike, displacement, or discrimination. Laws and practices were invoked that segregated people of colour, especially blacks, from full and equal participation in Canadian societies until the 1950s and 1960s (Walker, 1997). Racist groups like the Ku Klux Klan have also relied on violence to cultivate an environment of fear and hatred against minorities throughout the United States and Canada (Barrett, 1987; Pitsula, 2013).

As noted throughout this text, hate racism persists at present (Perry, 2015). Anti-Semitism remains an ongoing problem in Canada, while anti-black racism is routinely encountered by young males within the criminal justice system. Of particular concern—especially since 9/11 and the spread of jihadist terrorism in the name of Islam—is mounting hatred toward anyone perceived as Middle Eastern. This **Islamophobia** reflects deeply ingrained and largely unexamined anxieties, fears, and distrust of Islam and Muslim cultures (Gottschalk & Greenberg, 2008; Hennebry & Momani, 2013). With Islamophobia, the isolated acts of a small number of extremists tend to be amplified out of proportion by the media, in the process reinforcing people's worst expectations and darkest concerns, perpetuating prejudicial stereotyping of Muslim men as violent tyrants and Muslim women as emotionally crippled, while promoting the idea of the irreconcilable differences between the West and Islamic "other." To be sure, Islamophobia is not necessarily the cause of anti-Muslim racism but is its rationale and justification (Fekete, 2009; Sivanandan, 2009). Nevertheless, the end result of this rising tide of Islamophobia is a fundamental distrust and antipathy that borders on hate in solidifying the status of Arab Canadians as the "enemy within."

Of course, hate racism is no stranger to the United States. Canada is home to a host of hate groups, including white supremacist cells from the Aryan Nation and Western Guard movements to neo-Nazi skinheads in urban areas (Barkun, 1994; Kinsella, 1994). These groups are committed to an ideology of racial supremacy that asserts the superiority of whites and the hatred of non-whites. On the surface, white supremacists may not be explicitly anti-minority, preferring instead to see themselves as white Christians, fusing race and religion in a single nationalist crusade against the forces of evil (Jaret, 1995). People who endorse white supremacist ideology have become adept at reframing news items; for example, inner city looting is evidence of an imminent race war; or the indictment of police officers in the shooting of unarmed black males points to yet more white victimization (Blee & Creasap, 2010; Neyfakh, 2015). The trauma of 9/11 reinforced a renewed conviction of a pending global racial war (Barrett, 2007), prompting the racist right to actively seeking out converts to its cause. Disaffected youth are an obvious target because of perceived government indifference to their plight in a changing and diverse world (Li, 1995). The combination of music, pamphlets, disinformation by telephone hotlines, and the Internet—from chat rooms to websites that offer unique ways of spreading hate (Back, 2002; Rajagopal, 2006)—concocts an appealing mishmash of neo-Nazi philosophies, KKK folklore, pseudo-Nordic mythology, and survivalist slogans (O'Hara, 2005). Admittedly, there is no way of gauging the number of hardcore supremacists in Canada (according to the Southern Poverty Law Center, in the United States, there were 784 active hate groups in 2014, down from 1018 in 2011); nonetheless, even a small number of racist ideologues can destabilize a society, especially when the economy is sputtering or national anxieties are high.

Polite Racism Few people at present will tolerate the open expression of racism. Compare this with the past, when racism was openly articulated and socially acceptable. There was no need for pretense or politeness; everything was upfront and defiantly so.

The passage of constitutional guarantees such as the *Canadian Charter of Rights and Freedoms* and human rights codes, however, has eroded the legitimacy of hate racism from public discourse. But while blatant forms of racism have dissipated to some extent, **polite racism**—less candid expressions of bigotry and stereotyping remain in force. Instead of disappearing in the face of social reprisals and legal sanctions, racism is increasingly couched in a way that allows people to conceal their dislike of others by way of coded language (Wetherell & Potter, 1993). According to Peter Li (2007), Canadians assign social significance to race, despite its social and legal sanctions, in large part by relying on euphemisms to express racial views without appearing racist (see also Berry & Bonilla-Silva, 2007; Kobayashi & Johnson, 2007). In that this polite racism tends to be banal rather than blatant, obliquely couched in the language of political correctness rather than obtrusive, and sugar "coded" with higher principles to confuse or deflect, its detection is rendered more difficult (Coates, 2008).

Polite racism can be defined as a disguised dislike of or aversion to others manifested through behaviour that outwardly is non-prejudicial in appearance. These politely aversive feelings are not expressed through outright hostility or hate, but often through patterns of avoidance or rejection. It often manifests itself in the use of coded language ("those people") to mask inner feelings behind a facade of gentility (Blauner, 1994). This politeness is especially evident when racialized minorities are ignored or turned down for jobs, promotions, or accommodation. For example, when approached by an inappropriate applicant, an employer may claim a job is filled rather than admit "no blacks need apply." "Sorry, the apartment is rented," is another polite way of rejecting undesirable tenants when the unit in question is, in truth, still vacant. Polite racism would appear to be less hurtful than its hate equivalent; nevertheless, the effect on its victims is no less debilitating.

Consider as an example anti-Semitism as polite racism. Jewish people have long been targets of hate. But a new strain of anti-Semitism is increasingly directed not at Jews *per se* or their wealth—given the social unacceptability of such blatant dislike—but at Israel's relationship with Palestinians in the "occupied" or "reclaimed" lands. The acceptable face of anti-Semitism challenges Israel's right to exist as an equal member of the international community, its right to defend borders against enemies, and its human rights record in comparison to other countries (Cotler, 2007). As put by the Friends of the Simon Wiesenthal Center for Holocaust Studies (2008) in a letter to the president of the University of Toronto:

> Criticism of Israel is not of itself anti-Semitic. However, the specific targeting of Israel alone is anti-Semitic. Denying the Jewish people their right to self-determination by claiming that the existence of Israel is a racist endeavor is anti-Semitic. Applying a double standard by requiring of Israel behaviour not demanded of any of its neighbors is anti-Semitic.

No one is suggesting that Israel is above the law or unaccountable for human rights violations. However, unduly harsh and one-sided criticism of Israel may reflect a politely coded dislike of Jews (Bunzl, 2005; Cotler, 2007; Endelman, 2005; Weinfeld, 2005).

Subliminal Racism   A third type of interpersonal racism—**subliminal racism**—operates at an unconscious level. At its root, subliminal racism constitutes a deeply buried dislike of others that the perpetrator is generally unaware of (also Gorski, 2013; Tuch & Hughes,

2011). If this unconscious dislike is activated or exposed to the surface, this aversion to others is rationalized by appealing to rules or principled statements, in effect reflecting a willingness to criticize minorities or diversity by disguising the antipathy on loftier grounds. Not surprisingly, subliminal racism is found among that class of persons who openly abhor discriminatory treatment of minorities, yet appear incapable or unwilling to do something about it. The end result is a gap between what people say and what they do— between what values they profess to endorse and those they prefer to practice. When asked to justify this disconnect, they rely on rationalizations to oppose measures for remedying the problem of inequality (Augoustinos & Reynolds, 2001; see also Henry & Tator, 2009). In that a general principle is invoked to deny the legitimacy of specific instances, this opposition or criticism is coded in principled terms that politely skirt the issue by appealing to a higher sense of fair play or procedural justice.

There is no shortage of examples of subliminal racism—a racism that reflects a disconnect between conscious and unconscious beliefs, between thought and behaviour, and between principle and practice. Canadians generally are sympathetic toward refugees in distress, but less enamoured with those who are seen as breaking the rules by self-selecting themselves for entry into Canada, thus imperiling Canada's say over "who's in charge" (Fleras, 2014b). The so-called bogus asylum seekers are condemned not in blunt racist terminology; rather, their landed entry into Canada is criticized on principled grounds ranging from unfairness ("jumping the queue") and illegality of entry, to posing the threat of terrorism and criminality. Employment equity initiatives may be endorsed in principle but rejected in practice as unfair to the majority or inconsistent with the colour-blind principles of a post-racial society. Individuals may support a commitment to inclusiveness as a matter of principle, yet disapprove of equity measures to achieve that goal on grounds that in a meritocratic society everyone should be treated the same regardless of "colour" or consequences. Support for the principle of equality for minorities may be widely endorsed, but individuals balk at the prospect of moving over and making space, especially if costs or inconveniences are incurred (see Berry & Bonilla-Silva, 2007).

How, then, do we explain the subliminality of this "love–hate" relation toward minorities? Cynics might argue that Canadians are hypocrites whose racism is candy-coated by platitudinous pieties. In a Canada where open racism is socially unacceptable, coded opposition to multiculturalism or immigration is more acceptable than brazen expressions of intolerance (Li, 2007; Palmer, 1996). But unlike the deliberate euphemisms of polite racism, a subliminal racism reflects a largely unconscious dislike of others behind a folksy veneer of respectability. Context is critical: Canadians appear reluctant to criticize minorities or government minority policies unless the criticism can be rephrased and conveyed along principled grounds, thereby providing a "cover" for their racially-informed behaviour. That is, subliminal racists typically don't criticize or discriminate in situations where right or wrong are clearly defined and cannot be explained away without invoking a whiff of prejudice or racism. To express racial antipathy in a non-ambiguous situation would be obvious to others and to oneself. Rather, individuals will criticize or evade in safe situations that are not clearly defined so that a negative response can be justified, coded, or rationalized on the basis of some other principled factor other than race or racism (Dovidio, Gluszek, John, et al., 2010). For example, discounting the skills or credentials of foreign-born workers as an excuse to deny employment because they lack Canadian experience conveys the appearance of legitimate criticism rather than outright prejudice.

To be sure, criticism of racialized minority actions or government diversity initiatives is not necessarily racist, and it would be unfair to uniformly label critics as such. Nevertheless, principled opposition may well conceal a deeply seated unease over racialized migrants or minorities. Those who profess egalitarian attitudes yet refuse to act on this conviction because of principled excuses may be exhibiting subliminal racism by reinforcing those very inequities that need to be eradicated (Hochschild, 2002; hooks, 1995). After all, the act of doing nothing to bring about progressive change is not neutrality but a tacit acceptance of an unequal and racialized status quo.

Institutional Racism

Reference to institutional racisms shifts the sector of analysis to those racisms embedded in institutional designs, dynamics, and outcomes that secure both white privilege and a racialized status quo. Institutional racism is not about labelling individuals as racist but about organizational values and practices that create disproportionate outcomes for racialized minorities both in the workplace and in the community at large (Better, 2007). Nor is it necessarily the result of racist attitudes on the part of individuals who, in fact, may oppose racism but unwittingly perpetuate patterns of racial exclusion because they as institutional actors are compelled to act in a discriminatory manner due to institutional rules and business-as-usual practices (Desmond & Emirbayer, 2009). The concept of institutional racism refers to both overt and covert processes by which organizational practices and standard operating procedures adversely penalize minority women and men through rules, procedures, rewards, and practices that have the intent (systematic) or effect (systemic) of excluding or exploiting (Scheurich & Young, 1997). Institutional racism resides in those organizational policies, culture, and operations that reflect, reinforce, and advance differential access, treatment and outcomes pertaining to goods, services, and opportunities (Weiner, 2012). It also entails the collective failure of an institution to create a workforce that is representative at all levels, a working climate that reflects, respects, and responds to workplace diversity, and lastly, a delivery of services both accessible and available as well as culturally appropriate.

In some cases, this (dis)advantaging bias is deliberate (systematic racism); in other cases it exists in the very fabric of society (systemic racism) by way of agencies, governing bodies, and legal systems (Bruce-Jones, 2010; hooks, 2013). As a result, institutionalized discrimination and advantage can be sustained even if there is no deliberate intent to deny or exclude (systemic racism) (Chesler, Lewis, & Crowfoot, 2005). Bias against racialized minorities may persist because discrimination is so deeply ingrained within institutions ("institutionalized") that it becomes the automatic response ("the default option") even without conscious awareness or explicit intent (Mistry & Latoo, 2009:20). In all cases, institutions serve as a site where race and racism are constructed and maintained yet simultaneously obscured and normalized (Joseph, Darnell, & Nakamura, 2012).

Systematic Racism A racism that directly and deliberately prevents minorities from full and equal institutional involvement is known as **systematic racism**. This type of institutionalized racism appears when discriminatory practices are legally sanctioned by the institution (or the state) and carried out by employees who act on its behalf and with its approval (Milloy, 2001). Systematic institutional racism flourished in societies that endorsed racial segregation. The regime of apartheid in South Africa is a classic example, as was the pre-civil-rights United States. Canada was also tarnished by institutionally racist practices that directly and deliberately denied or excluded. Institutions at present can no longer openly discriminate against minorities, lest they attract negative publicity, encounter legal action, or incite consumer resistance. Nevertheless, systematic institutional racism continues to exist through discriminatory actions that the institutional culture discreetly endorses. For example, both Texaco and Denny's were hit with billion-dollar lawsuits in the 1990s for systematically discriminating against minorities. More recently, the US government paid out a $1.25 billion settlement to black farmers who had lodged a complaint of discrimination against the Department of Agriculture for refusing them loans and assistance (Christchurch Press, 2010).

Systemic Racism There is another type of institutional racism that is impersonal and unconscious, without much awareness of its presence or consequences except by those victimized. A **systemic racism** is predicated on the belief that institutional rules and procedures can be unwittingly racist in design, by practice, or in their effects, even if the actors are themselves free of prejudicial bias (Canadian Race Relations Foundation, 2003). It begins with the assumption that institutions are neither neutral sites nor passively devoid of agendas or consequences. Rather, they are socially constructed conventions both racialized and ideologically loaded, and consistent with beliefs and practices that reflect monocultural foundational principles and racialized assumptions that inadvertently advantage or empower some at the expense of others (Agocs & Jain, 2010; Pilkington, 2012). Predictably, racialized minorities find themselves disadvantaged within institutional contexts, not necessarily because of openly discriminatory barriers, but because mainstream institutions were neither designed to reflect their realities or experiences nor constructed to advance their interests or agendas.

Unlike other forms of racism whose existence can be criticized as departures from the norm, systemic racism involves normal institutional functions that, paradoxically, exert negative consequences for some. Institutional rules, expectations, and rewards may appear to be universally applicable and ostensibly colour-blind. But a commitment to a one-size-fits-all standardization (i.e., "we treat everyone the same around here") may discriminate against those who are disadvantaged through no fault of their own. Treating everyone the same when people's differences and disadvantages need to be recognized may exert a systemically biasing effect, that is, an unintended effect of inadvertently excluding those with different needs, goals, and values. In short, systemic racism embodies a bias that is normalized (inherent or institutionalized) within institutional structures, processes, and outcomes. A pervasive Eurocentrism that defines conventions and standards by which others are judged or serviced reinforces how the application of these rules or norms can exert unequal or harmful consequences for vulnerable minorities. This indirect discrimination arises when the outcomes of rules or protocols that apply equally to everybody, despite peoples' differences within unequal contexts, have the unintended effect of denying, controlling, or excluding others for reasons beyond their control.

With systemic racism, neither intent nor awareness count. (In this sense, racism defined as systemic advantage based on race (Tatum, 2003) resembles the institutional equivalent of subliminal racism.) The context and the consequences are critical, since even seemingly neutral policies and programs, when applied evenly and equally, can exert an exclusionary effect on those whose differences are disadvantaging. Institutional rules, priorities, and practices may not be inherently racist or deliberately discriminatory; that is, institutions do not go out of their way to exclude or deprive minorities. But once entrenched within institutions, racism is no longer intent-driven but is perpetuated by seemingly benign practices and programs (ERASE Racism, 2005). In that disadvantages are inherent within the system because the system itself is socially constructed by, for, and about the powerful and privileged, institutional rules that apply equally to all may have a discriminatory effect by disadvantaging those whose experiences, realities, and expectations do not coincide with the mainstream. Finally, systemic bias may arise because of the logical consequences of well-intentioned policies and initiatives that are based on faulty assumptions, ignore cultural differences, or fail to take context into account (Shkilnyk, 1985). A history of mismanaging Aboriginal peoples—from residential schools to forced relocation to the so-called "Sixties Scoop" that transferred aboriginal children to white families—is testimony to the deadly consequences inflicted by government assumptions that "We know what is best," "They want to be like us," and "White is right" (Truth and Reconciliation Commission Report, 2015). Admittedly, references to systemic racism have proliferated in recent years across a bewildering range of domains (see Kumi, 2008), in the process suggesting a tendency toward misuse (Fraser, 2006). Nevertheless, whether overused or not, systemic racism exists. In a one-size-fits-all world where a one-size-fits-all format can prove disadvantaging, failure to take differences into account creates consequences that are systemically biasing.

How do mainstream institutions exert a systemic bias against minority women and men? For years, a number of occupations such as police officers, firefighters, and mass-transit drivers imposed minimum weight, height, and educational requirements for job applicants. In retrospect, while not openly racist, these criteria proved systemically discriminatory because they favoured males over females and white applicants over people of colour. No deliberate attempt was made to exclude anyone; after all, equal standards were uniformly applied. Valid reasons may have existed to justify these restrictions; nevertheless, the imposition of these qualifications inflicted a set of unfair entry restrictions, regardless of intent or rationale. And these criteria have had the controlling effect of excluding racialized minorities who, as a group, lacked the criteria for entry or success *through no fault of their own.*

Consider also the systemic bias experienced by migrant agricultural workers from Mexico and the Caribbean who qualify under Canada's Seasonal Agricultural Workers Program (Fleras, 2010c). Like all Canadian workers, these migrant workers must pay premiums under the *Employment Insurance Act.* But unlike Canadian workers who don't have to leave the country upon completion of their authorized work terms (usually 6 to 8 months), seasonal agricultural workers cannot claim unemployment benefits or sick-leave benefits, because the Act stipulates that a claimant must be physically in Canada and available for work to receive benefits. In other words, the established rules of the *Employment Insurance Act,* when evenly applied to both categories of workers, have the effect of excluding migrant workers because of circumstances beyond their control. Other examples of systemic racism may include the following: an insistence on Canadian-only experience for job placement; the devaluation of minority experiences and credentials as a precondition for professional employment; unnecessarily high educational standards for entry into certain occupations; entry exams that do not take a candidate's cultural or racial background into account; and other demanding qualifications that discourage membership in professional bodies.

Finally, even academia is not exempt from the tarnish of systemic racism (Fleras, 1996; Samuel & Burney, 2003; Schick, 2008). As Henry and Tator point out (2006, 2009), universities perpetuate a culture of whiteness as the unquestioned norm in defining knowledge and ways of knowing, resulting in the privileging of Eurocentric interpretations of standards, teaching evaluations, criteria for tenure and promotion, and legitimate forms of publication (Fleras, 2014a). The following Box provides a hypothetical case study that illustrates both systemic and systematic bias at an academic level.

Alphabetism as Systemic Bias

A professor at the University of Ivory Towers taught a course which included a weekly test to gauge student knowledge of the readings and classroom material (adapted from Henry Yu, 2012; Fleras, 2014a). There was an insufficient number of textbooks, so some method of allocation had to be devised for divvying up the books. The professor decided to allocate books to students based on the alphabetical order of their last (family) name. Textbooks were than issued in order, beginning with students whose family names began with A and continuing until they ran out with last names that started with M.

Several weekly tests into the semester made it abundantly clear: Students who were given a book performed better than those without. Those whose last names began with N to Z protested over what they felt was unfair treatment, claiming an alphabet bias that confers an unfair advantage for some simply because of their last names. Chastened by this criticism of a systematic bias, the professor acknowledged the error of her ways and decided to differently re-distribute the textbooks. From now on, the professor explained, students will be evaluated on the grounds of merit rather than on the accidents of

a name assigned at birth. The books will be reallocated to the students with the highest grades, working down the ranking list until the supply of books is exhausted. The professor proudly announces the end of alphabetism since the books are now distributed to those most deserving based on their accomplishments. She then proclaims the dawn of new alphabet-free meritocracy in which underperforming students could no longer blame their failures on a systematically biased system of distribution.

Despite these changes, some students continue to express concerns about the unfairness of the arrangement. Those receiving low grades are concerned about the impact of poor scores on their careers. But the professor dismisses these complaints as unfounded. The system is now meritocratic, she argues, because an alphabetism bias no longer prevails in an alphabet-blind society. Furthermore, any poor results are the student's fault in an alphabet-blind meritocracy that treats everyone fairly and equally. Finally, the complaining students are urged to stop using history as an excuse, to take responsibility for their actions, and to get on with it.

(Continued)

This response does little to allay student concerns. They argue that the new system is fair in theory, and somewhat of an improvement over the alphabet-conscious arrangement. But a system that is theoretically fair, the students claim, has had the perverse effect of reinforcing the unfairness of the past. An alphabet-blind system not only accentuates past inequities by virtue of ranking students by criteria (grades) received during a period of inequality, but also continues to reward those who excelled under an inherently biased system. Worst still, by claiming the present system is fair and meritocratic, an alphabet-blind system conceals past unfairness and its effects (the poor grades from the first semester). In other words, a systemic bias has replaced a systematic bias, thereby perpetuating the injustices of the past into the present, yet without seeming to do so.

What lessons can be gleaned from this story in terms of how race as racialization works?

a. History matters because legacies of the past continue to have an impact on the present. The age-old analogy of a foot race is helpful; that is, two runners do not have an equal chance to cross the finish line at the same time if one of the runners is saddled with a ball and chain that is removed only near the end of the race (Bonilla-Silva, 2002)]. Or, to paraphrase William Faulkner's pithy insight into historical injustices, the past is never dead, it's not even the past.

b. Introduction of fairness or merit as concepts neither creates a just society nor erases an unjust society if the playing field is unequal because of an unjust history or a racialized society. An abstract or formal equality simply freezes the status quo, along with the prevailing distribution of power and privilege.

c. Inequalities and biases tend to systemic and institutional rather than systematic ("deliberate") and personal, in large because they are inherent within the opportunity structures of the system, yet masquerade as fair and just because they purport to treat everyone the same;

d. Replace the word "alphabet" with "race" or "colour," alphabetism with "racism," and "alphabet-blind" to "race-blind" to gain insight into how the principle of meritocracy in unequal contexts can prove systemically biasing to those hobbled by the disadvantages of a late start.

Ideological Racism

Ideological racism constitutes that sector of racism that permeates the general functioning of society. Ideological racism is the prevalence of cultural values and communication patterns that advance dominant interests as natural and normal at the expense of those defined as irrelevant and inferior. A distinction between the normative and everyday components of ideological racism is useful. **Everyday racism** consists of unconscious speech habits and everyday actions that have the cumulative effect of demeaning minority women and men. **Normative** racism, in turn, reflects a largely unconscious bias toward others because of prevailing cultural values.

Everyday Racism Contemporary racism is rarely directly expressed. More culturally acceptable ways that achieve the same effect without attracting negative attention are preferred instead (Sirna, 1996; Sue, 2010). **Everyday racism** consists of those micro-racist practices that infiltrate the routines of everyday life by becoming a normal part of what is accepted by society (Essed, 1991, 2002). With everyday racism, a dislike of others is created and reconstructed through daily actions that may be experienced by racialized minorities as micro-aggressions. For example, multiple forms of racism are played out in the everyday working lives of nurses (Barbee, 1993; das Gupta, 2009; Willmot, 2010; also Mapedzahama et al., 2012). Tania das Gupta (2009) writes of racist treatment in the day-to-day workplace life of nurses that includes (among others) tokenism, infantilization, denial of promotions, work allocation bias, targeting, scapegoating, excessive monitoring, lack of accommodation, segregation, and nurses being subjected to verbal abuse because of their race and ethnicity. Unconscious biases related to perceptions of race play a role in medical diagnosis (e.g., from paying less attention to and patient symptoms to interrupting patients or making patients feel less involved in health decisions, resulting in racially biased treatment and medical harm, despite claims by medical practitioners they harbored no negative attitudes or preferences (also Hoberman, 2007, 2012; Terrell, 2012). Racism in the nursing workplace also cross-cuts gender and class discrimination (das Gupta, 2009), while intersecting with other negative identity markers such as race, gender, class, further devaluing the lived realities of racialized nurses.

The role of language in perpetuating everyday racism is widely recognized (Blauner, 1994; Essed, 1991; Wetherell & Potter, 1993). Many think of language as a delivery service equivalent in function to a postal system; namely, a relatively neutral system of exchange between sender and receiver for the transmission of messages created independently through a process called thinking. To the contrary, words and language are neither a passive nor mechanical transmitter of information. They are "loaded" instead with values and preferences that define some aspects of reality as normal and acceptable while drawing attention away from other aspects as inconsequential. Words are not neutral; rather, they have a political dimension by virtue of conveying negative images beyond what is intended. Ideas and ideals are "trapped inside" language, in effect influencing patterns of thought and behaviour without our awareness. The two-edged nature of language is unmistakable. On the one hand, language can be used to enlighten and inform; on the other hand, as a discourse it can be employed to control, conceal, evade issues, draw attention, or dictate agendas that perpetuate patterns of power.

Language can be readily manipulated to express intolerance toward the other (Minikel-Lacoque, 2013). In reflecting and recreating processes that include or exclude others as legitimate members of a community (Modan, 2007), language possesses the potency to socially construct reality by highlighting differences and enlarging distance, as well as by criminalizing deviancy and sanctioning normalcy (Sirna, 1996). As Michael Pickering (2001) writes in *Stereotypes*, the boundaries between normal and deviant are constructed by words that define and demonize the other as an object yet simultaneously confirms the privileged position of the normal and natural subject. Robert Moore (1992) writes to this effect in his oft-quoted article on racism in the English language, by way of obvious bigotry, colour symbolism ("black" = bad), loaded terms ("Indian massacres"), and seemingly neutral phrases that are infused with hidden anxieties ("waves of immigrants"):

Some may blackly (angrily) accuse me of trying to blacken (defame) the English language, to give it a black eye (mark of shame) by writing such black words (hostile) . . . by accusing me of being black-hearted (malevolent), of having a black outlook (pessimistic; dismal) on life, of being a blackguard (scoundrel) which would certainly be a black mark (detrimental fact) against me.

To be sure, the racism implicit in words and metaphors may not be intentional or deliberate (see the Box on micro-aggression). Nor will the occasional use of derogatory words transform into full-blown racism. However the cumulative effects of "linguistic death by a thousand word cuts" should never be underestimated (Derald Wing Sue in Fitzgerald, 2015). And while it's an exaggeration to say that language determines our reality, it certainly provides a cultural frame of reference for defining what is desirable and important by stigmatizing differences through invisible yet real boundaries (Sirna, 1996). Or, as Bourdieu (1991) would likely say, the micro-aggressions in language are not about words that hurt, but *about those patterns of power perpetuated through language use in everyday discourses and daily practices.* That alone makes it doubly important to be aware of language as power of control in defense of dominant ideology (Fleras, 2014c).

Normative Racism Normative racism involves the perpetuation of racism by way of prevailing norms, values, standards, and beliefs. Certain ideas and ideals within a dominant culture are widely circulated that explicitly or implicitly assert the superiority of some people at the expense of others. Or, alternatively, dominant cultural beliefs, values, and norms tend to privilege mainstream patterns as the norm, whereas other cultural systems are devalued as irrelevant or inferior. An ethnocentric tendency to see and interpret "others" through a conventional cultural lens ensures that "they" come across as abnormal or unacceptable. Admittedly, it's rarely the case that mainstream cultural values explicitly reject or denigrate the "other" as racially inferior. Rather, "others" are defined as culturally inferior because of their incommensurability with conventional norms, values, and standards (Berry & Bonilla-Silva, 2007; Li, 2007). For example, consider how the principle of liberal universalism can prove culturally detrimental to those who espouse deep differences. Under the universal humanity espoused by liberal universalism, our commonalities as morally autonomous individuals are thought to supersede (at least for purposes of recognition or reward) whatever may divide us as members of racially different groups. However commendable such a commitment in many contexts, diminishing differences to the level of "pretend pluralism" does an injustice to those minorities whose deep differences matter and must be addressed accordingly.

There is little question that normative racisms mattered in the past. Normative racism contributed to Canada-building by facilitating expansion of the settling population by rationalizing the control and exploitation of the "other". Historically, racism in Canada was normatively entrenched within those policies and programs that justified the invasion and continuing occupation of territories occupied by the original inhabitants (Loppie, Reading, & de Leeuw, 2014). Racism was normatively reflected in the treatment of immigrants and racialized minorities in building Canada, from laying down tracks to domesticating the resource-rich expanses of Canada. The normativity of racism also proved useful in defining which class of foreigners to keep out of Canada and who were admissible. A normative racism is continues to be played out in a Canada that sometimes exploits temporary migrant labour for bolstering Canada's standard of living. Finally, racism plays out in a Canada whose normative principles continue to govern the foundational principles and assumptions of Canada's Eurocentric constitutional order—even while asserting cultural neutrality under the guise of universalism (Maaka & Fleras, 2005). In that these normative standards continue to reflect and reinforce patterns of white privilege and supremacy, racism is embedded in the very notion of "what Canada is for."

Contemporary references to normative racisms are reflective of broader ideological changes unleashed by neoliberal ideologies. How then do we explain the *shifting nature of racism within the context of neoliberalism* (Davis, 2007)? Scholars generally agree that neoliberalism can be broadly defined as the penetration of free market principles into all facets of life—economics, politics, society—the assumption being that markets are the most efficient way of organizing human life or establishing social order (Birch, 2015). Under neoliberalism as normative ideology, the concepts of community and public good are discredited and discarded in the hope of expanding the virtues of individual responsibility and self-sufficiency through (1) more market (including trade liberalization, free trade agreements, deregulation and privatization, and borderless capital flows and investment), (2) less government involvement in both the economy and in the distribution of a society's resources, and (3) global hegemony through worldwide homogeneity (Birch, 2015; Roberts & Mahtani, 2010; Wallis, Sunseri, & Galabuzi, 2010). For neoliberalism, the path to the "good life" reflects a commitment to the principle of colour-blindness, on grounds that true equality can only be achieved if both law and individuals become blind to race in advancing a free-wheeling market ideology (Bonilla-Silva, 2015; Giroux, 2006).

Notwithstanding this prognosis in freeing individuals from racism and race identity, the reality is different (Davis, 2012).Under the proposed colour-blindness of neoliberalism, racism is sharply redefined in the hopes of limiting its power as a legitimate grievance and explanatory framework (Davis, 2007). According to neoliberalism, a post-racial era is thought to prevail because: (a) race and racism have declined in significance as determinants of life chances; (b) racial conditions, ideologies, and practices have been abolished in justifying patterns of inequality; or (c) the racism of race no longer fuses power with ideology in shaping the distribution of valued resources. Despite denials, however, racism remains an inescapable component and an inevitable consequence of neoliberalism since racialized migrants and minorities continue to bear the brunt of neoliberalisms' downside. Consider the costs: a belief in more market is racist in consequence by virtue of assigning advantage to those with the benefit of a head start; a belief in less government and more austerity disproportionately impacts the poor and racialized; and a belief in more individual responsibility defines human agency as a series of individual choices yet glosses over those structural exclusions that limit, oppress or discriminate, while blaming the most vulnerable if they fail by assigning responsibility for the effects of racism on those who are its casualties (Davis, 2012). In other words, the privatization of race and racism means the deprivations that confront racialized migrants and minorities are framed as reflecting their own lack of initiative and responsibility rather than that of society's systems and structures (Simon-Kumar, 2015)

Clearly, then, neoliberalism represents a fundamental shift in how racism is played out in Canada. A racism without racists under neoliberalism functions not through overt state-sanctioned bigotry as in the past, but through the morality of the marketplace and the primacy of individual solutions to social and economic problems (Mascarenhas 2012:123). Endorsement of post-racial society under neoliberalism is consequential insofar as the mainstream can safely blame minorities for their predicament without being labelled as a racist. No one should underestimate the significance in shifting the blame from racism as an intentional act to racism as an invisible disadvantage embedded in society (from policy to ideology to economy). The mutedness of an implicit racism (i.e., racism without direct reference to it [Davis 2007]) is proving to be every bit as potent and politicized as its bigoted and blunt counterparts. Such a shift also demonstrates how the normative ideology of "racelessness" both obscures yet reinforces both a white superiority complex and minority disadvantages without seeming to do so or without general awareness of the hegemony at play (Alexander, 2012; Henry & Tator, 2009; Manning, Hartmann, & Gerteis, 2015; Mascarenhas 2012; Williams, 2011).

Infrastructural Racism

Racisms are never just about individuals, even if people are the perpetrators and carriers as well as beneficiaries or victims. More importantly, racisms are foundationally embedded within the structure, functions, and processes of society (Lentin, 2004). The origins and evolution of complex societies embodied a racialized distinction between groups, while the creation of the modern nation-state depended on securing patterns of inclusion and exclusion along a racialized divide. Racisms both in the past and at present were also inextricably linked with state policy and the political climate engendered by state and government actors. This link made it difficult to disentangle the societal racisms from the role of the state in preserving the prevailing distribution of power, privilege, and wealth. Or as Lentin and Lentin (2006) write, the drawing of connections between racisms and the state also reinforces the importance of framing racism as political rather than pathological (Cassin, Krawchenko, & VanderPlaat, 2007; Lehrman, 2003).

All complex societies are raced (or racialized). Inasmuch as societies conceive of themselves as racially configured with respect to emergence, formation, and development (Goldberg, 2002; Lentin, 2004), they make a distinction between superior and inferior groups (either racially or culturally defined); assign a corresponding division of power, privilege, and resources; and imbed these distinctions of inequality and inferiority within the foundational structures and cultural values of society. In some cases, a racist state/society explicitly endorses a racist ideology (such as apartheid) by erecting formal laws or official initiatives that segregate classes of citizenship and compromise civil rights. In other cases, open racism is rejected in favour of policies and practices that convey the illusion of inclusion. Nevertheless, the tacitly assumed principles of white supremacy and white privilege continue to justify the racialized distribution of power and wealth (Leonardo, 2004) not as something incidental to the functioning of the state but as integral and inevitable (Bonilla-Silva, 2015; Goldberg, 2002). What is the end result? Just as societies are gendered by virtue of androcentric mindsets and patriarchal structures, so too are they racialized insofar as society is infrastructurally *by, for*, and *about* "pale male" interests, experiences, and priorities.

Infrastructural racism refers to a sector of racism deeply implicated within the constitutional framework of society. According to dictionary sources, "infrastructure" (the Latin prefix *infra* means "below, beneath, underneath, invisible") can be loosely defined as those deeply embedded and tacitly assumed values, agendas, and priorities that underpin society's constitutional order—in the same way that infrastructures (i.e., basic installations and facilities from roads to power plants) contribute to the continuance, operation, and growth of communities. Infrastructural racism is predicated on the premise that the founding assumptions and foundational principles of society's constitutional order are neither neutral nor value-free. On the contrary, this foundational framework is infused with a tacitly assumed set of Eurocentric values and beliefs that advantage some and disadvantage others. For example, the principle of universal liberalism is hardly neutral or value-free. A commitment to valuing our commonalities as individuals puts an emphasis on doing rather than being, on privileging the content of a person's character rather than the colour of their skin, and a preference for reason rather than emotion (or violence) as a way of getting things done. References to the ideals of progress (movement upward and forward) at individual and societal levels not only constitute a foundational (if unstated) principle of Canada's infrastructural order, but also justify the prevailing distribution of power and privilege along racialized lines. In that the priorities, principles, and practices of a racialized constitutional order continue to be organized in ways that advance white interests at the expense of minority disadvantages, infrastructural racism is real and powerful in shifting from coercion-based systems (such as enslavement) to hegemonic domination through consent and acquiescence of the subdominant groups (Bonilla-Silva, 2015). The Debate Revisited at the end of this chapter will explore this more extensively.

THE BIG PICTURE: COSTS, ORIGINS, PERSISTENCE, CAUSES

Costs

Racism costs all Canadians. But the costs of racism are absorbed unevenly across Canada, with some capitalizing on racism as a basis for preserving privilege or power while others suffer the consequences of being disadvantaged (Bonnett, 2000). The perpetuation of racism is nothing less than a blot upon Canadian society, with untold capacity to squander Canada's potential and reputation as a progressive and prosperous country. A toxic environment is created where existing prejudices are articulated, legitimized, and defended as a basis for white privilege and advantage (McKenna, 1994). Mixed messages are conveyed that often contradict the ideals of a socially progressive society, despite Canada's constitutionally protected human rights code and commitment to the principles of multiculturalism. As well, racism diminishes the number of people who can contribute to Canada, whilst useless energy is expended that otherwise could be funneled into more productive channels. The consequences are costly: Racialized minorities live in perpetual fear of physical retaliation; they experience a loss of personal security that, in turn, intensifies isolation and self-defensive behaviours; and their self-worth plummets accordingly. Not surprisingly, racism remains a principal cause of alienation and marginalization due to its isolating and polarizing effect, creating tensions within the social fabric of society while precluding minority identification with the nation-state (Onyeji, 2010; Wood & Wortley, 2010). Finally, institutions that cannot capitalize on a diverse workforce are destined to lose their competitive edge in the global marketplace.

How is racism a problem? Those whose lives are generally untouched by racism may wonder what all the fuss is about. Sure, blatant expressions of racism or racial discrimination are painful, stigmatizing, and exclusionary. But what's the big deal about ethnic jokes or racial slurs, especially when celebrities or stand-up comedians achieve popularity by parodying others through racial stereotypes (but see Wright, 2007)? In reality, racism inflicts a cost on all Canadians, but especially on racialized minorities. Racism not only perpetuates patterns of inequality and violates the rights of minority Canadians by boxing them into a corner because of preconceived notions of how they should fit into Canadian society (Benjamin et al., 2010; RVH Project, 2002/03). Exposure to racism also may contribute to the poor health of minority women and men (Alvarez & Juang, 2010; Daniel & Cukier, 2014)—with corresponding costs to Canada's increasingly beleaguered healthcare system (Hannah, 2009; Hyman, 2009; Maioni, 2003; Nestel, 2012; Picard, 2005). According to Dalhousie University's Racism, Violence, and Health (RVH) Project (2002/03; also Benjamin et al., 2010), racism is a disease that can make people sick (physically, emotionally, and psychologically). Studies routinely indicate that repeated exposure to discrimination and racism typically generate high levels of stress which, in turn, induce health problems such as diabetes, hypertension, and strokes (Kim, 2006). In addition, token minorities in the workplace confront performance pressures: they cannot afford to make a mistake, are under continuous scrutiny to prove how smart they are, and find themselves questioning their own self competence (Benjamin et al., 2010; RVH Project, 2002/03:14). In the end, there is only so much negativity and self-hatred bred by racism that the body and mind can take before the onset of health problems, self-destruction, or the eruption into violence (T. Coates, 2015).

Origins, Persistence, Causes

Why, then, does racism exist if it comes with such high costs? What are its causes? Do we look to biology, culture, social structure, or personality as the major sources? Should it be defined as a sickness, a bad habit, a conspiratorial plot, a cultural blind spot, a structural flaw, a historical act, or a relic from the past? What about the origins of racism in human history—evolutionary adaptation, genetic hardwiring, tool of domination and control, strategy of exploitation? Why does racism persist despite its public disapproval as a practice inimical to the aspirations of a multicultural and inclusive society? How to explain its persistence in the face of government initiatives to condemn, curb, and control it? Is it because of fear, greed, ignorance, or arrogance? Is it because of societal inertia or public indifference, irrespective of its dysfunctional effects on society? Or is it because racism is so embedded within the institutional structures of society that moves to eradicate it are bound to fail? Responses to these questions are necessarily varied, in the main because the reasons behind the origins of racism are not the same as those that account for its persistence over time or across space, despite some degree of overlap; nor are its origins identical to the causes of racism both immediate and root or at interpersonal or institutional levels (Fleras, 2014a).

Some attribute the origins and persistence of racism to our biogenetic hardwiring from an evolutionary past. A fear of outsiders may have elicited a flee-or-fight response that remains in effect, so that recoiling from what is different seems only natural. This visceral dislike of out-groups may explain the universality of racism. Others see racism as the byproduct of ignorance or fear of the unknown. In that improper socialization is perceived as an origin, persistence, and cause of racism, improving people's knowledge about diversity will gradually diminish its spectre and scale. Still others believe that racism persists because of its psychological benefits (Dovidio, Gaertner, & Kawakami, 2010). While no demographic is exempt as perpetrators of racism, racial discrimination and prejudicial attitudes toward minority out-groups tend to be expressed by those with lower education, income, and employment levels, as well as by older folk and those with strong religious or conservative convictions (Semyonov, Raijman, & Gorodzeisky, 2008). Racism has a way of making a threatened mainstream feel good about itself in part by bolstering a collective self-image of superiority. This notion of racism as "functional" for white folk is captured in these words by Julian Bond of the National Association for the Advancement of Colored People (NAACP) when referring to the tenacity of white supremacist racism (as cited in White, 1998):

> It's still white supremacy. It still means so much to those who practice it. It defines who they are. It makes them feel that they are better than others. It ensures them positions in employment and college admissions they otherwise might not have. It still puts a lid on the dreams of black people. (p. 25)

In other words, and to paraphrase Derrick Bell of New York University (2006): Racism is of such value to the mainstream that, if minorities didn't exist, whites would have to invent them. Every society needs its scapegoats whose presence presents the majority with a target for projecting fantasies, fears, and frustrations. Without racism to bond all whites into an unspoken alliance, inter-white fighting would be endemic and anarchy an ever-present reality (also Mills, 1997; Le Guin, 1975).

Each of these explanations of racism bears merit. But reference to racism as a function of biology or psychology (either individually or collectively) cannot be divorced from its social dimensions. Most sociologists would argue that individuals are not biologically programmed to act in a racist manner. There are no genes that express themselves in racial discrimination; no compelling reason exists to believe that people are genetically hardwired with a propensity to hate. Nor does racism exist solely in the minds of poorly socialized individuals. Rather than an error of perception or belief, people are conditioned to be racist by environments that foster ethnocentrism, out-group antipathy, and hate. They are conditioned to be racist as part of a broader process of social control for preserving the status quo in complex societies. Simply put, whites represent a social collectivity with an overarching racial interest in preserving privilege and a racialized status quo in the competition for scarce resources without drawing unnecessary attention to the contradictions and dysfunctions of a so-called meritocratic system (Bonilla-Silva, 2015; Galabuzi, 2006).

Others argue the origins, persistence, and causes of racism are rooted in the material conditions of social life (Bolaria & Li, 1988; Bonilla-Silva, 2015; Satzewich, 1998). Neither a transient phenomenon nor an anomalous and unpredictable feature, racism is pivotal to

Canada's historical and economic development, embedded within the institutional structures of an unequal society, endemic to core Canadian values, and integral to Canada-building. Racism arose to explain and justify patterns of conquest, settlement, land appropriation, and economic domination (Cote-Meek, 2014; Green, 2014; Macedo & Gounari, 2006). Canada's economic prosperity and standard of living were fostered by a racism that facilitated rail construction, the domestication of the west (Daschuk, 2013), the extraction of timber and mineral resources, and work on the assembly lines. The quality of life for most Canadians continues to be supported by racialized minorities who toil in low-paying and dangerous jobs to underwrite the costs of cheaper goods and services (Bishop, 2005; Goldring & Landolt, 2013). Racist ideologies were, and continue to be, employed for securing ready access to a cheap and disposable labour supply; to destabilize labour movements by under-mining any potential show of unity or strength; to justify intrusive devices for controlling troublesome minorities; and to secure controlling functions in support of ruling-class inter-ests. In short, racism originated and continues to persist within a capitalist Canada because of its usefulness in advancing class interests (Bolaria & Li, 1988).

The evidence is compelling: Racism cannot be reduced to individual attitudes born of prejudice and ignorance. Rather, racism as a political project emerged within the context of European colonialism (see Lentin, 2004; Mills, 1997). Racism persists not because it constitutes a set of fallacious beliefs or personality flaws, but because it supports patterns of (in)difference, privilege, and power that bolster Canada's vested and national interests (Macedo & Gounari, 2006; Paolucci, 2006). Its persistence can be attributed to the material, social, and psychological advantages a racialized system provides for mainstream members (Wellman, 1993). Nor is racism an anomaly in society and its ideals—a kind of irrational or dysfunctional feature of an otherwise rational and sound system—but a true expression of "what society is for." Instead of seeing it as an unfortunate aberration from the norm of what constitutes Canada, racism *is* the logic behind a system constructed by, for, and about whites. There is much to commend in the rephrasing of racism as perversely "logical" or has having a "rationality" (Bonilla-Silva, 2015) for its work in preserving a pro-white social order. It confirms the centrality of racism within the broader context in which it is embedded, expressed, and nourished. Solutions to the problem of racism must be adjusted accordingly.

ANTI-RACISM: ROOTING OUT RACISM

Most Canadians are no longer racists in the classic sense of blatantly vilifying minority women and men. The "bad old days" of openly denying and excluding others because of appearances are long gone and unlikely to return in light of numerous checks and balances to prevent a repeat occurrence. Yet, as we have seen, racism continues to flourish in unob-trusive ways, deliberately or unconsciously, by way of action or inaction. Racism is rarely directly experienced, although the continued presence of anti-Semitic incidents and hate crimes in Canada would suggest otherwise (Allan, 2015). More frequently, it is endured through the cumulative impact of polite putdowns and micro-aggressions that quietly accu-mulate day by day into a "tonne of feathers." Recognition of racism as a major social prob-lem puts the onus on Canadians to do something about it (Bishop, 2005). As Tim Wise (1999), a renowned American anti-racism educator, puts it:

[T]hose persons called "white" have a particular obligation to fight racism because it's *ours* [emphasis added], created in its modern form by us, for the purpose of commanding power over resources and opportunities at the expense of people of color. Furthermore, all whites . . . have to address the internalized beliefs about white supremacy from which we all suffer. No one is unaffected by the daily socialization to which we are all subjected—specifically with regard to the way we are taught to think about persons of color in this society. (p. 17)

Clearly, a mindset shift is required for any progress to be made on the racism front. Most of us would agree that to do something to someone because of their skin colour is racism and something should be done about it. But doing nothing to confront racial discrimination may be no less racist; after all, fence-sitting (through inactivity or silence) is not impartiality or neutrality but tacit acceptance of a racialized and unequal status quo (Trepagnier, 2007). The only option is to take a stand, if only to be part of the solution rather than part of the problem.

The range of activities that directly challenge racism and racial discrimination is known as anti-racism. Yet the concept of anti-racism is not necessarily self-evident: Just as racism is multi-faceted and dynamic, so too is anti-racism seen as having no singular meaning but shifting over time and between contexts (Bakan & Dua, 2014; Burnett, 2015; Pitcher, 2009). If racism is primarily about attitudes (racism as race) or beliefs (racism as ideology), then individual-based strategies are in order. But institutional models are required if racism entails patterns of power and structures (both systemic and systematic). And if racism reflects infrastructure (foundational principles of society) and ideology (including language and culture), the onus shifts to more comprehensive ideological changes. Mindful of this definitional span, **anti-racism** can be defined as the process that challenges racism through direct action at different levels. A commitment to anti-racism is all-consuming by challenging white advantage and eradicating structural barriers to full participation and equal citizenship rights (Dei, 2005). Active involvement is necessary to dislodge the cultural values, personal prejudices, discriminatory behaviours, and institutional structures of society that perpetuate racism. Two general anti-racism strategies can be discerned: individual and institutional. One is concerned with modifying individual attitudes and behaviour through law, education, or interaction; the other with changing the institutional structural through the removal of discriminatory barriers. Combining both creates the possibility of a more inclusive anti-racism strategy.

Individual Anti-Racism

Taken at its most obvious level, racism is normally envisaged as a personal problem of hatred, fear, or ignorance. There is an element of truth to this assertion. Racism is often expressed through the thoughts and actions of individuals who dislike others because they perceive them as different or threatening. Thus, anti-racism strategies tend to focus on modifying defective attitudes related to prejudice, ethnocentrism, and stereotyping. Three of the more common personal anti-racism strategies for improvement are *interaction*, *education*, and *law*.

Interaction Learning through contact and interaction represents one technique for individual anti-racism change. Interaction with others is proposed for removing barriers that stem from a knowledge gap and replacing it with insight and sensitivity. But interaction on its own is not necessarily beneficial (Harell & Stolle, 2010). It is doubtful if interpersonal racism is diminished by the thousands of tourists who flock to the Caribbean each winter. Improvement is unlikely in contexts in which interactional patterns tend to reinforce the gap between the haves and have-nots. Under these potentially degrading circumstances, the degree of resentment and contempt escalates in tune with the reconstituting of colonialist patterns of servitude and deference.

The effectiveness of reducing racism through interaction varies with the quality of interaction. Cooperative models of interaction may result in less fear of the other, whereas competitive models involving deference or servitude may intensify tension and the potential for confrontation. For any positive effect, interaction must be conducted between individuals who are relatively equal in status, who collaborate on a common endeavour in a spirit of trust and respect, whose interaction receives some degree of institutional and societal support, and who derive mutual benefit from cooperation of sufficient frequency and duration to foster a working relationship (Jaret, 1995). Interaction between unequals outside a supportive context simply upholds the status quo by perpetuating stereotypes in a negatively charged environment.

Education It is widely assumed that education (or training) can reduce racism (Government of Canada, 2005). According to this line of thinking, racism arises when individuals are locked into ignorance or irrational beliefs. Therein lies the cure—educating people to realize the errors of their ways. People are deemed sufficiently rational to make the appropriate adjustments, once aware of their mistakes. This notion of enlightenment through anti-racism learning puts a premium on educational institutions. Milder versions of multicultural education propose modifying individual attitudes through exposure to diversity. Yet there are difficulties in defending the transformative properties of education and training in challenging racism. According to Ontario's Human Rights Commission (2005), success or change are unlikely if the training is isolated from other initiatives; if it emphasizes cultural sensitivity or the celebrating of cultures; and if it ignores the dynamics of racism by reducing discrimination to cultural misunderstandings. Gloria Yamato (2001) captures the futility of quick-fix solutions to a complex problem that has taken centuries to grow, take root, invade space, and morph into variations:

> Many believe that racism can be dealt with effectively in one hellifying workshop, or one hour-long heated discussion. . . I've run into folks who really think that we can beat this devil, kick this habit, be healed of this disease in a snap. In a sincere blink of a well-intentioned eye, presto—poof—racism disappears. "I've dealt with my racism. . . (envision a laying on of hands) . . . Hallelujah! Now I can go to the beach." Well fine, go to the beach. (p. 152)

Stronger versions of multicultural education encourage individuals to look inside themselves, to examine their own racism and privileged positions, to see how the dominant sector exercises power over racialized minorities, and to take responsibility for the disempowerment of others (Ghosh & Galczynski, 2014; McIntosh, 1988). Admittedly, while most white people can see and sympathize with victims of racism, fewer are capable of seeing the benefits and advantages that flow from whiteness. Many are equally reluctant to see how their privilege is directly connected with the disempowerment and disadvantage of those at the wrong end of racism (Bishop, 2005; Mistry & Latoo, 2009). In other words, people need to be educated about the advantages of whiteness by painting themselves into the picture of minority disadvantage.

For example, how would you respond if a colleague makes a racist joke? Do you ignore it? Refuse to laugh? Walk away? Bristle with indignation? Openly criticize the joke as offensive and racist? Regardless of your actions, there is a cost. Doing nothing implies a condoning of the behaviour. Doing something may elicit a range of defensive responses, from hostility and aggression to a breach in your working relationship. The best response should achieve three goals: (1) communicate that this behaviour is unacceptable, (2) indicate that the joke is racist, and (3) inflict as little damage as possible to the relationship. An interesting and recommended strategy is to *play dumb*. Put on a bewildered expression and ask the joker to explain the joke because you don't understand. The joker cannot explain the joke without invoking a racist stereotype. You can then question the validity of the stereotype, in the process pointing out the racism in the joke without being confrontational or humiliating your colleague. Why does this approach work? Racist jokes rely on a shared knowledge of stereotypes. Without stereotypes, there is no humour. Thus, when you play dumb and ask someone to explain the joke, the racist stereotype is drawn out into the open, where it's absurd and offensive nature can be openly dissected. And because you are feigning ignorance, the lesson/message can be conveyed without sabotaging your relationship with the joker (based on van Kerckhove, 2009).

Law Recourse to law is sometimes upheld as an effective personal deterrent. Laws exist in Canada that prohibit the expression of racial discrimination against vulnerable minorities. The scope of these laws is broad. Some legal measures entail protecting identifiable minorities through restrictions on majority behaviour. For example, the Supreme Court of Canada has ruled repeatedly that prohibiting hate literature is a justifiable and reasonable limitation on the freedom of speech. Other measures are aimed at removing the discriminatory barriers that preclude minority participation within society. On the assumption that most individuals are law-abiding because of the threat of punishment or social ostracism, passage of anti-racist laws focuses on outward compliance with the letter of the law. Passage of these and related laws is not intended to alter people's attitudes or conviction, at least not in the short run. A democratic society such as Canada entitles people to their own private thoughts, even if they are repugnant or anti-social. But behaviour can be monitored and modified. Over time, moreover, people may realign their beliefs to match behaviour in hopes of reducing the dissonance they experience between their thoughts and actions.

Institutional Anti-Racism

There is room for cautious optimism when discussing the effectiveness of individually tailored anti-racist programs. But are these initiatives of sufficient scope to remove racism? Racism may be expressed in and through people (who may be regarded as precipitating causes), but individuals are merely the conduits of racial antipathy. With individual anti-racism, the symptoms—not the cause or source—are addressed. Worse still, an individual anti-racism program tends to rely on multicultural platforms or attitude modification to ideologically cloak the structural supports of institutional racism (Scheurich & Young, 1997). Not surprisingly, personal solutions such as anti-racist training are criticized as the equivalent of applying a bandage to a gaping wound—compassionate and well-meaning to be sure, but ultimately inadequate to staunch the bleeding.

An institutional anti-racism approach draws attention to structural determinants of racism. According to this line of thinking, racism can be resolved only by attacking it at its source, namely, within the institutional structures that support patterns of power and inequality (Zine, 2002). Put bluntly, racism is not just about individuals with regressive beliefs or dormant prejudices. Rather, it is sourced in institutional structures that provide justifying ideologies and practices in those contexts organized (racialized) around the placement of minorities into racial categories (Bonilla-Silva, 2015; Lopes & Thomas, 2006). The problem of racism must be addressed within the wider confines of political domination and economic control, in large part by focusing on the systemic and institutional dimensions of white power, privilege, and the rationales for justifying domination, exclusion, and denial (Dei, 2005). Not surprisingly, a commitment to changing behaviour and contesting structures instead of modifying individual attitudes requires a different set of assumptions and tactics than those focusing on personal initiatives. Such tactics may include fighting racist hate groups, direct action through protest, or civil disobedience, boycotts, and litigation (Jaret, 1995).

Toward an Inclusive Anti-Racism

It is relatively easy to reduce racism to a personal problem. Common sense dictates that people are the cause of racism. As individuals, people must reflect critically upon their degree of complicity in perpetuating racism through their daily actions. But it is equally tempting to situate racism within a system of vast and impersonal institutional forces that are largely beyond individual control. However valid, such an approach runs the risk of absolving individuals of any responsibility. Neither of these positions is entirely correct. Individuals are not necessarily the cause of racism; nevertheless, racism is located within and carried out by the person. Institutions may be root causes; nonetheless, they do not exist apart from individuals who interact to create, express, support, and transform patterns of racism. The tension between agency and structure is palpable: Each of us must be held accountable for our actions, despite the presence of a broader social context over which we have less control.

Only an inclusive (or integrative) anti-racism approach can deliver the goods with any hope of success (Samuel, 2006). Too often, efforts to eliminate racism focus on surface differences such as race or attitude modification, in the process bypassing the root of the problem of the deep-level value system and those systemic biases that underpin racism (racism is thus defined as the outward manifestation of entrenched values and embedded structures [Rosado, 2013]). More inclusive strategies acknowledge as source and solution the interplay of social structures and individual experiences. In rejecting an either/or approach for a both/and perspective with its embrace of contextuality, connectedness, and simultaneity of unequal relations, an inclusive anti-racism acknowledges the interplay of structure with agency (Dei, 2005). The personal may be political but in need of an institutional focus, while the institutional is structural but demands a sense of individual agency.

The interlocking nature of racism must also be acknowledged (Bishop, 2005). Racialized minorities do not find themselves excluded because of race or class or gender. Rather, each of these inequities intersects with the other to amplify overlapping patterns of exclusion and denial within the broader context of a value system of denial and exclusion that advantages some at the expense of others. What can we conclude? The interdependence of race, class, and gender as intertwined strands of a wider, more complex, and self-perpetuating system of privilege and power makes it abundantly clear: The purging of racism must be confronted comprehensively in advancing an inclusive society based on the principle of treating people equally, yet as equals.

DEBATE REVISITED

Deep Racism in a Racialized Canada

Is Canada as "racist to the core," as critics say (Thobani, 2007)? Or is Canada essentially an open and tolerant society, with only isolated and random expressions of racism by misinformed individuals (Satzewich, 2011)? Some argue that racism and racial discrimination are relics from the past, excepting, of course, the actions of few knuckle-dragging Neanderthals. Any existing racisms in a post-racial Canada are, therefore, reflective of minority failures. Others contend that racism remains a key discriminatory barrier, although Canada prefers to mask its many racisms behind a myth of racelessness and under a blanket of whiteness (Backhouse, 1999; Cannon & Sunseri, 2011; Chazan et al., 2011; Das Gupta et al., 2007; Kobayashi, 2003; Razack, 2002; also Michael Brown, 2005). True, Canadians may not be racists in the blatant sense of confederate flags, swastika graffiti, and cross burnings. Rather, racism in Canadian society is increasingly covert and subtle; embedded in normal operations of institutions; beyond the direct discourse of racial terminology; and masquerades behind colour-blind and race neutral principles (Gillborn, 2006; Gilroy 2004; Li, 2007).

So, whose perspective is more accurate in debating the nature and scope of racism in Canada? Let's create a context and a perspective. What might come to mind in imaging the concept of a racist society? At minimum, a racist society is one in which racism is integral to the emergence, development, and governance of the modern state. This racism is (1) deeply embedded in the design, organization, and operations of society; (2) reflected in and reinforced by official cultural values; (3) expressed through widely accepted social norms; (4) tacitly approved by the state or government; (5) codified into laws and policies that openly discriminate against minorities; (6) reflected in restrictive policies of membership and citizenship; and (7) inseparable from the normal functioning of society (Aguirre & Turner, 1995). In a racist society, prejudice toward others is institutionally entrenched as part of the normal functioning of society, while formal boundaries are drawn around racialized groups to segregate them from the exalted mainstream (Thobani, 2007). The complicity of central authorities in solidifying racism is crucial: The government does little or nothing to prevent the outbreak of racist

(Continued)

incidents at individual or institutional levels; even less is done to "arrest" these transgressions when they occur.

According to these criteria, South Africa would have qualified as a racist society (or state). South Africa's apartheid regime explicitly endorsed a state ideology that established a set of laws or initiatives for formalizing separate classes of citizenship which, in turn, compromised civil rights based on racial criteria. Under an official apartheid, a system of race-based segregation was introduced that separated whites from blacks, including an archipelago of homelands that ringed the perimeter of white South Africa. Blacks were ruthlessly exploited as miners or domestics, thereby securing power and privilege for the white ruling class. Both the United States and Canada could also be defined as racist societies prior to the mid-1950s in light of state-endorsed colour bars that kept blacks from challenging white privilege (Horton & Horton, 2004). As well, racism was used to justify the conquest and colonialization of Indigenous peoples in both these countries, resulting in persistent patterns of in-group domination and the self-inflicted destruction of the out-group (Coulthard, 2014; Mills, 1997). But how valid is such an indictment of Canada at present?

An ideal-typical distinction between "racialized society" and "racist state" is advised. The modern state is tantamount to a racialized state because it is racially configured with respect to its emergence, formation, and development. The racialized state in which race and nation are mutually constitutive of each other is implicated in the reproduction of racist exclusion through its manifestations in justice and law enforcement; the power institutions of politics, legislation, and bureaucracy; and the assertion of white supremacy in justifying the control of those racialized as inferior (Goldberg, 2002). Canada is no exception in terms of its founding assumptions and foundational principles which continue to uphold a racialized constitutional order. It no longer subscribes to the attributes of an openly racist society as listed above (at least in theory if not always in practice); nevertheless, it remains racialized with respect to the tacitly assumed rules of what is normal and necessary, acceptable and desirable (Fleras, 2014a, b). In upholding the white superiority principles of a white supremacist society, a racialized Canada is indeed a systemic racist society.

In other words, Canada may be defined as a racist society not because it contains a lot of racists or racisms. If anything, police-reported incidents of anti-Semitism and hate crimes suggest a relatively modest number in proportion to Canada's 36 million population. More accurately, Canada is a racialized society whose political, cultural, and economic foundations are overwhelmingly a reflection of and controlled by white power, resources, and a sense of entitlement that, in turn, generates values, agendas and practices which may be interpreted as racism in reinforcing the advantages of whiteness at the expense of minority disadvantage across a broad array of institutions and interactions (Ansley, 2004; Gillborn, 2006; Kobayashi, 2009). Consider the ways in which Canada is racist because of its racialized status: Canada is racialized as racist because the racism of a white supremacism permeates Canada's colonial history, is institutionalized in those rules and practices that normalize "pale male" privilege and a white superiority complex, and permeates the language, laws, and rules of Canadian society yet appear invisible because of their normalcy. Canada is racialized as racist because deep differences are deemed to be disadvantaging if they don't advance mainstream advantage. Just as female differences are transformed into female disadvantages in a male-centred world, to rephrase Sandra Bem (1994), so too are minority differences defined (or racialized) as disadvantageous in a world designed and organized to reflect, reinforce, and advance "white-stream" interests. Racialized migrants and minorities may possess the same formal rights as all Canadians; however, they must exercise these rights and attain a level of success in a racialized Canada designed neither to reflect their realities nor advance their interests (Fleras, 2014b). Finally, Canada is a racialized and racist society because Canada-building continues to be grounded on exploiting those perceived as racially inferior and culturally different. For example, temporary foreign workers and irregular migrants are rendered expendable because of their precarious status, and subject to dismissal or removal for reasons that advance Canada's interests (Goldring & Landolt, 2013).

In short, Canada is not a racist society *per se*. More accurately, by virtue of reinforcing white privilege within the context of a systemic white supremacy, it constitutes a racialized society whose foundational principles and principled practices are racist in consequence rather than inherent or intentional. And Canada as a racialized society will continue to resonate as long as the principles of Canada's constitutional order reflect, reinforce, and advantage the interests of some but not others in a Canada that, despite post-racial claims to the contrary, is structurally organized by, for, and about a Eurocentric whiteness as normal, important, and inevitable.

Chapter Highlights

- Racism exists and has always existed in Canada, although its magnitude and scope as well as depth and intensity have varied over time. Unmasking the many faces of racism, both past and present, is the central theme of this chapter.
- Racism is more than a simple expression of individual prejudice; it is a complex system of structures, ideologies, discourses, and vocabularies in which the advantages of power, privilege, and resources are distributed unequally.
- Definitions of racism fall into five main categories: racism as biology, racism as ideology, racism as culture, racism as structure, and racism as advantage.
- The constituents of racism include prejudice, discrimination, and power. Power underpins all forms of racism: without it, racism is indistinguishable from a host of negative attitudes and practices.
- The sectors of racism comprise (1) interpersonal racism (hate, polite, and subliminal); (2) institutional racism (systematic, systemic); (3) ideological racism (normative,

everyday); and (4) infrastructural racism (society). The different sectors of racism can be compared on the basis of select criteria.

- A variety of social and psychological explanations may account for the pervasiveness of racism in Canada. Racism persists because it provides positive advantage for some in a racialized society organized around the principles of profit and white privilege.
- Anti-racism is concerned with the elimination of racism through direct action at personal and institutional levels. An inclusive anti-racism promises a more comprehensive attack on the racism problem.
- Responses to the question of whether Canada is a racist society depend on how racism is defined, how it's measured, and what exactly constitutes a racist governance.

Review Questions

1. Compare and contrast the different sectors of racism that have been discussed in terms of underlying assumptions and patterns of expression.

2. Discuss why it's so difficult to address in a principled way the question of whether Canada is a racist society.

3. Indicate the value of reframing racism as a "verb" rather than as a "noun."

4. Demonstrate how prejudice and discrimination represent key components of racism as defined in this chapter.

5. Compare the strategies of anti-racism at the individual level with those at the institutional level in terms of underlying assumptions and anticipated outcomes.

CHAPTER 4

Ethnicity Matters: Politics, Conflict, and Experiences

LEARNING OBJECTIVES

After reading this chapter, you will be able to:

1. Define ethnicity and understand the characteristics, causal explanations, and expressions of this concept at different levels and across diverse domains.

2. Identify why ethnicity matters—for better or worse.

3. Describe why the reference to "ethnic" in "ethnic conflict" may conceal more than it reveals as an explanatory framework.

4. Explain how the politics of ethnicity in Quebec are situated within the framework of an intercultural ("post-ethnic") nationalism.

5. Interpret how Canada's official Multiculturalism policy seeks to neutralize ("depoliticize") ethnicity.

DEBATE

Problematizing the "Ethnic" in "Ethnic Conflict": Inherent or Constructed?

If there is an iron law of ethnicity, it is that when ethnic groups are found in a hierarchy of wealth, power, and status, then conflict is inescapable. (Steinberg, 1989, p. 170)

If the postwar era could be described as the age of ideology involving capitalist and communist superpowers, the last decade of the twentieth century exposed yet another epoch in the making—the era of ethnic conflict (Crawford, 2006; Habyarimana et al., 2008; Shaykhutdinov & Bragg, 2011). With several major exceptions, virtually all global conflicts since 1990 have involved civil confrontations between and among ethnic groups within their existing borders (Arbatli, Ashraf, & Galor, 2015; Gurr, 2001; Taras & Ganguly, 2009). This observation hardly comes as a surprise: The so-called end of history (or the end of the Cold War) not only lifted the lid off political alignments, but also unleashed explosive ethnic revivals and animosities across the globe that have proven disruptive at best, destructive at worst (Hutchinson & Smith, 1996). From the Congo to Chechnya, from Somalia to

(Continued)

the Basque region, from Rwanda to Kashmir, and from Bosnia to Myanmar (Burma), the proliferation of ethnically driven civil wars, genocides, sectarian violence, and secessionist movements during the 1990s proved dismaying and destructive. Millions have been displaced or killed—mostly civilians rather than soldiers, and mainly from starvation or disease rather than from bullets or land-mines (Crawford & Lipschutz, 1998).

The prognosis for the twenty-first century is not much better (Taras & Ganguly, 2009). Although the number of countries experiencing conflict has declined from a peak in the early 1990s, as many as 35 countries since 2010 con-tinue to be afflicted by civil conflict and sectarian violence (Arbatli, Ashraf, & Galor, 2015:1). The catastrophes in the Darfur region in Sudan and, more recently, inter-group clashes in the Ukraine and Syria attest to its prevalence, while US-led invasions of Afghanistan and Iraq have unleashed internal conflicts that eventually may prove more debilitat-ing than the bloodbath that accompanied the occupations. The ascendancy of these ethnic conflicts is no longer seen as an international exception. Conflicts as clashes between culturally different groups appear to have evolved into a global norm, with no reason to believe an end is in sight to the destruction and death. Admittedly, ethnic differences *per se* do not necessarily culminate in large-scale violence and pitched battles (Habyarimana et al., 2008); nevertheless, there is potential for conflict and confron-tation over a host of factors including social identity, territory, natural resources, self-determination, holy places, economic gains, cultural values, and personal and collective security (Ward, 2004).

But a problem of analysis persists: However disruptive to the governance process or deadly in its consequences, the meaning of ethnic conflict is not readily transparent (Taras & Ganguly, 2009). For some, the term "ethnic conflict" conjures up images of violent confrontations between tribes over pent-up hatreds. For others, it entails a clash of interests (both political and economic) involving cleav-ages within and competition between major ethno-religious clusters (Caselli & Coleman, 2006/2010). For still others, ethnic conflict is synonymous with any expression of violence between non-Western groups originating, in part, from the political vacuum created by collapsed states and stagnant economies. Curiously, incursions by the coalition forces (NATO/USA) and their "peacekeeping missions" into domains such as Serbia in 1999 are never framed as ethnic conflicts. Even reference to the "conflict" in "ethnic con-flict" is problematic: Does the "conflict" in "ethnic conflict" refer only to armed confrontations between ethnically differ-ent groups, or can it be applied to any low-intensity competition involving dif-ferent groups over valued resources (Steinberg, 1989)? For example, is Que-bec's messy relationship to the rest of Canada a case of ethnic conflict or is it one of federal-provincial politics? No less puzzling is the concept of "ethnic" in "ethnic conflict" as an explanation. Is ethnicity *per se* a primary cause of hostilities? Or is ethnicity invoked after the fact to justify and explain a range of complex activities involving diverse groups? Should the origins of ethnic conflict be framed along instinc-tual ("primordial") grounds (see Arbatli, Ashraf, & Galor, 2015)? Or should reference to ethnicity be one of several feasibility factors or situational circumstances that construct conflicts? Or is the concept of ethnicity in a conflict manipulated as a smokescreen to achieve political goals or justify personal ambitions?

In theory, the persistence, salience, and intensity of ethnic conflicts should be an anomaly in this era of globalization and global citizenship. In reality, instead of diminishing, as might be expected because of an increasingly globalized world, ethnic-defined conflicts have escalated to the point where they are second only to international terrorism as a global security problem (Pieterse, 2007).

Factor religious intolerance into the equation and these hostilities often invoke a passion and fury that unsettles an abiding faith in the human condition (Tishkov, 2004). In short, ethnic conflicts (however defined) constitute a grave danger that threatens social cohesion, endangers public order, disrupts peaceful relations, and violates human rights and fundamental freedoms. That alone makes it doubly important to deconstruct the "ethnic" in ethnic conflicts to unravel what is going on and why. A set of responses to these dilemmas will be reexamined in the Debate Revisited box.

INTRODUCTION: GLOBAL IMPLOSION/ETHNICITY EXPLOSION

Two distinct but seemingly contradictory dynamics are in play at present. On the one hand are the imploding forces of globalization: Nation-states are inexorably drawn into the vortex of a single global economy, with its diversity-dampening commitment to rationality and universalism, conformity, and consumerism. The local and the national are conflated into a single world system that compresses and homogenizes, thanks to the interplay of mass communication, mass travel, mass consumerism, and mass education. But fears are mounting over a pending "McDonaldization" of societies—a kind of one-size-fits-all standardization in which differences are commodified as "ethnic chic" or, alternatively, a residual category to fall back on as a default option (Hutchinson & Smith, 1996).

On the other hand is an equally robust dynamic. The centripetal (the inward-leaning and pulling in) forces of globalization are in conflict with the centrifugal (outward-leaning and pushing out) dynamics of ethnicity. A powerful movement has evolved that transforms ethnicity into a cutting edge for collectively challenging the status quo. Ethnicity is now positioned as a potentially powerful (if enigmatic) social force capable of transformative disruptions that perplex as they provoke. The proliferation of ethnicity-based identity groups has proved equally unsettling, as ethnic minorities become increasingly assertive in capitalizing on ancestral differences for expressive and instrumental purposes. The **politicization** of ethnicity has not only redefined conventional intergroup relations; it has also eroded the rhythms of an established global order. The certainty and consensus that once prevailed is increasingly pervaded by uncertainty and confusion because of politicized ethnicities whose past clashes with the present, with no foreseeable resolution in the future (Castles & Miller, 2009).

Paradoxically, however, the surge in ethnicity may be directly related to the realities of globalization. That is, the greater the pressure for conformity because of standardization, the greater the incentive for promulgating ethnic differences. The very globalization that threatens a loss of distinctiveness may also spark a renewed interest in ethnic attachments in two ways: first, by creating new hybrid identities that oscillate between the "here" and the "there" by way of the "in-between" (Gillespie, 1996; Hall, 1996; Wiwa, 2003); and second, by uncoupling ethnicity from place because of global population movements, resulting in vastly more fluid identities that are increasingly transnational in scope and definition (Simmons, 2010). The corresponding dynamic is hardly inconsequential. A new set of "transnational" identities increasingly contests conventional notions of governance, in the process posing the question of whether it still makes sense to talk about multiculturalism or citizenship as place-based governance models when peoples' notions of identity and affiliation are often unlinked from any fixed point of location (Fleras, 2014b).

The politics of ethnicity in shaping human behaviour and intergroup dynamics has elicited mixed reaction (Yinger, 1994). For some, ethnic experiences are dismissed as "regressive" because of their capacity to unleash dormant hatreds for settling old scores. The cult of ethnicity is demonized as an inexcusable reversion to "tribalism" that panders to humanity's basest instincts. The "ethnification" (fragmentation) of society into squabbling ethnic communities also clashes with society-building imperatives, prompting some central authorities to dispose of this disruption by expulsion, extermination, cleansing, forced assimilation, or segregation (Taras & Ganguly, 2009). For others, ethnicity is seen as "progressive" in that it provides a community of like-minded individuals whose commitments and convictions secure an oasis of stability in a changing, confusing, and competitive world. Still others take a resigned view of ethnicity as a persistent presence in human affairs, with the potential to harm or help, depending on the circumstances. Societies that historically have championed ethnicity as an asset will flourish; conversely, those in arrears for managing ethnicity still struggle to balance the particular with the universal without spiraling into chaos or suppression. Not surprisingly, the preferred option lies in putting ethnicity to good use, without capitulating to a worst-case scenario of division or destruction. Or to put it differently: the challenge lies in making society safe *for* ethnicity as well as safe *from* ethnicity as grounds for living together with ethnic differences (Schlesinger, 1992).

Scholarly perceptions of ethnicity are also undergoing a conceptual shift (Simmons, 2010: 201). Ethnicity was once perceived as a relatively static and bounded category of ancestrally linked people whose shared distinctiveness isolated them from others. Classifying people into ethnic groups tended to "essentialize" ethnicity around fixed and uniform categories that not only determined how all members should think and act but also ignored the multidimensional nature of people's identities. Metaphorical references to the Canadian multicultural mosaic solidified this line of thinking. But ethnicity is less frequently framed along these essentialized and reified lines of ancestry. It tends instead to be defined in non-essentialist terms as a fluid and flexible dynamic instead of a separate state of being into which differences are slotted into preexisting categories (Howard-Hassmann, 1999). It is increasingly framed as a contextual and contested process constructed and reconstructed through interaction and adjustment across porous and overlapping boundaries at multiple levels and within a globalized world. No longer is ethnicity defined as a stable point of reference that determines how everyone will think and act (Fleras, 2015a). The focus now is on how ethnicity may inform a person's identity rather than boxing them into ways of thinking and acting that uniformly applies to everyone in the group. And instead of treating ethnicity as an insulated and isolated social phenomena rooted in a single place, ethnicity is situated within transnational and global contexts. As Rogers Brubaker (2002:167) points out:

> Ethnicity, race, and nation should be conceptualized not as substances or things or entities or organisms or collective individuals . . . but rather in relational, processual, dynamic, eventful, and disaggregated terms. This means thinking of ethnicity not in terms of substantial groups or entities but in terms of practical categories, situated actions, cultural idioms, cognitive schemas, discursive frames . . . contingent events. It means thinking of ethnization, racialization, and nationalization as political, social, cultural, and psychological processes . . . taking as a basic analytical category not the "group" as an entity but groupness as a contextually fluctuating conceptual variable.

The end result? Static and homogeneous, or "mosaic," models of ethnicity (ethnicity as a thing, or noun) are ceding ground to more dynamic and hybridic discourses, or "kaleidoscope" models for framing the ethnic experience ("kaleidoscope" used in the sense of constantly moving shapes, thus 'doing ethnicity' as a process, or verb) (see Table 4-1; see also, Hall, 1996; Simmons, 2010).

As well, ethnicity is no longer framed as a cuddly nostalgic blanket or as an irrational and embarrassing relic from the past that—like religion—is largely incommensurable with the modernist project. On the contrary: Far from drifting into oblivion, ethnicity has catapulted to the forefront of intergroup dynamics and politicized claims as interest groups capitalize on ethnic attachments to mobilize and engage. Canada is no stranger to ethnic politics and the politics of ethnicity. A convergence of controversies and challenges associated with ethnicity attests to the turmoil. The politics of aboriginal ethnicity have challenged the very foundational principles that govern Canada's constitutional order. The open conflicts at Ipperwash and Caledonia, Gustafsen Lake, and Burnt Church—and more recently the Idle No More movement—have seen to that. Québécois ethnicity continues to provoke English-speaking Canadians, many of whom are perplexed or apoplectic over Quebec's brand of nationalism (discussed later in this chapter). **Multicultural minorities**

TABLE 4-1	**Rethinking the Concept of Ethnicity**
CONVENTIONAL MOSAIC MODEL	**NEW KALEIDOSCOPE MODEL**
Ethnicity Matters: as thing or noun	Ethnicity Matters: as a process or verb
Situated in fixed field of location	Situated in fluid field of connections and flows
Separated and bounded	Relations between porous boundaries
Uniform and essentialistic	Multiplicity, contested, constructed, intersecting
Deterministic	Informs, not determines
Canada = mosaic of ethnic communities	Canada = dynamic kaleidoscope of ethnicized belongings and identities

have been no less adamant in leveraging their ethnicity in the competition for scarce resources. Moreover, ethnic diversity is not only about numbers, although the growing ethnic composition of Canada's population confirms the mobility of migrants and the mobilization of ethnic identities and enclaves (Belkhodia, 2014). Equally important are peoples' subjective feelings as they relate to ethnicity. To the extent that ethnicity matters, the Centre for Research and Information on Canada (2006) found that 59 percent of all respondents in a study claimed that ethnicity was "important" or "very important" to their personal identity. Another 28 percent acknowledged the importance of ethnicity when selecting a spouse. Among racialized minorities, 75 percent asserted that ethnicity was "important" or "very important" for personal identity, another 37 percent said that ethnic background was "important" or "very important" in choosing a spouse. As well, a sense of ethnic attachment and its importance to people's identity varies with length of time in Canada. Seventy-one percent of those who arrived in Canada after 1991 said it was "important"—as did 65 percent of those who arrived prior to 1991; 57 percent of those defined as second generation; and 44 percent of those defined as third generation (both parents born in Canada) (Statistics Canada, 2007). Clearly, ethnicity matters at individual levels, although its salience in terms of belonging and identity is highly varied and showing signs of decline over time (EKOS, 2013). Some want to preserve or promote their ethnicity at all costs; others can't wait to discard their ethnic "straightjacket"; still others want to fully participate in society without discarding what makes them distinctive; and yet others don't want to be boxed in by their ethnicity without necessarily discarding a sense of who they are (Malik, 2012, 2013).

This chapter explores the politics of ethnicity as a formidable dynamic in the creation of communities, identities, and activities. The chapter is organized around the theme that ethnicity once mattered, continues to matter even if many believed it wouldn't or shouldn't, and will continue to matter in the foreseeable future (albeit in forms that differ from the present and past). Ethnicity matters in two ways: First, it represents a key variable ("a difference that makes a difference") that increases the probability of making something happen; second, it provides an explanatory framework for understanding behaviour, predicting success or failure (or justifying who gets what), mobilizing people into action groups, and legitimizing claims-making activities (Karner, 2007). Framing ethnicity in terms of "it matters" raises a series of questions: Why do individuals and groups turn to ethnicity for expressive or instrumental goals? What is it about this powerful force that threatens to dismantle the conventional in exchange for the unorthodox? Why has ethnicity assumed such salience in shaping Canada's destiny? How do the politics of ethnicity pose a challenge to Canada-building? Answers to these questions are complex and contested; nevertheless, the quality of our responses will determine how adroitly Canadians can finesse ethnicity politics in advancing a cooperative coexistence.

More specifically, this chapter focuses on the politics of ethnicity when applied to a changing and diverse Canada. Canada's ethnic relations (used in the broadest sense to include Aboriginal peoples) are shown to be predominantly relations of inequality. How, then, does ethnicity contribute to the creation and maintenance of inequities as well as to challenging and changing patterns of power and privilege? The chapter is organized accordingly: (1) What is ethnicity? (2) Why does it exist? (3) How is it expressed? (4) What are its impacts on and implications for Canada-building? Attention is focused on the different expressions of ethnicity: (1) ethnicity as *community*, (2) ethnicity as *identity*, including lived, situational/symbolic, hybridic, transnational, and insurgent, and

(3) ethnicity as *activity*, including social movements such as ethnic nationalism. Reference to the concept that "ethnicity matters" is sharply played out in Quebec where the politics of ethnicity and nationalism intermesh to create a zone of instability. Quebec's distinctive brand of nationalism may be evolving toward greater inclusion of racialized minorities and migrants, although the process is proving trickier than many thought, given Quebec's ambivalent status as a majority/minority society. The chapter concludes by discussing how the depoliticizing of ethnicity under Canada's Multiculturalism banner establishes a governance model that makes Canada safe from ethnicity, yet safe for ethnicity.

CONCEPTUALIZING ETHNICITY

Most societies are composed of racially and ethnically diverse groups (Isajiw, 1999). The range of variation is almost limitless. Some societies are relatively homogeneous in terms of ethnic composition (Japan and Korea); others have a single dominant majority with numerous minorities in different stages of assimilation (United Kingdom); others consist of dominant and subdominant groups that are locked in competition for power (Fiji); still others, including Australia and New Zealand, are constitutive of white settler colonies with immigrant populations superimposed on increasingly powerful indigenous nations (Fleras & Spoonley, 1999).

On the surface, it might appear hopeless to extract a pattern from this seeming disarray. Nevertheless, two patterns can be discerned across societies. First, a dominant ethnic group prevails whose culture, language, values, and social patterns are privileged as normal and desirable. Those in control possess the power and resources to establish institutional arrangements and ideological systems consistent with their interests. Ethnocultural minorities have suffered as a result of this mistreatment, and many have reacted accordingly. A second pattern involves the proliferation of ethnically diverse groups who are increasingly restive because of their marginal status. Options open to these subdominant groups may be limited and limiting. Many endure constant pressure to absorb prevailing values, norms, and institutions. Others are kept securely in place to ensure a reserve pool of largely exploited labour. And still others are encouraged to retain diversity, but find themselves penalized or ostracized as a result. Needless to say, the prospect of defining ethnicity under such varied circumstances is daunting.

Defining Ethnicity

References to the term "ethnicity" continue to baffle and confuse as well as to infuriate and inflame. Ethnicity has evolved into an imprecise mélange of contested meanings that can be stretched to mean everything yet nothing, in the process acquiring the status of a cliché without much analytical clout. The term itself seems immune to rational analysis, thanks to its complexities and scope (Clarke et al., 2008): How can a single term encompass everything from ethnocide in the Darfur region of Sudan, to Québécois ethnic nationalism, to the contrived ethnicity of Kitchener-Waterloo's annual Oktoberfest celebration? What can be done with a word that people often use as a more polite euphemism for "race?" As well, the term is subject to additional overuse. For example, consider how reference to ethnic conflict is routinely employed to describe intergroup hostilities in Africa, but never applied to Western intervention in the Middle East—even though ethnicity may well prove pivotal in explaining the conflict.

Still, any definition must reflect certain prerequisites. A working definition must be sufficiently broad to capture the politics of ethnicity as principle and practice, yet not so sprawling as to lose this focus. A distinction between race and ethnicity provides a useful starting point. Whereas race connotes biological variation, genetic determinism, and imposed classifications, ethnicity differs in emphasizing self-generated cultural differences related to values, lifestyle, and world view (Durie, 2005). Definitions must also acknowledge both subjective and objective dimensions at either individual or group levels. Or, as Yinger (1994) notes, three components must prevail: (1) members of a so-called ethnicity see themselves as different; (2) others see them as different; and (3) people participate in shared activities with the intent of affirming their distinctiveness. With ethnicity, individuals experience a sense of belonging to a community of like-minded individuals who share a common attachment to identity markers such as language, history, birthright, kinship, and homeland. Broadly speaking, then, **ethnicity** can be defined as a principle and process in which a *shared awareness of a people's ancestral linkages and perceived commonalities serves as a basis for community, identity, and activity*. This definition captures the multidimensionality of ethnicity as (1) embodying a consciousness of being different because of tradition and transmission, (2) an awareness of differences as socially constructed yet grounded in historical origins and structural realities, (3) a recognition that people perceive themselves as different and are seen by others as being different, and (4) an acknowledgment that ethnicity matters in securing recognition (identities), rewards (entitlements), or relationships (engagements).

There is some value in distinguishing ethnicity from ethnic groups and ethnic minorities. Ethnicity consists of a principle whose distinctive attributes distinguish members of one category from another because of beliefs, values, emotions, and practices. Under the ethnicity principle, persons who are related by birth, loyalty, culture, or homeland have the "option" of joining goal-directed action groups in pursuit of instrumental or expressive ends. **Ethnic groups**, by contrast, refer to lived-communities of people who are socially and culturally distinct, who see themselves and are seen by others as distinct from other communities, and who are separated from others because of ancestries and boundaries. As widely noted, ethnic groups constitute a form of social organization with boundaries, a shared and transmitted culture, and a sense of identity among members that fosters patterns of belonging. The extent to which ethnic groups maintain a strong consciousness among members will fluctuate, too; that is, some ethnic groups seek rapid assimilation and are quickly accepted by the mainstream, while others may stoutly defend their identity because of mainstream rejection or a desire for distinctiveness (see discussion on dualisms in Chapter 1). Finally, the concept of "ethnic minority" refers to a group of culturally distinct people who occupy (or are seen to occupy) a marginal status in society, even though they may outnumber those of the dominant sector. In other words, references to ethnicity involving minority versus majority—as well as dominant versus subdominant—are about power and differences, not about numbers and proportions.

Attributes of Ethnicity

To ensure ethnic distinctiveness, boundaries are required. Ethnic boundaries can be defined as socially constructed barriers that provide a protective buffer by regulating of movement between ethnic groups (Barth, 1969). Neither totally impenetrable nor excessively permeable, these boundaries can be likened to "membranes" that simultaneously inhibit yet permit the interflow of particles. In some cases, these boundaries are vigorously maintained for keeping some people in and others out. This boundary maintenance is especially true when group members consider themselves under threat because of racist legislation, restricted economic opportunity, restrained cultural expression, or social rejection. In other cases, boundaries are relatively porous-fluid, contested, context dependent, and increasingly complex (Cornell & Hartmann, 1998). But difficulties arise in maintaining a degree of bounded distinctiveness, especially in a country such as Canada, with its official Multiculturalism and absence of official assimilationist pressure (Weinfeld, 2001).

Consider how the politics of boundary maintenance are played out in light of Quebec's commitment to the principles of interculturalism (Fleras, 2013). Quebec's endorsement of interculturalism as ethnic governance was first introduced in the early 1980s, although not fully articulated until the 1990 Policy Statement on Immigration and Integration (Leroux, 2014). An intercultural governance model proposes a distinct political community whose cultural and language priorities supersede the salience of ethnic diversities. According to interculturalism as ethnicity governance, newcomers and their contributions are welcome, but their entry activates a "moral contract" involving a reciprocal exchange of rights, duties, and obligations between newcomers and the Québécois. Newcomers must agree to abide by the primacy of speaking French, acknowledge Quebec as a free and democratic society as well as secular and pluralist (within limits), governed by the rule of law, and committed to gender equality (Gagnon & Iacovino, 2007; Montpetit, 2011). Quebec, in turn, cultivates a pluralistic notion of society that is sensitive to immigrant rights; preserves the creative tension between the diversity of minority differences and the predominance of French culture; and emphasizes the centrality of integration and interaction to the Quebec-building project (Bouchard-Taylor Commission, 2008:121). Quebec has also proposed an obligatory seminar to instruct newcomers about the province's common values, while cities such as Gatineau provide a statement of values to assist newcomer integration (Peritz, 2011). In short, an interculturalism commitment reflects what is metaphorically equivalent to an "arboreal" model of ethnic/immigrant governance; that is, the tree trunk is unflinchingly French in language and culture, while minority cultures constitute the branches grafted on to the trunk. With interculturalism, in other words, limits to diversity are explicit—you can be Haitian but always a Haitian in Quebec, with a corresponding commitment to its values, institutions, and norms as set out in laws, ideals, and constitution.

This emphasis on objective ethnic content has waned in recent years. In its place has emerged an interest in the subjective experiences that embrace and the symbolic boundaries that encircle. A subjectivist orientation rejects the notion of ethnicity as a clearly articulated cultural category with an easily defined set of objective features. Ethnicity instead is informed by a shared "we feeling" that infuses the members of a particular group with a sense of who they are, where they originated from, and where they are headed. Emphasis is focused on ethnicity as an intersubjective activity, that is, a flexible resource for crafting patterns of meaningful interaction (Barth, 1969; Isajiw, 1999). In acknowledging that people may manipulate ethnicity to adapt, gain, or play, there is an unmistakable shift away from conventional notions that embrace static and homogeneous models.

But just as a laundry-list approach to ethnicity has proven inadequate, so too has an overemphasis on subjective experience. Ethnicity is more than a feeling of apartness or a sense of shared awareness; it is also grounded around those visible cultural symbols deemed essential to group survival. Select tangible markers such as patterns of kinship, descent, and obligations are required to validate a sense of continuity, collectivity, and commitment. Of those characteristics that shine as indices of ethnicity, from appearances to dietary habits, the most prominent are birthright, homeland, and language. Birthright is critical: Only persons with proven (or perceived) descent from a common source can claim membership to a particular ethnicity. No less crucial is a powerful attachment to a territory or homeland that may have been lost or left behind. Ethnic homelands are valorized as an embodiment of the past whose value must be defended at all costs. Language often represents the quintessential component of group distinctiveness. It also serves as a powerful symbol of distinctiveness, cohesion, and integrity that performs integrative and identifying functions, as point out later in this chapter.

EXPLAINING ETHNICITY: WHY?

Ethnicity is evolving into one of the world's most powerful dynamics. Its salience in defining, shaping, and advancing group relations within multicultural contexts such as those found in Canada is beyond doubt. Not surprisingly, many regard as a major challenge the construction of a society that is safe for ethnicity, yet safe from ethnicity. But such a concern was not always the case. The inevitable dissolution of ethnicity was widely predicted and anticipated as recently as two generation ago. Both socialism and liberalism attacked the particularist attachments associated with ethnicity as atavistic survival at odds with universal progress and modernization. Ancient tribal hatreds would melt into memory because of a modernist belief in liberal universalism, with its attendant notion that, for purposes of reward and recognition, peoples' commonalities as individuals are more important than what divides them because of membership in racial or ethnically distinct groups (Maaka & Fleras, 2005).

Ideological considerations were no less dismissive of ethnicity. Capitalism rejected ethnicity as anathema to progress or prosperity. With its backward-looking attachments to tribes and traditions, ethnicity would imperil the unfettered flow of labour, capital, and markets. A Marxist perspective was equally dismissive. If class relations constituted the fundamental dynamic in society, everything else, including ethnicity, was deemed to be derivative or residual. To think or to act otherwise, namely, in terms of ethnicity, perpetuated the false consciousness that bolstered the principles of capitalism. In short, both functionalism/capitalism and conflict/Marxist theorists pounced on ethnicity as inferior, irrelevant, doomed to obscurity, and an obstacle to progress and prosperity.

Predictions of its demise have been premature, to say the least. Ethnicity has proven both resilient and tenacious, with no signs of diminishing or disappearing, despite powerful pressures to the contrary. Perpetuated at times by individuals as genuine culture (i.e., enjoyed in its own right); as an impetus for mobilizing people into goal-directed action (i.e., employed as a means to an end); and as a source of meaning, identity, and solidarity (Karner, 2007), the ethnicity "revolution" has profoundly redefined the notion of what society is for. People have turned to ethnicity as a means of protecting their immediate interests, especially when central authorities are unable or unwilling to offer protection. No longer are ethnic attachments dismissed as archaic survivals from the past—quaint and colourful, perhaps, but quite irrelevant to contemporary realities. On the contrary, ethnicity matters, and this renewal of ethnic pride and identity has revealed a double-edged capacity not only to enhance or empower, but also to destroy or dispossess.

The rejuvenation of ethnicity in Canada and elsewhere raises many questions: How do we account for the popularity and proliferation of ethnicity in contemporary societies? Why might people prefer to affiliate along ethnic lines rather than associate with political parties or trade unions? How can the visceral appeal of an inward-looking ethnicity possibly supersede the cosmopolitan lure of a modern society? Or rephrased along more grounded lines: Why would anyone want to be thought of as a Québécois or Aboriginal or Lithuanian-Canadian when they can identify solely as non-hyphenated Canadians? Three explanatory frameworks help to isolate the factors that underscore the popularity and persistence of the ethnicity experience, namely: the *primordial*, the *constructivist*, and the *instrumentalist*.

Primordial Explanation

The **primordial explanation** argues that the boom in ethnicity is essentially an extension of powerful and immutable instincts that cannot be indefinitely suppressed. People appear to have a genuine preference for aligning themselves with closely related blood kin; as a result, ethnicity represents an ancient and deep-rooted impulse for being with your "own kind." Suppression of these ascribed statuses for belonging with similar others, given at birth, and perceived as fixed and permanent, doesn't make ethnicity go away (Clarke et al., 2008). Rather, this ethnicity is forced to go underground, only to re-emerge in an often explosive rage when the lid is lifted. These bonds are primordial because they appear to have been hardwired by evolution into the human species for survival purposes. This intrinsic dimension may help to explain the intensity of passions and emotions associated with the ethnic experience. Consider this statement by a Serbian-Canadian in rationalizing his loyalties during the 1999 NATO-led bombings of Serbia: "I'm a Canadian by birth and a Serbian by blood. I think family values come ahead of values or loyalties to your country . . . It's not a question of loyalty to Canada or Serbia" (as cited in Sarick, 1999). The primordiality of ethnic attachments may also explain the popularity of staunchly ethnic social movements in advancing collective interests (Bell-Fialkoff, 1993).

Within the primordialist camp are various biologically informed theories of ethnic bonding, the most popular of which is sociobiology. According to this slant, ethnicity is biogenetically "wired" into the human species as a mechanism for maximizing the transmission of genes from one generation to the next. Pierre van den Berghe (1981), for example, traces the origins of ethnic bonding to an extension of kinship group solidarity. Any kinship group tends to act in a self-preservative manner by providing mutual aid and cooperation for those related because of a common ancestor. Involvement with related others ensures the long-term survival of the kin groups—albeit at some expense to any specific individual. It follows from this that even ostensibly altruistic actions have the effect of protecting and promoting the evolutionary survival of one's own ethnic kin.

There is something of value in sociobiological explanations of ethnicity. Situating ethnic experiences within our genetic and evolutionary past captures the tenacity and the intensely emotional appeal of ethnicity (Brown, 1989). But sociologists are divided over the merits of sociobiology as an explanation, especially as many reject those frameworks that exclude the social as primary cause. Many are unsettled by the political implications of reductionist arguments that conflate biology with culture. True, we may be genetically "hardwired" to identify with our "own kind"; nevertheless, definitions of what constitutes our "own kind" will vary over time and across space. The fact that people are also free to choose otherwise, and that many have done so by repudiating their ethnic heritage is a strike against primordiality.

Constructivist Explanation

Opposing the primordial explanation is a **constructivist explanation** that focuses on the creation of ethnicity through meaningful interaction. The constructivist approach tends to see ethnic identity and affiliation as a complex and contested process whose construction cannot be understood outside the context of situational circumstances (Koenig & de Guchteneire, 2007). The "construction" in a social constructivist position confirms how there is nothing natural or normal about the world we live in, despite continued efforts by vested interests to make it seem so. Social conventions that guide or organize are continually constructed and reconstructed through a process of meaningful engagement. Similarly, ethnicity is not a natural feature of society but a constructed response to challenges such as material exclusion, a search for social meaning, a quest for identity, the relief in being with "one's own kind," and a struggle for creating culturally safe spaces. Inasmuch as ethnicity represents a social construct, it is "imagined." But its effects on the lives and life chances of minority women and men are far from imaginary.

The identity thesis represents a variant of a constructivist explanation. According to the **identity thesis**, ethnicity persists because it provides a coping mechanism for addressing the globalizing demands of contemporary urban society. An identity perspective points to ethnicity as a buffer for insulating individuals from the pressures of an impersonal and competitive world. A commitment to ethnicity secures a source of stability in a world of diversity, uncertainty, and change; as an oasis of tranquility, it restores a measure of meaning in an increasingly meaningless world. Appeals to ethnicity foster a sense of relief, continuity, belonging, importance, security—and even enjoyment—especially for those at the margins of society without alternative channels for coping with societal stress caused by intense global competition, radicalized individualism, a disintegrating civil society, increasingly porous territorial borders, the erosion of the nation-state as the primary source of legitimacy, and cultural upheavals created by the proliferation of digital technologies. The dissolution of the familiar and reassuring may undermine a people's sense of social belonging, including a rootedness in traditional collectivities such as kinship or community. The confluence of uncertainty and change may also induce individuals to withdraw into ethnic shells both familiar and emotionally satisfying (Littleton, 1996). As Manuel Castells (1997) writes:

> When the world becomes too large to be controlled, social actors aim at shrinking it back to their size and reach. When networks dissolve time and space, people anchor themselves in places, and recall their historic memory. (p. 66)

Ethnic involvements, in other words, permit meaningful identity to be crafted when meanings are in short supply. A "quasi-kinship" community is sustained that provides a buffer against the backdrop of unremitting rationality, standardization, and central control (Scott, 1998). This binding and bonding dimension also helps to explain the universal appeal of such affiliation for people whose cultural moorings have been cut adrift by the relentless pressure for conformity and integration.

Instrumentalist Explanation

An **instrumentalist explanation** views ethnicity as a resource for the pursuit of diverse goals (Hutchinson & Smith, 1996). One version refers to elite competition for scarce resources, in which ethnic symbols are manipulated to secure mass support. A second version refers to a process by which both leaders and followers maximize preferences, since pooled resources provide a competitive advantage in advancing vested interests. An instrumentalist approach is firmly grounded in a sociological understanding of group competition and rational choice theory; that is, ethnicity is designed to maximize in-group advantage by excluding others. The drawing power of ethnicity provides a competitive edge in the struggle for scarce and valued resources as groups rely on their ethnic attachments to mobilize, challenge, and change. Especially in contexts in which an ethnic division of labour persists (Hechter, 1975), dominant sectors tend to monopolize wealth and power at the expense of ethnically different subdominant groups, many of whom are locked into a position of inferiority because of their unskilled status. Resentment over this differential treatment boils over when expectations soar but the means to achievement are blocked, resulting in escalating frustration, hostility, or conflict. These conflicts are further bolstered by the actions of opportunistic elites who often cloak personal interests behind a facade of altruism.

Two questions arise from an instrumentalist approach to ethnicity: First, why do ethnically like-minded persons prefer to act collectively, rather than as individuals, to achieve their goals? Put simply, a collective basis is superior for coping with the demands of a complex and bureaucratized society. According to **resource mobilization theory**, large-scale social movements possess the human resources and critical mass to compete effectively in the competition for scarce resources. Second, why are ethnic attachments important in securing the loyalty and commitment of members? What is the tactical advantage of relying on ethnicity as a basis for mobilizing people into groups? The best answer may be the most obvious: Recruitment by appealing to ethnicity is perceived as more natural and durable than the "artificial" linkages associated with political or economic ties. Ethnic bonds are consolidated by emotional involvement with persons of one's own kind, a kind of quasi-kinship that needs no justification beyond its own existence. These quasi-kinship ties also infuse the movement with the commitment for waging a protracted struggle against even seemingly insurmountable odds.

To sum up: Each of these three explanatory frameworks described above may be partially correct in that each provides insights into aspects of the ethnic experience that others prefer to ignore, including (1) ethnicity as an inherent affiliation that reflects an intrinsic need for belonging to one's own kind (primordial), (2) ethnicity as a constructed buffer for securing meaning and continuity in a changing and uncertain world (constructivist), and (3) ethnicity as a tool for the attainment of goals through collective action (instrumentalist). That said, there is no reason why primordial explanations cannot be incorporated into a broader explanatory framework (including the constructivist and instrumentalist explanations) in securing a multi-textured insight into the complexities of the ethnicity experience.

EXPRESSING ETHNICITY: HOW?

Ethnicity can be expressed at different levels of reality. At one level, ethnicity is manifested in ethnic groups who live together in relatively self-sufficient communities. At another level, ethnicity manifests itself through different expressions of identity, including lived, symbolic and situational, hybridic, insurgent, and transnational. At a third level, ethnicity reflects activity best expressed through social movements with nationalistic overtones. These different expressions of the ethnic experience—*community*, *identity*, and *activity* (see Table 4-2)—may be analyzed separately; in reality, however, they tend to coexist, overlap, and intersect in complex ways.

Ethnicity as Community

Ethnicity refers to a principle of potential group/community formation. Persons with shared and felt identification may be classified into a category that mobilizes ancestrally related persons into action groups to advance individual or collective claims. Ethnicity also provides a basis for relatively permanent communities with clearly defined rules for living together. Preference for being with one's own kind may foster a commitment to community. Or pressures from the outside may also compel a closing of the ranks along community lines to cope with unfriendly environments. Quebec, for example, represents an ethnicity and ethnic group/community as well as a nation and distinct society with its own distinct language, culture, and culture that distinguishes it from the rest of Canada and North America.

   Parts of urban Canada are composed of a mosaic of ethnic communities, including the widely celebrated Chinatowns in Vancouver and Toronto, South Asian communities in Brampton, and the relatively self-sufficient Hasidic Jews in Montreal. Or consider the town of Markham, located just north of Toronto, where nearly 72 percent of the population, according to 2011 data, identified themselves as ethnic—including one ward where 95 percent of the population self-identified as ethnic. According to Qadeer, Agrawal, and Lovell (2009), the percentage of South Asians residing in their respective ethnic

TABLE 4-2	Expressing Ethnicity: Community, Identity, and Activity	
Ethnicity as community	**Ethnicity as identity**	**Ethnicity as activity**
Enclaves	Lived	Nationalistic movements
	Situational/symbolic	Ethnic nationalism
	Hybridic	Civic nationalism
	Transnational	Intercultural nationalism
	Insurgent	

enclaves in Toronto's Census Metropolitan Area in 2006 was 49.6 percent, followed by Chinese at 48.2 percent and Jewish at 40.6 percent. These ethnic communities can be conceptualized in different ways—either as segregated ghettos that intensify downward spirals or as vibrant ethnic enclaves both distinctive and prosperous (Qadeer, Agrawal, & Lovell, 2009).

An important study of ethnocultural minority enclaves in Montreal, Toronto, and Vancouver by Daniel Hiebert (2015) uncovered interesting trends and developments. First, the proportion of racialized migrants and minorities living in enclaves has remained stable in Montreal, but enclave landscapes are increasingly more prevalent in Toronto and Vancouver. Second, racialized groups vary in their likelihood of living in an enclave, with some members residing in enclaves and another component living in other parts of the city. Certain racialized minorities and more recent migrants are more likely to settle in enclaves. Third, the socioeconomic characteristics of persons living in enclaves is difficult to generalize. In Montreal, enclaves are sites of relatively more poverty and unemployment, but the situation is much more complex in Toronto and Vancouver, with some indicators pointing to socioeconomic marginalization and other indicators indicating relatively high home ownership, a middle class commitment, and conformity to core values. Evidence also indicates that more members of a racialized minority who experience poverty live outside enclaves than those who live in them. Fourth, even those enclaves dominated by a single dominant group are not monocultural domains but characterized by high levels of internal diversity owing to the presence of other ethnocultural minorities. In short, unlike the situation in many parts of Europe, as Hiebert (2015) concludes, the existence of ethnocultural enclaves do not necessarily lead to residents leading "parallel lives" in terms of socioeconomic disadvantage or social isolation from the rest of Canada—although exceptions and departures from patterns do exist.

Ethnic communities can also be seen as complex matrices of intergroup relations and intragroup dynamics. They consist of communities that offer emotional and material support for facilitating the transition from the society of origin to urban Canada. Recent immigrants may find economic and cultural refuge in ethnic communities because of organizations that assist in the preservation of language and transmission of culture. In providing a framework for collective activities, they also establish a power base for advancing political consciousness and action. These communities may attract resources and influence if local leaders can command community loyalty and deliver this "commodity" as electoral support for government initiatives. Still, internal tensions may threaten community solidarity or consensus on issues. Despite a constructed facade of unity, social fissures are readily apparent as vested interests jockey for position, resulting in a high potential for factional infighting and political cleavages among community members because of politicized differences in age, sex, income, education, and length of residence.

Ethnicity as Identity

One of the identities open to Canadians is that of ethnicity. In a multicultural society such as Canada, many individuals regard their ethnicity as important in defining their self-identity (see Cornell & Hartmann, 2007; Liu et al., 2006; Muir & Wetherell, 2010). Identity entails how a person defines who he or she is by seeking a degree of consistency in responding to questions such as these: How do I see myself? How would I like to see myself? How do I think others see me? How would I like others to see me? (As we shall see in the next chapter, ethnicity also serves as a critical determinant of "who gets what.") Ethnic identities can also be broadly defined as personal attachments involving a subjective sense of belonging to or identification with a group or tradition over time, based on commonalities with similar others (Driedger, 1989; Satzewich & Liodakis, 2013). In certain cases, ethnic identities are imposed by outside sources; in others, they are voluntarily adopted on the basis of how individuals or groups feel about themselves. Some identities, such as "white ethnicity," are somewhat muted since whites rarely express a conscious awareness of their whiteness unless challenged to do so. Other identities may be active in that individuals are conscious of them and act accordingly to protect or promote them. Still other identities are politicized in securing the basis for collective action to achieve goals. In all cases, identities are relational in that they are constructed through meaningful interaction rather than psychologized as labels that are inherent or maturational (Drummond, n.d.).

Expressions of ethnic identities are varied (Simmons, 2010). Some Canadians reject their ethnic background except for on special occasions, preferring instead to be identified only as Canadians for purposes of recognition, relationships, and rewards. Others maintain a dual (or "transnational") identity without much difficulty: Modern communication and transport technologies allow ethnic minorities to transcend national borders by participating in the internal affairs of the homeland without relinquishing a commitment to Canada. Such a dynamic makes it difficult to think of Canada as a collection of self-contained localities. Rather, the intensified transnational exchanges between localities and the homeland have altered how people think about identity, place, and borders (Fleras, 2015b; Papillon, 2002). Still others thrive on multiple identities. They flit in and out of different ethnic identities without a sense of a crisis of confusion. Their identities are fluid and contextual—even contradictory—in coping with the many opportunities that a complex society has to offer, especially as individuals and groups are drawn into an ever-expanding nexus of networks and linkages (Handa, 2003). And yet still others remain locked into an "old country" identity with neither the intent nor energy to alter who they are. Five expressions of ethnic identity can be discerned, at least for the purposes of analysis, namely *lived*, *situational/symbolic*, *hybridic*, *transnational*, and *insurgent*.

Lived Ethnic Identity Individuals with common cultural values or religious beliefs may strongly identify with a particular ethnic group. Under a **lived ethnic identity**, individuals are born into these primary groups, membership is irrevocably assigned at birth, and the group remains a virtually exclusive source of identity throughout an entire lifetime. An attachment to the norms, values, and institutions of the group constitutes a serious statement about personal affiliation. Anabaptist sects such as the Hutterites are ethnic communities governed by rules, values, and sanctions. Here, the principle of ethnicity reflects and reinforces the organization of viable groups, with a corresponding powerful influence in shaping members' lives. These individuals admit that their identification with the cultural past makes a difference in how they think and behave. Involvement at this level presupposes a framework of constraints, demands, and responsibilities that cannot be casually discarded as moods shift or personalities change.

A lived ethnicity represents a difference that makes a difference in defining "who we are." There is no option or choice; either people conform or they are shunned or expelled.

Not surprisingly, this "old-fashioned" style of ethnicity is disappearing. Restricted largely to rural areas and certain urban enclaves of Canada, conventional ethnic groups have lost much of their moral authority as arbiters of correct human behaviour. Many of these groups can no longer supply a common set of shared values, enforce mutual obligations or responsibilities, offer incentives or impose sanctions, or secure compliance from members. Furthermore, a lived ethnicity rarely appeals to those who want to fully participate in an achievement-oriented society; they prefer a more flexible arrangement.

Situational/Symbolic Ethnic Identity Ethnicity in a multicultural society takes on a different dynamic. Ethnic identities may shift toward the part-time, focus on symbols rather than substance, and become situation-specific. The obligations of a lived ethnic identity are discarded in exchange for the flexibility associated with symbolic commitments and situational adjustments. This situationally specific and symbolically loaded identity often takes the form of a strategic personal resource that allows individuals to improve their life chances without rejecting their life sources. References to ethnic identities as situational or symbolic are not intended to trivialize or demean the ethnic experience as inauthentic or contrived. Emphasis instead is on its adaptiveness and resilience across time and place.

An ethnic identity based on situation and symbols reflects a uniquely distinct process of immigrant adaptation. Through involvement in their adopted country, incoming immigrants may become increasingly estranged from their cultural heritage—especially in terms of language use, friendship circles, and residential patterns—preferring instead to identify with the values and lifestyle of the host society. Ethnic attachments to the homeland culture begin to dissipate in light of host-country pressures to adapt and integrate. Involvement in ethnic organizations declines (except on isolated occasions or in favourable circumstances) to the point of insignificance—if measured by the frequency or intensity of institutional participation. Yet there is a reluctance to casually discard tradition, given its former importance as a blueprint for identity and relationships, with the result that many new Canadians may retain a strong emotional connection to the symbolic aspects of their cultural past. In resisting the lure of wholesale assimilation, they reveal an affective attachment to the community as a reference group, but reject as unacceptable both the restrictions and responsibilities of a lived ethnicity (Roberts & Clifton, 1990).

The emergence of this "part-time" ethnicity is known as **situational or symbolic ethnic identity**—situational because its expression is context-dependent rather than constant across time and space; and symbolic because identity is informed by an attachment to symbols rather than the substance of ethnicity. Ethnic salience is not measured by levels of participation in ethnic clubs, knowledge of ethnic language, circle of friends, place of residence, or marital patterns. Importance instead is attached to identifying with the symbols of that ethnicity, with a willingness to activate those symbols when appropriate or for advantage. Individuals do not so much belong to an ethnic group as they voluntarily affiliate with relevant cultural symbols as preferences dictate and situations demand (Amarasingam, 2008). Admittedly, not everyone possesses a choice of options. The centrality of racialized visibility make this option less applicable to people of colour, who may find ethnic identities imposed on them against their will, rather than something they can opt into or out of when they please.

The situational and symbolic nature of ethnic identity provides insights into (and questions about) the ethnicity experience. First, can distinct ethnic identities survive in situations where the traditional culture has disappeared? Second, can individuals continue to identify themselves as "ethnics" long after abandoning all involvement in group activities? According to the logic of situational and symbolic ethnicity, the answer to both questions is "yes." The decline of a particular lifestyle will not necessarily diminish the validity of the ethnic experience. What is critical for ethnic identity is the identification with select aspects of that cultural lifestyle—not the scope or intensity of affiliation. Needless to say, this style of identity is relatively painless and voluntary; moreover, its abstract and effortless style makes it well suited to the needs of an upwardly mobile society.

A third question is also of interest: Is a hyphenated Canadian a contradiction in terms? Is it possible to identify and participate as a Canadian, yet retain an affiliation with a certain ethnic heritage, such as Lithuanian (or New Zealander or German)? Again, the answer is in the affirmative. A hyphenated identity entitles people to compartmentalize their identities, then activate the appropriate identity according to the demands of a particular context. Dual (even multiple) identities are not mutually exclusive; rather, they may complement each other in fulfilling diverse personal needs and goals. Nor does identification with select symbolic elements necessarily compromise the business of making a living. As long as identification is restricted to the cognitive rather than the behavioural level, everyone can regard themselves as an "ethnic" without relinquishing a commitment to Canada.

Hybridic Ethnic Identity Most perspectives on ethnicity reflect a modernist or "structuralist" approach. Structuralists tend to see social groups or institutional arrangements as the fundamental building blocks of society, a primary source of human identity, a critical factor in shaping behaviour, and the key determinant of intergroup relations. According to structuralist thought, for each identifiable group there is a single ethnoculture with a unique and unchanging essence that can be categorically grasped independently of context. Ethnicities are envisioned as reflecting separate and fixed states of being into which individuals are slotted, with an attendant belief that everyone in this ethnic group will think and act in the same way.

But the seemingly locked-in identities of the modern era are giving way to the emergence of the **postmodern** self as relatively free-floating and detached from conventional structures of identity (Fleras, 2015a; Paradies, 2006). Individuals move into and out of so many different contexts and identities that it no longer makes sense to categorize people into stable ethnic groups (Uitermark, Rossi, & van Houtum, 2005). People are known to define themselves in terms of multiple national attachments involving identities that are both contested and contextual as well as fluid and flexible (Simmons, 2010). As personal resources for coping with diverse realities, ethnicities are increasingly evolving as hybrid identities that oscillate between the past and present, involving a multiplicity of crossovers and contingencies in a world where people live their paradoxes without fears of contradiction (Handa, 2003; Wiwa, 2003).

Hybridic ethnic identities reflect the predicaments and opportunities of a contemporary era. The increasingly postnational world we live in is a diasporic and transmigrant reality where (1) immigrants mingle with national minorities and Indigenous peoples; (2) increasingly porous cultural boundaries are constantly being invented or renegotiated; and (3) migrants and minorities assert multiple and overlapping patterns of belonging based on intersecting lines of gender, sexual preferences, homeland, and ethnicity. As a result, ethnic identities may no longer reflect stable points of reference for pre-slotting individuals into fixed boxes. Rather, ethnic identities reflect situational dynamics that come into being through interaction—continually changing and reinventing themselves by fusing the old with the new alongside other ethnicities, to create new and provisional hybrids that are neither stable nor coherent. Instead of being fixed in some kind of essentialized past, they are evolving, highly adaptive, involve crossings and connections, and are subject to the continuous play of context (Hall, 1996).

Transnational Ethnic Identity Both symbolic/situational and hybridic ethnicities reinforce the constructed nature of ethnic identities. References to **transnational ethnic identities** also follow this path. The concept itself acknowledges an emergent and fundamental reality: Globalization has challenged the conventional notions of belonging that linked a person's identity to a particular place (Fleras, 2014b). No longer is it useful to frame homeland and host country as an either/or dichotomy in winning an immigrant's sense of identity and belonging. New notions of multiple homelands and multiple attachments in light of diasporic movements of people are emerging instead, with a corresponding fresh perspective on how online ethnic identities can be imagined and constructed across national borders (Fleras, 2011b; Simmons, 2010).

Reaction to transnational identities is understandably varied. Some see multilocal identities as beneficial for society by providing linkages of value that span the borders of a global market economy. For others, however, these seemingly divided identities conjure up images of split loyalties, thus compromising the potential for political governance, societal integration, and assumption of citizenship responsibilities (Duncan, 2006). Place-based governance models such as multiculturalism become unsettled when peoples' notions of identity and belonging are no longer linked to a specific locale but splintered across diverse domains (Fleras, 2015b). For example, addressing a sense of belonging and attachment beyond Canada's borders may well undermine what it means to be Canadian. For still others, benefits come with costs, making it doubly important to understand how and why diasporic populations maintain ties with real and imagined homelands, what this means at the personal and community levels, and what kind of impact this has on society and culture (Satzewich & Wong, 2006; Sommerville, 2008).

The mixed reaction to transnational identities makes one thing abundantly clear: There is a growing acknowledgment of ethnic identities as a *process* or *verb* ("doing ethnicity") rather than a *thing* or a *noun*. Ethnic identities are no longer defined as rigid or fixed, especially as online ethnicities from around the world regroup into new points of being and becoming (Marotta, 2011). Because of transnational mobility, these diasporic experiences are not defined by essences or purity, but by the dynamics of hybridity and heterogeneity that define both the construction and negotiation of identities as well as how they are practised and experienced (Braziel & Mannur, 2003; Vertovec, 2006).

Insurgent Ethnic Identity Both lived and situational/symbolic ethnic identities appear to be relatively innocuous. Hybridic identities are equally harmless because of their preoccupation with the discourses of authenticity rather than the politics of power. Abiding by the liberal slogan of "agreeing to disagree," each of these identities upholds the multicultural axiom of "live and let live." But not all ethnic identities are so accommodating. **Insurgent ethnic identities** are much more assertive about what they believe is right or wrong, are highly politicized in terms of what they want, and appear more aggressive in achieving their goals. In transcending mere identification or celebration, an insurgent ethnicity projects an exaggerated notion of a shared and conscious attachment to a people, tradition, or territory. Cooperative coexistence is replaced by a politicized assertion of peoplehood that establishes a new political order reflecting and reinforcing their superiority. An intense dislike of others may be actively fostered, especially when issues pertaining to religion, language, or homelands are factored into the equation. Such collectivities are willing to take whatever measures necessary to achieve their goals, including the revival of dormant grievances and recourse to violent measures, if necessary (Taras & Ganguly, 2002).

Ethnicity as Activity: Nationalist Movements

Ethnicity as activity involves the process by which ideas and ideals are put into practice for goal attainment. Nowhere is this more evident than in the reality of ethnically related peoples engaging in organized action to achieve the political goals of identity, voice, or land. Appeals to ethnicity provide a criterion for mobilizing individuals into collective action; they also furnish the motivation and rationale to achieve ethnically defined goals. This surge of ethnic-based movements has come about for various reasons. The UN-based principle of national self-determination articulated a normative basis for making ethnically based political claims against the state. The collapse of superpower colonialism realigned social-political formations that emphasized ethnic loyalties rather than the abstractions of statehood (Ignatieff, 1994). Inter-tribal hatreds, once suppressed by colonialist control or Cold War politics, have created fertile conditions for a robust ethnicity to flourish (Snyder, 2000). Or as Michael Ignatieff wrote in 1994, the "key narrative of the new world order is the disintegration of nation states into warring factions. The key architects of that order are warlords; and the key language of our age is *ethnic nationalism* (emphasis added)."

   Nationalism constitutes the political expression of a **nation** whose peoples claim a common ancestry and shared destiny to govern themselves in a place they call a homeland. The nineteenth century gave rise to ideologies of nationalism in Europe, resulting in the birth of modern Germany, with its rallying cry of "Germany for the Germans," but also in the dismissing of Slavs, Jews, and Gypsies as unwelcome residue from past empires (Guibernau, 2007). Defining the nation-state around a shared language, culture, and identity (Smith, 1999) demonstrates how all expressions of nationalism remain grounded in a coherent ideal: namely, the ideas of group exclusiveness, cultural superiority, and collective loyalty against outside threats. The ideology of nationalism asserts the divisibility of the world into fundamentally autonomous political communities by peoples who define themselves as a nation. They claim the status of an actual or potential nation, with corresponding rights to self-determination over homeland, identity, and political voice, either as independent entities (nation-states or countries) in their own right or as subunits within society (nations) by vesting political sovereignty in a people's right to self-rule (see Pearson, 2001). In making this claim for self-determining autonomy, unity, and identity, nations are seeking to establish jurisdictional control over a defined homeland, in addition to reclaiming the sovereignty denied to them as a subject people.

   Nationalisms can be classified by who is entitled to join and belong. Two ideal-typical patterns of belonging are discernible—ethnic and civic—based largely on divergent patterns of belonging as criteria for group membership (Medrano & Koenig, 2005).

Ethnic nationalism assigns membership on largely ascriptive characteristics such as kinship ties and blood lines to include or exclude. It is aimed at building nationhood by strengthening a "people" (or nation) at the expense of others, if necessary. This focus on ascription, bloodlines, and descent restricts membership in the nationhood to those who can demonstrate common roots rather than shared attachments to key institutions and central values. A moral community is proposed in which members express an emotional commitment to each other with a passionate attachment to a homeland as the site of preexisting ethnic entitlements (Mead, 1993). Membership defined on the basis of birthright and descent privileges loyalty to the group or the homeland as paramount over any commitment to the **state** or to social classes. The territorial rights, distinctive language, and shared ethnicity of this imagined political community must be defended from hostile interlopers, both internal and external, by whatever means necessary (Pettinicchio, 2012).

By contrast, **civic nationalism** bases its appeal on loyalty to a set of political ideals, rule of law, the principle of inclusiveness, and institutions that are perceived as just and effective (Heath & Tilley, 2005; Snyder, 2000). Civic nationalism maintains that society should be composed of all individuals, regardless of race or ethnicity, as long as they subscribe to the norms of this constructed community. This nationalism is usually called civic: It envisages society as a constructed community of equal rights-bearing citizens organized around a commitment to the rule of law (although some civic nationalisms have proven more ruthless than ethnic nationalism in advancing their goals). Ethnicity is largely irrelevant in determining belonging or inclusion, as membership is open to anyone who abides by core values and constitutional principles.

To be sure, the distinction between these nationalisms is problematic. Few, if any, nationalisms qualify as purely ethnic or civic: Ethnic nationalisms have proven more civic-oriented than theory suggests; civic nationalisms, in turn, have proven more ethnically grounded than theory suggests (Kymlicka, 2001; Resnick, 2001; Vickers & de Seve, 2000). The case of Quebec is instructive in debating the definition of nation and nationalism: Does it include all Quebecers or only those of French-Canadian descent? Historically, Quebec's political aspirations (as were those of English-speaking Canada at large) were equated with ethnic nationalism because of a historical tendency to promote a predominantly white French character (Ignatieff, 1994). But Quebec's drive for autonomy within the Canadian state is now defended as a kind of civic nationalism, in that it's broad, tolerant, and inclusive of all who make the commitment to construct a modern political community without compromising its distinctiveness (Piche, 2010). The emergence of a hybrid (or "post-ethnic") nationalism around the principle of interculturalism points to a conceptual framework that is neither a defensive reaction nor a delusional embrace.

Québécois Intercultural Nationalism: Towards Hybridity?

The proliferation of ethnonational conflicts may pose a definitive challenge for the twenty-first century (Maclure, 2004; see also Gagnon, Guibernau, & Rocher, 2003). Canada is hardly exempt from these challenges: French-English relations (or, more accurately, French- and English-speaking relations) have coexisted uneasily since 1841, when Upper and Lower Canada combined into an incipient nation-state, a tinderbox aptly described by Lord Durham as the equivalent of "two nations warring in the bosom of a single state." Insofar as Confederation constituted a response to these internal rifts (LaSelva, 2004),

Quebec entered into the agreement with assurances that it would retain its status as a nation and its entitlements as a founding member of the Confederation. Quebecers continue to see themselves as a "peoples" with a shared language, culture, and homeland rather than as another province with equal rights or an ethnic group whose differences are quaint but superficial. They claim to constitute an ethnic nation-within as well, not only deserving of recognition of their differences, but also entitled to those self-governing powers equivalent to that of English Canada (Harty & Murphy, 2005; McRoberts, 2003). Predictably, then, the language of nationhood remains at the forefront of Quebec's interests because (1) it provides a standing and legitimacy within the international community, (2) it distinguishes Quebec's claims from those of ethnic minorities, (3) it imparts a sense of history and authenticity to Quebec's demands, and (4) it equalizes the bargaining power between Quebec and Ottawa (Kymlicka, 1998b). In November 2006, the House of Commons voted in favour of a motion introduced by Prime Minister Stephen Harper to recognize the Québécois as a "nation within a united Canada" (Thompson, 2006).

Quebec's emergent nationalism would appear increasingly liberal and tolerant. In shifting from a defensive, inward-looking community to a more open and cosmopolitan society (Salee & Coleman, 1997), this new nationalism is couched in secular and universalistic terms without abandoning an overriding commitment to the primacy of the French language, culture, and values (Harty & Murphy, 2005). Unlike conventional ethnic nationalisms, Quebec's more civic-oriented nationalism reflects a willingness to integrate immigrants as equals into society (Simon and Piche, 2011). Such a transition is not without its glitches: Quebec's dual status as a minority/majority society—a politically mature majority in its homeland (72 percent of Quebec is francophone), but a fragile minority within the broader North American context (Ha, 2007)—creates a social climate that breeds a suspicion of those minorities whose culture, religion, and commitments appear contrary to the Quebec consensus (EKOS, 2013). As a result, debates in Quebec vacillate between democratic impulses for inclusiveness and universal citizenship versus xenophobic anxieties over losing its distinctiveness, identity, and political relevance as an isolated ethnic outpost in North America.

Quebec is also regarded as one of the more socially liberal provinces. Social policies such as low university tuition fees and provincially subsided day care make Quebec the envy of many progressive-minded Canadians. In other words, a seemingly pejorative attitude toward religious minorities and diversity often appear at odds with its liberal principles and Canada's multicultural agenda (Conway, 2012). Points of controversy range from the controversial Herouxville code of conduct aimed at (Muslim) immigrants, to the equally controversial Bouchard-Taylor hearings on reasonable accommodation. More recently, Quebec's proposed secular charter has projected a ban on all conspicuous religious symbols for public sector employees, while fully veiled women are threatened with a denial of access to government services. Other evidence is equally damning. On the surface, it would appear that Quebecers possess more negative attitudes toward ethnocultural religious minorities than do Canadians in general (Christiano, 2013). An Angus Reid Global poll (2013, September 16) indicated that nearly two-thirds of Quebecers believe that Quebec is too accommodative of religious/cultural diversity and that laws should not be modified to accommodate diversities. Just over three-quarters take the view that reasonable accommodation poses a risk to Quebec's values, while over two-thirds of those polled in 2013 hold an unfavourable view of Islam (compared to just over half in the rest of

Canada)—up from just under half in 2009. It is interesting to note that a Privy Council Office poll of 3000 Canadians in mid-March of 2015 found that, while 82 percent of the respondents agreed with the federal government's stand to ban the full veil during the citizenship oath ceremony, the figure increased to 93 percent of respondents in Quebec (Levitz, 2015). (See Chapter 6 for additional discussion on the niqab and citizenship.) Of course, it's quite possible that Quebecers are no more biased or anti-religious than other Canadians; they simply are more open in admitting their biases. Concerns appear to be exacerbated by a belief that too much freedom of religion (which is a protected right under the Charter of Rights and Freedoms) may be used to justify practices incommensurate with core Quebec values.

Quebec continues to struggle with the politics of accommodating ethno-religious expression in the public domain, most recently with the controversy over a proposed Charter of Quebec Values (Brosseau, 2013). In late 2013, the Parti Quebecois released plans for a values charter (Bill 60) that would impose restrictions on religious clothing (from niqabs and kippas to turbans) and conspicuous religious symbols (large crucifixes) across all government institutions such as schools, hospitals and courts. Ostensibly, the Parti Quebecois argued, this ban extolled progressive intentions, namely, (a) ensuring gender equality by rejecting any accommodation for public service employees at odds with the rights of women; and (b) keeping Quebec secular and neutral (separation of church and state). The Charter was marketed as part of an ongoing struggle to liberate Quebec from the grip of religion in general, Catholicism initially, Islam more recently, amidst fears that any religious accommodation runs the risk of a slippery slope.

Reactions varied, with some such as David Rand (2014) supporting the Charter as a reasonable measure to limit religious privilege and influence. For him, ensuring the neutrality of the state and denying privileges to religions is not a threat to religious freedom, but protects everybody's freedom. Others saw it differently, arguing that the Charter was really an electoral ploy—a political wedge issue that distracted public attention from the government's mishandling of economic issues, at the same time appealing to Quebec nationalists and xenophobes to bolster waning electoral approval (Frappier, 2013). Criticism of the Charter by English-speaking Canada was subsequently framed in Quebec as an affront to the sovereignty of Quebecers, the Parti Quebecois contended—yet again "proving" the fundamental and irreconcilable differences between Quebec and the ROC. Finally, the Charter was deemed to be a discriminatory rights violation. Prohibiting many racialized and religious minorities from working in the public domain put Quebec's civil authorities and public servants in the awkward position of choosing between a career or religion (Hamilton, 2014). The defeat of the Parti Quebecois as the governing party in the spring of 2014 put the initiative on hold, although support for the Charter remains steady, according to a poll by Leger Marketing (Jedwab, 2014), despite sharp distinctions in outlooks between young and old, francophone and non-francophone, and Montreal and the rest of Quebec. Nevertheless, the underlying issues remain unresolved.

Does establishing a social code of conduct or charter of secular values constitute a reasonable restriction on the rights of migrants and minorities? Or should such draconian measures be seen for what they really are: A socially acceptable discourse for marginalizing those who do not fit into Quebec's normative framework, espoused by that sector of the population that resents public displays of difference or fears that society has gone too far in accommodating religious and cultural practices (Whyte, 2007)? Debates must be situated within the context of Québécois nationalism and Quebec's status in Canada (Cairns, 2007).

Insecurities over Quebec as a beleaguered francophone minority engulfed by a giant English-speaking sea are seen to intensify the province's discomfort with religious and cultural minorities (Ha, 2007). Yes, francophones in Quebec constitute a majority within the province, albeit with an extremely low birth rate, but the 5 million or so francophones also constitute a minority within English-speaking Canada and North America. In other words, Quebecers as a North American minority believe they cannot let their guard down if they want to preserve their language and culture against Anglo predations. The ambiguities associated with a majority/minority status generate a heightened sensitivity and defensiveness to any perceived threats to their identity and integrity as a French-speaking island in an English-speaking North American sea. Or as Bouchard and Taylor (2008) concluded as the quintessential lesson from the accommodation "crisis": "Moreover, it is quite possible French-speaking Quebec is a minority culture and needs a strong identity to allay its anxieties and behave like a serene majority."

Clearly, then, appearances may be deceiving. Quebecers, especially in urban areas, may not be any more prejudiced than other Canadians toward religious and cultural minorities. The Bouchard-Taylor Commission concluded as much, claiming there is no evidence that Quebecers are less accommodating or more racist/xenophobic than other Canadians (see also EKOS, 2013). To the extent that Quebecers appear to be more racist, the issue is blown out of proportion by opportunistic politicians both in Quebec and in the ROC. As well, the English newmedia fixation with the negative and conflicting tends to inflate the perception by conveying the impression that Quebecers are intolerant or unreasonable. Not surprisingly, says Valerie Raoul, professor of women's studies and French at the University of British Columbia, the English media sensationalize anything in Quebec that even remotely suggests a whiff of racism or xenophobia (cited in Delaney, 2008). Daniel Weinstock, professor of philosophy at the University of Montreal, points to a hidden agenda:

> When you're in a political conflict with someone else or a situation where you have to compromise, it's much easier to view the other side as being unreasonable, because that way you don't even have to think about how to accommodate them (cited in Delaney, 2008).

DEPOLITICIZING ETHNICITY: MAKING CANADA SAFE *FOR* ETHNICITY, SAFE *FROM* ETHNICITY

Ethnicity can no longer be dismissed as some primitive relic or primordial rage. Ethnicity goes beyond an obsessive craving to discover "roots" in the hopes of uncovering the past or collecting compensation. Nor should it be trivialized as a transient whimsy or a cultural backwater on the path to rational progress and democratic governance. Rather, ethnicity matters—for better or worse—in making things happen that advance collective interests and maximize social advantages (Gross, 1996). Recourse to ethnicity provides an anchor of security in a highly impersonal and mechanized society by buffering the old from the new, the individual from society, and the familiar from the strange.

Ethnicity's potential for greatness or depravity is further magnified when coupled with the conflicting demands of a new global order. The new millennium is proving to be a bewildering place (Taras & Ganguly, 2009). Gone are the global certainties of the past: The relatively simple verities of an established order have been superseded by a complex and multipolar world of moral ambivalence, shifting allegiances, and political ambiguity. With the obvious exception of the United States, no comparable political or military power has reclaimed the political vacuum created by the disintegration of the USSR, thus encouraging both intermediate powers and ethnic nationalisms to compete for vacated space. Not surprisingly, the very forces that many thought would reduce the risk of group conflicts have, paradoxically, increased inter-ethnic strife (Snyder, 2000). The politics of ethnicity are here to stay, whether we like it or not. And as the global competition for scarce resources intensifies, more ethnic conflicts are inevitable.

Canada is not unaffected by these political and cultural upheavals. Just as international relations are animated by a clash of competing and often incommensurable world views, so too does Canada's ethnicity agenda reflect both conflict and confusion (Kymlicka, 2001). Rules that formerly defined right from wrong are openly challenged or dismissed as irrelevant. What once were defined as virtues are now vices, and vice versa. Aboriginal peoples are no longer willing to abide by colonial paradigms (Alfred, 2005); the Québécois are looking for a foundationally different kind of partnership with the rest of Canada (Gibbins & Laforest, 1998); and multicultural minorities want to re-contour Canada along inclusive lines (Fleras, 2014a). The politics of ethnicity are proving double-edged: Canada may be enriched by weaving national unity from the strands of diversity. Alternatively, ethnic forces may ignite a chain reaction that could derail Canada's society-building aspirations. This paradox—how to make Canada safe from ethnicity, yet safe for ethnicity—raises the question of Canada's resolve in the face of potentially divisive forces.

An official Multiculturalism represents Canada's answer to the politics of ethnicity. Multiculturalism as ethnic governance pivots on the premise that a Canada of many different cultures and diverse peoples is possible, provided that ethnic differences don't get in the way of living together with differences. With Multiculturalism, this seemingly implausible balancing act is possible, in part by transcending the specifics of cultures to ensure that no one is excluded from full and equal participation in society for reasons beyond their control (namely, their ethnicity); in part by acknowledging the legitimacy of ethnic differences as long as they stay within limits; and in part by taking these differences into account when necessary to ensure full participation and equal citizenship rights.

But there is a catch in endorsing ethnocultural diversity as grounds for living differently together. Canada's official Multiculturalism is not concerned with promoting ethnic diversity or ethnic communities. Few societies could survive the strain of multiple competing groups, with clearly demarcated political boundaries, separate power bases, and parallel institutions. Even fewer are equipped to address the society-busting demands of ethnic nationalism. This aversion to a politicized ethnicity is evident in Canada, where the politics of ethnicity threaten to dismember or dissolve. Ethnicity under Canada's multicultural commitments is justified when stripped of its potency to divide or incite. In rejecting those politicized ethnicities that compete for scarce resources, Multiculturalism as policy endorses the symbols of differences at personal or private levels. Or differently put, an official Multiculturalism accommodates the appearance of ethnicity and endorses "pretend pluralism" rather than taking its substance seriously.

In other words, an official Multiculturalism as ethnicity governance is not about promoting ethnic cultures as distinct and coherent lifestyles (Modood, 2007). More accurately, a multicultural commitment to creating an inclusive Canada by integrating migrants and minorities into the existing status quo promotes a depoliticizing ("neutering") of ethnicity by removing its potency to challenge or change. Under an official Multiculturalism, ethnicity is rendered tolerable to the extent that (1) people identify only with the symbols of their difference; (2) this identification is restricted to the personal and private rather than the public realm; (3) this affiliation does not violate the laws of the land, interfere with the rights of others, or contravene core Canadian values and constitutional principles, and (4) ethnicity is deployed to bolster people's sense of belonging to Canada rather than for erecting inward-looking communities. Put bluntly, then, Canada's official Multiculturalism does not exist to "celebrate" ethnicity. More to the point, official Multiculturalism is concerned with neutering ethnicity as a framework for living together with what's left of our differences. Or to put it more finely, under Multiculturalism, all Canadians can belong to, and identify with, Canada through their ethnicity.

Herein, then, lies the appeal of hybridic, transnational, and situational/symbolic ethnic identities within a multicultural society. In contrast to insurgent or lived ethnicities, they (a) do not directly challenge the status quo, (b) are more concerned with the symbols of attachment, and (c) are more diffuse because of their potential to combine identities. Endorsing ethnic identity at these levels comes across as relatively innocuous, since the recognition of multiple and complementary identities does not fundamentally alter the political landscape and economic status quo. Depoliticizing the potential of ethnicity as a destabilizing force under an official Multiculturalism puts Canada firmly ahead of the governance curve in *making society safe for ethnicity, as well as safe from ethnicity*. Time will tell whether Canada's multicultural response for engaging ethnicity will be sufficient for those politicized ethnicities who want to reverse the governance formula by *making ethnicity safe from Canada, yet safe for Canada*.

DEBATE REVISITED

Ethnic Conflicts or Conflicts That Are Ethnicized?

The debate at the beginning of this chapter posed some tricky questions. Are ethnic conflicts really about ethnicities at loggerheads with each other? Or is it more accurate to say that certain conflicts are "ethnicized"; that is, ethnicity inserted into the equation to justify or advance a variety of political or economic purposes? If ethnicity is a factor, which theories of ethnic expression are most apt: primordialism, constructivism, or instrumentalism?

Which of the following responses appears most credible in light of this chapter's content?

- The conflict that erupts between mutually antagonistic groups may

be motivated by historically deep-seated hatreds (Crawford, 2006). Tribal- or clan-based impulses that once were dormant or suppressed may be activated when the grip of central control is relaxed. Once unleashed and whipped into a frenzy by manipulative leaders, these primordial forces are difficult to stop, especially in clan- or tribal-based societies (since people trust only their own kind), while collective interests are defined in opposition to other group interests. In other words, the tribe (or clan) is everything— mutual aid, protection, source of trust—while dangers await life outside the tribe (Clarfield, 2007; Kay, 2007).

- Ethnicity is one of many variables driving the dynamics of intergroup competition for scarce resources (Shaykhutdinov & Bragg, 2011). Consider Africa, where states and boundaries between states were created for political, military, economic, and diplomatic reasons, with little regard for ethnic differences and tribal borders. With decolonization, these artificially constructed and politically expedient nation-states proved brittle and prone to fracture from within by tribal groups who sought a degree of autonomy or advantage at the expense of others (but see Bass, 2006). The risk of ethnic conflict is amplified when governments collapse and there is no state capable of guaranteeing personal security. Patterns of intergroup inequality (including poverty, corruption, and tribalism [Perry & Blue, 2008]) can also generate ethnic conflict, especially in those contexts where globalization unsettles an established **social contract** that once normalized access to scarce resources or power relations along ethnic lines. Disruptions to these social contracts produce new ethnic patterns of discrimination and exclusion; in turn, resentment over the new arrangements provides fertile ground for opportunistic leaders to mobilize public support around ethnic identities for advancing vested interests (Crawford, 2006).

- Ethnicity may not be a direct factor in the conflict; nevertheless, it may be invoked to impart a sheen of legitimacy by concealing political motives and economic interests. Most ethnic conflicts are not about ethnicity per se. Contexts involving sharp inequalities in power and wealth often foster coalitions along ethnic lines in the competition for scarce resources, with the result that ethnicity serves as an identity marker in sorting out winners from losers (Caselli & Coleman, 2006/2010). Conflicts in this competitive context often become "ethnicized" via political elites, who apply an ethnicity spin as a propaganda tool for self-serving reasons (Collier, 2007; Marger, 1997). Power-hungry elites will readily exploit ethnic tension during times of political uncertainty and social upheaval, such as the wave of democratization and institutional change that swept through Asia and Africa during the 1990s (Carment, 2007). In short, ethnic conflicts do not just erupt; they are constructed (Bass, 2006).

- Perhaps references to the ethnic in ethnic conflict are largely "fictional." Without first-hand accounts, people's knowledge about ethnic conflict is conveyed by mainstream media, who perhaps unwittingly impose an ethnic-conflict spin in defining situations that may have little to do with ethnicity or conflict. Complex issues are framed into simple—even simplistic—binary formats that intensify North American stereotypes of tribal life as nasty, brutish, and short (Taras & Ganguly, 2002). The tendency to frame conflicts in ethnic terms—to "ethnicize" conflict by casting it as a conflict between ethnic

(Continued)

groups—is not without consequences. Labelling these disputes as ethnic may legitimize and amplify the claims of ethnic militants by playing into the hands of those who have ethnicized the conflict in the first place. In other words, a heightened sense of ethnicity may not cause conflict, but is a likely consequence of conflict (Taras & Ganguly, 2009).

Let's put all this into perspective: The phrase "ethnic conflict" is generally deployed in a descriptive and explanatory sense (Collier, 2007). As a description, it is unexceptional; as an explanation, it leaves much to be desired. Caution must be exercised in assuming that ethnic conflicts consist of "tribal" groups with uncontrollable instincts and insatiable urges to slaughter the demonized "other." Although spontaneous or irrational outbursts cannot be dismissed as immediate causes, ethnic conflicts often involve a calculated opportunism in the competition over identity, autonomy, or resources. Moreover, references to ethnic conflict may be misleading in yet another way: Hatred and conflict against ethnic others reflect the manipulations of a small cadre of calculating militants (rather than the actions of entire ethnic community) who claim to act on the group's behalf (Crawford, 2006).

The debunking of myths about ethnic(ized) conflict cannot come too soon if there is any hope of solving problems that many perceive as quintessential challenges to our existence. Ethnic conflicts are real enough; nevertheless, most conflicts involving an ethnic dimension speak to broader issues pertaining to power and inequality. The question, then, is how and why do conflicts become *ethnicized*, especially in contexts involving competing yet legitimate claims to the same territory or valued resources? In that conflict appears to be an inescapable feature of the human species, particularly in those societies marked by shifting patterns of power and privilege, the challenge is before us. The solution is not in eliminating the "ethnicity" in ethnic conflict. The key to success is in channeling the "conflict" part into more constructive avenues (Marger, 1997).

Chapter Highlights

- Ethnicity matters because it increases the probability of something to happen. Ethnicity represents a key variable in shaping people's identities, experiences, and outcomes. It also provides a framework that helps explain patterns of behaviour at individual and group levels.
- Ethnicity can be defined as a shared awareness of ancestral differences as a basis for community, identity, and activity. Both subjective experiences and objective properties are integral for mobilizing individuals into action groups.
- The *why* behind ethnicity can be explained by reference to primordial, constructivist, and instrumentalist approaches, while the *how* behind ethnicity is expressed in three ways: communities, identities, and activities.

- The politics of ethnicity in Quebec tend to focus on establishing an intercultural ("hybrid") nationalism that respects diversities without sacrificing the primacy of French language and values.
- In looking to make Canada safe *from* ethnicity and yet safe *for* ethnicity, official Multiculturalism provides a framework for depoliticizing ethnicity as a basis for living together with ethnic differences.

Review Questions

1. Three major approaches—primordial, instrumentalist, and constructivist—have historically been used to explain the power and popularity of ethnicity. Compare how each frames the nature and extent of the ethnic experience.

2. Compare ethnic nationalism and civic nationalism as ideal types with respect to their underlying logic in creating a new society. Which nationalism best describes Quebec's commitment to preserve and protect the ethnic nation?

3. How is ethnicity expressed? Focus on the notions of community, identity, and activity.

4. Indicate the role played by an official Multiculturalism for managing ethnicity in Canada's continuing efforts to make the country safe *for* ethnicity as well as safe *from* ethnicity.

5. Ethnicity is seen by sociologists as a key variable that accounts for patterns of human behaviour. Explain, with reference to the concept of ethnic conflict, to demonstrate how ethnicity matters.

CHAPTER 5

Racialized Inequality

LEARNING OBJECTIVES

After reading this chapter you will be able to:

1. Explain how Canada remains stratified by race and immigration status despite its *bona fides* as a post-racial and pro-multicultural society.

2. Define what is meant by racialized inequality with respect to exclusion and stratification.

3. Appreciate the magnitude of racialized inequality with regards to income, employment, and poverty levels.

4. Compare and contrast how two sociological-based models may account for racialized inequality.

5. Describe how Canada's employment equity program may be interpreted as a solution (reversing discrimination) or a problem (reverse discrimination).

DEBATE

Employment Equity: Reverse Discrimination or Reversing Discrimination?

Canada is widely acclaimed as an egalitarian society whose commitment to inclusiveness is globally admired and occasionally emulated (Fleras, 2016; Grabb & Guppy, 2010; McMullin, 2010). Canada's global status as the world's 6th most socially progressive society (and highest ranked G-7 country) attests to its lofty stature as a "go-to" country (Social Progress Imperative, 2015). Yet Canada has proven a paradox in engaging diversity along more inclusive and equitable lines. Yes, most major institutions now have policies and programs in place to foster a more accommodative environment. Both the federal public service and federally regulated institutions from banks to Crown corporations and telecommunications firms have incorporated inclusiveness principles for doing business in the twenty-first century. Even the private sector is banking on inclusivity as a platform for attracting new talent and tapping into new markets.

But there is a less flattering narrative, as well (Jedwab & Satzewich, 2015). However well-intentioned this push for inclusiveness, the results of Canada's commitments are modest at best, with many migrants and minorities continuing to experience discrimination in terms of access, representation, and equity (Galabuzi, 2006; Toronto Board of Trade, 2010). Both Aboriginal peoples and racialized ("visible") minorities (including new Canadians) as a group tend to earn less, are underrepresented in higher management, default into dirty, dull, and dangerous jobs ("precarious employment"), and confront an undervaluation of their skills, contributions, and credentials. To overcome this potentially embarrassing situation within the federal public service, the federal government's "Embracing Change" program of 2002 stipulated a 20 percent target in the hiring, training, and promotion of racialized minorities. But modest improvements in the proportion of racialized minorities under this program neither matches rapid demographic changes nor addresses shifts in Canada's labour market composition (Said, 2013; Xu, 2009).

The principles and practices of employment equity represent an official policy response to this iniquitous state of affairs. In place since 1986 for the federally regulated private sector and updated in 1996 to include the federal public service, the *Employment Equity Act* was designed to achieve equality in the workplace by increasing the representation of members from the following designated groups: Aboriginal peoples, racialized (or "visible") minorities, persons with disabilities, and women (Statistical Analysis Unit, 2010). Terms of the Act apply to all federally regulated, private-sector employers with 100 or more employees (e.g., banking), federal public services (e.g., Health Canada), public-sector companies (e.g., the RCMP), Crown corporations, and federal contractors

with at least 100 employees who bid on government goods or services contracts worth $200 000 or more. These companies are obligated to file and submit annual reports on the composition of their workforce to ensure appropriate levels of workplace representation, with particular reference to overall numbers and the type of work performed by members from the four targeted groups. To put these objectives into practice, the Act instructs all employers to address four core obligations: (1) survey the workforce in terms of hires, occupation, salaries, promotion, and retention; (2) analyze the under-representation of targeted minorities in each occupational group; (3) identify and remove employment barriers; and (4) introduce positive policies and programs (hiring, training, promotion, retention) to improve representation through reasonable accommodation. In contrast to America's Affirmative Action program, Canada's *Employment Equity Act* rejects the idea of government-mandated quotas and deadlines, including the idea of a rigid and externally imposed system of fixed percentages to be achieved within a certain timeframe. Under Affirmative Action, American companies felt compelled to hire even unqualified personnel, if only to comply with the letter of the law, to circumvent penalties for non-compliance, or to secure government contracts at all costs. By contrast, goals under Canada's employment equity program are much more flexible as planning and evaluation tools, involving "reasonable expectations" about hiring and promotion of individuals from qualified groups when available for employment. In short, goals are preferred over quotas,

(Continued)

timetables over deadlines, and reasonableness over ultimatums.

With its commitment to improve minority access and representation at all levels, employment equity should be a proven winner in the accommodation sweepstakes. Yet few issues have elicited as much admiration or hostility. For some, this exercise in preferential hiring is nothing less than "reverse" discrimination against white males, thus creating more problems than it solves; for others, it is seen as a bold venture in **"reversing" discrimination**; for still others, it can take on different meanings—"reverse" or "reversing"—depending, of course, on the frame of reference. To what extent do the promises and provisions of employment equity help to right historical wrongs by "reversing" discrimination? Are employment equity interventions the most effective way of achieving a proportional number of racialized minorities at all institutional levels? Or, is this "Pandora's box" of pitfalls really an exercise in political correctness that—despite good intentions—violates core cultural values and compromises human rights (reverse discrimination)? The Debate Revisited Box at the end of the chapter will assess the debate over employment equity as a case of reverse versus reversing discrimination.

INTRODUCTION: CANADA'S "RACIALIZED MOSAIC"

Canada cherishes its image as an egalitarian society. Canadians like to see themselves as citizens of a proudly post-racial and pro-multicultural society that disdains the evils of prejudice, discrimination, and racism (Fleras, 2014a). There is some truth to this collective self-perception. Admittedly, Canada has yet to come to grips with its racist history and exclusionary past; nevertheless, it has evolved into an open and tolerant society with a powerful commitment to equality and inclusion, regardless of a person's background or beliefs. Blatant forms of discrimination are no longer tolerated or condoned. Racialized minorities rarely endure the kind of flagrant inequalities that once prevailed in the not-too-distant past (Walker, 1997). In turn, new Canadians are making their mark in transforming Canada along more cosmopolitan lines (Bricker & Ibbitson, 2013). A commitment to the principles of multiculturalism not only secures a basis for living together with differences in dignity and equitably; it also endorses diversity as a strength rather than a liability in fostering creativity and improving this country's competitive edge in a global economy. Even Aboriginal peoples—long the targets of misunderstanding and hostility in Canada—are making significant political and economic strides in overcoming the structures and strictures of colonialism, while securing the rights to indigenous models of self-determining autonomy over land, identity, and political voice (Coates & Crowley, 2013; Fleras & Maaka, 2009; Maaka & Fleras, 2005).

This bucolic portrayal is arguably true in a relative sense, as well. But appearances are deceiving because of polite fictions that routinely gloss over inconvenient truths. Ideally, all the diversity tiles in Canada's multicultural "mosaic" are envisaged as contributing equally to the whole. Each component is also viewed as deserving in a fair share of the entitlements and rewards. But Canada may also be portrayed as an unequal and stratified society—a racialized and "sticky" mosaic—with wealth, power, and privilege concentrated in the hands of the few (Kunz, Milan, & Schetagne, 2001; Pendakur & Pendakur, 2011; Teelucksingh & Galabuzi, 2005). Income and opportunity gaps that privilege some while disempowering others have culminated in a pattern of racialized stratification that says a lot about the power of national self-deception. Racialized minorities continue to be stratified unequally against a vertical mosaic of raised (dominant) and lowered (subordinate) tiles (Porter, 1965; Public Service Alliance of Canada, 2010; Tepper, 1988). Pyramids of privilege exist that elevate the "pale-male stream" to the top of the heap and lower racialized others to the bottom—often through no fault of their own. Neither Canada's official Multiculturalism nor its employment equity program for racialized minorities have appreciably altered this arrangement (Senate Standing Committee on Human Rights, 2013), with some measures having had the somewhat perverse effect of perpetuating yet more inequality. A paradox is at play: As Canada becomes more diverse, mainstream institutions are under increased pressure to standardize by adopting universal (that is, colour- and culture-blind) standards that transcend the claims of any specific group except, of course, that of the dominant group (Sowell, 2004).

In other words, all the deeply ingrained myths in the country cannot disguise the obvious: Canada remains a racially stratified society where differences because of race and ethnicity continue to make a difference in who gets what and how much (Block & Galabuzi, 2011; Kazemipur, 2014; Nakhaie, 2007; Pendakur, 2005). Racism is a deeply embedded and defining characteristic of Canadian history despite a whitewashing that ignores the injustices and degradations of the past (Backhouse, 1999; Daschuk, 2013). Moreover, while attitudes toward racialized migrants and minorities have changed, socioeconomic outcomes haven't, and the gaps may be increasing. Such an observation raises a number of questions for discussion and debate: How do we account for these disparities in a Canada that abides by the principle of inclusiveness and multiculturalism? What causes **racialized inequality**? Is it caused by racism and racial discrimination; personal failure on the part of migrants and minorities to take advantage of opportunities; a lack of human capital (from education to work experience to language competence); or the play of market forces that restrict economic opportunities (Reitz & Banerjee, 2007)? Is the problem attributable to minority cultures and values that discourage initiative and success? Or should the finger be pointed at mainstream structures, from systemic biases to economic restructuring, that compromise minority and migrant prospects (Heath & Cheung, 2007; Yu & Heath, 2007)? What constitutes a just and equitable society—is it one that treats everyone the same regardless of differences? Or is it one that takes differences into account to ensure equality? Equal treatment, or treatment as equals? Answers to these questions remain at the forefront of vigorous debate, with varied and contradictory responses reflecting different visions of race, ethnic, and aboriginal relations as fundamentally unequal relations.

This chapter is predicated on the assumption that racialized inequalities are neither natural and inevitable nor healthy and productive. On the contrary, they are highly toxic and counterproductive because of their corrosive effect in fraying the social fabric of society (Wilkinson & Pickett, 2009). The devaluations and put-downs associated with low social status, dominance hierarchies, racialized realities, and dysfunctional communities can prove dangerously stressful for people's health and life chances (Nestel, 2012). This chapter draws on these themes by looking at the patterns and politics of racialized inequality in Canada. The chapter explores the inequitable relationship of racialized minorities to the distribution of valued resources, in the process demonstrating how inequality in Canada is not randomly distributed but shown to be stratified along racialized lines ("racialized stratification") and embedded within a broader institutional framework. These racialized disparities are not simply the result of antediluvian mindsets amenable to attitude modification; on the contrary, they are entrenched within the founding assumptions and foundational principles of Canadian society, from its unwritten constitutional order to its core values and institutional frameworks (Fleras, 2014a). Such a macro-perspective puts the onus on analyzing how racialized inequities are created, expressed, and sustained, as well as challenged and transformed by way of government initiative, institutional reform, ideological shifts, and minority assertiveness. Issues up for discussion include (1) a conceptualizing of racialized inequality from a sociological perspective, (2) the expression of racialized inequality at the level of income, employment, and poverty, (3) explanatory frameworks that account for the origins and persistence of racialized inequality, and (4) competing models for reducing those inequities that engulf racialized minorities.

DEFINING RACIALIZED INEQUALITY: EXCLUSIONS & STRATIFICATION

Canada's role in advancing multiculturalism and human rights deserves commendation. No less commendable is its commitment to positively managing diversity in an inclusive Canada in which no one is excluded or denied because of race, ethnicity, or national origins. But national studies reinforce what many "intuitively" know: Not all Canadians are created equal when it comes to distributing the power, privilege, and property, with the result that Canada is characterized by layers of racialized inequality (Galabuzi, 2006). Race has long proven a key variable in predicting success or shaping unequal outcomes. First, racialized groups may be singled out as inferior or irrelevant, and dismissed accordingly. Second, racialized groups are criticized for embracing social patterns and cultural values that may prove disadvantaging in the competition for scarce resources (see Porter, 1965). Finally, a racialized inequality acknowledges how inequities go beyond individual prejudice. They instead are embedded within the foundational principles and structures of society, most notably at the institutional levels of hidden agendas and systemic biases. In brief, Canada is not always the egalitarian utopia often promulgated by polite fictions. It is also a society of racialized inequalities and race-based exclusions that reinforce patterns of stratification at odds with Canada's ideals (Clement & Helmes-Hayes, 2015).

What is meant by "inequality"? What is the relation of inequality to stratification? A careful analysis is required; after all, the major theme of this book is animated by the notion of race, ethnic, and aboriginal relations as *unequal* relations, with a corresponding commitment to deconstruct their origins, expression, and maintenance, in addition to examining those interventions that challenge and change. Inequality itself can be framed in two ways: First, as people's differential access to the good things (power, privilege, property) in life ("equality of opportunities"); second, as differential distribution of these valued resources among members of society ("equality of outcomes or conditions"). Defining inequality as both differential access ("who gets what") and differential distribution ("what goes where") reinforces a perception of inequality as differential access to valued recourses resulting in differential distribution of power, privilege, and property (Fleras, 2016). Or as Olsen (2011:13) writes:

> Inequality refers to the unequal access people have to a wide range of material and non-material resources, supports, provisions, and opportunities that are widely held as valued and desirable in society and are consequential to our lives. It also refers to the asymmetrical distributions that this unequal access fosters and perpetuates across many sites (such as the family...) and spheres (economic. . .)

Put succinctly, inequality is about the politics of entitlements in regards to "who gets what," how, and why; that is, differential access to or differences in people's share of valued resources. This preferential access to the good things in life is stratified around those human differences defined as socially significant and aligned accordingly for purposes of reward and recognition (Grabb & Guppy, 2009). Reference to inequality also embraces the politics of distribution with respect to "what goes where," when, and how; that is, differential distribution or differences in the allocation of valued resources related to power, privilege, and wealth/income. These inequities of access or distribution are of particular interest to sociologists when they are (1) pervasive and persistent, (2) patterned or clustered around certain groups, (3) harmful or exploitative, and (4) resistant to reform (Fleras, 2005). Lastly, sociological perspectives on inequality are known to vary. For some, inequality is a regrettable but necessary component of a modern complex system; for others, inequality is inevitable yet odious in regimes that pivot around profit and private ("productive") property. Many see inequality as the culmination of individual shortcomings; others blame inequality on structural barriers embedded in society. But most sociological takes on inequality acknowledge the centrality of exclusions in these debates.

Inequalities as Exclusion

Many definitions of inequality lean toward a narrow economist perspective, with its focus on income or wealth that are relatively easy to measure or quantify. For sociologists, inequality is more attuned to the social dimensions pertaining to group membership (such as membership in particular identity-based social groups) and social exclusions from both material resources and non-material resourcefulness that preclude integration, involvement, and contribution (Bastia, 2013; Fleras. 2016). Social inequality is reframed through the prism of exclusion—an umbrella term for a variety of social disadvantages related to powerlessness, discrimination, political participation, institutional involvement, health outcomes, and quality of life factors, as well as vulnerability to violence, deprivation, and violation of peoples' rights (Green & Kesselman, 2006; Levitas et al., 2007; Saloojee, 2003; Wilkinson & Pickett, 2009). The concept of social exclusion consists of those unequal conditions that preclude opportunity and access to social citizenship (notions of belonging, engagement, and identity); services and resources as well as rights and capabilities (the lack of which culminate in material deprivation and social alienation); active participation in social, cultural, political, and economic activities; and opportunities to make meaningful contributions as valued and respected members of a community of shared experiences, mutual understandings, and reciprocal respect (Labonte, Hadi, & Kauffmann, 2011; Saloojee, 2003; Teelucksingh & Galabuzi, 2010). It refers to those members of society who (a) suffer real deprivation due to lack of food, shelter, and clothing; (b) are precluded from full and equal participation owing to a lack of social capital; (c) trend toward power-lessness and marginalization; (d) are underappreciated and undervalued; and (e) are prone to anti-social behavior because of early childhood deprivations and restricted opportunities (Crouch, 2011; Sarlo, 2013). The concept of social exclusion also empha-sizes those denials and discriminations that preempt peoples' full potential to function as human beings ("self-actualization"), with its attendant notion of belonging, participa-tion, recognition, representation, respect, and valued contribution ("social capital") (Fraser, 2008; Richmond & Saloojee, 2005; Saloojee, 2003; Therborn, 2013; Winlow & Hall, 2013).

Stratification

Just as inequality and exclusion are closely associated, so too is the concept of inequality inextricably linked to stratification, with its concomitant notion of layers and strata (Fleras, 2016). It is widely conceded that a society of perfect equality is a contradiction in terms. No human society is "equal" in the sense that everyone is ranked equally in possessing the same access to valued resources (Tepperman, 2012). All human societies are unequal and stratified to some extent. Some individuals are higher ranked than others because they have more of what is valued related to (a) material or ideological resource distribution, (b) biological traits that are imbued with cultural meanings, and (c) membership in groups based on shared characteristics. Both simple and complex societies are ranked/stratified along the lines of age or gender, yet only agricultural-industrial societies possess the tech-nology and organization to support extremes of stratified inequality. Groups of individuals in stratified societies are classified into different layers of status ("status hierarchy") according to shared commonalities in occupation, income, wealth, class, and race or eth-nicity, then ranked ("stratified") *vis-à-vis* one another. Class and caste systems provide two popular and ideal-typical expressions of stratification. A person rank (or status) in a caste systems is ascribed (assigned at birth), whereas people's status in class systems is generally acquired through achievement in what is commonly called a meritocracy (a system of stratification based on the principle of merit that rewards individuals on the basis of what they deserve (Crompton, 2008; McNamee, 2014). These systems of stratification are persistent, patterned, and resistant to change; they are also supported by a legitimating ideology that rationalizes away the differential distribution of persons or goods (Breen & Rottman, 1995).

Reference to stratification refers to a division of society into unequal layers known as "strata." Or, to expand on this notion: stratification can be defined as a hierarchical ranking of groups of individuals in ascending and descending order, based on (1) different family background with respect to power, privilege, and property, including income and assets or (2) different relationship to the means of production (class location as worker, manager, or owner (also Olsen, 2011). Stratification as a ranking process can be differentiated along two separate yet mutually overlapping lines (Ferguson, 2012). For Marxists, patterns of stratification reflect an economic dimension involving a layering of class relationships (from workers to owners with fractions in between). For Weberians (followers of the German sociologist, Max Weber), peoples' position in a system of stratification (or status hierarchy) reflect their "market situation" (from family background to education to life chances) rather than a specific relationship to productive property (Breen & Rottman,

1995). According to Weberians, systems of stratification are multidimensional and over-lapping rather than based on a single factor (as posited by Marx) reflecting a combination of class, status ("prestige" and "privilege"), and party ("power"). Patterns of stratification can also be expressed in terms of identity markers such as (a) social class, with its basis in mate-rial wealth, (b) race (inequality due to visibility), (c) ethnicity (inequality from culture and symbols), (d) gender (inequality based on perceived sex differences), and (e) aboriginality (inequality reflecting the logic and legacy of colonialism). The interplay of these hierarchi-cally ranked strata overlaps and intersects to create or intensify existing patterns of power, privilege, and property (Ferguson, 2012).

In short, society is said to be stratified when socially defined categories of individuals (based on class, race, gender, or aboriginality) differ from other groups owing to the amount of valued resources they possess. These de/valued groups are then ranked higher or lower along a hierarchy of ascending and descending order of importance, superiority or rewards. This stratified access to scarce resources is not randomly distributed, as far as sociologists are concerned. Differential access to valued goods tends to cluster around the achieved and ascribed status of historically disadvantaged groups, such as racialized minorities, new-comers to Canada, and Aboriginal peoples. In acknowledging that society is stratified along racialized lines, the term **racialized stratification** is instructive in two ways: First, it refers to hierarchical systems in which scarce resources are unequally distributed among migrants and minorities of colour, who are disproportionately under-represented in terms of the "good things in life"; and second, it refers to highly segmented systems involving minority groups in occupational statuses that reflect a racial(ized) division of labour (See & Wilson, 1988). To be sure, patterns of racialized stratification are not of a transitory nature; that is, they go beyond the "costs" of initial adjustment. These differences are patterned and pervasive insofar as they are socially significant, deeply embedded, and have proven difficult to dislodge. The next section demonstrates the validity of this statement by looking at racialized inequality along income, employment, and poverty lines.

RACIALIZED INEQUALITIES IN CANADA

Canada takes pride in its reputation as a colour-blind society in which no one is purport-edly denied or excluded because of race or ethnicity. As a society that endorses a merit-based system of rewards, Canada likes to consider itself relatively open and tolerant, with equal opportunity for all regardless of who they are or where they came from. Canada's commitment to the principle of inclusiveness is no less commendable, even if the realities of accommodation do not always align with the rhetoric. But repeated references to Canada as multicultural, inclusive, and egalitarian have not translated into equal outcomes for migrants and minorities when measured by indicators such as income, unemployment, or poverty rates (Block & Galabuzi, 2011; Nakhaie & Kazemipur, 2013). Canada remains highly stratified along racial(ized) lines, with race continuing to matter not because it's objectively real or naturally occurring, but because people act "as if" it were real, with corresponding effect in predicting success or failure. Moreover, despite claims to the contrary, the gap between the haves and have-nots is widening, becoming increasingly racialized and gendered, and seemingly impervious to reform because of its embeddedness in society (Block, 2010; Pendakur & Pendakur, 2010; Teelucksingh & Galabuzi, 2005).

Income Differences

Inequality remains a fact of life in Canadian society when assessed by income differences (Block 2013; Green, Riddell & St. Hilaire, 2015; Hou & Picot 2014; Jedwab 2012; Pendakur & Pendakur, 2011). Income measures have historically been used to gauge inequality between groups—that is, to determine if there is labour market discrimination—by comparing the annual earnings of racialized minorities with those of white Canadians. Admittedly, income as a measure of inequality may conceal as much as it reveals (Hum & Simpson, 2000; Jedwab & Satzewich, 2015). Averages don't tell the story of the range of disparity between the richest and the poorest, with the result being that internal variations within the category of racialized minorities are concealed (Pendakur, 2005). Nor do they take into account differences in the cost of living between large and small cities or between remote and metropolitan regions. Important variables that account for the disparities may be excluded as well, including gender, place of birth, length of stay in Canada, levels of work experience, educational levels, number of hours worked, language competence, and sample size (see Statistics Canada, 2007). Inequities pertaining to power and privilege are ignored as are those pertaining to ownership of wealth or assets in breaking the cycle of poverty (Shapiro, 2004). Still, in the absence of more measurable indicators, income differences remain the index of choice for measuring inequality.

Consider the results of a recent Statistics Canada study, presented in Table 5-1, that looks at average employment income, visibility of Canadians (racialized versus all Canadians), and gender and age. Generalized patterns can be detected (Statistics Canada, 2003). Racialized women do more poorly than women in general and racialized men; racialized young men do less well than men at all other age levels; and older males and females, except for those in the retirement bracket, generally outperform younger men and women. A 2007 essay by Jeffrey Reitz and Rupa Banerjee reported that the wage gap between whites and racialized minorities was $9581 (whites were $1895 above the local average, whereas racialized minorities were $7686 below the local average). Other studies confirm that race matters: Canadian-born blacks face a statistically significant wage gap, once other variables such as education are controlled (Hum & Simpson, 2000; Jedwab, 2004), earning about 69 percent of what whites earn (blacks in the United States earn about approximately 70 percent of white wages).

TABLE 5-1	Income, Visibility, Gender, and Age, 2000			
	Racialized minorities		**All Canadians**	
Age*	**Men**	**Women**	**Men**	**Women**
15–24	$22 394	$20 707	$23 696	$19 634
25–44	$41 638	$32 462	$47 611	$35 048
45–64	$46 626	$33 664	$55 754	$37 407
65 and over	$41 568	$23 663	$44 661	$28 171
All	$42 377	$32 143	$49 224	$34 892

*Includes only those in full-time, full-year employment

Source: Statistics Canada (2003).

Yet there are dangers in making such simple income comparisons. Such studies are incomplete—perhaps even misleading—because they lump all racialized minorities into a single category without distinguishing those born in Canada from those who are foreign-born (Hum & Simpson, 2000). An important study by Jean Lock Kunz and associates (2001) for the Canadian Race Relations Foundation focused on the earning disparities between whites (or non-racialized groups) and visible minorities (racialized groups) with regard to average annual income, gender, and immigrant status (foreign-born), as set out in Table 5-2. The table clearly demonstrates how labour market disadvantages exist for racialized immigrants (Hum & Simpson, 2000; see also Alboim & McIsaac, 2007). Canadian-born men, both racialized and non-racialized (i.e., whites), outperform foreign-born racialized males but not foreign-born whites. Men across all categories do better than women, regardless of visibility and place of birth, whereas Aboriginal peoples rank at the bottom for both genders, although recent evidence suggests that aboriginal women have made significant strides in the labour market in recent years (DePratto, 2015). Paradoxically, higher education levels may not improve income levels. Racialized immigrants have generally higher levels of education than the general population (there is also a larger percentage whose highest attainment is a primary level of education), yet they tend to trail behind Canadian-born whites and minorities with regard to employment, income, and access to professional/managerial jobs (Kunz et al., 2001; Picot & Coulombe, 2007).

Among immigrants, there is an unexplained wage gap (Statistics Canada, 2007; Walters, Phythian, & Anisef, 2006). Immigrants appear to be losing ground in the income-earning sweepstakes in both initial income and income earnings over time. But a failure to distinguish between recent immigrants (those here less than five years) and more established immigrants underscores the limitations of any study (Gee, Kobayashi, & Prus, 2007). In 1980, according to Statistics Canada data, male and female immigrants who had lived in Canada for 10 years earned about the same as Canadian-born workers. In 2000, immigrants who were in Canada for 10 years were making much less than Canadian-born workers. A male immigrant's earnings as a percentage of earnings of a Canadian-born male had dropped to 79.8 percent, while a female immigrant's earnings had fallen to 87.3 percent. Recent data seem to support these figures, especially if distinguishing recent immigrants from more established immigrants. According to the 2006 Census data issued by Statistics Canada (2008), in 1980, recent

TABLE 5-2	**Earnings* by Gender, Racialization, and Place of Birth**		
	Male	**Female**	**Average**
Racialized minority (CB)	$42 433	$33 519	$38 582
Racialized minority (FB)	$35 329	$27 075	$31 829
Whites (CB)	$43 456	$31 150	$38 529
Whites (FB)	$46 457	$31 627	$40 854
Aboriginal peoples	$32 369	$26 361	$29 290

*Full-time, full-year earnings for those aged 25 to 64.

CB = Canadian-born

FB = Foreign-born

Sources: Adapted from Kunz et al., (2001); 1996 Census, Public Use Microdata File.

TABLE 5-3	**Earnings by Place of Birth, Education**	
	1980	**2005**
Recent immigrant males with university degrees	$48 581	$30 332
Canadian-born males with university degrees	$63 040	$62 556
Recent immigrant females with university degrees	$24 317	$18 969
Canadian-born females with university degrees	$41 241	$44 545

Source: Statistics Canada. (2008). Median Earnings, using 2005 constant dollars for full-time wage earners (self-employed individuals excluded).

immigrant males with some employment income had earned 85 percent of what their Canadian-born counterparts earned; by 2005, that figure had dropped to 63 percent. For recent immigrant women, the figures are even more pronounced, plummeting from 85 percent in 1980 to 56 percent in 2005. Nor does possessing a university degree make much difference: As shown in Table 5-3, in 2005 recent immigrant men with degrees earned 48 percent of the wages of their educated Canadian-born counterparts, whereas recent immigrant women with degrees earned 42 percent of what was earned by Canadian-born women with degrees (Perkel, 2008).

How do we account for this growing disparity? Barriers persist in converting international credentials and expertise into comparable occupational status and compensation in Canada (George & Chaze, 2014; Teelucksingh & Galabuzi, 2005). Human capital skills do not transfer well and are discounted once in Canada, with the result that one year of overseas experience is deemed equivalent to one-third of a year of domestic experience, while foreign education is worth about 75 percent of a comparable education for a Canadian-born person (Finnie & Meng, 2002). Others suggest a three-fold factor in the earning gaps: (1) a shift in source countries since the 1960s that has enhanced the potential for prejudicial discrimination and concerns over language competence; (2) declining income returns from foreign work experiences and educational levels among non-European immigrants; and (3) a general dip in labour market outcomes for new employees, especially as immigrants are treated as recent entrants in competition with a growing pool of Canadian graduates (Aydemir & Skuterud, 2004; Statistics Canada, 2006a).

To be sure, measuring income differences across broad analytical categories such as immigrant or racialized groups can be misleading (Jedwab & Satzewich, 2015). Such crude measures blur important differences related to class, race, gender, and ethnic differences within each category (Satzewich & Liodakis, 2013). Table 5-4 demonstrates how certain ethnic and racialized groups outearn others; for example, Japanese Canadians are among the highest earners, whereas Koreans in Canada are one of the lowest. Placing both groups into a single category as racialized ("visible") minorities mistakenly implies that both Japanese Canadians and Korean Canadians are equally disadvantaged in the Canadian labour market. In addition, conceptualizing the category of racialized minorities in monolithic terms for statistical purposes underplays the complexities of peoples' real-life circumstances (Jedwab & Satzewich, 2015). Note, the table does not take into account immigrant status (foreign-born vs. Canadian-born; recent or established).

TABLE 5-4	Mean Income for Canadians in 2011 by Ethnic Origin, Aged 45–54 Years, with University Degree or Diploma
Ethnic Origin	Mean Income $
Total	64 070
Highest Earners	
Jewish	87 261
Japanese	76 215
Italian	73 323
Hungarian	72 493
British	70 641
Lowest Earners	
Filipino	36 804
East African	34 071
Pakistani	34 008
Iranian	33 914
Korean	28 182

Source: Adapted from Statistics Canada, National Household Survey, 2011; also Jedwab & Satzewich (2015).

Or consider the differences that can be discerned when men and women are considered separately (as in Table 5-5). Whereas racialized women of colour on average earn less than non-racialized white women, women of Chinese and Japanese origins are an exception. Moreover, some second-generation Canadian-born racialized women earn

TABLE 5-5	Average Employment Income in 2010 Based on Visible Minority Status and Gender		
	Total$	Male$	Female$
Total Population	61 996	69 692	52 178
Not Racialized	63 404	71 427	53 109
Racialized	56 209	62 466	48 409
Highest Earners			
Japanese	70 397	86 269	54 020
Chinese	61 979	67 967	55 018
Korean	61 346	70 315	49 528
Lowest Earners			
Southeast Asian	51 675	59 089	42 858
Black	50 909	54 436	46 935
Filipino	47 693	54 682	42 540

Source: Adapted from Statistics Canada, National Household Survey, 2011; also Jedwab & Satzewich (2015).

more than first-generation racialized immigrant women as well as white Canadian-born women (Hum & Simpson, 2007; Jedwab & Satzewich 2015). Clearly, then, a different picture of income inequality emerges when focusing on differences within ethnic and racialized groups rather than on simply differences between groups (Jedwab & Satzewich, 2015).

To sum up: Migrants and minorities endure income differences that are inconsistent with Canada's egalitarian commitments. But these disparities need to be disaggregated to expose a more nuanced and accurate picture. First, not all racialized minorities or newcomers to Canada are doing poorly when it comes to income and wages. Second, gender differences are noticeable, with males out-earning females by a significant amount. Third, failure to make a distinction between new and established immigrants distorts the picture of income inequality. Fourth, racialized immigrants start with a distinct earning disadvantage relative to the Canadian-born, a gap that admittedly narrows over time, although in recent years this initial earning gap has widened and the catch-up rate is slower. Fifth, income differences are one thing, differences in wealth (assets) are often more significant as indicators of inequality.

Employment/Unemployment

Another key indicator of racialized stratification entails levels of unemployment. Generally speaking, both racialized and recently arrived immigrants tend to be more unemployed than non-racialized (white) immigrants. Consider the results from a recent Statistics Canada study, presented in Table 5-6.

TABLE 5-6	Unemployment Rates for Immigrants Aged 25 to 54 by Region of Birth and Landing Period, 2006	
Region of Birth	**Landing Period**	**Average Unemployment Rate (%)**
Canadian born	—	4.9
Latin American	2001–2006	10.5
	1996–2005	6.5
	Before 1996	6.1
African	2001–2006	20.8%
	1996–2005	13.6%
	Before 1996	7.6%
Asian	2001–2006	11.1%
	1996–2001	7.3%
	Before 1996	5.5%
European	2001–2006	8.4%
	1996–2001	5.1%
	Before 1996	4.0%
North American	Before 1996	2.8%
	(other figures not available)	

Source: Statistics Canada (2008).

The figures nearly speak for themselves. Compared to others, immigrants from Europe and the United States are less likely to be unemployed. According to Queen's University professor Charles Beach (2008), European immigrants are less likely to be subject to discrimination, whereas immigrants from "non-conventional sources" are perceived to lack the education, workplace experience, and language skills to mesh smoothly into the labour market. Europeans who arrived before 1996 are also less unemployed than the national average, reflecting a pattern of greater adaptability with the passage of time. Interestingly, immigrants born in Southeast Asia—particularly those from the Philippines—had the strongest labour market performance of all immigrants to Canada, regardless of when they landed, with rates comparable to Canadian-born workers (Statistics Canada, 2008). Their extended exposure to colonial domination may have predisposed them to greater competence in the English language and western culture (Beach, 2008).

Patterns of employment are no less ambiguous than patterns of earnings. Many university-educated immigrants fail to land employment consistent with their credentials or expertise, although 80 percent of new Canadians between the ages of 25 and 44 had found at least one job within two years of arrival in Canada. Among those that do, however, 60 percent end up working in areas other than those in which they are qualified, often in jobs described as precarious, that is, either dirty, dull, or dangerous or, alternatively, of a contingent nature (e.g., part-time) (Fleras, 2014b). Failure to translate overseas work experience and educational qualifications into Canadian equivalents reflects bottlenecks in the licensing and accreditation process, a resistance to hiring those with international credentials, and an insistence on Canadian experience, even when that experience is not job related (Sakamoto et al., 2013). No less a contributing factor is a persistent prejudice that produces discriminatory employment outcomes as the following Box discussion demonstrates.

Names Matter

It's widely acknowledged that prejudice and discrimination continue to mar immigrant entry into the labour market. But these prejudicial attitudes and discriminatory practices are now much more subtle than they were in the past. Nevertheless, they are real and exert an exclusionary impact, regardless of intent or awareness. Consider this field experiment by Philip Oreopoulos (2009) a University of Toronto Labour Economist. Oreopoulos sent out 6000 fictitious CVs for online job vacancies in the Toronto area during the economic boom. The first CV described a Canadian-born individual with Canadian education and experience, as well as addition to a Canadian sounding name.

Another set of CVs differed slightly: (a) some had a name change to a common Chinese, Indian, and Pakistani name (b) others had a name change and only foreign work experiences, and (c) still others had a name change, foreign work experiences, and foreign education credentials. The number of call backs for interviews were then recorded and sorted accordingly. Three findings emerged:

1. Interview request rates for English-named applicants with Canadian credentials were three times higher (16% vs. 5%) than for resumes with foreign sounding names and foreign credentials.

(Continued)

2. Foreign-named resumes that included only Canadian experience increased call back rates to 11 percent.
3. Applicants with English-sounding names received 40 percent more interview requests than those with similar credentials but foreign sounding names (16% vs. 11%).

The conclusion is inescapable: Employer discrimination persists against those applicants whose metrics do not fit into a conventional Canadian mold (see also Skaggs & Bridges, 2013). That alone should suggest that any public policy meant to enhance immigrant integration must move beyond improving the human capital of migrants and minorities. The focus should instead be on changing the mindsets and behaviour patterns of those whose decisions determine "who gets the work." After all, in a multicultural Canada, racial discrimination represents an affront to the principle and practice of equality for all its citizens. Discrimination also constitutes an inefficient way of allocating human resources by imposing an economic cost on both racialized minorities and Canadian society (Teelucksingh & Galabuzi, 2005).

Racializing Poverty

Poverty in Canada is becoming increasingly racialized (Wallis & Kwok, 2008). That is, patterns of poverty are neither colour-blind nor randomly distributed across all Canadians, but clustered around certain historically disadvantaged minorities (Galabuzi, 2006; Picot & Coulombe, 2007). In 2006, according to the National Council of Welfare (2011), the overall poverty rate in Canada was 11 percent. For racialized persons it was 22 percent compared to 9 percent for non-racialized white Canadians. Of those racialized persons living in poverty, 24 percent identified as Chinese, South Asian (20%), and blacks (18%). A study by Michael Ornstein (2006), based on racialized groups in Toronto, found that the 20 poorest groups were non-Europeans, with Somali, Afghan, and Ethiopian groups displaying poverty rates in excess of 50 percent. Another study based on National Household Survey data in 2011 arrived at similar conclusions as the 2006 study. The incidence of poverty for racialized minorities was 21.5 percent (median income, $20 153) using LIM-AT (Low Income Measure, After tax and Transfers), compared to 13.3 percent for whites (median income, $29 649) (Jackson, 2014). Children of racialized minorities are particularly vulnerable According to the Colour of Poverty Campaign (2007), 43 percent of minority children in Ontario live in poverty, in part because of barriers that prevent their parents from finding and keeping good paying jobs. No less disturbing is the feminization of colour-coded poverty. The 2005 Statistics Canada report, "Women in Canada" indicated that poverty informed the lives of 28.8 percent of racialized minority women in Canada, compared with women in the general population at 15.9 percent, including 33.8 percent who are under the age of 15.

For newcomers to Canada, especially more recent immigrants, the situation is equally grim. In 2004, according to 2007 Statistics Canada data, low income ("poverty") rates for immigrants during their first year in Canada were 3.2 times higher than for Canadian-born persons. Increased levels of educational attainment among immigrants and a shift toward increasingly skilled immigrants do not appear to have made much difference (Picot & Coulombe, 2007). More recent studies indicate that 36 percent of immigrants who have been in Canada for less than five years live in poverty, a figure that singled out immigrant men and those over 50 years of age (Dungan, Fang, & Gunderson, 2012; also Dodd, 2013). Not surprisingly, concluded the 2006 Ontario Hunger Report by the province's food bank association, new Canadians accounted for nearly one-third of the 320 000 Ontario residents who depended on food banks every month—an increase of 14 percent since 2001—many of whom could not find affordable housing or access to well-paying jobs, despite the province's then booming economy.

EXPLAINING RACIALIZED DISPARITIES

This overview of racialized inequalities is dismaying when assessed against the backdrop of Canada's commitment to an egalitarian society. Two theoretical perspectives provide an explanatory framework for these patterns of racialized inequality, exclusions, and stratification: Functionalist perspectives tend to blame inequality on ethnicity and individual shortcomings (the ethnicity model), whereas radical conflict perspectives situate the problem within institutional frameworks, systemic biases, and opportunity structures (the critical race model). These explanatory models differ in how they analyze racialized inequality in terms of underlying assumptions, problem source, proposed solutions, and anticipated outcomes.

Functionalist Perspectives/Ethnicity Models

The existence of an economic division of labour is a starting point for functionalist models. For society to operate smoothly, functionalists argue, positions in the economic structure must be appropriately filled with suitable personnel. As these jobs differ in skill level and importance, people need to be rewarded appropriately for doing tasks of differing complexity. The occupational prestige hierarchy is the result of these differential rewards. Many accept as "natural" that physicians are compensated more for their services than are plumbers, even though, arguably, both are crucial for Canada's collective well-being (Davis & Moore, 1945). Leading sports figures are paid more than common labourers (in the United States, the average major league baseball player earned about US$4.2 million annually at the start of the 2015 season), while the typical childcare worker continues to earn minimum wage. This earnings discrepancy arises not because one skill is more important to society than the other: Salary and status gaps exist because certain skills are in short supply compared with the demand.

Functionalists do not treat all inequalities equally. Inequality is "good" when generated by the "rules of the game" (i.e., on the basis of merit, credentials, and equal opportunities); it is "bad" if unfairly acquired by excluding others because of irrelevant ascriptive attributes (such as race) outside a person's control. Functionalists believe that a commitment to "colour-blindness" boosts the bottom line by capitalizing on a broader pool of brainpower for competing in a global market economy. To be sure, a degree of inequality is inevitable; after all, people are not all equally equipped in the competition for scarce resources. Functionalists may accept the inevitability of innate differences, albeit not necessarily in a racial way, but in terms of the skills an individual brings to the marketplace. For functionalists, then, inequality is necessary, normal, and desirable in a complex, merit-based, and openly competitive society. This perspective is also consistent with ethnicity models in accounting for racialized inequalities.

A generation ago, references to racial(ized) stratification were couched within the discursive framework of an ethnicity paradigm (Fleras, 1993). Canadian society was envisaged as an open and competitive marketplace in which individuals competed as equals and were rewarded because of their skills or production. Individual success or failure reflected a person's level of human capital: Those with training, skills, and education succeeded; those without, did not. Ethnic differences were pivotal. On one side, ethnic minorities had to discard the debilitating aspects of their ethnicity that precluded participation (Porter, 1965). On the other side, those in charge also had to discard those prejudgments that precluded inclusiveness. Not surprisingly, the inception of a Multiculturalism policy in 1971 sought to depoliticize the relevance of ethnicity in defining who got what by eliminating its salience as a basis for recognition, relationships, and reward (Fleras, 2009a).

An ethnicity model argues that racialized minorities and new Canadians are largely responsible for the predicament in which they find themselves. While studies suggest that market conditions may account for 40 percent of the decline in newcomer earnings since the 1980s (e.g., changes in the labour market related to economic globalization, the interplay of outsourcing and downsizing, and the growing prevalence of digital technology), the remaining 60 percent is related to variations in the human capital of immigrants (from deficient language skills to lack of Canadian experience) (Jedwab, 2012). Of particular importance is an immigrant's proficiency in one of Canada's two official languages (Tal, 2012). Most studies conclude that the strongest predictor of economic and labour market success is neither credentials nor degrees, but competencies in one of Canada's two official languages—not just basic French or English competencies in reading and writing, but a nuanced level of sophistication for solving problems, communicating effectively, and getting along (Banting, Courchene, & Seidle, 2007). Yet many immigrants have neither French nor English as a first language (nearly 27% in 2010 [Citizenship & Immigration Canada, 2011]). According to this line of thought, the failure of minorities to penetrate the market may reflect a lack of human capital (from language to Canadian experience) because of their ethnicity (also Porter, 1965). Efforts to boost their "human capital" must focus on improving minority "skills" consistent with competitive labour force needs.

Radical Conflict Perspectives/Critical Race Models

Radical conflict perspectives share with functionalists the view that complex societies are differentiated by inequality. Where the models differ is in their assessment of inequality as value, process, and outcome. The inevitability of inequality—a basic tenet of functionalism—is anathema to radical conflict theory. For radical conflict theorists, society is envisaged as a site of inequality involving competitively different groups in a struggle for valued resources such as power, privilege, and property. Society (including its institutions, values, and relations) is designed and organized in a way that reflects, reinforces, and advances the interests and experiences of the rich and the powerful. Patterns of inequality are neither natural nor normal, but rather "naturalized" or "normalized" in those societies organized around the relentless pursuit of profit. Inequities stem from the different class locations occupied by groups of people—owners versus workers—in relationship to the means of production. The ruling class does everything in its power to secure its power and privilege, including sowing the seeds of dissension to destabilize the working classes. The working classes, in turn, struggle to redefine the status quo with the resources at their disposal.

Class relations in a capitalist society inform Marxist versions of radical conflict perspectives (Velez, 1998). (Feminist versions are addressed in the next chapter). But shared experiences notwithstanding, the working class is neither homogeneous in composition nor uniform in outlook. It is internally divided inasmuch as some workers are more exploited than others because of gender or race. White male workers are often better paid than non-white workers, while males in general earn more than females from all racialized groups. In addition to income differentials, males generally have access to more secure types of employment with greater opportunities for promotion and power. These class factions can also be manipulated to foster what Marx termed "false consciousness": Instead of directing their hostility at the source of their exploitation and domination (i.e., the capitalists), workers displace their antagonism by scapegoating the minorities among them. In other words, inter-group hostility is fostered by the ruling class to distract oppressed classes, mask the underlying relations of production, and conceal or mystify the primary source of exploitation. Fomenting racial prejudice and out-group hostility helps to perpetuate the status quo, prevents the formation of worker solidarity, improves capital formation, destabilizes counter movements, militates against the development of class consciousness, and justifies the exploitation of a cheap and disposable labour force by stigmatizing groups as inferior (Velez, 1998).

Under radical conflict perspectives, the true source of racialized inequality is not race or ethnicity; rather, it's the logic of capitalist systems. Racialized differences and confrontations are simply aspects of the wider struggle between and within classes. Minority concerns merely complicate the issue by distorting the reality of domination and the cause of exploitation. In that this text begins with the premise that race, ethnic, and aboriginal relations are essentially unequal relations, a radical conflict perspective provides a richer insight into how these racialized inequalities are constructed and maintained as well as challenged and changed. Moreover, in contrast to functionalist models of social reality that tend to blame the victim for racialized inequalities (the ethnicity model), a radical conflict perspective pins the blame on society as an unequal system.

The concept of racialized inequality as a discourse underwent a shift in emphasis from the 1980s onward (Agocs & Boyd, 1993). It was apparent that the attainment of formal equality rights failed to generate the increased equality of outcome that many had anticipated (see also Squires, 2007a). What sounded good in theory—a commitment to formal equality—did not pan out into positive outcomes at the ground level. Awareness also shifted from a focus on blaming individuals (the ethnicity model) to a growing concern with discriminatory barriers that often are deeply institutionalized and systemically embedded. This cognitive shift was driven by a concomitant increase in immigrants arriving from developing countries. Multicultural commitments that focused on ethnicity no longer resonated with the language of relevance. Proposed instead were new equity discourses based on the principle of institutional inclusion, removal of discriminatory barriers at structural levels, and eradication of racism that precluded full and equal participation in society. References to racialized inequality shifted accordingly in their focus—from individuals to structure, from ethnicity to race, from equality of opportunity to equal outcomes, and from a commitment to formal (abstract) equality to that of **substantive equality (equity)**.

Of particular note in explaining racialized inequality was the shift from an ethnicity model to a critical race model (see Abrams & Moio, 2009; Chandra & Airhihenbuwa, 2010; Thobani, Razack, & Smith, 2010). As an analytical lens for analyzing the interplay of race, power, and inequality in society, this model commits to actively pursuing social justice by interrogating issues of race and racism in a Canada that purports to be post-racial and abide by pro-multicultural principles (Fleras, 2014a). According to this model, the race concept must be refracted through the prism of racialization since race is not a naturally occurring biological reality but a socially constructed convention that is imposed to the advantage of some, and disadvantages others. Neither society nor its institutions are race-neutral or colour-blind, as critical race theorists argue, but are ideologically loaded to reflect, reinforce, and advance the interests and agendas of a white supremacist regime. Institutional racism is pervasive and ingrained within the fabric of deeply Eurocentric society, including the founding assumptions and foundational principles of its unwritten constitutional order (Bell, 2008). The significance of race in constructing law and the role of law in maintaining social domination plays a key role in securing white power, privilege, and property (Aylward, 1999; Odartey-Wellington, 2011). And yet the centrality of race in racialized inequalities is obscured by the gloss of multiculturalism discourses, which, in turn, perpetuates patterns of racialized exclusion by whitewashing uncomfortable truths. In other words, instead of something aberrant or random, racism is an everyday occurrence for racialized minorities, given its systemic entrenchment in the social fabric of society (Abrams & Moio, 2009). Finally, a critical race commitment to the principles of intersectionality points to the multidimensional and interlocking nature of oppressions—colonization, racism, sexism, and classism—that amplify the inequalities of exclusion (Razack, Smith, & Thobani, 2010). Table 5-7 provides a brief comparison of these models.

In contrast to the once-dominant ethnicity model, the critical race model emphasizes the bigger picture as an explanatory framework. According to the critical race model, the problem is not about individuals or attitudes *per se*. Rather, the source of the problem is embedded in the institutional *structures* of society (Bonilla-Silva, 2015; Skaggs & Bridges, 2013). Inequality and barriers to advancement reflect structural constraints that are largely systemic in advancing "pale-male" interests. That is, while the system pretends to be value-neutral under the guise of universality and colour-blindness, the very notion of a level playing field is discriminatory by virtue of its treating racialized migrants and minorities the same as dominant group members. To apply the metaphor of a competitive footrace with staggered starting blocks, it is obvious that not all contestants are equally positioned to compete in the labour market. The race is rigged because of ascribed characteristics that handicap some because of skin colour or gender, while privileging others for precisely the same reasons. Yes, racialized minorities may possess the same rights to equal opportunity; however, they must exercise these rights and achieve success on an unlevel playing field that was neither designed to reflect their experiences and realities nor constructed to advance their interests (Fleras, 2015).

TABLE 5-7	Explaining Racialized Inequality: Ethnicity versus Critical Race Models	
	The Ethnicity Model	**The Critical Race Model**
Problem	Individual ("blaming the victim")	Institutional ("blaming the system")
Root cause	Ethnicity	Discriminatory barriers
Focus of solution	Increase human capital	Improve institutional inclusiveness
Means of solution	Market forces	Government intervention
Sociological perspective	Functionalism	Radical Conflict

TOWARD EQUALITY

That most migrants and minorities aspire to social inclusion and economic equality is surely beyond dispute or debate. Many Canadians would also agree that equality is to be preferred over an inequality that is unfairly achieved. But the concept of "equality" is itself subject to diverse interpretations: as sameness, as proportional equivalence, and as equity. For some, equality is synonymous with sameness—everyone is treated the same regardless of background or circumstances, because true equality is based on acknowledging our common humanity. No one is explicitly accorded special privileges in a market system designed around the principles of equal opportunity, equality before the law, and credential-based merit. For others, equality is used in the sense of numerical, or "proportional," equivalence. Under systems of preferential hiring and promotion, each group is allocated positions according to their numbers in society or the workforce. For yet others, the concept of equality pivots around the principle of equity. References to equality as equity acknowledge the need to take seriously difference-based disadvantages. The unique circumstances of a person or group are taken into account to ensure "customized" treatment by way of institutional adjustments or exemptions from general rules. Emphasis is on the attainment of equal outcomes (or conditions) rather than the abstract principle of equal opportunity.

Consider, for example, the so-called special treatment accorded to individuals with disabilities. Concessions such as wheelchair ramps, closed-caption TV, and designated parking spots can hardly be thought of as special or preferential. On the contrary, removing disability barriers ensures equality of opportunity by providing reasonable accommodation. Likewise, minorities encounter barriers as real and as debilitating as physical impediments. Just as building ramps for the wheelchair-bound creates a more level playing field, so too does a similar logic apply to racialized minorities. In both cases, those with socially defined disabilities require special/different treatment, if only to ensure their right to equal opportunity. A commitment to reversing discrimination by way of customized treatment makes it doubly important to treat unequals differently. To do otherwise, that is, to treat everyone the same in contexts of inequality, perpetuates the prevailing distribution of power, privilege, and resources.

Two models of equality exist as they pertain to racialized inequalities of exclusions, each of which differs from the other at key points of comparison. **Formal (equal) equality** is concerned with mathematical equivalence and a market-driven means for establishing who gets what. According to this model, no one is entitled to differential treatment (either positive or negative) since everyone is equal before law, regardless of their race or ethnicity. Any criterion that rewards individuals on grounds other than merit or competition is criticized as unfair, racist, or counterproductive. More substantive versions of equality (or equity) disagree. This more equity oriented equality argues that seemingly neutral rules applied evenly and equally may exert an adverse, if unintended, impact on racialized minority groups. A one-size-fits-all mentality can produce unequal results and perpetuate group-based inequities of exclusions, according to the Ontario Human Rights Commission annual reports, especially when everyone is treated as asexual, deracialized, and classless, without a history or context for the purposes of reward (McIntyre, 1993). Strict and equal application of a seemingly neutral rule or standard (which in fact reflects and reinforces deeply embedded majority worldviews and values) may infringe on a person's right to true equality. Insofar as treating everyone the same regardless of their circumstances is not

TABLE 5-8	Comparing Equality Models	
Formal (or Equal) Model	**Substantive (or Equity) Model**	
Formal (abstract and mathematical equivalent)	Substantive (context and consequences)	
Everyone should be treated equally (the same)	People should be treated as equals (differently)	
Pretend pluralism	Taking differences seriously/into account	
Same treatment as a matter of course	Customized treatment when situation arises	
Equal opportunity	Equitable outcomes	
Discipline of the market	Government intervention	

equality, but is the privileging of a racialized and unequal status quo, the politics of solutions must be judged by the actual effect that they exert rather than by abstract legal principles (Cohen, 1999).

The distinction between equal and equity is captured by the debate between formal versus substantive models of equality (see Table 5-8). A formal or equal model focuses on the rights of individuals to be free from discrimination when competing for the good things in life. By contrast, an equity or substantive model concentrates on the rights of historically disadvantaged individuals to a fair and equitable share of the goods and services. A commitment to an equal model openly advocates competition, inequality, and hierarchy as a natural and healthy way of allocating rewards and entitlements; by contrast, an equity model is concerned with controlled distribution and egalitarian outcomes for members of disadvantaged groups. This perspective recognizes the need for collective considerations over individual rights when the situation demands it. After all, the unintended consequences of even seemingly neutral practices may lead to the exclusion of qualified personnel, regardless of motive or consciousness. It also endorses the principle of social intervention for true equality, as equal outcomes are unlikely under competitive market forces. In other words, it embraces the inclusivity principle that people should be treated the same ("equally") as a matter of course, yet be treated as equals ("differently") precisely because of their differences when the situation demands it.

Which version of equality should prevail? Is one more important than the other, or is it a case of one serving as a necessary precondition for the other? By itself, the principle of equal opportunity structures cannot overcome the debilitating effects of systemic discrimination and institutional racism. For true equality to take root, additional measures are required over and above those available to the general population. Context and consequences are as important as abstract principles in righting the wrongs. Taking context into consideration may justify differential treatment in some cases, to achieve an equality of outcome. Taking consequences into account suggests that focusing on the outcomes of even well-intentioned programs is more important than their intent. In short, equity-based equality hinges on a key principle: Treating everyone the same is not equality or justice. References to equal opportunity may sound good in theory but rarely stand up to scrutiny when the unlevel playing field is structurally tilted, the game is rigged by the rich and powerful, and the rules are always changing to accommodate those in charge. What is required is a commitment to an outcome-based equality, one that recognizes the need to take differences seriously. To be sure, an equity equality is not opposed to equal opportunities in defining equality. On the contrary, a commitment to the principle of equal opportunity is acknowledged as a preliminary step in overcoming entrenched racism and discrimination. But ultimately, such a commitment cannot achieve a fair and just equality in deeply racialized contexts. Only a dual commitment to equitable outcomes and equal opportunities can foster the conditions for living together differently. To what extent, then, does employment equity help or hinder the achievement of equality and equity?

Is Employment Equity a Problem or a Solution?

How should employment equity be assessed—as a solution or as a problem? Is Canada's employment equity program to promote racial equality through increased minority representation a case of reversing discrimination? Or does it promote artificial quotas and political correctness at the expense of merit, fairness, and qualifications (reverse discrimination)? For supporters, employment equity is a first step in reversing past discrimination, eliminating discriminatory preferences and favouritism in hiring, and improving employment levels for the historically disadvantaged (Public Service Alliance of Canada, 2010). They point out that gaps in the representation of historically disadvantaged workers have narrowed over the past 20 years, so that most groups are better represented in the labour market than in the past (Statistical Analysis Unit, 2010). The latest statistics updated to the end of 2012 using 2006 data indicate that women, people with disabilities, and Aboriginal peoples are better represented in the federal public service than as per their workforce availability, but racialized minorities continue to be underrepresented (i.e., 12.1 percent of the federal service, up from 6.1 percent in 2002) (Said 2013; Standing Senate

Committee on Human Rights, 2013). For critics, employment equity is primarily a euphemism for reverse discrimination that not only penalizes deserving white males but also undermines the principle of meritocracy (Loney, 1998). They argue that these advances for some have come at the expense of others. In replacing one form of discrimination with another, employment equity initiatives are less about removing discriminatory barriers but more about displacing qualified white men with quotas of racialized minorities and Aboriginal peoples (Loney, 1998). The logic of the argument is fairly straightforward: Just as it is unfair to discriminate against minorities, critics say, it is just as wrong to give preference to minorities in the process unfairly penalizing whites. All distinctions based on race, gender, or ethnicity are discriminatory and wrong, according to this line of thinking, especially when this exercise in social engineering is little more than government-endorsed discrimination under the guise of fairness or equity.

Others disagree: Reference to context and consequences is important in evaluating the "rightness" of employment equity. In opposition to those who believe that no Canadian should be

(Continued)

barred from employment because of race or ethnicity, others argue that those once excluded because of race now require a race-based solution to level the playing field. Admittedly, equity measures that seemingly privilege race over merit may appear like reverse discrimination insofar as they discriminate against whites, while securing preference for equity target groups. In reality, however, employment equity is aimed at "reversing" discrimination through the removal of discriminatory barriers, thereby expanding the pool of formerly excluded but qualified applicants. Instead of explicitly excluding "pale males" from the competition—although the unintended consequences (or collateral damage) of doing so are inevitable when obligating people to move over and make space—a commitment to "reversing" discrimination fosters a workplace dynamic that is both inclusive and equitable, as well as progressive and productive. In short, appearances are deceiving because words like "discrimination" do not always mean what they seem to. A discrimination aimed at removing (or reversing) exclusion in order to foster inclusiveness differs sharply from a discrimination that excludes by reinforcing a racialized status quo.

Chapter Highlights

- Canada remains stratified by race and immigration status despite its *bona fides* as a post-racial and pro-multicultural society.
- Racialized inequality is deeply ingrained in the concepts of exclusion and stratification.
- Racialized inequalities are readily apparent at income, employment, and poverty levels.
- Two major models can account for racialized inequality (Ethnicity and Critical Race) and the sociological perspectives that underpin these models (Functionalism and Radical Conflict, respectively).
- Two models were proposed for addressing the problem of racialized inequality: the Formal (or Equal) Model and the Substantive (or Equity) Model.
- Canada's employment equity program may be interpreted as a solution (reversing discrimination) or a problem (reverse discrimination).

Review Questions

1. How and why does racialized inequality persist in a Canada that commits to both a post-racial and pro-multicultural society?
2. What is meant by the racialized inequalities of exclusion (as opposed to racial inequality)?
3. Compare a functionalist/ethnicity model with a radical conflict/critical race model as competing models to explain racialized inequality.
4. Moves to address racialized inequalities tend to focus on two models: Formal (equal) versus substantive (equity). Discuss.
5. Employment equity has been described as both "reverse" discrimination as well as a case of "reversing" discrimination. Discuss.

CHAPTER 6

Gender Minorities, Gendered Exclusions

LEARNING OBJECTIVES

After reading this chapter, you will be able to:

1. Explain how a sociological perspective may account for the violence directed at aboriginal women.

2. Outline the relationship between gender differences and gendered exclusions in a gendered society.

3. Describe how and why minority women continue to experience patterns of exclusions that differ from minority men and white women.

4. Clarify the importance of an intersectional analysis in framing gendered violence.

5. Deconstruct the category of minority women to demonstrate how and why this deconstruction matters in creating gendered exclusions.

DEBATE

Murdered and Missing: The Crisis of Aboriginal Women in Canada

Violence against aboriginal and indigenous women remains a persistent and pervasive problem (Legal Strategy Coalition on Violence Against Indigenous Women, 2015; National Citizens Observatory on Femicide, 2012; Romero et al., 2013). A 2009 General Social Survey by Statistics Canada (Perreault, 2011) indicated that aboriginal women were three times more likely than non-aboriginal women to be victims of spousal violence. Aboriginal women were also eight times more likely to be killed than non-aboriginal women (Canadian Women's Foundation, 2012; Report, 2014). Both the incidence and the severity of the violence is reflected in the shocking number of murdered and missing aboriginal women who happen to live in a society "that poses a risk to their safety" (Oppal, 2012:7). An RCMP Report (2014) found that between 1980 and 2012, 1181 aboriginal women were murdered or reported missing to the police—nearly double the number that had

(Continued)

been previously circulated by Native Women's groups and Amnesty International. To put this figure into perspective: Women represented 32 percent of homicides in Canada during this time period, although they comprise less than 2.1 percent of the national population. The RCMP subsequently revealed that family violence accounted for approximately 70 percent of solved cases of murdered aboriginal women, including 62 percent of the victims killed by a spouse, an intimate relation, or a family member. While the national homicide rate continues to dip downward to 1.56 victims per 100 000 of Canadian population, according to 2012 Statistics Canada data, the homicide rate for the Inuit-based territory of Nunavut was 14.84 victims for every 100 000 population (a gender breakdown is not available). Provincial variations are significant, as well (Perreault, 2011), with aboriginal women representing 55 percent of all homicides in Saskatchewan and 49 percent of those in Manitoba. It should be noted that police-reported violent crime against women was highest in the Territories and Manitoba and Saskatchewan—domains that also happen to have higher than average aboriginal populations (Sinha, 2013).

What is going on? How can we account for this appalling state of affairs? Why are aboriginal women and girls more likely to be victims of violence and homicide than women in the general population? Is it a case of men in general, aboriginal men in particular, acting badly whose violent impulses are best controlled through criminal justice intervention (police, courts, and jails)? Or should the blame be directed in part to those women who gravitate toward risky behavior—from substance abuse to plying the sex trade industry—that render them susceptible to victimization? Or is it case that the most marginalized members of society are vulnerable to systemic violence? As many indigenous groups point out, violence against aboriginal women is steeply rooted in poverty, discrimination, and the legacy of colonialism, resulting in a greater probability of pursuing dangerous lifestyles and at-risk occupations. Should we blame the victim or blame society? Is this a criminal problem or a social problem? Can the crisis be reduced to the level of "crime," as the Harper government was prone to do? Or is time to "commit to sociology" by upping the ante to incorporate broader context, feasibility factors, and root causes (Singh, 2014)? The Debate Revisited Box will try to untangle the debate—criminal or sociological—that informs the controversy over the crisis of murdered and missing women.

INTRODUCTION: THE DYNAMICS OF GENDER IN A GENDERED CANADA

It is commonly acknowledged that all human societies are gendered. Four dimensions account for a **gendered society**. First, all societies make a distinction between male and female (although some societies condone more fluid notions of gender, including intersexed and transgendered persons). Second, societies tend to endorse a division of labour, with men monopolizing the public domain of politics (from diplomacy to armed conflict), while women are expected to gravitate toward the private realm of the maternal and domestic. Third, male public-domain activities are usually valued as superior, whereas the private (maternal, domestic) world of women is devalued as inferior or irrelevant. Fourth, this devaluation eventually becomes deeply embedded within the framework of society (patriarchy) by way of values and structures that become defined as normal, necessary, and neutral (rather than constructed, contingent, and gender-based) in defining notions of what is right, acceptable, and desirable.

To be sure, there is little agreement on whether these male–female differences are fundamental and innate or superficial and situational. For some, gender differences are experienced as maximal, inherited, and difficult to dislodge or redefine; for others, gender differences are considered contextual, reflecting specific socio-historical circumstances, and amenable to revision (Nelson, 2009). Most sociologists, however, acknowledge the socially constructed nature of gender and gender relations. That is, there is nothing natural, inevitable, or normal about the concepts of masculinity or femininity. These constructs reflect how a gendered society defines what it means to be female and male at a specific point in time and place. As a result, what constitutes maleness and femaleness in any given society must be seen as relative, evolving, contested—and unequal.

Gender relations are invariably unequal relations because gender remains a key variable in shaping negative outcomes (Jiwani, 2006). This gendered inequality may be neither deliberate nor conspiratorial; rather it may reflect the logical, yet negative, consequences of ostensibly neutral (or even well-intentioned) rules that remain anchored in androcentric assumptions of right, normal, and acceptable. Or, a gendered inequality may reflect the systemic biases inherent in the founding assumptions and foundational principles of a society's patriarchal constitutional order. Patriarchy refers to a society that is designed, organized, and oriented by, for, and around men. Under patriarchy, male interests, priorities, and experiences are reflected, reinforced, and advanced by an arrangements in which (1) the social, political, economic, and cultural domains are controlled by men; (2) masculinity is more highly valued than femininity; and (3) males have preferential access to power and privilege because of their gender. Patterns of gender stratification are established that perpetuate patterns of "pale-male" power and privilege over females and children while reinforcing a gendered status quo (Boyd & Pikkov, 2008). The cumulative effect of such a patriarchal bias toward women is exclusionary. In rephrasing Sandra Bem's (1994) classic title, in a male-centred and male-dominated world, female differences are often transformed into female disadvantages and dismissed or disparaged accordingly.

Few sociologists would deny the asymmetry of gender relations in Canada (Nelson, 2009). Despite claims that we are at the "end of men" (Rosin, 2012), women continue to be "put down" because of institutional and systemic bias, "put in their place" by way of outright violence or harassment, or "put out of sight" as inferior or irrelevant. Many are denied equality in the workplace or deprived of the support to compete equitably with men in the corporate boardroom. Women working full time in full-year employment continue to earn significantly less than men—despite the fact that women are more educated, are working in greater numbers and for longer hours, and are having fewer children with less time away from work. They are also more likely than men to confront a narrower range of high paying occupations; to work on a part-time basis, in precarious conditions, and at a minimum wage; and to perpetually juggle the constant challenges of balancing care responsibilities with career ambitions. At times these inequalities of exclusion are deliberate (systematic): Examples include occupational segregation; the undervaluing of women's work and their status as the principal caregivers for children and the elderly; the restructuring of women's work because of privatization, downsizing, and outsourcing; and a lack of access to afford-able childcare. At other times, inequities are systemic; that is, they stem from a system informed by those foundational principles that promote "pale-male" interests at the expense of those of others (Canadian Feminist Alliance for International Action [CFAFIA], 2008). Or as Susan Pinker argues in her 2008 book *The Sexual Paradox*, women are unfairly penalized because ". . . they're expected to play by the same testosterone-charged rules men do, rules that men made up decades ago while women were kept barefoot, pregnant, and even illiterate."

More precarious still is the situation for minority women (or, more accurately, "minori-tized" women to emphasize a definitional process rather than naturally occurring category [Mukherjee, Mukherjee, & Godard, 2006]). Racialized women of colour, immigrant and refugee women, and aboriginal women continue to be denied or exploited because of their social status within a predominantly "white man's" world. As a group, they confront denial and experience exclusion with respect to power, privilege, and property (income and assets) because of brick walls, revolving doors, glass ceilings, and sticky floors. Table 5-2 in Chapter 5 clearly demonstrates how both foreign- and Canadian-born racialized minority women in full-year, full-time employment earn on average just over 75 percent of what racialized males earn (Block, 2010). Onsite discrimination, double standards, and gender stereotypes may account for the gender income disparities within the workplace. However, a more plausible reason may reflect the much narrower range of occupations open to minority women, most of whom are lower paid and offered fewer chances for promotion. Even those with credentials may default into low-paying employment when lacking the requisite amount of Canadian experience or language expertise. This situation is com-pounded by the marginality of class status. After all, to be poor in a society that values wealth is in itself marginalizing. To be poor and different—and a woman—intensifies the marginalization.

That racialized minorities experience exclusion and endure exploitation because of race, ethnicity, and social class is widely acknowledged (Henry & Tator, 2009; Jedwab & Satzewich, 2015). But minority women (including women of colour, immigrant women, and aboriginal women) are additionally disadvantaged by discriminatory barriers that are specifically related to their circumstances and experiences. As a group, they tend to earn less than their minority menfolk, experience discrimination and harassment at work, shoul-der domestic responsibilities, and are largely excluded from the corridors of power (CFAFIA, 2008; Wallis & Kwok, 2008). Until recently, the literature on the inequality of minority women was neither well established nor taken seriously. Academics often tripped over the trap of approaching minorities as if they were a homogeneous category of people—regardless of age, socioeconomic status, origins, or gender (see Tastsoglou & Preston, 2006). Despite their diversity of identities, concerns, and experiences, all minority women (including aboriginal women, racialized women of colour, and immigrant and refugee women) were indiscriminately squeezed into an all-purpose category. Such reductionism had a controlling effect by reinforcing the invisibility of minority women at the expense of their lived realities and aspirations (Zinn, Hondagneu-Sotelo, & Messner, 2011). Studies were further marred by a dearth of analytical sophistication. Instead of situating gender within an interactional context of race, ethnicity, and class, each of these indicators of inequality was separately analyzed in an additive rather than interactional manner (see Stasiulis, 1990, 1999). Such an approach made it difficult to appreciate how the interlocking nature of gendered inequality intersected with other indicators of inequality to amplify exclusion or exploitation (Jiwani, 2006; Signs, 2013; also McMullin, 2010; Zawilski, 2010).

The invisibility of gender in the study of race, ethnic, and aboriginal relations is no longer the case. Awareness is growing that women are both minorities and minorities-within-minorities. Excluding minority women from analysis diminishes a comprehensive understanding of social inequality—in the same way that excluding men from gender studies does society a disservice. This chapter takes advantage of this conceptual shift by exploring the politics of **gendered inequality** in terms of what, why, and how. A simple but profound premise predominates: Race, ethnic, and aboriginal relations are neither gender-neutral nor gender-passive. On the contrary, the assumptions and principles that inform and underpin society (Abraham, Chow, Maratou-Alipranti, & Tastsoglou, 2010) are fundamentally gendered and deeply stratified by way of asymmetrical relations of power, privilege, and resources (Boyd & Pikkov, 2008). Inasmuch as the gendered basis of female–male relations reflects a separate dynamic with a distinctive history, rationale, and expression, minority women experience reality differently than minority men do. But minority women also experience a different reality than white women because they are differently located with respect to the devalued and interrelated statuses of race, class, and ethnicity. In addition, the category of "minority women" must be disassembled: Aboriginal women, immigrant and refugee women, and racialized women of colour also differ experientially from each other because of their unique social locations and lived-realities.

The objectives of this chapter are doubly articulated: (1) to examine the politics of race, ethnic, and aboriginal relations through the conceptual framework of gender; conversely, to examine the politics of gender by filtering it through the lens of race, ethnicity, class, and aboriginality; and (2) to explore how gender intersects with race, ethnicity, and class to create interlocking systems of inequality; conversely, to explore how race, class, aboriginality, and ethnicity intersect with gender to intensify unequal relations. The chapter begins by conceptualizing gender minorities as a framework for analyzing gendered inequality. Gender is shown to be differently organized, experienced, and expressed when refracted through the prism of minority women's lived realities (Zinn, Hondagneu-Sotelo, & Messner, 2011). The impact of gendered inequality on minority women's lives and life chances puts the onus on deconstructing how and why these gendered inequalities are constructed, expressed, and maintained as well as challenged and transformed. The chapter concludes by demonstrating how gender is superimposed on and intersects with race, class, and ethnicity to variously shape realities and outcomes for racialized, immigrant/refugee, and aboriginal women. Conceptualizing violence along intersectional lines provides a fitting if disturbing application of the concept (Rajiva & Batacharya, 2010).

A word of caution: A chapter on gendered inequality tends to be long on problems and short on optimism. Emphasis is on the "bad" things that are done to minoritized women, either by misogynist/sexist males or by systemically biased institutions within a patriarchal regime. But there is another narrative that warrants attention: Contrary to popular belief, aboriginal women have displayed a tenacious resilience and remarkable pragmatism in responding to multiple burdens and challenges as guardians of tradition in protecting their cultures while promoting their communities (Anderson, 2009; Castellano, 2009; DePratto,

2015; Kino nda niimi Collective, 2014; Valaskakis, Dion Stout, & Guimond, 2009; Wesley-Esquimaux, 2009). Minority women's histories and contemporary realities incorporate narratives of contestation, resistance, struggle, and triumph in defending women's rights, equality, independence, job marketability, and socioeconomic conditions (Cummings, 2007; Hassan, 2008). In short, minority women cannot be reduced to the level of a dependent variable or a control group; instead, they are active agents in constructing their world—subjects rather than objects—coping with the sometimes competing demands of community and Canada on one side, and a commitment to gender and minority equality on the other.

GENDERED INEQUALITY: WOMEN AS MINORITIES, MINORITIES AS WOMEN

The concerns of racialized minority women and men often converge. Both are looking to forge productive and satisfying lives, to settle into Canada without forsaking their distinctiveness; for an end to discrimination in housing, employment, education, and delivery of social services; for protection of their fundamental human rights without enduring excessive bureaucratic interference; and for the best for their children without loss of their cultural heritage. But for racialized minorities, aspirations are one thing—reality may be quite another. They routinely endure denial or exclusion because their race, ethnicity, and social class are obstacles to equality (Galabuzi, 2006). Visibility continues to compromise their hopes of full and equal participation: Discrimination remains a factor in controlling minority lives, albeit more covertly than in the past. The lives and life chances of minorities are also controlled by a pervasive Eurocentrism that imposes restrictions in defining what is acceptable and desirable. Pressures to succeed are formidable, yet opportunities—from jobs to training—may be lacking. Even those with overseas credentials, foreign experience, and professional status may be consigned to menial and demeaning jobs. With such pressures, some individuals see little option except to reject the system by withdrawing into their ethnic enclaves or resorting to criminal lifestyles.

Minority Women, Minority Men

Both minoritized women and men suffer exclusion and exploitation because of factors beyond their control. For men, including fathers and husbands, coping with cultural differences can prove a jolting experience (Gordon, 2008). Males may have been raised in cultures in which their roles were largely authoritarian and centred on their status as the breadwinner and decision maker. In Canada, however, they are expected to assume the role of nurturer and equal partner, while trying to find work and secure settlement within a context of discrimination and diminished social and economic status. As wives expand their social circles and children effortlessly soak up the language and culture, fathers begin to lose their confidence as positive role models, with a corresponding loss of face. For immigrant males who are unemployed or underemployed, the effect is even more debilitating. According to David Este (2008), a lead researcher for the Father Involvement Initiative, a cross-Canada research project on immigrant dads, this emasculinization not only undermines self-esteem while instilling a sense of hopelessness; anxieties over procuring the family's needs are intensified as well. Men who are humiliated by their diminishment in status and authority may lash out violently at daughters, sisters, or wives.

Minority males may confront many challenges, but minority women are doubly jeopardized because of their membership in yet another historically devalued category, namely, female. Racialized women of colour, immigrant and refugee women, and aboriginal women confront the same problems as minority men, but they are additionally disadvantaged because of their gender status in a patriarchal society. To be sure, patriarchy does not exert a similar impact on all women. Aboriginal women, racialized minority women, and immigrant and refugee women may experience the disadvantage differently because of their respectively diverse histories, social locations, and legal statuses (Zinn, Hondagneu-Sotelo, & Messner, 2011). As a result, conclude Vickers and de Seve (2000), the unique yet unequal experiences of minority women may outweigh the commonalities of experience that they share with their menfolk. Just as racialized differences must be taken into account in crafting a multicultural Canada, so too must the different experiences of minority women be taken seriously in a gendered society. A Canada committed to the principle of inclusiveness cannot settle for anything less.

White Women, Minority Women

Women as a group may share common experiences of disadvantage because of male dominance and patriarchal infrastructures. Yet not all women are similarly disadvantaged at work or in the public domain. Nor do women represent a homogeneous group whose experiences are universally filtered through patriarchy. Minority women endure different patterns of control and domination that reflect their distinct status and social location as aboriginal women, women of colour, and immigrant and refugee women (Gillespie, 1996). Aida Hurtado (1996) describes how gender disparities are experienced differently. Whereas white women are increasingly striding the corridors of power, minority women continue to mop corridor floors. White women are largely concerned with projecting private-sphere issues (such as accessible daycare for women in management positions) into the public realm; by contrast, minority women tend to focus on bread-and-butter issues related to discrimination, healthy children, and daily survival.

A conflict of interest results: Racialized women of colour, aboriginal women, and immigrant and refugee women confront similar issues as white women, but they engage these challenges differently because their realities are refracted through the prism of racism, ethnicity, and class. Minority women have difficulty identifying with mainstream **feminist** theories that ignore racial hierarchies, discrimination within the workplace, and oppressive patterns within their own ethnic communities. Moreover, the interlocking of gender with race, ethnicity, and class generates such a different set of outcomes that reference to "sisterhood" as an all-encompassing category is both unrealistic and reductionist. As Daiva Stasiulis (1999) writes,

> [T]o speak about or for "women" was no longer a liberating politics but a homogenizing gesture that masked the race privilege of racially dominant women and the racial oppression and marginalization of women of colour. (p. 355)

Even strategies for change differ. Unlike white women, minority women are rarely in a position to divorce themselves from their male partners, since neither can exist without the other in the struggle against oppression (hooks, 1994, 1995). Nor are they in a position to compartmentalize their politics from broader struggles for inclusion and equality. Racialized minority women are caught in a double bind. They may be tempted to identify with white women with whom they share sexist discrimination; yet they may have little choice except to affiliate with their sometimes sexist menfolk, with whom they share a common experience of racism, ethnocentrism, and classism. To the extent that white women do not experience race and racism, they are free to focus on sexism. To the degree that minority women must confront racism, ethnocentrism, and classism in addition to sexism, they cannot afford to "cherry-pick" gender over race, class, and ethnicity as a preferred site of struggle.

Racialized Women of Colour

Racialized women of colour have long endured discrimination and exclusion in Canada. Numerous studies using different measures and samples appear to converge and confirm that racialized women of colour confront discrimination, both systematic and systemic (Reitz, Phan, & Banerjee, 2015). Black women were excluded from nursing in Canada before the 1940s, and continue to experience racism and discrimination in Canadian hospitals, often at the hands of white female nurses who collaborate with management to monitor, control, and harass them (das Gupta, 2009; Hagey, 2004). Muslim women in Quebec who insist on wearing a niqab will find that under Bill 94 they can no longer receive government services, public employment, educational opportunities and even most medical care (Orwin, 2010; Perreaux, 2010). Outside of Quebec, the federal government intended that fully veiled women be precluded from participating in Canadian citizenship ceremonies on the grounds that covering their face constitutes an affront to Canadian values (see the Dog Whistle Racism? Box). Yet these same women may find themselves victims of honour killings or arranged marriages, while continuing to be stuck in media-driven representations of passivity and victimhood (Hennebry and Momani, 2013; Phillips & Saharso, 2008). Both the critique of multiculturalism as too accommodating and a corresponding clash of values between "East" and "West" are played out on the bodies of Muslim women. In other words, Muslim women appear to have evolved into a litmus test of tolerance and civilization in a Quebec and Canada that claim to be secular yet tolerant. As a result, debates over the niqab in citizenship ceremonies or in government workplaces may well serve as code or proxy for larger anxieties about Muslims in Canada (Daro, 2015).

Consider income differences: Both Canadian-born and foreign-born racialized minority women earn less than minority men or white women (Kunz, Milan, & Schetagne, 2001; see also Table 5-1 in Chapter 5). But women of Japanese and Chinese origins on average earn more than non-racialized white women in Canada (see Table 5-5 in Chapter 5; also Jedwab & Satzewich, 2015). To be sure, earning differences can measure only the tip of the discriminatory iceberg. Differences in earnings are contingent on many factors, including qualifications, experience, seniority, and number of hours, all of which need to be statistically controlled if labour market discrimination is to be proven (Hum & Simpson, 2000). Nevertheless, racialized women of colour find themselves ghettoized in occupations that are dangerous or unprotected; they experience the trauma of role overload because of both paid and unpaid labour; and they must endure both racism and sexism in the workplace that devalues their contributions. As well, human rights laws have proven somewhat ineffective in eliminating systemic discrimination, resulting in the under-representation of racialized women of colour in political office, academia, corporate management, and mainstream media in terms of dominant and distorted images (CFAFIA, 2008; Fleras,

Dog Whistle Racism? Veiling, Citizenship, and the Politics of Expediency

What a difference a piece of cloth can make. The outcome of Canada's (no, not Yemen's or Pakistan's [Majka, 2015]) 2015 federal election pivoted around a woman's insistence to remain fully veiled during the citizenship oath ceremonies (Coyne, 2015). In 2011, Zunera Ishaq, a 29-year-old Pakistani woman who come to Canada in 2008, successfully challenged the government's proposed ban on face coverings during the citizenship swearing-in formalities (Southey, 2015). Ms. Ishaq had indicated a willingness to confirm her identity by unveiling privately just prior to taking the oath, but the government—long a proponent that all things Muslim are to be smeared as security issues [Fisk, 2015])—dismissed this concession to reasonable accommodation as unCanadian. In mid-September 2015, the Federal Court of Appeal again ruled against the government's determination to ban the practice of "oathing while veiling" (Selley, 2015), arguing the ban was unlawful and contravened the *Citizenship Act*. In what may have amounted to a carefully orchestrated act of political theatre, the government promised to take the banning of the ban all the way to the Supreme Court by requesting for a stay of the decision, but the Federal Court of Appeal refused to suspend its earlier rulings (Fine, 2015).

The government ostensibly justified its stand on the grounds that no person should be allowed to hide their identity or compromise their loyalty at the very moment they commit to join the Canadian family. According to the government, citizenship is a privilege, not a right, and everyone should comply with convention as a sign of loyalty. But critics accused the government of a politically expedient attack on individual and minority rights and freedom of religious expression that not only pandered to the lowest common denominator but, as a diversion, also distracted from more serious political and economic issues (Wente, 2015).

The Canadian public appeared to be on the side of the federal government. A government-funded poll conducted by Leger on behalf the Privy Council Office in March, 2015 of 3000 Canadians, found that 82 percent of respondents agreed that people should unveil during the citizenship ceremonies (Levitz, 2015). Another survey in late September 2015 from the polling firm Forum Research found that 64 percent of the 1499 respondents oppose fully veiled women from swearing the oath of citizenship (26% support it), including 79 percent in Quebec (Vincent, 2015). The poll also found that 56 percent of respondents believe the niqab oppresses women (29% disagree). Not surprisingly, a government that is prone to playing the wedge politics of fear and division thought they had hit the electoral jackpot by taking a hard stand in opposing the niqab.

So what's going on? Is this about generalized anti-niqab sentiment or about opposition to a niqab at citizenship ceremonies? Perhaps widespread negativity toward the niqab reflects high levels of closet bigotry, especially now that the politics of accommodating cultural diversity are increasingly problematized through the Muslim question (Dedi, 2015). How unflattering: Canadians may imagine themselves as beacons of multicultural enlightenment, but the politics of veiling have lifted the veil from the phobias and bigotries that lurk beneath our vaunted tradition of tolerance (Cohn, 2015; Dedi, 2015). In other words, what we have amounts to "dog whistle racism": just as a dog whistle produces a high pitched sound that only dogs, not humans, hear, so too does dog whistle racism consist of coded language such as "Jane-Finch," "those people," or even "immigrant" often employed by politicians that secretly insult or demonize minorities and is understood as such by those constituents in the know "in the know," even though the words sound normal to the general public (Lopez, 2015). Perhaps public opposition is more about the niqab as a proxy or code for wider worries over cultural incompatibilities or Islamist extremism, in addition to concerns about social change, values, equality, tolerance, and accommodation (e.g., should newcomers accommodate

to Canada or should Canadians accommodate religious and cultural diversities [Wente, 2015]?).

The governance of Canada's race and ethnic relations should NOT be swayed by polls, fear, or wedge politics, for in the final analysis, Canada is founded not on the tyranny of majority rule or public apprehension; rather, its foundations rest on the rule of law and the principle of individual rights. Furthermore, Canada is a multicultural society that purports to abide by the principles of multiculturalism. Not only is the ban unlawful (and possibly unconstitutional in violation of Charter rights), but wearing the niqab is also consistent with Canada's multicultural principles, since the covering does not break the law, violate individual rights or inflict harmful consequences, or contravene core constitutional values. In other words, as Andrew Coyne (2015) writes, unless a practice inflicts some identifiable harm rather than simply discomfort or outrage, there is no basis in Canadian law for restricting someone's rights during citizenship protocols.

On October 5, 2015, wearing her full veil, Zunera Ishaq was formally sworn in as a Canadian.

2011a; Littlefield, 2008). Finally, racialized women of colour experience racism differently from racialized men of colour, and differently among themselves, depending on their age, class, ability, sexual preference, and place of residence. They also experience gender discrimination differently from white women because of racism.

Aboriginal Women

It's tragic but true: Indigenous peoples who have experienced colonialism, systemic genocide, and exploitation may internalize that hatred, then project it outward through violence and abuse on those most vulnerable among them (Black et al., 2012; Deveaux, 2006; RCMP, 2014). For example, the violence that infused the residential school system not only disrupted traditional family life but also initiated a cycle of domestic abuse that continues to haunt aboriginal communities today (Pauktuutit, 2006). Aboriginal women in Canada are particularly vulnerable to colonialism and its legacy, from a diminuation of status and power to a loss of culture and language (Statistics Canada, 2006b; Report, 2014; Valaskakis et al., 2009). For Aboriginal peoples, the intersection of gender with colonialism has proved both complex and destructive (Green, 2007; Leigh, 2009, Turpel-Lafond, 2014; Voyageur, 2011). Aboriginal gender relations and family organization underwent major changes with the imposition of racist and sexist laws and legislation (i.e., the *Indian Act* of 1876). In contrast to the more fluid and open precontact gender roles in aboriginal societies, which authorities and agents may have perceived as impediments to the colonizing project, the imposition of colonization and settler values reinforced the primacy of European gender norms along Victorian lines. Under the *Indian Act* of 1876, which infantilized Aboriginal peoples in general, aboriginal women were further marginalized when their legal status was folded into that of men and marriage. Under colonization, aboriginal societies were reorganized along patriarchal lines, in the process displacing aboriginal women from government and power, while aligning the interests of male-dominated aboriginal families with those of colonial powers (Leigh, 2009). Accordingly, the forced sterilization of aboriginal women during the 1900s must be situated within the colonial context of an assimilationist Indian policy which sought to divest Aboriginal peoples of their land while reducing their dependency on the Canadian state (Stote, 2015).

Aboriginal women's vulnerability to exploitation and victimization both within and outside their communities is precipitated by several factors. The interplay of racism and discrimination with that of inequality and a generally precarious status in society compromises their safety and security (Green, 2008; Mann, 2005). Of particular salience is their exposure to socioeconomic marginalization; a coercive assimilation that disrupted traditional gender relations and cultural identity; and a perception that they are "easy targets" because of their over-involvement in the sex trade. The internalization of these pressures may instill a mood of depression and self-hatred among aboriginal women which, in turn, can induce high rates of suicide, alcohol dependency, and neglect of children. Compounding this volatile mixture is the pressure of derogatory stereotypes that reinforce their marginalization and disposability (Fleras, 2011a).

Historical and social factors also militate against the adequate recognition and rightful status of aboriginal women. Those who married non-Aboriginal males were penalized through a loss of status and corresponding benefits (aboriginal men who married non-aboriginal women retained their status). Even the 1985 repeal of the offending passage (section 12(1) (b) of the *Indian Act*) by Bill C-31 did not remove all barriers. Although women who had lost their status and that of their children the Act were reinstated, resource-strapped bands have refused them membership and residence for political and economic reasons. Moreover, despite reinstatement, C-31 women could not pass on full status to their children; accordingly, if the offspring of a C-31 woman married a non-status person, the status of any resulting children would lapse because of successive out-marriage (Mann, 2005). (An amendment to Section 6 of the 2009 *Indian Act* overturned this discriminatory bias.) The effects of this loss of status and lack of rights are incalculable.

> Aboriginal women do not enjoy the same rights as Aboriginal men with respect to passing their Indian status to their children and grandchildren. Nor do Aboriginal women living on reserves enjoy the same rights to the division of matrimonial property as their Aboriginal and

non-Aboriginal counterparts who live off reserve. This discriminatory treatment of Aboriginal women at law affects their enjoyment—and the enjoyment of their children and grandchildren—of their right to culture, ancestral lands, the benefits of land claims, and other social and economic benefits provided to Indians. (CFAFIA, 2008:10)

And yet, despite success at the legislative front (for example, passage of *The Family Homes on Reserves and Matrimonial Interests or Rights Act*, which came into effect in late 2013), efforts by aboriginal women to remove blatant forms of discrimination encounter resistance on the grounds that tampering with the status quo is both disruptive and disloyal (Weaver, 1993a). Consider the controversy generated over the Kahnawake Band Council's "marry out, get out" ruling based on a 1981 membership law which stipulates that any Mohawk forfeits their rights (to residence, local elections, and band services) if they marry a non-aboriginal, justified on the grounds that an influx of outsiders could scuttle limited resources and erode Mohawk culture (Curtis, 2015). The controversy pits federal authorities versus Mohawk Band Council (each of whom argue that they have the right to determine membership), group rights of the Mohawk versus individual rights as set out in the Charter, and aboriginal rights versus non-aboriginal citizenship rights.

Both formal studies and personal testimonies indicate that aboriginal women rank among the most severely disadvantaged people in Canada (Mann, 2005; Native Women's Association of Canada, 2004). Aboriginal women are known to experience a double oppression: As Aboriginal peoples who happen to be women, they must confront the foundational bias that governs the constitutional order of a capitalist and patriarchal society. As women who happen to be aboriginal, they suffer from repressive practices because of the *Indian Act* and Canada's colonialist project. Economically, in terms of income levels and employment options, they are generally less well off than both non-aboriginal women and aboriginal men; as a result, the feminization of poverty bites deeply, especially for lone-parent aboriginal women in cities (Monture, 2004; Wallis & Kwok, 2008). Social hardships for aboriginal women are staggering in scope, with reports of abusive male family members, sexual assaults and rapes, inadequate and overcrowded housing, squalid living conditions, unhealthy child-raising environments, and alcohol and drug abuse. For many, jails have evolved into a second home. A Justice Department report found that aboriginal women may constitute about 4 percent of women in Canada, yet they represent 40 percent of women in the provincial and federal prisons. The near doubling of the incarceration rate over the past decade is not necessarily the result of more aboriginal offending. It's quite possible that aboriginal women are more likely to be charged, arrested, and incarcerated since they lack the financial resources to properly navigate the legal system. In that violence against aboriginal women remains a persistent and pervasive problem within society at large and households in particular, the prospect of healthy aboriginal communities in the foreseeable future does not look promising.

Immigrant and Refugee Women

Gender is a key variable in analyzing international migration (Fleras, 2014b; Piper, 2008). Immigration laws and policies affect women and men differently, resulting in both gendered patterns of immigration and gendered outcomes. Modes of entry into Canada are bimodal in pattern (Boyd & Pikkov, 2008). Women often enter Canada as wives or dependents of men who sponsor them; they also arrive as autonomous labour migrants, highly skilled professionals, and the undocumented (Khoo et al., 2008). Settlement programs for integrating immigrants into society also affect men and women differently, with corresponding diverse implications for livelihood, rights, and entitlements. Female immigrants encounter a gender-stratified labour market that ignores their credentials and expertise by slotting them into "women's work" (Khoo et al., 2008). Gender intersects with other social categories such as class and race to create complex systems of stratification with their own power dynamics and patterns of exclusion in both the origin (leaving) and destination (entry) societies.

In short, too much of what passes for theorizing regarding immigration and immigrants tended to ignore gender as a key variable (Vickers & de Seve, 2000; Willis & Yeoh, 2000; but see Piper, 2008). In the past, immigrants were assumed to be gender-neutral beings with similar immigration experiences, but recent research has highlighted the gendered basis of Canada's immigration policy with respect to entry requirements, access to skills training and employment, and definitions of family and sponsorship (Boyd, 2006; Citizenship and Immigration Canada, 2010; see also Hyndman, 1999). Immigrant women routinely experience a more sexist reality than do their fathers, husbands, brothers, and sons. The pervasiveness of sexism in the lives of immigrant women is graphically captured by Himani Bannerji (2000) who depicted the fear, anxiety, humiliation, and anger that accompanied her transition into Canada. In the final immigration interview, she faced a white and balding elderly male:

> [H]e asked me—"Do you speak Hindi?" I replied that I understood it very well and spoke it with mistakes. "Can you translate this sentence for me?" he asked, and proceeded to say in Hindi what in English amounts to, "Do you want to fuck with me?" . . . I gripped the edge of my chair and stared at him—silently. His hand was on my passport, the pink slip of my "landing" document lay next to it. Steadying my voice I said, "I don't know Hindi that well." . . . My interview continued.

Immigrant women encounter additional problems because of social class (Bannerji, 2000). They not only find themselves restricted to the lower echelons of the Canadian labour force, including low-paying job ghettos such as manufacturing, service industries, and domestic work, but the employment status for immigrant and religious minority women also reflects lower levels of labour force participation (Reitz, Phan, & Banerjee, 2015). According to Debbie Douglas (2005), executive director of the Ontario Council of Agencies Serving Immigrants and winner of the Social Action and Justice Award, many immigrant women in Toronto work in modern-day equivalents of nineteenth-century sweatshops, including many racialized women of colour who earn slightly more than minimum wage in jobs without union protection, benefits, or security. If undervalued and underpaid work isn't stressful enough, tradition may dictate double duty for women, with outside employment superimposed on maternal and domestic responsibilities that may go underappreciated and unrewarded. Or as sharply put by the *Report of the Ontario Joint Task Force on Immigration and Women*, a Canadian-born woman may have difficulty reconciling the conflicting demands of homemaking and motherhood with paid employment, but immigrant women must face these same problems, in addition to learning a new language and adjusting to a different culture.

For immigrant women, Canada is proving an elusive and illusory destination. Promises and opportunities notwithstanding, they must endure loneliness stemming from isolation (limited language, lack of training opportunities, child-rearing and school-related problems, racial prejudice, underemployment, lack of "Canadian" experience, and limited services to cater to their unique situations). Women are expected to know their place—or else: Actions by women that do not conform to conventional norms or male privileges—although consistent with Canadian normative standards—may be criticized as a betrayal or irresponsible. For the sake of appearances, women will often defer to male authority, even if such deference may inhibit the acquisition of skills for societal success. For those who defy convention or authority, the consequences may prove costly. The family, the community, and the culture are often regarded as bastions of privacy from prying eyes; as a result, those women who go public to authorities with damning information may be shunned, ostracized, or physically punished.

The case of temporary foreign workers in Canada is instructive as a lesson in migrant vulnerability. Migrant labour has become a structural necessity in a neoliberal and just-in-time economy, so that Canada is increasingly reliant on temporary workers as a form of disposable and subservient labour (Fleras, 2014b). The exploitation of migrants as cheap labour to do Canada's "dirty work" applies to men and women; nevertheless, only women are "recruited" for gender-specific jobs pertaining to the sex trade, child rearing, and domestic labour (Macklin, 1999). Nowhere is this more evident than with Canada's Live-in Caregiver Program. This program allows a family to hire a live in caregiver for a minimum of 30 hours per week of care to children under 18 years of age, seniors over 65 years of age, and persons with disabilities—provided of course that no qualified Canadian citizens or permanent residents are available (HRSDC, 2012). The terms of the arrangement obligate caregiver workers to live in their employers' homes without supervision for at least two years (or 3900 hours) over a four-year period. As live-in nannies, they are legally classified as temporary workers and are subject to deportation upon termination of their contract, unless they apply for landed immigrant status. Upon completion of their residency requirement, they can then sponsor children and partners to come to Canada. In 2011, just over 11 000 caregivers and their dependents were granted permanent residency in Canada (Manicom, 2013), while a total of 5033 caregivers were admitted, with most admissions consisting of trained nurses from the Philippines (Atanackovic & Bourgeault, 2013). The number of admissions increased to 8797 in 2013, compared to a high of 13 773 in 2007.

However benign-looking on the surface, the program is not without its darker side. The combination of temporary work permits and the program's "live-in" requirements strips domestic workers of the power to complain about punishing work schedules, unpaid wages (especially for overtime work), and unlawful confinement at the hands of their employers (Diocson, 2005; Stasiulis & Bakan, 1997). Yes, there are labour laws in place for the protection of live-in workers. Yet their vulnerable status as "foreign" and "domestic" workers creates an institutionalized power imbalance whereby they face the risk of overwork and underpay, the possibility of sexual assault, and the threat of deportation. Moreover, labour laws are of marginal value if live-in workers are unable to understand and exercise their rights or to seek redress. Of course, not all domestic workers are exploited; nevertheless, as Audrey Macklin (1999) concludes, the potential for exploitation is bolstered by the combination of unregulated work environments, the constant spectre of expulsion and deportation if they complain, and a perception among employers that they "own" these "indentured" workers.

Refugee women are no less vulnerable. The 1951 Convention on the Status of Refugees clearly defined a refugee as a person who is outside his or her country, who has a well-founded fear of persecution for reasons of race, religion, nationality, political opinion, or group membership, and whom the state is unwilling or unable to protect. Definitions of persecution were typically based on male experiences: A focus on the violation of fundamental freedoms pertaining to expression, association, or conscience emphasized the public domain as the site of persecution. Predictably, then, a refugee was typified as a male political dissident who was jailed or harassed for espousing anti-government views of a repressive regime (Ramirez, 2001). The definition excludes those women's experiences that fall outside conventional (i.e., male) definitions of persecution—even though women and children account for about 80 percent of the world's refugees (Canadian Council for Refugees, 2001). Minimal attention was paid to the fact that refugee women faced not only the risks and dangers that men confronted in flight, resettlement, and exile, but also threats of sexual assault and exploitation (Matsuoka & Sorenson, 1999).

In short, the dangers of flight experienced by women differ from those of men (Status of Women Canada, 2007). Women's experiences of persecution often take place in the "private sphere" of home and community and may include rape, infanticide, genital mutilation, forced abortion, compulsory sterilization, sexual slavery, trafficking in women, and domestic violence (Ramirez, 2001). The evidence that women use in support of their refugee claims may be more difficult to validate or quantify. To its credit, in 1993, Canada became the first country to issue guidelines on female refugee claimants fleeing gender-related persecution, including female genital mutilation. The recognition of gender-based violence is now well established within Canada's refugee determination system.

Finally, "trafficking" in women remains big business, although reliable statistics are difficult to access; after all, human trafficking is, by definition, a clandestine operation with few victims and survivors willing to come forward and testify for fear of retaliation or embarrassment; or, alternatively, they lack an understanding of what is going on (US Department of State, 2014). On the basis of mainly open source information, the International Labour Organization (ILO) estimates that 21 million persons globally are thought to be victims of human trafficking and involuntary servitude from slavery to debt bondage (cited in United Nations Office on Drugs and Crime [UNODC], 2012). **Human trafficking** may be defined as the use of coercion or deception to recruit a person in order to exploit them against their will for sexual purposes or forced labour. According to the UNODC (2012), 58 percent of all worldwide trafficking is for the purpose of sexual exploitation, while trafficking for forced labour accounts for 36 percent. Women and girls are believed to account for up to 75 percent of all trafficked victims and survivors. And while 132 countries and territories have criminalized trafficking laws in line with UN protocols, the number of convictions remains low, with 16 percent of jurisdictions without a single conviction between 2007 and 2010 (UNODC, 2012).

EXPLAINING GENDERED INEQUALITY: OVERLAPPING, INTERSECTING, AND INTERLOCKING

How do we account for gendered inequalities? Are they the result of innate differences or social conditioning? Does the blame lie with the structures of society or with the discipline of the market? Do we blame the victim or blame the system? Sociological theories emphasize the social and the structural as key explanatory variables. Of those social variables most responsible for gendered inequality, the most relevant hierarchies of exclusion are race, ethnicity, (including aboriginality), class, and gender. In the analytical language of sociologists, these social categories constitute "variables" that impact differently on minority women. Admittedly, these identity markers may be treated as analytically distinct for purposes of analysis; nevertheless, their conceptualization as interlocking and mutually reinforcing social categories is increasingly central to social analysis (Jiwani, 2006; Signs, 2013). Each of these social categories of identity interacts with the others to construct a complex set of interlocking and overlapping patterns of domination and control whose cumulative impact creates a multiplier effect that amplifies the exclusion or exploitation (Devine, Savage, Scott, & Crompton, 2005). As Pragna Patel notes,

> The idea of "intersectionality" seeks to capture both the structural and dynamic consequences of the interaction between two or more forms of discrimination or systems of subordination. It specifically addresses the manner in which racism, patriarchy, economic disadvantages and other discriminatory systems contribute to create layers of inequality that structures the relative positions of women and men, races and other groups. Moreover, it addresses the way that specific acts and policies create burdens that flow along these intersecting axes contributing actively to create a dynamic of disempowerment. (as cited in United Nations, 2010:42)

Theoretical efforts to understand race, ethnic, and aboriginal relations increasingly acknowledge the intersectionality of social categories involving race, class, gender, and ethnicity (Aylward, 2009; Signs, 2013; Zinn, Hondagneu-Sotelo, & Messner, 2011). According to Daiva Stasiulis (1999), feminist intersectional analysis demonstrates how the inequalities of exclusions are "*multiply, simultaneously, and interactively* determined by various significant *axes of social organization*" (p. 347). An **intersectional analysis** goes beyond an additive model approach that (a) sees race and ethnicity as fixed and static, (b) ignores diversity within groups, and (c) glosses over the interactive elements of devalued identities. Intersectional analysis proposes a theoretical framework that incorporates the inseparability and simultaneity of race, ethnicity, class, aboriginality, and gender as interlocking and overlapping axes of inequality, while acknowledging how the impact of one particular source of subordination will be intensified when interposed with other subordinating sources (Denis, 2008; Johnson et al., 2012; Penner & Saperstein, 2013). An intersectional analysis thus provides an alternative analysis to (1) the reductionist tendencies that characterize Marxist/socialist thought (which emphasizes the centrality of class relations in shaping dynamics and outcomes); (2) feminist thought that posits the "categorical hegemony" of gender as pivotal in explaining patterns of power and privilege over time and across space; and (3) anti-racist thought that "privileges" race and racism as the bane of minority women's existence (Stasiulis, 1999).

Clearly, then, there is much value in promoting the multiple, interactive, and concurrent experiences of race, class, and gender as intersecting systems of privilege or inequality rather than as discrete categories that stand in a mechanistic relationship to each other (United Nations, 2010). The centrality of social location is integral to an intersectional analysis (Rajiva & Batacharya, 2010); that is, where minority women are socially located in society with respect to race, ethnicity, aboriginality, and class will profoundly influence their identities and experiences, opportunities, and outcomes. Predictably, then, minoritized women experience reality differently from white women, because they are differently located in terms of how race intersects with gender, ethnicity, and class (also age and sexual orientation) to create interlocking and overlapping hierarchies of inequality that intensify patterns of exclusion or exploitation. Similarly, minority women experience reality differently from minority men, because they are differently located in terms of how gender intersects with race, ethnicity, and class to create overlapping and interlocking hierarchies of inequality that intensify exploitation and exclusion.

Finally, there are also patterns of intersectionality within the intersections. That is, rather than treating gender minorities as a singular category, emphasis must focus on the reality of differences-within-differences within the gender minority category. Aboriginal women, immigrant and refugee women, and racialized women of colour experience reality differently because *each* is differently located with respect to how race, ethnicity, and class intersect with gender to deny and exclude. For example, Muslim women confront dilemmas that other minority women do not because of their appearance and their placement as the "other" caught between their suspicions of the West and the criminalization of extremists. Aboriginal women confront a legacy of colonialism as a major barrier within both their communities and Canadian society at large. In short, there is much value in acknowledging the complexity of intersecting and intrasecting realities for minority women—especially when it comes to violence.

Violence and Visibility: Intersectionality at Work

Violence against women remains a social problem of grisly proportions in Canada and abroad (Black et al., 2011; LSC 2015; McInturff, 2013; RCMP, 2014; Statistics Canada, 2006b; True, 2012; Turpel-Lafond, 2014; United Nations, 2010). Women worldwide between the ages of 15 and 44 are more likely to die or be maimed by male violence (hence the expression, "femicide") than to succumb to cancer, malaria, war, and traffic accidents combined (Kristof, 2013). It is estimated that about one-third of women around the world have been physically or sexually assaulted at some point in their lives by a current or former partner according to the World Health Organization (2013). Rates of assault range from 23 percent of women in North America to 37 percent in Africa, the Middle East, and South East Asia. Another World Health Organization (2012) study concluded that domestic and sexual violence afflicts up to 70 percent of women aged 15 to 49, with most countries falling into the 29% to 62% range (see also UN News, 2015). In Canada, police-reported data indicate that 173 600 women aged 15 and older were violent crime victims, resulting in a rate of 1 207 per 100 000 women in the Canadian population—a slightly higher level than the rate of violent crime against men (Sinha, 2013; also Perreault, 2011). To be sure, rates of spousal homicide continue to decline, from 16.5 per 1 million spouses in 1974 to four per million spouses in 2007—the lowest ratio in 30 years. Nevertheless, women continue to be four times more likely to be killed by a current or former spouse (Department of Justice, 2012; Canadian Women's Foundation, 2012).

Although violence in general is to be abhorred, its expression in intimate relations is particularly deplorable, in part because it entails ongoing incidents, long-standing relationships, deep emotional attachment, acts of betrayal, and negative effects on innocent victims, such as children (McInturff, 2013b; Sinha, 2012). Violence toward girls and women inflicts devastating consequences. Its persistence and pervasiveness curtails the liberty of women and girls, exploits their unequal status in society, and results in unspeakable harm to lives and life chances (CFAFIA, 2008). Spousal violence is costly, as well. A Justice Canada (2012) report indicated that, of the 50 000 incidents of spousal violence reported to the police, females accounted for 80% of all victims. The cost to Canada is staggering—at least $7.4 billion in 2009, from policing and health care to funerals and lost wages. The cost to women is no less crushing: Colleen Varcoe, the lead investigator for the 2011 Justice Canada study, acknowledged the difficulties of putting a dollar value on intangibles such as victim suffering and pain. Still, she emphasized how victims are susceptible to costly and long-lasting physical disfigurement, emotional pain, psychological distress, and financial consequences.

Minority women in Canada (including aboriginal, immigrant and refugee, and racialized) are particularly vulnerable to violence in their lives (Department of Justice, 2009; Jiwani, 2006; RCMP, 2014). They are violated and abused for many reasons, including (a) a devalued status that legitimizes personalized violence within the community (including exposure to rape and domestic abuse), (b) institutionalized state violence (such as policing) directed at communities, and (c) racism within society at large that interlocks with other systems of exclusion to engender violence in its own right (Jiwani, 2010, 2001; INCITE, 2006). In the case of aboriginal women, the pathway to becoming a missing or murdered female most often includes persistent abuse and neglect (for example, aboriginal children constitute about 8 percent of the children in BC yet more than 50 percent of children in welfare care are aboriginal [Turpel-Lafond, 2014; Report, 2014b]). As well, racialized and immigrant women continually confront racial stereotypes that routinely diminish their status as less than human and undeserving of respect. In addition to concerns shared by all victimized women, immigrant and refugee women must endure the prospect of violence because of their newcomer (and often precarious) status in Canada. The threat of violence is intensified by a lethal combination of financial, legal, language, and cultural exclusions (Smith, 2004).

Racialized minority communities are painfully afflicted. In October 2006, Canada's South Asian community was shocked by reports of six violent incidents in British Columbia and Ontario that left five women dead and another in critical condition (Leong & Mapp, 2006). In some cases, daughters, sisters, and partners were killed for dishonouring the family, community, or religion; in other cases, women were murdered for daring to exercise choices or engage in actions beyond the acceptable range of permissible behaviour. These grotesquely misnamed "honour" killings are anything but honourable. More accurately, these "dishonourable killings" involve the murder of girls or women for daring to "defile" the family's honour through sexual infidelity or refusal to comply with an arranged marriage (Deveaux, 2006). The murder of women also reflects impulses of control and male domination, an obsession with ethnic or religious purity at any cost, and a slavish commitment to outdated templates of gender relations that commodified women as property to be pushed around with relative impunity (Caplan, 2010; Khoday, 2007; Papp, 2010).

In a tragedy that shocked Canadians, Aqsa Parvez, a 16-year-young Muslim woman from Brampton, Ontario, was killed just before Christmas in 2007; her father was charged with and eventually convicted of murder (as were her mother and brother; a similar scenario was tragically played out in the 2009 Shafia killings of three daughters and a first wife by the husband and wife and son—subsequently found guilty in 2012 [Tripp, 2012]). The two had repeatedly clashed over curfews and clothing (especially Aqsa's refusal to wear a traditional headscarf known as a hijab). Reaction to the Aqsa's being murdered for wanting to be normal and fitting in prompted fierce debates over root causes: For some, the young woman's death could be attributed to a *culture clash* between Western and Islamic cultures, with multiculturalism shouldering some of the blame for tolerating such intolerance (hence, criticism of multiculturalism as bad for women [Papp, 2010]). Others preferred to frame it as a *religious issue* involving strict Islamic rules at odds with Canada's liberal and secular values (interestingly, many of the debates over the limits of religious accommodation revolve around the rights and regulation of women [Shachar, 2005], suggesting that a commitment to gender equality may be manipulated as an excuse [or smokescreen] to criticize minorities such as Muslims rather than out of any sense of outrage or commitment to justice). For others, it was best interpreted as an *intergenerational conflict*, often exacerbated within immigrant contexts between rebellious teens and "skittish" parents. For still others, it was about *peer pressure* to conform versus parental pressure to comply (e.g., young South Asian women routinely find themselves living double lives because of the double standards imposed on them by their fathers, brothers, or partners [Handa, 2003]. And yet others saw the issue as one of domestic violence within the context of a patriarchal framework without necessarily excluding the aforementioned factors (see Alcoba, 2007).

Is there a pattern to the indiscriminate killing of aboriginal, racialized, and immigrant women? Can its prevalence and pervasiveness be explained by reference to misogyny (hatred of women [Sheehy, 2010]), or sexism (belief in the inferiority of women), or androcentrism (a tendency to see the world from a male normative standard), or patriarchy (a system designed by, prioritized for, and organized around male interests)? Some believe the source of the problem is rooted in the uncritical relativism of a misguided multicultural commitment that mistakenly tolerates sexist cultural practices by subordinating the universality of women's human and equality rights to the patricentric specifics of a singular culture (Papp, 2010; United Nations, 2010). Others think a political economy model should prevail in which violence is rooted in structural exclusions related to material production and ideological reproduction (True, 2012). Still others see the violence as a spontaneous and arbitrary outburst of male rage. Yet others want to frame it as a strategic component of a broader social framework for collectively controlling women. For some, the murder of women is an extreme manifestation of a more banal violence that women confront on a daily basis in a patriarchal system (Rebick, 2014). For others, women suffer abuse because of gender (sexism) or poverty and powerless (class) or race (racism) or cultural values (ethnicity) within those ethnocultural communities who commit to honour as a core cultural value (Dogan, 2011; Korteweg, & Yurdakul, 2010; Schliesman, 2012). Perhaps the emphasis must focus on how these seemingly independent variables intersect in interlocking ways to exponentially intensify the vulnerability of minority women to violence and victimization. Rajiva and Batacharya (2010:10) frame the murder of Reena Virk along the lines of a multiplier effect:

> As a young South Asian woman, Reena was on the losing end of many of the binaries that secure social hierarchies. She was not just "different" but, rather, inferiorized according to hierarchies that privilege white skin and hairless thin bodies that are unequivocally middle class, heterosexual, and able-bodied; bodies that, in short, conform to the hegemonic definitions of gender and respectability.

The politics of control also come into play. Societal messages routinely convey an impression that men are more important than women and more deserving of power. Such an inequality narrative makes it easier for men to believe they have the right to be in charge and in control over women even if violence is required to exert domination (Canadian Women's Foundation, n.d.). Ambitious and upwardly mobile immigrant women may become targets of domestic violence by tradition-bound males who expect servitude, deference, and submissiveness. This violence would appear to reflect cultural traditions that (1) normalize male abuse of women without necessarily condoning it, (2) naturalize abuse as a male entitlement to dominate, (3) discourage public disclosure for fear of airing "dirty laundry," and (4) so uphold the primacy and tradition of family honour that only death can remove the defilement and restore patriarchal pride.

To be sure, references to "tradition" or "culture" to explain violence against immigrant and racialized women is problematic (United Nations, 2010). Too often this pattern of violence is blamed on some cultural defect in need of an enlightened Western intervention. By contrast, the problem of violence against mainstream women is attributed to disturbed and/ or controlling individuals rather than as structurally embedded or culturally endorsed (Deckha, 2010). As a result, according to Maneesha Deckha of University of Victoria, there is a mainstream tendency to criticize minority cultures as patriarchal and its practices as violent, yet conveniently self-exempt itself from these labels. For example, consider the overheated media hype over the dozen or so honour killings in Canada between 2002 and 2010 (3 between 1954 and 1983, none between 1984 and 2001 [Singh, 2012]), compared to the lukewarm coverage of over 212 spousal deaths in Ontario alone between 2002 and 2007 (Caplan, 2010). Police reported 82 intimate partner homicides across Canada in 2012, according to Statistics Canada, with the vast majority involving a female victim. Mainstream media may frame these killings as domestic homicides, yet this homicidal violence may be motivated by the same twisted logic as honour killings: namely, to dominate and control women perceived as chattel ("property") by aggrieved men with a pathologically inflated sense of entitlement and importance (Khan, 2013). The double standard is unmistakable: Non-western cultures are framed in deterministic and essentialized terms, thereby reducing the problem of domestic violence to a simplistic and singular explanation (a "patriarchal culture") (United Nations, 2010). By contrast, a focus on individual motives to explain actions exempts cultures of the global north from scrutiny and criticism.

Immigrant and racialized women remain the "hushed-over" victims of violence. Many may not know that spousal abuse is a crime in Canada, where they can go for help (if you can't speak English, how can you dial 911?), or they may fear deportation if they complain (United Nations, 2010). The experience of domestic abuse is painfully intensified because of loneliness, dependency, homesickness, lack of knowledge of English or access to services, and the threat of social ostracism. As Ekuwa Smith (2004) writes:

> These women can be incredibly isolated in an unfamiliar environment where there seems to be no safe place, not even at home. The loss of traditional supports of extended family, friends, and advisors from their home country of origin weighs heavily on some of these women and compounds their isolation. Some wives have never experienced abuse until they come here, when the trauma of adjusting economically and socially to the new country disrupts family life.

However useful as a stop-gap measure for victims of domestic violence, many shelters are neither equipped nor prepared to provide culturally sensitive services, nor do they have the commitment or resources to get to the root of the problem. No less daunting in looking for help is a victim's wariness toward the criminal justice system, especially when involvement may prove as traumatizing as what triggered the response in the first place. Women may then be re-victimized (or re-traumatized) by the very system they turn to for help. Finally, even escaping from abusive relations may not prove a panacea. The dearth of job prospects because of prejudicial attitudes and institutional barriers—not to mention the loneliness and estrangement—further intensifies the prospect of yet more poverty and isolation.

No one is suggesting that domestic violence is more prevalent in immigrant communities. Abuse and violence are about power, and the abuse of power is displayed across all cultures and groups regardless of ethnicity, race, or class. But domestic abuse impacts immigrant women differently because of the unique social location they occupy in a Canada that that is largely unfamiliar to them (United Nations, 2010). Without access to knowledge or resources, few options for escape exist; moreover, alternatives often lead to more shame, physical retaliation, and isolation. The cumulative effect of such a patricentric bias becomes even more punitive when escaping an abusive relationship, especially if friends, relatives, priests/ministers, and others exert additional pressure to stay put. Foreign-born women are told to "learn to deal with it and make sacrifices." Mindful of less-than-viable alternatives, immigrant women and their children stay in abusive relationships for protracted periods of time, resulting in more mental health and physical injury issues (Alaggia, Regehr, & Rishchynski, 2009).

Class matters, too: Immigrant and racialized minority women often occupy a socioeconomic/ class status below that of white women. Lower class status is not necessarily indicative of greater victimization, but minority women confront a doubly articulated class hierarchy— one based on their subordinate status within their communities in addition to their subdominant status in society at large (see Jiwani, 2006). Thus, violence against minority women reflects their unequal status in society together with the abuse of power by those in control. Their ghettoization in dangerous and low-paying jobs—including that of prostitution and other sex work activity—may expose them to greater danger in the workplace. Certain occupations are also more vulnerable to violence, including foreign domestic workers secluded in private homes, without recourse or relief, and threatened with deportation if they complain of abuse (Statistics Canada, 2006b).

Paradoxically, what is most "striking" may be the class status of those who perpetuate the violence. Foreign-born males are victims as well. Those males who migrate to Canada may come from global regions where abuse of women may be formally forbidden but often tolerated in practice. The possible persistence of such practices in Canada should not be casually dismissed. In addition, the stress of making a "go of it" in a decidedly difficult labour market may intensify conditions that incite yet more violence. Males who once wielded economic power and political clout in their homeland now find themselves marginalized and ignored—even emasculated. Making matters worse are those humiliations and disappointments resulting from under/unemployment or loss of domestic authority. That makes it imperative to understand how the challenge of eradicating violence must begin by understanding logic behind the twisted beliefs and constraints of the perpetrators (see African Canadian Legal Clinic, 2006).

The gender-based violence experienced by immigrant and racialized minority women within their communities is compounded by the institutionalized racism and sexism they encounter on a daily basis (Jiwani, 2006). But just as none of the variables in isolation (gender, race, class, age, or ethnicity) can explain what happened to Aqsa Parvez or

Reena Virk or Helen Betty Osborne, so too is it impossible to isolate a single factor to account for the pervasiveness of violence toward aboriginal and minority women. Violence against minority women involves multiple oppressions sustained by gendered power relations along varying axes of social difference (United Nations, 2010). Gender intersects with the variables of class, ethnicity, and race to create complex and interlocking systems of vulnerability that renders women more susceptible to harm (Piper, 2008). With race, women of colour and aboriginal women are targets of violence by virtue of their visibility. The often impoverished and disempowered class status of racialized and minority women draws them as pawns into high-risk occupations. The realities, rights, and experiences of immigrant and racialized minority women may be further compromised by a multiculturally-inspired commitment to the principle of culturalism: A (mistaken) belief that the integrity of cultural communities and their attendant beliefs and values must be protected and promoted at all costs, regardless of the harm or exclusion inflicted on the more vulnerable members of that community (Phillips, 2007; United Nations, 2010).

In short, the interplay of these factors demonstrates the importance of contextualizing violence along structural and situational lines rather than as individual pathologies. The image of cascading disadvantages is helpful in attending to how those already vulnerable along several fronts tend to experience yet more disadvantages (see also Shkilnyk, 1985). Emphasis must focus on those factors (variables) that expose the vulnerability of minority women to different forms of violence (because of gender, race, ethnicity, and class). The interplay of these dimensions also underscores the explanatory value of both an intersectional and intrasectional analysis in exposing violence and oppression toward racialized and immigrant minority women. A commitment to intrasectionality acknowledges the existence of differences-within-differences. Aboriginal women, immigrant and refugee women, and racialized women of colour tend to experience reality differently because each is differently located with respect to how identity markers (race, ethnicity, and class) intersect with gender to create a multiplier effect. For aboriginal women, gender intersects with race, class, and colonization to intensify exposure to violence and abuse (Jackson, 1999). For racialized women of colour, their gender intersects differently with race, ethnicity, and class to generate different patterns of violence (Rajiva & Batacharya, 2010). For immigrants and refugees, gender intersects still differently with race, ethnicity, and class to amplify patterns and potencies of violence. To ignore these differences-within-difference and the need to differently accommodate these diverse differences is to invisibilize and normalize the violence implicit in racism and sexism (Jiwani, 2006).

DEBATE REVISITED

Criminality or Sociology?

Responses vary in reaction to who or what is responsible for the national crisis of murdered and missing aboriginal women. To date, much of the debate over aboriginal women and girls who are disproportionately abducted, assaulted, and killed tends to fall into one of two camps: the recent Harper government's assessment of the situation ("It's a crime, stupid") versus those who "commit to sociology ('It's a sociological phenomenon')." The Harper government argued that violence toward aboriginal women is a crime (or a series of crimes) best addressed through the interventions of the criminal justice system. The government also rejected calls for a national public inquiry, pointing to the existence of numerous studies on violence toward aboriginal women and girls so that this is no time to "commit sociology" (as Harper opined in the spring of 2013) (LSC, 2015). Those critical of this position believe that the Harper government was reluctant to commit sociology or launch a national inquiry for fear of exposing Canada's complicity or indifference in creating and sustaining conditions that increase the likelihood of violence toward aboriginal women. The government's neoliberal agenda was also inconsistent with any sociology-based explanatory framework preferring, instead, to individualize responsibility and sidestep any proactive intervention beyond a criminal justice response (Singh, 2014).

In opposition to Harper's position, others have argued that the issue is deeply sociological, insofar as all crime is social, and must be situated within a broader context that acknowledges root causes (LSC, 2015; Singh, 2014). A sociological lens on crime advances the concept of a sociological imagination, one that links personal experiences (or troubles) to the wider society. That is, a single homicide may be interpreted as an individual and random act, although even individualized actions do not occur in a void. Nearly 1200 homicides constitute a public concern whose causal factors are societal and require a sociological explanation since, as Durkheim once noted, only a social fact can explain another social phenomenon. The overrepresentation of aboriginal women as victims of violence and homicide indicates a problem whose causes are structurally embedded in ongoing colonialism, institutionalized racism, and systemic biases (Monture-Angus, 2003; Jackson, 1999; Turpel-Lafond, 2014). Their vulnerability to exploitation and victimization both within and outside their communities is reinforced by their socioeconomic marginalization; a coercive assimilation including residential schools that disrupted gender relations and cultural identity; and a host of debilitating factors including abusive male family members, sexual assaults and rapes, inadequate/overcrowded housing, squalid living conditions, unhealthy child-raising environments, and alcohol and drug abuse. The pathways toward violent victimization most often include early childhood abuse and chronic neglect. The internalization of these pressures too often results in depression and self-hatred among aboriginal women which, in turn, is reflected in high rates of suicide, alcohol dependency, and child neglect. In addition, as Christine Welsh (2006) contends in her moving documentary, *Finding Dawn*, the tragedy of murdered and missing aboriginal women persists because of (a) societal and institutional indifference to those who are poor, aboriginal, and work in high-risk occupations, (b) a belief by predators that nobody will miss the weakest and most vulnerable

(Continued)

members of society, (c) a perception they are easy targets because of their over-involvement in the sex trade, and (d) a worldwide culture of impunity that allows perpetrators of gender violence to literally get away with murder.

Paradoxically, the criminal justice system itself is a contributing factor, given an indifferent court system to discriminatory policing. Police officers are known to be guilty of failing to provide appropriate protection or, worse still, to be complicit in committing sexual assault against aboriginal women because some officers use their authority inappropriately in the mistreatment of aboriginal women (Price, 2012). The Human Rights Watch Report (2013) drew attention to how the RCMP proved neglectful and unresponsive to concerns of aboriginal women, and, in some cases, were abusive to the point of assault and excessive force. And because aboriginal women have nowhere to turn for protection, they live in a constant state of insecurity and fear, especially when they endure domestic and community violence on the one hand yet confront police indifference or mistreatment on the other. Lastly, the courts remain lax in their application of the Gladue principle of finding alternatives to sentence or by taking aboriginality into account when sentencing (NWAC, 2011). In this sense, the national crisis of missing and murdered aboriginal women is indeed a crime, but a crime perpetuated by the criminal justice system. And while it may be true that aboriginal men are the dominant perpetrators in violating aboriginal women, their actions do materialize in a social vacuum but must be contextualized against the broader framework of colonialism, systemic genocide, aggressive assimilation, the *Indian Act*, the residential school system, forced relocations, and loss of identity and culture.

In short, crime itself is sociological since the link between criminality and social inequality is widely accepted (Fleras, 2016; Singh, 2014). Economic and social marginalization adversely affects aboriginal women by rendering them more susceptible to violence and less capable of escaping violent circumstances (LSC, 2015). Put bluntly, the only way to stem the violence against aboriginal women must target the root causes rather than simply crime fighting (LSC, 2015). The Inter-American Commission on Human Rights (2014) has confirmed Canada's legal obligation to prevent violence—in accordance with established principles of international law—by addressing the institutional and structural inequalities (poverty, housing, education, employment) that confront aboriginal women and girls. But as many have implored and as the film, *Finding Dawn* (Welsh, 2006), movingly entreats, women can march and demonstrate to bring about systemic change, but it is men who must do the changing. That, in turn, reinforces the importance of delving into the root causes that animate male violence—as well as into those feasibility factors that propel aboriginal women into risky behaviour. A discursive shift that acknowledges the sociological dimensions of violence and crime is reason enough to justify a national commission of inquiry and a national action plan that addresses the crisis of missing and murdered aboriginal women and girls.

Chapter Highlights

- Both minority women and men tend to be exploited or excluded because of race, ethnicity, or class. Minority women are additionally handicapped because of gender discrimination.
- Two principles underpin this chapter on gendered diversity: First, race, ethnic, and aboriginal relations are ultimately gendered relations; second, gendered relations are relationships of inequality.
- Aboriginal women, racialized women of colour, and immigrant and refugee women face similar issues, but the particular ways in which these issues are refracted through the prism of race, ethnicity, and class tend to amplify their effects.
- Gendered inequality is experienced differently by aboriginal women, racialized women of colour, and immigrant and refugee women because of the different demands imposed by their specific location in society.
- Intersectional analysis involves the notion that gender is superimposed on and intersects with race, ethnicity, and class to create interlocking and overlapping hierarchies of privilege/disprivilege.
- Minority women experience violence differently because gender for aboriginal women, racialized women of colour, and immigrant and refugee women intrasects differently with race, class, and ethnicity to create different patterns and outcomes.

Review Questions

1. The concept of minority women includes Aboriginal women, racialized women of colour, and immigrant and refugee women. Compare the different experiences, concerns, and aspirations of each of these differently located women.

2. The concepts of race, aboriginality, gender, and class are widely perceived as having a differential impact on minority women. Each of these variables is determining in its own right, yet each intersects with the others to create interlocking patterns of inequality. Taken together, they create systems of gender inequality that have proven difficult to dismantle. Explain by way of an intersectional analysis.

3. Canada is widely regarded as immigration society that abides by the principles of multiculturalism and inclusiveness. Yet immigrant women and racialized women of colour continue to confront patterns of inequality and exclusion. Compare the concepts of misogyny, sexism, androcentrism, and patriarchy as the basis for the unequal treatment of migrant and minority women in Canada.

4. Commit to sociology by discussing the causes that intensify the pattern of violence toward minoritized women in general, aboriginal women in particular.

5. Indicate why the concept "gendered exclusions" is preferred over "gender inequality."

PART 2

Diversities and Difference in a Multicultural Canada: Peoples, Migrants, and Minorities

Canada encompasses a rich tapestry of complex diversities. Over 200 racialized and ethnic groups can be identified in Canada, including descendants of the British and French settlers. Aboriginal peoples are no less internally diverse, with over 600 First Nations groups (excluding Métis and Inuit) who speak 60 different languages (International Working Group on Indigenous Affairs [IWGIA], 2015). Efforts to classify this astonishing array of diversities and difference into a coherent framework have proven perplexing. Who should be included in the framework, and why? Should the focus of any typology be based on commonalities of colour (race) or culture (ethnicity)? Should it focus on shared features reflecting national origins or migration status; or group similarities with respect to who is entitled to what, and why; or general sameness in terms of major challenges and proposed solutions? Or should emphasis be on how different groups see their collective status in society, in addition to their relationship to the Canadian state and other groups in Canada?

Of the many proposals for solving this conceptual impasse, few have met with as much success as a typology that divides Canada's multilayered diversities into a limited number of categories based on commonalities in relational status (Elliott, 1983). *Unequal Relations* follows this format. Canada's racial, ethnic, and aboriginal composition is partitioned into three major "Diversities"—Aboriginal peoples (Indigenous peoples), charter groups (national minorities such as the French-speaking in Quebec), and multicultural minorities (immigrants, descendants of immigrants, and racialized minorities). Each of these major Diversities is associated with a distinctive yet shared set of attributes; each also confronts a host of unique problems because of its constitutional and sociological status in Canadian society; and each is likely to espouse solutions and anticipate outcomes commensurate with its priorities (see also Jenson & Papillon, 2001; Kymlicka, 2001; Roth, 1998). As a result, these Diversity categories can be compared on the basis of the following criteria: (1) constitutional status in society, (2) core problems, (3) proposed solutions, (4) anticipated outcomes, and (5) sociological framework.

The table below clearly demonstrates how Canada's major Diversities differ in terms of who they are, what they want, why they want it, how they propose to get it, and where they hope to end up.

- The politics of aboriginality are inseparable from Aboriginal peoples' constitutional status as the "first peoples" whose occupation on Turtle Island (North America) preceded European colonization. In contrast to immigrant minorities, who voluntarily migrated to Canada and are thus anxious to "get in," Aboriginal peoples were forcibly incorporated into the Canada-building project; accordingly, they are anxious to "get out," primarily by decolonizing their relational status around a postcolonial social contract based on aboriginal models of **self-determining autonomy** over land, identity, and political voice. For Aboriginal peoples, prevailing discourses pertain to issues such as treaty rights, inherent aboriginal rights, land title, self-governance, and sovereignty.

- Multicultural minorities confront a different set of challenges in staking out a place in Canada. They are disinterested in revamping the foundational principles of Canada's constitutional order. Their concerns are directed at "getting in" through the removal of discriminatory barriers to insure inclusive institutions. The central focus for migrants and minorities is captured by the narratives of accommodation, multiculturalism, tolerance, citizenship, and integration (Banting et al., 2007:650).

These broad sets of Diversity claims provide a framework for analyzing race, ethnic, and aboriginal relations as unequal relations. They secure a blueprint for fundamentally different governance structures that not only construct a "complex architecture for Canada-building" (Banting et al., 2007:650), but also transform Canada into a contested

CANADA'S DIVERSITY MODEL: THE TWO MAJOR ETHNICITIES

	Aboriginal Peoples	Multicultural Minorities
Sociological Framework	Forcibly incorporated (colonized)	Voluntary minorities (by migration)
Constitutional Status	Original occupants	Citizens
Core Problem	A broken relationship (Internal colonialism)	Discrimination
Proposed Solution	Repairing the relationship along postcolonial lines	Equity programs/ Multiculturalism
Anticipated Outcome	Power-sharing partnership through aboriginal models of self-determining autonomy	Inclusive society

site of competing interests over valued resources. Exceptions abound in this kind of ideal-typical typology, including anomalous status minorities such as Hutterites and francophones outside of Quebec. However, the goal of any typology is not to replicate reality in its exactitude—after all, the very complexity of reality makes it immune to simplification or reductionism—but to render it intelligible for the purposes of description or analysis. The classification of Canada's ethnicities into the major Diversities solves several problems in one fell swoop. Recurrent themes and prevailing patterns in group behaviour can be foregrounded without lapsing into a welter of detail. Specifics are sacrificed along the way; still, much can be gleaned from exploring the inner logic behind the "bigger picture" instead of getting lost in the minutiae. This "big picture" approach also reinforces a macro-sociological view of society as a dynamic of competitively different groups in ongoing struggles over power, privilege, and property. Finally, acknowledging the different sociological and constitutional status of each major Diversity helps to explain why some ethnicities are more entitled than others in terms of who gets what and why.

Part 2 is organized around this macro-level analysis of Canada as a multilayered and multicultural society of competing groups, opposing agendas, and contested models for living together differently. Chapter 7 explores the politics of Aboriginal peoples—state relations within the context of repairing a broken relationship. It focuses on the tensions between a still colonial Canada and Aboriginal peoples who claim status as political communities with an inherent right to aboriginal models of self-determining autonomy—albeit within the framework of Canadian society. Chapter 8 looks at a variety of concerns that confront immigrant minorities as they cope with the challenges of "getting in," "settling down," "fitting in," and "moving up." Primary attention is given to various issues pertaining to immigrants and immigration, including an overview of current immigration policies, immigration patterns in the past and at present, debates over the pros/benefits and cons/costs of immigration, and insights into the immigrants' experiences in Canada. Particular attention is devoted to the politics of Canada's refugee determination system in light of ongoing changes to tighten the program. Chapter 9 on Canada's official multiculturalism as diversity governance deals more specifically with the politics of institutional inclusiveness in addressing the needs and demands of new and racialized Canadians.

CHAPTER 7

Aboriginal Peoples in Canada: Repairing the Relationship

LEARNING OBJECTIVES

After reading this chapter, you will be able to:

1. Explain and acknowledge the importance of repairing a broken relationship if there is any hope of reconciling settler Canadians with Aboriginal peoples.

2. Demonstrate how and why Canada's *First* peoples are generally *last* on all major socioeconomic indicators.

3. Compare three major models that account for the disenfranchisement of aboriginal individuals and communities.

4. Define the principles of aboriginality, aboriginal title and treaty rights, and aboriginal models of self-determining autonomy as preconditions for relations-repair.

5. Understand why any progress in repairing the relationship is contingent on adopting a postcolonial model of power-sharing partnership.

DEBATE

Canada's "Indian Problem" or Aboriginal Peoples' "Canada Problem"?

Let's situate the status of Canada's Aboriginal (or Indigenous) peoples against a global backdrop. Canada may be perennially ranked by UN measures as one of the world's best places to live. But if Canada's on-reserve peoples are disaggregated from the population at large and assessed independently, according to a human development index, Canada's ranking plummets into the mid-60s range. That Aboriginal peoples live shorter lives in often substandard conditions puts aboriginal communities on par with medium-developing countries, such as Mexico and Thailand. No less disturbing are patterns of aboriginal poverty and powerlessness shockingly inconsistent with Canadian values and its vaunted global reputation. Factor in deplorable levels of violence turned inwards (suicide) and outwards (homicide)—nine of Canada's ten most violent communities are aboriginal, as pointed out by Statistics Canada violent crime index—and what emerges is a toxic cocktail of depression, disarray, and destruction (McMahon, 2014; Reputation Institute, 2012). These and other data are a blistering indictment of Canada's inability to address the so-called "Indian problem" (or perhaps, more accurately, the *"Indians' Canada problem"*). To add insult to injury, various human rights committees, including the UN special rapporteur for indigenous rights, have roundly criticized Canada's mistreatment of Aboriginal peoples as a hidden shame; as contrary to international law; and as its most egregious human rights violation (Anaya, 2014; Fontaine & Farber, 2013; Olson, 2013). Despite this condemnation at international levels, national surveys indicate any commitment to improving the standard of living for Aboriginal peoples hovers near the bottom of Canada's national agenda (IWGIA, 2015; Nanos, 2012). The irony is unmistakable: As John Ralston Saul (2014) argues in his book, *The Comeback,* the growing power and prosperity of Canada's Aboriginal peoples is offset by the current government's Victorian-era mentality towards aboriginal affairs and the appropriation of indigenous lands in advancing economic interests.

The impoverishment and disempowerment that wracks aboriginal communities is a scathing critique of the status quo (Manuel & Derrickson, 2015). Aboriginal peoples tend to score poorly on those indicators that positively count, including income, education, and employment levels, but soar on the negativity index; namely, safe housing, clean water and sanitation facilities, and health outcomes—with few indications of immediate improvements. To be sure, there are risks in fixating on Aboriginal peoples only as "problem people" who have or create problems. Framing Aboriginal peoples as "troublesome constituents" tends to gloss over the broader context of colonization and its ongoing legacy for many aboriginal communities. Moving beyond such a frame raises questions about what are the causes behind the so-called "Indian problems," why do these inequalities of exclusion persist, who is responsible, what are the proposed solutions, and what are the anticipated outcomes, as follows:

1. What is the root cause of problems within Aboriginal communities— individuals (blaming the victim), society (blaming the system), or the context (blame the situation)? Too much external pressure (assimilation) or not enough of it (too much separation or special treatment), or too much of the wrong assimilation yet not enough of the right assimilation? Some believe that Aboriginal peoples have brought inequality on themselves by choosing to live in regions of little employment or on reserves whose traditional economies have been decimated by remoteness and relocation. For others, the legacy and continuing impact of colonialism is thought to be the prime culprit (Palmeter, 2015). For still others, any assessment of who's right or wrong is more complex than a simple either/or position, but entails a both/and evaluation.

2. Who is ultimately responsible for solving these problems? If it's an "Indian problem," responsibility should rest with Aboriginal peoples and communities. If it's a "Canada problem," Canada must take responsibility for taking charge.

(Continued)

If it's a Canada-Indian problem, a commitment to co-responsibility and mutual adjustment should prevail.

3. Should solutions focus on modernizing aboriginal communities by discarding practices inconsistent with contemporary realities ("to become more mainstream")? Or must modernization-induced patterns that lead to dependency and underdevelopment be discarded for more indigenous-controlled levels of self-determining autonomy ("to become less mainstream")? Or does a commitment to accommodation acknowledge the simultaneous value of both "more" and "less" like the mainstream?

4. What should a proposed outcome look like? Should Aboriginal peoples assimilate by becoming individual citizens with the same rights, duties, and obligations as ordinary Canadians? Or should they reinforce their status as "the Nations Within" (Fleras & Elliott, 1992) with corresponding collective and inherent rights to aboriginal models of self-determining autonomy over land, identity, and political representation (Maaka & Fleras, 2005)? Is the best route that of accommodation so that Aboriginal peoples are both citizens yet nations with "citizen-plus" rights (Cairns, 2000)?

In response to these questions and challenges, contradictions and gridlocks abound. And yet there is so little agreement over a crisis so formidable in its reach and depth that few know where to begin (McMahon, 2014). The Debate Revisited box at the end of this chapter provides a principled set of responses to these complex issues and vexing questions.

INTRODUCTION: AN UNSETTLED RELATIONSHIP

Four hundred years of colonial contact has plunged many **Aboriginal peoples** into disarray, destruction, and despair. The largely dysfunctional relationship between the colonizers and the colonized can be crudely captured by this blunt assessment by Duncan Campbell Scott, a Superintendent of Indian Affairs, who proclaimed, "I want to get rid of the Indian problem. . . . Our objective is to continue until there is not a single Indian in Canada that has not been absorbed into the body politic." The colonizers sought to eliminate aboriginal peoples as a distinct population through a process of assimilation into "civilization"—resulting in the "taming" and "caging" of the indigenes that proved every bit as restraining as physical constraints (Churchill, 2004; Porter, 2005). In some cases, government policies deliberately destroyed the viability of aboriginal communities in the relentless quest to divest them of their land, culture, and tribal authority (Carter, 1990; Daschuk, 2013). In other cases, the demise of Aboriginal peoples came about through unobtrusive but equally powerful assimilationist measures, such as education and proselytism. In still other cases, the often unintended consequences of possibly well-intentioned, but ultimately destructive, government policies and programs, such as reserve relocation or the residential school system, have proven equally marginalizing (Miller, 1999; Shkilnyk, 1985; Truth and Reconciliation Commission Report, 2015; also Moseby, 2013).

But times are changing. As recently as 1969, Canada's Aboriginal peoples were poised on the brink of legal extinction because of the assimilationist intent of the government's draft **White Paper**, under then Indian Affairs Minister, Jean Chrétien. Prior to this, aboriginal concerns had focused largely on basic survival strategies, in response to the government's long-standing assimilationist commitments, with most seemingly resigned to life under powerful outside forces beyond their control. But aboriginal protest mobilized in reaction to the White Paper, which many perceived as a pretext for cultural genocide. By the late 1970s, a palpable sense of revolt was mounting because of government waffling over aboriginal issues, a crisis that nearly derailed Trudeau's efforts at repatriating the Constitution. The constitutional entrenchment of aboriginal and treaty rights in 1982 clearly confirmed the ascendant political clout of Aboriginal peoples. A new era dawned when, in 1995, the Liberal government acknowledged the "inherent right" of Canada's Aboriginal peoples to self-government, followed by ratification of the Nisga'a Final Agreement in 2000. But it was the Tsilhqot'in Ruling in mid-2014 that confirmed what the Supreme Court of Canada has repeatedly called for: A reconciliation that entails an interplay of pre-existing aboriginal sovereignty with assumed crown sovereignty, in part because Canada has never proved its legal jurisdiction over Aboriginal peoples' territory. An implicit awareness that Canada is relying on the racist doctrine of discovery to justify its sovereignty and legitimacy and that its national prosperity is built on land unjustly appropriated may yet prove a game-changer in unsettling—and resetting—settler–Aboriginal peoples relations (IWGIA, 2015; also Barker, 2009; Keenan, 2014; Regan, 2011).

One of the major themes in this chapter is the distance travelled by Aboriginal peoples in reclaiming legal and constitutional space (Belanger, 2008; Bird, Land, & Macadam, 2002; Long & Dickason, 2011). Decades of political, legal, and constitutional activism have elevated their status from that of wards of the state to self-determining peoples, from a minority group with needs to a people with rights, and from passive observers on the margins of Canada to robust actors on Canada's political stage with unprecedented power and authority (Saul, 2014; Kino nda niimi Collective, 2014). But another theme in this chapter is less hopeful; namely, the enormous distance that has yet to be traversed before Aboriginal peoples assume their rightful place in Canada. Or, as posed by Australian Aboriginal activist, community leader, and lawyer, Noel Pearson (2014; also Manuel & Derrickson, 2015), is there a proper and rightful place for Canada's original peoples to survive and prosper as distinct nations in the country forged into existence 150 years ago from their ancestral lands? To date, Canadians have been slow in addressing aboriginal demands; even slower in acknowledging their realities as a basis for "living together separately"; and slower still in recognizing the transformative dynamic of aboriginality. They also appear reluctant to recognize the central reality that must inform Aboriginal peoples–Canada relations, namely, the principle of **aboriginality** (or aboriginal difference [Macklem, 2001]). Aboriginal peoples possess inherent and collective rights that not only set them apart from the mainstream in terms of entitlements but also articulate a framework for re-priming their relationship to Canada (see McCaskill, 2012). Yet even when rights are formally recognized, the government retreats behind a "rights ritualism"; that is, embracing the language of human and aboriginal rights without any serious commitment to implementation in the hope of buying time or deflecting international scrutiny (Charlesworth & Larking, 2015). Moreover, the founding assumptions and foundational principles that govern Canada's **constitutional order** are resistant to change because of vested interests and systemic bias; as a result, *conventions that refer to the rules may change, but rules that inform the conventions rarely do.* Not surprisingly, the lived-relationship between Canada and Aboriginal peoples continues to be dictated by the colonialist logic of a predominantly Eurocentric constitutional order, while central authorities predictably resist those claims to land and self-determining autonomy that undermine the authority and legitimacy of the Canadian settler state (Barker, 2009; Douglas & Lenon, 2014).

It is not coincidental, then, that Part 2 begins with an analysis of Canada's First Peoples. The term "first" in First Peoples is not to be taken lightly. The term "Aboriginal" itself refers to the original or "first" occupants of this country (or at least those immediately prior to European contact and conquest [Waldron, 2002]). Their status as original occupants (or more accurately, descendants of the original occupants) secures a moral legitimacy as first among equals in defining who gets what. The term "first" can also be used in a less flattering way. **Aboriginal peoples** are "first" in those social areas that count least (unemployment, under education, suicide, and morbidity rates), but rarely score first in realms that matter most, including wealth, power, and privilege. They may be first as Canada's largest landowners, yet they are last in measures of prosperity (Flanagan, Alcantara, & Le Dressay, 2010). The colonialist structures that thwart aboriginal aspirations have succeeded only too well in ensuring that the "first" are often the "last" (Alfred & Corntassel, 2005). In his report to the Human Rights Council in 2014, James Anaya, UN Special Rapporteur on the Rights of Indigenous peoples, writes to this effect:

> Canada faces a continuing crisis when it comes to the situation of indigenous peoples of the country. The well-being gap between aboriginal and non-aboriginal people in Canada has not narrowed over the past several years, treaty and aboriginal claims remain persistently unresolved, indigenous women and girls remain vulnerable to abuse, and overall there appears to be high levels of distrust among indigenous peoples towards government at both the federal and provincial levels.

However badly treated and maligned, Aboriginal peoples have not stood by as passive and powerless victims (Ashini, 2002; Belanger, 2008; Cannon & Sunseri, 2011; Palmeter, 2015; Maaka & Andersen, 2007; Ominayak & Bianchi, 2002). As human actors with the desire and power to shape destinies (Niezen, 2003; Willow, 2012), many have taken the initiative in recalibrating their relationship to society along innovative lines. The content of this chapter is informed by these "initiatives" for moving forward rather than on the "inertia" of looking back. An awareness that change is overdue but undervalued redoubles the need to focus on Aboriginal peoples–Canada relations in terms of underlying logic, hidden agendas, competing interests, and future outcomes. This chapter neither unfolds as a history nor reads as a description. Nor is it intended to obsess over social problems in aboriginal communities, as if Aboriginal peoples were the sole architects of their misfortune. Rather, the chapter addresses the politics of "aboriginality" ("being aboriginal" as a framework for challenge, resistance, and transformative change) by analyzing the evolving and contested relationship of Aboriginal peoples to Canadian society. The chapter also addresses the challenges of repairing a broken relationship along postcolonial governance lines for living together separately as power-sharing partners.

Two narratives capture the reality of Aboriginal peoples in Canada at present (Fraser, 2004). One tells of the growing recognition of aboriginal rights, court decisions that uphold

Aboriginal peoples' claims to self-determining autonomy, and constitutional changes to the political architecture for framing the relationship (see Abele, 2004). The other narrative speaks of dispossession, disempowerment, degradation, and despair at individual and community levels. In acknowledging the concurrent reality of both narratives, this chapter begins with a brief overview of Aboriginal peoples with respect to their legal/constitutional and socioeconomic status. Canada's Aboriginal policy and programs are shown to have generated as many problems as they set out to solve, partly because of faulty premises that have induced negative outcomes and partly from privileging "national interests" over aboriginal concerns (Shkilnyk, 1985). Those preconditions for renewing the relationship are discussed at three levels of engagement: (1) taking aboriginal difference ("aboriginality") seriously, (2) recognizing aboriginal title and treaty rights, and (3) promoting aboriginal models of self-determining autonomy. The chapter concludes by exploring the politics of constructing a new relationship based on the postcolonial principles of power sharing, partnership, property return, and participation.

A few words of warning to the reader: First, neither of the original authors (Augie Fleras and Jean Leonard Elliott) is of aboriginal ancestry, so we cannot speak from an aboriginal perspective by tapping into aboriginal experiences. Such an outsider status can be a strength or a weakness, but invariably necessitates a certain deftness in approach—if only to avoid the trap of treacly sentimentality, overgeneralization, indignation, or defensiveness (see also Weisberger, 1999). Second, limitations of space cannot be ignored. Indians (as defined by the Constitution and generally registered under the *Indian Act*) are an extremely diverse group of more than 600 First Nations, including 80 nation groups who speak up to 60 different languages, in addition to the Métis and Inuit, each with their own set of priorities and aspirations (IWGIA, 2015). Such diversity makes it impossible to compress into a single chapter the entirety of knowledge about Aboriginal peoples, either in the past or at present. Nor can their diverse concerns be squeezed into a singular position, especially when differences within aboriginal communities may be as striking as differences between non-aboriginal Canadians. Priorities vary widely. The political aspirations of aboriginal "elites" may be widely endorsed in principle within aboriginal communities, but their concerns do not always resonate with more pragmatic local concerns such as raising healthy children and having indoor plumbing (EKOS, 2004). On one side are those willing to work within the system without sacrificing their identity in the process; on the other side are those committed to more "radical" indigenism who will work outside the system until it's transformed along postcolonial lines (Alfred, 2005). Some Aboriginal leaders prefer the language of victimization by focusing on accusations and grievances; others reject this discourse because they eschew any notion of themselves as oppressed or victimized, preferring instead to see themselves as self-sufficient participants in Canadian society (Aboriginal Economic Progress Report, 2015; Louie & Madahbee, 2015). The necessity to be selective reduces our options to a focus on the macro-dimension of Aboriginal realities, namely, the evolving political relationship of Aboriginal peoples with Canada through the prism of a relationship both in disarray yet also under repair.

In short, references to Aboriginal peoples are confined herein to general terms. Such a level of generality increases the risk of glossing over the historical and cultural specifics of different aboriginal communities. Aboriginal peoples constitute an extremely diverse constituency, with numerous tribes of varying size, access to resources, development levels, ecological adaptations, and community health; as well as individual differences based on age, education levels, location, and socioeconomic status (Monture-Angus, 2002). Clearly, then, numerous traps await any discussion dealing with Aboriginal peoples as if they were a relatively homogeneous entity with a shared sense of community and commitment. (To some, even the term "aboriginal" is a misnomer that bureaucratizes and homogenizes differences [Alfred, 2008].) Common sense will dictate that they are as heterogeneous as non-aboriginal Canadians in political outlook, socioeconomic status, and personality types. Readers must insulate themselves against the temptation to impose a uniform explanatory framework across domains of astonishing complexity.

CANADA'S ABORIGINAL PEOPLES: DIVERSITY IN DISTRESS

Indian, Native, Status Indian, Aboriginal, Treaty Indian, Non-treaty Indian, Registered Indian, C-31s, Non-status Indian, Inuit, Métis—about all these different terms have in common is the unilateral manner in which they were imposed on the original inhabitants of Turtle Island, resulting in one of the most arbitrary yet oppressive classifications ever devised by a government to categorize and control (Sawchuk, 1998). Rather than reflecting cultural or historical distinctions, each of these terms describes a legality for political and bureaucratic reasons. Political authorities have reacted accordingly. While the Inuit and on-reserve First Nations possess entitlements and rights, those who live off-reserves and the Métis were perceived—until recently—as having needs rather than specific rights. These divisions not only make it difficult for Aboriginal peoples to speak with one voice; but they are also likely to lead to legal challenges, internal conflicts, intergovernmental disputes, and administrative snafus. Not surprisingly, perhaps, different national organizations have been established to promote the interests of specific Aboriginal peoples, reflect their distinctive world views, and reinforce their historical experiences.

Constitutional Status/Legal Distinctions

Canada's Indigenous peoples are commonly and collectively (and controversially) referred to as Aboriginal peoples. The term "Aboriginal peoples" in the Constitution describes the descendants of the original occupants whose constitutional status can be further subdivided into the categories of Status Indians (or First Nations), Métis, and Inuit. The *Indian Act* of 1876 established the criterion for defining an Indian. This criterion did not reflect the realities of race or culture as much as the principle of patrilineal (on the male side) descent (Sawchuk, 1998). Not until 1951 did the *Indian Act* define an Indian as "a person who, pursuant to the *Indian Act*, is registered as an Indian or entitled to be registered as an Indian." The current definition of "Indian" embraces the rank of "status" or "registered" Indian. The federal government acknowledges responsibility for providing services and programs, albeit only for registered (status) Indians and the Inuit, despite a 2013 Supreme Court ruling that both Metis and non-status Indians qualify as "Indians" under the *Constitution Act* and fall under federal jurisdiction. Status Indians are further divided into treaty versus non-treaty Indians, depending on whether their ancestors signed a treaty with the federal government. Entitlements by status could be offset by loss of status for different reasons. Prior to 1985, aboriginal women who married non-aboriginal men lost their status. With reinstatement of status on the basis of Bill C-31, many have returned to their reserve communities, with full access to housing and services; others, however, have been less fortunate since legal status and band membership and entitlements do not always correspond. In that the Bill C-31 amendment to the *Indian Act* also redefined membership codes (i.e., transmission of status from one generation to the next), several classes of Indians now exist, including (1) those with registered Indian status and band membership, (2) those with registered status but no band membership, (3) those without status but with band membership, and (4) descendants of registered Indians but who are entitled to neither status nor membership (INAC, 2004).

With some exceptions, membership as a status Indian is defined by (1) registration in a general registry in Ottawa, (2) affiliation with one of 633 bands, (3) entitlement to residence on band reserve lands, and (4) jurisdiction under the *Indian Act* (Frideres & Gadacz, 2012). Registered or status Indians can apply for postsecondary tuition support, are entitled to on-reserve social programs such as assisted living and income assistance, are beneficiaries of Non-Insured Health Benefits which cover some prescription medication and health services not covered by the province, do not pay taxes on income earned on-reserve, and are exempt from paying goods and services tax on items purchased on the reserve (Curry & Ha, 2013). Status Indians are associated with one of about 2500 reserves across Canada, ranging in population size from less than a dozen to over 22 000 at the Six Nations Reserve near Brantford, Ontario. But while status Indians may be entitled to live on reserves because of treaties signed with the Crown, about 45 percent reside off-reserve in rural, urban, or remote areas. Finally, responsibility for status Indians rests with the federal government, which allocates around $9 billion per year for programs and administration. The national interests of status Indians are represented by the band chiefs who collectively comprise membership in the Assembly of First Nations.

Non-status Indians constitute a quasi-official category of Aboriginal peoples. Persons of Aboriginal ancestry are classified as non-status if their ancestors failed to register under the *Indian Act*, never signed a treaty with federal authorities, or lost their Indian status in exchange for the right to vote, drink alcohol off the reserve, or (in the case of Aboriginal women prior to 1985) marry a non-Indian. Unlike status Indians, non-status Indians do not qualify for recognition or rights under the *Indian Act*, although Canada's Supreme Court has ruled that they may be defined as "Indian" for purposes of federal entitlements, albeit on a case-by-case basis, thereby removing constitutional uncertainty over jurisdictions. The exact number of non-status Indians is unknown, but estimates range up to 400 000. Non-status Indians do not live on reserves (only status Indians are entitled to reserve life and band entitlements), but are scattered in small towns and large cities across Canada. Despite this formal estrangement from their roots, many non-status Indians continue to self-identify as Aboriginal peoples because of shared affinities. Nevertheless, relationships between non-status and status Indians remain fraught with tension because of competition over limited federal resources. Currently, non-status Indians are represented by the Congress of Aboriginal Peoples.

The second class of Aboriginal peoples, the Métis, constitutes a contested category. Comprising the descendants of mixed European-Aboriginal unions, the Métis peoples initially were defined as those inhabitants of the Red River Settlements in Manitoba who identified with the Métis nation. But reference to the Métis now includes anyone of mixed heritage who is recognized as such or who lives in Métis communities, in effect connoting a hybrid culture that cannot be associated with a particular culture or language but a "cultural, linguistic, and territorial mosaic" with which a population has identified and continues to

evolve (Guimond, Kerr, & Beaujot, 2004; see also Sawchuk, 1998). Such a broad definition of Métis as "mixed race" or hybrid off-shoot of two groups does not sit well with those
who want a strict definition of "Métis-ness" as a basis for advancing political claims along
Indigenous peoples/nationhood lines (Anderson, 2014). Until recently, a lack of judicial
recognition on par with status Indians has undermined their legal authority to negotiate
claims over traditional lands. But the Ontario provincial court has ruled that Métis have the
same right as status Indians to hunt and fish for food without a license (Blackwell, 2000).
The ruling also confirmed the Métis as full-fledged Aboriginal peoples with constitutionally protected rights to self-determining autonomy because of a shared culture, collective
identity, and communal life (Harty & Murphy, 2005). The Métis National Council provides
national representation and a lobby voice for Métis at the federal level.

The Inuit constitute the final category of Aboriginal peoples. They enjoy a special status
and relationship with the federal government, despite never having signed any treaty arrangements or registered under the *Indian Act*. A Supreme Court ruling in 1939 defined the Inuit
as Indians for purposes of federal jurisdiction and entitlements, although the federal government subsequently revised the *Indian Act* to exclude the Inuit (Cudmore, 2001). At local
levels, the Inuit are governed by municipal councils, with various committees to discharge
responsibilities for health and education. Inuit interests at national levels are represented by
the Inuit Tapirisat of Canada (an association of various Inuit leaders). The Inuit have concluded successful land claims settlements with Ottawa for control over their homeland in the
Eastern Arctic. The territory of Nunavut, which came into being in 1999, shows great promise in self-determining growth, but confronts numerous problems, ranging from punishing
rates of suicide to a dearth of employment opportunities outside the government sector.

Socioeconomic Status

No matter how they are evaluated or assessed, Aboriginal peoples as a group cluster near the
bottom of the socioeconomic heap (Cooke & McWhirter, 2010; Frideres & Gadacz, 2012).
Aboriginal communities comprise 92 of Canada's poorest 100 communities based on a
community well-being index (income, housing, employment, and education). (Note:
Aboriginal is capitalized when referring to Aboriginal peoples as a nation, otherwise the
lowercase is employed.) Child poverty is punitively high, according to a report by the Canadian
Centre for Policy Alternatives based on 2006 data (Macdonald & Wilson, 2013). Nearly one
half of status Indian children live in poverty based on one set of poverty measures, including
64 percent of aboriginal children in Manitoba and Saskatchewan (McMahon, 2014),
compared to 27 percent of children from Métis, Inuit, and non-status groups (the report
indicated that 33% of immigrant children and 25% of racialized minority children also
were poor, whereas the overall rate is 12% for children outside all these demographics).
Compounding the poverty problem is the housing situation on many reserves, where basic
standards of amenities are often unmet (e.g., nonexistent sewer outlets and unclean water
connections). For example, in what must amount to a contradiction of baffling proportions,
aboriginal communities across Canada confront a host of water-related problems, despite
Canada's status as one of the world's premier fresh water sources (Beaton, 2013; Mascarenhas,
2012). Remote reserves, such as Marten Falls First Nations, 500 kilometres north of Thunder
Bay, continue to rely on flown-in bottled water since Health Canada imposed a water-boil
advisory *a decade ago* (Angus, 2014). Almost 80 percent of homes on the Six Nations

Reserve near Brantford Ontario have no access to water lines but rely on wells or cisterns, most of which are contaminated because of toxic field runoff or buried contaminated waste (Pecoskie, 2013). The potable water crisis is not exclusive to this locale. About half of Ontario's aboriginal communities remain on a water boil alert, while the federal government confirmed that in 2011, about 75 percent of water systems on aboriginal reserves posed high or medium risk to human health (Health Canada, 2013).

Good health and access to health care services also pose a problem (Allan & Smylie, 2015; Wilk & Cooke, 2015; Wynne & Currie 2011). On-reserve peoples are exposed an array of serious health problems more reminiscent of depressed communities in the global south (McMahon, 2014; Statistics Canada, 2013). Compared to non-aboriginal Canadians, they are more likely to suffer chronic ailments, addiction and substance abuse, higher obesity and diabetes rates, and chronic food shortages. A study of Inuit families in Arctic Quebec found that hunger and food insecurity was so severe that many children were below average height (Pirkle, 2014; Trovato & Romaniuk, 2014). Despite these adverse conditions, many residents are reluctant to abandon reserves for fear of losing band entitlements, resulting in what critics call a "subsidies-to-stay" program whose perverse effects are thought to foster an unhealthy dependency (Fiss, 2004; Flanagan 2001)—for those who rely on social assistance (McMahon, 2014). The lives and life chances of those living off-reserve are also under pressure. Urban aboriginal folk encounter patterns of discrimination in accessing housing, employment, education, and social services that, frankly, pose an embarrassment to a country as bountiful as Canada.

Equally worrying is the ticking demographic time bomb in many aboriginal communities. The combination of a relatively high (albeit declining) birth rate with a youthful population creates uncertainty in divvying up limited reserve resources, such as housing and jobs. The aboriginal population is much younger (average age, 28 years) than the non-aboriginal population (41 years average). Just under 400 000 children are aged 14 and under (or 28% of the total aboriginal population), with less than half (49.6%) living in a domestic arrangement that includes both parents (biological or adoptive), while nearly half of the 30 000 children in Canadian foster care are aboriginal (Johnson, Faille, & Barr, 2013; Métis Nation of Ontario, 2013; Statistics Canada, 2013b). Economic projections do not bode well: The fact that the aboriginal population is relatively younger with fewer educational qualifications and less labour market experience exposes the vulnerability of this demographic to economic slumps and job layoffs (Delic & Abele, 2010). The awkward location of many reserves and their limited resources lowers the prospect of employment or development (see the Attawapiskat Box, below). With rates nearly three times the national average, unemployment is a major cause of poverty and powerlessness. The jobless rate for non-aboriginal Canadians was 6 percent in 2011, whereas the aboriginal unemployment rate stood at 13.0 percent and 22 percent for those living on reserves (DePratto, 2015). In 2011, according to the National Household Survey, the employment rate for non-aboriginal Canadians was 76 percent, whereas the figure for the aboriginal population was 63 percent, but 55 percent for those on reserve (DePratto, 2015; also National Aboriginal Economic Development Board Report, 2015, which pegged on-reserve employment rates at 35.4%). Even these figures are misleading: On some reserves, up to 95 percent of the population are so un- or underemployed that government transfers are primary income sources. The Box below on the crisis in Attawapiskat illustrates the dystopian situation of many aboriginal communities.

Attawapiskat First Nations: "Where Dying in Slow Motion is a Way of Life".

> Attawapiskat is the tip of the iceberg for the numerous Bantustan-style homeland of the far north. Years of chronic underfunding and bureaucratic indifference has created a Haiti north where dying in slow motion on ice-filled shantytowns is considered the norm. (Charlie Angus, 2011)

What comes to mind when you think of aboriginality? For some, the first images consist of those of militant warriors in camouflage fatigues whose disruptive tactics—from armed confrontation to blockades or occupations—are denounced as inconvenient and costly. Both activists and their misguided leaders tend to be labelled as trouble makers with unacceptable agendas and impossible demands. Others prefer to romanticize Aboriginal peoples as eco-mystic tree-huggers whose iconic status as environmental guardians may be laudable but impractical and obstructionist. For still others, a less flattering vision zooms into view. Aboriginal peoples are perceived by some as "problem people" who have or who create social, economic, and cultural problems that cost Canada or inconvenience Canadians. This framing of Aboriginal peoples as troublesome constituents is often conveyed and reinforced by a sensationalist media in search of the negative, conflicting, and the abnormal as newsworthy (Simpson, 2013). However accurate this indictment of the media, there is another perspective (Fleras, 2011b). Both mainstream and social media can work as allies in drawing attention to the abysmal living conditions of Canada's first peoples. The Attawapiskat housing crisis in late 2011 was a case in point. The crisis not only proved a flashpoint for relations between the Harper government and the local community, but the housing crisis that triggered a state of emergency also uncovered the intractability of those structural exclusions in remote aboriginal communities. It also demonstrated how diametrically opposed positions over causes and blame can often induce the equivalent of a paralysis by analysis via turf wars, brinkmanship, and grandstanding.

A humanitarian disaster unfolded in the fly-in community of Attawapiskat First Nations, situated approximately 500 km north of Timmins along the western shores of James Bay. Federal indifference to their pleas for assistance—namely, a severe housing shortage that forced several dozen families into temporary shelters without insulation or plumbing—prompted the 1800 strong community of Mushkegowuk (Cree) peoples to declare a state of emergency (Toulouse, 2011). (This state of emergency was the third in three years, including massive diesel leak and a sewage backup in 2009 [Robson, 2013]). Hardly anyone paid much attention to the calamity-in-the-making until a video of the community's plight went viral in late November (Angus, 2011). Few were unmoved by the spectre of Canadian citizens living under developing world conditions of the global south. Images displayed rampant overcrowding, with people crammed into wood-frame tents heated by oil-drum stoves (a fire hazard), while nearly 90 individuals dwelt in a construction trailer abandoned by a diamond mining company. No less unnerving was the plight of aboriginal Canadians shivering in unheated and decrepit plywood shacks without indoor plumbing (using slop pails for toilets), insulation, or hydro hookups. The convergence of squalid living conditions with the lack of hygiene and sanitary facilities proved catastrophic in intensifying major health problems, ranging from respiratory/gastrointestinal infections and scabies/lice, to mental health issues such as depression and suicide (Brennan, 2011).

Media attention and public discourses accelerated into overdrive with images that showcased neglect, poor management, and the logistics of operating in an isolated northern community. Canada's already declining global image was further sullied by media coverage of the Red Cross supplying generators, insulated sleeping mats, blankets, and clothing for winter survival. If the housing crisis wasn't cringe-worthy enough, Attawapiskat was plunged into state of emergency because of floodwaters and sewer backups that overwhelmed a damage-prone infrastructure, resulting in the evacuation of hospitals and the closure of schools. Outrage was further fuelled by a growing awareness that the situation in Attawapiskat was neither isolated nor anomalous; to the contrary, hundreds of Attawapiskats were strung out in remote regions across Northern Canada (Galloway, 2011). Similar crises prevail on numerous reserves in Northern Manitoba and Northern

Saskatchewan, few of which ever attract attention without a concerted media campaign to incite embarrassment (Scoffield, 2011). The scope of this neglect was mindboggling: About 80 000 new homes are needed across aboriginal Canada; at the current pace of construction, however, it may take up to 800 years to resolve the housing backlog (Carlson, 2011). As well, nearly 50 percent of houses on reserves are substandard, often without running water, toilets, and even electricity. Nevertheless, people continue to live under derelict conditions because they have nowhere else to go.

In short, the wretched state of housing in Attawapiskat should have touched a collective nerve. Sadly, however, debates got sidetracked, in part because politicians and bureaucrats are so averse to being labelled as racist that many refuse to criticize band mismanagement or challenge government policy—or to engage in any straight talk about the problem-solution nexus—on the mistaken assumption that saying nothing equals neutrality while saying something may derail a promising career (Blatchford, 2011; Gunter, 2011). Yet neither white guilt nor political correctness should preclude Canadians from asking some sharp questions about the dysfunctionalities on many aboriginal communities, including Attawapiskat. Of course, there was plenty of finger-pointing blame to go around in manipulating the plight of Attawapiskat for scoring political points, with the very people in need of assistance lost in a welter of mutual recriminations (Beardsley, 2011). In ramping up the rhetoric for electoral gain, opposition

> parties blamed the Harper Govern-
> ment; Stephen Harper blamed poor
> band governance for fiscal impropri-
> ety; the UN blamed a colonialist
> Canadian state for its intransigence;
> aboriginal leaders blamed the
> paternalistic *Indian Act*; critics of
> government policy blamed the reserve
> system (especially in remote locales),
> chronic underfunding, and bureau-
> cratic indifference; and the Canadian
> public didn't know who to blame or
> what to blame because of ignorance,
> confusion, or indifference. Even the
> people of Attawapiskat couldn't agree
> on the who, how, and why behind the
> predicament (Scoffield, 2011; also
> Wagamese, 2011). However inconve-
> nient or awkward, failure to ask (and
> answer) the right questions makes it
> abundantly clear: Canadians will
> again be bombarded next year with
> images and polemics that replay the
> tragedies of Attawapiskat at yet
> another remote and unpronounceable
> dot on the map.

Income inequality poses a problem for those persons disproportionately ranked among the poorest in Canada (Wilson & Macdonald, 2010). According to the 2015 National Aboriginal Economic Development Report, the median income for Aboriginal peoples was $20 701, or 30 percent less than the median income for non-aboriginal Canadians ($30 195). Average incomes in 2010 were no less glaring: $18 586 for on-reserve aboriginals, $30 226 for aboriginals living off-reserve, and $41 052 for non-aboriginals (see Friesen, 2015, for similar patterns in Alberta). In another study that looked at wage growth between 2007 and 2014 (DePratto, 2015), aboriginal males who lived off reserve earned a weekly wage of $973 in 2014, compared to $1024 for non-aboriginal men; off-reserve aboriginal women earned $697 per week compared to $773 for non-aboriginal women. Gender clearly makes a difference: Data from Pendakur and Pendakur (2011b) concluded that income and earning gaps for aboriginal women from 1995 to 2005 was 10 to 20 percent lower than for non-aboriginal women of British origin and controlling for age and education (registered Indian women fared worst, followed by non-status Indian women and Métis women, with Inuit women an exception). For aboriginal men, the income and earning gap was about 20 to 50 percent below the figure for non-aboriginal males of British origin with similar age and education characteristics, but the gap for non-status Indians and Métis men was significantly less (10 to 20% bracket) (Pendakur & Pendakur, 2011b). Despite these earning gaps, persons with aboriginal ancestry (descent) did better income-wise than those who self-reported aboriginal identity or who were registered with Ottawa (Pendakur & Pendakur, 2011b).

Higher education levels matter (Wilson & Macdonald, 2010): In terms of income, for example, only $648 separated those aboriginal persons with university degrees from non-aboriginal Canadians with a BA (although admittedly, there are far fewer aboriginal individuals with degrees. According to Delic & Abele [2010], 43.6 percent of the total aboriginal identity population had less than high school education in 2006, while 5.6 percent possessed a university degree or certificate [but see DePratto, 2015]. By contrast, the comparable figures for the non-aboriginal population stood at 23.5 percent and 18 percent, respectively). Recent evidence points to overall improvement in the number of aboriginal graduates; however, progress on the postsecondary front is slow, with the result being that the achievement gap between aboriginal and non-aboriginal Canadians has widened between 1996 and 2011 (Parkin, 2015). A catch-22 is at play: Attainment of higher education may secure an escape from dire straits (Richards & Scott, 2009), but it is precisely the straitened circumstances of those with low socioeconomic status who are least likely to possess the resources or resourcefulness to capitalize on educational opportunities (Mendelson, 2006).

The interplay of powerlessness and poverty stimulates inner- and outer-directed violence. Domestic abuse is endemic within aboriginal communities, according to Dawn Harvard, President of Ontario Native Women's Association, with many aboriginal women being the victims of extreme violence (Hill, 2012; Legal Strategy Coalition on Violence Against Indigenous Women [LSC], 2015; also Samuelson, 2012). Nearly 21 percent of the population experienced spousal violence compared to 6 percent for non-aboriginal population; not surprisingly, few aboriginal children grow into adulthood without first-hand experience of interpersonal violence (Drost, Crowley, & Schwindt, 1995; Government of Canada, 2010 [see also Chapter 6]). Aboriginal peoples not only suffer trauma-induced injuries and violent deaths at four times the rate in Canada (Picard, 2012), including nearly one quarter of the 516 police-reported homicides in Canada in 2014, but they also represent one of the most self-destructive groups in the world at present, with a suicide rate of six to eight times the national average for age-specific groups. Remote communities are particularly vulnerable to deprivations that speak volumes of lives that are nasty, brutish, and short. In Davis Inlet, Labrador, the Innu suicide rate is the equivalent of 178 per 100 000 of an admittedly small population base, in contrast to the Canadian average of about 11 per 100 000 of population. (The tiny Baltic country of Lithuania has the dubious distinction of ranking first in the world at 35 per 100 000.) Nunavut's suicide rate is 15 times the Canadian average (most involving single, unemployed, and poorly educated men), even though suicides were rare prior to the 1980s (Alexander, 2014). The 1000 member fly-in community of Shamattawa, Manitoba saw four young adults take their lives in the first few months of 2015, in addition to four suicide attempts in only one week in late March (Taylor, 2015). Consider also Pikangikum—a small reserve with just over 2000 residents about 300 kilometres northeast of Winnipeg. Given a rate of 250 per 100 000 in 2011 (note that a small sample can grossly inflate ratios), British suicide expert Colin Sampson has labelled Pikangikum Canada's suicide capital (Patriquin, 2012).

The devastation of suicide goes beyond the immediate family. The entire community is ripped apart by the ripple effect of trauma that can destroy closely knit groups (Patriquin, 2012). Dysfunctional communities often serve as incubators of youth suicides in the absence of those protective factors that mitigate against suicidal tendencies (Chandler & Lalonde, 1998). Studies in Canada and abroad indicate the importance of good governance (including both rule of law and property rights) in creating positive conditions for economic development (Cornell & Kalt, 2003; Flanagan & Beauregard, 2013; MacDonald, 2014). Aboriginal communities with some form of self-government arrangement displayed the lowest suicide rates, followed by communities with settled land claims and educational services. The lack of effective parenting has also contributed to this breakdown in community life. But "bad parenting" itself may reflect earlier negative experiences, ranging from intergenerational poverty cycles to the painful legacy of residential schools. The situation is exacerbated when combined with root factors related to a lack of opportunity, boredom and despair, confused identities, and a dearth of positive role models to assist in meeting life's challenges. A void whose emptiness and ennui is conducive to anti-social behavior is the lot of those aboriginal youth who are trapped between exclusion from mainstream society yet alienated from an idealized version of traditional life—that is, strung between two cultures yet psychologically in neither (Royal Commission on Aboriginal Peoples, 1996a, b). The conclusion is inescapable: Communities that fail to provide boundaries and coping skills are ticking time bombs.

Aboriginal violent crime victimization is of pandemic proportions (Monture, 2011). Aboriginal peoples are victimized at a rate of 319 per 1000 population, including 461/1000 for those in the 15 to 34 age bracket, compared to 101/1000 for non-aboriginal Canadians (Government of Canada, 2010). Of particular concern are shockingly high imprisonment rates: Although just over 4 percent of Canada's population, aboriginal offenders account for up to 22 percent of federal penitentiary admissions and 19 percent of provincial custody admissions (Sapers, 2013). Among female offenders, one in three federally sentenced offenders is aboriginal. Provincial rates for aboriginal women are even more alarming, including 80 percent of admissions in Saskatchewan, despite comprising a small percentage of that province's population (Roberts & Melchers, 2003; Samuelson, 2012). Young aboriginal men aged 12 to 17 represent about 3 percent of the young males in Ontario; yet they account for 15 percent of male admissions to Ontario youth facilities (Sapers, 2013). Not surprisingly, overall aboriginal rates of incarceration are now approaching nine times the national average (Office of the Correctional Investigator, 2009). Worse still, those with prison records may be doubly penalized in the search for post-prison employment (also Alexander, 2012). That on-reserve aboriginal youth are more likely to go to jail than to graduate from high school is a scathing indictment of the exclusions at play. And yet the federal government appears reluctant to invest in programs to rehabilitate federal aboriginal offenders (for example, Correctional Services of Canada employs 19 000 workers, yet only 12 are assigned to work with aboriginal inmates [Sapers, 2013]).

To be sure, these incarceration figures have prompted a response on the judicial front. The Gladue Supreme Court Decision of 1999 ruled that the courts had to take aboriginality into account when sentencing aboriginal offenders, including disadvantaging factors such as colonialism, domestic abuse, dislocation, unemployment, and racism. The federal government's Aboriginal Justice Strategy is also contingent on "doing it differently," such as alternative sentencing strategies informed by the holistic and healing principles of restorative justice. But principles and promises aside, incarceration appears to be the response of first resort in dealing with social problems (Saper, 2013; see also Davis, 1998). The inequalities of exclusion that range from unemployment, poverty, mental illness, substance abuse, and endemic violence are often concealed from (or disappear from) public view when conveniently lumped together under the default category of crime, the automatic linking of criminal behaviour to a marginalized peoples, and the warehousing of "criminals" into prisons. But as Angela Davis (and others such as Alexander, 2012) conclude in response to skyrocketing rates of black imprisonment in the United States (where nearly 2 million people are locked-up in America's private-for-profit prison system, 8 times the number from as recently as 30 years ago, with 70 percent consisting of people of colour—mainly blacks and Native Americans), *"prisons do not disappear problems, they disappear humans."*

Demoralizing data on the socioeconomic front should not distract from more hopeful narratives (Long & Dickason, 2011; Saul, 2014). Not all indicators on the aboriginal front are distress signals; for example, increases in life expectancy for both aboriginal women and men are a promising sign. As well, aboriginal education outcomes based on 2011 Census data (Richards, 2014) indicate that those aged 20 to 24 who identified as Métis and off-reserve aboriginals attained higher rates of secondary school graduation than they did in 2005. According to data from the 2011 National Household Survey, the share of women with post-secondary education was 52.7 percent for non-aboriginal women compared to 35 percent for aboriginal women in general and 42.6 percent for Métis women (DePratto, 2015). (On the downside, despite improvements, the incompletion rate for this demographic is still 3 times higher than for non-aboriginal youth, thus reinforcing a widening achievement gap (Parkin, 2015); for on-reserve aboriginal youth it's 58 percent higher (with provincial variations)—with little improvement since 2006). Nor should all communities be tarred as dysfunctional, despite media coverage to this effect (also Newhouse et al., 2012). For example, whilst many communities experience punishing rates of suicide, those communities with a solid governance structure in place and actively engaged in defending their culture and territory appear relatively immune to the scourge (Alcantara & Whitfield, 2010; Chandler & Lalonde, 1998). Moreover, not all Aboriginal peoples are destined to fail, even when measured by Eurocentric standards. Nor should success be evaluated exclusively along mainstream lines. There is no shortage of aboriginal individuals who possess secure and satisfying prospects and enriched lives without rejecting one or both cultures—as demonstrated in the Spotlight, below.

SPOTLIGHT

Robust Economic Growth in "Indian" Country: Osoyoos Indian Band

Aboriginal communities are not unaccustomed to success stories. Moreover, aboriginal economic growth is impressive and critical to Canada's future prosperity (the National Aboriginal Economic Development Board, 2015; also Newhouse et al., 2012). Aboriginal land base has grown to 3.2 million hectares (a 25% increase since 1990) thanks to the infusion of revenue from successful land claim settlements. As pointed out by lawyer and author Bill Gallagher (2012), aboriginal claimants have won over 150 court case victories involving control or ownership of resources and projects vital to Canada's economic future (also Ivison, 2012). The surge in aboriginal enterprises and entrepreneurs is substantial: From airline companies and construction firms to wineries and technology consulting firms, aboriginal entrepreneurship is thriving like never before, according to Roberta Jamieson, CEO of the National Aboriginal Achievement Foundation (Freeland, 2010). This includes 37 000 aboriginal-owned and operated businesses (First Nations,

(Continued)

Métis, and Inuit) according to the 2006 Census, in addition to 50 financial institutions, and an aboriginal trust company and bank (Grant, 2013). Aboriginal communities increasingly play the role of economic drivers who are cashing in on (a) developments in energy, forestry, and mining resources, and (b) earnings as landlords of on-reserve condos and high-end golf resorts (Coates & Crowley, 2013). In short, Aboriginal peoples have arrived as a natural resource superpower in a Canada that is banking on a resource attraction boom (Crowley & Coates, 2015; Newman, 2015). That kind of clout exerts pressure to establish an equal economic partnership involving power sharing and meaningful partici-pation, in which aboriginal communi-ties benefit from the value created by their involvement and expertise (Crow-ley & Coates, 2013).

The list of success stories includes the Membertou First Nations who employed a strategic approach to economic development and self-government (NCFNG, 2010). But few have achieved the level of accomplish-ment as has the Osoyoos Indian Band. Situated on 32 000 acres of prime real estate in the Okanagan region with a population of about 400, the Osoyoos Indian Band is one of 7 bands that comprise the Okanagan Nation of British Columbia. Under the leadership of Chief Clarence Louie, a commitment to create a community-based eco-nomic self-sufficiency has paid divi-dends through a series of profitable economic projects in agriculture, eco-tourism, and commercial, industrial, and residential buildings. The annual net benefits of $26 million in business revenue and $2.5 million in profits have proven beneficial in eliminating unemployment for the 520 band mem-bers (MacDonald, 2014). Successful business ventures include a multimil-lion dollar expansion of a resort-golf course, a partnership with Vincor (Canada's largest wine producer), and joint ventures with the timber industry. The band operates its own health, social, educational, and municipal services, in addition to businesses that provide financial independence for preserving tradition and culture. Clearly, then, the combination of tools, vision, and commitment, coupled with good governance (from removing mismanagement to instituting sound corporate structures) can translate into sustained economic development and cultural renewal (MacDonald, 2014; NCFNG, 2010).

Urban Experiences

Contrary to a widespread perception, Aboriginal peoples are increasingly city folk. As noted in Chapter 1, about 45 percent of all registered Indians live off-reserve, as do 75 percent of non-status Indians, 71 percent of Métis, and 46 percent of Inuit in rural areas (AANDC, 2013). In 2011, Winnipeg boasted the largest urban Aboriginal population at 78 420 (the highest percentage per total population of all major cities in Canada), while Toronto was fourth at 36 995 (.05% of its population) (AANDC, 2014). Several factors account for this movement. Generally speaking, it reflects a combination of "push" factors (lack of resources, opportunity, or excitement) and "pull" forces related to family, employment, education, lifestyle, and availability of services and amenities (Environics Institute, 2010b). It was once assumed that aboriginal patterns of migration to cities was more circular than linear (Peters, 2004; see also Dosman, 1972), with the promise of urban potential offset by a powerful sense of connection and commitment to communities of origin (Monture-Angus, 2002). But according to an Environics Institute (2010b) study, only 2 in 10 have ever returned to their community of origin or plan to return permanently—thus reinforcing the fact that Aboriginal peoples' sense of place (home) is defined as much by their city of residence as by their community of origin. Finally, the growing critical mass of Aboriginal peoples in cities is not just about numbers. It's also about the distinctive and enduring realities that urban Aboriginal peoples are constructing in terms of social patterns and cultural forms just as authentic and valid as traditional forms (Newhouse & Peters, 2003). Or, as expressed by the project manager for the 2010 Environics Institute study in a news release on the publication:

> When urban Aboriginal peoples are researched, it's often about problems like homelessness and sexual exploitation. There are hundreds and thousands of us living in cities, and there are a lot of interesting things happening in our communities; it's not all crises. (Environics Institute, 2010a)

Too often, Aboriginal peoples in cities are ignored in debates over "who gets what" (Cairns, 2003; Dinsdale, 2009). Reserve communities continue to receive a disproportionate share of the federal funding, despite a rapidly growing urban aboriginal population (Murphy, 2005). The resultant policy void at the centre of Canadian politics (Dinsdale, 2009) ensures that government institutions are poorly equipped (both in terms of resources and needs assessments) to offer culturally sensitive services to aboriginal clients. As a result, aboriginal-run voluntary agencies and friendship centres have been established in urban centres to address a wide range of issues related to healthcare, traditional healing, shelter, education and training, and criminal justice (Abele, 2004; Warry, 2007). These programs incorporate a strong cultural dimension; they also range widely in funding and outreach, from aboriginal head-start incentives to assistance for aboriginal mothers. But jurisdictional wrangles are inevitable: The federal government disclaims any responsibility for providing services to off-reserve Aboriginal peoples, citing jurisdictional wrangles with the provinces as a stumbling block. (The federal government has jurisdiction and responsibility for "Indians and Lands reserved for Indians," while the *Constitution Act* of 1982 allocates responsibility for the provision of social services to the provinces [Dinsdale, 2009].) Needless to say, neither the federal government nor the provinces are anxious to assume more financial responsibilities.

The conclusion is inescapable: The impoverishment that confronts Aboriginal peoples is a blistering indictment of an unequal status quo. An unacceptable number endure punitive conditions that evoke gut-wrenching images of grinding developing-world poverty and the powerlessness of the underclass. The aftermath of the colonialism continues to infuse and distort the lives of Aboriginal peoples who also remain victimized by racism and racial discrimination (Paul, 2012). To be sure, there are risks in framing Aboriginal peoples only as "problem people" who have or create problems of inequality. Framing aboriginality as "troublesome constituents" tends to gloss over the broader context of colonization, its ongoing legacy, and its persistence into and pervasiveness at the present (Coulthard, 2014; Simpson, 2013; Warry, 2009). References to Aboriginal peoples as "problem people" may also reinforce stereotypes (such as blaming the victim) that do little to improve public empathy (Harding, 2010). But a number of questions about the origins, causes, and persistence of aboriginal inequalities must be asked, given that Canada's Aboriginal peoples (as well as the Maori tribes of Aotearoa/New Zealand and the First Australians) showed negligible improvement between 1981 and 2006 at the level of employment, education, and income (Cooke et al., 2014). That these exclusions appear to be structurally based speaks volumes about the need for rethinking and repairing the relationship.

RELATIONS REPAIR: DIFFERENCE, LAND, GOVERNANCE

"The history of indigenous peoples in the modern era is, fundamentally, a story of struggle to overcome the effects of colonization." Taiaiake Alfred and Lana Lowe (2006:4)

Aboriginal peoples do not like to see themselves as a social problem. Without denying the many challenges that confront aboriginal communities, they contend that material poverty is not necessarily responsible for their marginalization. The powerlessness associated with (neo-)colonization and the denial of aboriginal rights is just as problematic (Adams, 1999). Equally demoralizing are stereotypes that portray Aboriginal peoples as hopeless welfare dependents or helpless slaves of customs, whose cultures preclude a secure and satisfying coexistence in Canadian society. Contrary to popular perception, Aboriginal peoples have struggled to halt the vicious cycle of exclusion and demeaning clientelism that has historically entrapped them. Collectively and individually, they have explored ways to survive by asserting control over their lives (Willow, 2012). They reject those political and social arrangements that once colonized and controlled, proposing, instead, innovative arrangements that not only advance aboriginal interests but also challenge and transform those colonial principles that govern Canada's constitutional order (Maaka & Fleras, 2005). In other words, it is not a case of solving the "Indian problem," but one of fixing a broken relationship. Three key planks secure a platform for renewing the relationship along postcolonial lines: (1) taking aboriginality ("aboriginal difference") seriously, (2) promoting self-determining autonomy through aboriginal models of self-governance, and (3) acknowledging aboriginal title and treaty rights by way of specific and comprehensive claims.

Taking Aboriginal Difference ("Aboriginality") Seriously

Aboriginal peoples define themselves as different and deserving of differential status and treatment (Macklem, 2001). They categorically reject the view of themselves as Canadian citizens who happen to live on reserves. Nor do they approve of being labelled as just another ethnic or immigrant minority. In contrast to immigrants, who voluntarily chose to be part of Canada, Aboriginal peoples were forcibly incorporated into the Canada-building project and now want to "get out" by reconfiguring their relational status. They claim to be a *de facto* sovereign political community (peoples) whose inherent and collective rights to self-government (nationhood) are guaranteed—not because of need, disadvantage, or compensation—but by virtue of aboriginality as principle and their rights as Aboriginal peoples. As the original occupants, whose inalienable rights have never been extinguished by treaty or conquest, Aboriginal peoples do not seek sovereignty *per se*. Rather, they *are* sovereign because of ancestral occupation; in turn, they *have* sovereignty because of aboriginal and treaty rights. All that is required are appropriate arrangements to put this principle into practice for purposes of recognition, reward, and relationships.

The centrality of **Aboriginal (peoples') rights** underpins the notion of aboriginal difference (Alfred, 2005; Belanger, 2008; D. Turner, 2006). According to Canadian law, the concept of aboriginal rights protects pre-contact activities; that is, the activity in question must have continuity with an activity that was integral to traditional aboriginal culture and society (R. v. Van der Peet, (1996) 2 S.C.R., 507). Aboriginal rights encompass those activities and entitlements that ensure their survival as peoples, including the right to ownership of land and resources; the right to protect and promote language, culture, and identity; the right to political voice and self-governance; and the right to aboriginal models of self-determination (McKee, 1996). The rights of Aboriginal peoples are regarded as *sui generis*, that is, they differ from ordinary citizenship rights by virtue of Aboriginal peoples' status as the original occupants (Borrows & Rotman, 1997) of the land. These *sui generis* rights are collective and inherent: *collective* in that Aboriginal communities can exercise jurisdiction over the individual rights of members of these communities; *inherent* in that they are not delegated by government decree but are intrinsic to Aboriginal peoples because of first principles, reflecting either natural law or spiritual decree. Inherency suggests that the legitimacy of aboriginal governance does not flow from sources such as the Crown, Parliament, or the Constitution. Legitimacy is derived instead from original occupancy, is bequeathed by the Creator, reflects the consent of the people, complies with treaties or international law, and may never be extinguished even with explicit consent (Bell, 1997). According to Elijah Harper,

> Self-government is not [something] that can be given away by any government, but rather . . . flows from Creator. Self-government . . . is taking control and managing our own affairs, being able to determine our own future and destiny . . . It has never been up to the governments to give self-government. It has never been theirs to give (as cited in the Royal Commission on Aboriginal Peoples, 1992:19).

The concept of aboriginality underlies the notion of taking aboriginal difference seriously (Maaka & Fleras, 2005). Strictly speaking, the word "aboriginality" is the nominalization of the adjective "aboriginal" (refers to the state of being aboriginal or pertaining to Aboriginal peoples). With aboriginality, aboriginal difference is justified on grounds of original occupancy, together with the corresponding rights and power that flow from this status. Aboriginal peoples have long insisted on recognition of their difference, including: (1) Aboriginal peoples are constitutionally different from non-aboriginal Canadians and entitled to group-differentiated rights because of their unique status as original occupants; (2) aboriginal difference must be protected in constructing a new postcolonial social contract; (3) aboriginal difference must be taken seriously as grounds for living together separately as the Nations Within; (4) it must be taken into account as the basis for rewards, recognition, and relations-repair (Macklem, 2001). Aboriginal difference is key; without it, Aboriginal peoples have no more moral authority than other Canadians to challenge the political agenda and transform the constitutional order.

Aboriginal Models of Self-Determining Autonomy

Aboriginal peoples are in the midst of a drive to regain control over their lives and life chances. This commitment is predicated on the premise that Canada remains colonialist in terms of the founding assumptions ("rights of discovery") and foundational principles

(Eurocentric structures, values, and ideology) undergirding its constitutional order (Kulchyski, 2013). Then, as now, Aboriginal peoples continue to be hobbled by the consequences of forcible incorporation into Canada's colonial project (Hedican, 2013; Neeganawedgin 2012; Newhouse & Belanger, 2011; Warry, 2009). The powerful expression of aboriginality rejects the legitimacy of existing political relations and mainstream institutions as a framework for living together. It also repudiates the relevance and moral authority of those structures that were once used to colonize Aboriginal peoples. Proposed instead is the restoration of an inherent and collective right to Aboriginal models of self-determining autonomy over land, identity, and political voice (Alcantara & Whitfield, 2010). Key elements of this self-determination project include control over the process and power of local governance, sharp curtailment of state jurisdiction in deference to aboriginal control, the attainment of cultural sovereignty, and a realignment of political relations around a nation-to-nation format in key jurisdictional areas related to power, privilege, and resources (Maaka & Fleras, 2008; Tomsons & Mayer, 2013).

Aboriginal leaders have endorsed the principle of self-determining autonomy. Its value lies in breaking the cycle of deprivation and dependency, in moving beyond the colonialist mentality of the *Indian Act*, and in its embrace of an aboriginal renaissance as a spearhead for renewal and reform. Aboriginal models of self-determining autonomy will vary and are expected to evolve in line with community needs (social, economic, cultural) and local circumstances (rural or urban). Some communities will reflect a government model, others an aboriginal model, and still others will combine elements of both, with differences being contextual rather than categorical, that is, in accordance with community levels of local development rather than ideology. A few aboriginal models are looking for complete independence; others want a fundamental restructuring of their relationship within a reconstituted Canada; many want some kind of accommodation within the existing federal system because they lack any viable alternatives; and still others want a limited autonomy involving negotiated agreements that are mostly administrative in nature, that is, delegation of government power to manage local services (Kulchyski, 2005).

Four models of self-determining autonomy as governance can be theorized: (1) statehood, a sovereign country with absolute independence, no external interference, and a final say over both internal and external affairs; (2) nationhood, a *de facto* sovereignty with province-like powers and jurisdiction over all internal matters; (3) municipality-hood, a community-based level of self-determining autonomy, retaining control over local affairs but limited by interaction with comparable mainstream bodies; and (4) institution-hood, having meaningful decision-making powers through institutional inclusion or parallel institutions (see also O'Regan, 1994). Table 7-1 summarizes these possibilities with respect to varying categories of self-determining autonomy and its expression through levels of self-governance.

TABLE 7-1	Models of Self-Determining Autonomy: Different Self-Governance Levels
Statehood	**Nationhood**
absolute (*de jure*) sovereignty	relative (*de facto*) sovereignty
Community/municipality-level	**Institution-level**
nested (community-based) sovereignty	nominal (as if) sovereignty

Generally speaking, aboriginal claims for self-determining autonomy are consistent with the "nationhood" model of "domestic dependent nations" in the United States. American First Peoples do not possess external sovereignty (e.g., they cannot raise an army or establish diplomatic relations with foreign countries). Nevertheless, these "domestic dependent nations" retain considerable control over their internal affairs, at least in theory if not always in practice, subject to certain restrictions at the federal and state levels. To date, with the possible exception of the Nisga'a settlement, the Canadian government has proposed a level of self-determining autonomy with authority somewhere between a municipality and a nation or province. Aboriginal leaders publicly endorse a model somewhere between nationhood/provincehood and statehood but appear willing to compromise, depending on particular circumstances.

However progressive sounding, all claims to self-determination are not created equally (Coulthard, 2014; Maaka & Fleras, 2008; Manuel & Derrickson, 2015). State-centered models define self-determination in ways that reflect, reinforce, and advance state interests over those of Indigenous peoples. Too much of what passes for state determination endorses policies, laws, and agendas at odds with the post-colonizing realities of the twenty-first century. A statist agenda promotes the self-sufficiency of Indigenous peoples, albeit within the confines of an existing institutional framework. Such a governance agenda cannot allow any self-determining arrangement that challenges the principles of territorial integrity and the final authority of the state as the supreme sovereign over the land. In contrast to those top-down state determination models for managing aboriginality are aboriginal models of self-determining autonomy that advocate engaging aboriginality in a spirit of power-sharing partnership. Aboriginal models of self-determining autonomy propose a radical governance alternative by extolling the principle of engaging aboriginality from below as basis for relations repair. Predictably, central authorities dislike this discursive framework for precisely the same reason, namely, a fear that too expansive a recognition of self-determining autonomy rights may incite a legitimacy crisis by eroding Canada's authority to dominate and control (Charters, 2005). By contrast, Aboriginal peoples demand the broadest interpretation of self-determination on the grounds that all other rights flow from this first principle.

A commitment to the aboriginal self-determining autonomy approach to governance articulates the following principles: (1) recognition of Aboriginal peoples as possessing distinctive ways of looking at the world; (2) respect for indigenous difference and distinctiveness through its incorporation into policymaking; (3) an acknowledgement that they alone possess the right to decide for themselves what is best; and (4) endorsement of their status as sovereign in their own right, yet sharing in the sovereign of society at large (Fleras, 2009b). Aboriginal models of self-determining autonomy aim to bring relations-repair into the forefront not only by establishing innovative ways for living together separately (Blaser et al., 2011) but also by reinforcing their distinct and profound relationship with land, territories, and resources (Barelli, 2012). The focus is on challenging those founding assumptions and foundational principles that initially created the problem, first, by resisting the centralizing tendencies of top-down ("one size fits all") policymaking model; and second, by advancing the principle of mainstreaming indigeneity that indigenizes policymaking as grounds for a new governance framework. Such a transformative commitment stands in contrast to Eurocentric governance notions, understood as one-size-fits-all initiatives that are imposed from above in the "best interests" of those defined as problem people or people with special needs (Poole, 2008). The challenge is unassailable. Indigenous peoples rights to constitutional status as original occupants and sovereign political communities conveys a corresponding right to self-determining autonomy, not in the absolute sense of complete independence but in the relative and relational sense of relations-repair (Woons, 2015). In other words, the concept of aboriginal self-determining autonomy as a third order of governance is not about separation but about incorporation—about "getting in" on their terms rather than "getting out" in hopes of completing the "circle of confederation" (as cited in Hawkes, 2000:142).

Aboriginal Title and Treaty Rights

Moves toward a new social contract are anchored in the recognition, definition, and implementation of aboriginal title and treaty rights (Russell, 2005). Enforcement of federal treaty obligations is particularly important in advancing aboriginal interests and aspirations. **Treaties** were seen as a fundamental component of Aboriginal diplomacy with European powers. The British, in particular, insisted on observing legalities. Treaties represented practical nation-to-nation relationships between European colonizers and tribes. They also demanded a principled approach to determining ownership of private property, as only land that had been properly acquired (without encumbrances) could be sold, mortgaged, used as collateral, or employed in a productive manner in a free enterprise economy (Walkom, 1998). Treaties continue to be regarded as ongoing and organic agreements that reaffirm the distinctive legal status of Aboriginal nations. With treaties, Aboriginal peoples possess a constitutional right to carry on traditional harvesting practices for moderate livelihood, with governments having to justify any restrictions they wish to impose on this right by way of consultation, consent, and compensation (Manfredi, 2004).

Perceptual differences and a conflict of interest informed the treaty-making process (McKee, 1996). European authorities tended to see treaties as legal surrenders of aboriginal land and authority in exchange for reserves, goods, and services. Treaties would provide the Crown with legal title to underoccupied land, foster peaceful settlement, avoid costly wars, and deter foreign annexation or expansion (Price, 1991). In short, treaties extinguished Aboriginal peoples' sovereignty. But others see it differently: For Aboriginal peoples, treaties reaffirmed their autonomy as political communities. According to international law, a treaty is a formally ratified agreement incorporating a nation-to-nation relationship between sovereign entities. Treaties were viewed as semi-sacred and mutually binding contracts involving a reciprocal exchange of rights and responsibilities. As far as aboriginal leaders are concerned, governments remain bound to honour the contractual obligations of these treaties—if only to preserve the honour of the Crown. To date, Canada's courts have shown little inclination to see treaties as international agreements, preferring, instead, to define them as unique contractual agreements involving mutually binding obligations and the exchange of rights (Brooks, 1998).

Specific Treaty Claims Two types of treaty rights exist. One is based on specific claims to existing treaty violations, and the other involves comprehensive modern-day land claims (or regional settlements). A series of treaties was signed between 1763 and 1867 involving representatives of the Crown and Aboriginal nations. The earliest treaties resembled peace and friendship compacts to facilitate trade, secure allies, and pre-empt European rivals (McKee, 1996). Later treaties involved exchanges of land for goods and services. Between 1867 and 1923, 11 numbered (1–11) treaties were signed, involving a surrender of aboriginal interest in land to the Crown across much of the Prairies and parts of the Northwest Territories, British Columbia, and Ontario. These historical Indian treaties set out the obligations and benefits for both parties to the agreement. Aboriginal peoples surrendered title to land and resources. In return, they received reserve lands, agricultural equipment, ammunition, annual payment, access to services, and clothing. Their right to hunt and fish on Crown land remained in effect as long as these lands remained unoccupied. The Crown also promised schools on reserves or teachers when requested. As an example, consider the terms of an agreement between the Crown and the First Nations of Manitoba and the Northwest Territories:

- Aboriginal tribes would relinquish all their rights and title to the great region from Lake Superior to the foot of the Rocky Mountains.
- Land would be set aside as reserves for homes and agriculture. This land could not be sold without Indian consent and then only for their benefit.
- Tribes and bands would be granted the right to hunt and fish over these Crown lands until sold into private hands.
- An annual payment of $5 would be made for each man, woman, and child ($25 for chief, $15 for councillor). Suitable clothing, medals, and flags to the chiefs would be provided.
- To assist in agricultural endeavours, each band would receive implements, herds, and grain.
- Schools would be established on reserves.
- Sale of alcohol on reserves would be prohibited (see Price, 1991).

Noble intentions were one thing; implementation proved another. The treaty process was often marred by such willful duplicity and callous expediency that it hardly seemed worth its weight in paper (Price, 1991). Most grievances reflected federal failures to abide by treaty promises. With the passage of time, benefits were pared back or simply ignored. Miserly payouts proved a sore point. Another source of grievance entailed the unauthorized and uncompensated whittling away of reserve lands because of fraud, expropriation, or government theft. Disputes over reserve boundaries proved a constant source of friction. No less devastating was the misappropriation of aboriginal monies from government sale of resources or mineral rights held in trust by the Crown.

Specific treaty claims are aimed at righting historical wrongs associated with treaty deception and double dealing on the part of Crown agents. To restore Crown honour in redressing past violations, the courts have instructed the federal government to display a "fair, large, and liberal interpretation" of treaty provisions by giving Aboriginal peoples the benefit of the doubt. In the words of Chief Justice Beverley McLachlin: "Put simply, Canada's Aboriginal peoples were here when Europeans came, and were never conquered" (as cited in Fenwick, 2005), thus putting the onus on the "honour of the Crown" to deal generously with aboriginal claims. Settling a specific land claim entails a four-stage process: (1) review (a submitted claim is vetted by Indian and Northern Affairs Canada to determine its validity, then forwarded to the Justice Department to determine its chances of winning in court. The vast majority of claims filed since 1973 are mired at this preliminary stage); (2) negotiation; (3) ratification (once a deal is struck it must be ratified by the First Nations community, and sometimes requires provincial approval, and finally, federal ratification), and (4) implementation (funds and land are transferred to the community). Hundreds of outstanding specific claims exist, ranging in scope from expropriations for hydro lines to reserve boundaries and actual land parcels, including much of downtown Toronto (Maccharles, 2005). In May 2008, the House of Commons gave final approval to establish an independent Specific Claims Tribunal, including $2.5 billion over ten years for resolving specific claims of $150 million or less (Curry, 2008). Unlike the advisory Indian Claims Commission, the Specific Claims Tribunal is an independent body empowered to make binding decisions about specific violations of agreements such as treaties or government mismanagement of aboriginal assets held in trust (Delic & Abele, 2010). According to AANDC data, 108 specific claims were resolved between 2007 and March of 2014, despite criticism that the Tribunal lacks the resources and independence to function properly (IWGIA, 2015).

Comprehensive Land Claims Comprehensive land claims consist of modern-day treaty arrangements for establishing certainty over disputed ownership of land (Alcantara, 2013). For those aboriginal groups without a treaty or alternative arrangement, a comprehensive land claims protocol provides a method of redress for land rights violations or land dispossession (IWGIA, 2015). Since 1973, 29 modern treaties have been negotiated, beginning with the James Bay and Northern Quebec Agreement in 1976 for most of the territorial north, particularly the Yukon, most of northern Quebec, and parts of British Columbia (AADNC, 2015). Rather than redressing the specific claims of existing treaties, comprehensive (land claims) treaties address the need to establish broadly based agreements over *who owns what* with those aboriginal nations without a treaty (Purvis, 1999). Securing certainty of control over "untreatied" land and resources is imperative. For the Crown, certainty of ownership is a prerequisite for investment and development purposes. For Aboriginal peoples, clarifying the rights of ownership secures a potential economic base for prosperity and survival. Negotiated settlements provide aboriginal communities with constitutionally protected rights to wildlife harvests, resource management, some subsurface mineral rights, and regulated development (Land & Townshend, 2002). Economic benefits can be derived by renting out lands and resources at rates that are favourable to aboriginal interests. Benefits can also be achieved through local development (in tandem with public or private interests) at a pace that reflects community priorities and developmental levels.

The resolution of land claims settlements in Canada is predicated on the principle of **aboriginal title**. Broadly speaking, aboriginal title specifies Aboriginal rights of use over land and resources whose ownership (title) has not yet been legally extinguished and transferred to the Crown (Knafla & Westra, 2010). The principle itself revolves around the question of who occupied the land prior to the unilateral assertion of Crown ownership. If Aboriginal peoples can prove that they had continuous and exclusive occupation of the land prior to European contact, they can claim aboriginal title; otherwise, the land reverts to Crown ownership. Because it has no counterpart in English common property law, aboriginal title is unlike other forms of property ownership, hence it is *sui generis*: Aboriginal title cannot be surrendered or transferred to any individual but only to the Crown, is sourced in original occupancy, and is collectively held in perpetuity for the benefit of future owners.

How does aboriginal title apply to Canada? The Calder decision of 1973 may have acknowledged the possibility of aboriginal title to unceded (unextinguished) land. A Supreme Court ruling (the Sparrow decision) in 1990 gave practical effect to constitutional guarantees of existing treaty and aboriginal rights (Rotman, 2004). But it was the Delgamuukw ruling in 1997 that really advanced the cause of aboriginal title, when the Supreme Court overturned an earlier British Columbia court decision that dismissed aboriginal claims to land title as impossible to determine, even if they existed. Under Delgamuukw, the court ruled that Aboriginal peoples have a constitutional and exclusive right of use and ownership to land, if they can prove that they occupied it prior to European arrival. Until aboriginal title is settled, in other words, not a single tree can be felled by Crown authorities without *consultation, consent, and compensation*—even in cases where infringements on aboriginal title lands are for public purposes or national interests. Finally, rather than restricting land use to traditional hunting and foraging practices, aboriginal claimants can use the land or resources in almost any way they wish, except in a destructive sense that may imperil future use. Delgamuukw also advanced the concept of aboriginal title by expanding the support base for proving ownership. To assist in proving claims, oral traditions are now admissible as evidence in deciding aboriginal title, in effect tipping the burden of proof over to the Crown.

Subsequent Supreme Court rulings have also strengthened the aboriginal hand with respect to aboriginal title. None have been as important as the Tsilhqot'in decision in late June 2014 which marked the first time a Canadian court legally recognized aboriginal land title based on tribal traditional use and control of the lands (IWGIA, 2015). The decision acknowledged the existence of aboriginal title on a specific parcel of traditional land covering a large swath of central British Columbia. It also conceded aboriginal ownership, control, economic benefits, and future use of land they have historically and continually occupied ("aboriginal title") unless signed away through treaties with the government (Fine, 2014). Finally a principled framework was established (IWGIA, 2015) for recognition of aboriginal land rights in Canada, including:

a. Rejection of the both *terra nullius* and rights of discovery doctrine. Aboriginal peoples prior to European contact owned and controlled traditional lands as a result, colonizer assertion of sovereignty did not extinguish this legal interest.

b. Aboriginal rights to ownership and control of title reinforces the importance of Aboriginal peoples' consent. If consent is not forthcoming, the government's only recourse is to justify its proposed incursion as in the national interests as per S. 35 of the 1982 *Constitution Act*. And should the Crown initiate a project without consent prior to the establishment of aboriginal title, it must discontinue the project if continuation would infringe on the spirit of the decision.

c. Aboriginal title extends beyond simply small tracts of land in continuous intensive use. Rather it's conceivable that title could be established by those groups who exercised control over large territories.

d. The Crown possessed a legal obligation to negotiate in good faith to resolve issues of aboriginal title. The governing ethos is one of reconciliation and engagement rather than sharp dealing and competing interests.

Aboriginal peoples have greeted the Tsilhqot'in ruling as an historic game changer; however, both government and industry have been slow to respond to the Supreme Court ruling.

REMAKING CANADA: RETHINKING THE RELATIONSHIP

Canada, like other settler societies, sought to eliminate the "Indian problem" by way of assimilation, forced migration, bureaucratic indifference, or outright suppression (Lowman & Barker, 2015; Churchill, 2004; McRoberts, 2003). The present may be no less single-minded, albeit more subtle and indirect (Palmeter, 2015). In reaction, Indigenous peoples in Canada and throughout the world have taken the initiative in politicizing their demands for a radical restructuring of society along the lines of a new governance contract (Fleras & Elliott, 1992; IWGIA, 2015; Niezen, 2003). Emphasis has shifted from a governance that seeks survival to one that challenges the distribution of power and resources within a new constitutional order whose foundational principles include aboriginal rights. The terrain is increasingly contested. Aboriginal leaders have relied on various tactics and strategies to get the message across. Political authorities, ever distrustful and fearful of losing power or control, have responded with a host of delaying or defusing tactics (Sissons, 2005).

Aboriginal Initiatives: Tactics and Strategies

The politics of "relations repair" are sharply contested. Principles and philosophies span the spectrum from "radical" to "moderate": At one end are those who believe in revolutionary changes for advancing Aboriginal peoples' claims to self-determining autonomy (Alfred, 2005; Mercredi & Turpel, 1993). At the other are the moderates who endorse a conciliatory, incremental approach that cuts deals, enhances local autonomy, improves job opportunities, and fosters dialogue with private sectors (Fontaine, 1998; see also Gray, 1997). In between are those who don't know, who don't care, or who are more concerned with "getting on" than with "taking a stand."

Aboriginal initiatives tend to focus on land and resources (Kulchyski, 2005). Without land, any hope of economic development is seriously compromised, as is Aboriginal peoples' capacity to protect language and culture, speak the language of nationhood, or assert self-determining autonomy in any meaningful fashion. Aboriginal initiatives for reconciliation, reform, and renewal are generally pursued through conventional channels of dialogue, consultation, and persuasion, with central policy structures. Tactics include recourse to Parliament, the existing court system, public opinion polls, and special interest/lobby groups, such as the Assembly of First Nations (AFN). Courts are the preferred venues for exerting pressure on the government to honour its constitutional obligations, while also providing a forum for articulating aboriginal issues. Lacking the reach of wealth and government power, Aboriginal peoples must rely on the powers of persuasion and moral rectitude through the courts, litigation, and the law (Wilkins, 2004). And court decisions, from Calder to Sparrow to Delgamuukw to Tsilhqot'in, have secured redress for historical inequities as grounds for advancing collective interests. Aboriginal leaders have also relied on international fora and agencies for assistance, including the United Nations, Britain, and the Vatican in the hopes of righting historical wrongs. These tactics have attained a measure of success, partly because of Canada's sensitivity to international criticism and censure.

Alternative strategies have been adopted, as well. This cannot come as a surprise: after all, the use of conventional channels involves working within a colonialistic framework that (1) historically oppressed Aboriginal peoples, (2) is constructed in a way that systemically advances mainstream interests, and (3) is prone to protecting the system against challenge and change (see Green, 2003). Failure of political and constitutional channels to adequately address local grievances and national concerns has culminated in activist protest, ranging from acts of civil disobedience to threats of violence in some cases. Flamboyant and theatrically staged protests involving the mass media are particularly important in tweaking the conscience of a publicity-conscious government. By startling a complacent public into awareness or action, the use of negative publicity to embarrass the government has proven especially effective because of Canada's much ballyhooed commitment to human and individual rights (see the Box below). Finally, there have been occasional threats to employ violence, if necessary. Yet the threat of violence has rarely moved beyond rhetoric and, when employed as at Oka, Burnt Church, or Caledonia, is often defensive in nature. How long this non-violence will persist is open to conjecture, given the urgency of Aboriginal grievances, the impatience of younger activists, and perceptions of federal foot dragging and stonewalling.

Idle No More: Challenging the Relationship

The Occupy Wall Street Movement made it abundantly clear: A relatively small number of media savvy folk possess the power not only to mobilize the masses into action, but also to galvanize public awareness of social injustice issues. A similar logic applies to the Idle No More (INM) movement that originated in late 2012, then accelerated into prominence in 2013, drawing on a history of indigenous nationalist movements for asserting aboriginal sovereignty in opposition to settler colonialism (Barker, 2015). A pan-aboriginal grassroots movement was ignited that, unlike more localized struggles with definable leadership, reflected a nation-wide constituency whose concerns generated a critical mass of energy which capitalized on the revolution of rising expectations, especially among aboriginal youth and

women (Kino-nda-niimi Collective, 2014). Outside a general frustration with the status quo (Coates, 2014), a shifting package of demands and diffuse grievances prevailed over a clearly articulated policy framework (Gibson, 2013). The mainstream media and political pundits may have lamented the dearth of consensus as problematic (it complicates the challenge of determining who speaks for Aboriginal peoples [Coyne, 2013]). But the diversity of aboriginal voices both young and female—thanks to the movement's fluidity in content and organization— could just as easily be interpreted as a healthy sign of a deep democracy from below (Fournier, 2013; Kino-nda-niimi Collective, 2014; Simpson, 2014). If nothing else, the INM movement drew attention to the complexities and contradictions that infuse aboriginal issues, in addition to the faultlines that complicate the politics of aboriginality (Wotherspoon & Hansen, 2013). And like the OWS movement, it too was popularized by social media and online activism, in the process bypassing the corporate media as the primary source of representation and dissemination (Donkin, 2013; Coates, 2014; Simpson, 2014).

The Idle No More movement originated in Saskatchewan when four aboriginal woman challenged the Federal government's Omnibus Budget Bill that bundled together a large number of changes, including reduced environmental protection for waterways across traditional lands (Hopper, 2012). The proposed Omnibus bill C-45 dismantled a 130-year-old environmental statute by removing federal oversight of over 99% of Canada's 32 000 major lakes and 2.25 million rivers (Doucet, 2013). The Bill also made changes to the *Indian Act* to stream-line the leasing of federally protected reserve lands to resource-hungry development companies without community consent or majority support, thus empowering the Aboriginal Affairs minister (an agent of the federal government) to circumvent community opposition to leasing of land without adequate safeguards (Douglas & Lenon, 2014). The bill, that proposed legislative changes to ramp up federal plans for gas and oil extraction on reserve land by bypassing aboriginal rights, was subsequently passed in December (*Jobs and Growth Act*, 2012). Not surprisingly, the thrust of the INM movement was fuelled by anger over perceptions

of Harper's government as a dismissive and assimilationist colonial power (Palmater, 2014). In an effort to encourage solidarity, activism, and education, INM coalesced around several broad motivations or objectives (Coates, 2014; Kino-nda-niimi Collective, 2014), most notably, a rejection of the colonial state that suppressed Indigenous peoples' rights while challenging Canadian sovereignty and settler identity by insisting on a nation-to nation partnership anchored in the spirit and intent of treaties (i.e., including control over traditional territories and sharing of resources) (Barker, 2015). The movement eventually gravitated to more specific concerns: the squalid state of many aboriginal communities, government intransigence toward fulfilling treaty agreements, legislative erosion of aboriginal rights, and demands for more equitable sharing of resource development proceeds across traditional aboriginal lands. But the most recurrent theme focused on the principle of repairing a broken relationship—from one rooted in a colonial mentality of cooptation and control to that of a postcolonial model for living together differently as power-sharing partners (Kino-nda-niimi Collective, 2014; Smith & Campion-Smith, 2013).

It's too early to gauge the success, consequences, and implications of the Idle No More movement. Despite its profile and persistence, the movement does not appear to have gained much traction with the Canadian population. An Ipsos Reid poll in mid-January, 2013, indicated that most

Canadians reject the legitimacy of INM, agreeing in principle with the grievances raised, but objecting to the means (from blockades to traffic disruptions) to resolve the issues. But another perspective is helpful as well. As perhaps the largest and most important outpouring of grassroots aboriginal anger since the late 1960s (Dobbin, 2013), the cumulative impact of the INM movement promises to be transformative (Coates, 2014; Wotherspoon & Hansen, 2013) in curbing corporate Canada's headlong rush to extract natural resources without appropriate pause for consideration of the long-term consequences. Pam Palmeter (2013) put it aptly in defending the benefit of INM for Canada, especially in protecting Canadians from Harper's destructive environmental agenda: "Canadians need to realize that we are their last best hope at saving the lands, waters, plants, animals and resources for future generations because our Aboriginal and treaty rights are constitutionally protected" (cited in Rebick, 2013b).

Finally, the INM movement shares much in common with the Civil Rights and feminist movements that, too, were ridiculed or dismissed by mainstream media and politicians as idealistic and misguided (see Killian, 2013; Rebick, 2013), but which in the end, ushered in fundamental changes by linking the personal with the sociopolitical, while empowering the once powerless to challenge, resist, and change. To be sure, there are differences. The more recent movements are deeply anarchistic, that is, driven by grassroots democracy from below ("anarchy"). They also are propelled by the historically disenfranchised— young people and aboriginal women— who increasingly dismiss (and are dismissed by) both mainstream politics (Kurlantzick, 2012) and traditional leadership (such as the AFN) as co-opted and too establishment-friendly (Dobbin, 2013; Freisen, 2013; Kino-nda-niimi Collective, 2014). The lesson is clear: As Franz Fanon recognized many years ago, colonization and oppression work best when the colonized have internalized a sense of helplessness and inferiority. Shatter that ideology, it is argued, and people will no longer sit by idly.

Aboriginal demands are consistent with their articulated status as "Nations Within." Fleras & Elliott 1992 Central to their aspirations is the middle way—to strike a balance between extremes of separatism/fragmentation and absorption/assimilation (see Pearson, 2014). Aboriginal peoples don't want to separate from Canada in the territorial sense, yet they also reject any move toward assimilation with a corresponding diminution of their unique status as self-determining political communities. What is proposed instead is a mutually respectful partnership involving a sharing of jurisdiction in some areas such as health, but exclusive jurisdiction in other areas such as culture— with just enough room to ensure self-rule and control over their lives (Erasmus & Sanders, 2002). In other words, balance and compromise are key. Aboriginal peoples want to be modern by capitalizing on political and economic power for rebuilding strong communities. But "being modern" is not the same as abandoning traditional values and the practices of the past as a framework for the present (Alfred, 1999, 2005; Dean & Levi, 2006). Aboriginal peoples are pragmatists who want a working balance between the cultural and spiritual values of the past without rejecting the technological benefits of modern society. They are not against development *per se* (unless attained at the cost of sacrificing uniqueness, authenticity, and spirituality), but they insist on controlling the benefits derived from local developmental projects (Coates, 2015). The goal is to ensure the survival of future generations by regenerating the basis of indigenous nationhood; to secure a collective sense of self by reconnecting individuals to land, identity, and cultures, and to secure the foundations of an authentic community life (Alfred, 2009).

To be sure, the unconventional nature of Aboriginal peoples' proposals may unduly concern non-aboriginal Canadians. But their demands are not radical when compared to the alternatives: They rarely invoke the overthrow of political institutions, since it's hardly in their best interests to destroy the fiduciary (special) relationship that informs their existence. Few actively espouse the dismemberment of Canadian society or the imposition of aboriginal cultural values. A restructuring of the relationship is endorsed instead to ensure that (1) aboriginal difference and rights are taken seriously, (2) aboriginal models of self-determination by way of self-governance are implemented, and (3) aboriginal title and treaty rights are recognized. If these demands appear threatening to Canadians or if they seem unrealistic in light of contemporary realities, consider the options: A continuation of ineffectual government interference and paternalistic handouts is not the answer. No more effective is throwing more money at the problem or expanding the legion of experts for yet more top-down solutions. In short, the costs of re-priming the relationship may be formidable; however, they're nowhere near as daunting as the costs of doing things the same way they've been done until now.

Government Responses/Communication Breakdown

Central authorities, for the most part, have stumbled in repairing the relational status of Aboriginal peoples. Political sectors have come under attack for caving in to aboriginal demands while sacrificing national interests through restitutional expenditures and power giveaways. Conversely, they have also been criticized for sacrificing aboriginal interests in pursuit of national goals (Adams, 1999). The promises of lofty rhetoric notwithstanding, there remains a noticeable lack of political will for "walking the walk" (Macklem, 2001; Weaver, 1993b). A hollow-ritualism persists (Charlesworth & Larking, 2015): Instead of a principled approach to addressing the issues, what prevails is the equivalent of a political samba: Every step forward is matched by one step back and two steps sideways. Politics and initiatives continue to be driven by public opinion polls, despite known deficiencies in mass surveys (Ponting, 1997; Purvis, 1999). Canadians appear to be broadly supportive of Aboriginal concerns and sympathetic to Aboriginal problems (Environics Institute, 2010b). But public support may be superficial, tentative, and conditional, thus making any government fearful of moving too quickly. Inasmuch as the intent is to simply rearrange the furniture without altering the floor plan of a sinking relationship, the government's aboriginal agenda appears more concerned with appearances than with substance—of talking the talk of promises rather than walking the walk through implementation and enforcement.

Political authorities appear receptive to aboriginal claims—if only to avert a crisis of legitimacy and restore some semblance of political tranquility—albeit without enthusiasm or commitment. Awareness and acceptance are growing in acknowledging that Aboriginal peoples (1) are a distinct society, (2) possess a threatened culture and society, (3) depend on government trust and responsibilities for survival, (4) desire more control in line with local priorities, and (5) prefer to achieve their goals in partnership with central authorities. But enthusiasm wanes with the prospect of putting the principles of power-sharing and partnership into a meaningful reality and measurable practice. Policy officials are understandably wary of dissolving conventional patterns of domination for the uncharted waters of a new constitutional order. The Crown is often unwilling to negotiate aboriginal issues except when compelled to do so by the threat of unfavourable litigation (Rotman, 2004). The principle of aboriginal self-governance is endorsed not as an independently sourced inherent right, but as a political concession, both contingent (qualified) and delegated on a band-to-band basis, with accountability to Parliament and the Constitution. Claims to aboriginal self-governance may be politically acceptable, but only when they do not (a) affect most Canadians, (b) involve exorbitant sums of money, or (c) endorse any fundamental shift in power (Widdowson, 2003).

In brief, aboriginality as principle and politics poses an unprecedented challenge for the balancing act in any society constructed around compromises. Few politicians can afford to cavalierly dismiss aboriginality or deny the existence of Aboriginal peoples' rights. By the same token, they can't afford to be seen as capitulating to aboriginal demands. A willingness to compensate Aboriginal peoples for historical wrongs does not extend to bankrupting Canada. What prevails instead are debates over how to re-calibrate the relationship without shearing Canada's social fabric in the process. And although the most egregious expressions of colonialism have been abolished, the debate over the place of Aboriginal peoples in Canada remains so steeped in the foundational principles of a colonial constitutional order that many despair of transformational change (Alfred, 2001; Denis, 1997). The legacy of "whiteness" continues to shape how the legal system identifies, interprets, and enforces Aboriginal rights—proof, yet again, that Canadian law is neither neutral nor impartial, but an instrument for advancing mainstream interests under the guise of neutrality and fairness (Asch, 1997). The words of Noel Lyons (1997) are especially timely in emphasizing the contradictions of working within the very system that created the problem:

> As long as the process continues to be defined by rules and standards set by the dominant society, no measure of real self-government is possible because the process itself is a denial of the inherent rights of self-government of Aboriginal peoples. In other words, we cannot de-colonize peoples by relying on the rules and standards that were used to colonize them in the first place.

How is this neo-colonial relationship expressed (Denis, 1996, 1997)? Neo-colonialism works on the assumption that people may appear to be free by virtue of living in a system that is ostensibly neutral and based on universalistic principles. But this neutrality is an illusion because hidden agendas continue to control and contain, albeit in an indirect manner (Adams, 1999). For example, take the notion of aboriginal title as a legal burden on the Crown. Why not assert that the Crown imposes a burden on unsurrendered aboriginal land that has been long occupied and unceded, thus shifting the onus of proof on the Crown to prove its case? The Delgamuukw ruling may have acknowledged aboriginal title as an exclusive and collective right to ownership of land and its use, but this entitlement does not come into play without aboriginal proof of title to land—an often expensive and lengthy undertaking (Christie, 2005). An extraordinarily high level of proof is required. According to Chief Justice Beverley McLachlin (R. v Bernard, 2005; R. v Marshall, 2005), aboriginal claimants must prove exclusive physical possession, establish a substantial connection to the land, demonstrate direct lineage with the original inhabitants of the land, and avoid claims that do not reflect a "logical evolution" of activities from traditional times. As a result, a right to fish or hunt for moderate livelihood may be acceptable because of its traditional nature—constructing casinos or bingo halls is not.

Clearly, then, Aboriginal peoples–Canada relations remain rooted in the colonialist assumption that the Crown knows what is best and is the final authority with the last say in defining what counts as aboriginal difference, and what difference counts. Canada's claim to sovereignty over Aboriginal peoples and their lands is disputed since it rests on different forms of violence, ranging from the violence inherent in the unilateral assertion of dominance over Indigenous nations that long occupied territory prior to European contact/invasion, to the violence of an expanding settler occupation that created a coercive context in which seemingly honorable treaties were forcibly negotiated and fraudulently signed (Douglas & Lenon 2014; Thielen-Wilson 2014; Truth and Reconciliation Commission Report, 2015). As Sharon Venne (1998) points out, there is no legal proof for ascertaining the legality of the Crown's unilateral assertion of sovereignty over Aboriginal peoples and their lands. Such neo-colonial arrogance, Venne asserts, is nothing more than political mumbo-jumbo dressed up in "hocus pocus" rules and regulations designed by the colonizers to dispossess Aboriginal peoples of their land and resources.

Even the courts are complicit in upholding unilateral Crown assertions of sovereignty over Aboriginal peoples and their territories. How could it be otherwise? Both the Crown and the judicial system are systemically rooted in the foundational principles of a Eurocentric and colonial constitutional order. Court judges consist of persons who are by training, personal history, and inclination more in tune with mainstream rhythms, ordering principles, and institutions rather than with aboriginal realities (Wilkins, 2004). To be sure, the courts have proven allies: They have conferred on Aboriginal peoples a "*sui generis* legal status" based on their occupation of Canada prior to the Crown's unilateral assertion declaration of sovereignty over Canada (Murphy, 2001:110). They have ruled for the need to reinforce Crown fiduciary obligations by restricting Crown infringement on aboriginal rights. Such an admission is particularly evident with the 2014 Tsilhqot'in ruling that protected aboriginal title from federal infringement except under conditions involving pressing national interests. Nevertheless, they are not prepared to challenge the colonialist assumptions that privilege the undisputed primacy of the Crown's claims to absolute sovereignty (Harris-Short, 2007).

In short, the foundational premises of a colonial social contract are doing a disservice in establishing an agenda for living together differently. This social contract is based on a brand of liberal universalism that leaves little room for taking differences seriously, distrusts the notion of self-determining autonomy for aboriginal communities, and privileges individual rights to choose over collective rights to survive (Peach, 2005). The application of universal norms and individualistic values embodied in the Charter to self-governing aboriginal communities are fundamentally at odds with their social and cultural values (Harris-Short, 2007). The pervasive Eurocentrism that informs a neo-colonial political architecture has had the effect of (1) dismissing aboriginal rights, values, or traditions as irrelevant or inferior; (2) normalizing Eurocentric ways of seeing and doing as natural and inevitable; and (3) asserting the superiority and dominance of conventional patterns and institutional structures. The framing of issues from a Eurocentric perspective draws attention to some aspects of reality as normal and necessary, but others as not; defines some aspects of reality as acceptable and desirable, but not others; and imposes a preferred reading of reality by emphasizing commonalities and similarities at the expense of deep differences (Maaka & Fleras, 2005). But for Aboriginal peoples to be equal they must be different, and their aboriginality must be taken seriously as a blueprint for relationships, rights, and recognition (see Denis, 1996). Otherwise, there is a risk of being muscled into agreements that say more about securing a neo-colonial status quo rather than advancing a postcolonial social contract (Venne, 1998).

TOWARD A POSTCOLONIAL SOCIAL CONTRACT: TWO STEPS FORWARD . . .

> Canada is a test case for a grand notion—the notion that dissimilar people can share lands, resources, power, and dreams while respecting and sustaining their differences ("A Word from the Commissioners," in Highlights from the Report of the Royal Commission on Aboriginal Peoples, 1996b:ix).

Indigenous peoples around the world are in the midst of a powerful social movement to reclaim what rightfully belongs to them (Maaka & Fleras, 2005; Editorial, IWGIA, 2015). In many cases, land and natural resources are of primary concern; in other cases, reclamation of culture, spirituality, and language are central; in all cases, repairing the relations is central in constructing a postcolonial social contract (Maaka & Andersen, 2007). Canada, too, is struggling to recast its relationship with Aboriginal peoples. Growing awareness of massive disparities has combined with mounting resentment and emergent political realities to intensify political and public awareness of Aboriginal issues. Government initiatives to engage with Aboriginal peoples to improve their collective lot reflect an interplay of principle and ideology with realpolitik ("pragmatism") and appeasement (in which political authorities appear to act from fear of aboriginal extremism in order to ensure peace at any cost [Widdowson & Howard, 2008]). Not surprisingly, projections vary regarding transforming the relational status of Aboriginal peoples from colonized subjects to self-determining nations, with some advocating to work within the system, others outside of it, and still others proposing to transform it along postcolonial lines.

A sense of perspective is useful. A generation ago, most Canadians would have cringed at the prospect of discovering some aboriginal ancestry; at present, they are scouring their closets in hopes of unearthing an ancestor they can claim as their own (Kulchyski, 2005). Not long ago, Canada believed it had moral authority and developmental progress on its side; after all, Canada saw itself as a white-man's country, with a God-given duty to control, co-opt, and convert those less fortunate. How times have changed: In rejecting the notions that "white is right" and "white is might," Aboriginal peoples now claim the high moral ground once occupied by those who justified their superiority by reference to "white" or "might" (Cairns, 2003). The distance travelled has been impressive. In the space of just over four decades, Aboriginal peoples have recoiled from the brink of legal extinction to reclaim a pivotal role in the reconstruction of Canadian society (Saul, 2014). Such a reversal originated and gained legitimacy when the "costs" of excluding Aboriginal peoples from the national agenda proved unacceptably high in social, political, and economic terms (Fleras & Krahn, 1992).

But while the rhetoric of transformation may be compelling, it may also be premature. Aboriginal moves to redefine their relationship with the people of Canada are fraught with ambiguity and confusion because of competing paradigms, hidden agendas, and entrenched interests. The most egregious colonialist practices and structures may have been discarded; nevertheless, Canada's constitutional order continues to promulgate principles that compromise aboriginal rights. Of particular relevance is the imposition of one legal and sovereign political authority in a given territory under a single nationality, and universal citizenship that reduces all differences to equal status before the law (Harty & Murphy, 2005; McRoberts, 2003). Political authorities continue to call the shots by endorsing the founding assumptions and foundational principles of a neo-colonial settler society, while aboriginal values and aspirations are overwhelmed by the priorities and constraints of the majority "whitestream" (Denis, 1996). And while Canada's colonialist approach to aboriginal affairs is explicitly repudiated, the fundamental objective of government policy—to eliminate the "Indian problem" by fostering neo-colonial arrangements—has barely budged with the passage of time (Alfred, 2005; Ponting, 1986). Only the means have changed, with crude assimilationist strategies replaced by more sophisticated tactics that not only co-opt Aboriginal discourses for self-serving purposes but also have the neo-colonial effect of advancing a corporatist agenda.

Recent developments are pointing to yet another governance turn in Aboriginal peoples–Canada relations. This proposed paradigm shift is gathering momentum partly in response to escalating aboriginal pressure, and partly to deflect a growing crisis in state legitimacy. In that no consensus prevails as to what should replace the paternalism of a patronizing past, instead of a paradigm shift, what we have is a paradigm "muddle." On one side is the dead weight of the *Indian Act*; on the other side are the progressive themes enshrined in the 1996 RCAP report and the Truth and Reconciliation Commission Report, 2015. On one side are the "old rules of the game," many of which appear to be drawing to a close, but not without a struggle; on the other side is a new postcolonial paradigm that lacks both the political will and the critical mass of support to take hold (see Table 7-2). To no one's surprise, proposals for change are imbued with an air of ambivalence as colonialist paradigms grind up against postcolonizing realities, as the old collides with the new without displacing the other—resulting in discordant amalgams of progress with regress. Such a neo-colonial state of conflict is likely to persist until such time as conventional thinking accepts a unifying "vision" of Canada as a multilayered partnership of two founding peoples—Aboriginal and non-Aboriginal (French and English colonizers)—each sovereign in its own right yet sharing in the sovereignty of postcolonial Canada.

TABLE 7-2	Towards a Postcolonial Social Contract: Evolving Paradigms in the Relational Status of Aboriginal Peoples		
	COLONIAL GOVERNANCE (old social contract of direct rule–from *Indian Act* to White Paper)	**NEO-COLONIAL GOVERNANCE** (current social contract based on the principle of indirect rule)	**POSTCOLONIAL GOVERNANCE** (proposed social contract based on principles of Aboriginal peoples' self-rule)
Status	Perceived as children	Citizens plus	Peoples/nations/political communities
Rights	Defined as wards of the state	Delegated rights and responsibilities	Inherent and collective indigenous rights
Entitlements	Framed as social problems with needs	A minority problem with rights	Indigenous peoples with rights
Nature of Relationship	Parent-child guardianship	Participation in government initiatives	Nation to nation; government to government; peoples to peoples
Rules of Engagement	Paternalistic (government "doing for" Aboriginal peoples)	Partnership (senior-junior partners)	Equal partnership
Power Distribution	Power deficit	Delegate power	Power sharing
Policy Approach	Canada knows what is best (obey/conform)	Canada knows what is best but has duty to consult	Indigenous peoples know to what is best in defining outcomes
Policy Goal	Assimilation (protection until absorption and normalization)	Integration (conditional autonomy + state determination)	Relational self-determining autonomy without domination
Underlying Policy Assumptions	Absorption	Modernize	Indigenize—indigenous difference as basis for rewards, recognition, and relations
Animating Logic	Eliminate "Indian problem"	Control problem by devolving responsibilities	Seek co-sovereign coexistence
Anticipated Outcomes	Individual self-sufficiency	Community self-sufficiency	The Nations Within

Solving the Problem, Repairing the Relationship: Assimilationism? Autonomism? Accommodationism?

As noted at the outset of this chapter, Aboriginal peoples often live in a world of problems. These problems range from the socioeconomic and the cultural to those involving health issues related to well-being and violence. To be sure, variations in socioeconomic status, gender, age, proximity to major centres, and location (off-reserve or on-reserve) ensure that some individuals and communities experience problems more intensely than others, who lead healthy and prosperous lives. The range of problems confronting Aboriginal communities raises a number of questions: What are the causes? Who is responsible? Why? How can solutions consistent with the problem definition be achieved? While all agree that a broken relationship is key in the breakdown of Aboriginal peoples–Canada relationship, there is little agreement on how and why this relationship is broken and what to do about it. For some, Aboriginal peoples are widely thought to have brought inequality on themselves by choosing to live in regions of little employment on remote and barren reserves whose traditional economies cannot possibly thrive and new economic opportunities cannot take root; by embracing traditional cultural values at odds with a modern economy; and by insisting on social patterns of interaction and community life that disrupt or destroy. Others rightly believe the legacy and impact of colonialism (from legislated segregation to systemic violence) is driving an exclusionary wedge between Canada's ideals and Canadian practices (Wilson & Macdonald, 2010). Actions easily defined as crimes against humanity (or even genocide) such as starving Aboriginal peoples into submission played a key role in Canada-building (Daschuk, 2013; MacDonald, Dan, & Farber, 2015). The lasting trauma of the residential school system has scarred generations of aboriginal adults and parents with a corresponding impact currently being played out in the lives of their children (Rolfsen, 2008). The erosion of aboriginal cultural values under (neo)colonialism has compounded the difficulties of identity and adjustment, with many aboriginal languages on the brink of extinction (only three languages—Ojibwa, Cree, and Inuktitut—are on a relatively solid footing). In addition, more than a century of patronizing submission and paternalistic servitude has instilled a host of psychological barriers and social impediments that amplifies patterns of helplessness, powerlessness, and hopelessness (Adams, 1999; Alfred, 2005; Cannon & Sunseri, 2011). Finally, there are those who believe these inequalities of exclusion are largely the result of situational circumstances in which both Aboriginal peoples and Canadian society must assume co-responsibility. The broken relationship can only be fixed if there is mutual accommodation and compromises involving all parties. In short, three ideal-typical models can be discerned for addressing the "Indian problem": *assimilationism* ("more modernization"), *autonomism* ("more autonomy"), or *accommodationism* ("both more and less mainstream/ autonomy").

The Assimilationism Model: Living Together Similarly

At one end of the debate continuum are those who endorse an assimilationism model as a solution to the "Indian problem" (Fiss, 2005a, 2005b; Flanagan, 1999; Gibson, 2009a, 2009b). The assimilationism model is predicated on the assumption that Aboriginal peoples are themselves the architects of their misfortune because of their refusal to assimilate into Canadian society. They must take responsibility for solutions by becoming more thoroughly modern through exposure and involvement in the mainstream, while discarding those social patterns and cultural values at odds with contemporary Canadian realities.

No less problem inducing is the special status enjoyed by Aboriginal peoples (see Widdowson & Howard, 2008). Assimilationists argue that for true equality, the racist and counterproductive edifice of laws and programs for Aboriginal peoples (from reserves to Aboriginal Affairs and Northern Development Canada) must be abolished in favour of normal citizenship. Insofar as all Canadians are fundamentally alike and equal before the law (Gibson, 2005), preferential treatment on the basis of race is morally wrong, bad policy, and socially divisive (Fiss, 2004). The *Indian Act* comes under special criticism by assimilationists because of its imposition of outdated property rights that hobble reserve

residents from using their land and houses in economically productive ways (Flanagan & Beauregard, 2013). Moreover, these critics argue, the Canadian government spends up to $9 billion per year shoring up aboriginal difference, with little to show for the expenditure except third-world living standards, a glaring lack of accountability and transparency in spending, and increasingly strident Aboriginal demands for more and more (Fiss, 2005b). Worse still, a culture of dependency prevails. According to Calvin Helin (2006), the federal government has created a situation whereby all wealth in Aboriginal communities reflects transfer payments or welfare, thus reinforcing a dependency mindset at the expense of self-reliance as a community value.

For assimilationists, then, the solution to the so-called "Indian problem" points to absorption into Canadian society: The strategies are three-fold: First, to eliminate the collectivist mindset that underpins these special provisions and preferential status, while exposing Aboriginal peoples to the balm of modernist values pertaining to individualism, competition, and private property rights (Fiss, 2004; Flanagan, 2001). Second, to wean Aboriginal peoples away from those "artificially preserved" cultural values and social patterns that no longer resonate with meaning in a twenty-first century society but preclude their ability to participate in a modern economy (Widdowson & Howard, 2008). Third, to expose Aboriginal peoples to the discipline of the market—most notably, a conversion into a municipal level of elected

(Continued)

government that generates income from taxing individualized property rights rather than relying on federal transfers for wealth creation (Fiss, 2005b).

The Autonomism Model: Living Separately Together

At the other end of the debate is the autonomist model (see Alfred, 2005). In that Aboriginal peoples continue to suffer the consequences of being forcibly incorporated into someone else's political project, the "Indian problem" is really the Indians' "Canada problem," hence, any solution must begin by challenging those (neo-) colonialist arrangements that created the problem in the first place, including those constitutional barriers that continue to box in aboriginal communities along neo-colonial lines, while conditioning aboriginal minds to think like the colonizers (Alfred, 2005; Hedican, 2013; Newhouse & Belanger, 2011). Autonomists not only radically challenge Canada's political economy, national identity, and unilateral assertion of sovereign jurisdiction over its vast territory and its original inhabitants (Barker, 2015). They also endorse Aboriginal peoples' claims as sovereign political nations with inherent and collective rights to aboriginal models of self-determining autonomy over land, identity, and political voice (see Asch, 2014). Government policy must play its part in securing the inherent and treaty rights of Aboriginal peoples, according to the autonomists. That is, the federal government is pressured to honour its fiduciary responsibilities; protect the legitimacy of aboriginal difference as a basis for recognition, reward, and relationship; and uphold the principles of aboriginal sovereignty as basis for repairing the relationship.

The logic behind the autonomist claim is consistent with the principles of dependency theories: That is, sustained contact with the West, with its corresponding pressures to assimilate and modernize, creates more problems than solutions through dependencies that generate underdevelopment (see also Helin, 2006). Poverty and powerlessness will not disappear with better opportunities or increased expenditures. A "throwing of money at a problem" approach may be effective in the short run, yet it downplays the structural (and more costly) roots of aboriginal problems, namely, the lack of power and resource control. Significant improvements will materialize only when Aboriginal peoples secure a degree of autonomy, including access to power-sharing, an equitable share of revenue from reserve resources, and aboriginal title to land—as aptly captured by Matthew Coon Come, former Grand Chief of the Grand Council of the Crees in Quebec:

> But without adequate access to lands, resources, and without the jurisdictions required to benefit meaningfully and sustainably from them . . . no number of apologies, policies, token programs, or symbolic healing funds are going to remedy this fundamental socio-economic fact. (as cited in Barnsley, 1999:1)

Different models of autonomy can be discerned. A "soft" autonomy model proposed by Cornell and Kalt (2003) and Graham and Levesque (2010) is based on a nation-building approach to development. It proposes a degree of *de facto* sovereignty, in which aboriginal communities take charge of what happens on reserves to create sustainable growth that addresses the causes of problems, not just the symptoms. Others reject this materialist model of autonomy. For Alfred (2005), the route to autonomy lies in rejecting co-optation into mainstream society by political concessions or economic development. In asking the question of how to decolonize a Canada constructed on colonialism, Alfred emphasizes instead the need to delegitimize colonization by decolonizing Aboriginal minds through the rejuvenation of tradition ("heeding the voices of the ancestors") and spirituality. In the words of Taiaiake Alfred and Jeff Corntassel (2005:297–298) in writing of the need to move beyond "white ways" as basis for renewal and resurgence:

> . . . the struggle to survive as distinct peoples on foundations constituted in their unique heritages, attachment to their homelands, and natural ways of life is what is shared by all Indigenous peoples, as well as the fact that their existence is in large part lived as determined acts of survival against the colonizing state's efforts to eradicate them culturally, politically, and physically. The challenge of "being Indigenous" in a psychic and cultural sense, forms the critical question facing Indigenous peoples today in the era of contemporary colonialism—a form of post-modern imperialism in which domination is still the Settler imperative, but where colonizers have designed and practice more subtle means . . . of accomplishing their objectives.

Finally, a radical self-determining autonomy model is endorsed by the Mohawk Nation of the 150 000 strong Iroquois (Haudenosaunee) Confederacy whose communities straddle the territories of Ontario, Quebec, and New York state. Mohawk peoples argue that they are neither Canadian nor American citizens because the Mohawk nation never relinquished by treaty or agreement their sovereign status as an independent nation with exclusive jurisdiction over their territory and peoples.

The Accommodation Model: Living Together with Differences

In between these positions are those who endorse the principle of Aboriginal autonomy but within the framework of Canadian society (see Cairns, 2005). An accommodation model represents a compromise that balances the strengths of autonomy and assimilation models while rejecting the weaknesses of each. Aboriginal problems reflect an interactional frame: Although aboriginal communities are the site of social problems, it's neither an "Indian problem" nor a Canada problem, but rather an "Indian–Canada" problem. According to accommodationists, there is some truth in acknowledging that Aboriginal peoples must assume responsibility for the choices they make and the predicament in which they find themselves. However, as sociologists are prone to say, peoples' options and choices do not originate in a political, historical, or economic vacuum, but within the broader context that fosters restrictions and impositions. A degree of autonomy is critical in breaking the bonds of dependency and constructing self-reliance—not in the individual sense but through interdependence with other

(Continued)

Aboriginal communities and with society at large (Helin, 2006). For example, the indigenous law scholar John Borrows (2010) has proposed a multi-juridicial Canada, one that accommodates the coexistence of indigenous legal traditions with Canadian civil and common law within a single system. In other words, for accommodationists, aboriginal communities suffer from too much of the wrong kind of assimilation and autonomy but too little of the right kind of autonomy and assimilation.

Consider the accommodation solution proposed by Alan Cairns (2000) in his book *Citizens Plus: Aboriginal Peoples and the Canadian State*. The term "citizen plus" was first articulated in the *Hawthorne Report* of 1966 (Cairns participated in the commission that produced the report). The report emphasized that Aboriginal peoples have not only the same rights as all Canadians but also additional rights because of their historical and treaty status (Hawkes, 2000). According to Cairns (2000:86), a commitment to "citizen plus" provides the framework for solving complex aboriginal problems without dismantling Canada in the process. In rejecting a nation-to-nation paradigm, it provides a middle ground that recognizes both aboriginal difference and rights (thus rejecting assimilation) without forsaking a commitment to belonging and citizenship in Canada and the legitimacy of the Canadian state to survive (thus rejecting autonomy). In doing so, a citizen plus model provides a vehicle for Aboriginal peoples to ameliorate the conditions imposed by colonialism without relinquishing the benefits of citizenship in a modern state.

To sum up: Three ideal-typical explanatory frameworks provide competing models for defining and solving the so-called Indian problem. The assimilationist model argues which the most workable solution entails normalizing the status of Aboriginal peoples as citizens and taxpayers, together with their absorption into mainstream society. According to the autonomy model, Aboriginal peoples' problems arise from too much absorption into a system that doesn't work for them. As a result, the solution rests in advancing an aboriginal right to self-determining autonomy by establishing as much distance as possible from mainstream society. The accommodation model seeks a compromise to these two options. Aboriginal peoples require a degree of autonomy to ensure self-determination and the protection of their rights, but not at the expense of disengaging from mainstream society in terms of belonging and commitment.

All three models concur that problems exist in Aboriginal communities, but disagree in framing the issue. Are Aboriginal peoples a *minority* with needs? A *peoples* with rights? Or *citizens* with rights and responsibilities? For assimilationists, the problems are seen as *needs* that require modern solutions; for autonomists, the existence of problems reflects a violation of their rights that must be restored for any sustainable renewal; and for accommodationists, solving the problems is all about repairing the *relationship* in ways workable, necessary, and fair. Table 7-3 compares these models by way of select criteria pertaining to problem, solution, and outcomes. It should be noted that other models exist that do not necessarily fit into one of these three models.

TABLE 7.3	Framing the Problem, Repairing the Relationship: Assimilationism, Autonomism, Accommodationism		
MODEL	**ASSIMILATIONISM**	**AUTONOMISM**	**ACCOMMODATIONISM**
NATURE OF THE INEQUALITY PROBLEM: "Who's to blame?"	"Indian" problem: Blaming the victims	"White" problem: Blame the system	"Indian–white" problem: Blame the situation/ interaction
SOURCE OF THE INEQUALITY PROBLEM	Broken relationship because of not enough assimilation and too much special status/treatment	Broken relationship because of too much assimilation and not enough autonomy	Broken relationship because of too much of the wrong kind of assimilation/ autonomy, too little of the right kind of assimilation/ autonomy, resulting in insufficient accommodation on the part of both whites and Aboriginal peoples
SOLVING THE INEQUALITY PROBLEM	Repair the relationship by **modernizing** (becoming *more like us as basis for getting in*): Primacy of inclusion (fit into system)	Repair the relationship by **indigenizing** (becoming *less like you as basis for getting out*): Primacy of inclusivity (reform system)	Repair the relationship through **mutual adjustment** (becoming both *more like you YET less like you as basis for getting on and getting along*) Inclusiveness (adjust system + modify Aboriginal mindsets)
MEANS	Address *needs* by eliminating special status (*Indian Act*) and preferential treatment	Recognize Aboriginal *rights* to self-determining autonomy at cultural, political, economic levels	Acknowledge mutual interdependence: Aboriginal peoples as citizens but with distinct rights
RESULTS	Common citizenship (same)	Separate citizenship as the Nations Within	Citizen-plus
OUTCOMES	Living together similarly	Living separately together	Living together with differences

Chapter Highlights

- Canadians often perceive Aboriginal peoples as "troublesome constituents" who create problems or have problems in need of solutions through government intervention. Yet the depressed social and economic conditions that confront many aboriginal communities may be a "Canada problem," insofar as Aboriginal peoples were forcibly incorporated into a colonial system that continues to deny, exclude, or exploit.
- The overall status of Aboriginal peoples can be summarized in the expression, "diversity in inequality." Aboriginal peoples are highly diverse in terms of demographics, constitutional status, and cultural differences. They tend to be united in patterns of inequality pertaining to socioeconomic indicators such as income, employment, education, poverty, housing, and general living conditions.

- Aboriginal resistance has shifted from a focus on cultural survival and formal equality to a highly politicized demand for radical renewal through relations-repair, based on recognition of aboriginal title and treaty rights, aboriginal models of self-determining autonomy at self-government levels, and a commitment to taking aboriginal difference seriously.
- Efforts to decolonize the aboriginal agenda are widely anticipated as necessary and overdue; nevertheless, proposals for re-constitutionalizing the foundational principles of Aboriginal peoples–state relations must contend with political and bureaucratic interests, both of which resist fundamental change for fear of destabilizing the status quo.
- It remains to be seen if the creation of a more positive Canada–Aboriginal peoples relationship along postcolonial lines (i.e. partnership, power-sharing, meaningful participation, and property return) can overcome the founding assumptions and foundational rules of a (neo-)colonial constitutional order.

Review Questions

1. Outline the current demands of the Aboriginal peoples with respect to improving their relational status in Canadian society. How do aboriginal demands compare with the solutions proposed by the federal government?

2. Demonstrate how and why the assimilationists differ from the autonomists in defining and solving the so-called Indian problem. Indicate the underlying assumptions, problem definition, proposed solution, and anticipated outcome. Does a commitment to accommodationism provide a compromise position in repairing the relationship?

3. Relations repair is at the heart of renewing the relationship between Canada and Aboriginal peoples. Indicate how and why this is case and briefly indicate the relevance of a commitment to recognizing aboriginality, aboriginal title and treaty rights, and aboriginal self-determining autonomy as basis for relations-repair.

4. While most Canadians dismiss colonialism as an unfortunate relic of the past, Eurocentric attitudes and discriminatory practices continue to reinforce Aboriginal realities at present. Only the means have changed, according to aboriginal critics (Alfred, 2005; J. Green, 2003), with open assimilation strategies giving way to more covert strategies of control that consolidate a neo-colonialist framework of containment. Explain, with examples.

5. Explain what is meant by the concept of "aboriginal models of self-determining autonomy over land, identity, and political voice." What is the political significance of this concept?

CHAPTER 8

Immigrants and Immigration

LEARNING OBJECTIVES

After reading this chapter, you will be able to:

1. Describe the nature of the debate over the issue of inland refugee claimants in Canada.

2. Discuss the implications of Canada as an "immigration society."

3. Compare and contrast Canada's pre-1960s immigration model with the current immigration model.

4. List the basic elements of Canada's immigration program at present.

5. Provide insights into the mix of experiences and aspirations of newcomers to Canada.

DEBATE

Canada's Inland Refugee Determination System: Is It Working?

Debates over refugee claimants and asylum seekers perplex and provoke as few other issues can or have. The global crisis in displaced persons says it all: In 2014, according to the United Nations High Commissioner for Refugees (UNHCR) annual Global Trends report (2015) figures, the number of people around the world uprooted against their will stood at the 59.5 million mark—an increase of 8.3 million over 2013, driven largely by the war in Syria where estimates indicate a displacement of up to 65 percent of the country's 22 million people. (The UNHCR was established in 1950 with a three-year mandate to process European refugees.) Yet another example of an ongoing crisis that shows no signs of abating is the much-publicized movement of migrants across the Mediterranean from both Africa and the Middle East in search of opportunity and safety, yet often experiencing hardship and death during the passage (an estimated 1900 lost their lives in the first half of 2015). More recently, media attention has spotlighted the continuing displacement of peoples such as the Rohingya from Myanmar and the world's ongoing indifference to their pleas (UNHCR, 2015).

The numbers continue to amaze: One of out of every 122 humans is now forcibly displaced as a refugee or asylum seeker, or is internally displaced, which if this was the population of a country, would make it the world's 24th most populous. This total includes:

(Continued)

239

- 38.2 million internally displaced persons (forced to flee their homes but remain within country borders).

- 19.5 million refugees, with the biggest refugee populations by source country (apart from 5 million Palestinians who fall under the jurisdiction of the UN Relief and Works Agency for Palestinian Refugees [UNRWA] established in 1949) being Syria (3.8 million), Afghanistan (2.6 million), and Somalia (1.1 million); in turn, the biggest refugee hosting countries are Turkey, Pakistan, Iran, and Lebanon. About half of all refugees of concern to UNHCR live in Asia, with another 28 percent in Africa, according to the 2014 Global Trends report, under widely varying conditions from well-established camps to unsheltered compounds. As well, half the world's refugees are children who travel alone or in groups, and often fall prey to the clutches of increasingly sophisticated networks of people traffickers and human smugglers.

- 1.8 million asylum seekers ("**refugee claimants**") awaiting the outcomes of their claims for asylum, with the vast majority lodged in developed countries. Six hundred twenty-six thousand people requested asylum in Europe in 2014, a jump of 45 percent from 2013, whereas North American registered 134 600 asylum seekers, a 42 percent increase (Kauffmann, 2015). The United States boasts the largest resettlement program, having accepted two-thirds of the 98 000 UN-based refugees who were permanently resettled in 2013 (Capps & Newland, 2015).

Clearly, then, the global displacement crisis is real, its impact on countries and the international order is inestimable, and its omnipresence is unlikely to dissipate very soon. The asylum and refugee crisis involves debates over constructing a system that not only deters "unwanted" claimants but also establishes a transparent protocol for deciding who is a refugee. Canada is not exempt from this crisis of undocumented movement of people. But while other countries are struggling to staunch the flow of refugee claimants, including Australia with its hardline policy of interdiction and shipboard screening, mandatory detention and forced relocation of massed ship arrivals, off-shore processing, and overseas resettlement of recognized refugees (Frelick, 2015), Canada has a framework in place that ostensibly provides a principled way of determining who is or is not a refugee. On the surface, establishing a refugee determination system that is fair, fast, and final would seem simple enough (Showler, 2005, 2009). And in many ways, many admire the inland refugee determination system Canada has in place (namely, the Immigration and Refugee Board [IRB]). The United Nations High Commission for Refugees (1998) has called Canada's protectionist system with its high recognition rate and expansive definition of a refugee "a model to be emulated" (also Soennecken, 2014:110). In reality, the system continues to reflect structural and procedural weaknesses that render its subject to relentless scrutiny and withering criticism (Bissett, 2009; Gallagher, 2008b; ImmigrationWatch, 2011; Moens & Collacott, 2008; Stoffman, 2002, 2009), as the following questions imply:

- Can the inland refugee determination system distinguish genuine refugee claimants from bogus applicants? Is the refugee determination system subject to abuse and breakdown, resulting in a safe-haven for terrorists and a quick-fix channel for the so-called "queue jumpers"?

- How do we distinguish refugees fleeing persecution from asylum seekers originating in those grey zones where discrimination is rife, the state has collapsed, and the economy is in dire straits, thereby making it nearly impossible to disentangle motives (Refugees, 2007)?

- Has the inland determination system proven effective in balancing national interests with the rights of those seeking refugee status (Adelman, 2004)?

- Can a principle to protect asylum seekers established to process a trickle of Cold War dissidents address a burgeoning caseload involving new and bewildering complexities (Spencer, 2003)?

- Does the IRB possess a degree of principled integrity in determining whose inland claims qualify them as a refugee, or is it prone to patterns of subjectivity that makes a mockery of its role in rendering life–death decisions (Rehaag, 2013, 2015)?

How should the inland refugee determination process be assessed—is it in disarray, or is it as good as it gets? Opinion is mixed: Many, including the United Nations High Commissioner for Refugees, believe Canada's inland refugee determination process to be one of the world's most generous, although the

2015 UN annual asylum trends report put Canada at the bottom of the world's top 15 refugee receiving countries, down from a high of fifth in the world five years previous. For some, this generosity is to be celebrated as a source of pride (Mawani, 1997); for others, it proves that Canadians are being taken for a ride (Collacott, 2006). Those who think the system is excessively generous point out that Canada accepts refugee claimants at six times the international norm. Of the 95 500 refugees who made claims to the Immigration and Refugee Board of Canada between 1993 and 1997, 42 percent were accepted (down from 84 percent in 1989), 33 percent were rejected, and 25 percent were neither finalized nor ineligible. In 2003, the figure for acceptance remained at 42 percent, with 40 percent rejected and 18 percent abandoned. In 2010, the acceptance rate dipped to 38 percent, but by 2014, acceptance rates had rebounded to almost half of the 19 960 claims processed, including 61 percent for new post-2012 claims (but 34% for backlog claims) (Keung, 2015), in part because of proportionately fewer applicants from the 42 countries now deemed to be "safe" and free from persecution.

The best spin on the 42 percent acceptance rate endorses these numbers as a reflection of Canada's commitment to assist the world's most unfortunate. The worst spin suggests that Canada's refugee determination system is absurdly dysfunctional—especially since Canada does not share a border with a refugee-producing country, thus negating any justification for such low numbers. Others, including refugee lawyers and advocacy groups, see the 42 percent

(Continued)

acceptance rate as exceptionally low for such a rich and spacious country. Canada's refugee determination system is accused of turning its back on the world's most desperate by adapting a European (i.e., restrictive- and security-driven) "turn" toward asylum policies (Soennecken, 2014). So who is right? Is the 42 percent acceptance figure too high or too low? Does Canada, as an affluent society, have an obligation to be more generous when dealing with refugees? Or should priority be assigned to protecting Canada's national interests related to security, prosperity, and sovereignty? Is the system too strict or not restrictive enough? On what grounds can any assessment be made? Who says so, and why? The Debate Revisited box at the end of this chapter will provide some additional insights in assessing whether Canada's approach toward refugee determination under the IRB is working and fair.

INTRODUCTION: THE PARADOXES OF IMMIGRATION

The conclusion cannot be avoided: In this globalized era of human uprootedness and migration, the movement of people is not an anomaly but a normal process that may prove impossible to curb or control. (Pecoud & de Guchteneire, 2005)

The twenty-first century may well become defined by the movement of peoples from one country to another, from one continent to another (Castles, de Haas, & Miller 2013; Guterres, 2007). With up to 235 million people on the move outside of their homeland—a population equivalent to that of Brazil, the world's fifth most populous country—it is safe to say that few countries have been untouched by international migration (Kapur, 2005; Papademetriou, 2003; Simmons, 2010). Humans from around the world are in a constant quest to improve their lives, to flee from confining environments, and to escape from natural and social disasters. People are being "pushed" from their homelands because of political oppression, ethnic conflicts, demographic pressure, and economic stagnation (Fleras, 2014b). They also are "pulled" to other countries to take advantage of opportunity and freedom—or to seek out adventure and excitement. In some cases, people are seeking asylum by fleeing persecution, human rights abuses, and armed conflicts; in other cases, they are escaping hardship and the uncertainties of life in developing countries with weak economies and unstable political systems (also Spoonley & Bedford, 2012). The foreseeable future will prove even more challenging: Climate change and natural disasters will make human existence increasingly unsustainable, while the growing awareness of gaps between the rich and poor will induce many to pull up roots and seek their fortunes elsewhere, despite exposure to risks and disappointments (Guterres, 2007).

In short, the world is increasingly inundated with new and more complex patterns of displacement and migration (Massey, 2009; Pecoud & de Guchteneire, 2005). As the nature of these border crossings varies, so too does the proliferation of terms to account for the variety, as Table 8-1 shows. The politics of immigration are especially striking in Canada (Fleras, 2014b; Hansen, 2013). As Stephen Gallagher (2008b) observes, Canada may be the only country in the world where mass (employed in the sense of massive rather

TABLE 8-1	Types of Migrants

Immigrants

- Born elsewhere
- Arrive voluntarily
- Entitled to permanent status
- Associated with economic benefits or family reunification

Refugees

- Forced to flee their home country
- Cannot return because of a well-founded fear of persecution based on race, ethnicity, etc. (convention refugees)
- In need of protection (seeking asylum) and cannot be returned because of safety concerns (protected persons)

Convention Refugees

- Designated as such according to the 1951 Geneva convention
- Normally living in refugee camps around the world
- Awaiting resettlement by host country selection
- Arrive as government assisted or privately sponsored ("resettled" refugees)

Inland Refugee Claimants

- Claim refugee status through self-selection
- Claim is made at port of entry or from within Canada's borders
- Are subject to a quasi-legal process to determine legitimacy of claims
- Also known in Canada as persons in need of protection

Refugees Landed in Canada

- Claimants whose claims for refugee status approved by the IRB
- Entitled to apply for permanent residence status

Asylum seekers

- Seek sanctuary or refuge (safe keeping) in another country, but have not yet received refugee status.

Internally displaced persons

- Uprooted and forced to flee their home, but remain located in their home country

Stateless persons

- Not considered a national by any state

Evacuees

- Temporarily evacuated from a crisis zone, but must return once hostilities subside

Guest workers/temporary foreign workers

- Foreign nationals who enter another country on a temporary basis and are expected to leave upon completion of their job or expiry of their work visa

than undifferentiated) immigration constitutes an article of faith, embodies a policy norm, and informs national identity. Canada's immigration program has garnered widespread popularity and public support, in addition to praise as an international success story (Reitz, 2010). On the whole, Canada has become a more vibrant and dynamic society because of immigrants and immigration. Immigration and immigrants have not only contributed to Canada's national identity and character (Bauder, 2011; Cliplef, 2014), but have also bolstered the Canadian economy in their role as Canada-builders, both abroad and domestically (Halli & Driedger, 1999; Hiebert & Ley, 2006). Immigrants may provide a solution to the problems of an aging population, shrinking birth rate, diminishing tax base, and skills shortage in a global and information-based economy. They have also proven pivotal in re-energizing Canada's economy by virtue of consumer spending, optimistic outlook, and entrepreneurial spirit (Walton-Roberts, 2011). In other words, a fundamental mindset shift is overdue in light of increased global competition for the brightest and the best: *Canada needs immigrants more than immigrants may need Canada.*

Canadians, for the most part, have embraced immigration with the kind of civility and open-mindedness that is becoming a national trademark (Adams, 2007; Bloemraad, 2014). Whereas many European countries are rethinking their commitment to immigration in light of post-9/11 security concerns and the Mediterranean migrant crisis, Canada continues to maintain historically high admission levels. Canada's intake of about 250 000 migrants on average per year over the past 20 years (including nearly 281, 000 in 2010—the highest single year total in 50 years) constitutes about 0.7 percent of the total population—making Canada one of the largest per capita immigrant-receiving countries in the world relative to the size of its population. Canadians also appear favourably disposed to immigration (but see Graves, 2015). Polls routinely convey a positive message: Canadians overwhelmingly support immigration as part of a Canada-building project; immigration and immigrants are thought to strengthen the economy; and immigrants do a good job of fitting into Canada (Environics Institute, 2015; Nanos, 2010).

As well, Canada remains a destination of choice for international immigrants. According to an international survey of nearly 19 000 adult respondents commissioned by the Historica-Dominion Institute (2010) in partnership with the Munk School of Global Affairs and Aurea Foundation, more than half the people (53 percent) from the world's 24 leading economies say they would abandon their homelands and move to Canada if they could. This tilt toward Canada is most noticeable in the emerging economies of the G20: A whopping 77 percent of Chinese would immigrate to Canada if they had a choice, followed by 71 percent of Mexicans, 68 percent of Indians, 64 percent of Turks, and 62 percent of both the Polish and South Africans. Respondents to the survey expressed overwhelmingly positive attitudes about Canada's welcoming and tolerant treatment of newcomers. A full 86 percent of respondents embrace Canada as a country that respects rights and freedoms; 79 percent believe Canadians are tolerant of those from different racial and cultural backgrounds; 79 percent said that Canada has one of the best qualities of life in the world (in 2009, the UN Human Development Index ranked Canada fourth, behind Norway, Australia, and Iceland); and 72 percent said Canada is welcoming to immigrants. Moreover, unlike many European countries, Canada possesses neither an anti-immigrant political party nor an active far right movement. The conclusion seems inescapable: Canada remains a country of choice for those looking to improve fortunes, to reunite with family and relatives, and to escape political repression. Such praise bodes well for Canada's efforts to attract talent and the talented in the looming global talent wars (Reputation Institute, 2015).

But there is a darker side to this bucolic picture: Canada may be a land of immigrants, yet it remains sharply conflicted over the pros and cons of immigration. Put bluntly, Canada's immigration policy is thought to be out of control with respect to "how many," "what kind," "where from," and "what for," with a corresponding negative impact on both new Canadians and Canadian society (Bissett, 2008; Grubel & Grady, 2011). Those on the right complain of too many of the "wrong kind"; those on the left complain of not enough of the "right kind"; and those in the middle may be confused over "what kind" or "how much." Still others criticize Canada's immigration program as one in need of a major overhaul, despite a glowing international reputation as a principled framework that is being copied elsewhere, including the United Kingdom (Canadian Press, 2007a) and more recently in Germany. Not surprisingly, perhaps, recent polls suggest a hardening of Canadian attitudes in general toward the admission of immigrants, but especially toward those who are racialized (Graves, 2015; also Environics Institute, 2015).

Criticism over immigration paradoxes cannot be brushed off. Immigration may be inseparable from the quality of life in Canada; after all, Canada's standard of living will depend on immigration to offset the diminishing returns of an aging population and the declining birth rate. The labour of irregular migrants and temporary foreign workers is critical in shoring up the middle-class lifestyle that Canadians crave (Hiebert, 2006). Yet the promise and productivity of immigration are lost in a welter of debates over fiscal uncertainty, corporate downsizing, job losses, economic restructuring, and political expediency (Li, 2003). Immigration may have facilitated a robust consumer economy in Canada's gateway cities of Vancouver and Toronto, but associated costs cannot be discounted, including congestion, shortage of affordable housing, and strains on social service delivery (ImmigrationWatch, 2011). Double standards are no less unmistakable: Immigrants are rebuked for stealing jobs from "real" Canadians, yet rejected as "freeloading parasites" if on the dole or on welfare. Put bluntly, Canadians remain "reluctant hosts" who appear welcoming at times, truculent at other times, but whose ambivalence—even hostility— toward certain foreign-born nationals is palpable beneath a folksy veneer of tolerance. (See controversy over the niqab and citizenship in Chapter 6.)

Of those immigration issues that generate controversy, few can match the staying power of debates over the refugee question. A key distinction is required: Criticism of refugees does not revolve around resettled UN-defined refugees who are selected either privately or by governments from UN-based camps around the world. Much vitriol is directed at those asylum seekers who self-select to enter into Canada and claim inland refugee status. Canada's attempt at determining the legitimacy of inland refugee claimants (or protected persons) by way of the IRB has also drawn criticism and prompted questions (Rehaag, 2015). Is the system working? Is it fair? Is the system too generous or not generous enough? Is it too restrictive or not restrictive enough? Is it too inclusive or not inclusive enough? Criticized as well are recent government moves to tighten up the inland refugee determination program, which critics denounce as unfair and inhumane—and in contravention of international protocols on the rights on asylum seeker and refugees.

Just as Canadians are perplexed by the politics of immigration, so too are newcomers experiencing glitches in the transition-to-Canada trajectory (Bauder, 2012; Kazemipur, 2014). "Getting in" is one thing. "Settling down," "fitting in," and "moving up" have proven more challenging than most would have imagined. Immigrants come to Canada with the best of intentions for making a positive contribution to Canada and for themselves (Isajiw,

1999). Yet Canada has not always proven itself the haven that many had expected. True, both immigrants and refugees possess the rights of citizenship and the multicultural right to inclusiveness, in addition to an assortment of various government programs to facilitate integration and settlement (Halli & Driedger, 1999; Wayland, 2006). Nevertheless, many continue to encounter obstacles that intensify levels of immigration frustration, up to and including violence turned inward (suicide) or outwards (domestic abuse)—in large part because they must exercise their formal equality rights in a Canadian context neither designed to reflect their realities nor constructed to advance their interests (Fleras, 2014a). Formidable barriers exist in a society whose welcome mat is yanked out from underneath at the slightest provocation. Furthermore, Canada's much-vaunted tolerance has been put to the test in the aftermath of 9/11 amidst fears that loose entry regulations and lax enforcement may foster a haven for terrorist groups (Immigration Watch Canada, 2011). As a result, antipathy toward new Canadians sometimes borders on the xenophobic or apoplectic, with calls for rigorous screening procedures, including DNA testing, immigrant and citizenship tests, and vigorous deportation procedures.

Problem or solution? Cost or benefit? Good or bad or in between (see Chomsky, 2007; Swain, 2007)? It is within the context of concern and criticism, of progress and stalemate, of conviction and confusion that this chapter delves into the politics of Canadian immigration and immigrants to Canada. Its central focus aims at those recurrent debates over the political and social dimensions of immigration both in the past and at present with respect to principles and politics, patterns and programs, and impacts and implications for Canada-building. The chapter begins by theorizing the concept of Canada as an **immigration society**, followed by a brief discussion of Canada's immigration model. It continues with a closer examination of the laws and policies that govern the entry of immigrants into Canada. Particular attention is aimed at the politics of "entry," as this category has evolved over time, thus raising the question of whether the current model of admission works best in light of emergent realities. Many of the controversies associated with immigration are discussed as well, including responses to the following key questions (also Legrain, 2007):

- Why should Canada accept immigrants?
- Who should be encouraged to come to Canada?
- How many immigrants should be accepted?
- Which category of immigrant is preferred: family, economic, or refugee?
- What kind of diversity can immigrants bring with them? How far should immigrants go to adapt to society, and vice versa?
- How much immigrant diversity can a society embrace? How much commonalities does it need?
- How do we balance long-term goals for Canada-building with short-term responses to labour specific needs?
- In what way do immigrants contribute to or detract from Canada-building?
- What is the best way of integrating immigrants—by incorporating differences or emphasizing commonalities?
- Should immigrants be left to their devices in settling down or should government intervention be promoted?

The chapter also provides a review, assessment, and criticism of Canada's inland refugee determination process by asking the key questions: Who is a refugee? How do we find out? Is the system fair? Is it working? How can it be improved? Has it shown improvement with recent changes? The difficulties endured by immigrants in adjusting to Canadian society—that is, settling down, fitting in, and moving up—confirm what many suspect: From afar, Canada's status as an immigration society sparkles; up close, it loses some of its lustre.

A word of caution: A chapter on immigration, immigrants, and refugees could not possibly address all topics without stretching its resources to the point of superficiality and gloss. Emphasis is directed primarily at the challenges and concerns of immigrants and their descendants from the so-called non-conventional countries of origin, in terms of their adjustment to Canadian society under a bewildering array of policy circumstances, institutional barriers, and social pressures. Specific groups are not dealt with *per se*. Admittedly, the intent to provide a comprehensive overview of immigrants and refugees *as if* they constituted a relatively uniform category for analytical purposes runs the risk of oversimplification, reductionism, or essentializing (treating everyone in a category in a fixed, homogeneous, and deterministic fashion). Still, there are many benefits in embracing the big picture while acknowledging the range of internal diversity because of race, ethnicity, age, gender, sexual preference, and social class. Finally, the sensitivity of the topic can generate hostility because immigration politics upset cherished notions of national unity, identity, and belonging (Spoonley & Bedford 2012); require difficult political decisions and tradeoffs at individual or institutional levels; and may expose hypocrisies of governance or political commitment (Papademetriou, 2003). Nevertheless, answers to these questions and debates require a level of deliberation that goes beyond political slogans or public posturing (see also Swain, 2007).

CANADA: AN IMMIGRATION SOCIETY OF IMMIGRANTS

Canada embraces a tapestry of diversity from around the world. Its robust immigration program creates a staunchly heterogeneous society whose reputation as a multicultural mosaic needs little propping up. Canada's diverse composition has undergone a radical transformation since the passage of the *British North America (Constitution) Act* of 1867 when 92 percent of people living in Canada were neither of British nor French ancestry (Palmer, 1975); that is, in 1867, the overwhelming majority of the population was Aboriginal. Between 1896 and 1914, the balance began to shift when up to 3 million immigrants—many of them from Central and Eastern Europe—arrived to domesticate the West. Immigration increased substantially prior to the First World War, reaching a peak of just over 400 000 in 1913. Both the Great Depression and the Second World War had a dampening effect on immigration into Canada, resulting in an all-time low intake of less than 8000 admissions in 1942. The post-World War II period resulted in yet another "exodus" from the war-devastated countries of Europe, but sources of immigration since the 1970s have shifted as well—in the process rekindling controversy over the politics of "who gets in, why, and how." Despite some criticism (Immigration Watch, 2011), Canada's immigration program remains as lively as ever, with annual averages in the 250 000 range over the past 20 years, with remarkably little in the way of public backlash or political back pedaling.

Canada can be described as a society of immigrants. It's also one of the few countries in the world that qualifies as *an immigration society* in the normative sense of the expression

(Fleras, 2014b). With nearly 235 million migrants on the move (some voluntarily, others forcibly), such a statement may strike one as odd. But the centrality of immigrants to contemporary existence notwithstanding, few societies have addressed the reality and importance of immigration, in part out of fear of disrupting national identities, exposing weaknesses in national governance and security, and undermining state capacity for enforcing unpopular laws (Spoonley & Bedford, 2012). Not surprisingly, migrants in search of jobs or a new life tend to be seen as problems to be solved through programs or services rather than as victims of "failed societies" related to the larger issue of transnational global capital and its impact on those that are most impoverished (Simmons, 2010).

In other words, many societies may qualify as a society of immigrants if defined along descriptive lines; few, however, can claim to be a prescriptively immigration society in terms of normative standards. The United States, Australia, and New Zealand are normally regarded as immigration societies, as are Brazil and Argentina, several other Latin American countries, and possibly Israel (Spoonley & Bedford, 2012). An immigration society can be defined as one that takes a principled and proactive approach to immigration based on four distinguishing criteria (see also Ucarer, 1997; Reitz, 2014):

- Policies and principles regulate the entry of immigrants into the country.
- Programs are in place to facilitate immigrants' integration and settlement.
- Immigrants are entitled to all rights, including the expectation of permanent residence and citizenship.
- Immigration and immigrants are embraced as assets for society-building and central to national identity.

These criteria form the basis of what might be called Canada's immigration model. Reference to Canada as an immigration society with a distinctive immigration model is captured in Table 8-2. Content that appears in the right hand column will be expanded on throughout this chapter.

Canada clearly subscribes to each of these attributes, at least in principle, if not always in practice. Immigration and immigrants are defined as part of Canada's national character, immigrants are framed as crucial to Canada-building, their admission is based on principled rules, they are expected to permanently reside as citizens with rights, and programs are in place to facilitate their integration and participation (Fleras, 2014b). By contrast, countries such as Germany tended to deny a dependency on immigrants, although guest workers were imported to address the post-Second World War reconstruction boom. If anything, these countries defined themselves as "complete societies" (Castles & Miller, 2009)—as ethnically rooted with a shared sense of history, culture, and destiny; an exclusive concept of citizenship that excluded outsiders from contributing to the national identity or to society-building in general; and as emigration countries that exported surplus populations (Sykes, 2008:11; Zick, Pettigrew, & Wagner, 2008). Policies were devised to stabilize inflows, limit long-term stays, discourage permanent residence, restrict participation and involvement, label newcomers as guest workers, and withhold citizenship and attendant rights (Pecoud & de Guchteneire, 2005). For example, children of foreigners were generally excluded from citizenship even if they were born and raised in Germany; paradoxically, those of German parentage (ancestry) were automatically granted citizenship regardless of how long they had lived *outside* of Germany (Modood, 2003).

TABLE 8-2	Canada's Immigration Model
Immigration and Immigrants Define Canada	– National identity
Rules/Protocols to Regulate Admissions	– Managed immigration/Canada must be in charge of admission
	– Principled and proactive
	– Transparent/objective/accountable/ non-discriminatory
	– Balance of family, economic, humanitarian classes (self-interest + humanitarian)
	– Balance short term labour needs with long term Canada-building citizens
	– Until recently, based on principle of first come, first serve, (i.e., those who qualify are automatically allowed entry into Canada)
	– Increasingly a shared jurisdiction (feds, provinces, private interests)
	– Protect health, security, and safety of Canadians
Immigrants = Society Building Assets	– Solution to problems
	– Crucial to sustained economic growth
	– Labour market + human capital models
	– International linkages as key to global economy
	– Cultural enrichment
Immigrants = Permanent residents with rights and rights to citizenship	– Settlement model of Immigration (not just market correction/contract labour)
	– Relatively easy path to citizenship = based on commitment to principles/idea/ideals
	– Social contract between migrants and state;
	– A thin national identity that makes Canada more accommodative
Programs for Settlement/Integration	– Multiculturalism, Employment Equity
	– Immigration settlement services such as ESL programs, Welcoming Communities Initiative
	– Respect for differences, removal of discriminatory barriers
	– Inclusive principle—no one is excluded

To be sure, this mindset is changing across Europe. Formerly anti-immigrant emigration countries have little option now except to embrace immigration to offset the effects of an aging population, a plummeting birth rate, costly welfare programs, a shortage of skilled professional workers, and obligations under EU membership (Munz & Ohliger, 2003). Germany is now the second most popular migration destination in the world, second only to the United States, with one of every five persons having some ancestral roots outside of Germany (Bloomberg, 2014). Since 2000, the restrictions for citizenship in Germany have been lifted for children born of lawfully resident foreign parents (Macklin &

Crepeau, 2010). Passage of the *Immigration Act* of 2005 also established provisions for a single statutory framework for managing immigration into Germany, including the *Residence Act* in regulating the residence status and integration of foreigners (Germany.info, 2007). Chancellor Angela Merkel's commitment in 2015 to admit an unlimited number of newcomers in response to the European migration crisis points to Germany's emerging status as an immigration society, although there are mounting signs of public unease and political backlash over this proposed shift (*Economist*, 2015a, b). In short, any transitioning from a society of immigrants to an immigration society will prove challenging, as both mindsets and institutions must rethink the paradox of needing immigrants but not wanting them (*Economist*, 2010).

WHO GOT IN? EXCLUSIONARY PRACTICES

Canada is frequently praised—or occasionally pilloried—as an immigration society of immigrants (Foster, 1998). With the exception of Aboriginal peoples, all Canadians are immigrants or descendants of immigrants. Immigration has played a pivotal role in Canada's national development and will continue to do so in the foreseeable future (Ibbitson, 2005b). The increasingly unfettered movements of capital, ideas, elite labour, and investment because of globalization will see to that. But Canadians seem curiously ambivalent about immigration and immigrants, despite a long-standing reliance on immigrant labour as a catalyst for development and capitalist expansion (Bolaria & Li, 1988).

The content and direction of Canadian immigration practices have evolved over time (Kelly & Trebilcock, 2010; Knowles, 2007; Siemiatycki, 2015). Initial moves for governing the admission of foreign individuals reflected a combination of ideological considerations, political expediency, international obligations, and the colonialist requirements of a hinterland economy. Outcomes were decided by an interplay of factors, including racism and ethnocentrism, the agricultural bias of Canada's early immigration policies, the pivotal role of private and business interests, Canada's Commonwealth commitments as part of the British Empire, and high levels of out-migration to the United States. Historically, the Canadian state grappled with conflicting interests, that is, how to preserve its whiteness while securing an adequate supply of migrant labour without embracing an overtly racist immigration program (Thobani, 2000b, 2007). This conflict of interest transformed immigration policy and practice into a contested site, with competing interests jockeying to impose their agenda.

Immigration into Canada until the late nineteenth century was largely informal and highly discretionary (Meyers, 2002). Initial practices regarding whom to let in and whom to keep out could be described as essentially racist in orientation, assimilationist in objective, nativist in content, and exclusionary in outcome (Abu-Laban, 1999; Wallis & Fleras, 2008). To the extent that rules existed, immigration regulations reflected a distinction between preferred versus non-preferred "races" (Elabor-Idemudia, 1999; Thobani, 2000b). A preference for more assimilable whites, namely, those from Britain and Northern Europe, contrasted with the dismissal of inferior "races" as contrary to Canada's climate or cultural values (Simmons, 2010). As much energy was expended in keeping out certain "types" as was in encouraging others to settle. The 1869 *Immigration Act* and subsequent amendments, including the 1910 *Immigration Act*, excluded undesirables, such as criminals, the mentally unfit, the diseased, nationalities unlikely to assimilate, and city dwellers. Strict limitations were imposed on the Japanese, Chinese, and East Asians, in part through head taxes or regulations such as the Continuous Journey Rule that required all immigrants to travel directly from their country of origin or citizenship with a through ticket purchased in the home country. The fact that steamships required refueling at some point before arriving at Vancouver or Halifax ensured a *de facto* exclusion behind a facade of formal neutrality.

A "racial pecking order" of preference prevailed (Lupul, 1988; Walker, 1997). A prevailing perception of Canada as "a white man's country" ensured that preferred immigrants were drawn from the so-called superior stock of Western Europe. This category was virtually exempt from entry restrictions except for certain formalities that precluded those defined as diseased, deranged, and dangerous. At the bottom of this pecking order were blacks and Asians, both of whom were seen as inherently inferior and ultimately unassimilable. The Irish, too, were deemed to be culturally and economically dangerous people—a poor, ignorant, and knavish people with "papist" religious convictions and prone to crime and joblessness. Between these two poles were the non-preferred classes, consisting of immigrants from Eastern and Middle Europe and Russia. Canadians also harboured a degree of suspicion toward these "dangerous foreigners," despite admiration for their brawn and industry, particularly those Bolsheviks who dared to challenge the principles of free enterprise (Avery, 1995). A special "restricted" permit class controlled the entry of Jews and Mediterranean peoples.

Once preferred sources dwindled, other Europeans began to look better. Canada's first immigration minister, Clifford Sifton, made virtue of necessity in 1896 when he encouraged immigrants from Eastern Europe to settle the west, despite a chorus of criticism over compromising national interests. Sifton resolutely opposed the import of urban factory workers, many of whom were seen as degenerate, susceptible to economic unrest, or fodder for radical agitators. Most immigrants were expected to settle, to farm, and to secure a rural economic base for Canada (Knowles, 2007). The agricultural bias of early immigration was eloquently expressed when Sifton mused about "stalwart peasants in a sheepskin coat, born on the soil, whose forefathers had been farmers for 10 generations, with a stout wife and a half-dozen children."

But not all immigrants saw themselves as tillers of soil. Over time, migrants shifted from agriculture to wage employment in labour-intensive industries such as railroad construction, mining, and construction work (Avery, 1995). Nor did all immigrants look to Canada as the Promised Land. It took a lot of convincing to get people to come; even more inducements were required to make them stay, considering the vagaries of Canada's physical terrain and climatic rigors. Many new Canadians promptly emigrated to the United States; for instance, between 1851 and 1948, almost as many left for the United States as immigrated to Canada (Beaujot, 1999; Isajiw, 1999). Or consider how during the 1971 to 1981 decade, there were almost half as many long-term departures (636 000) as permanent arrivals (1 429 000)—in effect reinforcing a perception of Canada as essentially a transfer point between America and Europe (Whitaker, 1991). This trend persists into the present, according to a Statistics Canada study, with the departure of many male immigrants within 20 years of arrival (Thompson, 2006).

A commitment to immigration for Canada-building exposed two thorny problems: the need for cheap labour and the necessity of a means for rapid removal of immigrants when no longer required (Walker, 2001b). Political parties engaged in endless polemics over who was desirable or assimilable, preferred or non-preferred (Thobani, 2000a, b). But all agreed that Canada's survival depended on excluding those workers who were perceived as unsuitable to Canadian conditions, who were thought to be incapable of assimilating into prevailing norms of decency and democracy, and who posed a threat to Canadian values and institutions. Non-preferred immigrants were tolerated as long as they quietly toiled away in remote regions and at tasks deemed too demeaning and demanding for white Canadians (e.g., railways, mines, lumber camps, domestic work). Nowhere was this more evident than in the treatment of Asian "guest workers" or "sojourners," such as the Chinese and Indians, many of whom were tolerated merely as "fodder" for Canadian capitalist expansion—a tap to be turned on when needed, turned off when not.

Three insights can be gleaned from this overview of early migration. First, diverse interests tended to sway public reaction and political response to immigrants and immigration. For example, business and powerful transportation companies supported immigration on the grounds that a prosperous local economy required a steady supply of migrant labour. By contrast, organized labour and public sentiment generally favoured a restriction of those immigrants who depressed wages, increased job insecurity, and threatened to "lower [the] Canadian standard of living" (Avery, 1995; see also Stoffman, 2003). The government found itself sandwiched in between, sometimes aligning with one side, then the other; at other times capitulating to private or to public interests as the circumstances dictated.

Second, early immigration practices reflected practical considerations that coincided with Canada's economic needs. Immigrants were selected on the basis of their ability to fill slots in the expanding economy, resulting in a "taps-on," "taps-off" approach to admissions. When Chinese migrants were required for railroad building, the taps were turned on; when they were no longer required, the taps were turned off. The expediency of a taps-on and taps-off approach assured an uneven immigration intake for advancing national interests. Settlement of the Prairies required large numbers, with immigration peaking at 400 870 in 1913; by contrast, wars and Depression conditions resulted in declining figures, bottoming out in 1942 at 7576 immigrants. This stop-and-go mentality exposed Canada to criticism that it was merely operating a guest worker system; that is, foreigners were welcome when the economy boomed, but unwelcome otherwise.

Third, the acceptance of immigrants was driven by a hard-boiled pragmatism. Canada "needed" workers and settlers for the backbreaking toil of taming the wilderness and "manning" industries. The practical aspects of Canada's immigration policy remain in effect at present. Canada wants immigrants for largely self-serving reasons, including to (1) offset the effects of an aging population and the declining birth rate, (2) ensure a sufficient tax base to underwrite increasingly costly services, (3) expand the size of the domestic market, (4) establish profitable international linkages, and (5) stimulate sustained economic activity through production and consumption. Those business immigrants who are willing to invest in Canada or to create jobs for Canadians are actively courted under a series of programs that come and go. No less critical a factor is the need for cheap and disposable labour to address short-term labour needs in the quick-service, hospitality, and extractive industries (Hennebry, 2010; Goldring & Landolt 2013). The importation of temporary foreign workers and domestic live-in caregivers are but two instances of how Canada creates a convenience pool of just-in-time workers (Fleras, 2010a). Canada, of course, is not the only country whose immigration practices reflect political calculation and economic expediency. European countries have demonstrated all too readily their eagerness to accept immigrants as guest workers to feed a labour-starved economic boom, but an equal level of disdain for retention during the downturn.

OVERHAULING THE PROGRAM

Immigration into Canada remained expansionist beyond World War I. Entry criteria in 1931 embraced British subjects, American citizens, dependents of permanent residents in Canada, and agriculturalists, while discouraging migrants from Southern and Eastern Europe and the near total prohibition of Asians between 1923 and 1947 (Castles & Miller, 2003). To take advantage of the postwar economic boom, a 1947 immigration policy specified who could get in, namely: (1) British subjects and American citizens, if they met standards of health and character; (2) those who were qualified to work in labour-starved primary industries; (3) sponsored relatives from those European countries such as Greece or Italy with strong family connections; and (4) refugees and displaced persons under international supervision. Guilt over Canada's heartless denial of sanctuary for Holocaust victims during the war also helped to fuel the immigration boom (Thompson, Herd, & Weinfeld, 1995). Nonetheless, immigration was locked into a cycle of exclusion that privileged whiteness in making the distinction between preferred and non-preferred races. Orders to maintain an eye on Canada's absorptive capacity were strictly enforced, with quotas still applying for most non-Europeans, despite a growing demand for skilled and unskilled labour (Foster, 1998).

By 1962, Canadian immigration laws experienced a shift of paradigmatic proportions. Canada became one of the first countries in the world to announce that " . . . any suitable, qualified person from anywhere in the world" would qualify for entry, based primarily on personal merit and societal contribution. Embracing an ostensibly colour-blind commitment meant that Canada's immigration selection process was deracialized by shifting the selection criteria from national origin and ethnicity to those of skills, education, and experience (Gwyn, 2000; Hawkins, 1974; Mackey, 1998). Regulations were introduced emphasizing labour market needs and family relations, while independent-class immigrants were admitted on the strength of their technical/professional qualifications. With further reforms in 1967, criteria for entry were justified on four major immigrant classes: family, assisted relatives, independents, and refugees. A points system of evaluation was introduced that minimized the relevance of race as a criterion for entry: Both independent and assisted-relative applicants were numerically assessed in light of occupation, education, and language expertise. Still, the system was not entirely free of systemic bias. A points system continued to favour class-advantaged male applicants with educational credentials from countries with Canadian embassies facilitating the process of applications (Abu-Laban, 1999; Thompson, 2006).

For the most part, Canada's immigration program was largely reactive in responding to domestic realities and international pressures. But passage of the *Immigration Act* in 1978 formalized a shift in rationale. The Act not only codified the grounds for admission into Canada, but also articulated a principled framework for balancing the goals of (1) reunifying families, (2) protecting legitimate refugees, and (3) enhancing Canada's national interests related to prosperity and global competitiveness. A further realignment was reflected by the passage of the *Immigration and Refugee Protection Act* in 2002. As the first major change to Canada's immigration program since 1978, the Act sought to tighten up the immigration program by (1) imposing more restrictions on entry; (2) focusing on the recruitment of immigrants with the human capital to integrate quickly into the workplace and society; (3) shifting from a strict points system to an emphasis on flexible and transferable skills and income-generating potential; (4) insisting on knowledge of an official language; and (5) firming up sponsorship rules to ensure a more evenly shared burden of the costs of resettlement. Changes to the processing of refugees were introduced as well, including a one-step process involving single-member panels with limited avenues of appeal (Dauvergne, 2004). Dennis Coderre (2003), then Minister of Citizenship and Immigration, defended the rationale behind the new immigration law:

> Our strategy is designed to strike a balance between attracting workers with flexible skills, reuniting families, and being tough on those who pose a threat to Canadian security, all the while maintaining Canada's humanitarian tradition of providing a safe haven to people in need of protection. (p. 5)

Passage of the Act was not without criticism (*Canadian Issues*, 2005). Not everyone endorsed the focus on human capital attributes rather than occupational demand as the basis for admission into Canada. Critics charged that the system was elitist and counterproductive, resulting in a shortage of skilled tradespeople and blue-collar workers such as truck drivers, but a surplus of foreign-trained professionals unable to crack a highly regulated job market without Canadian experience. Critics also questioned the Act's emphasis on security as compromising the basic civil rights of immigrants and refugees (Crepeau & Nakache, 2006). Passage of Bill C-36 and the issuing of security certificates enable the government to detain, arrest, and deport immigrants or refugees based on suspicion of terrorism or secret evidence that suspects cannot access (Beare, 2003).

Overview of Who Got In: Historical Trends

An overview of immigration history demonstrates how the content, dynamics of, and rationale behind immigration into Canada have evolved over time (Knowles, 2007). The logic governing immigration today differs in terms of focus, rationale, underlying assumptions, and anticipated outcomes from the dynamic that drove immigration in the past. The nature of immigrants with respect to their origins, requisite skills, and expectations has shifted, as well. Immigration patterns are more transient and complex than they were in the past in a world of circular migration, dual citizenship, and transnational communities (Willis & Yeoh, 2000; also Spoonley & Bedford, 2012). Comparing the past with the present yields the following historical trends (see also Boyd & Vickers, 2000; Fleras, 2014b):

- From a highly subjective emphasis on racial and national origins as criteria for selection to an immigration program that is principled, transparent, and espouses the principle of colour-blindness in attracting the best and brightest.
- From a reliance on European sources of immigrants to those from Asia and other so-called non-conventional origins.
- From emphasizing the importance of rural-based agricultural/primary industry immigrants to focusing on those designer immigrants who are globally connected, highly educated, and professionally skilled; and who do not require costly resettlement services (Simmons, 2010).

- From a focus on immigration in terms of an absorptive capacity model ("taps-on, taps-off" approach to admissions) to immigration as a model for advancing "sustained economic growth" through consumer purchases, international connections, and entrepreneurial spirit.

- From a labour market model of immigration to that of a "human capital model," thus shifting the emphasis from matching immigrants with worker shortages to that of attracting newcomers with education, flexible and transferable skills, and language competence who can smoothly integrate into a knowledge-based economy or quickly adapt to changing economic environments (Beach, Green, & Reitz, 2003; Weber, 2005).

- From a loosely monitored administrative system concerned with who to keep out, to a tightly regulated and politically charged system preoccupied with who to let in involving both the private sector and federal/provincial levels of government.

- From a settlement immigration model based on immigrants as potential citizens and Canada-builders to a more proactive and customized immigration model, including a growing reliance on temporary foreign workers required to achieve short-term economic results (Fleras, 2010a).

Despite these shifts in trends, three themes prevail throughout (also Siemiatycki, 2015) First, immigration remains a response to Canada's demands for labour (see Li, 2003). The prime objective has never wavered: to supply a labour pool, first for agriculture and settlement, then for industrialization, and currently for professionally skilled jobs. The fact that the preferred requirements have varied from one historical context to the next does not invalidate this underlying logic. A bimodal dynamic prevails: Whereas the immigration program is focused on recruiting the best and the brightest from the global south, businesses in Canada are also interested in securing cheap labour to pare costs and remain globally competitive (Hiebert & Ley, 2006). Second, the nature and characteristics of immigration and immigrants reflect both internal and external pressures often beyond federal control. Unlike the past when national or vested interests determined who got in (Canada's membership in the Commonwealth notwithstanding), current immigration programs and patterns are influenced by global labour shortages in key economic sectors, competition in the global markets, the demands of an aging population, a shrinking labour force, and improvements in communication and transportation networks (Simmons, 2010). Third, much of the political and public discourses behind immigration reflect an unspoken assumption: immigrants are often perceived as a social burden on Canadian society whose costs must be minimized for ongoing acceptance, in part by keeping a lid on intake numbers and ensuring admission of those who are a "fit" for Canada (Friesen, 2015). As a result, there are "good" immigrants who are economically productive, readily self-sufficient, and can easily integrate without draining public resources (Abu-Laban, 1999). But other immigrants are increasingly criticized as social problems who inflict a cost and do a disservice to Canada (Bissett, 2008; also www.immigrationwatchcanada.org). Such a polarization is reflected in the politics of who gets into Canada.

WHO GETS IN? CANADA'S IMMIGRATION PROGRAM

Immigration to Canada divides along a permanent basis or temporary grounds to work, visit, or study. Canada's immigration program for permanent residency is guided by three broad objectives: to reunite families, fulfill Canada's international obligations and humanitarian traditions, and promote a vibrant economy. These objectives are reflected in the three main admission categories for entry into Canada on a permanent basis, namely, family-class immigrants, refugee class immigrants, and economic (or independent) class immigrants (Schellenberg & Maheux, 2007). The year 2013 saw 258 953 permanent resident admissions, with the People's Republic of China leading the way at 13.1 percent of the total, followed by India (11.8%), the Philippines (10.5%), Pakistan (4.4%), and United States (4.1%) (Citizenship and Immigration Canada [CIC], 2014). Of the permanent residents admitted in 2013, 67 percent self-identified as having knowledge of English or French or both (for economic immigrants, 91 percent of the principal applicants indicated a knowledge of at least one official language [CIC, 2014]). In terms of gender, women comprised 51 percent of new permanent admissions over the past 10 years, including 38 percent of all principal applicants under the Economic category. The past decade has also seen the Conservative Government shift the immigration program from a passive instrument to a dynamic and interventionist model to improve immigrant selection (more economically salient migrants), integration of newcomers, and border control (Reitz, 2014; also Simon-Kumar, 2015). The government has also modified the program in the hope of better aligning immigration with the goals of neo-liberalism, including increased emphasis on economic class admissions, reduced family and refugee class admissions, increased reliance on temporary foreign workers, and firming up both federal and provincial control of the selection process (Root et al., 2014; Siemiatycki, 2015). But others are critical of the government's pragmatic approach toward immigration with an emphasis on short-term interests but indifference toward human rights (Cliplef, 2014). Table 8-3 provides an overview of Canada's immigration program in 2013 by way of admission class and totals.

Categories of Admission

There are three main immigration admission categories for permanent entry into Canada, namely, family-class, economic (or independent) class, and refugee class.

Family Class The family class recognizes the need for families to stay together to improve their integration into Canada. Families can employ two basic entry strategies (Thomas, 2001). They can migrate as a unit by relying on the skills and resources of the principal applicant to qualify for admission under the skilled worker point system (see Table 8-4). Or, one member of a family (or domestic unit) might migrate first, then send for the remaining members once citizenship or permanent residency is established. Under this chain migration strategy, immediate members of the family—a spouse (or fiancé), parents, grandparents, dependent and unmarried children under 18 years of age, and orphaned brothers, sisters, nieces, nephews, and grandchildren—are allowed automatic entry into Canada provided, of course, they are of good health, pass security checks, and are without a criminal record. Processing times for family-class sponsorship can vary: 50 percent of cases involving spouses/partners and dependent children are finalized within six months. By contrast, according to Citizenship and Immigration Canada, it takes 30 months to finalize 50 percent of admissions related to parents or grandparents (Australia, New Zealand, and the United States do not normally permit grandparent sponsorships [CIC, 2014]) (Wayland, 2006). To assure CIC that family relationships are authentic, especially for those from Africa, the Caribbean, India, and Pakistan, individuals may require additional proof (see Satzewich, 2015). Sponsors must agree to support their sponsored family after

TABLE 8-3	Permanent Resident[1] Immigrants by Admission Class and Totals, 2013	
		% of all immigrants
Family class (total)	81 831	31.6%
Spouses, children and partners	49 513	
Parents/grandparents	32 318	
Economic (independent) class (total)	148 181	57.2%
Federal skilled workers	52 877	
Business immigrants (investors, self-employed, entrepreneurs)	5 098	
Provincial/territorial nominees	39 915	
Live-in caregivers	8 797	
Canadian Experience Class	7 216	
Quebec-selected Skilled Workers/ Business	34 278	
Total of principal applicants under the economic category	(64 765)	
Total of spouses and dependants under the economic category	(83 416)	
Refugees and protected persons class (total)	24 049	11.2%
Government assisted	5 756	
Privately sponsored	6 277	
Inland Protected Persons	8 149	
Refugee dependents	3 714	
Other	4 892	
Total	258 953	100%
Temporary foreign workers and foreign students		
Temporary foreign workers	221 310	
International students	111 865	

[1]Permanent residents are persons with permission to permanently live, work, or study in Canada provided they meet residency requirements and do not violate the conditions of their status (e.g., serious criminality). Permanent residence status is a precondition for Canadian citizenship (CIC, 2014).

Source: (CIC, 2014).

TABLE 8-4	The Skilled Worker Point System	
Maximum points allowed	**Criteria for points**
Education—25 points	25 points for education (maximum for Ph.D. or M.A., 5 points for high school diploma)
Language skills—24 points	24 points for language proficiency (up to 16 points for first official language—reading, writing, speaking, understanding; up to 8 points for the second official language)
Work experience—21 points	21 points for work experience (top points for four years of experience in a highly skilled occupation, 15 points for one year)
Employment status—10 points	10 points for arranged employment in Canada
Age—10 points	10 points for age (maximum points for those between 21 and 49; 2 points less each year over 49 or under 21 years of age)
Adaptability—10 points	10 points for adaptability (5 points for full-time job experience in Canada; 5 points for full-time study in Canada; 5 points for having a close relative in Canada, 5 points for a spouse with a university degree)

they become permanent residents. Non-immediate members of a family as defined by Canada, such as aunts or uncles, must partially rely on points for entry. In lieu of permanent residence, parents and grandparents of permanent residents or citizens of Canada may apply for a 10-year super-visa which entitles them to visit Canada for up to two years at a time. In 2013, 15 000 super-visas were issued (CIC, 2014).

Economic (Independent) Class The economic class (including federal skilled workers and business people such as entrepreneurs, self-employed individuals, and investors) has emerged as a major source of landing for immigrants. Until recently, most immigrants entered Canada on the strength of family relations; now, however, nearly 60 percent of immigrants currently fall into the economic category. This trend is likely to continue as Canada increasingly looks for those designer immigrants with higher skill levels whose costs of training and education are borne outside this country (Simmons, 2010; Weinfeld & Wilkinson, 1999). Keep in mind that, strictly speaking, the totals for the economic class include spouses and dependents who are not preselected on a skills basis. As a result, in 2013, principal applicants accounted for about 40 percent of admissions under the economic class or just under 25 percent of the total immigrant intake for 2013.

A point system is applied that assesses the principal applicant on the grounds of job-related experience, age, official-language knowledge, and education. (As of January 1, 2015, the Express Entry program replaced the existing point system, although pre-existing applicants (prior to 2015) will continue to be assessed along points-based lines). The candidate may also undergo an assessment for adaptability. The number of points required for entry under the point system is 67 points for skilled workers and the self-employed. Applicants from the business class (both investor and entrepreneur) can earn up to 35 points for their commercial experiences and connections. Assisted relatives also receive credit as nominated immigrants (5 points), but require additional points elsewhere to qualify. Everyone in this category must pass the usual health, criminal, and security clearances. Each adult applicant must also pay an application fee (including a fee for children), in addition to a right-of-landing fee to a maximum of four members per family. The landing fee was waived for refugees in 2000. The point system is outlined in Table 8-4.

In response to criticism that a human capital model of immigration isn't working, Canada's immigration program adopted a more strategic approach to render the system "faster, more flexible, and more responsive" to the changing needs of the economy and labour market (Alexander, 2014). In 2008, Citizenship and Immigration Canada established rules that restricted the entry of federal skilled workers to those (a) with an offer of arranged employment, (b) applicants legally residing in Canada for at least one year, or (c) with demonstrated skills in one of 38 (now 29) priority jobs in hopes of unblocking an unmanageable backlog and processing delays (Alboim, 2009; Nakache & Kinoshita, 2010). Passage of Bill C-50 enables the immigration minister to prioritize applicants from the Federal Skilled Workers Program in response to labour shortages in select occupations. Applicants who fall outside of these three categories are not processed, while those already in the queue but lacking one of the 29 occupational designations are put on hold. The then Immigration Minister Jason Kenney justified this move as a game-changer when he claimed,

> . . . when he claimed that in the past Canada was mandated to process every application for admission. This commitment resulted in a growing backlog since more individuals applied for admission than the system could possibly process. But in processing only those applicants who meet specific criteria, the government is making significant strides in reducing the backlog while ensuring the entry of those positioned to address Canada's labour market needs.

In a move that promises to revolutionize the immigration program along more decentralized, demand-driven, and employer-instigated lines (Boyd, 2013), Ottawa has introduced a two-stage system for selecting federal skilled workers that came into effect in January 2015. An Express Entry system is not an immigration program *per se* (there are over 60 Canadian immigration programs), but rather a protocol employed by CIC to select candidates following an assessment and invitation to apply. Its introduction is intended to transform the immigrant admission process from a passive processing of applicants (a "queue" in which everyone who passed the points test received automatic admission into Canada, pending health, security, and criminal checks) to a more proactive system (a "pool") for in-demand workers with the skills that employers want and Canada needs (Canadian Association of Professional Immigration Consultants [CAPIC], 2013; CIC, 2013d). Under Express Entry, prospective candidates are asked to send in an online job application by electronically submitting a resume of their skills and work experience as well as education levels and language ability (Ibbitson, 2014). Those who meet the eligibility criteria will be pre-screened (points assigned and applications ranked) for placement into a pool of candidates for employers to peruse (Keung, 2014). The expression-of-interest pool does not constitute an application for admission *per se*; rather, it's an *invitation* for candidates with valued skills or job offers to apply for admission into Canada upon notification to do so (CIC, 2013). (In July 2015, an invitation to apply for permanent residence required just over 460 points out of a possible 1200; in addition, the majority of candidates invited to apply lacked a qualifying job offer or a provincial nominee certificate [CIC News, 2015]). Once an invitation to apply has been offered, the candidate has 60 days to file a complete application with all supporting documents (CIC, 2015). In the second stage, the federal government and provinces will dip into this "expression-of-interest pool" to select applicants that best match Canada's labour needs (Mas, 2014). Those who qualify will then be accorded priority processing for rapid admission into Canada. Those applicants not selected after a period of time may be removed from the database to prevent a backlog and ensure timely processing times (CIC, 2013d).

Reaction to the Express Entry system has yet to be fully gauged. For the Government, the Express Entry admission model promises to provide greater flexibility and responsiveness to regional labour shortages for which there are no available Canadian workers. This neo-liberal-driven system ensures the selection of skilled candidates; namely, those with a valid job offer; those who are provincial nominees; and those who are highly skilled or possess relevant work experience most likely to succeed in Canada under one of four economic immigration streams: the federal skilled worker program, Canadian experience class, the federal skilled trades program, and the provincial nominee program (CIC News, 2015). A two-step and just-in-time approach to admissions also revamps the selection and processing of skilled workers by transforming the one-size-fits-all, points-based approach into a designer-driven approach with an increased role for employers in deciding who gets in; enhancing Canada's control over the type and number of skilled workers who apply and enter; ensuring a higher level of proactivity in selecting applicants with in-demand skills; and attracting newcomers who are more resilient and self-sufficient because they possess those human capital resources to compete, adapt, and succeed (Alberta Association of Immigrant Serving Agencies [AAISA], 2013; Boyd, 2013). Others are concerned about throwing out the points-based baby with the Express Entry bathwater. The danger lies in mothballing the current point system that seemingly is more focused on recruiting those newcomers whose long-term commitments are more attuned to Canada-building rather than simply growing the economy (Beiser & Bauder, 2014).

The economic class includes the *business subcategory*—namely, investor, entrepreneur, and self-employed. The "entrepreneurial" program selects immigrants with an ability to establish a new business or buy equity (at least 33 percent) into a qualifying business that they must manage and that will create at least one full-time job for a non-family member. To qualify under the self-employed category, an applicant must possess (1) an appropriate business acumen, (2) artistic qualifications, or (3) a net worth to be able to either establish or buy a business that will make a contribution to the Canadian economy or to Canada's artistic and cultural (sports) life. Under the "investor" program, applicants must meet the usual immigration criteria in addition to demonstrating a net worth of $1.6 million legally acquired. In exchange for investing $800 000 in a Canadian fund for five years (the principal amount is then returned) a business applicant receives permanent resident status. Thousands of applicants have taken advantage of this program since its inception in 1986, including just over 3400 in 2009. But the program has also been plagued by charges of fraudulent abuse, cumbersome delays (up to five years to process applicant files), and gross mismanagement that undermines its potential benefits (Ley & Hiebert, 2001). In 2014, the government announced its intention to replace the investor program with a new pilot program (CIC, 2014).

Canada and the United States: Doing Immigration Differently

Canada and the United States may be described and prescribed as immigration societies. And yet the immigration patterns with respect to number and types in Canada and the United States continue to reflect striking differences despite the two countries sharing many commonalities (Bauder & Shields, 2015; German Marshall Fund, 2015; Vineberg, 2015) (see Table 8-5).

TABLE 8-5	Annual Immigration to the United States, 2013
New Arrivals	459 751 (or 46% of LPR)
All new lawful permanent residents (LPR)	990 553
Employer sponsored	16% of LPR
Family sponsored	65% of LPR
Other	2% of LPR
Diversity	5% of LPR
Refugees and Asylum Seekers	12% of LPR

Source: Zong & Batalova, 2015.

- The total US immigration population in 2013 stood at 41.3 million, or 13 percent of the total US population (Zong & Batalova, 2015). In 2011, the foreign born accounted for just over 20 percent of Canada's population.

- Mexican-born migrants accounted for 28 percent of the total immigrant population in 2013, making them the largest immigrant group in the United States, followed by India, China (Hong Kong but not Taiwan), and the Philippines. Forty-six percent of all immigrants reported having Latino/a origins.

- The average annual number of arrivals for the past 20 years is about 420 000 (Auclair & Bata-lova, 2013). Canada's intake is smaller at about 250 000 per year, but Canada's population is one-tenth the size of the US population.

- Immigrants are defined as foreign-born persons with lawful permanent resident status. About 60 percent of immigrants (permanent residents) to the United States are not new arrivals but those adjusting their status from within, from temporary to permanent status. (Status adjusters account for the difference in numbers between New Arrivals and New Lawful Permanent Residents). With few exceptions, such as those in the Canadian Experience Class, those on temporary permits in Canada must apply from outside.

- Unlike in the United States, with its focus on family sponsorship, most immigrants to Canada arrive via economic class. There is a high degree of provincial involvement in Canada's admission program (Vineberg, 2015).

- The United States attracts a disproportionately higher number of undocumented persons than Canada. It is estimated there are 11.4 undocumented persons as of 2012, with about half from Mexico (Pew Research Center, 2014).

- Canadians and Americans appear to possess fundamentally different attitudes toward immigration and immigrants. In contrast to respondents in the United States, Canadians are not only more predisposed to see newcomers as opportunities and assets, but also tend to support the government's management of Canada's immigration program (German Marshall Fund, 2015; Transatlantic Trends, 2010).

Another subcategory of the economic class is *provincial nominees*. Provinces and territories may nominate individuals for permanent admission to address specific regional labour market needs (Alboim, 2009) while redistributing the benefits of immigration to areas that are not traditional immigrant destinations (CIC, 2014). (The *Constitution Act* of 1867 makes jurisdiction over immigration a joint federal/provincial responsibility.) The program's success can be assessed by the numbers. The number of provincial nominees has grown exponentially in recent years from fewer than 500 in 2000 to just under 40 000 in 2013—in part because the program is designed to overcome long delays and a backlog of immigrants via the federal pipeline (Taylor, 2009). Under the Provincial Nominee Program (PNP), all provinces and territories (except Nunavut) have entered into an agreement with the federal government that permits each of them to tailor nomination programs for their specific needs (Paquet, 2015; CIC News, 2015). The program also allows employers to recruit foreign workers based on their ability to contribute to province-specific economic development. To apply under the PNP, applicants must be nominated by a Canadian province or territory; possess the necessary skills, experience, and education to make an immediate economic contribution; and be prepared to assume permanent residency in Canada. The federal government continues to maintain control over PNP admissions by stipulating that all applicants must pass a medical examination and security and criminal checks (Nakache & Kinoshita, 2010).

It should be noted that Quebec possesses a relatively autonomous and distinctive immigration program for skilled workers and professionals (CIC, 2011b). It has the authority to determine the volume and composition of permanent immigration to the province, as well as control over the creation and implementation of federally funded social and linguistic integration programs (Jedwab, 2012; Rodriguez-Garcia, 2012). Skilled workers and professionals are selected on the basis of a different set of criteria than applicants who wish to settle elsewhere in Canada. Any applicant can qualify under any occupation listed in the Quebec Skilled Worker category, with or without a job offer from a Canadian employer. A two-step process is entailed: Applicants under Quebec's immigration selection system are issued a Quebec Selection Certificate which entitles the bearer to a Canadian Permanent Resident (Immigrant) Visa. To qualify for a Quebec Selection Certificate, a single applicant must score at least 49 points based on the criteria below, whereas an applicant with a partner or spouse must score at least 57 points. An additional six points may be awarded for adaptability upon an interview. A single person then requires at least 55 (49 + 6) points to obtain a certificate, while a married person or an applicant living in common law requires 63 (57 + 6) points.

The introduction of the *Canadian Experience Class (CEC)* in 2008 entitles skilled temporary foreign workers and international student graduates with full-time work experience to stay in Canada permanently (CIC, 2014; Simmons, 2010; Sweetman & Warman, 2010). Under the CEC, international students who have graduated from a Canadian university and temporary workers with the qualifying work experience and competence in English or French can apply for permanent residency without having to leave Canada (Government of Canada, 2011). To qualify for permanent residency, a highly skilled temporary worker must have two years of full-time (or equivalent) Canadian work experience in a managerial, professional, or technical/skilled occupation (e.g., carpenter, welder, pipefitter). But the program has come under criticism because the transition to permanent residency is only at the high end, thus excluding those with "lower skill levels" (e.g., meat packers, food plant workers, kitchen staff). For a foreign graduate from a Canadian post-secondary institution (with at least two years of full-time study), the program requires one year of full-time (or equivalent) skilled work experience in Canada. International students are a main target for CEC; after all, they are highly skilled, possess Canadian credentials, and reduce settlement costs due to their familiarity with Canadian society (Simmons, 2010).

Finally, the live-in caregiver program also provides a pipeline to permanent residency. The program allows Canadian families to hire temporary domestic workers from abroad to provide live-in home care for children, older parents, persons with disabilities—provided they meet certain residency requirements and that no Canadians are available to fill these positions. (See Chapter 6 for more detail.) In 2013, 4671 caregivers were admitted into Canada on a temporary basis; 8797 received their permanent residence status; and a total of 16 927 live-in caregivers lived in Canada (CIC, 2014).

Refugees and Protected Persons Class The refugee category is the third category of landing. Refugees are accepted as part of Canada's humanitarian and legal obligations to the world community. Since 1951 (or more accurately 1969, when it signed the 1951 UN Convention on Refugees), Canada has performed admirably in protecting refugees, especially in comparison with countries that perfunctorily deny entry or routinely deport those seeking asylum. Canada has officially admitted over half a million refugees during this period of time, with recent annual intakes ranging from 20 000 to 35 000 (from 54 073 in 1991 to 24 398 in 2013 [Ibbitson, 2014])—an impressive total in its own right, but a modest dent in global volumes.

Two categories of refugees exist, neither of which requires points for entry. One category consists of sponsored refugees who are selected for resettlement from overseas, UN-based camps. These "resettled" refugees are selected either by government officials on their ability to establish themselves in Canada (Government Assisted Refugees) or by private agencies, individuals, clubs, or church groups (Privately Sponsored Refugees), with private sponsors obligated to provide support for them for up to 20 years. Both government and privately sponsored refugees automatically receive landed immigrant (or permanent residence) status upon arriving in Canada. They also receive assistance through government programs once they arrive. The UNHCR has acknowledged that Canada accepts a relatively high number of resettled refugees (those being transferred from an asylum country to a permanent home), with just over 12 000 admissions in 2013 (including 2374 Syrians) (Hopper, 2015).

The second category consists of inland refugee claimants (also known as Landed in Canada Refugees if approved by the IRB, or inland protected persons) who seek protected person status in Canada as a result of a positive refugee claim (CIC, 2014). According to the Canadian Council of Refugees (2007), most (62 percent in 2006) claims in Canada are made from within Canada at an immigration office (about one-third of these are made at the Etobicoke office, which covers Toronto). Only about 20 percent of claims are made at a land border (i.e., a port of entry). Once asylum is claimed, a set of refugee determination protocols is activated (see Wayland, 2006). The current three-step system—(1) eligibility determination, (2) refugee status determination, and (3) permanent residency—consists of a so-called simplified procedure that purports to balance fairness with efficiency (see the Box below). In contrast to sponsored refugees, refugee claimants are not entitled to all the benefits and social services until their claims are cleared and they apply for permanent residency status. The third category involves those rejected refugee claimants who are granted protection under a Pre-Removal Risk Assessment (i.e., protected persons will not be deported to their home country if the removal exposes them to danger) (Wayland, 2006).

Temporary Foreign Workers: Visible yet Invisible

Temporary foreign worker (TFW) programs and contract migration schemes are experiencing something of a global revival (Castles, 2006; Fudge & McPhail, 2009; Goldring & Landolt, 2012; MacLaren & Lapointe, 2010; Piper, 2010; Thomas, 2010).

Processing Refugee Claimants: Immigration and Refugee Board (IRB)

Canada provides protection for refugees in two ways. First, refugees are selected from overseas centres and resettled in Canada by government or private sponsorship. Second, inland claims occur when asylum seekers claim refugee status once in Canada because they need protection from dangers or risks (Amnesty International, 2009). According to well-known immigration lawyers, Lorne Waldman and Max Berger (Aulakh, 2010), the processing of refugee claimants in theory is relatively straight forward: A person applies for refugee status, shows identification, and is allowed to go free provided they are not a health/security/flight risk or a danger to the public. In addition to making a promise to appear for a hearing before the IRB, a refugee claimant must also file their "history"/personal information form to the Board, followed by a hearing within 60 days to determine eligibility of status or need for protection. In reality, the process is much more complex and entails a 3-step procedure that purports to balance fairness and justice with efficiency and effectiveness: (1) make an eligibility determination, (2) determine if claimants are Convention refugees or persons in need of protection, and (3) decide whether to grant permanent residency or remove the claimant from Canada.

Step 1—Eligibility Determination

An asylum seeker can claim status as a refugee on entry into Canada at the border or at any immigration office if already in Canada (Showler, 2006). Within 72 hours of entry, claimants are photographed, finger printed, and interviewed by an immigration official from Citizenship and Immigration Canada (often with the assistance of an interpreter) to solicit information on their personal identity, criminality and security risks, and grounds of persecution. This information is used to assess the eligibility of the claim for referral to and evaluation by the Refugee Protection Division of the Immigration and Refugee Board (IRB) (about 90% of claimants are eligible [Showler, 2006]). Eligibility for referral to the IRB may be denied on grounds related to security, human rights violations, serious criminality, and costly health concerns (Showler & Maytree Foundation, n.d.). Or, admissibility may be revoked if the claimant lied or new information emerges to discredit the application. Also ineligible are those who have made a previous refugee claim in Canada, possess refugee status in another country, or have passed through a safe third country enroute to Canada (Canadian Council for Refugees, 2008; Waldman & Berger in Aulakh, 2010). To discourage false claimants from entering Canada, the government insists on proper documentation as proof of identity. Without documents, refugees may be temporarily detained until their identification is established. The number of detainees in 2013 stood at 7300, with almost one third held in provincial jails for some period of time (Macklin, 2015). But unless they pose a serious criminal, security, or health risk, or have been previously deported, inland claimants are free to go, pending an IRB hearing to adjudicate their claims for refugee status (Crepeau & Janik, 2008). This perceived laxity, critics argue, increases the risk of releasing refugees with terrorist links who evade detection or deportation.

Step 2—Refugee Determination

Once identity has been established and forms completed by Citizenship and Immigration Canada or Canadian Border Services Agency, refugee claimants must attend a formal hearing by the Refugee Protection Division of the Immigration and Refugee Board (IRB). The IRB constitutes a quasi-independent tribunal and quasi-judicial decision-making body independent of the CIC whose primary function is to hear refugee status determination claims (Crepeau & Janik, 2008). Created in 1989 following a scandal involving political and diplomatic interference in the refugee determination process, this administrative tribunal is less formal than its judicial counterpart, and allows claimants to present their case in a simpler manner (Fleury, 2004). Members of the IRB used to be political appointees appointed by Order in Council for a period of seven years, but are increasingly selected from the civil service and are presumably less susceptible to political influence (Quan, 2015). Following extensive training and access to the refugee documentation centre for assistance in making decisions, board members are charged with determining whether asylum seekers

(refugee claimants who arrive unannounced) are convention (fleeing persecution as per UN definition) or in need of protection because of dangers to their lives if returned to their homeland. Refugee hearings are conducted by one IRB official who may operate without the assistance of a Refugee Protection Officer (a civil servant cognizant of refugee laws) (Bauer, 2009).

The difficulty of the job should not be underestimated (Showler, 2006). IRB members require knowledge of the country of origin and solid legal skills in addition to good listening and communication skills for conducting interviews and writing coherent reasons for their decisions (Showler & Maytree Foundation, n.d.). Many of the claims are complex, allegations are often difficult to document or verify, and many claimants must speak through an interpreter. Making a refugee claim is a dicey proposition (Jones & Houle, 2008). The sole witness is the refugee, and he or she may prove unreliable. Much of the evidence and many of the witnesses for the defence of the refugee claim remain inaccessible in the refugee's home country. Refugees must normally testify through an interpreter; they must describe events elsewhere about which little is known; they are frightened, traumatized, and haunted by their own persecution; they can't remember key events or even find the words to make a credible presentation (Jones & Houle, 2008); and they don't understand the legal procedure involved. The quality of their legal representation varies from the heroic to the incompetent and unethical. Given the radically different experiences

(Continued)

between refugee decision makers and claimants, IRB members have difficulty distinguishing between the frightened the confused as well as between the manipulated and the manipulating (Stadelmann-Elder, 2011:1). Not surprisingly, subjectivity and arbitrariness remains a problem: Refugee approval rates not only vary from city to city but also from board member to board member, with some granting asylum in less than 10 percent of the cases, whereas others grant asylum in 90 percent of cases (Colaiacovo, 2013; also Rehaag, 2015). Not surprisingly, the practice of refugee determination appears to be dictated more by political expediency and personal politics than by humanitarian concerns, and a tendency to treat refugees as a social problem rather than as humans in distress (Dench, 2004).

Once an oral hearing is approved, each refugee claimant schedules a meeting before a single member of the IRB Refugee Protection board. Claimants must first fill out a lengthy personal information form that is submitted to the IRB (Showler, 2006). The interval between the date of this initial claim until the claim is heard is usually several months to a year. Those claimants who are almost certain of entry receive an "expedited hearing" (an interview rather than a full hearing) to hasten the process and prevent a backlog. If the claimant is not given expedited treatment, a hearing is convened before an IRB member. The claimant has the right to be represented by legal counsel (legal aid is provided in four provinces) and the services of an interpreter. The average time to complete this step is 12 to 18 months, during which claimants can apply for temporary work or study

permits. Most cases are decided on the credibility of the claimants, supporting evidence about their country of origin, and the quality of the submission by the legal representative (Showler, 2006). The Board member renders a decision based on law or evidence either in writing (in the case of a rejected claim) or orally from the bench.

Step 3—Permanent Residency

Conferral of "protected person" (refugee) status entitles the claimant to apply for permanent residency. Those granted permanent resident status are issued a social insurance number and a record of landing (identity papers) which allow them to open a bank account, apply for employment, and travel freely within Canada. They can also qualify for basic income support, health care, and social services if they possess a valid work permit (although both employment and rental accommodation may prove difficult to obtain because of their insecure status). But others find themselves in a legal limbo, especially those claimants who are accepted as refugees but not conferred permanent resident status, usually because of minor criminality (Showler, 2006). They must wait for additional security and medical checks, confirmation of family relationships, and payment of processing fees. Delays in processing can occur for a variety of reasons, resulting in lengthy waiting times. The entire 3-step process may take upwards of 3 years (Wayland, 2006), although 18 months is an average figure (Showler & Maytree Foundation, n.d.).

Not all claimants are successful, with acceptance rates in recent years hovering around the 38 to 42 percent mark, a wildly contested figure high by global measures but low by traditional Canadian standards (Black, 2012). If the IRB rejects the application, the claimant must leave within 30 days or face arrest and deportation. Claimants may also appeal by applying for a judicial review in the federal court within 15 days, albeit only on matters of procedure (serious mistakes in law) rather than on the merits of the case. In theory, those who have exhausted all appeal routes are destined for deportation. In reality, they may be exempted on the basis of humanitarian and compassionate grounds (e.g., they married a Canadian with children born in Canada), administrative bungling, and a Pre-Removal Risk Assessment to determine the probable risks of serious harm from returning home (assuming, of course, that the country of origin will allow failed claimants to re-enter in the first place). But unless deportees indicate their exit plans—and the time lapse between rejection and removal can take years in which no one assumes responsibility for the file (Peter Showler in Keung, 2010b)— Immigration Canada has no way of confirming who leaves or who stays.

In recent years, the Conservative Government has passed a number of controversial laws to tighten up the IRB process and the processing of inland refugee claimants (Fleras 2014b; Ibbitson, 2014; Soennecken, 2014). Passage of the *Balanced Refugee Reform Act* in 2010 reinforced a commitment to (a) address the massive backlog of refugee claimants, (b) facilitate flow of genuine refugees through the system, (c) fast-track the claims

of asylum seekers from countries presumed to be safe (i.e., countries with traditionally low acceptance rates), (d) remove failed claimants more quickly, (e) offer more protection for victims of torture and persecution, (f) propose a new Refugee Appeal Division for failed claimants from non-DCO countries, and (g) resettle or sponsor more refugees from refugee camps (McDowell, 2010). Refugee claims are sorted into two streams: Those from democratic countries deemed to be *safe* (Designated Countries of Origins or DCO) versus those from more dangerous domains. A list of safe countries (DCOs) is continually updated, based on a combination of rejection/withdrawal/abandonment rates and/or a qualitative checklist to determine the democratic foundations of the country (in mid-December 2012, Immigration Minister Kenney listed 29 safe countries (now 42), most of them in Europe [Cohen, 2012, 2013]). Asylum seekers from safe countries will now be fast tracked to facilitate a more expeditious removal (including an initial IRB hearing within 45 days of their arrival). They will still have access to a full IRB hearing but will be stripped of access to any appeals (such as the promised Appeal Division) except to the Federal Court on matters of law (Cohen, 2012). The *Cracking Down on Crooked Consultants Act* and the *Preventing Human Smugglers from Abusing Canada's Immigration System Act* (Little, 2010) mandated the imposition of stiffer penalties for smugglers (from ship owners to organized crime smugglers). As well, those asylum seekers who are part of an irregular arrival will be detained without review and put on probation with

(Continued)

no right to travel outside Canada, to sponsor families, or to apply for permanent resident status for five years.

No less contentious is Bill C-31, *Protecting Canada's Immigration System Act* which became law on June 28, 2012. The Act was intended to hasten the sorting out process for those in need of genuine protection, while curbing (disincentivizing) the number of frivolous, costly, and fraudulent claims, especially from EU countries. It reiterated the principle of a Designated Country of Origin (DCO) rule designed to dissuade those from safe countries from gaming the system to the detriment of quick approval for "genuine" refugee claimants. It also ended supplemental benefits such as vision and dental care under the Interim Federal Health Programs for most claimants, although Public Safety Health Care Coverage for DCOs and failed claimants awaiting deportation was retained to protect Canadians from a communicable disease. Finally, Bill C-31 established automatic detention for irregular arrivals over the age of 16, subject to periodic reviews until a final decision is made that does not imperil the safety and security of Canadians (Centre for Israel and Jewish Affairs, 2013). Those irregular migrants who are smuggled in are subject to immediate expulsion if their claims are rejected (Department of Justice, 2012; Leblanc, 2012).

The Conservative government has touted its reforms as timely and overdue in providing faster and fairer protection for those in genuine need, whereas failed asylum claimants are removed more quickly (Alexander, 2014). Applications for asylum from those entering from safe countries have declined by 80 percent since the introduction of the reforms to expedite their processing and removal (Ibbitson, 2014). Under the new system, according to the CIC (2014), processing times for asylum claimants are down to about 3 months, compared to the 18 to 20 months wait before the reforms, while a failed asylum claimant is removed from Canada within 4 months rather than the 4½ years it took in the past because of unsuccessful appeals.

Not everyone concurs with these reforms either in principle or in practice. Crackdowns on bogus refugee claimants, unscrupulous consultants, and human smugglers reflect a punishment-oriented model that may generate adverse consequences (Dauvergne, 2013). Attempts to curb and punish human smuggling and trafficking may prove much more complex. According to the UNHCR (as cited in Scoffield, 2010), almost all of the world's asylum seekers depend on human smuggling rings at some point along the way (Kaushal & Dauvergne, 2011). In other words, the solution (if there is one) must focus on those factors that are driving asylum seekers into the hands of sophisticated smuggling networks increasingly run by organized crime. What is required instead of tighter migration controls are reforms for building a refugee program that is humanitarian (rather than restrictive), demonstrates compassion, respects international protocols, and works to strengthen Canada's social fabric (Soennecken, 2014). Other reform criticisms include the timeline for assessment, appeal, and removal; for example, under the new proposed timeline, DCO claimants find that their claims are assessed in an accelerated fashion, with tight procedural timelines and little time to find a lawyer and prepare their defence (Canadian Council of Refugees, 2013; Cliplef, 2014; McDowell, 2010; Soennecken, 2014). They are ineligible for health care or work permits while they wait (Quan, 2015). Much criticism is aimed at the concept of a safe country; for instance, Mexico would be regarded as a safe country since it has a democratically elected government and generally subscribes to international agreements on human rights. Yet for many, Mexico is anything but a safe country, considering the level of gang violence and generalized criminality the state seems incapable of controlling (Showler in Galloway, 2010). What is the logic in designating Mexico a safe country, yet granting asylum to 568 Mexicans in 2012 (similarly, 448 Hungarians granted asylum despite Hungary's designation as a DCO country, including an acceptance rate of 68% for the first half of 2015 [Quan, 2015]) (Canadian Council for Refugees, 2013; also Cohen, 2013)?

Canada is no exception to this global trend: In 2013, Canada admitted over 221 000 new TFWs, increasing the overall TFW total to around 385 000, under a variety of arrangements and admission portals, and with varying degrees of entitlements once in Canada (Elgersma, 2014). According to Jason Kenney, Minister of Employment and Social Development (2014), only 20 percent of the 221 000 TFWs who entered Canada in 2013 filled low-skilled jobs at the request of employer, of which 62 percent were farm workers. By contrast, a much larger number of temporary foreign workers enter Canada through the now separate stream called the International Mobility Program (IMP) (Elgersma, 2014). Admission under IMP is based on advancing Canada' s broad interests rather than filling a particular job (IMP entrants receive "open permits")—unlike the TFWs who enter at the request of a specific employer upon approval by Employment and Social Development Canada (Lemieux & Nadeau, 2015). The use of TFWs taps into Canada's historical roots, as well: Throughout the nineteenth and twentieth centuries, Canada adopted a variety of "guest-worker" programs for jobs that the Canadian-born disdained as too dangerous, dirty, or dull (Siemiatycki, 2010); for example, importation of Chinese sojourners into British Columbia during the 1880s for the precarious task of laying railway track across rugged terrain.

The contemporary antecedents that justify the right of foreign nationals to work temporarily in Canada has been in effect since 1973 (Austin & Bauder, 2012), following the implementation of the Non-Immigrant Employment Authorization Program (NIEAP) (both the Seasonal Agricultural Worker Program and the Live-in-Caregiver Program were inaugurated earlier). Originally designed as a temporary fix for employers in need of critical skills, the TFW program evolved into a path of least resistance for employers who needed cheap and reliable workers (Lemieux & Nadeau, 2015). A rotational category of TFW tied specifically to non-permanent employment was established, with various restrictions that continue to inform the core of today's TFW program, including (a) time-limited work permits tied directly to employment status, (b) the legal right to stay in Canada only during the period of authorized employment (with some exceptions), (c) constraints on labour mobility rights without formal authorization to do otherwise, and (d) restriction on applying for work permits, family reunification, or immigrant status from within the country (Fudge & McPhail, 2009; Jason Foster, 2012; Nakache & Dixon-Perera, 2015; Taylor & Foster, 2014).

The current TFW program entails four entry streams (Elgersma, 2014). They include (1) the Live-in-Caregiver Program, (2) the Primary Agricultural Stream including the Seasonal Agricultural Worker Program (SAWP), (3) the Low-Skilled Worker Program, and (4) the High-Skilled Worker Program. In theory, the program is intended as a last and limited resort when qualified Canadian workers are not available (Alexander, 2014). Those employers who want to hire TFW must have authorization from the Canadian government—namely, a Labour Market Impact Assessment (previously called a Labour Market Opinion). Those TFWs who do not need a LMIA (including those who arrive under the International Mobility Program) enter on the basis of advancing Canada's economic and cultural interests (Lemieux & Nadeau, 2015). Of the 221 000 foreign nationals who entered as a TFW in 2013, about 84 000 required a LMIA (or LMO); the rest were exempt. All TFWs must satisfy Citizenship and Immigration Canada's medical, criminal, and criminal checks. TFWs are issued a two-year work permit, renewable once, but are then ineligible for another permit for four years (Jason Foster, 2012). This work visa constitutes a labour contract that restricts TFWs to a particular occupation, location, or employer (there is some wiggle room to change jobs) (Hennebry, 2012; Nakache, 2010; Thomas, 2010). The tethering of workers to a job prompted one critic to write: "Migrant workers represent the perfect workforce in an era of evolving capital-labor relations: commodified and exploitable; flexible and expendable" (Walia, 2010:76).

In reality, TFWs constitute a just-in-time post-Fordist workforce (Fudge, 2011) who are attractive for a variety of reasons: (1) They are utilized to offset deficiencies in the domestic workforce by matching them with employers across a narrowly defined range of labour shortages; (2) they address labour market needs by quickly responding to an expanding economy without requiring employers to absorb the costs of maintaining unemployed workers during a downturn or the costs of training and settlement; (3) they can be prescreened prior to selection as permanent residents (Thomas, 2010); (4) they provide a relief valve that staunches the flow of irregular (undocumented) migrants; and (5) they constitute largely unfree labour to perform the drudge work that Canadians eschew by doing it cheaply and uncomplainingly (Abella, 2006; Sharma, 2006). Predictably, the TFW program in general, the SAW program in particular, have morphed into a structural necessity and a business model for a vast range of industries and services both in Canada and in the United States (Grez, 2008; Hennebry, 2012; Thomas, 2010). Clearly, then, the expression TFW is a bit of misnomer from a management perspective: It is anything but transient and temporary, but an increasingly permanent component of the Canadian labour force. Even that most iconic of Canadian institutions, Tim Hortons, admits that many stores could not stay open or operate full-time without a steady supply of TFWs (Carletti & Davison, 2012; Yalnizyan, 2012).

The increased reliance on unfree labour as a core employee supply stream instead of a stop-gap measure to alleviate short-term localized deficiencies is not without consequences. The shift from a stable program that plugged short-term labour needs in highly skilled occupations to a broader-based labour market tool for lower-skilled occupations creates a permanent TFW pool reminiscent of European guest/migrant worker programs of the past (Jason Foster, 2012). A reliance on temporary and unskilled foreign workers as "indentured labour" incurs the risk of entrenching an underclass of marginalized individuals whose prospects for citizenship are sharply curtailed (Siemiatycki, 2010). To be sure, the TFWP was initially intended for skilled workers from the global North (Lemieux & Nadeau, 2015), with 57 percent of TFWs employed in skilled occupations such as management, university teaching, or engineering (mostly from Europe, the United States, and Japan), whereas 26 percent were low-skilled. By 2010, the number of high-skilled temporary workers had dropped to 37 percent, whereas that of the low-skilled increased to about 30 percent (mostly from Asia, particularly the Philippines; and Latin American countries, such as Mexico) (Government of Canada, 2011), but back to about 20 percent following moves to tighten the program by rooting out abuse (Kenney, 2014). Finally, women account for about 40 percent of TFWs, many of whom are slotted into low-paying and low-skilled sectors, such as caregiving, domestic and hotel work, and entertainment (TFWs cannot be paid less than Canadians working in similar jobs [Kenney, 2014]). These occupational ghettoes render women more vulnerable to abuse and exploitation while diminishing their chances of permanent residency, with only the Live-in-Caregiver Program providing a principled path for permanent status (Gibb, 2010). The fear of deportation or banishment from the program silences complaints and makes it difficult for TFWs to exercise their right to challenge dangerous work conditions, to enforce labour laws, and to guarantee workplace safety (Basok & Ilcan, 2013; Goutor & Ramsaroop, 2012; Lenard & Straehle, 2012).

In short, Canada now embraces a guest worker program in all but name to address its labour needs—a kind of just-in-time migration policy for a neoliberal era, one that generally pigeonholes TFWs into a particular occupation, location, or employer as a condition of their admission (Thomas, 2010). This shift constitutes a fundamental departure from traditional notions of immigrants as permanent Canada builders to that of hastily hired fill-ins (Lorne Foster, 2012; Omidvar, 2013). Reaction to Canada's TFWP is mixed (Canadian Centre for Immigration Policy Reform, 2010; Lenard & Straehle, 2012; Worswick, 2010), ranging from criticism as "modern day slavery" (McMurtry, 2013), "indentured labour" (Lenard & Straehle, 2012) or contrary to Canada's long-term national interests (Hennebry & McLaughlin, 2011; Hennebry & Preibisch, 2010; Piché, 2011), to those who see it as a market solution to a labour problem—one that bypasses a slow and cumbersome point-driven system, privileges the principles of human capital to predict employability, and more actively responds to actual labour market needs (Nakache & Kinoshita, 2010). For others, the principle of the TFWP is defensible, at least in the short run, provided a balance is struck between long-term national goals and short-term economic interests (Conference Board of Canada, 2008). Yes, the contribution of TFWs deserve commendation. Yet Canada has gone too far in favouring (a) short-term fixes over long-term solutions and objectives, (b) opting for temporary entrants instead of responding to labour shortages through higher wages, (c) devolving responsibility for selection to provinces, educational institutions, and employers rather than using a national grid, and (d) prioritizing commodified labour over future citizens (Alboim, 2009; Alboim & Cohl, 2012). To that end, Ottawa has gradually overhauled the program by reinforcing its status as a tool of last resort when qualified Canadians are unavailable, tightening the rules on temporary work permits, establishing restrictions on the number of TFWs hired by a single employer, and limiting their numbers in regions of Canada with high unemployment rates (Marr, 2015).

ASSESSING IMMIGRATION: BENEFITS AND COSTS

Immigration has long proven a defining characteristic of Canada (Clipsen, 2014; Ibbitson, 2014). From Canada's earliest days as a nation through to its involvement in the global transformations of recent decades, immigration has advanced Canada's social, economic, and cultural development. Canadians have reacted to immigrants and immigration in different ways, ranging from enthusiasm and endorsement on the one hand to resentment and hostility on the other, with a combination of indifference, resignation, and indecision in between. As well, there are difficulties in trying to determine what it is about immigration or immigrants (including refugees) that Canadians dislike or disapprove of—is it the diversity or the politics or the processing system?

Immigration Benefits

For some, Canada's immigration and refugee programs are positively endorsed as a model of decorum, reflecting both the epitome of Canada's values and its maturity as a nation. Immigrants and refugees built this country, according to this line of thinking, and Canada's prosperity and identity will continue to depend on their industry and enthusiasm. Studies in other immigration societies such as Australia, New Zealand, and the United States, confirm that, on balance, immigrants are a net contributor to society—demographically, socially, culturally, and economically (Castles & Miller, 2009; Fleras & Spoonley, 1999; Spoonley & Bedford, 2012). The same conclusions apply to Canada (Halli & Driedger, 1999): Immigrants create more jobs than they take; as consumers, they provide markets for Canadian goods; they are more likely to start businesses than other Canadians; they are better qualified in terms of education; they realign the demographics by offsetting the effects of an aging population and declining birth rates; and they pay more in taxes than they accept in social services. Immigrants not only do the drudge work that Canadians disdain but also ease labour shortages during phases of capitalist expansion (it is estimated that all new labour market growth will come from immigrants [CIC, 2014]). Immigrants tend to possess drive and vitality, with boundless energy and optimism, and a willingness to take entrepreneurial risks by capitalizing on international links to improve Canada's competitive position in a global economy. Finally, despite the financial and social costs related to initial settlement in Canada, immigrants are the same people who will keep the economy afloat so that Canadians can retire comfortably (Hiebert & Ley, 2006). In general, then, rather than crippling the economy, immigrants inject a much-needed kick-start because of their commitment, connections, and cash.

The Costs of Immigration

Others disagree with this positive picture and point out how arguments cited in defence of immigration neither stand up to empirical scrutiny nor have a logical basis (Centre for Immigration Policy Reform, 2010; Francis, 2002; Paquet, 2011; Stoffman, 2003). Criticisms of immigration include: (1) Immigration rules are unjust, prone to abuse, and difficult to enforce (e.g., they are open to the reckless issuing of ministerial permits in exchange for favours or to facilitate entry or stay [Francis, 2005]); (2) the immigration program is manipulated to accommodate crass political considerations rather than national interests (e.g., electoral politics may help explain why political parties maintain high levels of immigration in Canada while avoiding any reference to immigration issues or any criticism of immigrants); (3) newcomers continue to be duped and exploited by unscrupulous immigrant consultants (CIC, 2011); and (4) immigration is feared as a portal for entry of extremists and terrorists (Moens & Collacott, 2008). The security-conscious concerns of the post-9/11 era justify accusing immigrant of using Canada as a launching pad for recruitment, fund raising, and staging grounds for terrorist attacks, both abroad and at home (Moens & Collacott, 2008). Immigrants are also criticized for the "problems" they allegedly bring into Canada. They are singled out for using their ties abroad to establish illegal international distribution systems for contraband drugs, loan-sharking, extortion rackets, prostitution, and the smuggling of "human cargo" into Canada. (Studies indicate that immigrant youth are less likely to commit crime because of bonds and commitments [Dinovitzer, Hagan, & Levi, 2009].) For critics, then, immigrants and immigration are essentially an investment option for Canada, to be measured in cost–benefit terms and evaluated accordingly (Bissett, 2008): If the costs are too high, Canada should pare back or bail out.

One of the more contentious aspects of immigration is its highly urbanized character. Nearly all immigrants settle in urban centres (primarily the MTV cities of Montreal, Toronto, and Vancouver), while avoiding wide swaths of Canada that are in need of what immigrants have to offer, prompting debate over how to spread the wealth more evenly across Canada. That immigrants and refugees are drawn to large urban regions is understandable (Hiebert, 2000). Cities provide the networks, supports, and resources that facilitate the adjustment and integration of immigrants and refugees. Thus, they prove to be a magnet for incoming immigrants and refugees. For example, about one-half of all immigrants to Toronto cite family and community as the chief reason for selecting that city (only about a quarter cite economic or work reasons). By contrast, immigrants are reluctant to settle in the Atlantic provinces because the cities lack a critical mass of their "own kind." To date, efforts to create a more geographically balanced distribution of migrants have proven futile, although the Provincial Nominee programs have shown some capacity to redistribute newcomers more evenly across Canada (CIC, 2014). Recent evidence also indicates a modest growth of newcomers to cities such as Charlottetown and Moncton, with a corresponding decline in numbers to the MTV cities.

Benefits and Costs: A Balanced View

The success of an immigration program can be assessed by gauging the balance of its benefits *and* costs. For example, economic benefits are not distributed equally; some regions and sectors receive a disproportionate share of both costs and benefits. Some parts of the economy (e.g., real estate or immigration lawyers) benefit from immigration and others (e.g., manual workers) suffer (Stoffman, 2003), but the average person may be largely unaffected. Immigrants may grow Canada's population and the size of its economy, but their presence does not necessarily increase its standard of living (Centre for Immigration Policy Reform, 2010). Certain immigrants provide immediate benefit (especially economic-class immigrants), while some may not (refugee class) because of their circumstances, and others do so indirectly or over time (family-class immigrants) (see Hou & Picot, 2014). Despite the undeniable long-term gains of immigration, the short-term costs may sting and are often offloaded by Ottawa to provinces, municipalities, and institutions (Grubel & Grady, 2011). Moreover, immigration policies and patterns cannot be a benefit to all: Migration may be good for the host country, which wants the brightest and the best, but less than ideal for those sending countries who are depleted of the very personnel they need for their own societal improvement (Kapur, 2005; Pecoud & de Guchteneire, 2005). Such a complex assessment makes it doubly important to appreciate the pros *and* cons of immigration.

In short, just as the benefits of immigration are unmistakable, so too are the costs. Those who obsess about the negative (threats to national unity, identity, and security) are no less ideologically myopic than those supporters who rhapsodize about the positive (Castles & Miller, 2003). Nor should the response or assessment be based entirely on utilitarian terms of "liability" or "asset." The importance of immigration to Canada goes beyond the question of demography or economy; issues related to Canada-building are implicated as well (Halli & Driedger, 1999; Ibbitson, 2005). Evolving patterns of immigration have irrevocably transformed the very concept of Canada as a British colony. The watering down of the historical duality that once defined "Canadianness" because of immigration has re-sculpted the political contours of Canada's social landscape along a cosmopolitan kaleidoscope of cultures, colours, and connections, with striking implications for national unity and identity. In the process of making over Canada, immigrants are more likely than non-immigrants to express a very strong sense of belonging to Canada (67% vs. 62%) without necessarily abandoning a strong connection to their country of origin (Statistics Canada, 2015b).

Attitudes toward Immigrants and Immigration

Attitudes and reactions toward immigrants and immigration vary. Many people are supportive of immigrants and refugees as hard-working and positive contributors to society (Nanos, 2008). But Canadians are openly critical of immigrants who do not add "value" to Canada or, worse still, prove a drain on its resources (Blackwell, 2004). The changing ethnic mix is endorsed as enriching the Canadian landscape; yet fears mount over possible social friction when immigrants are thought to reject core Canadian values (see Adams, 2007). Canadians may resent the presence of refugees who jump the queue to get in, but approve of their availability as cheap and disposable labour in factories, restaurants, fields, and homes (Canadian Council for Refugees, 2000). Canadians may be generous about offering assistance to those UN-mandated refugees who wait in camps and apply for protection from overseas, but bristle at the prospect of asylum seekers who self-select themselves and arrive *en masse* (Ibbitson, 2014). Context is critical in making these assessments: Canadians may not be unduly upset over immigration when the economy is booming; however, concerns escalate when the economy cools and (1) competition intensifies for good jobs and scarce resources; (2) immigrant labour becomes a permanent underclass; and (3) imbalances appear in education, welfare, service demands, and income distribution (Goldsborough, 2000).

To date, surveys indicate that Canadians are generally supportive of immigration and the benefits that immigrants bring (Bloemraad, 2014; Nanos, 2010; Reitz, 2014; Transatlantic Trends, 2010). A survey conducted by the Research House for the CBC involving 1500 adult Canadians and 260 racialized minorities in October of 2014 reinforced what most polls have confirmed: Canadian attitudes toward immigrants are generally positive but remain conditional, are conflicting and contradictory, and vary along socioeconomic and regional lines (CBC Poll, 2014; also Graves, 2015). For example, consider this poll by The Environics Institute (2015) which conducted a telephone survey of 2003 adult Canadians in June of 2015 to gauge their opinions about immigration and multiculturalism, integration, and discrimination: In general, the survey found that Canadian attitudes toward these issues have remained steady or have grown more positive over the past five years. Yet Canadians also remain sharply divided and deeply conflicted in assessing the positives and negatives, pros and cons, benefits and costs of immigration. Canadians with the least positive outlook on multiculturalism, immigration, integration, and anti-discrimination tend to be older Canadians, of lower socioeconomic status, live in smaller cities, and are more likely to support the Conservative Party. More specifically:

Multiculturalism

- 54 percent of Canadians regard multiculturalism as an important symbol of Canada's national identity, a figure similar to findings in 2010 and 2000. This view is most widespread in Ontario, among young women, and in Toronto, and least so in Quebec and for those who would vote Conservative. Of the nine symbols included in the survey, the health care system came in first (88%), followed by the Charter of Rights (81%), public education (78%), RCMP (65%), and Aboriginal peoples (62%). The Queen is at the bottom with 21 percent seeing her as an important symbol of Canadian national identity.

Immigration

- 38 percent of Canadians agree that "overall, there is too much immigration in Canada," down from 61 percent in 1977. 57 percent disagree with this statement, up from 35 percent who disagreed with this statement in 1977.
- 82 percent believe that "overall, immigration has a positive impact on the economy of Canada," up from 56 percent in 1993. 14 percent disagree with this belief, down from 39 percent in 1993.
- 30 percent believe that immigrants take away jobs from other Canadians. 54 percent disagree with this statement.
- 47 percent believe that "most people claiming to be refugees are not real refugees," down from 79 percent in 1987. 35 percent disagree with this statement, up from 13 percent in 1987. 17 percent are uncertain.
- 59 percent agree that "Canada is doing a good job of keeping (suspected) criminals out of the country," up from 28 percent in 1993. 32 percent disagree, down from 62 percent in 1993. 9 percent are unsure.
- 65 percent agree that "there are too many immigrants coming into this country who are not adopting Canadian values," down slightly from 72 percent in 1993. 30 percent disagree, down from 23 percent in 1993.
- 40 percent believe that Canada should accept political refugees who otherwise would not qualify for immigration, up from 32 percent in 1981. 50 percent disagree with this statement, down from 60 percent in 1981. 10 percent are uncertain.

Integration

- 75 percent believe that "ethnic groups should try as much as possible to blend into Canadian society and not form a separate community," down from 81 percent in 1985. 22 percent disagree, up from 15 percent in 1985.

- 47 percent believe that "it is more difficult for non-whites to be successful in Canadian society than it is for other groups," down from 60 percent in 1985. 49 percent disagree with this statement, up from 32 percent in 1985.

- 55 percent believe that "ethnic and racial groups should take more responsibility for solving their own economic and social problems," down from 80 percent in 1985. 39 percent disagree, up from 12 percent in 1985.

- 95 percent believe that "someone born outside Canada can be just as likely to be a good citizen as someone born here," up from 91 percent in 2011. 3 percent disagreed, down from 6 percent in 2011.

Discrimination

- 51 percent believe Muslims often experience discrimination (up 9% since 2011), whereas 36 percent believe it rarely happens and 7 percent believe it occurs occasionally.

- 47 percent believe Aboriginal peoples often experience discrimination (up 5% from 2011), whereas 37 percent believe it rarely happens and 10 percent think it happens occasionally.

- 31 percent believe blacks often experience discrimination; 30 percent believe South Asians often experience discrimination; 14 percent believe Jews often experience discrimination (32% occasionally); and 13 percent believe Chinese often experience discrimination (30% occasionally).

Clearly, then, this survey provides a counterpoint to the negative narrative in Chapter 1 that criticized the management of race, ethnic, and aboriginal relations in Canada. That narrative was blanketed by references to white supremacy, colonialism, racialized, structural exclusions, systemic biases, racism, and a white superiority complex. By contrast, this survey's endorsement of multiculturalism, support for immigration, integration of new Canadians, and greater awareness of discrimination toward racialized minorities points to a radically different narrative—at least in theory (attitudes) if not in practice. It also raises the question of whether other narratives are possible: (1) Canada's commitment to positively managing diversity and aboriginality lies somewhere in between extreme narratives; that is, the reality in Canada is not nearly as dismal as critics would have us believe, but neither is it as progressive as surveys on attitudes indicate; (2) both narratives are in play and reflect the fact that Canada and Canadian attitudes continues to evolve from Canada's historical status as a white society to one that is more open, tolerant, and inclusive; (3) that both points (1) and (2) are equally valid, depending on the context, criteria for assessment, and consequences of unintended actions.

To be realistic, no person, no matter how opposed to immigration in principle or practice, is without some sympathy for the plight of the world's poorest. Similarly, no person, regardless of his or her pro-immigrant sympathies, can dismiss its negative impact on some sectors of society (Millman, 1997). Somewhere between the "yeas" and the "nays" are those who see the interplay of immigration's costs and benefits. The in-between sector takes a practical outlook on immigration. With an intake of approximately 250 000 new Canadians each year, some with clearly different cultures, experiences, and expectations, a degree of friction and annoyance is inevitable. So too is the likelihood of crowding, pressure on existing services, inflated markets, sporadic crime surges, and congested roads. The costs cannot be ignored: A country cannot expect to have a policy of immigration-driven sustained economic growth without some negative repercussions. A sense of proportion is badly needed. If Canadians value the cultural and economic benefits associated with immigration, they must be prepared to shoulder the costs. In short, immigration *is* a benefit that invariably accompanies a cost for someone, somewhere, sometimes.

For the in-betweens, then, immigration is neither a sacred cow immune to criticism nor a convenient scapegoat to blame for Canada's problems. People who occupy an informed middle ground acknowledge the partial validity of arguments both for and against immigration. They acknowledge that costs accompany benefits; for example, there is much of value in Canada's principled (rule-based, transparent, and accountable) approach toward immigration; nevertheless, a proliferation of rules can create bureaucracy, red tape, and inflexibility because of high volumes, in the process eliminating room for discretionary decisions except at political levels where such interference can prove costly (Thompson, 2005). Canadians tend to be comfortable with immigrants who are poor, appear to be grateful for the opportunity, and are willing to start at the bottom as cooks, labourers, and farmhands. Immigrants are largely deemed "acceptable" if (1) their cultural practices are compatible with Canada's; (2) they know their place by acknowledging their status as "guests" in Canada and fit in accordingly; and (3) they appreciate that immigration must advance national interests rather than cater to minority demands. Canadians are less sure of how to "cope" with those immigrants who are affluent, confident, assertive, and highly qualified; unwilling to put up with slights or slurs as the price of admission or staying; and, as professional transnationals, are willing to barter their talents wherever the global economy will take them. In other words, assessments about the costs and benefits of immigration are rarely right or wrong, but both right and wrong, depending on the context, criteria, and consequences, with the result that inflated claims on both sides of the debate often conceal whatever truths they contain.

IMMIGRANT EXPERIENCES: SETTLING DOWN, MOVING UP, FITTING IN

> Every act of immigration is like suffering a brain stroke: One has to learn to walk again, to talk again, to move around the world again, and, probably most difficult of all, one has to learn how to re-establish a sense of community. (Vivian Rakoff, as cited in Fulford, 2003)

The model of immigration settlement based on the European experience may no longer apply (Frideres, 2005; Suarez-Orozco & Suarez-Orozco, 2001). The European (or national) model saw immigration settlement as a one-way upwardly mobile journey resulting in permanent residence in the adopted country. But in a world of globalization and transnational localities, immigrants are increasingly expressing complex attachments, fluid identities, and multiple homelands (Cheng, 2005; Satzewich & Wong, 2006), in the process creating new wrinkles in the adjustment process as some groups rapidly integrate while others don't. The new global context demands a fresh outlook on immigration—from new explanatory frameworks to innovative policy responses—one that acknowledges its multidimensional and dynamic nature when applied to cross-border movements and transmigrant networks (Fleras, 2011b; Massey, 2009; Simmons, 2010; Spoonley, 2010).

Put succinctly, it's no longer acceptable to see immigration as a fixed and linear pattern of relocation between A and B (Fleras, 2014b). Current immigration patterns reflect complex and fluid fields of flow involving different actors, across different domains, and at different levels (Simmons, 2010). Rather than a simple one-way movement of people in search of permanent residency, immigration must be framed as a complex and drawn-out transformational process across a host of political and social factors, with economic and cultural consequences for both the sending and receiving country (Castles, deHaas, & Miller, 2013). The process itself can be envisaged as falling along a continuum from pre-migration preparation at one end to post-migration integration at the other end, with transitional phases in-between, as demonstrated in Table 8-6.

TABLE 8-6	Settlement Process: Life Course Transition of an Adult Immigrant with Children		
Pre-migration >	**Settlement >** "Settling down"	**Adaptation >** "Moving up"	**Integration** "Fitting in"
Conditions in homeland (political, economic, etc.)	Basic language	Language skills	Citizenship
Status and experiences in home country (social class, education level, resources, resourcefulness)	Housing	Career	Participation in politics and civic life
Skill sets (labourer, entrepreneur, professional)	Employment	Networks	Adjustment to host country (from marginalization to acceptance)
Reasons for leaving the country (push and pull)	Education	Community	
Necessary attributes: (a) motivation to move (b) resources to do so, and (c) be admissible	Social services	Sense of identity	
Transition experiences (good, easy, etc.)	Readiness of receiving country (policies, programs, opportunities)	Knowledge of Canada	
Entry formalities, including application	Immigrant resources for settling in (supports, language competence)	Implications for the human services sector	
Sources: Kunz (2005); Segal et al. (2010); Simmons (2010).			

Canada's immigration policy continues to emphasize the settlement of new Canadians in terms of settling down, moving up, and fitting in. Settlement itself involves a three-stage process: (1) immediate needs for assistance and reception; (2) intermediate needs for accessing the labour market, housing, health services, and so on; and (3) long-term needs in which immigrants strive for integration into Canadian society and the economy (see Table 8-6) (Wayland, 2006). In hopes of equipping migrants with the tools to settle down, both the governmental and non-profit sectors offer language training, employment counselling, and translation services, in addition to a normative framework known as multiculturalism to facilitate immigrant integration through mutual adjustment (Winter, 2015). Settlement services are predominantly delivered by immigrant-serving groups such as the Kitchener-Waterloo Multicultural Centre, who rely heavily on government funding to defray the costs of service delivery. Admittedly, there are glitches: In most provinces, settlement services are available only to permanent residents or **convention refugees**; as a result, years of residence may be required of a refugee claimant before eligibility for these services kicks in (Wayland, 2006; Zaman, 2006). As well, the federal government has waffled over increased funding for settlement and language services, preferring instead to devolve responsibility for settlement to the private sector or the provinces.

The emergence of a new immigrant experience acknowledges how the settlement process reflects a dynamic mix of success and failure (Halli-Vedanand, 2007; Pendakur & Pendakur, 2004). It also reflects the layered realities and varying complexities of immigrant lived-experiences (Bauder & Shields, 2015). Some immigrants are primed for success; others are being squeezed out of the picture because of discrimination, racism, and prejudice; and still others are just muddling through. For some immigrants, the immigration process is filled with hope and opportunity; for others, it is fraught with danger and disappointment; for still others, it is a combination of hope and despair (Suarez-Orozco & Suarez-Orozco, 2001). The immigrant experience may prove less gratifying than originally anticipated—particularly as elders drift apart from the junior generation, as younger women chafe over traditional roles and pervasive paternalism, and as educated elites become estranged from the community at large (Handa, 2003). No less immobilizing are the pangs of homesickness. Andrei Codrescu (1995) writes of the bittersweet, near-death experiences of his Romanian mother:

> Most people come here because they are sick of being poor. They want to eat and they want something to show for their industry. But soon enough it becomes evident to them that these things are not enough. They have eaten and they are full, but they have eaten alone . . . This time they are lacking something more elusive than salami and furniture. They are bereft of a social and cultural milieu . . . Leaving behind your kin, your friends, your language, your smells, your childhood, is traumatic. It is a kind of death. (p. 47)

For others, the immigrant experience provides a payoff but is not without penalties. Newcomers realize opportunities exist in Canada that are unavailable back home, but they still miss their homeland; certain Canadian values are muchly appreciated, yet they long for the values from home that can't be found in Canada; they like their new friends but ache for the closeness of family and kin they have left behind.

Many new Canadians appear to be relatively satisfied with the quality of life in Canada (Adams, 2007; Clarkson, 2015). The General Social Survey (see Omidvar, 2010) indicated that 84 percent of immigrants who arrived between 1990 and 2003 expressed strong or somewhat strong feelings of belonging to Canada, compared with 85 percent of all Canadians (The Dominion Institute, 2008). They appreciate the opportunities and services available to them and their children, the promise of human freedom, and sufficient market transparency to succeed. According to the 2005 Longitudinal Survey of Immigrants to Canada (see Schellenberg & Maheux, 2007), what immigrants like best about Canada are the climate and physical environment (19.1%), cultural aspects (freedom, rights, etc.) (14.4%), safety (11%), peace and political stability (10.4%), and educational opportunities (9.9%). Paradoxically, however, what they most dislike (aside from the 19% who do not dislike anything) are the climate and physical environment (26.7%), lack of employment opportunities (17.4%), and high taxes (11.1%). Yes, material well-being and quality of life are perceived to have improved compared with their homelands, but many immigrants will confront a series of problems that have accompanied them into Canada or encounter problems upon entry and settlement (Jimenez, 2006). Few could possibly anticipate the obstacles that need to be surmounted, including culture shock, psychological stress, lack of political power, loss of economic well-being, personal isolation, lack of support from the homeland, and discriminatory barriers that preclude entry or acceptance (Fleras, 2014b). Surveys repeatedly indicate that securing employment (preferably jobs in one's field of experience or expertise) is the largest settlement-related problem for new Canadians (BMO Report, 2014; Wayland, 2006). Other common obstacles include learning a new language, acclimatizing to the weather, adapting to new cultural values, and accessing language training, housing, and healthcare services (Schellenberg & Maheux, 2007). Immigrants confront numerous challenges and criticisms; after all, living in a new country can be daunting, especially in the context of major cultural differences.

Patterns of settlement may expose immigrants to double standards (damned if they do, damned if they don't). If economically successful, they are criticized for taking jobs from the Canadian-born; if unemployed or unsuccessful, they are castigated as a drain on the system (Esses, 2015). They might be inclined to maintain some semblance of their traditions and culture to temper the culture shock because of a need for continuity, and in the search for meaning at a time of rapid change. But doing so may subject immigrants to criticism for sticking with their own kind and own ways at the expense of integrating into Canada. Yet if they integrate and immerse themselves in the host community at the expense of their ethnicity, they may be accused of "selling out" to the system. The persistence of immigrant enclaves has also raised questions about Canada's "welcome mat." Are these enclaves the result of racist and exclusionary practices such as housing discrimination, or do they reflect an immigrant preference for familiar community (Hiebert, 2015; Novac, 1999; Yelaja & Keung, 2005)? In either case, the challenges of integration are mounting as more new arrivals speak neither French nor English and increasingly find themselves isolated in suburban enclaves (Bauder & Shields, 2015; Reinhart, 2007; Siemiatycki, 2007).

Settling Down

Generally speaking, the primary concerns of new Canadians are practical and survival-related. Unlike the more political demands of Canada's founding peoples for self-determining autonomy, immigrants and refugees are more concerned with the pragmatic issues related to "getting in" by way of equality, participation, and acceptance. They don't want a separate existence that rejects their new adopted homeland, but they are also leery of an assimilation that robs of them of their authenticity. What they want is an inclusiveness without assimilation—even if that means opting for residence in their own immigrant communities because of convenience or comfort, while pressuring institutions to accommodate their cultural and religious identities through removal of the discriminatory barriers that impede full and equal participation (Fleras, 2014b). Foremost is the desire to "put down roots" by "settling down," "fitting in," and "moving up" in Canadian society, without necessarily severing ties with their cultural traditions. More specifically, immigrant concerns and aspirations can be itemized as follows:

1. A labour market with opportunity and a workplace without discrimination,

2. Conferral of full citizenship rights, including the right to move, participate, and criticize,

3. Improved access to housing, government institutions, social services, and mass media without diminishing their sense of cultural identity,

4. The capability to express themselves in terms of their cultural distinctiveness without paying a penalty in the process, and

5. Respect for their differences as a legitimate and valued part of society.

In short, newcomers to Canada want the best that both worlds have to offer. They want to be treated as individuals by being accepted for what they *do* rather than being lumped together into an amorphous mass on the basis of who they *are* perceived to be. Conversely, they also want appreciation for who they are culturally, without sacrificing equal and meaningful involvement in society. Full Canadian citizenship rights are important, but no less so is respect for their cultural worth as individuals with a meaningful past.

But what new Canadians want is not necessarily what they get. Immigrant qualifications continue to be dismissed, education degrees devalued, and overseas experience discounted as next to worthless (Drummond & Fong, 2010; Finnie & Meng, 2002). Foreign education counts for about half of the value of Canadian schooling in terms of earning power, while foreign experience often has little market value in Canada (one year overseas equates to about one-third of a year in Canada). Refusal to recognize the credentials of new Canadians costs Canada billions in lost revenue (Conference Board of Canada, 2004), in effect reinforcing the idea that non-recognition is really a Canada problem rather than an immigrant problem (Wayland, 2006). In other words, immigrants may be selected for their skills, credentials, and work experiences; yet Canadian employers don't want to or don't know how to use these. Not surprisingly, as noted by many (Hansen, 2013; Reitz, 2005), the success of Canada's immigration policy will be measured by institutions that link workers to jobs by providing for an international transferability of skills, credentials, and experience. Or, in the pithy phrasing of Randall Hansen of the University of Toronto at a conference at Augsburg University, Germany in December 2010, "Immigration works when immigrants work."

The much-hyped reference to Canada as a land of opportunity has not paid dividends. Thousands of immigrants can't find meaningful work in Canada (Basok & Bastable, 2009; Schellenberg & Hou, 2005). As noted earlier, the most common barriers to working include: (1) lack of Canadian work experience, (2) lack of recognition of foreign credentials and work experience, (3) lack of knowledge about the Canadian economy and the unwritten labour market codes that take time to learn, and (4) increased competition with a growing educated Canadian labour force (Alboim & McIsaac, 2007). Employers in the regulated professions, from engineering to dentistry, confront the challenge of not wanting to discriminate against foreign born professionals yet, at the same time, are under pressure to protect public safety (Barnett, Nicol, & Walker, 2012). Not surprisingly, highly skilled immigrants find themselves segregated in menial and unskilled occupations with little in the way of security or prospects for promotion. A Longitudinal Survey of 12 000 immigrants who arrived in Canada in 2000/1 found that only 40 percent of skilled principal applicants found work in the occupations for which they were trained (Alboim & McIsaac, 2007). Understandably, frustration levels mount:

> Many individuals feel that they were duped into coming to Canada, but do not want to face the shame of returning to their homelands. They settle for underemployment and hope that their children's luck will be better. Other migrants move to the United States where accreditation processes are perceived to be swifter. (Wayland, 2006:77)

No less harrowing for skilled and professional immigrants is the closed-shop mentality of licensed occupations that continue to impose restrictions and deny accreditation (George & Chaze, 2014). This bottleneck that prevents professionals from gainful employment may reflect a fundamental disconnect: The federal government controls immigration, but the provinces control the licensing, while the professional bodies control who gets in.

Moving Up

Equally demanding are the challenges in moving up (Ruddick, 2003). Income earnings among new immigrants increase over time after initial arrival, but no cohort of immigrants since 1980 has matched (or caught up with) the earnings of the immigrant cohort that preceded it, controlling for length of residence in Canada (Simmons, 2010:144). If anything, earning gaps between recent immigrants (many of whom are highly educated) and Canadian-born workers continue to widen. In 1980, recent immigrant males with some employment income earned 85 cents for every dollar earned by a Canadian born male; by 2005, the ratio had dropped to 63 cents. The corresponding numbers for recent immigrant women were 85 cents and 56 cents (Statistics Canada, 2009). To be sure, the picture is more complex than many critics realize. According to a Statistics Canada study of Canada's immigrant labour markets in 2006, new immigrants (fewer than five years in Canada) have unemployment rates three times higher than Canadian-born residents, despite much higher educational levels for those between 25 and 54. However, within 10 years of their arrival, immigrants possess the same job prospects as Canadian-born workers, thanks to increased experience and improved language skills. In other words, foreign credentials matter, of course, but employers may be more interested in those competencies (speaking without a foreign accent) for which qualifications often serve as a proxy. Not surprisingly, the strongest predictors of economic success are neither credentials nor degrees but competence in one of Canada's two official languages. And not just basic French or English competencies in reading and writing, it is argued, but a nuanced level of sophistication for solving problems and getting along (Banting, Courchene, & Seidle, 2007).

How do we account for these disparities? Lower entry-level earnings are determined as much by institutional structures, local labour market conditions, and protectionism on the part of employers and professional bodies as they are by prejudicial attitudes and lack of human capital (Reitz, 1998). Foremost among structural factors are the changing racial and ethnic composition of the immigrant population, the attendant racism that seemingly comes with diversity, the inability of employers to evaluate foreign credentials and educational degrees (resulting in a corresponding discounting of these skills), communication problems for non-English and non-French-speaking immigrants, and changes in the labour market because of economic globalization and knowledge-based economies (Biles & Burstein, 2003). Increased employment and earnings are often linked with language proficiency in one of Canada's two official languages. Yet many immigrants have neither French nor English as a first language (around 33 percent in 2013 [CIC, 2014]), even as the federal government is scaling back access to its English as a second language (ESL) program (Wayland, 2006). Finally, the managers of unionized workplaces may find their hands tied when it comes to hiring skilled workers with overseas experience. Collective agreements with entrenched seniority rights stipulate that they recruit from within the bargaining unit when filling positions (James, 2005). Clearly, then, settlement structures and reception models are key to reducing poverty and improving productivity: The better the reception models in terms of integration into social and economic networks, the greater the success of immigrant adaptation (Abu-Laban, Derwing, & Mulder, 2004).

Fitting In

The challenges of fitting in are no less complex. Customary family relations and status are challenged and transformed in the new country, resulting in intergenerational conflicts (Tyyska, 2008). For immigrant youth, the pressures may be intimidating (Handa, 2003): They must adjust to a new country, cope with the pressures of prejudice and racism during their formative years of identity construction, become involved with new routines and friendships, and learn a new language quickly enough to finish high school and compete with their Canadian-born peers for places in post-secondary education (it generally takes five to seven years to develop English language equivalency for success at school). Immigrant and refugee schoolchildren are subject to a host of conflicting demands and pressures. Some may perform poorly because of racial stereotyping, low teacher expectations, curricula and textbooks at odds with minority experiences, and lack of positive role models among school staff (L. Brown, 2005). And most need to negotiate the demands of a mainstream peer culture whose values of independence and competition may conflict with the cultural norms (from interdependence and cooperation to obedience) of family and community (Anisef & Kilbride, 2003; Handa, 2003; Tyyska, 2008). Young women, as the moral guardians of the culture and nation, are particularly vulnerable, as Mythili Rajiva (2005) says:

> Girls are expected to maintain cultural practices that are sometimes no longer relevant in their homeland countries, and are certainly not widely accepted in Canadian society. This includes concerns with dress and behaviour; peer socializing (at night, at parties, and school dancing); growing independence at adolescence (which is often not part of immigrant community understandings of adolescence); and perhaps most importantly, interacting with members of the opposite sex and having romantic relationships with boys who are not part of the community. (p. 27)

Intergenerational family tensions are inevitable as parents and offspring struggle to find a working balance between Canada's permissiveness and the more conservative traditions of new immigrant groups (Handa, 2003). In many cases, the immigrant story contains two broad narratives: adult immigrants who falter in making the transition versus their offspring who successfully adjust (Sykes, 2008). Immigrant parents may feel alienated from a language and culture that confuses them, especially when their parental authority is questioned, whereas their immigrant children assimilate rapidly, which enables them to assume an assertiveness, control, and independence that inverts conventional roles (Lupa, 1999). Parents are forced to strike a Faustian bargain: All parents desire a better future for their children, nevertheless, attainment of this success tends to undermine parental authority and family cohesion (Suarez-Orozco & Suarez-Orozco, 2001). And immigrant women may be the real victims (Rajiva, 2005). Thousands of new Canadians are living in quiet desperation and depression, suffering in silence behind walls of social alienation, financial pressure, family turmoil, and cultural mores that isolate and foreclose avenues of help (Reinhart & Rusk, 2006). Clearly, there is much value in understanding immigrants as gendered subjects who are differently located with respect to identity construction, experiences, and opportunity and outcomes (Tastsoglou, Ray, & Preston, 2005; Zaman, 2006).

For both convention and inland refugees, the situation is decidedly grimmer. Traumatized by emotional and psychological abuses before and en route to Canada, refugees are still expected to adapt to Canada's unique social, cultural, and geographic climate with only minimal outside assistance. Refugees may have complex needs, widely varying educational and literacy levels because of disruptions to schooling (Sirin & Rogers-Sirin, 2015), and much to learn in a relatively short period of time, ranging from awareness of community support agencies to lived-issues of housing and employment (Bauder, 2012). The impact of the cultural shock may be unsettling because of exposure to radically different lifestyles, mixed messages and conflicting expectations, rapid social change, and an inhospitable climate. Worse still, refugee families may remain separated for lengthy periods of time because of delays in acquiring permanent residence for the sponsoring family member or an inability to pay the processing fees that must accompany each application (Wayland, 2006). The transitional stresses that accompany refugee claimants are compounded by their language difficulties, shame at their inability to work, and low self-esteem because of loss of control over their destiny. As expressed by one refugee from Central America who fell into an abusive relationship: "I was from a country where I was the daughter of a middle-class professional. Here, I was no one. Refugee is such a negative word. People saw me as garbage" (as cited in White, 1999).

PROSPECTS: NEEDING IMMIGRATION, EMBRACING IMMIGRANTS?

From 2006 to 2015, the Canadian government transformed Canada's immigration program by favouring immigrants over refugees while limiting refugee claims; discouraging family class reunification in favour of economic class migrants; promoting a TFWP that prioritized economic expediency (such as on-demand labour) at the expense of citizenship and

Canada-building; and encouraging new arrivals who could quickly integrate into society without government assistance and generate economic outputs (Ibbitson, 2014; Root et al., 2014). How, then, should we assess Canada's record as an immigration country? Few countries have demonstrated the same degree of generosity, inclusiveness, and tolerance that Canada has, especially with the introduction of the *Canadian Charter of Rights and Freedoms* and its official policy of Multiculturalism (Bloemraad, 2014). Canada's commitment is reflected in the positioning of immigration within the context of Canada-building. Canada's record may not be perfect in this regard, but surely it is less imperfect than other countries in living up to an historic ideal, as articulated by this 1862 pamphlet to entice prospective German settlers:

> Canada is the land of peace, order, and abundance . . . The immigrant when he arrives is protected and guided by government officials . . . Canada is about the only country in which the . . . immigrant practically as well as before [the] law is seen as immediately equal to the native born. (as cited in Avery, 1995:239)

The immigration process activates a "social contract" between immigrants that involves a two-way process of mutual accommodation (Frith, 2003; Parekh, 1997; Spencer, 2003). Canada expects immigrants to identify with core cultural values, make a positive contribution, participate through involvement, and abide by the laws of society. Immigrants, in turn, expect fair treatment through the removal of discriminatory barriers, the conferral of citizenship rights, the creation of welcoming communities, and the right to identify with the cultural tradition of their choice (Volpe, 2005). In short, coming to Canada activates a social contract in which immigrants trade talents for responsibilities, while Canada exchanges safety and security for rights.

Yet another dimension to assessing immigration requires attention: Canadians for the most part have not yet fully confronted the reality and challenges of immigrant integration as a two-way process of mutual adjustment (see Modood, 2003). Reluctance to endorse measures that encourage inclusiveness and accommodation of ethno-religious practices is but one sign of this indecisiveness. Another sign is a belief that some immigrant groups are making demands perceived as culturally, socially, and politically unacceptable, although Tariq Modood (2005) argues that these groups are only seeking exemptions from general rules to ensure social space and respectful endorsement of their cultural heritage—a right that is implied in an official Multiculturalism. Growing anti-immigrant sentiment is a possibility, although any backlash would likely be constrained in its expression by (1) human rights codes that prohibit the public articulation of racist views, (2) a pervasive liberalism within the political culture, and (3) a lack of institutional power base to fortify racist exclusion. In other words, there is not much likelihood of reverting to an openly racial basis for either the selection of immigrants or their treatment once they are in Canada. Still, immigrants continue to experience barriers that deny or exclude. They may not be second-class citizens under the law, nevertheless, they remain so in public perception and within national discourses. Moreover, they may possess formal equality rights, but must exercise these rights and achieve success in contexts neither designed with them in mind nor constructed to advance their interests or realities. Such mixed messages of denial and exclusion reflect badly on Canada's much-vaunted reputation as an immigrant society that abides by the principles of multiculturalism.

The IRB as a Functioning Dysfunction?

Canadians appear to be of mixed minds when it comes to the refugee question. Support is overwhelming for resettled (in camps) refugees or for those who are seen as legitimate victims of state oppression. For example, for its work with international refugees, especially in resettling those fleeing from communist rule in Vietnam, Laos, and Cambodia, Canada received the UN Nansen medal in 1986—the first and so far the only country to earn such an accolade. But the welcome mat is fraying for refugees who are smuggled in, arrive unannounced without documentation, who appear to be shopping around for the best deal, who come across as economic opportunists circumventing conventional channels of entry, and who abuse the system through endless appeals and delays. Perceptions of control appear to be critical: As long as they are in charge of "who gets in," Canadians admire themselves as generous patrons to genuine victims. But with any departure from the norm—for example, asylum seekers who self-select themselves for admission based on *their* needs (Simmons, 2010)—Canadians bristle at the prospect of being taken advantage of.

Canadians are also conflicted over the concept of inland refugee claimants and the system in place (IRB) to assess the situation. Much of the conflict over the politics of inland refugee claims pivots around two philosophical axis points (Plaut, 1989).

- A *restrictive* perspective that endorses a skeptical mentality toward refugee claims. According to this "guilty until proven innocent" approach, measures must be put in place to thwart the entry of "bogus" asylum seekers who imperil Canada's national interests, while expediting a summary expulsion for unfounded claims (Collacott, 2006; Gallagher, 2004). According to critics, unlike countries that vigorously weed out "fake" asylum seekers, everyone who lands in Canada is entitled to due process by a tribunal (Gallagher, 2004), including claims from citizens of countries such as the United States, the United Kingdom, and Germany. Numerous loopholes and vulnerabilities are exploited that can prove costly once legal, welfare, and administrative costs are factored in (Stoffman, 1997). The entire process is inundated with excess capacity; case workers are overworked; claimants encounter lengthy delays; and the system itself not only is prone to gaffes and subject to abuse because of political patronage in staffing the IRB, but also exposes Canadians to security risks (Collacott, 2006; Francis, 2002). Those who take a restrictive perspective propose three options for tightening the admission and determination process: (1) detain undocumented asylum seekers until proof of person is established; (2) establish a firewall that excludes as many refugees as possible, then deal with genuine cases as they arise; or (3) redesign Canada's refugee program by selecting (sponsoring) only those from refugee camps around the world (Stoffman, 2002). Recent changes to the inland refugee determination process as pointed out earlier in the chapter are clearly consistent with a more restrictive perspective (Fleras, 2014b).

- An *expansionist* mindset disagrees, proposing, instead, a generous acceptance of refugees in line with Canada's humanitarian and human rights commitments. The expansionist objective is to cast as wide a net as possible for asylum seekers, then dispose of those who don't fit. According to this line of logic, all refugees should be assumed innocent and given the benefit of the doubt until they are proven guilty. After all, there is no such thing as an illegal migrant, since all asylum seekers are within their rights by international law to claim asylum. Admittedly, proof of authenticity may be awkward without identity papers; yet playing by the rules by patiently standing in a queue is rarely an option. Such is the nature of any flight from persecution and chaos that few can afford the luxury of asking for papers or permission. The necessity to produce "satisfactory identity documents" negatively affects those refugee groups who come from countries where no government authority exists to issue such documents; certain groups such as women or rural residents cannot access such documentation; and simply asking for such documentation is likely to arouse suspicion or incur reprisals. (Keep in mind that it is often the refugee's identity that put him or her at risk in the first place [Canadian Council for Refugees, 2000]). In short, refugee claimants as protected persons

deserve the benefit of the doubt, on the assumption that it is better to err on the side of generosity (i.e., to accept 99 bogus refugees) than to incorrectly reject a genuine case.

In keeping with this expansionist ethos—at least until recently—Canada cast its refugee net ever more broadly. A 1986 Supreme Court decision ruled that everyone who landed in Canada was entitled to due process when claiming refugee status. There is growing acceptance of certain groups who do not strictly comply with the definition of persecution, but need *protection* because they experience refugee-like conditions, such as political oppression or environmental disaster. In May 1997, Canada expanded its definition of refugee status to include those internally displaced because of war or terrorism and in need of temporary protection from a dangerous situation (Stoffman, 1997; Waldie, 1998). Refugee status may be granted to minorities, such as the European Roma, who fail to receive state protection from public discrimination. Gender is also proving to be grounds for refugee status, reflecting patterns of persecution that affect women only, including cases of abusive domestic situations, exposure to mutilation, or forced marriage and sterilization (Kumin, 2001). Finally, even rejected claimants or those who commit a serious crime may escape deportation if they risk injury upon return, fear becoming victims of crime in their homeland, or if their Canadian-born children would suffer from their removal. Table 8-7 captures the gist of arguments between the "expansion" (optimist) versus "restriction" (pessimist) camps.

(Continued)

TABLE 8-7	Competing Perspectives on Refugees and Inland Refugee Determination System	
RESTRICTIVE/PESSIMISTS	**EXPANSIVE/OPTIMISTS**	
Claims = Bogus (most asylum seekers are fake)	Claims = *Bona Fide* (most asylum seekers are genuine)	
Claimants = Guilty until proven innocent	Claimants = innocent until proven guilty	
Strict interpretation of the law for admission	Looser interpretation of the law (protected persons) for admission	
National interests must prevail in sorting out who gets in	Human rights must prevail in defining who gets in	
Case-by-case adjudication to determine merits	Spread net wide to ensure no one is excluded	

Flaws and glitches notwithstanding, Canada's refugee processing program is globally admired for its openness and generosity in providing the benefit of the doubt to those in need. There is much to commend in Canada's refugee determination system; nevertheless, improvement is necessary if Canada is to maintain its status as the true north, strong and free. The challenge is no longer how to design the perfect inland refugee determination system (Kumin, 2004); rather, the focus now is on how to create one that is politically, socially, and ethically acceptable to rule over matters of life and death, without compromising Canada's national interests. Moral quandaries abound: Canadians do not want Canada to become a haven for terrorists because of misplaced generosity or inadequate screening procedures, yet they squirm at the prospect of sending people back to torture or death. Canadians may resent refugees who prove to be a social or medical burden, particularly those refugees who self-select to arrive in Canada without proper identification (Simmons, 2010), yet they balk at the prospect of deporting them to a cruel fate (Duffy, 1999). It ultimately boils down to choices: As Janet Dench (2007) points out, refugees are people who have no choice except to flee. Canadians by contrast do have a choice: to welcome refugees as human beings in need of protection or to abandon them by pulling up the drawbridge. The decision by the Trudeau Government in late 2015 to admit 25 000 Syrian refugees from camps in the Middle East goes a long way toward restoring Canada's gold-plated status as a refugee-friendly country.

Chapter Highlights

- Canada is sociologically regarded as an immigrant society. That is, it has an immigration program in place, sees immigrants as a national asset, confers rights to immigrants, and encourages settlement and citizenship.
- Canada routinely ranks high among countries with respect to immigration on a per capita basis, with the result that the foreign born account for just over 20 percent of the population.

- Immigration currently averages about 250 000 people per year, with the majority arriving from Asia, Africa, and South and Central America. Most immigrants prefer Ontario and British Columbia; cities such as Toronto, Montreal, and Vancouver remain major immigrant targets.
- In the past, immigration practices were highly racist in defining who got in. At present, Canada's immigration policy can be described as relatively colour-blind, with a focus on sustaining economic growth through a proactive and designer immigrant selection process.
- Immigrants can be admitted on three grounds: family-reunification class, economic class, and refugee class.
- The spectacular expansion of the temporary foreign workers program elicits praise from Canadian businesses but criticism from those concerned that Canada's long-term interests are sacrificed for short-term gains.
- Canadians appear divided in their reaction to immigration, with some seeing it as a problem, others as a solution, and still others as both a problem and a solution, depending on the context, consequences, and criteria.
- Immigration comes with benefits and costs. Benefits are numerous but resonate differently on different sectors of society and the economy. The costs are no less real for some Canadians.
- Immigrant needs and aspirations tend to be basic. Most want to put down roots in their adopted country, contribute to its growth, receive the benefits that all Canadians are entitled to, and insist on the best for their children without loss of attachment to family, community, and culture.
- The refugee program continues to be seen as a problem, especially with regard to those refugee claimants who make inland claims for asylum. Canada may have a relatively high rate of acceptance of refugee claimants, but most agree that concerns prevail over the issue of "Who is a refugee?" "How do we find out?" "Is the current system working?" and "Can the system be improved?"

Review Questions

1. Briefly compare the concept of immigration in the past with the current (post-1978) immigration policy in terms of underlying assumptions, goals, methods, and outcomes.

2. Discuss the aspirations of immigrants in terms of needs and goals. What kinds of barriers exist that preclude attainment of these goals?

3. Point out the issues and debates that contribute to a "refugee status determination crisis" in Canada.

4. Is the current immigration model of immigration the best one for Canada, in light of emergent realities? If you were the Immigration Minister, what *principled* changes would you make, based on doing what is workable, necessary, and fair?

CHAPTER 9

Multiculturalism as Canada-Building Governance

LEARNING OBJECTIVES

After reading this chapter, you will be able to:

1. Summarize the different models of multiculturalism as diversity governance.

2. Outline the ways in which reference to multiculturalism in Canada reflects five distinct levels of meaning.

3. Identify the four overlapping phases through which Canada's official multiculturalism has evolved.

4. Demonstrate how the practice of putting multiculturalism to work at institutional levels entails a commitment to the principle of inclusiveness.

5. Describe patterns of bias in public attitudes and general criticism of multiculturalism.

DEBATE

The Politics of Multiculturalism: European Rejection, Canadian Embrace

References to Multiculturalism as policy and philosophy have come under intense scrutiny. From the Antipodes to Europe, multiculturalism is experiencing a crisis of legitimacy as both the public and political elites have opted to reject (at least in rhetoric, if not necessarily in practice) a multicultural model for managing complex diversities (Bevelander & Taras, 2012). Policies and ideologies that once embraced multiculturalism as a framework for cooperative coexistence are now dismissed as irrelevant or inferior, a failure or a threat (Gregg, 2006; Mansur, 2011). In the aftermath of 9/11, the Madrid and London bombings, and politicized

assassinations of high-profile Dutch personalities including Pym Fortune and Theo van Gogh, multiculturalism in Europe is criticized for everything from the spate of terrorist attacks to the fostering of cultural separatism, political fragmentation, and social ghettoization (Ossewaarde, 2014). A resonant note of dismay was captured by Trevor Phillips, chair of Britain's Commission for Racial Equality, when, in 2005, he accused the British of "sleepwalking into segregation": "We've focused far too much on the "multi" and not enough on the common culture—thereby allowing **tolerance** to solidify into isolation rather than insisting on sharing common values without losing a sense of uniqueness." More recently, in an address to the country's conservative Christian Democratic Union in October 2010, German Chancellor Angela Merkel dismissed "multikulti" as a failure for its role in aborting the integration of immigrants—sentiments similarly echoed in early 2011 by French President Sarkozy and British Prime Minister Cameron.

In brief, multiculturalism may have reigned supreme in Europe for 20 years, but not anymore, and a commitment to multicultural governance is increasingly ridiculed as a deadly liability instead of an empowering solution. Having outworn its welcome and ostensibly outlived its usefulness, multiculturalism is increasingly maligned as either a good idea gone bad or, alternatively, as a bad idea that has unfolded precisely as predicted. But while Europe's love affair with multiculturalism has tanked, the situation in Canada differs sharply. Canada's multiculturalism appears to be relatively untouched by criticism or backlash, while public support for immigrants and immigration remains at an all-time high, albeit with strings attached (Environics Institute, 2015; Graves, 2015; Jedwab, 2006; Nanos, 2010; Soroka & Roberton, 2010). For example, a 2014 survey by the Canadian Race Relations Foundation (CRRF, 2014) confirmed a general endorsement of multiculturalism in principle, but less enthusiasm over its limits when applied to the principle of reasonable accommodation and the place of religious diversity in the public domain. But relatively few Canadians openly express concern that an official multiculturalism would weaken national identity, strengthen ethnic attachments and compartmentalize ethnic enclaves, and unleash a clash of civilizations (EKOS, 2013). Not surprisingly, Canadians are genuinely puzzled by the intensity of European vitriol, especially since core Canadian policies related to multiculturalism and immigration enjoy substantial public consensus, while sporadic criticisms rarely yield much political traction (Soroka, Johnston, & Banting, 2006).

How do we account for this multicultural divide (Fleras, 2009a)? Why is Canada seemingly immune to calls for retrenchment of multiculturalism, whereas European jurisdictions are circling the proverbial wagons against what many perceive as excessive (proxy for Muslim) immigration and a misguided multiculturalism (Hage, 2006; Joppke, 2007)? How reasonable is the backlash in Europe? Is the backlash little more than a code for Islamophobia, which is prompted by a combination of fear of Muslim terrorism, concerns over Muslim rejection of gender and gay rights, and worries about being "swamped" by Muslims should Turkey enter the European Union (Hage, 2006)? Should Canada be worried as well and begin to reassess its much-ballyhooed commitment to an official Multiculturalism before all hell breaks loose (Paquet, 2008)? Is there something about Canada—its people or its policies or its priorities or placement—that transforms multiculturalism into a source of pride, a defining characteristic, and a national symbol (Environics Institute, 2015)? Or is Canada riding a lucky streak because of a fortuitous combination of history and geography (Kymlicka, 2004)? The Debate Revisited box at the end of this chapter provides some possible answers based on the issues raised in this chapter.

INTRODUCTION: LIVING TOGETHER WITH DIFFERENCES: PUZZLES, PARADOXES, AND PROSPECTS

The upsurge of racial pride and ethnic affiliation in Canada and abroad is well documented (Isajiw, 1997). Religious and ethnocultural minorities are demanding respectful recognition of their identities, seeking the right to full and equal participation in society, and insisting that institutions make reasonable accommodations to ensure inclusiveness. Yet these spiraling and sometimes contradictory demands create a dilemma for pluralistic societies in pursuit of cooperative coexistence. A principled framework must be established for constructing a functioning society out of culturally diverse populations without compromising a commitment to either common values or individual rights (Little & Macdonald, 2015; Sellers, 2005). But the interplay of competing agendas may disrupt the dynamics of any balancing act: To one side is a liberal commitment to the individuality of autonomy and equality; to the other side is a society-building imperative to impose a uniformity of language, culture, and identity over a heterogeneous population (Baubock, 2005; May, 2004; Pearson, 2001); to yet a third side is a multicultural adherence to the principle of respecting differences without undermining a commitment to inclusiveness and equality in the process (Guo & Wong, 2015).

Countries such as Australia (May, 2004) and New Zealand (Pearson, 2001; Spoonley, 2005) confront a host of challenges related to diversities and difference. They include (1) the influx of immigrants, (2) the proliferation of identity politics, (3) the politicization of ethnicity as a social force, (4) the appearance of anti-racism movements, and (5) the ascendancy of ethnic and indigenous nationalisms. Central authorities have responded to this unprecedented surge of diversities and difference in a variety of ways, ranging from indifference or rejection to tolerance or acceptance (Fleras, 2009a; Kobayashi, 1999; Willett, 1998). Historically, many believed the presence of cultural diversity posed a threat to effective governance. Recognition of cultural differences was thought to culminate in social fragmentation, block the creation of a cohesive and stable society, and jeopardize the attainment of national identity and unity. Predictably, state authorities tended to either ignore, isolate, or suppress differences in the hopes of enhancing a ruling class hegemony (Jakubowicz, 2005). Strategies to bolster national unity and identity were varied, but invariably included (1) the centralization of political power to ensure mainstream control; (2) the imposition of a dominant legal tradition and judicial system; (3) official language laws; (4) a nationalized system of compulsory education; (5) the adoption of state symbols for celebrating the dominant group's history; (6) the seizure of the so-called "empty lands" in the name of progress or national interests; and (7) a selective immigrant intake.

But the self-evident truths of the past are being increasingly contested at present. New ground rules are emerging that challenge a belief in good governance and cultural diversity as mutually incompatible. Under consideration is the possibility that good governance is impossible without respect for and recognition of cultural diversity—in part because traditional formats such as assimilation no longer offer a moral compass for living together amiably—and in part to defuse minority challenges to the prevailing status quo. Assimilation as a governance framework for managing diversity has been displaced by a commitment to the principles and practices of **multiculturalism** (Fleras, 2014a, b). In acknowledging that national unity and identity do not require a singular identity or denunciation of diversity—after all, people are known to have multiple identities and conflicting affiliations without relapsing into personal incoherence or social chaos—a commitment to multicultural principles has resulted in government programs to assist in the settlement of migrants, to acknowledge their contribution to society, and to educate the general public about the benefits of a pluralistic society (May, 2004).

Of those societies at the vanguard in advancing a multicultural governance, few can match Canada's blistering pace (Government of Canada, 2015). With the emergence of Toronto and Vancouver as dynamically cosmopolitan cities, Canada has transformed itself into one of the world's most ethnically diverse societies without collapsing into a welter of inter-ethnic conflicts. The entrenchment of multiculturalism at constitutional and statutory levels has not only reinforced Canada's legacy as a pacesetter in advancing intergroup harmony (Foster, 2005; James, 2005), but 45 years of **official multiculturalism** have also confirmed what many now routinely endorse: the right of individuals to identify with the cultural tradition of their choice without relinquishing access to full and equal participation because of ethnic differences. Canada's official multiculturalism has served admirably as a catalyst for defusing intergroup tensions by promulgating the once unthinkable—that diversities and difference are compatible with good governance, provided that ground rules are in place. A commitment to multiculturalism embraces the notion that people possess multiple identities, that equitable outcomes can be achieved without denying cultural differences, that culturally diverse people can coexist without conflict if an overarching vision prevails, and that respect for differences cannot transpire without a commitment to social justice, political equality, and full and equal participation (see also Rodriguez-Garcia, 2010). To be sure, Canadians are not nearly as multicultural as their collective pride would imply (CRRF, 2014). Bigotry and bias-motivated violence expose fissures in the multicultural façade, (Perry, 2015), while both ethnicity and faith-based communities continue to be viewed with some suspicion for seeming to erode national unity and identity (Guo & Guo, 2015). Still, the promotion of multiculturalism has accelerated a reshaping of Canada in ways that have evoked international acclaim, in effect reinforcing Canada's lofty ranking as a leading light in advancing a living together with differences without the differences getting in the way of living together.

Originating in part to harmonize competing ethnicities without losing control of the overall agenda, official multiculturalism has been perpetuated for a variety of political and economic considerations involving state functions, private interests, and electoral survival (Wood & Gilbert, 2005). Multiculturalism continues to provide an aspirational blueprint: it serves as a normative framework for "managing" diversity by seeking to reconcile (balance) cultural diversity with social inclusion, economic equality, and political cohesion (also Rodriguez-Garcia, 2010). A combination of demographic and political upheavals in recent years has further reconfigured Canada's multicultural agenda in ways inconceivable even a generation ago (Hiebert, Collins, & Spoonley, 2003; Kymlicka, 2007; Moosa, 2007; Ujimoto, 2000). Not surprisingly, reaction is mixed to what many perceive as one of the world's most powerful social forces at present (Savard & Vignezzi, 1999). As Tyler Cowen (1999) concludes:

> Based on the dual ideals of peace and *multiculturalism*, Canada is one of mankind's greatest achievements. It is comparable to the notable civilizations of the past, and indeed exceeds most of them in terms of stability, living standards, and civil liberties. (emphasis mine)

For some, multiculturalism represents a late-twentieth century experiment for rewriting the rules of social and political engagement in an age of migration (Gagnon & Iacovino, 2007). Others prefer to dismiss it as a modernist anachronism in a postmodern world of fluidity, multiplicity, and unpredictability (Duncan, 2005). Still others recognize both its potency and impotence in addressing the challenges of "getting along." For some, official multiculturalism may advance the society-building goals of cultural identity, social justice, citizenship, national unity, societal integration, and equality. For others, a state multiculturalism may have the sincerest intentions of creating a just and inclusive Canada, but its logic can be manipulated to foster inequality, separate ethnic silos, and intergroup friction (Kostash, 2000; Valpy, 2007). In light of these disparities in reactions, who can be surprised when multiculturalism is pilloried by some as Canada's "biggest mistake" (Hitchens, 2010; Kay, 2008), yet triumphalized by others as a "quiet revolution" equivalent in status and stature to three other societal transformations—the French, American, and Russian revolutions (Sandercock, 2006)?

This chapter responds to these challenges by exploring the politics and practices of multiculturalism within the context of proactively managing diversities as "different" yet "equal." The chapter emphasizes the status and role of multiculturalism as policy and practice for creating an inclusive Canada by improving the integration of minorities and migrants into the existing framework. Attention is devoted to (1) theorizing multiculturalism as governance (conservative, liberal, plural), (2) examining it at different levels of meaning, (3) analyzing diverse perceptions, public attitudes, and critical reactions, and (4) evaluating its role in Canada-building. Different levels of meaning are unpacked, including multiculturalism as (1) fact (what empirically is); (2) ideology (what ought to be); (3) policy (what it proposes to do); and (4) practices (what really happens) (Fleras, 2002). Particular attention is devoted to the concept of putting multiculturalism to work in fostering more inclusive institutions. Initiatives are in place to (1) improve minority access, representation, and equitable treatment at institutional levels, (2) create institutions that are reflective of, respectful of, and responsive to differences, and (3) formulate institutional services that are available, accessible, and appropriate. The chapter concludes by demonstrating how multiculturalism can be interpreted as a progressive yet flawed social experiment for democratic governance that has proven both constructive and integrative (a benefit), yet fractious and controversial (a cost).

THEORIZING MULTICULTURALISM AS GOVERNANCE

To say we live in a multicultural world is surely an understatement. Our world is characterized by immigrant-driven demographic diversity, a growing commitment to accommodation as a basis for living together differently, and the codification of pluralist principles for managing difference. To be sure, the post-9/11 epoch has played havoc with the principles and practices of multiculturalism, with reactions ranging from outright hostility to studied indifference, including:

- Can an official Multiculturalism provide a bulwark against the sense of alienation and exclusion that many believe motivates disaffected second-generation youth into anti-social activities?

- Can Multiculturalism be held accountable for the so-called integration failures related to home-grown terrorism (Jakubowicz, 2007; see also Biles & Spoonley, 2007)?

- Is Multiculturalism meant to address racialized and immigrant inequality, or is it a cynical ploy to disguise inequities behind a facade of orchestrated platitudes (Thobani, 2007)?

- How potent is Multiculturalism as an instrument of change: Does it promise more than it can deliver (a kind of "sheep in wolf's clothing") or, alternatively, does it accomplish more than it is willing to admit ("a wolf in sheep's clothing") (Fleras, 2007c)?

The dearth of consensus in responding to these questions makes it abundantly clear: Theorizing multiculturalism has proven an enigmatic and elusive exercise (Ryan, 2010). Too often, debates over multiculturalism are a matter of semantics rather than of substance because of its uncanny knack for meaning everything, yet nothing, given its status as both multidimensional and a moving target, with the result being that it does not always mean what it says or say what it means (Colombo, 2015). Political and philosophical debates over multiculturalism are so fractured—ranging from questions of how to balance collective and individual rights to debates over establishing a framework for equality between groups without sacrificing individual freedoms within groups—that agreement is virtually impossible. Confusion is further sowed by people's seeming inability to distinguish between the ideal and the real; that is, between what an official Multiculturalism says it's doing and (1) what it really is doing, (2) what people think it's doing, (3) what people think it should be doing, and (4) what a state-endorsed multiculturalism can realistically do. Any theorizing of multiculturalism is compromised by the failure to distinguish between and among each of these operative levels.

Despite continued popularity and support (at least in Canada), repeated reference to multiculturalism has not congealed into any agreement over definition, attributes, or applications (Biles, 2002). Instead, references have revealed an uncanny knack of meaning different things to different people, depending on whatever the context allows (Fleras, 2002). This should come as no surprise; after all, if the concept of culture is widely regarded as one of the most complex concepts in the English language, it stands to reason that *multi*culture should prove equally elusive. Championed yet maligned, idealized as well as demonized, the term itself has absorbed such a mélange of meanings that many despair of any clarity or consensus. To break free of this conceptual gridlock, the concept of multiculturalism in this text is framed at the level of governance. Multiculturalism as governance entails a framework that establishes a governing relationship between the rulers (the governing) and the ruled (the governed) for living together with differences in ways workable, necessary, and fair. The range of models that fall under a multicultural governance umbrella are three-fold: conservative, liberal, and plural (Fish, 1997; Fleras, 2009b; Sandercock, 2003):

- At one end are *conservative* models of multiculturalism as governance. This largely assimilationist and weaker version of multiculturalism is anchored in the need (whether by submission or absorption) to respect common values and shared monocultural principles as the basis for a cohesive society, although cultural diversities are tolerated in the private sphere (Rodriguez-Garcia, 2010). According to a culture-blind equality that defines everyone as equal regardless of race or ethnicity, a conservative model of multiculturalism believes that a society of many cultures is possible as long as cultural differences are ignored as grounds for recognition and reward. After all, if everyone is equal before the law, then everyone is entitled to the same treatment—no more, no less (Neill & Schwedler, 2007). Three premises inform this multiculturalism-as-melting-pot model of governance:

(1) our similarities as individuals outweigh our differences as group members; (2) nobody should be denied or excluded because of racial and ethnic differences (and by the same token, no one should receive special privileges or preferential treatment because of their differences); and (3) within reasonable limits and the rule of law, a commitment to commonalities can craft a progressive and prosperous society.

- Stronger models point to a *liberal* multiculturalism. With its lukewarm endorsement of diversity and difference along the lines of liberal universalism, a liberal model of multiculturalism believes that a society of many cultures is possible as long as people are treated the same as a matter of course, but differently when situations dictate otherwise, for example through exemptions from general rules. This multiculturalism-as-a-kaleidoscope model of governance acknowledges the need to recognize and respect cultural differences (within limits) without sacrificing minority rights to equality and opportunity. However important in advancing reasonable accommodation and institutional inclusion, any acceptance of diversities must (1) conform to mainstream values and constitutional principles, (2) neither break the law nor violate people's rights, and (3) comply with the principle of agreeing to disagree because an intolerance of tolerance is unacceptable in a multicultural society.

- Finally, *plural* models of multiculturalism endorse a no-holds-barred allegiance to embracing difference as a basis for multicultural governance. A plural multicultural model takes cultural differences seriously even if they challenge existing patterns of power and privilege while fostering different group rights, differential citizenship, illiberal outlooks, separate institutional development, and hermetically sealed communities (May, 2002). This "radical" multiculturalism recognizes the legitimacy of cultural differences and ethnoreligious communities in the public sphere (in institutions, for instance) (Grillo, 2007). In that all cultures are seen as equally worthwhile under a multiculturalism-as-mosaic model of governance, a coexistence of culturally different communities is endorsed, with or without bridging devices to unify. (It could be argued that a plural multiculturalism can also include segregationist or exclusionary versions characterized by separation between communities, essentialist readings of difference that foster inequality, and restrictive access to citizenship [Rodriguez-Garcia, 2010]). It remains to be seen if any society can flourish under the radical relativism of such a strong multiculturalism: Survival would be at best provocative; at worst, precarious. Table 9-1 provides a quick comparison of the three models of multiculturalism as governance.

In short, models of multiculturalism as governance span a spectrum of meanings, implications, and scenarios. Multiculturalism itself is loosely defined as a normative framework and political program to improve the incorporation/integration of migrants and minorities along conservative, liberal, or plural lines. Admittedly, the distinctions among these models of multicultural governance are more categorical (analytical) rather than contextual (lived), with the result that most jurisdictions embody an inconsistent package of multicultural do's and don'ts. Nevertheless, distinctions exist. Both liberal and (to a lesser extent) conservative models tend to create conditions for securing the status quo by facilitating a more gentle integration of newcomers and minorities into the existing social and cultural framework. By contrast, plural models tend to promote the long-term maintenance of multiple and separate cultures by allowing minority communities a degree of control over internal religious, political, and cultural affairs. Clearly, then, competing models make it difficult to theorize

TABLE 9-1	Models of Multiculturalism as Governance		
Conservative Multiculturalism	**Liberal Multiculturalism**	**Plural Multiculturalism**	
"Melting pot model = difference-blind"	"Kaleidoscope model = difference-tolerant"	"Sticky mosaic model = difference-conscious"	
A belief that a society of many cultures is possible, but only if ethnocultural differences are rejected as irrelevant for attainment of full equality and participation. Differences are permissible but only in the private or personal spheres. True equality arises from treating everyone the same (equal treatment), regardless of their racial or ethnocultural differences. In that everyone is fundamentally the same and the same before the law, no one should be excluded because of their differences; nor should anyone be accorded special treatment on that basis.	A belief that a society of many cultures is possible when cultural differences are tolerated or respected; but normally such differences are rejected as a basis for advancing equality or special treatment unless circumstances dictate otherwise. Members of culturally diverse minorities are treated equally (the same) as a matter of course, but treated *as equals* (differently or equivalently) when necessary by taking their differences into account. In short, a liberal model endorses a commitment to universalism as a rule; a commitment to accommodate through exemptions as an exception.	A belief that a society of many cultures is possible, but only if people's cultural differences are taken seriously as well as taken into account up to and including (1) special treatment, (2) autonomous institutions, (3) separate communities, and (4) collective group rights. In other words, differences matter and society must be reconfigured accordingly to ensure that minorities are treated *as equals* (equivalently).	

multiculturalism, given the plethora of conflicting discourses and hidden agendas that abound. Still, there is no paucity of questions pertaining to multiculturalism as governance:

1. Is multiculturalism primarily about culture-conscious equity or culture-blind equality? Is it about treating people equally regardless of their differences, or about treating people as equals precisely because of those differences that are disadvantaging?

2. Is multiculturalism about society-in-difference or difference-in-society? Does multiculturalism as governance endorse a particular vision of the good society and then ask how much difference can be incorporated within the limits of this vision? Or does it accept the priority of cultural differences, then redesign the good society accordingly (Sandercock, 2003)?

3. Is multiculturalism about difference or disadvantage? About recognition or redistribution (Banting et al., 2007)? Does multiculturalism as governance celebrate differences as ends in themselves? Or does it emphasize the removal of discriminatory barriers to ensure inclusiveness for those whose cultural differences have proven disadvantageous?

4. Is multiculturalism a major policy departure (a new normative framework for integrating minorities into society along more equitable lines) or more of the same, albeit with fancier labels (that is, a kind of assimilation in slow motion)?

5. Can a commitment to multiculturalism tolerate intolerance? That is, can a multicultural governance thrive in a context in which people agree to disagree? Can it flourish when certain groups disagree with the principle of agreeing to disagree?

6. Is multiculturalism about promoting cultural identity or social equality or national interests? Is the issue one of fostering a social climate conducive to the retention of cultural identity? Should the focus be on social equality by ensuring that everyone is equal before the law, regardless of race or ethnicity? Or should multiculturalism be concerned primarily with advancing national interests by combining respect for diversity within a framework of shared values (Granatstein, 2007; Runnymede Trust, 2000)?

7. How gender neutral is multiculturalism as governance? Do some versions of multiculturalism embrace an androcentric tendency to condone cultural and religious practices that compromise women's **gender equity** rights (Reitman, 2005; Stein, 2007)?

8. Is multiculturalism about universality or particularity? Does a multicultural governance endorse the universality principle, that what we have in common as rights-bearing individuals is more important—at least for purposes of entitlement and recognition—than what divides us into culturally distinct groups? Or does it reject the universality of liberalism by privileging the particularism of ethnicity and group rights as a basis for belonging and governance (Hall, 2000)?

9. Is multiculturalism about "us" or "them"? Should a multicultural governance focus on addressing the concerns of minority women and men? Or should it aim at sensitizing the mainstream mindset by removing those prejudicial and discriminatory barriers that preclude minority integration?

10. Is a commitment to multiculturalism relevant or irrelevant? Has multiculturalism outlived its usefulness as a twentieth-century modernist project? In a globalizing world of transmigration and diaspora, does it still make sense to endorse a multicultural governance when immigrant realities are no longer tied to a single place (Fleras, 2015a, b)?

11. Is it possible to create a more "religion-friendly" model of multiculturalism? Or must a commitment to religion as a publicly legitimate player be rejected because of Canada's commitment to secularism and separation of church and state (Bramadat & Seljak, 2005, 2008; Kymlicka, 2015; Modood, 2003; Seljak, 2009)?

12. Should the multiculturalism in a multicultural governance be concerned with making society safe *from* diversities, yet safe *for* diversities? Or should it focus on making diversities safe *from* society as well as safe *for* society?

To the extent that no consensus prevails, disagreement persists. Multiculturalism may be seen as a blueprint for facilitating the integration of minorities into an inclusive-leaning society. Yet there is no agreement over the role of multiculturalism in promoting integration, whether multiculturalism fosters or obstructs the integration process, and how much each side needs to concede as part of the mutual accommodation process (Jedwab, 2005). In other words, if minority-majority relations are fundamentally unequal relations, does multiculturalism create or reinforce this inequity, or does it challenge and change it? There is even less agreement regarding what multiculturalism is doing, what it's really doing, and what it should be doing or is capable of doing in a liberal-capitalist society (Duncan, 2005). Responses will vary with the frame of reference (official Multiculturalism versus popular multiculturalism), the level of analysis (micro versus macro), a proposed vision of society (a **mosaic** or kaleidoscope or melting pot), and the role of multiculturalism in advancing an inclusive society (positive or negative).

The conclusion is inescapable: multiculturalism is experiencing an identity crisis (what is it in the context of the twenty-first century?) and a crisis of confidence (what should it be doing in light of post-9/11 realities?) (Hartmann, 2015). Multiculturalism can mean whatever people want it to mean—a kind of "floating signifier" in which many meanings and references can be absorbed or dispersed without much fear of contradiction (Gunew, 2004)—and it is precisely this ambiguity that is proving both a strength and a weakness in theorizing multiculturalism (Modood, 2005; Willett, 1998). Any theorizing must begin by a distinguishing of the general (multiculturalism as the informal, the interpersonal, the contextual) from the specific (multiculturalism as the formal, the official, the principled). At the general level, multiculturalism can be defined as a belief that people can live together with their differences at personal, institutional, and national levels, provided that an overarching vision is in place, as are a set of rules for constructively *engaging differences as different yet equal.* More specifically, official Multiculturalism can be defined as a package of policies and programs for society-building around the institutional integration of minorities through the removal of discriminatory barriers (also Kivisto, 2015). That's the theory; what about the reality in Canada?

MULTICULTURALISM IN CANADA

How would you respond to the question, "Is Canada a multicultural society?" To qualify, a multicultural society is one that minimally subscribes to the following attributes: (1) differences are defined as an asset and opportunity; (2) minorities are seen as contributing to society-building; (3) policies and programs supporting the inclusion of differences are in place at institutional levels; (4) governments not only endorse differences as part of the national identity, but also take an active role in facilitating the integration of migrants and minorities; and (5) sufficient resources are available for transitioning diversity ideals into daily practice. Yet framing Canada as a multicultural society will also vary with how multiculturalism is defined, including these different levels of meaning:

1. An *empirical fact* (what is)
2. An *ideology* (what ought to be) with a corresponding array of ideas and ideals
3. An explicit government *policy* and programs (what it proposes to do)
4. A set of *practices* for promoting political and minority interests (what it really is)

Failure to separate these analytically different levels of meaning can create confusion because of the tendency people have to talk past each other—using the same words but speaking a different language.

Multiculturalism as Fact

As fact, multiculturalism makes an empirical statement about "what is." It may be stating the obvious, but the obvious is sometimes overlooked for precisely that reason; that is, most countries are ethnically diverse, composed of people from a variety of different backgrounds who speak, think, worship, and act differently. Nearly all countries comprise different racialized and ethnic groups whose identities are stoutly defended and demanding of recognition or resources. Members of these minority groups often wish to retain aspects of their culture, yet are equally anxious to reap the benefits of full societal involvement. Reference to multiculturalism as fact also attests to growing interest in the analysis of everyday encounters in diverse urban contexts through which cultural differences and social cooperation are produced and negotiated (Colombo, 2015).

Employed in the descriptive sense of the term, few would dispute the "fact" of Canada as a multicultural society. The existence of Aboriginal peoples, French and English charter group members, and multicultural minorities attests to this empirical fact of reality (Elliott, 1983). Canadians have been drawn from 170 different countries, comprise over 200 diverse ethnic communities, and speak over 200 different languages (Kalbach & Kalbach, 1999). Recent immigration patterns suggest a continuation of this diversity trend (see Chapter 1 for an overview of ethnic diversity in Canada).

Multiculturalism as Ideology

Unlike its descriptive counterpart, multiculturalism as an **ideology** refers to a prescriptive statement of "what ought to be." It prescribes a set of beliefs about creating a society of many cultures in which people cooperatively coexist without capitulating to chaos. Canadians have long prided themselves on being a tolerant society, with numerous national polls demonstrating consistent public support for Canada's multicultural mosaic. To be sure, this endorsement varies with time and place, often lacks enthusiasm, is conditional, and is easily revoked when costs outstrip benefits. Nevertheless, multiculturalism remains pivotal as one of Canada's defining characteristics, an embodiment of "Canadianness," and proof that living in a pluralistic society provides a richer experience than does living in a monocultural society (Kymlicka, 2005). In general, a multicultural ideology purports that a society of many cultures is better than monocultural society; a commitment to multicultural principles is preferred over assimilation as a policy alternative; and culturally diverse communities can coexist as long as certain ground rules prevail.

Several assumptions underlie a multicultural ideology, the first of which is a belief that people are social beings whose well-being depends on a shared cultural identity. Minority cultures constitute living and lived-in realities that are valued in their own right, while imparting a sheen of security during times of stress or social change (Kymlicka, 1995). Affiliation with one's cultural kind does not imply an element of mental inferiority, stubbornness, or lack of patriotism. Rather, these differences are important and of benefit to both individuals and society at large if properly "managed." Second, multiculturalism does not dismiss difference as contrary to the goals of national unity or societal progress. Instead, cultural differences are endorsed as integral components of a national mosaic, a reflection of the Canadian ideal, and a source of unity and strength. Third, a multicultural ideal builds upon the principles of **cultural relativism**. This doctrine holds that all cultural practices are relative to a particular time and place, take their meaning from this context, and must be understood accordingly. That is not to say that everything *is* equally good; nor is anyone espousing the philosophy that "anything goes." On the contrary, a critically informed relativism approaches diversity *as if* it were an equally valid expression of the human experience. Fourth, a commitment to multiculturalism is predicated on the premise that those confident in their cultural background will concede a similar tolerance to others (Berry, Kalin, & Taylor, 1977). Or, as Trudeau explained back in 1971, if national unity is to mean anything in the deeply personal sense, it must be anchored in confidence in one's own identity, for it is out of this respect for others that a sharing of ideas and assumptions is fostered (see Forbes, 2007).

There is yet another ideological slant to multiculturalism. Rather than a "happy face" ideology based around the virtues of tolerance and celebrating diversity, an official Multiculturalism can be interpreted as a hegemonic discourse in advancing the dominant ideology ("ruling elites controlling unruly ethnics"). Much of what passes for multiculturalism is little more than an exercise in conflict resolution and impression management whose primary goal is to "cool off" those troublesome constituents who are problems or create problems (Bannerji, 2000; Fleras, 2012; Thobani, 2007). On one side, the ideas and ideals associated with multiculturalism are critical in securing an unequal status quo behind the folksy facade of national interests. On the other side, an ideology is embraced that promotes the interests of vested groups at the expense of the population at large. In short, the ideological aspect of multiculturalism reflects its status as false consciousness. Multiculturalism not only dulls the public senses to the continuing marginalization of migrants and minorities—a kind of opiate of the masses—but also lulls people into a false sense of security by conveying the "illusion of inclusion." Emphasis on the "culture" in multiculturalism also has the effect of papering over the structural sources of division and disadvantage in society. In that little of substance happens under a multicultural watch, no one should underestimate the power of a hegemonic ideology to obscure and distract (see Ley, 2005).

Multiculturalism as Policy

Policy considerations are central to any official Multiculturalism (Griffith, 2013; Magsino, 2000). Governments throughout the world have embarked on official strategies for controlling immigration, managing ethnic relations, accommodating differences, "cooling off" troublesome constituents, and integrating ethnocultural minorities into the mainstream (Fleras, 2012; Hudson, 1987). Policy frameworks such as assimilation or segregation, which may have worked in the past, are increasingly inadequate for addressing contemporary minority demands. By contrast, multiculturalism represents an aspirational blueprint for living together with differences. It provides a principled framework for specific government initiatives to transform multicultural ideals into official programs and practice. In that Multiculturalism promotes the right to be different yet the same, as well as the right to be the same yet different, a new symbolic order is projected, one that addresses the integration of migrants and minorities by respecting differences while removing discriminatory barriers (Banting et al., 2007). Multiculturalism can also be interpreted within a broader normative framework that justifies the promotion of diversity programs without fear of inciting public concern over yet more government intrusion. This normative framework may not be openly articulated; nevertheless, it supplies the "underlying agenda" that legitimizes policy initiatives for enhancing a multicultural society-building project.

To say that Canada is officially Multicultural is extolling the obvious. Yet the irony is improbable. From its inception in 1971, when it barely garnered a paragraph in Canada's national newspaper, official Multiculturalism has evolved to the point where it constitutes a formidable component of Canada's national identity, profoundly altering how Canadians think about themselves and their relationship to the world (Forbes, 2007; Kymlicka, 2015; Temelini, 2007; see also Henshaw, 2007, for the 1930s origins of multicultural thinking). Forty-five years of official Multiculturalism have proven pivotal in orchestrating a national consensus around majority acceptance of minority participation. Multiculturalism as a policy originated in the quest for integrative society-building functions. It continues to persist for precisely the same reasons, namely, to create an inclusive Canada through the integration of migrants and minorities into the existing system by modifying the rules of inclusion and settlement (Fleras, 2015c). The goal of Multiculturalism has never wavered from its underlying commitment, which is the possibility of living together with differences without the differences getting in the way of equal involvement or social order. Only the means for achieving the "cultural," the "social," and "national interests" have changed, evolving in response to demographic upheavals and political developments, with ethnicity-based solutions giving way to equity-grounded reforms and, more recently, the promotion of citizenship, belonging, and cohesion. For the sake of simplicity, these shifts can be partitioned into four overlapping policy stages: *ethnicity*, *equity*, *civic*, and *integrative*.

Ethnicity Multiculturalism Canada's official Multiculturalism arose following the publication of the Report of the Royal Commission on Bilingualism and Biculturalism in 1969. The findings of the Royal Commission concluded that Canada comprised a multicultural commonwealth of "other ethnics," albeit within the bicultural (or binational) framework of two founding peoples. Various ethnic minority groups, especially the Ukrainians and Germans, had lobbied vigorously, arguing that their languages and cultures were as vital as Quebec's to Canada-building (Jaworsky, 1979; see also Lupul, 2005; Temelini, 2007). They rejected the notion of Canada as the union of two founding nations, with its implication that some Canadians were more deserving than others. Proposed instead was a descriptive ideal that captured the contribution of the "other ethnics" to the cultural enrichment of a bicultural Canada. Pressure to create a symbolic multicultural order was further heightened by the need to depoliticize the autonomist forces of Québécois nationalism in the aftermath of the Quiet Revolution (Breton, 1989). Finally, with "Britishness" losing its saliency in Canada and elsewhere (see Jakubowicz, 2005), Multiculturalism emerged as an ideological glue for bonding Canadians, based on a vision of Canada as a multicultural mosaic of equality-seeking individuals rather than a colonial outpost.

A commitment to multiculturalism within a bilingual framework was subsequently articulated by the Liberal government when Prime Minister Pierre Elliott Trudeau rose in Parliament on 8 October 1971 and declared his government's intentions to embrace "multiculturalism within a bilingual framework." As many have noted, multiculturalism originated in response to Trudeau's disdain for both British and French nationalism, whose ethnonational tyrannies compromised individual rights and the right of choice. Trudeau sought to abolish culture and rootedness as justification for superior entitlement. By putting all Canadians on an equal footing regardless of their culture or immigrant status, Trudeau's goal was a Canada in which members of different nationalities intermingled as neighbours on a common territory, without discarding their distinct cultural identities *if they chose to do so* (Cameron, 2004; Forbes, 2007). For Trudeau, the linking of individual rights with equal status under multiculturalism would "strengthen the solidarity of the Canadian people by enabling all Canadians to participate fully and without discrimination in defining and building the nation's future." Four major principles secured this aspirational aim to realign Canada along multicultural lines:

- *Equality of status*: Canada does not have an official culture; all cultures are equal.
- *Canadian identity*: Diversity lies at the heart of Canadian identity.
- *Personal choice*: Individuals have the right to identify with the cultural tradition of their choice.
- *Protection of individual rights*: Individuals have the right to be free from discrimination.

To put these principles into practice, the government proposed initiatives to (1) assist those cultural groups that demonstrated a commitment to share and contribute to Canada; (2) assist the members of all cultural groups to overcome cultural barriers to full participation in Canadian society; (3) promote creative encounters and exchanges among all Canadian cultural groups; and (4) assist immigrants to acquire at least one of Canada's official languages to ensure full and equal participation.

In short, an ethnicity multiculturalism was not about celebrating ethnocultural differences; if anything, it hoped to eliminate those cultural prejudices that denied or excluded. A commitment to ethnocultural preservation was not high on the multicultural agenda—at least not beyond an initial commitment when powerful ethnic lobbyists prevailed. Ethnicity multiculturalism went beyond a simple "be nice to different people" focus, with emphasis instead on improving minority and migrant integration into an inclusive society (Donaldson, 2004). It sought not only to promote national unity, in the belief that those secure in their culture would reciprocate accordingly, but also to simultaneously make ethnicity irrelevant as an indicator of privilege or a marker of identity for ranking Canadians or allocating power (Kruhlak, 2003). To the extent that cultural diversity was respected and protected, ethnicity multiculturalism focused on integrating new Canadians through their ethnic identity rather than offering unqualified preservation of their differences. Conditions applied to this social contract, including: (1) all new Canadians should have a primary commitment to Canada; (2) all new Canadians must accept Canada's fundamental structures, principles, and values; and (3) all new Canadians had the right to identify with the culture of their choice, provided these choices were freely chosen, did not violate people's rights, break the law, or contravene core constitutional values (Cardozo & Musto, 1997).

Equity Multiculturalism The focus of official Multiculturalism shifted noticeably by the early 1980s. Instead of emphasizing the centrality of identity and ethnicity, Multiculturalism discourses centred around the more equity-driven concerns of racialized immigrants. The often different requirements of visible minority immigrants, compared to those of European "ethnics," proved more perplexing. For new immigrants, their visibility complicated the process and prospect of integration; as a result, the need for dismantling racial barriers to opportunity had to prevail over the celebration of their cultural differences (McRoberts, 1997). The earlier emphasis on ethnicity and identity as keys to integration was subsequently replaced by a commitment to equity, social justice, and institutional inclusiveness (Agocs & Boyd, 1993; Donaldson, 2004). Funding allocations were adjusted accordingly. Rather than simply doling out vast sums to ethnocultural organizations or events, as had hitherto been done, authorities shifted toward equity goals related to anti-racism, race relations, and removal of discriminatory barriers at institutional levels.

Subsequent developments further advanced the political profile of official Multiculturalism. Passage of the *Canadian Charter of Rights and Freedoms* constitutionally entrenched Multiculturalism as a distinguishing feature of Canadian life. The emergence of Multiculturalism as a tool of interpretation at the highest levels of constitutional decision making reinforced its status as a fundamental characteristic of Canada. Its prominence was further advanced when Canada became the world's first and only officially Multicultural country with the passage of the **Canadian Multiculturalism Act** in 1988. Passage of the Act aspired to promote cultures, reduce discrimination, and accelerate institutional inclusiveness through the "preservation and enhancement of Canadian multiculturalism." In that the *Canadian Multiculturalism Act* completed the Canada-building project associated with the passage of the *Official Languages Act* of 1969, the Statement on Multiculturalism in 1971, and its enshrinement in the *Constitution Act* of 1982, its significance cannot be understated. Each of these initiatives converged to create a distinctly Canadian society based on the integrative principle that individuals are self-defining and morally autonomous agents who should participate equally, regardless of their differences (Breton, 2001).

Civic Multiculturalism   The fortunes of official Multiculturalism began to decline in 1993 following the election of a new government. The stand-alone but short-lived Department of Multiculturalism and Citizenship was subsequently deprived of its lofty status and folded into the super-ministry of Canadian Heritage under a Secretary of State (Multiculturalism and Canadian Identity). In an era of government cutbacks, Multiculturalism proved a soft target, attracting criticism from both the right and the left (Bibby, 1990; Bissoondath, 1994), despite its ongoing commitment to social equality and cultural respect. Concerns that Multiculturalism was losing its popularity because it lacked relevance for both mainstream and racialized Canadians prompted calls for rethinking the multicultural agenda. A more inclusive multiculturalism—civic multiculturalism—began to emerge, directed at a shared national unity by "break[ing] down the ghettoization of multiculturalism," as aptly phrased by Hedy Fry (1997), former minister for Multiculturalism.

A repackaged Multiculturalism program was formalized in 1996 around three strategic goals: (1) civic participation (full and equal involvement), (2) social justice (equitable treatment), and (3) identity (fostering a Canada in which all Canadians feel a sense of attachment and belonging regardless of their background). In 2002, four priority objectives were articulated: (1) fostering cross-cultural understanding and awareness of racism, (2) combating racism and discrimination, (3) promoting shared citizenship, and (4) developing more responsive and representative institutions (Department of Canadian Heritage, 2005). To achieve these objectives, the Multiculturalism programs adopted the following goals: (1) institutional change (inclusiveness through removal of discriminatory barriers); (2) federal institutional change (integrating diversity into policies, programs, and services); (3) combating racism (including removing discriminatory barriers, and promoting anti-racism programs and cross-cultural understanding); and (4) civic engagement (promoting active and shared citizenship as well as building capacity for minorities to participate in public decision making) (Canadian Heritage, 2005/6). In short, a **civic multiculturalism** was oriented toward Canada-building by way of shared citizenship, with an emphasis on fostering a sense of belonging, a civic engagement, an active involvement in community life, and a shared awareness of Canadian identity and Canada's national interests.

Integrative Multiculturalism Multiculturalism has evolved into a new phase whose operative focus is integration. In reacting to perceived fears of social fragmentation and ethnic isolation because of differences in immigrant values and social patterns, the minister for Citizenship, Immigration, and Multiculturalism, Jason Kenney, has proposed a fundamental shift toward immigrant integration and community cohesion in hopes of depoliticizing diversities and difference while defusing the threat of homegrown extremism (Freeze, 2008; Kunz & Sykes, 2007). In a speech entitled, "Good Citizenship: The Duty to Integrate," Kenney argued that any embrace of diversity must be balanced by a prior commitment to value consensus, that is, ". . . on the political values that are grounded in our history, the values of liberal democracy rooted in British Parliamentary democracy that precisely have given us the space to accommodate such diversity" (as cited in Marwah & Triadafilopoulos, 2009). Not surprisingly, according to the *Annual Report on the Operation of the* Canadian Multiculturalism Act *2013-2014* (Government of Canada, 2015), the government has implemented a unity and diversity approach to multiculturalism around three main policy objectives: (1) to build an integrated and socially cohesive society by promoting civic literacy and engagement among all Canadians; (2) to make federal institutions more responsive to Canada's diverse populations through removing discriminatory barriers and fostering intercultural understanding; and (3) to promote Canadian values abroad by engaging in international discussions on multiculturalism and diversity (Citizenship and Immigration Canada, 2010).

To sum up, Canada's official Multiculturalism represents a complex and contested policy that has evolved over time in response to social and political changes (Seiler, 2002). Despite shifts in emphasis—from ethnicity to equity to civic to integrative—Canada's official Multiculturalism has never wavered from its central mission: an inclusive Canada-building through immigrant integration (Kymlicka, 1998a, 2001). An official Multiculturalism as governance represents a politically driven commitment for building an inclusive society through the removal of prejudice and discriminatory barriers so that no one is excluded from full and equal participation because of race or ethnicity. Only the means have changed over time. Table 9-2 compares and contrasts the different stages in the evolution of Canada's official Multiculturalism, keeping in mind the inevitability of simplification when comparing ideal-typical categories in a world that is contextual rather than categorical.

This policy overview exposes another dimension of Canada's official Multiculturalism: State-backed Multiculturalism is *not* about (1) celebrating differences, (2) promoting ethnic minorities or group rights, (3) fostering parallel communities, (4) transforming structures or challenging liberal democratic principles, (5) addressing politicized or deep differences, or (6) advocating an "anything goes" mentality. Rather, it tends to promote a principled governance framework for creating an inclusive Canada through the integration of migrants and minorities by (1) establishing the rules for living together with differences without the differences getting in the way of living together; (2) making society safe for differences and safe from differences; and (3) creating an

TABLE 9-2	Policy Shifts in Canada's Official Multiculturalism: A Work In Progress			
	Ethnicity multiculturalism (1970s)	Equity multiculturalism (1980s–early 1990s)	Civic multiculturalism (1995–2005)	Integrative multiculturalism (2006–present)
Dimension	Cultural	Structural	Social	Societal
Focus	Respecting differences	Fostering equality	Living together	Integration
Mandate	Ethnicity	Race relations	Civic culture	Citizenship
Magnitude	Individual adjustment	Institutional accommodation	Full engagement	National safety/ security
Problem	Prejudice	Racism/ discrimination	Exclusion	Segregation/ extremism
Solution	Cultural sensitivity	Removal of barriers	Inclusion	Shared Canadian values
Outcomes	Cultural capital	Human capital	Social capital	National community
Key metaphor	"Mosaic"	"Level playing field"	"Strengthening the bonds"	"Strangers becoming neighbours"

accommodating social climate and responsive institutional framework that (a) rejects racism and racial discrimination, (b) endorses the principles of equity regardless of ethnic background, and (c) fosters an environment in which newcomers feel a sense of interconnectedness to Canada and other Canadians. And most important, in advancing the principle of inclusion through the removal of discriminatory barriers and a respect for cultural differences, an inclusive multiculturalism emphasizes the centrality of political equality, social justice, and full participation as the governance model for living together with diversities and differences (Rodriguez-Garcia, 2010).

Multiculturalism as Practice

Glowing accolades about celebrating and sharing cannot disguise what many have long suspected: The implementation of multiculturalism as ideology does not always translate into practices consistent with policy principles. Multiculturalism as practice refers to its application for advancing a broad range of goals, agendas, and priorities. Politicians and bureaucrats look upon multiculturalism as a resource with economic or political potential to be exploited at national or international levels for practical gain. A hardly surprising conclusion since, Canada's official Multiculturalism originated as a political program to achieve political goals in a politically astute manner (Peter, 1978). The governing apparatus of the Canadian state relied on Multiculturalism to fulfill a variety of legitimating functions involving national unity, economic prosperity, and electoral survival (see also Bharucha, 2000). At its inception, official Multiculturalism hoped to formulate a new founding myth of Canada as a land of opportunity and equality, thus uniting all Canadians at a time of political turmoil, but without any fundamental redistribution of power (Helly, 1993). It also sought to shore up electoral strength in urban Ontario, to counterbalance Western resentment over Ottawa's perceived favouritism toward the Québécois, to preempt the encroachment of American cultural values, and to thwart intergroup strife because of competing priorities. In short, official Multiculturalism parlayed a potential weakness into strength by bolstering a commitment to social cohesion, national identity, domestic peace, economic advantage, and global status (Kurthen, 1997).

The politics of multiculturalism are closely linked with party politics. From nomination struggles to ethnic coalitions, multicultural politics at the crassest level reflect a belief in ethnic support as relevant for (re-)election. The vast majority of Canada's multicultural minorities are concentrated in the MTV centres of Montreal, Toronto, and Vancouver—a trend likely to be amplified by future immigration patterns. The continuing heterogeneity of Canada's population will further prompt political parties to pursue the multicultural vote through promises of increased representation, funding, and employment equity initiatives. Also widely touted is the commercial potential of multiculturalism. Former Prime Minister Brian Mulroney promoted a business model of multiculturalism rooted in economic rationality and self-interest in his "Multiculturalism Means Business" speech at a Toronto conference in 1986. The commercial value of multiculturalism remains stronger than ever because of the demands of a global economy. Diversity and the market are closely intertwined because capitalizing on differences is seen as good for the economy, especially when 40 percent of Canada's GDP is export based:

> The ethnocultural diversity of Canada's population is a major advantage when access to global markets is more important than ever to our economic prosperity. Protecting this advantage means that steps to eradicate racism are essential. Canada cannot afford to have any of its citizens marginalized. As a knowledge-based economy in an increasingly global marketplace, every mind matters. All Canadians must have the opportunity to develop and contribute to their full potential. (Canadian Heritage, 2001)

Multiculturalism continues to be promoted as a valuable export, just as staple products were in the past (Abu-Laban & Gabriel, 2002). By enhancing Canada's sales image and competitive edge in a global economy—particularly by cultivating and tapping into the lucrative Asian market—references to multiculturalism are touted as having the potential to harness lucrative trade contracts, establish international linkages and mutually profitable points of contact, attract members of the transnational elite, and penetrate export markets. By playing the "ethnic harmony card," the promotion of multiculturalism as an ideology of cooperative coexistence and worldly cosmopolitanism provides reassurance for nervous investors and fidgety capital (Mitchell, 1993). Finally, as the globalization of capitalist market economies continues to expand, multiculturalism may well provide the networking for confronting the challenges of a shifting and increasingly borderless reality that informs twenty-first century commerce. The conclusion seems inescapable: In that multicultural priorities will continue to be driven by an economic agenda more interested in improving Canada's competitive advantage than in securing institutional inclusiveness, the business side of Multiculturalism should never be discounted.

Migrants and minorities are no less inclined to adopt multiculturalism as a resource for attaining practical goals (Burnet, 1981; Qadeer, 2007). Newcomers to Canada have basic needs: As a group, they want to become established, expand economic opportunities for themselves and their children, eliminate discrimination and exploitation, and retain access to their cultural heritage without loss of citizenship rights. Multiculturalism is employed as a tool for meeting these needs through elimination of discriminatory barriers in employment, education, housing, and criminal justice. After all, racialized minorities and immigrants may have the same rights as all Canadians, including the right to be free of discrimination. But they must live (from survive to prosper) in a racialized Canada that is *neither designed for their use or advancement nor reflective of their experiences, realities, or aspirations.* With official Multiculturalism, minority women and men are empowered with a platform and a tool for staking out their claims while articulating their demands alongside those of Aboriginal peoples and the Québécois. Multiculturalism also empowers an otherwise powerless sector with the leverage to prod or provoke central policy structures. By holding central authorities accountable for their failure to connect multicultural ideals with everyday results, appeals to official Multiculturalism are thus calculated to extract public sympathy and global scrutiny—in the same way as Canada's Aboriginal peoples have relied on international fora (such as the United Nations) to leverage concessions from the federal government. For minorities, then, the driving force behind multiculturalism is equality, not diversity; integration, not isolation; and inclusion, not separation.

Putting Multiculturalism to Work: Institutional Practices

There is much to commend in institutions becoming more multiculturally responsive. At a time when both the workforce and the community at large are increasingly diverse and demanding, only the pace of change or the scope of adjustments should remain open to debate (Diller, 2004). Public and private institutions are increasingly anxious to enhance overall effectiveness by including all Canadians who have something to contribute, no more so than in Canada's cities, where the vast majority of immigrant and racialized Canadians live (Andrew, 2004; Frideres, 2006). Municipalities are under pressure to create welcoming communities through governance programs that not only remove discriminatory barriers but also enhance access, participation, and inclusivity (Our Diverse Cities, 2004, 2006, 2007). For urban service organizations, a commitment to multiculturalism can reap institutional dividends by easing workplace tensions, generating creative synergies, and facilitating community access by improving the quality of service delivery. For private companies, the inclusion of diversity is tantamount to money in the bank. Corporations increasingly rely on the language skills, cultural knowledge, life experience, and international connections that people of diversity bring to the workplace. Diversity connections can also provide the catalyst for internationalizing domestic businesses, thus improving their competitive advantage in global markets.

However valued and overdue, preliminary efforts at putting multiculturalism to work at institutional levels have proven uneven. The commitment may be there, but with neither the political will for implementation nor the resources for enforcement, a reality gap looms. Of particular note are service-oriented institutions such as media, education, and policing, each of which is under pressure to move over and make institutional space. Their mandate as agencies of socialization and social control not only strikes at the hub of social existence but also influences the degree to which people are in harmony with or alienated from their communities. Media and education furnish the "blueprint" for acceptable behaviour; the police, in turn, control the limits of unacceptable behaviour by enforcing the rules. Failure of each of these institutions to balance multicultural imperatives with organizational realities runs the risk of marginalizing untapped talent, shortchanging the delivery of services, and compromising institutional effectiveness and efficiency.

The emergence of "inclusive" or ("inclusiveness") as a popular buzzword poses a key question: What exactly is meant by the term? Is it about assimilation or integration? About diversity or disadvantage? About culture-blind or culture-conscious initiatives? About reform or radical change (Fleras, 2014b)? The politics of inclusiveness can prove a veritable minefield of unanswered questions. Minimizing the relevance of diversity when required to level the playing field may be as discriminatory as overemphasizing it when not. Excluding minorities from full and equal involvement can generate conflict, yet incorporating differences can be equally disruptive to intergroup relations—at least in the short run (see Putnam, 2007). Fostering an inclusive workplace climate requires a careful reassessment of rules, procedures, and outlooks; nevertheless, changes of this magnitude may imperil the bottom line. The adjustment process must not only occur at the level of institutional structure and individual mindsets but also concentrate on the relationships within (the workplace environment) and connections without (clients). Finally, institutions must balance employment and equity concerns with an equally legitimate Charter-right requirement for institutions to reasonably accommodate worker needs. Such varied demands confirm the complexities of incorporation in a world where accommodating reasonably does not come naturally.

Having good intentions is one thing—putting inclusiveness principles into institutional practice is another. Institutions are complex, often baffling landscapes of domination, power, and control, often pervaded by prejudice, nepotism, patronage, and the "old boys" network. Mainstream institutions are neither neutral in design nor value-free in process, but structurally Eurocentric and constructed for advancing majority interests and priorities, either deliberately or systemically (Harris, 1995). Moves to inclusivize are rarely simple or straightforward; rather, they are fraught with ambiguity and tension because of individual resistance, structural barriers, and institutional inertia. Conservatives confront progressives in a struggle for control of the agenda. Despite both internal and external pressures to change, conventional views remain firmly entrenched as vested interests balk at discarding the tried and true. Newer visions are compelling but lack the critical mass to scuttle traditional ways of "doing business." The interplay of these juxtapositions can be disruptive as institutions evolve into a "contested site" involving competing world views and opposing agendas.

Generally speaking, five criteria define institutional inclusiveness, namely: *workforce representation*, *organizational rules and operations*, *workplace climate*, *service delivery*, and *community relations*.

1. An institution's workforce should be representative, that is, relatively proportional to the composition of the regional labour force, acknowledging, of course, both extenuating social and cultural factors to account for discrepancies. Such a numerical accommodation applies not only to entry-level jobs but also across the board to include all occupational and managerial levels.

2. Institutional rules and operations cannot hinder minority recruitment, selection, training, promotion, and retention. This commitment to rooting out both open (overt) and closed (covert) forms of discrimination demands a careful scrutiny of company policy and procedures.

3. The institution must foster a workplace climate conducive to minority well-being and success. At minimum, such a climate cannot tolerate harassment of any form; at best, diversity is actively promoted as normal, necessary, and beneficial to productive functioning (Wrench, 2007).

4. An inclusive institution ensures a delivery of services that are community-based, culturally sensitive, and multiculturally responsive. This multicultural commitment to culturally sensitive services entails an institutional willingness to engage as partners in genuine dialogue with the community at large. Outcomes must be based on bilateral decision-making rather than be unilaterally imposed.

5. Finally, institutions do not operate in a social or political vacuum. Some degree of community input, power sharing, and public accountability is critical if productive lines of communication are to be secured.

Attainment of these criteria for institutional inclusiveness yields two analytically distinct models of diversity governance: inclusion and inclusivity (Fleras, 2014b). Inclusion as institutional accommodation is predicated on the principle of removing discriminatory barriers to ensure the integration of migrants and minorities into the existing system. It is based on the belief that no one should be excluded because of their differences; as a result, everyone should be treated the same under the inclusion principle. The principle of inclusivity differs: Inclusivity can be broadly defined as a process and framework for modifying institutions to make them more inclusive of difference-based needs. Institutional design, organization, assumptions, operations, outputs, and opportunity and reward structures are modified to reasonably accommodate ("within limits, without undue hardship") the needs (the realities, values, and concerns) of the historically disadvantaged. More specifically, inclusivity entails a commitment to reasonable accommodation for improving minority access, representation, and equity—in part by creating a workplace that is reflective of, respectful of and responsive to diversity and difference, in part through the delivery of community services that are available, accessible, accountable, and appropriate (Fleras, 2012). Inclusivity as principle endorses the value of diversity, neither as a problem to solve nor a challenge to surmount, but as an asset for improving workplace climate and the delivery of social services (Fleras & Spoonley, 1999). Or, put a bit differently: A commitment to inclusivity insists that everyone should be included by incorporating their differences-based needs when necessary through interventions that enhance the concepts of belonging, participation, recognition, and contribution (see also Senate, 2013; Richmond & Saloojee, 2005). A commitment to inclusivity/equity (as equals) invariably draws attention to the principle of differential accommodation, namely, accommodating different ways of accommodating differences for successful outcomes.

In theory and as ideal-typical constructs, inclusivity and inclusion embody competing models of institutional inclusiveness (Fleras, 2014b). One (inclusivity) is concerned primarily with changing the system to accommodate the needs of an internally diverse and changing demographic, whereas the other (inclusion) is about changing the individual to facilitate their integration into the prevailing institutional framework (Council of Europe, 2011). Inclusion models of inclusiveness begin with the assumption that the existing system is essentially sound and equitable, although a few tweaks may be required to level the playing field. Any inequalities or exclusions are largely the fault of individuals or groups who must be fixed if they are to be fit into the existing system (Harmon, n.d.). By contrast, inclusivity models entail a fundamentally different principle: The system must be restructured to accommodate, creating a more level playing field. Whereas inclusion (or inclusive) is about including everyone by fitting them into the dominant framework regardless of their differences, inclusivity promotes an accommodation model for modifying institutions to ensure that everyone is included precisely because of differences arising from their needs or values. Instead of simply adding to something that already exists, inclusivity promotes the principle of breaking with the past and beginning anew by changing the culture, structure, environment, and social-organizational life (Dei, 2010). According to this line of thinking, a commitment to inclusivity must go beyond developing skills or modifying mindsets as the basis for fundamental change. The focus instead is on structural changes in how service institutions view their role and in the actions they take (Council of Europe, 2011). Cosmetic changes to institutional conventions such as minority hires or sensitivity sessions are a good start, according to inclusivity principles, but unlikely to dislodge those foundational rules that reinforce power structures and institutional culture. Little of permanence prevails in advancing a more equitable workplace without a corresponding removal of discriminatory barriers and systemic biases (Wilson, 2009). In short, a fundamentally different pattern of inclusiveness is proposed: While inclusion as principle is focused on modifying the conventions that refer to the rules, a commitment to inclusivity as governance logic entails changing the rules that inform the conventions. Taken to its logical conclusion, a commitment to inclusivity proposes the creation of a new game with a different set of rules for belonging in (not just to) society.

The following table captures the distinction between inclusion ("incorporation") and inclusivity ("accommodation") as competing governance models. A commitment to institutional inclusivity proposes a governance model that questions existing arrangements, posits a relational and multiversal view of culture, and frames diversities within contexts of power and inequality (Glasser, Awad, & Kim, 2009). Access to services is rooted in rights rather than needs or cultural differences so that the focus is on mainstreaming equitable provisions rather than perfunctory add-ons to mainstream services. Particularly noteworthy is a distinction between the principles of differences-in-society versus society-in-differences (Sandercock, 2003). An inclusion integration model is likely to pose the question, "what is the good society," then accommodate differences corresponding with that vision (differences-in-society). By contrast, an inclusivity model of integration will begin with the primacy of diversities and differences as good, then adjust society accordingly to foster accommodation (society-in-differences). Table 9-3 outlines the distinctions.

PUBLIC PERCEPTIONS/CRITICAL REACTIONS

Of the conceptual tripwires and cultural landmines strewn across the Western landscape in recent years, few have triggered as much vitriol or controversy as multiculturalism (Gilroy, 2004; Possner, 1997). Timing in particular has played politics with a modernist project that many regard as passé for the post-9/11 (and 7/7 in London) realities of the twenty-first century. The introduction of multiculturalism as a popular and political discourse may have originated in an era of optimism and reform, but it is badly listing at present because of concerns over security (Rex & Singh, 2004; see also Gregg, 2006). What started out as a society-building idea with noble intentions (to assist newcomers into Canada) has evolved

TABLE 9-3	Institutional Inclusiveness: Inclusion vs. Inclusivity as Models	
Inclusion Models	**Inclusivity Models**	
People must fit into existing system	System must change to accommodate diversities	
One way process of incorporation	Two way process of mutual accommodation	
Diversities – challenge or problem	Diversities = asset	
We/they mentality	Us/our mindset	
Living together with diversity	Living together in/with/though diversities	
Make society safe from, safe for, differences	Make differences safe from, safe for, society	
Differences-in-society Incorporating (whitewashing) differences = One size fits all treatment (colourblind)	Society-in-differences Accommodating differences within differences = customizing treatment (colour-conscious)	
Everyone treated the same (equal treatment)	Difference-based needs taken into account	
Minority hires + sensitivity training = create the right change	Structural changes through removal of discriminatory barriers	
Change conventions that refer to rules ("adding to what already exists")	Change rules that inform conventions ("breaking with existing order and starting fresh")	
Top down approach to decision making ("we know what's best")	Bottom up decision making ("listen & learn" dialogue)	

into a flashpoint for tension. On one side are those advocates who continue to worship at the altar of multiculturalism; on another side are those who recoil at the very prospect of foisting yet more multicultural mumbo-jumbo on an unsuspecting public (Paquet, 2008); on yet another side are those critics who sneer at something they deem to be irrelevant or counterproductive (see Ley, 2005).

Public Perceptions

Public perception of multiculturalism in Canada is varied. Some Canadians are vigorously supportive; others are in total rejection or denial; still others are indifferent; and yet others are plainly uninformed (see Cameron, 2004; Cardozo & Musto, 1997). For some, multiculturalism is at the root of many of Canada's problems; for others, multiculturalism is too often scapegoated for everything that goes wrong when minorities are involved (Kymlicka, 2007; Siddiqui, 2007). The majority appears to be caught somewhere in between, depending on their reading of multiculturalism and its contribution (or lack thereof) to Canadian society. Variables such as age, income, level of education, and place of residence are critical in gauging support, with higher levels of approval among the younger, more affluent, better educated, and urban (Anderssen & Valpy, 2003). While many may be critical of Canada's official Multiculturalism—after all, it's a proven scapegoat for the sins of a society undergoing rapid changes and increased diversity (Ley, 2007)—few Canadians actually know what federal and provincial governments are doing to promote the idea, prompting this reaction from Jack Jedwab, the executive director of the Association for Canadian Studies: "People don't know that much about the policy. There's a giant leap—probably one of the biggest public policy gaps that I've seen—between the extent to which people know about the policy and the regular criticism of it" (as cited in Boswell, 2010). To the extent that many Canadians are unsure of what Canada's official Multiculturalism is trying to do, how, and why, the prospect of living differently together equitably and in dignity is compromised.

Public support for official Multiculturalism is open to debate. Opinion polls are known to provide different answers, depending on the kind of questions asked. Nevertheless, national surveys on multiculturalism suggest a solid base of support often in the 60 to 70 percent range (ACS/Leger Marketing, 2015; Angus Reid Group, 1991; Berry, 2006; Cardozo & Musto, 1997; Dasko, 2005; Jedwab, 2005; Nanos, 2010; Soroka & Roberton, 2010; Environics Institute, 2015). Yet support for official Multiculturalism is not as transparent as the data suggest. First, Canadians may be supportive of multiculturalism, but only on principle or as a demographic fact: At the same time, they may reject Multiculturalism as official policy or mistakenly conflate it with unpopular government programs such as employment equity. Second, support is not the same as enthusiasm: Canadians appear to embrace Multiculturalism as a reality to be tolerated rather than an ideal to be emulated or a passion to be pursued. Third, support or rejection tends to be selective and inconsistent: Most Canadians support some aspect of Multiculturalism, but are conflicted over issues of assimilation versus accommodation (Collacott, 2006; Jedwab, 2004; Soroka & Roberton, 2010) or its unintended consequences; they may harbour worries over Multiculturalism as the thin edge of the wedge for justifying practices at odds with mainstream values or for fostering conditions that breed terrorism, discourage integration, or encourage ghettoization (Baubock, 2005; Friesen, 2005). Fourth, support is conditional: Canadians are prepared to accept Multiculturalism if costs are low and demands are reasonable for assisting new Canadians to settle in, removing discriminatory barriers, learning about others, and promoting tolerance (Gwyn, 1996). Support is withdrawn when endorsement is seen as eroding Canada's sense of national unity and identity, challenging authority or core values, curbing the integration of cultural communities, criticizing the mainstream, breaking the law, or acquiescing to the demands of particular groups through special rights (Soroka & Roberton, 2010).

Critical Reactions

Official Multiculturalism is unevenly supported across Canada (Duncan, 2005). Residents of Ontario and western Canada appear receptive to Multiculturalism, but the Québécois and Aboriginal peoples have spurned it (Bouchard & Taylor, 2008; Breton, 2001; Ignace & Ignace, 1998; Kymlicka, 2001). The concerns of "nations within" go beyond those of disadvantage or difference but focus, instead, on the injustices and disempowerment resulting from Canada's society-building project (Baubock, 2005). Instead of self-defining themselves as immigrants who want to "get in" (using the language of multiculturalism), both Aboriginal peoples and the Québécois prefer the language of nationalism, that is, "getting out" (Maaka & Fleras, 2005; Murphy, 2005). An official Multiculturalism cannot possibly address the demands of fundamentally autonomous political communities; nor is it equipped to handle the highly politicized discourses of challenge and transformation (McRoberts, 2001). Still, Quebec possesses its own program of official multiculturalism entitled *interculturalism*, with its connotation of an interactive process of participation, engagement, and social exchange (Rodriguez-Garcia, 2010).

Many political observers and social critics have criticized Canada's multicultural agenda (Paquet, 2008; 2011; Perry, 2015; Mansur, 2011). Multiculturalism is seen as divisive because of its tendency to tolerate practices incompatible with Canada's central core. It is also accused of hypocrisy in offering the illusion of tolerance while punishing behaviour at odds with core values (Stoffman, 2002, 2007). Some dismiss official Multiculturalism as a bad idea that's performing as poorly as many had predicted. It originated to pander to ethnic interests, persists as little more than an opiate for the masses, and remains a divisive force in Canadian society. Others are no less dismissive of Multiculturalism, calling it a good idea gone bad. Still others dismiss Multiculturalism as a largely aspirational document: It not only fails to clearly articulate objectives and expectations but also lacks the power of implementation and enforcement. Noble intentions aside, critics contend, Multiculturalism continues to undermine the common good, in large part because both politicians and minority leaders have hijacked it for ulterior purposes. Even the much-touted mosaic metaphor comes in for criticism. Canada's multicultural discourses remain rooted in an understanding of ethnicity as primordial and essentialized rather than flexible, dynamic, and relational. Membership and participation in this mosaic locks individuals into hermetically sealed groups that are isolated from the rest of society—to the detriment of Canadian unity (Fleras, 2015a, b).

Still others denounce on official Multiculturalism regardless of what it does or doesn't do. Multiculturalism has been accused of being too radical or too reactionary, of promoting too much or not enough change, of promising more than it can deliver (a sheep in wolf's clothing) or delivering more than bargained for (a wolf in sheep's clothing). And while Multiculturalism may be embraced by many as a strength to be admired, it may be demonized and dismissed by others as a weakness to be condemned or exploited, as noted by Irshad Manji (2005):

> As Westerners bow before multiculturalism, we anesthetize ourselves into believing that anything goes. We see our readiness to accommodate as a strength—even a form of cultural superiority . . . Radical Muslims, on the other hand, see our inclusive instincts as a form of corruption that makes us soft and rudderless. They believe the weak deserve to be vanquished. Paradoxically, then, the more we accommodate to placate, the more their contempt for our "weakness" grows. And the ultimate paradox may be that in order to defend our diversity, we'll need to be less tolerant. (p. A19)

Academic opinion is mixed (see May, 2002). Critics on the left have pounced on Multiculturalism as ineffective except as a mantra for politicians to trot out for publicity purposes (Perry, 2015). Multiculturalism is criticized as a colossal hoax perpetuated by vested interests to ensure minority co-optation through ideological indoctrination (false consciousness) (Thobani, 1995). Excessive emphasis on diversity and culture and insufficient focus on racism and racialized structures pose a serious challenge to inclusion and justice. As a capitalist plot to divide and distract the working classes, Multiculturalism is condemned for ghettoizing minorities into occupational structures and residential arrangements, thereby lubricating the prevailing distribution of power and wealth behind a smokescreen of well-oiled platitudes (Bannerji, 2000; Dei, 2000). Not surprisingly, Multiculturalism is rejected as little more than an interim measure for absorbing minorities rather than an authentic policy alternative—an "assimilation in slow motion" behind a facade of diversity intentions. Or to put a none too fine spin on it, Multiculturalism represents a clever device by ruling elites to control unruly ethnics (Hage, 1998).

Those on the right repudiate Multiculturalism as a costly drain on resources that runs the risk of eroding national unity. Worse still, Stewart Bell writes in *Cold Terror: How Canada Nurtures and Exports Terrorism around the World* (2004), the openness of Multiculturalism makes Canada vulnerable to infiltration by terrorists. Moderates may be unsure of where they stand. Official Multiculturalism may sound good in theory, but implementation may falter because of difficulties in balancing unity with diversity. For example, while its intent may be to facilitate the integration of immigrants and secure their loyalty, Multiculturalism may have the perverse effect of strengthening immigrants' attachment to their homeland by way of diasporic nationalisms (Kurien, 2006). Conversely, while Multiculturalism may provide minorities with a platform for promoting distinctiveness, the very act of participation may have the reverse effect of absorbing minorities into the dominant culture (Pearson, 2001). Or, put differently, Multiculturalism is long on principle and promise, but has proven short on delivery except to convey an air of mutual indifference in which Canadians share geographic and political space but little else (Ignatieff, 2001).

In its role as the self-appointed catalyst for social engineering, multiculturalism has attracted its share of criticism—even in the country where it was first articulated and is most fully institutionalized (Ley, 2005). National shortcomings tend to polarize around the multicultural management of minority relations (Siddiqui, 2007). This is hardly surprising, since criticism and controversy are generated by the disconnect between what an official Multiculturalism says it does versus (1) what it really means to do, (2) what it really does, (3) what it can realistically do, and (4) what the public and critics think it should be doing compared to what they think it is doing or is meant to do. For example, Multiculturalism is so ill-defined that immigrants are understandably confused about what is permissible and what is not, thus encouraging a belief that Canada is committed to accepting and adapting to whatever customs they bring with them into the country. Not surprisingly, when asked how he saw Multiculturalism 20 years after its inception, Trudeau responded that it had been twisted to celebrate differences rather than to improve newcomer integration into Canada—the original intent was not for newcomers to retreat into their ethnic corners, but to enjoy full participation through creative encounters (as cited in Cobb, 1995).

But while much of this criticism may be valid, it is not entirely accurate (see also Ryan, 2010). Criticism of Multiculturalism may not reflect a looming backlash any more than silence is proof of its acceptance. To the extent that criticism is vocal, the disgruntlement may arise from growing discontent among the already disenchanted rather than from a new legion of malcontents. And it is difficult to determine what exactly people dislike about Multiculturalism—the principle, the policy, or the practice? A sense of perspective is helpful: In that both critics and supporters gloss over the underlying logic of Multiculturalism, those who stoutly defend it at all costs are as ideological as those anti-multiculturalists who disparage it for lacking any redeeming value. In that there are many publics, all with different expectations and needs, the impact of official Multiculturalism is neither all good nor all bad; rather, it may be both good and bad, depending on the context, criteria, and consequences. In other words, as demonstrated below, Multiculturalism may be both good *and* bad simultaneously, liberating yet marginalizing, unifying yet divisive, inclusive yet exclusive, beneficial yet costly (also Wong, 2015). Consider the following paradoxes:

- On one side, an official Multiculturalism is dismissed as divisive in that it undermines the basis of Canadian unity and identity (see also Ryan, 2010). Too literal an interpretation of multiculturalism can generate reified and essentialist group distinctions that foster group stereotyping and negative out-group sentiments at odds with the attainment of social cohesion and national unity (see Verkuyten, 2007). On the other side, Canada's official Multiculturalism is unifying in that it creates a blueprint for an inclusive Canada. A 2011 study by the European Commission concluded that Canada ranked third among 29 countries for the strength of its integration policies and commitments (Jedwab, 2011). The virtues of sharing, interaction, and participation points to Multiculturalism as Canada-building by improving the process of integration for minorities rather than condoning the creation of segregated ethnic communities with separate power bases (Kostash, 2000; McRoberts, 2004).

- On one side, Multiculturalism may be seen as regressive in its ghettoizing or stigmatizing of minorities. Neil Bissoondath (1994) has castigated a Multiculturalism that aids in the containment and control of migrants and minorities while essentializing their identities in some frozen past. On the other side, Multiculturalism has proven integrative in reversing discrimination by creating a commitment to institutional inclusiveness. In building bridges rather than erecting walls, Canada's Multiculturalism encourages minority women and men to become involved, construct productive lives, and contribute to society (McGauran, 2005). Compared with immigrants in other countries, new Canadians are more likely to become citizens, engage in the political process, perform better in the economy (especially in the second generation), and experience social acceptance (Kymlicka, 2011). By incorporating efforts to remove discrimination, nurture civic engagement, foster cross-cultural understanding, and promote responsive institutions, Multiculturalism connotes a process for making the mainstream more inclusive rather than making minorities more multicultural (see Chan, 2003/4).

- On one side, Multiculturalism is criticized for not taking differences seriously because of preference for an empty pluralism. On the other side, Multiculturalism is criticized for taking differences too seriously, thus imperiling Canadian unity and identity. In reality, Multiculturalism is not about promoting diversity, but about fostering unity through the removal of differences-based discrimination. Multiculturalism provides a social climate that not only encourages an individual to affiliate with the cultural tradition of his or her choice but also ensures that cultural differences do not interfere with getting along, settling down, and fitting in.

- On one side, Multiculturalism may be accused of being a symbol without substance—a frivolous diversion with no power to challenge or transform. On the other side, Multiculturalism has presided over a radical remaking of Canada—from a transplanted mono-colonial enclave to a cosmopolitan society of many cultures and colours—in part by incorporating the symbols of diversity into the narratives of Canadian "nationhood" (see Gregg, 2006).

In short, the impact and implications of official Multiculturalism are double-edged. In the same way that ethnicity can empower or divide, depending on the particular frame of reference, so too can a commitment to Multiculturalism both enhance and detract as well as be a problem and a solution that simultaneously entails costs and benefits. That the benefits of Multiculturalism cannot be discounted reflects the ability of the powerless to convert the very tools for controlling them into levers of resistance and change (Pearson, 1994). Yet recourse to official Multiculturalism can depoliticize the potency of difference by channeling it into the private or personal. Far from being a threat to the social order, Canada's official Multiculturalism constitutes a discourse in advancing the 1867 *Constitution Act* principle of "Peace, Order, and Good Government." Depending on where one stands on the political spectrum, this is a cause for concern or contentment.

A sense of perspective is useful. Multiculturalism is not the cause of Canada's problems, any more than it can be the cure-all (Belkhodja et al., 2006). There is no risk of Canada unravelling because of Multiculturalism: The politics of a "distinct society" and the "nations within" will see to that first. Nor should we get worked up over the absence of a common culture, as if Multiculturalism destroyed what never existed except, perhaps, within the context of a transplanted British Empire. Perhaps Canada's core value is the absence of any common culture except those shared values pertaining to basic decency, a respect for rule of law, a commitment to individual equality, and a constant quest for identity (see Sajoo, 1994). Difference, not uniformity, is Canada's strength, and to expect otherwise is unrealistic in a multilayered and deeply divided society organized around diverse yet overlapping citizenships. Disagreement and conflict are inevitable in such a contested context. Just as shared ethnicity goes beyond a unanimity of vision (Bissoondath, 1994), so too can a multicultural society survive on a multiplicity of voices and visions—provided that we agree on the principle of agreeing to disagree.

MULTICULTURALISM: DOING IT THE CANADIAN WAY

A commitment to multiculturalism has contributed to Canada's image as a progressive society. Some measure of proof is gleaned from accolades by high-flying personalities, including Bono of U2, who claims the world "needs more Canadas," and the Aga Khan, who extols Canada as the most "successful pluralist society" in the world (see Biles, Tolley, & Ibrahim, 2005:25). Canada's lofty status as an enlightened multicultural society with an enviable standard of living is further confirmed by several UN panels. Finally, when compared with others, Canadians themselves seem to express markedly more positive attitudes toward immigration, multiculturalism, and difference, while taking pride in Canada's reputation as an open and inclusive society (Jedwab, 2005; Nanos, 2010).

Canada's worldwide reputation as a beacon of tolerance in an intolerant world is largely deserved. The fact that Canada has escaped much of the inter-ethnic strife that currently plagues many countries speaks well of its ability to proactively work through differences. The majority of Canadians, especially the younger and the well-educated, are relatively open to diversity, with pride in Canada's multicultural heritage as a long-term investment in constructing a more vibrant society (see Anderssen & Valpy, 2003; SBS, 2008). Canada's success in integrating immigrants scores high by international standards, while official Multiculturalism may well prove pivotal in facilitating successful outcomes (Kymlicka, 2008). This tolerance is paying reputational dividends abroad (Reputation Institute, 2015). Compared to the Canadian-born, newcomers to Canada display higher levels of pride in Canada (Adams, 2007) because of its freedom and democracy, quality of life, and tolerance for diversities—with the vast majority of newcomers taking out Canadian citizenship as soon as they qualify (Bloemraad, 2006).

Other markers of success include the following:

- Compared with immigrants in other countries, Canadian immigrants are much more likely to be involved in the political process as voters, party members, and candidates who are actively recruited by political parties.
- The children of immigrants in Canada have better educational outcomes than the children of immigrants in any other Western democracy; as well, these second-generation Canadians outperform children of Canadian parents in terms of educational outcomes.
- The absence of immigrant ghettos in Canada would suggest high levels of social/ geographical integration. To be sure, immigrant/ethnic enclaves are common, but they embody a fundamentally different logic and different dynamics than ghettoes (Hiebert, 2015).
- Increasing levels of inter-racial marriage attest to growing immigration integration along multiculturalism lines (Kymlicka, 2008).

A perspective is helpful: In contrast with the grisliness of reality elsewhere, Canada's commitment to multiculturalism stands as a paragon of virtue. But compared with the ideals enshrined in multiculturalism, Canadians could be doing better in the art of living together with differences. Furthermore, everyone agrees that there are enough loopholes in official Multiculturalism to dishearten even the most optimistic. Few would deny its vulnerability to manipulation by politicians and minority leaders. And when carelessly bandied about, its potential to deter, divide, diminish, or digress cannot be dismissed.

Carping criticism is no more helpful than unstinting praise. Evaluating multiculturalism is not simply a case of either/or, but both/and with respect to its costs and benefits. Multiculturalism cannot be reduced to either a cost or a benefit, but as a benefit that accompanies a cost, depending on the context, consequences, or criteria. Moreover, criticism is one thing; proposals for alternatives to multiculturalism are quite another. Critics may relentlessly attack multiculturalism as regressive or irrelevant, but critiques rarely offer constructive criticism in proposing positive alternatives that are workable, necessary, and fair (Ford & Delaney, 2008). If a commitment to multiculturalism is incompatible with living together with differences, what other options are there? Let's be candid: Multiculturalism is hardly an option in a postmodern Canada because of its politicized diversities, robust immigration programs, and competing citizenships. Neither assimilation nor isolation stands much chance of survival in our politicized era. A much-touted return to traditional values for cementing Canadians into a unified and coherent whole may sound good in theory (Bibby, 1990; Bissoondath, 1993, 1994), but in reality, such wishful thinking may camouflage a sentimental wistfulness for a golden age that never existed.

Forty-five years ago, Canada blazed a trail in establishing a framework for living together with differences. Has it been worth it? On balance, yes. Multiculturalism established a national agenda for engaging difference that strikes many as consistent with Canada's liberal-democratic framework. A governance framework has evolved that to date, has managed to balance difference with unity—even if that balancing act is a bit wobbly at times. Such an endorsement may not sound like a lot to those with unrealistically high expectations; nevertheless, the contributions of multiculturalism should not be diminished by unfair comparison with utopian standards. A sense of proportion is required. Just as multiculturalism cannot be blamed for everything that goes wrong in Canada, neither should Canadians bask in the glory of excessive praise in a country where equality and inclusiveness are unevenly applied. The nature of its impact and implications falls somewhere in between the poles of unblemished good and absolute evil. Multiculturalism is neither the root of all Canada's problems nor the all-encompassing solution to problems that rightfully belong elsewhere. It is but one component—however imperfect—for improving the integration of migrants and minorities by balancing the competing demands of diversity with unity.

Multiculturalism, in short, remains an option of necessity for a changing and diverse Canada (Ley, 2005). As a skillful blend of balances in a country built around compromises, multiculturalism symbolizes an innovative if imperfect social experiment for living together with differences. Multiculturalism has excelled in extricating Canada from its colonialist past and elevating it to its much-ballyhooed status as a trailblazer for constructive engagement. Under the circumstances, it is not a question of whether Canada can afford multiculturalism. More to the point, Canada cannot afford *not to* embrace multiculturalism in advancing political unity, social coherence, economic prosperity, and cultural enrichment. That is not to say that the coast is clear or that Canadians can rest on their laurels. Still, the entrenchment of multiculturalism has elevated Canada to the front ranks of global society—not a perfect society by any stretch of the imagination—but possibly one of the world's least imperfect societies.

DEBATE REVISITED

Accounting for the Transatlantic Divide: Has Multiculturalism Failed in Europe or Has Europe Failed Multiculturalism?

How do we account for the continued popularity of multiculturalism in Canada in contrast to its declining fortunes in European societies? Is it because of good luck, good foresight, sound policies, and historical trends? A bit of context might help to answer this question: The prevalent side-by-side/live-and-let-live multiculturalism of most European societies tended to disengage immigrants from full and equal citizenship rights. Immigrants were rarely seen as potential permanent residents, but rather as guest workers who would eventually leave upon completion of their work. Thus, Europe's embrace of multiculturalism was predicated on a removal logic: Guest workers and their families were encouraged to retain their cultural traditions and language skills to facilitate a readjustment upon return to their home countries. The benign neglect of immigrant communities was further justified on the grounds that European countries did not see themselves as immigrant societies and thus felt minimal responsibility to actively integrate immigrants (guest workers) into the social fabric.

(Continued)

The end result? The segregation of differences into semi-autonomous ethnic silos culminated in a visionless coexistence of separate groups with little or no inter-ethnic interaction (much less creative encounters) among them. Nor was there much incentive for migrants to identify with a Europe that denied them citizenship or exposed them to marginality. Without an overarching vision for living together differently, what eventually emerged was a living arrangement that amounted to a serial monoculturalism (Sen, 2006) A serial monoculturalism stalled (even precluded) the social and economic integration of migrants and minorities, resulting in the marginalization of too many immigrants—further reinforcing public fears that multiculturalism represented a slippery slope for the dismantling of liberal–democratic values (Hurst, 2006; Kymlicka, 2011).

The situation in Canada differs (Fleras, 2007c; Kymlicka, 2005). First, in contrast to European countries that tend to see themselves as complete societies with established identities (Verkuyten, 2007), Canada defines itself as an unfinished project in progress. Canada also defines itself as an immigration society: immigrants to Canada are seen as assets rather than burdens, crucial to Canada-building rather than a national liability, and as potential and productive citizens rather than as a permanent underclass. Multiculturalism, in turn, provides a tool to create an inclusive Canada by facilitating the integration of new Canadians in terms of settling down, fitting in, and moving up. Not surprisingly, as a low cost risk, Multiculturalism is more likely to enjoy public support when immigrants are seen as *bona fide* permanent residents with access to full and equal citizenship rights. Support is also bolstered when there are principled rules regarding the acceptability of immigrant cultural practices. Cultural differences may be respected under Canada's official Multiculturalism, but this commitment is conditional and comes with strings attached. Its legitimacy is all but assured since a commitment to Multiculturalism reflects and reinforces Canada's status as an immigration society while securing the creation of a national identity based on tolerance (Fleras, 2009a).

Second, the link between immigration and multiculturalism is mutually enhancing. A robust immigration program not only creates a need for multiculturalism governance, it also depends on multiculturalism for its success. Conversely, Canada's Multiculturalism program could hardly flourish outside the context of a proactive and comprehensive immigration program. Not surprisingly, the multicultural response to immigration represents a low-risk option for living together with differences (Kymlicka, 2005). The political and social architecture is in place to manage this risk by ensuring that immigrants are legal, liberal, and equipped. Immigrants to Canada arrive through conventional channels, most share liberal values with the rest of Canada, and many are well educated and primed to work in Canada's postindustrial economy. The fact that Canada does better than other countries when measured on the grounds of immigrant participation, citizenship, pride of country, and levels of trust attests to its popularity and success (Bloemraad, 2006). Compare this situation with those European countries that are in close proximity to poor, unstable countries from North Africa or the Middle East, whose young inhabitants want opportunities, whether as legal migrants, illegal workers, guest workers, or asylum seekers. Predictably, then, this disconnect undermines public support for multiculturalism when immigrants are associated with illiberal practices at odds with mainstream norms and values, when immigrants are viewed as illegal by entry or unwelcome for the long haul, and when they are perceived as ill-equipped for coping with the demands of contemporary society (see Calder & Ceva, 2011).

Third, Canada's continued embrace of multiculturalism may not reflect commitment, principle, or insight. Rather, the accidents of geography and history may prove the critical factor (Kymlicka, 2004). Canada is so geographically isolated from the mass migration centres of the world (e.g., North Africa, the Middle East, and Central America) that it rarely must worry about porous borders (but see Hier & Greenberg, 2002). Canada can afford to cherry pick whom it wants as new residents, while disbarring those whose differences are too different. As well, the serendipity of timing is pivotal: The emergence and entrenchment of multiculturalism came about in an era when most immigrants were from Europe with a seeming willingness to comply with Canada's liberal values and rights-based framework (Granatstein, 2007). As a result, once immigration shifted toward more culturally contentious non-European sources, Canadians had already internalized a familiarity with and fondness for multiculturalism and its role in managing diversity (Kymlicka, 2004/2007).

Fourth, support for multiculturalism is further bolstered by implicit rules for "drawing the multicultural line." Unlike the perceived anything-goes excesses of some multicultural regimes, Multiculturalism in Canada is about limits and boundaries. Difference may be tolerated under an inclusive multiculturalism, but this tolerance is conditional and principled: That is, cultural differences must be freely chosen, cannot break the law, violate individual rights, preclude individuals from full and equal involvement, or contravene core constitutional values. Furthermore, differences should not be expressed through inward looking ethnic enclaves or politicized for public power grabs, but de-politicized as a basis or dialogue, interaction, and understanding. Even passage of the 1988 *Canadian Multiculturalism Act* sought to integrate new Canadians into the mainstream through their ethnic identity rather than by offering unqualified preservation of their differences. Clearly, then, the multiculturalism in Canada's official Multicultural governance is not what it appears to be. More accurately, multiculturalism transforms differences into discourses about social equality and human rights rather than a fixation with celebrating diversity. In doing so, Multiculturalism embodies a classic Canadian contradiction: Canada may extol the benefits of diversity, but it also represents one of the world's most successful integration models (Rao, 2010). Multiculturalism is rendered an indispensable component in advancing Canada's inclusiveness agenda for living together with differences, in dignity, and equitably.

Chapter Highlights

- Reference to multiculturalism as a model of diversity governance can be interpreted along three analytical lines: conservative, liberal, and plural.
- Canada's official Multiculturalism should be interpreted as a political act to achieve the goal of creating an inclusive Canada by integrating migrants and minorities into the existing framework.
- Responses to the question of whether Canada is a multicultural society vary because of different levels of meaning; that is, multiculturalism as a sociological fact, an ideological system, a series of formal policies and programs, or as a set of practices that serve political and minority interests.
- Canadian Multiculturalism has evolved through a series of overlapping phases, from (1) ethnicity, (2) equity, (3) civic, to (4) integration.
- The practice of multiculturalism in Canada revolves around creating institutions that are more inclusive of migrants and minorities, either through inclusion practices or inclusivity commitments.
- Canada's multiculturalism may be interpreted as both a cost (divisive, regressive, or incompetent) and a benefit (unifying, progressive, and effective), in addition to eliciting a wide range of reactions, from acceptance to rejection.
- Canada remains a global outlier in continuing to explicitly endorse a formal multiculturalism as diversity governance.

Review Questions

1. Indicate how a commitment to institutional inclusiveness as diversity governance may embrace the concept of inclusion or that of inclusivity.
2. Compare and contrast the different phases in the development of Canada's multiculturalism policy in terms of objectives, assumptions, means, and outcomes.
3. Is Canada a multicultural society? "Yes," "no," "maybe," or "it depends"? Be sure to focus on the different levels of meaning associated with multiculturalism (consult the Debate Box in Chapter 1).
4. Demonstrate some of the benefits and costs associated with Canada's official Multiculturalism. Defend whether you believe multiculturalism is a solution to the problem of unequal relations, or more of a problem than a solution.
5. *Multiculturalism is about knowing limits and drawing lines as a basis for living together with our differences.* Explain, and provide an example to illustrate how much diversity a multicultural society can tolerate before self-destructing.

CHAPTER 10

This Adventure Called Canada-Building

LEARNING OBJECTIVES

After reading this chapter, you will be able to:

1. Describe the complexities of rethinking citizenship in a postnational Canada.

2. Identify the challenges of forging unity from diversity for Canada-building.

3. Demonstrate the value of the Canadian Way and Canada's Diversity Model in advancing a living together with differences.

4. Understand why an official multiculturalism may need an upgrading to address those complex realities related to transmigration and diverse-diversities.

5. Explain how Canada's imperfections as a diverse society may yet prove Canada-building strengths in a postnational era.

DEBATE

Rethinking Citizenship in a Postnational Canada

Canadians pride themselves as citizens of a widely admired society with an enviable international reputation (Clarkson, 2014; Reputation Institute 2015). Newcomers to Canada appear also to think along these lines: About 85 percent of all immigrants who permanently settle in Canada take the oath of **citizenship**, putting Canada at the forefront of the global citizenship sweepstakes (Kymlicka, 2003; Seidle, 2007a; Tran, Kustec, & Chui, 2005). This commitment is hardly surprising: A Canadian citizenship entitles its bearer to rights, entitlements, and privileges that may be unheard of in the

applicant's home country. They also gain access to membership in what many regard as one of the world's best places to live. Even recent moves to restrict the conditions for citizenship attainment ("harder to get, easier to lose" [Abu-Laban, 2015:3]) have not had much effect in deterring applicants, despite concerns over Bill C-24 (which received Royal Assent and now is law) which allows the revocation of citizenship for individuals convicted of specific crimes such as terrorism or treason (Amnesty International, 2014).

Until the *Citizenship Act*, which came into effect in January 1947, there

(Continued)

was no such thing as a Canadian citizen, apart from within a Commonwealth context. "Canadians" were defined as British subjects who happened to be living in Canada, with a corresponding obligation to conduct themselves accordingly. But passage of the *Citizenship Act* announced that Canada had acquired autonomous legal existence despite continuing linkages to Britain. Canadians, in turn, were no longer simply transplanted British "expats" or a subset of British subjecthood (Bloemraad, 2007; Macklin & Crepeau, 2010). A new kind of belonging was proposed, one that embraced the realities of Canada instead of those of the United Kingdom. The Act also sought to integrate all Canadians into a unitary body politic, in large part by ignoring any distinction between Canada-born and foreign-born as a basis for citizenship.

The boldness of this universalistic ("unitary") embrace cannot be underestimated. In an era when differences invariably invoked inferiority or exclusion, terms of the *Citizenship Act* established a precedent by embracing all lawfully residing Canadians as citizens, regardless of who they were or where they were from. A unitary citizenship proposed that both foreign- and Canadian-born individuals possessed the same rights and entitlements as well as similar duties and obligations, based on the universalistic principle that all individuals are equal before the law and must be treated equally (the same) without exception or favour. But however enlightened for its time, the concept of universal citizenship has come under attack (Bosniak, 2000; Harty & Murphy, 2005; Kernerman, 2005; Yuval-Davis, 2007). Citizenship frameworks that once worked in the past have proven cumbersome in addressing the highly politicized and collective claims of national minorities and Indigenous peoples. The challenges of globalization and cultural diversity have increasingly disrupted conventional assumptions pertaining to the primacy of the nation-state, the placement of individuals in terms of identity and belonging within a transnational context, and the relevance of a unitary citizenship in a world of coming and going. (Ang, 2011). Or, to put it more bluntly, it no longer makes sense to talk about a unitary citizenship as a place-specific model of governance when peoples' notions of identity and belonging are increasingly uncoupled from a single locale. In short, a world of transmigration and multiple identities renders the idea of a universal citizenship unsustainable, although some would argue that increased diversification intensifies the importance of commonalities (Kymlicka, 2003).

The concept of a universal citizenship has come under pressure to be split into (or differentiated into) a different set of rights and entitlements depending on the social category in question. Under a differentiated citizenship model, citizenship rights and entitlements would be customized in a manner consistent with the rights, realities, and status of Aboriginal peoples, racialized migrants and minorities, ethnoculturally and faith-based groups, and transmigrants with multiple affiliations. Yet the recalibrating of citizenship along customizing lines raises a number of questions: Is Canada ready for a more complex citizenship, one that is (1) differentiated by way of different entitlements and belongings, (2) inclusive of differences yet united in purpose, (3) responsive to both individual and collective group rights, and (4) reflective of a primary affiliation with the whole while retaining membership in the parts without incurring a penalty?

Not surprisingly, the politics of citizenship in Canada are attracting attention in the quest to balance a commitment to differentiated citizenship customized along particularistic lines, with the unifying framework of universal citizen rights (Abu-Laban, 2015; Wilkinson, 2005). Should the principle of a unitary citizenship prevail to ensure national unity and identity? Or is it time for a more differentiated citizenship consistent with contemporary dynamics, demands, and divisions of an increasingly postnational era? Is it possible to create a unitary yet differentiated citizenship in a global world of transnational communities and diasporic migrants (see also Harty & Murphy, 2005; Kernerman, 2005) without compromising a commitment to commonalities? The Debate Revisited box at the end of this chapter will further examine this possibility of a compromise arrangement that incorporates the strengths of unitary and differentiated citizenship into a more inclusive package.

INTRODUCTION: NEW RULES, NEW GAME, EVOLVING OUTCOMES

Adventure, n. a daring enterprise (*Concise Oxford Dictionary*)

That we live in a period of convulsive social change is surely beyond dispute. Canada is currently in the midst of a social and demographic revolution so profound in its impact and implications that it threatens to sever the very moorings that formerly anchored it into place. Everything is changing so quickly that nothing is certain or predictable except a pervasive sense of confusion or uncertainty. What once were endorsed as universal truths are no longer accepted as morally valid or socially relevant, while yesterday's heresies are now conventional wisdom. What once were defined as vices are increasingly embraced as virtues, whereas perceived strengths lapse into weaknesses as the politics of difference scuttles traditional assumptions about right and wrong. For example, in rejecting a belief that differences are incompatible with good governance, Canada now abides by the principles of an inclusive multiculturalism as a principled framework for living together differently (Fleras, 2009b). Admittedly, the transformational process has proven more bumpy than many imagined. Rules of the established order rarely apply in an age of difference and change; nevertheless, vested interests tend to resist the establishment of new rules. The old order may be eroding but retains a critical mass of inertia; by contrast, the new order is compelling yet lacks the critical mass to dislodge the old.

Transformative changes of such magnitude require a mastery of context and perspective. Compared to societies that are plagued by human and natural misery, Canada's relentless inspection of itself reflects the indulgence of a country that by any measure is a "solution in search of a problem." The challenge of **Canada-building** may pale in comparison to that of India. With its 1.25 billion people, 16 official languages, and 5 major religions, India's survival as a modern democracy is a twenty-first century success story. Or consider the jurisdictional quagmire known as Indonesia, with its 250 million people (2015) spread across 17 000 islands, representing 300 ethnic groups and 500 languages/dialects. Still, no one should casually dismiss the challenges that confront a deeply divided and multilayered Canada. Canada-building is complicated by factors as disparate as an expansive geography, the unhealthy dependencies imposed by colonialism, an unwieldy and fractious regionalism, a proximity to the United States, the potentially divisive politics of aboriginal and ethnic nationalism, and robust levels of immigrants and immigrant diversities (Hiller, 2000). A cooperative coexistence is complicated by the interplay of Aboriginal peoples' politics, the continuing solitude between Quebec and the rest of Canada, the politicization of racialized minorities, and the heightened expectations of newcomers to Canada. Canada's multicultural commitment to inclusiveness as grounds for living together further reinforces the country's status as a "contested site" involving a competitive struggle over power, privilege, and resources.

In short, Canada appears to be cresting the wave of a brave new adventure. This "adventure called Canada" (as a former Governor General of Canada once deftly put it) involves a series of interrelated but incomplete and competing society-building projects. The challenge lies in transforming this sprawling but narrowly populated land mass into a moral community of citizens with a shared sense of core values, a common vision, a sense of belonging, and a singularity of collective purpose. Foremost is the ongoing business of constructing a sense of cohesion, commitment, and identity from the threads of history, change, and diversities. Of equal importance to the national project is the sorting out of jurisdictions and entitlements around a three-nations model of Canada. The politics of Canada-building are sharply contested by the interplay of Canada's three major Diversities with respect to competing agendas, unique histories, distinct constitutional statuses, and varying rights and entitlements (see Jenson, 2002). Sorting through each of these different demand levels—and doing so simultaneously by accommodating diverse ways of accommodating difference—may pose Canada's definitive challenge yet also reflect its crowning glory.

Reactions over the politics of Canada-building vary. That much can be expected in a society in which the politicization of difference has profoundly challenged the very notion of "what Canada is for"—A nation of nations? A community of communities? A market-place of self-interested individuals? A category of convenience for people on the move? For some, the prospect of a multicultural society within the framework of a tri-national state equips Canada with the flexibility to cope with uncertainties, diversities, and change. Others disagree and continue to embrace attitudes and projections seemingly inconsistent with twenty-first century realities. They want to turn back the clock by fortifying Canada against the intrusions of a changing and diverse world. Still others fall somewhere in between. They may be mentally predisposed for change and accommodation, yet recoil at the prospect of applying yesterday's solutions to today's problems. There is mounting dismay that the promising diversity initiatives of the 1970s and 1980s—from multiculturalism to employment equity—have capitulated to a pessimism that nothing works and nobody cares (see also Friesen, 2005; Kitaro, 1997). With everything up for grabs and nothing taken for granted, Canada's **society-building** skills will be sorely tested in the attempt to reconcile the often competing demands of unity with those of difference in a freewheeling yet interconnected global world.

The politicization of diversities and difference have made it abundantly clear: If improperly managed or left entirely to market forces, they can provoke and partition. But create the appropriate governance architecture, and dissimilar peoples can learn to share land, power, and resources while respecting their differences as grounds for a sustainable coexistence. There is much of value with such an assessment, and this concluding chapter explores the possibilities of a Canada at a critical juncture in its evolutionary development from a closed and exclusive monoculture to a more open and tolerant multiculturalism that, in turn, is showing its age in an increasingly postnational era. The chapter will examine how this adventure called Canada-building is fraught with perils and pitfalls, yet full of promise and potential. Reference to the "**Canadian Way**" implicit within **Canada's Difference Model** offers a blueprint for addressing the challenges of complex diversities and diverse complexities. A reassessment of Canada's nation-building trajectory suggests the possibility of reframing Canada as a postnational society, with a corresponding push toward a postmulticulturalism as a governance model for managing diversities. This transformational dynamic is captured by debates over the politics of citizenship, involving proponents of a universal citizenship clashing with advocates of a differential citizenship without necessarily excluding the possibility of an inclusive citizenship. The chapter concludes accordingly. Canada is hardly perfect in managing race, ethnic, and aboriginal relations. Nevertheless, it may be less imperfect than the rest, partly because Canada possesses the right kind of "imperfections" for living together with differences, equitably and respectfully.

CANADA-BUILDING: AN UNFINISHED WORK IN PROGRESS

> Can a modern (European-based) constitution recognize and accommodate cultural diversity? This is one of the most difficult and pressing questions of the political era we are entering at the dawn of the twenty-first century. (James Tully, 1995:1)

Canada sits among a fistful of settler-based countries in the vanguard for constructing coherent yet pluralistic societies. Canada's status as a global trailblazer for constructively engaging differences stems from the unorthodox way it has gone about solving its largely atypical problems (see Saul, 1998). The contours of Canadian society are realigning along pluralistic lines, signaling a departure from earlier eras when government agendas routinely privileged the authority of mainstream rules, monocultural values, and dominant institutions (Guo & Wong, 2015). But the challenges of a diversifying and changing Canada are proving a governance conundrum. A proliferation of divided loyalties has complicated the search for national unity—especially when Canada's major Diversities envision their commitment to Canada as conditional and contingent on claims that must be differently accommodated (Kymlicka, 2001). Aboriginal peoples are no longer willing to remain on the peripheries of Canada. They instead are actively and openly competing for recognition and resources as part of an ongoing reformulation of Canada's Aboriginal peoples–state relations. The proposed restructuring of Quebec–Ottawa relations within a renewed federalism has proven frustratingly elusive, with little in the way of a permanent resolution. But both pairs of these uncomfortable bedfellows have such a vested interest in staying together that this mutual dependency may well yield the flexibility and compromise to shore up an awkwardly coherent coexistence. The politics of Canada's multicultural agenda are no less potent (Zachariah, Sheppard, & Barrett, 2004). Both migrants and minorities in a transnational and transmigrant world are increasingly demonstrating splintered loyalties, multiple identities, and fractured belongings that challenge the relevance of place-based governance models such as Canada's official Multiculturalism or Canadian citizenship (Fleras, 2014b).

The politics of working in/with/through differences has profoundly transformed Canada (Fleras, 2013; Magnet, 2004; Parkin, 2003). In ways unimaginable, the Canada of today differs from the country of a generation ago, much less that of a century ago. Many of the changes it has endured are reflected, reinforced, and advanced at (1) policy levels for constructing engaging difference, (2) institutional levels for reasonably accommodating diversities, (3) the level of a more tolerant cultural climate, and (4) the symbolic level, in terms of more inclusive citizenship. Even the discourses around race, ethnic, and aboriginal relations are changing. References to race, ethnicity, and aboriginality are no longer framed as a static "thing" (noun) but as a dynamic "process" (verb)—from a mosaic to a kaleidoscope—undergoing a fluidity of changes, challenges, and contestation. Consider the following discursive shifts in redefining Canada's evolving response to the dynamics of race, ethnic, and aboriginal relations:

- *National Vision: From British Colony to Cosmopolitan Canada.* From a vision of Canada as a tightly scripted "white-man's country," where everyone knew their place, to its emergence as a tri-national and multilayered work in progress where nothing is certain because everything is contested and negotiable.

- *Models of Governance: From Uniformity to Multiculturalism to Postmulticulturalism.* From monoculturalism as a framework for living together to the principles of multiculturalism for managing diversity, to the growing emergence of postmulticulturalism as governance model for engaging a Canada of diverse diversities. From a one-size-fits-all formula for Canada-building under an official multiculturalism, including a universal citizenship with similar rights and obligations, to the idea of customizing arrangements along a postnational line in response to Canada's multilayered differences-within-differences.

- *Status of Minorities: From Margins to Mainstream.* From the marginalization and inferiorization of those outside an Anglo-Canadian profile—including Aboriginal peoples, racialized minorities, and immigrant Canadians—to their centrality as key players in reshaping the political, social, and cultural contours of the national agenda.

- *Institutions: From Exclusion to Inclusion to Inclusivity.* From institutions that ordinarily and routinely excluded minorities because of their differences to an emphasis on institutional inclusion ("fit into the existing system") through reasonable accommodation, to the principle of inclusivity (adjust system to fit to individuals) that is respectful of, reflective of, and responsive to differences by way of services that are available, accessible, and appropriate.

- *Status of Diversity: From Indifference to Diverse Differences.* From a rejection of difference as irrelevant, inferior, and contrary to good governance, to its endorsement—albeit at a superficial level ("pretend pluralism")—in defining who gets what (Bannerji, 2000). The interplay of transmigration and transnationalism generates an awareness of a multiversal world of hyperdiversities and the need to differently accommodate accommodations (Fleras, 2011b).

- *Tolerance Levels: From Open Dislike to Openness.* From an intolerance of others as a badge of pride to an embrace of tolerance as profoundly central to Canada's identity as a multiculturally cosmopolitan society (Foster, 2005).

- *Patterns of Entitlement: From Inequality to Equality to Equity.* From an endorsement of inequality as inevitable, normal, and necessary, to the principle of equality that treats everyone the same (inclusion), to a commitment to the principle of equity, including recognition of collective rights and group-specific measures as well as the need to take people's differences into account for true equality (inclusivity).

- *From Race-Conscious to Race-Blind to Race-Sensitive.* From a Canada that explicitly excluded others because of race, to one that believes race no longer matters because of Canada's commitment to the principles of a colour-blind society. From an era when race mattered (stigma), to one where it shouldn't matter but it does (perception), to one with a growing awareness that it will matter because a colour-blind Canada neither exists nor should it exist if differences are taken seriously (race-sensitive).

- *Levels of Intervention: From Laissez-Faire to Macro-Management to Micro-Engaging.* From a government reluctance to get involved in managing the dynamics of race, ethnic, and Aboriginal relations, to the centrality of government intervention in macro-managing priorities. Growing awareness that a one-size-fits-all model for macro-managing diversity is creating space for the emergence of micro-engaging strategies consistent with the postmulticultural principle of multiversal inclusivity (Fleras, 2015a, b).

- *Expanding Rights: From Whites to Humanity.* From a Canada that routinely denied and excluded others because of national origins (as well as gender) to a Canada that many see as a pacesetter in protecting and promoting the principle of universal **human rights**, both individual and collective—at least in theory if not always in practice.

- *Rethinking Citizenship: From Exclusion to Inclusiveness.* From an exclusionary focus that restricted citizenship to those who qualified for British subjecthood, to a unitary model in which everyone possesses the same rights and obligations, to a more differentiated citizenship in acknowledging how different Canadians require a different set of rights and entitlements. Reference to the concept of an inclusive citizenship reinforces the idea of postnational citizenship as both universal and differentiated.

What is Citizenship? Legal and Social Dimensions

The concept of citizenship consists of two dimensions: the legal and the social. In legal parlance, citizenship entails formal membership in a politically constituted community (Delanty, 2000). A legal–political contract is established involving a transaction of mutual benefit to all parties, including a reciprocal exchange of rights and duties that connects individuals with membership in the state (Hebert & Wilkinson, 2002; Squires, 2007a). Individual citizens rely on the state to protect their rights and freedoms; in turn, the state expects that individual citizens fulfill certain duties, obligations, and responsibilities. For citizens of Canada, these rights and freedoms include equality rights, democratic rights, legal rights, mobility rights, language rights, a right of return to Canada from overseas travel, freedom of religion, freedom of expression, and freedom of assembly and association. In return, Canadian citizens are obliged to obey Canadian laws, participate in the democratic process, respect the rights and freedoms of others, and recognize Canada's linguistic duality and multicultural heritage.

(Continued)

People can acquire citizenship in two ways: at *birth* or by *naturalization* (Macklin & Crepeau, 2010). Citizenship by *birthright* is transmitted by descent from a citizen, with the result that citizenship is restricted to those who share a common bloodline or who can trace their genealogy to a citizen. All states allow their citizen parents to automatically pass their citizenship on to their children, according to Macklin and Crepeau (2010), but will vary in the number of generations across which a person living abroad can transmit citizenship by descent. Citizenship by birthright can also be acquired by birth on the territory of the conferring citizenship state. Relatively few states (Canada and the United States are exceptions) tolerate automatic and unconditional citizenship to anyone born on their territory regardless of parental "legal" status, citizenship, or nationality. Countries like the United Kingdom and Australia allow citizenship by birth, but only if one of the parents holds lawful resident status. By contrast, citizenship by *naturalization* involves the process of formal acquisition by someone who is not a citizen by birth. It is offered to those newcomers who are legal residents, fulfill certain residency requirements, make an effort to acquire citizenship, and acknowledge a commitment to the rule of law and shared values of the country in question.

But citizenship goes beyond the legalities of membership and relationship to the state (Brodie, 2002). Citizenship also incorporates a social dimension with respect to belonging, identity, and entitlements. The debate over belonging pivots on who can belong as citizens, how and why, what constitutes good citizens, and what kind of entitlements and expectations flow from this status (Sobel 2015; Simon-Kumar, 2012). Common to citizenship regimes such as Canada is the primacy of universality as a basis for belonging and entitlement. A **universal citizenship** can be defined as one that treats all citizens the same, since everyone is thought to belong in the same way. Each citizen is entitled to the same benefits and rights—and stands in the same relation to the state—regardless of race, origins, or ethnicity. Entitlements because of difference are ignored under a universal citizenship: Just as people's differences cannot be used to exclude, so too should their differences not entitle them to special privileges or preferential treatment. A universal (or unitary) citizenship also rejects any type of entitlement rooted in collective or group rights as contrary to the principle of individual equality before the law. Promotion of group differences on racial or ethnic grounds— even in the spirit of inclusiveness and progress—can only undermine bonds of loyalty, unity, and identity.

The concept of a universal citizenship has come under fire as increasingly inappropriate in a fluid, mobile, and hybridic world of complex diversities and diverse complexities (Conference Notes, 2013). The interplay of globalization with transmigratory connections ensures that many individuals retain meaningful links to more than one state, and acknowledge this reality through the acceptance of multiple or multidimensional citizenships (Fleras, 2011b; Macklin & Crepeau, 2010; Simmons, 2010; Sobel, 2015). Ethnic and racialized minorities prefer a citizenship that acknowledges their sometimes disenfranchised status in Canada, either marginalized in socioeconomic terms or threatened with the loss of their language and culture. Indigenous peoples and national minorities such as Canada's Aboriginal peoples and the Quebecois embrace a differentiated citizenship that recognizes their unique constitutional status with respect to rights and entitlements. Accordingly, four types of customized citizenship rights and entitlements can be discerned: *equity*, *multicultural*, *self-determining*, and *transmigratory* (or *transnational*)— each of which reflects a reading of Canada as a community of communities.

- *Equity Entitlements*: Historically disadvantaged migrants and minorities may require a different set of entitlements to ensure full citizenship rights. Equity citizenship entitlements are aimed at improving institutional access and societal integration through the removal of discriminatory barriers and the introduction of proactive programs, such as employment equity.
- *Multicultural Entitlements*: Both racial and cultural minorities may require some degree of official protection of their ethnocultural heritage. Multicultural citizenship goes beyond a demand for cultural rights or acceptance of cultural differences as a value; rather, it entails the assumption that membership in a living and lived-in cultural reality provides individuals with meaningful choices to maximize freedom (Allegritti, 2010; Kymlicka, 1992).
- *Self-Determining Rights and Entitlements*: Another type of citizenship entitlement involves Aboriginal peoples and the Québécois. Both Aboriginal peoples and minority nations like the Québécois have different group-specific needs, aspirations, status, and experience; as a result, citizenship entitlements must be customized accordingly. As peoples or nations, their demands as citizens go beyond the entitlements of universal citizenship. They include claims upon the state for control over land, culture, language, and identity; the right to self-government and jurisdiction over matters of direct relevance; access to power and resources that flow from their unique relational status; and the right to belonging indirectly to Canada through membership in their nations rather than through individual citizenship.
- *Transmigratory (Transnational) Entitlements*: Transmigratory citizenship refers to the possibility of dual or even multiple citizenships, both concurrently and without contradiction. The theory of a postnational (or transnational) citizenship in a global era is predicated on three realities: (1) the eroding sovereignty of states; (2) increased mobility and communication thanks to new technology; and (3) the capacity of people to maintain multiple links between their homeland and the host country (Simmons, 2010). In an age of migration where up to 235 million people may be on the move at any given time and connections are a mouse click away, new patterns of belonging may reflect concurrent loyalty to the home country as well as to the adopted country (Castles, de Haas, & Miller, 2013).

The Canadian Way and Canada's Difference Model: Differential Accommodation

> . . . Canada is a world leader in three of the most important areas of ethnocultural relations: immigration, Indigenous peoples, and the accommodation of minority nationalisms . . . That we have managed to cope with all these forms of diversity simultaneously while still managing to live together in peace and civility is, by any objective standard, a remarkable achievement. (Kymlicka, 1998a:3)

Canada is widely regarded both nationally and internationally as a world leader when it comes to constructively engaging diversity. Canada's experiment in accommodating differences—including Aboriginal peoples, Québécois, and increasingly politicized multicultural minorities—has produced 150 years of relatively peaceful coexistence (Kymlicka, 2004; LaSelva, 2004; see also Bickerton & Gagnon, 2004). As well, Canada is perceived as a model for managing intergroup differences in those countries that, too, are grappling with the politics of differences. The challenge is relatively straightforward: to balance these fundamental yet opposed differences in a way that most Canadians find acceptable, that provide a blueprint for living together despite deep differences, and that consolidate a commitment to the whole without undermining the integrity of its parts (McRoberts, 2003). Responses to this challenge point to the concept of the Canadian Way and Canada's Difference Model for addressing the key challenge of the new millennium: How can different ways of accommodating difference coexist in deeply divided and multilayered societies without a capitulation to chaos?

The Canadian Way: Principle and Process The Canadian Way entails a host of meanings, depending on the speaker, context, or intended audience, but most references involve *content* and a *process*. As content, the Canadian Way articulates a commitment to the principles of *differences, equality,* and *inclusiveness* as a basis for democratic governance. In contrast to the past, when a monocultural governance sought to uphold a white Canada while working to assimilate or exclude minorities and differences, the Canadian Way embraces the possibility of creating a prosperous and cohesive Canada by injecting a diversity dividend into the national agenda (Kymlicka, 2003). A principled commitment to diversity and difference does not necessarily compromise an equally strong attachment to national unity and respect for core Canadian values, as pointed out by Canadian Heritage (2001):

> Canada's approach to diversity is based on the belief that the common good is best served when everyone is accepted and respected for who they are, and that this ultimately makes for a resilient, more harmonious, and more creative society. This faith in the value of diversity recognizes that respect for cultural distinctiveness is intrinsic to an individual's sense of self-worth and identity, and a society that encourages achievement, participation, attachment to country, and a sense of belonging.

The Canadian Way also endorses a principled process for meeting the evolving challenges of diversities (Kymlicka, 2001). Mechanisms and arrangements have been introduced to facilitate engagement and community without violating individual rights and national interests. An extensive legal framework exists to promote the principles of diversity and individual rights—from official Multiculturalism to the *Canadian Charter of Rights and Freedoms* to the *Employment Equity Act*. Structures are in place so that disagreements can be resolved through negotiation and compromise instead of a rigid dogmatism. Individuals who believe their rights have been violated can appeal to federal and provincial human rights commissions for redress.

Two preconditions inform this process. First, there must be a society-wide commitment to the principle of agreeing to disagree, so that differences of opinion can be articulated, discussed, and adjusted accordingly. Second, the process of negotiated compromise requires an institutional framework that creates relatively open lines of communication. Or, as Will Kymlicka (2001) writes in defending process as the heart of the Canadian Way:

> Canada has a legal framework for discussing issues of diversity. Policies of multiculturalism, federalism, and Aboriginal rights give the relevant groups a seat at the table and constitutional legitimacy to their identities and interests. Many countries have no framework for the majority and minority to sit down and discuss how to live together. (p. A15)

In brief, reference to the Canadian Way connotes the pragmatic ways in which Canadians address the challenge of difference and diversities in ways workable, necessary, and fair. Canada's strength lies in differently working through problems rather than applying a one-size-fits-all solution, of seeking compromises rather than unilaterally imposing fixtures, and of balancing diverse interests in a state of creative tension rather than seeking definitive answers.

Canada's Difference Model: Differential Accommodation Canada may be one of the only countries in the world that must simultaneously address the interests, agendas, and demands of three major ethnicities—namely, Aboriginal peoples, charter groups, and multicultural minorities. The genius of Canada's Difference Model is its willingness to recognize the legitimacy of three mutually exclusive yet principled policy platforms. Canada's Difference Model for managing diversities is not just about accommodating difference. More to the point, it's about *accommodating different ways of accommodating difference.* In creating a society based on compromise, a Difference Model acknowledges that (1) Canada's major Diversities possess fundamental divergent agendas and priorities because of different sociological status, patterns of belonging, and corresponding entitlements; (2) any policy solutions must be customized to accommodate the difference between the voluntary minorities who want to "get in" versus the forcibly incorporated peoples who want to "get out"; and (3) proposed outcomes must coincide with the constitutional status of each major diversity without breaching the principle of unity within diversity. In addition, Canada's Difference Model must also balance oppositional tensions and choices resulting from competing values, including uniformity versus diversity; individual rights versus group rights; formal equality (symmetry or equal treatment) versus substantive equality (asymmetry or special treatment); and personal freedom versus national security (Jenson & Papillon, 2001).

Three levels of differential accommodation are addressed in Canada's Difference Model:

1. One level is represented by Aboriginal peoples, who claim to be sovereign peoples with the right of self-determining autonomy over land, identity, and political representation (Maaka & Fleras, 2008). A package of priorities is proposed whose foundational principles promote power-sharing and a partnership based on a government-to-government relationship. To the extent that Canada is grappling with decolonizing its relationship with the descendants of the original inhabitants, in part by promising a more positive alternative, the contours of a new postcolonial social contract are beginning to take shape.

2. Another level is represented by the Québécois, who, like Aboriginal peoples, claim to be sovereign in principle. Québécois demands pivot around putting this principle into

practice in a way that acknowledges a compact view of Canada, Quebec's status as a distinct society, and Québécois demands of mastery over their own house (Gagnon, Guibernau, & Rocher, 2003). English-speaking Canada appears to be moving in the direction of a more flexible federalism, one that recognizes Quebec as more than a province but less than a separate nation-state, although there is reluctance to constitutionally entrench this shift for fear of blowing out of proportion the fictions that paper over Canada's contradictions.

3. At yet another level are multicultural (immigrant and racialized) minorities. They want equality and inclusion yet respect for their cultural differences, without incurring a penalty in the process (James, 2005; see also Abu-Laban & Gabriel, 2002). The combination of initiatives, from anti-racism to employment equity, reinforce the notion of Canada as a society of many cultures, in which people's cultural differences cannot preclude full participation and equal citizenship rights as a matter of course, while still acknowledging that differences can be taken into account when necessary.

To be sure, references to Canada's Difference Model tend to overstate this country's outcomes in the diversity sweepstakes. The most egregious expressions of colonialism in Canada may have been eradicated; nevertheless, Canada's Difference Model is largely silent about challenging the foundational principles that govern the country's constitutional order. For example, Ontario's *Mining Act* of 1873 still allows mining companies (or any adult with a prospector's license) to prospect anywhere for subsurface minerals—even when trampling on aboriginal lands or yet-to-be-resolved land claims. In keeping with this colonial mentality, there remains a refusal or incapacity to take aboriginal difference seriously. Yes, aboriginal self-government is in place, but not necessarily aboriginal *models* of self-determining autonomy. True, Quebec is now recognized as a nation (in the "cultural" and "sociological" sense of the word) and a distinct society, but neither concession is constitutionally entrenched. Nor is there much enthusiasm for seriously re-engaging Aboriginal peoples or the Québécois as fundamentally autonomous political communities, both sovereign and sharing sovereignty by way of separate but interlocking jurisdictions. As well, a commitment to institutional inclusiveness may reflect the principles of multiculturalism, but too often, only in the very narrow sense of replacing white incumbents with minority hires within the existing framework of rules, structures, and priorities. Finally, a policy of Multiculturalism may be premised on the principle of respecting the cultural identities of Canadian citizens, but without addressing the racially stratified structures that embed these cultures (Henry & Tator, 2010). Inasmuch as the status quo remains largely intact, with changes only to the practices referring to the rules instead of foundational rules that inform practices and conventions, the challenge of living together with differences remains as complex as ever.

TOWARD A POSTNATIONAL CANADA: NATION OR NOTION?

Increasingly, we are cultural Canadians: Canadian by willpower rather than by policy. We feel attached to Canada because we like the smell of it. It is an affair of the heart. The process is ephemeral, not mechanical, but no less real. Get used to it. We live in an age of intangibles, and our love of country is as intangible as it is profound. (Edward Greenspon, editor of *The Globe and Mail*, 2001)

The world is engulfed by two mutually exclusive yet inextricably linked forces. On the one hand are the universalizing (and homogenizing) forces of a freewheeling global market economy. Transnational movements of goods and services are conducted with seemingly minimal regard for societal boundaries (Castles, de Haas, & Miller, 2014). Advances in information technology tend to render national borders increasingly porous and difficult to monitor and control. On the other hand, the fragmenting forces of insurgent ethnic identities are poised to dismember and destroy. Radical ethnicities and ethnic nationalisms appear to be largely indifferent or hostile to the legitimacy of the nation-state, preferring instead a commitment to challenge, resist, and transform regardless of consequences (Ignatieff, 2005). This interplay of centrifugal ("push out") and centripetal ("pull in") forces promises to reshape the political contours of societies large and small, in the process contesting the concept of "what society is for."

On the whole, Canada appears to have been relatively successful in balancing these global forces with those of national interests and minority rights, even if the juggling act tends to be wobbly at times. Such an achievement is not to be sneered at, given the enormity of the challenges. Unlike the more **complete (or civilizational) societies** of Europe (Castles & Miller, 2009), Canada represents *an idea and a set of ideals* (i.e., a notion) rather than a distinct people with a history, language, and culture, and it is this fundamental ambiguity that underscores the contradictions inherent in Canada-building. "Canada is not a real country," as former Quebec premier Lucien Bouchard once taunted English-speaking Canadians, but a collection of shreds and patches with no real historical or cultural reason to claim nationality or peoplehood. Outside of Quebec, Canadians have little in common—no shared ancestors or genetic pool, no origin myths, and few common rituals—except perhaps a commitment to public institutions such as universal healthcare. Or, rephrased, Canada is not so much a mosaic of culturally distinct tiles, but a complex matrix of wiggly lines and contested angles in response to the demands of multiple identities and competing sovereignties under a single polity. That is, it's a notion, not a nation.

This assessment of Canada as all "lines" and "angles" may not flatter. Yet these very vulnerabilities may yield a host of possibilities for crafting a new kind of Canada. Canada may be poised on the brink of becoming the world's first postnational society by eschewing conventional nation-building wisdom. Consider the contrasts: A "national" society embraces the principles of modernity and modernism as the basis for modern governance. As an Enlightenment project, modernity rejected religion as a legitimate form of social authority, endorsed reason and scientific inquiry as the organizing principle of social life, sought to develop universal categories of explanation and rationalization, strove for the attainment of absolute truth (universally valid foundations for human knowledge based on reason and science), and embraced a belief in history as having direction or purpose (Dustin, 2007). Applied to society, an embrace of modernity and modernism reflected the ideals and attainment of a unitary, centralized, and homogenized nation-state under the control of a dominant national group, which used its privileged status and power to impose nationhood through its language, culture, history, symbols, and so on (Kymlicka, 2004, 2007). A national (or modern) society also enlisted for society-building purposes a commitment to a master narrative (uniformity), a coherent state identity (homogeneity), universalism (rules apply to all), centrality (to ensure conformity and control), clarity (rather than ambiguities), a low threshold for uncertainties, and a belief in a merging nation (peoples) with state (a people) (Dustin, 2007). Or, put alternatively, society-building adhered to the principle of rational instrumentality, with its McDonaldized commitment to reducing costs by improving efficiency, predictability, and standardization (Ritzer, 2014).

By contrast, the world we inhabit at present is an untidy one. Established rules, values, and institutions are falling in line with more flexible modes of governance to cope with new and fluid realities that have yet to gain mainstream traction (Ang, 2011). The uncertainties and inconsistencies are numerous: In a globalizing world of capital flows and people movement, the nation-state may be losing its salience as an exclusive governance space for fostering human security and community, yet it's also proving impossible to ignore as an instrument of intervention and regulation. In a world of transmigration (transnationalism), hybridity, and diaspora, it no longer makes sense to talk of multiculturalism or citizenship as strictly place-based forms of governance when people's notions of identity and affiliation are increasingly disconnected from place. A static and categorical multiculturalism as governance and discursive construct is increasingly incapable of capturing the immensely more complex and dynamic world of diversities within diversities (multiversal or super-diversity) within shifting contexts of power and inequality (Fleras, 2011b). The interplay and dynamics of unsettled boundaries, uncertain loyalties, and fragile identities is consequential in deconstructing the monocultural ideal of the nation-state as a unity-in-diversity. As Ien Ang (2011) argues, it is now time to recast the nation-state as a socially constructed and imaginary ideal, both unstable and evolving with no foreseeable closure in sight.

Postnational society invokes the postmodernist principle of "doing things differently." In a postnational era of politicized differences within differences that challenges the foundational principles of a conventional societal order, it is futile or repressive to endorse the modernist goals of clarity, coherence, centralized authority, commonality, and consensus. The lofty position of a monocultural nation-state as the privileged unit of sovereign identity and agency—a bounded entity with territorial integrity and historical continuity—is sharply being eroded by rampant internal fragmentation and increasingly porous borders (Ang, 2011). Traditional criteria for defining a nation-state are contested, including the goal of matching territory ("state") with that of culture, identity, a people, and history ("nation"). In contrast to a monocultural nation-state, a postnational society espouses a multiculturality that repudiates (1) the idea that the state is possessed by a single national group (but rather espouses the idea that it belongs equally to all citizens); (2) assimilationist policies that force minorities to hide their identities (but rather accords equal recognition and respect for difference and diversity) and (3) institutional practices that exclude or deny (in favour of those that improve equal involvement and full citizenship rights) (Kymlicka, 2007). A centralized and fixed mono-uniformity is displaced by a sense of impermanence, fragmentation, and mutability, reflecting a radically skeptical world where everything is relative and contested because nothing is absolute and definitive (Bauerlein, 2001; Dustin, 2007; Gwyn, 1996). With postnationality, in other words, weaknesses morph into society-building strengths; conversely, strengths drift into weaknesses within contexts of transformative changes.

In short, by challenging the rules upon which convention is based rather than simply the practices that refer to the rules (Angus, 2002), a postnational society proposes a new game with a different set of rules for belonging, identity, and unity. This line of reasoning applies to Canada in how it manages the politics of difference without destroying itself in the process. Instead of a definitive centre that categorically defines and controls, Canada is constructed around a society-building process that accommodates different ways of accommodating

TABLE 10-1	The Nation-State versus the Notion-State
Modern nation-state	**Postnational society (notion-state)**
Society = striving completion	Society as ongoing social construction/ unfinished project in progress
All-encompassing narrative: "We are all one people"	Multiple voices, multiple identities, multiple loyalties
Making society safe from difference	Making difference safe from society
One-way adjustment: "Our way, the right way"	Inclusive two-way adjustment/reasonable accommodation: "You adjust, we adapt; we adjust, you adapt"
Coherent and singular national identity	Splintered and contested national identity
Conformity and standardization: "Treat everyone the same"	Inclusive diversity: "Treat others equally and as equals" + accommodate different ways of accommodating differences
Centralized command and pyramidal control	Decentralized and devolved (flattened) control
Conflate nation with state, including universal citizenship model of belonging, identity, and entitlement	Society as a nation of nations, community of communities, diversities within diversities, including customized citizenship models of belonging, entitlement, and identity
A monocultural society that acknowledges a pretend (superficial) pluralism	A difference-driven society that takes difference seriously
Society-building problem to be solved	Society-building tension to be managed/ negotiated
A commitment to a nation (a society with common history, cultures, peoples, territory)	A commitment to a notion (a society based on a set of ideas and ideals)

difference with respect to belonging, entitlements, and identity. Rather than something natural or normal with a shared history, geography, or ethnicity ("nation"), Canada is defined as an ongoing social construction ("notion")—a project or convention created by individuals and groups, evolving and relative to a particular time and place, and subject to reformative change—as this quote aptly conveys: "Canada is a kind of model for the 21st century, in which a nation defines itself not as a piece of geography or a race of people but as a political and cultural and existential concept" (John Gray, as cited in Whittington, 1998).

A brief comparison (see Table 10-1) demonstrates the ideal–typical contrasts between the modernist *nation*-state project and the postnational *notion*-state model—keeping in mind that Canada is only beginning to disengage from modernity toward postmodernity as a society-building blueprint.

Toward Postmulticulturalism: Moving Positively Beyond Multiculturalism 1.0

The world at present is an untidy and unruly place (Fleras, 2015a, b). Societies are no longer the ordered jurisdictions of centralized planning and social engineering that many imagined them to be, or to what they themselves aspired (Scott, 1998). To the contrary, they are complex, inconsistent, and contested, with a dizzying array of identities, perspectives, and belong-ings that cross borders, challenge conventional notions of citizenship, and compromise conventions of state sovereignty and national unity. Orthodox patterns of belongings and identities are increasingly contested in this diasporic and seemingly borderless world of both crossings and connections, yet also played out against a world whose regimes impose restrictive admissions, integration ("assimilation") tests, citizenship restrictions, and mili-tarized borders to offset the border-busting movements (Ang, 2010). No less disruptive to the national governance is the proliferation of diversities-within-diversities (Latham, 2008) in posing yet another layer of complexity to an already complex world (Kraus, 2011). The interplay of these dynamics raises a raft of governance dilemmas related to: (a) the rele-vance of place-based models of governance in a transmigrant and diasporic world of "here", "there", and "everywhere"; (b) the possibility of living together in a de-spatialized world when people's notions of identity and belonging are uncoupled from place but glob-ally linked; (c) creating more robust patterns of civic participation, citizenship identity, and meaningful commitment to neutralize the society-sapping effects of splintered loyalties, multiple identities, and hybridic affiliations; and (d) the possibility of a new analytic framework for engaging a "multiversal" world of diversifying diversities by way of differ-ential accommodation.

These emergent dynamics and contested projections unsettle the relevance of an official (or bounded) multiculturalism as a diversity governance model (Ang, 2010; Guo & Guo, 2015; Karim, 2007; Vertovec & Wessendorf, 2004). Consider the following points of con-tention: Canada's official multiculturalism may no longer be relevant as as a governance model for managing complex diversities in a diversifying Canada (also Mansouri & de B'beri, 2014). An inclusive multiculturalism may prove incapable of differently accommo-dating the non-linear realities and fragmented dynamics of a diversities-within-diversities universe (i.e., "multiverse"). A territorially-bounded multiculturalism (i.e., a national governance framework that is physically circumscribed, culturally specific, and spatially exclusive) may be irrelevant in a seemingly unbounded world of transmigratory movements, transnational loyalties, translocal linkages, fractured identities, and de-territorialized belongings (Carruthers, 2013; Walton-Roberts, 2011). Perhaps there is no point in invoking an official multiculturalism as a place-based governance model for micro-managing com-plex diversities when migrant notions of identity and belonging are increasingly delinked from a singular residency, identity, and citizenship (Karim, 2007; Mawani, 2008). The chal-lenge may lie in conjoining these oppositional dynamics—the centrifugal push of diversify-ing differences with the centripetal pull of securitization and surveillance—into a synthesis that weds the lived-politics of transmigrant hyperdiversities to the abstract principles of a bounded and inclusive governance.

The world's quintessential multiculturalism is experiencing a legitimacy crisis of confidence in a diversifying Canada of overlapping identities, transmigrant linkages, and intersecting belongings. The inclination of a static and categorical multiculturalism 1.0 to impose a one-size-fits-all straitjacket for managing diversity reinforces its inability to address the immensely complex diversities of migrants and minorities within a shifting and deterritorized context of transmigration and transnationalism (Fleras, 2014c; also Baker et al., 2013). Or to phrase it more emphatically, Canada's hyperdiverse and migrant-rich urban centres (or "mongrel cities" [Sandercock, 2003]) are outgrowing a bounded multiculturalism model that once informed and circumscribed peoples' lived-experiences (Sandercock, 2006;

Ley, 2005; Habacon, 2007; Fleras, 2011b). Ang (2011:29) points to those preconditions that amplify the growing irrelevance of a multiculturalism 1.0 platform:

> [Nation states] are de facto diverse in ways that can no longer be contained within the neat model of unity in diversity. After many generations of immigration history, migrants and their descendants are no longer containable within a fixed and internally homogeneous category of "ethnic community", as tended to be assumed in the formative years of a state-sponsored multiculturalism. Witness the second, third, and fourth generations, whose ethnic identities are increasingly fluid, hybridized and Westernized. Nor has there been a smooth process of integration of migrants into the national community, not because multiculturalism encouraged them to lead parallel lives, but because differences between people(s) – racial, cultural, religious – are very resistant to erasure: processes of inclusion and exclusion, the differentiation of the self and other, and the drawing of dividing lines between us and them are an enduring feature of the human way of life.

In short, a multicultural governance model is at the crossroads of a freewheeling yet networked global world of transnational connections and hyperdiverse diversities (Kymlicka, 2014; Walton-Roberts, 2011)? The politics of diversities-within-diversities, with its attendant need to differently accommodate the different ways of accommodating complex diversities, raises a set of governance challenges:

- The proliferation of identity politics and the politicization of faith-based communities creates inward-looking commitments that complicate governance. Concerns are mounting that multicultural coexistence may be impossible if migrants and minorities espouse sharply defined links to a primary affiliation, reject the legitimacy and authority of the prevailing governance, and endorse an unflinching loyalty that emanates from a religious or tribal source. For example, the prospect of integrating Islam into a secular and multicultural governance has unleashed debate over "whose rules rule":

  > For multiculturalism was always about finding a space for the culture of the other, in so far as that culture does not claim a sovereignty over itself that clashes with the laws of the nation . . . Multiculturalism has always had capacity to find a space for such minor laws within an all-encompassing national law. This is part of what defines it. However, for people who take their religion seriously, this situation is reversed. The laws of God are all encompassing, and the national laws of the host nation are minor. For a seriously religious Muslim migrant, to integrate into the host nation becomes a matter of finding space for these national laws within the all-encompassing laws of God. We then see how the very relationship between encompassing and encompassed cultures, on which multiculturalism is based, is here inverted (Hage, 2006).

  Pressure in multiculturally diverse societies is mounting to take differences seriously, although an official multiculturalism is ill-equipped to address deep differences except in the most superficial, static, and standardized ("one-size-fits-all") way.

- The globalization project has unleashed those transmigatory dynamics and transnational linkages that threaten to erode place-based models of immigrant integration. The interplay of unsettled boundaries, transnational loyalties, and multiple identities has proven consequential as well in dis-establishing the monocultural ideal of a unitary nation-state. More complex diversities confirm the futility of squeezing diverse complexities into those multicultural governance frameworks for managing diversity that once worked. Increased references to cosmopolitanism as a global governance further unsettle the politics of diversity management in a global order locked into the concept of territorial-based sovereignty (Brown, 2014; Kymlicka & Walker, 2012).

- Canada is no longer a diverse society. It's a hyperdiverse society (Hanlon, 2014) of multiple social universes ("multiversal"), with a vast range of diverse perspectives, premises, and lived realities (Latham, 2007/08). Differences in a multiversal context persist across many overlapping and intersecting universes, resulting in a proliferation of *fissions, fissures, and fusions*. *Fissions* within migrant and minority communities are increasingly compounded and crosscut by new axes of differentiation, distinction, and demands related to legal status, religion, gender age, nationality, class, and so on (Vertovec, 2007; also Vertovec & Wessendorf, 2004). *Fissures* within migrant and minority communities reflect social cleavages, both temporary and permanent, because of internal politics, conflicting agendas, and variable socioeconomic statuses. Canadian cities now exhibit the dynamics of hybridity, according to Daniel Hiebert (2011), a co-director of Vancouver's Metropolis Project, namely, a robust *fusion* of cultures, religions, homeland linkages, sexual orientation, and everyday experiences that are more complex yet harder to categorize (Baker et al., 2013). Predictably, a mosaic reading of multiculturalism may antagonize those Canadians whose ethnicity matters, but is not all consuming. Yes, ethnicity may inform their fluid and hybridic identities across multiple cultural spaces. Yet it should neither define who they are nor should it box them in (Habacan, 2007).

Living in an age of diversity—or more correctly an era infused by the challenge of managing complex diversities—yields an unprecedented level of complexity, contestation, and contradiction. It also raises the possibility of a pending postmulticultural "turn" in the governance of differences that want to be taken seriously, that want to differently addressed, and that want to be accommodated when necessary to do so. Although governments continue to rely on frameworks often at cross-purposes with the dynamics and demands of complex and proliferating diversities (Vertovec, 2012), awareness is mounting that conventional multicultural governances confront a crisis of credibility in managing complex diversities in a diversifying world (Prato, 2009). Too much of what passes for multicultural management of diversity is grounded in the metaphorical equivalent of a "multi cul de sac" multiculturalism, with its concomitant notions of singular, fixed, and homogenous mosaic of ethnocultures within a territorially bounded and monocultural nation-state. Too much focus on an uncritical preservation of essentialized and deterministic cultural differences privileges an official multiculturalism that micro-manages *diversity* in the abstract rather than engages *diversities* through the lived-humanity they have in common (Bauman, 2011; Mukherjee, 1989). Kenan Malik (3 June 2012) acknowledges as much in his Milton K Wong Lecture "What is Wrong with Multiculturalism" when pinpointing the schism between multicultural diversities as a lived experience versus multiculturalism as a political program for micro-managing diversity:

> As a political process, however, multiculturalism means something very different. It prescribes a set of policies, the aim of which is to manage and institutionalize diversity by putting people into ethnic and cultural boxes, defining individual needs and rights by virtue of the boxes into which people are put, and using these boxes to shape public policy. It is a case, not for open borders and minds, but for policing of borders, whether physical, cultural, or imaginative.

In short, a mosaic ("bounded") multiculturalism is poorly equipped to address the multiversal re-articulation of identity and belonging as multidimensional, fluid, and hybridic—against the backdrop of a hyperdiverse and interconnected world (Hoyos, 2014). The future looks grim for those multicultural governance models constrained by issues and arrangements within the confines of a particular nation state, a clearly bounded territory, and a singular citizenship (Ang, 2010; Kymlicka, 2014).

To date, there exists a dearth of theoretical frameworks with which to unthink and rethink core governance concepts for managing a complexity of diversities (Li & Juffermans, 2011; Blommaert, 2012). To offset this lacuna in theorizing, a newer "post-ethnic" governance model—multiculturalism 2.0, or postmulticulturalism—is proposed that (a) recognizes the realities of shifting group boundaries, (b) acknowledges new cultural hybrids and combinations, (c) capitalizes on diverse migration sources and diversities within immigrant groups, and (d) endorses multiple identities and hybridic affiliations at odds with conventional identity politics, group rights, deterministic communities of descent, essentializing cultures, and fixed identities (Hollinger, 2005). The principle of "multiversal inclusivity" within an emergent postmulticulturalism attends to the hyperdiverse realities of new (trans)migrants in addition to the dynamics of their cultural comings and goings beyond fixed borders and permanent locales (Carruthers, 2013). A postmulticulturalism framework is primed to engage the realities of those whose commitments and connections are transnational; who reject the prospect of being boxed into a homogeneous and essentialized ethnic category preferring, instead, to visualize identity as a cultural web to be negotiated and navigated (Habacan, 2012); who are on the lookout for arrangements that can differently accommodate the accommodation of diverse diversities; who insist their differences be framed *as assets* to treasure rather than as deficits to reconcile; and who expect to be engaged as valued contributors rather than micro-managed as social problems.

Clearly, then, a bounded multiculturalism may have addressed the needs and demands of a specific historic period—namely, the modernist drive for cohesion, respect, integration, and unity—in hopes of superimposing a shared "we" morality to displace an "us" versus "them" mentality (Hrushetska, 2013). Its fixation with the principle of liberal universalism (we are all basically alike) may have dismissed the salience of differences as superficial and secondary to our commonalities as individuals. Yet its commitment to inclusion represented a critical step forward from a racist and exclusionary past. But aspirations under an inclusive multiculturalism are now holding it back from meeting new challenges, in part because of the generality and singularity of its commitments as a normative framework for Canada-building at a specific point in time (also Hollinger, 2005). Nowhere is this gap between universalism and multiversality more evident than in an intergenerational perception of multiculturalism. The balm of a multicultural canopy may have entitled the first generation of migrants to become part of the national whole; however, a mosaic multiculturalism for the second generation is perceived as a cultural straitjacket that pigeonholes as it reifies and essentializes (Saunders, 2013; also New Canadian Media, 2013). First-generation immigrants may have endorsed a multicultural policy that embraced them as part of the national whole; however, children of these migrants tend to see multiculturalism as increasingly obsolete in a complex world of diverse complexities, an impediment that precludes their inclusion into Canada, and a hindrance that micro-manages their aspirations on the basis of ticking them into ethnic boxes for policy purposes (Saunders, 2013; also New Canadian Media, 2013). In that a bounded multiculturalism cannot possibly attend to the challenges and complexities of a multiversal world of hyperdiversities and transnationalism (Tunis, 2010), it's time to move on to a postmulticulturalism phase, given the increasingly transparent limitations of conventional governance models (Kymlicka, 2014; Heath, 2014).

Contrary to popular discourses in this domain (Fleras, 2015a, b), a postmulticulturalism project is not necessarily a rejection or retreat from multiculturalism. Governance flaws notwithstanding, it's unnecessary to toss out the multicultural baby with the postmulticultural bathwater. A commitment to postmulticulturalism should be framed instead as building on, yet moving beyond, a bounded multiculturalism model. After all, the benefits of an inclusive multiculturalism as diversity governance are unmistakable, although its governance strengths also embed governance weaknesses exposed by the demands of a postnational Canada of transmigration, transnationalism, and complex diversities. An official multiculturalism once symbolized a shift forward in fostering a social climate that facilitated the inclusion ("integration") of migrants and newcomers as equals into the existing status quo. It was premised on an inclusionary promise; that is, that no one would be excluded from full and equal citizenship rights because of their differences or for reasons beyond their control (Berry, 2014). Members from diverse ethnocultural groups would coexist through a process of multicultural integration (i.e., inclusion)—a kind of unity-within-diversity framework paralleled at the global level by the United Nations where each nation-state member possesses a separate seat at the table yet must abide by common rules (Ang, 2011:28). An inclusionary concept of a cooperative coexistence was endorsed (Habacan 2012), primarily by encouraging intercultural/interfaith understanding through dialogue and interaction; promoting shared values and civic pride in Canadian history and society; instilling a governance model that respects and accepts diversity; securing institutions responsive to the needs of Canada's diversity; advancing equal opportunities for all Canadians through removal of prejudicial mindsets and discriminatory barriers; relegating the practice of racism into the four-letter word-basket; and acknowledging the right of newcomers to become Canadian on their own terms (within limits) provided they comply with the law of the land, respect people's individual rights, subscribe to core constitutional values such as gender equality, and employ their ethnicity as a way of belonging to Canada. That these inclusionary commitments remain as integral to Canada in its 150th year of existence as they did in the past attests to the continuing value of a bounded multiculturalism.

To sum up, let's acknowledge the different governance logic between the "mosaic" inclusion of an official multiculturalism and the "multiversal inclusivity" of a postmulticultural turn. A multicultural inclusion model is concerned primarily with making sure that no one is excluded from full and equal participation because of who they are. This inclusion model focuses on fitting all individuals into the existing system, regardless of race, ethnicity, or aboriginality because in the final analysis, everyone is equal before the law and should not be excluded (or offered special treatment unless it's deployed to facilitate their fit into the existing system). By contrast, the inclusivity commitment of a multiversal multiculturalism (i.e., postmulticulturalism) is predicated on the principle of ensuring that everyone must be included precisely because of their difference-based needs, rights, or values and taking them into consideration. This inclusivity commitment asserts the importance of adjusting the system not only to ensure a recognition of differences-within-differences, but also to endorse the importance of differently accommodating a diversity of diversities. And if an official multiculturalism is focused on forging unity at the expense of diversity, a commitment to postmulticulturalism attends to the primacy of diversity as a precondition of unity. Table 10-2 provides a quick and ideal typical comparison of an inclusion multiculturalism and inclusivity postmulticulturalism as diversity governance models.

TABLE 10-2	**Multiculturalism versus Postmulticulturalism as Diversity Governance Models**	
	Multiculturalism Model for Managing Diversity	**Postmulticulturalism Model for Engaging Diversities**
Guiding metaphor	Mosaic	Kaleidoscope
Status of Diversity	Liberal Universalism	Multiversal Particularism
Governance Logic	Manage diversity	Engage diversities (-within-diversities)
Focus of accommodation	Standardized	Differential
Demographic Targets	Migrants and minorities	Transmigrants and Hyperdiverse migrants and minorities
Level of inclusiveness	Inclusion	Inclusivity
Model of society	National model	Postnational model

Put bluntly, neither an inclusion multiculturalism nor an inclusivity postmulticulturalism should be played off as mutually exclusive principles for managing diversity—complex or otherwise. They should be positioned instead as starting reference points for re-negotiating a new multiculturalism 2.0 governance model that engages with a diversity of diversities across a range of inclusivity channels (Latour & Balint, 2013; Pinder, 2010). In other words, postmulticulturalism is less a rejection of multiculturalism 1.0 but more of a recognition that an inclusive (inclusion + inclusivity) multicultural governance 2.0 model secures a better template for the complex realities of the twenty-first century:

> . . . [A] post-multiculturalism is not a rejection of multiculturalism as much as it is a recognition that renewed energies are needed to create a global understanding of diversity across multiple contexts and locales that can be an asset, and not simply a set of problems in need of better judgement. (Ley, 2005:15)

Yet another inescapable truth is reinforced in proposing a postmulticultural governance model that builds on yet transcends a bounded multicultural governance: Any reference to an official multiculturalism as governance must acknowledge its provisional status—not as a timeless ideal to defend at all costs—but as an unfinished project and an ongoing work in progress in need of periodic overhauls (Fleras, 2015a, b).

BUILDING CANADA: PERFECTING IMPERFECTIONS

A rewriting of the rules for differently living together allows Canada to claim status as one of the world's first postnational societies (see Gwyn, 1994, 1996). The lightness of being that is associated with Canada's postnationality may provide a prototype for the ideal twenty-first century society by the simple expedient of transforming weaknesses into strengths because of shifting circumstances. The fact that Canada represents a political union born out of economic necessity and political expediency rather than a national spirit or violent struggle may work in its favour. The endless debates over power and jurisdictions may have morphed into a kind of glue for binding Canadians together. Of course, debates over Canada's unity and identity often perplex and provoke, even infuriate those with a rigid sense of what Canada is for. But the paradox of a rolling Canadian identity provides a resiliency and flexibility that avoids being locked into the rigidities of the past (see Castles, de Haas, & Miller, 2013). This notion of Canada as "tension to be negotiated rather than a problem to be solved" mentality may have also bolstered its reputation as an open and tolerant society, with a commitment to constructively engaging difference as a virtue to be nurtured rather than a vice to be spurned.

In a world of diversity, uncertainty, and change, Canada's atypical circumstance may be its strength. Canada's seeming vulnerability—its decentralized unity and diversity-based identity—may prove a tower of strength in a world where rigidity and authority are incompatible with the freewheeling demands of a global market economy animated by the international movement of people and ideas (Simmons, 2010). Perhaps this penchant for snatching virtue from vice defines and distinguishes Canadians in promoting postnationalist ways of living together differently across a multitiered Canada. Canadians may well possess the kind of temperament best suited for the postmodern realities of the twenty-first century, namely, a dedication to pragmatism, a commitment to civility and tolerance, and a willingness to compromise for the sake of the whole. In a world where rules and conventions are being turned inside out, Canada's threshold for uncertainty and tolerance of ambiguity may provide just the right amount of resilience to bend, not break. In an era where a passionate attachment to homeland or culture may maim or destroy, Canada's redemption may reside in a willingness to "cut some slack" when necessary. In renegotiating the meaning of Canadianness by way of rights, principles, obligations, and rules of engagement, a commitment to compromise may prove our lasting contribution to world peace, as eloquently expressed by Adrienne Clarkson, former Governor General of Canada:

> It's a strength and not a weakness that we are a permanently incomplete experiment built on a triangular foundation—aboriginal, francophone, and anglophone. What we continue to create, today, began 450 years ago as a political project . . . It is an old experiment, complex, and, in worldly terms, largely successful. Stumbling through darkness and racing through light, we have persisted in the creation of a Canadian civilization (as cited in Canadian Heritage, 2001).

The conclusion is inescapable: This adventure called Canada-building remains a work in progress. Canada may not be a real country in the conventional sense of a complete society. It is better described as an ongoing and unfinished project that must be continually willed into action. As a social construction of ideas and ideals—a space of travelling cultures—Canada cannot rest on its laurels. On the contrary, as a work in progress, it must always define, modify, and change in line with changing circumstances (see also Sandercock, 2003). That it has managed to transform this indeterminancy into contemporary strengths—even if out of necessity rather than principle—must surely say something about Canada's commitment for constructively engaging difference (Clarkson, 2014). In other words, Canada appears to have just the right kind of imperfections for harnessing the resources and resourcefulness needed to meet the challenges of an increasingly postnational global era. The words of Professor Xavier Arbos, a Catalan and president of the International Council for Canadian Studies, strike as reassuring and rewarding: "Canadians have reasons to be proud of a country that is balanced, democratic, a country that cares, where there is less violence . . ." Canada may not be perfect, he adds, but it looks a lot better than most.

From Universal to Inclusive Citizenship: Postnationalism in Practice

Two ideal-typical citizenship models can be discerned: unitary (or universal) and differentiated. Some believe that a universal citizenship must prevail in Canada because only a universal citizenship can perform the twin tasks of protecting Canada's national interests while ensuring protection of the fundamental rights of all loyal Canadians. A differentiated citizenship splintered into "this" and "that" cannot possibly fulfill its basic function of creating shared loyalty, common identity, patriotic commitment, and those unifying symbols for linking citizens into a single framework. Without the shared values of a universal (common) citizenship for bonding and bridging, the danger of society splitting into a series of fractured communities is all too real. Moreover, for these people, the concept of a differentiated citizenship may be deemed un-Canadian since (1) some individuals are treated more equally than others, (2) special group rights are elevated over individual rights, and (3) the legitimacy of the political community at large is compromised.

Others think that a more differentiated citizenship is required in Canada. A one-size-fits-all unitary citizenship no longer resonates with relevance within the complex context of Canada's multilayered and deeply divided differences (Hebert & Wilkinson, 2002; Redhead, 2003). Entitlements and rights under a "universal" citizenship may reinforce the marginality of minorities when they privilege formal equality

rights (equal treatment) over substantive equity rights (treatment as equals), thus ranking all individuals as similar for political or economic purposes, regardless of circumstances or commitments (Schouls, 1997). As Iris Marion Young (1990) has argued, a universal citizenship is unfair when applied to unequal contexts, that is, treating all citizens—regardless of race, class, or gender—as disembodied individuals in the abstract rather than as disadvantaged minorities in a real world. Moreover, Canada can no longer be defined in terms of singularity—one nation, one identity, one culture, or one belonging (Hebert & Wilkinson, 2002). In a world of globalization and transnational connections, identities today are openly plural, with people belonging to many different groups and defining themselves in terms of these multiple affiliations without necessarily experiencing contradiction or rejecting commonalities (Karim, 2006; Mawani, 2008).

Clearly, then, both a unitary and differentiated citizenship possess strengths and weakness. Perhaps the challenge lies in conceptualizing a citizenship model that incorporates the strength of each while bypassing respective weaknesses (Bloemraad, 2015). An **inclusive citizenship** combines the rights of universal citizenship with the differentiated claims of Aboriginal peoples, national communities, and racialized migrants and minorities (Harty & Murphy, 2005). In visualizing citizenship as a rope of interwoven strands, one of these strands

(Continued)

emphasizes universal citizenship rights with respect to individual equality and equality before the law. Another strand focuses on those differentiated citizenship entitlements that take differences seriously, together with the need to take into account these differences based on the principle of differential accommodation. Admittedly, the balancing act implicit in fostering a "differentiated universalism" (Squires, 2007a) will prove difficult and awkward, as Ruth Lister (1997) concludes, since neither is sufficient in its own right but requires the other to complete it:

> [R]ejecting the "false universalism" of traditional citizenship theory does not mean abandoning citizenship as a universalist goal. Instead, we can aspire to a universalism that stands in creative tension to diversity and difference and that challenges the divisions and exclusionary inequalities which can stem from diversity. (p. 66)

With an inclusive citizenship, in other words, different patterns of rights and entitlements are endorsed without discarding the principle of universality or commonality. A globalized world of heightened migration, plural loyalties, and transnational patterns of association still require a robust form of geographically anchored citizenship to promote national identity and social cooperation (Motomura, 2006).

Like it or not, approve or disapprove, the future of a postnational Canada entails customizing different models of rights and entitlements. An era of transnationalism and diasporic dispersion means people no longer identify exclusively with one country, preferring instead multiple identities and intersecting allegiances that transcend national boundaries (Dijkstra, Geutjen, & De Ruijter, 2001; Satzewich & Wong, 2006). This is no time to impose the modernist notion of a unitary Canadian citizenship, with a dash of multicultural colour thrown in for good measure. Rather, Canada must acknowledge the reality of comings and goings if it wants to attract the brightest and the best. A one-size-fits-all citizenship is unlikely to appeal in a multidimensional and multilayered Canada where some are banging on the door to "get in" while others are breaking down the door to "get out." Yes, it will take time to convince Canadians that people are alike in different ways yet different in similar ways. Nevertheless, the postnational goal of belonging differently together without drifting apart will depend on accepting this seeming paradox—that true equality arises from treating people equally (the same, i.e., inclusion) as a matter of course but treating them as equals (differently, i.e., inclusivity) when the situation calls for adjusting the system.

Chapter Highlights

- Canada can be envisaged as an unfinished work in progress with respect to managing the diversities of race, ethnic, and aboriginal relations. It has evolved from an intolerant and exclusive British colony to a postnational society based on a commitment to managing diversity in a principled manner.

- Conventional ways of thinking about citizenship (universal citizenship) are being challenged by the concept of differentiated citizenship rights based on customized notions of belonging and entitlements. An inclusive citizenship seeks to combine the unitary with the differentiated as a basis for living together across a deeply divided and multilayed Canada.
- Canada's Difference Model and the Canadian Way are widely touted as Canada's main contributions to cooperative coexistence, in large part by acknowledging the principle of differential accommodation of complex diversities rather than relying on a single one-size-fits-all standard.
- Canadians possess a relatively high threshold for ambiguity and change because of historical precedents. Such flexibility not only allows weaknesses to be transformed into strengths but also may secure Canada's status as the world's first postnational society.
- A postnational Canada that commits to differently accommodating a proliferation of diversities-within-diversities will build on yet move beyond an official multiculturalism 1.0.

Review Questions

1. One of the key themes in this chapter is the notion that "this adventure called Canada" has transformed weaknesses into strengths. Describe what is meant by this claim, and provide several examples of how weaknesses-into-strengths are reflective of a Canada-building process.

2. Compare the concept of a universal versus inclusive citizenship in terms of underlying assumptions and anticipated outcomes.

3. What is meant by the expression "Canada's Difference Model"? How does reference to "Canada's Difference Model" relate to the concept of the Canadian Way?

4. Evidence suggests that Canada may be advantageously positioned to redefine itself as the world's first postnational society. Comment on what constitutes a postnational society, how a postnational society differs from a modern society, and how a post-Canada appears to fit this new model of societyhood.

5. Compare official multiculturalism 1.0 with postmulticulturalism 2.0 as competing models of governance in "managing" diversities. Reference to the concepts of inclusion versus inclusivity will be helpful.

Glossary

Aboriginal peoples Aboriginal peoples represent the descendants of the original (indigenous) occupants of Canada who have been forcibly incorporated into Canadian society, but now want to "get out" of this arrangement by redefining their relational status in society along nation-to-nation lines. The Constitution Act, 1982, employs this umbrella term to describe three distinct groups—Indians (or First Nations), Metis, and Inuit. *See also* Aboriginality; Aboriginal (peoples') rights.

Aboriginal (peoples') rights The entitlements that Aboriginal peoples possess by virtue of their original occupancy and ancestral use of the land for subsistence and survival. These rights are unique to Aboriginal peoples; secure the basis for rewards, recognition, and relationships; and acknowledge their right to aboriginal models of self-determining autonomy over jurisdictions related to land, identity, and political voice. *See also* Aboriginal peoples, Aboriginality.

Aboriginal self-governance Aboriginal peoples claim that, as fundamentally autonomous political communities ("nations"), they have a right to govern themselves ("self rule") in ways that reflect their realities, reinforce their experiences, and advance their interests. *See also* Governance, Self-government.

Aboriginal title A constitutional recognition that Aboriginal peoples continue to own those lands and resources that they have occupied continuously for centuries. The Crown cannot encroach upon lands that have not been lawfully surrendered without meaningful consultation, consent, and compensation.

Aboriginality Used in a descriptive sense, aboriginality ("being aboriginal") describes the principle by which a politicized awareness of original occupancy provides a moral basis for entitlement and recognition. The politicization of "being aboriginal" involves the politics of transformative change, not only in challenging the legitimacy of the sovereign state as the paramount authority, but also in advancing innovative patterns of belonging that embody the post-sovereign notion of the "nations within." *See also* Aboriginal peoples, Aboriginal (peoples') rights, Aboriginal self-governance.

Androcentrism A tendency for men to see the world from their point of view as normal and necessary; to assume that others are seeing the world in the same way or would like to if they could or if they knew better; and to dismiss other worldviews as inferior or irrelevant.

Anglo-conformity An expectation that minorities under British colonial rule must outwardly conform to mainstream (British) culture and society, with some leeway for privately held values and norms. *See also* Assimilation.

Anti-racism A commitment to identify, isolate, and challenge racisms through direct action at individual and institutional levels.

Assimilation A complex and dynamic process in which minorities begin to lose their distinctiveness through absorption into dominant society. As policy or political framework, assimilation can refer to those formal government initiatives for absorbing minority populations into the mainstream. *See also* Anglo-conformity.

Asylum seeker A person who flees one country and seeks refuge and protection in another country by claiming refugee status.

Bilingualism   The coexistence of two languages at *territorial*, *institutional*, or *individual* levels. Canada may be officially bilingual at federal institutional levels; however, of the ten provinces, only New Brunswick is officially bilingual. Under an official bilingualism, minority language rights (French outside Quebec, English in Quebec) are protected.

Canada-building   *See* Society-building.

Canada's Difference Model   Widely regarded as a progressive model for simultaneously accommodating different ways of accommodating racial, ethnic, and aboriginal difference, Canada's Difference Model acknowledges the need to customize policy and programs to meet the distinctive aspirations of Canada's three major "Ethnicities": Aboriginal peoples, the Québécois, and multicultural minorities. *See also* Canadian Way.

Canadian Charter of Rights and Freedoms
When it came into effect in 1985, the Charter constitutionally entrenched the right of individuals to be free of unnecessary state intrusion. The concept of collective rights is also endorsed as a reasonable limitation on individual rights if demonstrably justified in a free and democratic Canada.

Canadian Multiculturalism Act   *See* Official Multiculturalism.

Canadian Way   A discourse that espouses Canada's commitment to difference (content) and dialogue (process) as a model for living together with differences in a deeply divided and multi-layered society. *See also* Canada's Difference Model.

Capitalism   An economic (and social) system organized around the rational pursuit of profit.

Citizenship   A legal contract establishing a reciprocal exchange of rights and duties between a person and the state in which he or she lives. A social dimension of citizenship pertains to issues of belonging, identity, rights, and entitlements. *See also* Inclusive citizenship.

Citizenship Act   Passage of this Act in 1947 established citizenship as something distinctively

Canadian in terms of identity and rights, thereby replacing the earlier notion that defined Canadians as transplanted British subjects.

Civic multiculturalism   An emphasis on Canada's Multiculturalism policy and program that focuses on promoting inclusion by way of citizenship, belonging, and participation.

Class   An aggregate of persons who occupy a similar status or stratum in society because of similarities in power, wealth, or status. Marxists see class in terms of people's relationship to the means of productive private property (namely, owners versus workers). Those of a Weberian bent see class as a complex interplay of factors such as wealth, power, and prestige, in effect leading to different classifications, including the always-popular categories of upper, middle, and lower class.

Collective definition   A distinct if somewhat underutilized approach to the study of race and ethnicity, collective definition endorses a view of race, ethnic, and aboriginal relations as dynamic and contested. Factions ("dualisms") within both the dominant and subdominant groups compete with each other in privileging their definition of the situation, thereby creating complex intergroup dynamics that pull in seemingly opposite directions. *See also* Dualism.

Colonialism   A violent and traumatic process reflecting a specific era of European expansion and settlement over the so-called "underutilized" lands. European powers forcibly exploited indigenous peoples by appropriating land and resources, extracting wealth, and capitalizing on cheap labour, while invoking racial doctrines to justify and explain their removal, exploitation, or extermination.

Complete (or civilizational) society   A term that describes the settled countries of Europe. European societies tend to see themselves as culturally and demographically finished projects, with a corresponding rejection of society-building through immigration or diversity.

Comprehensive claims   A modern-day equivalent of nineteenth-century treaty agreements in which the Crown acquired certainty of ownership over large blocks of aboriginal land, while aboriginal communities received rights to smaller sections of land (reserves), allocation of services, money, and goods, and access to Crown land resources. In contrast to nineteenth-century agreements, however, comprehensive treaties tend to include protocols for establishing aboriginal self-governing arrangements as well as rights to co-manage natural resources and revenue-sharing from resource extraction.

Conflict theory   Based on the idea that societies are sites of inequality, with the result that confrontation, competition, and change are inevitable, in part because diverse groups compete for scarce resources in contexts that advantage some groups at the expense of others. *See also* Internal colonialism.

Constitutional order   A combination of founding assumptions, foundational principles, fundamental rules, and normative understandings that collectively establish a functioning governance in terms of what is normal, desirable, and acceptable. It also provides a framework for the expression of ordinary political debates while fostering a platform for decision-making over a sustained period of time.

Constructive engagement   A new (postcolonial) social contract for redefining the relationship of Aboriginal peoples to society at large. Constructive engagement is premised on the notion that competitive or confrontational models are not conducive to living together differently. Proposed instead is a model of cooperative coexistence that not only endorses Aboriginal peoples as fundamentally autonomous political communities—sovereign in their own right while sharing sovereignty over society—but also embraces the postcolonial principles of power-sharing partnership. *See also* Postcolonial social contract, Aboriginality.

Constructivist explanation   A framework for explaining ethnicity by reference to its socially constructed character. Rather than something real, natural, or inevitable, ethnicity constitutes a social convention created by individuals who make meaningful choices

within broader contexts to achieve particular goals. *See also* Primordial explanation.

Convention refugees   Individuals who are selected and sponsored for entry into Canada because they fulfill the UN criteria for refugee status.

Critical multiculturalism   A commitment to difference politics that promotes an agenda to challenge, resist, and transform those prevailing patterns of power and privilege that marginalize minority women and men.

Cultural relativism   A belief that the merit and worth of cultures and cultural practices are relative to the society in which they exist. As a result, all cultural practices should be analyzed and assessed on their own terms rather than by some arbitrarily selected external criteria. It is widely (but incorrectly) thought that, in the absence of absolute standards, cultural relativism embraces the idea that all cultural practices are good and valid—even those in violation of human rights. A critical cultural relativism argues that, for purposes of assessment and change, all cultural practices should be seen *as if* good and valid.

Depoliticizing ethnicity   A process by which the potency of ethnicity or difference is "neutered" by eroding its potential for intergroup strife. Ethnicity is relegated to the private or personal domain and is thus dislodged from the competition for power and privilege in the public sphere.

Difference   In contrast to the empirical descriptor "diversity," difference is employed in the more politicized sense to convey the placement of different groups along a hierarchy of dominance and subdominance within unequal contexts.

Differentiated citizenship   The idea that the social contract implicit in belonging to society must be customized to reflect the different realities, experiences, and needs of Canada's major ethnic groups. *See also* Citizenship, Inclusive citizenship.

Discourse   Ways of thinking and talking about the world based on how reality is framed (i.e., identified, named, classified, and interpreted).

Discrimination   Often viewed as the behavioural counterpart of prejudice (attitudes), discrimination consists of actions that have an adverse effect (whether deliberate or not) of denying or excluding someone because of who they are. This denial of equal opportunity or treatment for those perceived as different can be expressed at different levels, ranging from the personal, intentional, and direct to the impersonal, inadvertent, and systemic. *See also* Racism.

Discursive   *See* Discourse.

Distinct society   The concept of distinct society is usually applied to describe the political aspirations of the Québécois. The Québécois assert that they constitute a "distinct society," that is, a historical peoples with a unique language, culture, and identity, whose homeland of last resort is Quebec. *See also* Nation.

Diversity   A descriptive and depoliticized statement of demographic fact about differences, namely, a reference to separate states of being in which people are slotted into a pre-existing category. Compare with "difference" and its connotation of politicized diversity or the contextualizing of diversity within contexts of power and inequality.

Dominant group   The collectivity of persons in society with the institutionalized authority not only to preserve the prevailing distribution of power, privilege, and property, but also to impose its standard and culture as the norm by which to judge and evaluate others.

Dualism   A term at the core of collective definition perspective, the concept of dualism suggests a series of binary divisions (factions) within both the dominant and subdominant sectors of society that compete for control of the diversity agenda. *See also* Collective definition.

Employment equity   A principle (or philosophy) or a policy (or program) with a corresponding set of programs and practices. As a *principle*, employment equity embraces the notion of institutional inclusion by removing employment barriers for reasons unrelated to

ability, while improving the hiring and treatment of minorities through the implementation of proactive programs. As a *policy*, it refers to official government policy of Canada's *Employment Equity Act* of 1986/96, with its commitment to institutional representation for the historically disadvantaged.

Equity   The belief that true equality rests on recognizing the relevance of context, the importance of taking differences into account, and a balancing of individual with collective rights. A commitment to equity acknowledges the primacy of equal outcomes (not just equal opportunity) to ensure that members of a group have a fair share of scarce resources.

Essentializing   A belief in unchanging human characteristics that are (1) uniform and stable within a certain category of persons, (2) immutable and impervious to social context or historical modification, and (3) determinative of people's thoughts and actions. The fluidity and complexity of identity formation are ignored while the homogeneity of the group is emphasized.

Ethnic cleansing   As a variant of genocide, it involves a deliberate process to eliminate an ethnic group from a particular locale through either outright killing or forced expulsion.

Ethnic groups   Communities of "like-minded" individuals with a shared awareness of a common identity, language, history, and culture, together with a sense of group belonging based on perceived ancestral links.

Ethnic nationalism   People who share an ancestrally based identity can be mobilized into an action group (social movement) for defence of homeland, language, culture, and autonomy. Those related by blood can claim a right to speak the language of nationhood, express a fierce loyalty to their sense of peoplehood, and insist on their status as peoples with an inherent right to self-determining autonomy, including secession. *See also* Nationalism.

Ethnicity   A principle by which socially distinct groups of individuals are defined, differentiated, and organized around a shared awareness of their common ancestry because of culture, physical attributes, language, historical experiences, homeland, and birthright. Ethnicity not only secures a basis for community and identity, but also provides a rationale for mobilizing "like-minded" people into action for advancing social, political, and cultural interests.

Ethnocentrism   A universal tendency to see and interpret reality from a particular cultural perspective as normal, necessary, and natural, with a corresponding inclination to dismiss or denigrate others as inferior or irrelevant and to judge other practices or beliefs by one's own cultural standards. Ethnocentrism can also include a belief in the superiority of one's culture, values, assumptions, and world view. *See also* Eurocentrism.

Eugenics   A science and a social movement that attained considerable popularity during the first decades of the twentieth century, eugenics advocated improving the quality of the human species through selective reproduction. Eugenics encouraged the creation of large families among the socially superior, while discouraging breeding within the so-called inferior stock (i.e., the poor or minorities).

Eurocentrism   A belief in the moral superiority of European thoughts and practices as the norm or standard by which others are judged and interpreted. Also a tendency to see and interpret the world through European eyes as natural and normal, assume others are doing so as well, and dismiss those that don't as mistaken or a threat. *See also* Ethnocentrism.

Everyday racism   Largely unconscious speech patterns and daily actions that reinforce the denial and exclusion of those marginalized. *See also* Micro-aggression.

Feminism   A widely varied ideology and social movement that espouses the equality and worth of women. Feminisms range from those that reject the existing system as patriarchal, racist, or classist to those that are willing to work within the system by removing

discriminatory barriers to equality. Feminisms also vary, depending on whether the differences between men and women are perceived as absolute or relative, maximal or minimal.

Formal equality   An equality that is based on strict mathematical equivalence; that is, because everyone is equal before the law, everyone should be treated the same, regardless of their differences. Often associated with the principle of equal opportunity. *See also* Equity.

Functionalism   A sociological perspective (or theory) that sees society as a complex and integrated totality composed of interrelated parts that individually and collectively contribute to the stability and survival of society.

Gender equity   Acknowledges that achievement of *de facto* equality must entail special measures, such as institutional adjustments, to correct historical imbalances and social disadvantages that preclude women from participating as equals on a level playing field.

Gendered inequality   A belief that inequality between women and men goes beyond the expression of individual attitudes but is structural and structured; that is, is embedded within the design, organization, and functioning of society. *See also* Patriarchy.

Gendered society   An acknowledgment that all human societies are fundamentally informed by and divided along foundational lines that marginalize or exploit women while bolstering the interests, privilege, and power of men as natural and normal.

Genocide   An attempt to destroy a people in whole or in part. An orchestrated effort by the state or those acting on its behalf or approval to eradicate members from a devalued group occupying the same territory. The centrality of "intent" is seen as crucial to any definition; however, genocide in a broader sense can also be indirect, unintended, or unconscious, and not openly violent in process. *See also* Ethnic cleansing.

Governance   A political framework that defines the relationship between the ruled and the rulers in terms of how authority is divided, power is distributed, and valued resources are allocated within a particular jurisdiction. The term "government" refers to specific forms of this relationship. *See also* Aboriginal self-governance.

Harassment   A type of discrimination in which persistent and unwelcome actions are directed at individuals by those who ought to know better.

Hate racism   An open dislike of others because of who they are or what they do.

Hegemony   The changing of people's attitudes—without their being aware of it—whereby those in positions of power are able to secure control and cooperation through consent rather than coercion.

Human rights   Inalienable (inherent) entitlements that all persons have by virtue of their status as human beings.

Hybridic ethnic identity   *See* Postmodern ethnic identity.

Identity politics   Also known as politics of recognition, identity politics incorporates a broad range of attachments and activities based on the shared experiences of an identifiable group. Members of that constituency assert or reclaim their distinctiveness not only to ensure that they are recognized and accorded respect *on their own terms*, but also to challenge dominant group characterizations of them.

Identity thesis   An attempt to explain the surge in and popularity of ethnicity by pointing out how ethnic group membership provides a buffer for coping with the demands of an urban context.

Ideological racism   A racism that reflects, reinforces, and advances dominant group ideas and ideals (including beliefs and values about what is normal, desirable, and acceptable) that have a negative or controlling effect on a devalued group. *See* Ideology.

Ideology   Defined in its broadest sense, ideology refers to a complex set of ideas and ideals that attempts to explain, justify, and perpetuate a specific set of circumstances. Employed in a critical sense, ideology consists of those beliefs

that rationalize the prevailing distribution of power, privilege, and resources in society by bolstering the cultural patterns of the dominant sector as natural or normal, while dismissing or demeaning subdominant patterns.

Immigrant   Persons born overseas but voluntarily residing in a new country, with a right to permanent residency on the grounds of labour market contribution or family reunification. With the exception of Aboriginal peoples, all Canadians are immigrants or descendants of immigrants.

***Immigration Act,* 1978**   Although superseded by the *Immigration and Refugee Protection Act* of 2002, this Act continues to provide the ideological underpinnings of Canada's immigration policies, programs, and practices. The focus is on finding a working balance between humanitarian and pragmatic concerns while protecting Canada's national interests and international commitments.

Immigration and Refugee Board of Canada (IRB)   An agency of approximately 180 specifically trained civil servants (formerly political appointees) who sit in single-person tribunals to determine whether individual asylum seekers qualify for entry into Canada as legitimate refugees.

Immigration and Refugee Protection Act
This 2002 Act replaces the 1978 *Immigration Act.* Emphasis is increasingly aimed at addressing Canada's security concerns without sacrificing conventional humanitarian commitments and a commitment to Canada-building through immigrant-driven economic growth.

Immigration society   A society that takes a principled and proactive approach to immigration and immigrants. Policies and programs exist to regulate the entry of immigrants, programs are in place to assist the integration and settlement of immigrants, immigrants are entitled to all rights and privileges, and immigration is viewed as an asset or resource for society-building.

Inclusion   A subset of inclusiveness, inclusion entails a belief that, because everyone is equal before the law, nobody should be excluded from equal and full participation within the existing institutional framework for reasons beyond their control (i.e., race, religion, gender, etc.)

Inclusive   *See* institutional inclusiveness

Inclusive citizenship   A belief that citizenship in Canada must be customized to reflect the distinctive needs and aspirations of Aboriginal peoples, national communities such as the Québécois, and historically disadvantaged multicultural minorities. An inclusive citizenship is, in many ways, consistent with the core principle of Canada's Difference Model, namely, a commitment to accommodate different ways of accommodating differences.

Inclusive multiculturalism   *See* Integrative multiculturalism.

Inclusiveness   *See* Institutional inclusiveness.

Inclusivity   A subset of inclusiveness, inclusivity refers to the idea that everyone should be included in terms of full and equal participation precisely because of their differences that must be taken into account by way of institutional accommodation.

Indigenous peoples   Refers to those descendants of the original inhabitants who possess a historical continuity with the territories and ancestral societies that predated European colonialism. *See also* Aboriginal peoples.

Indigenous rights   *See* Aboriginal (peoples') rights.

Institutional inclusiveness   The idea that mainstream institutions must move over and make space for the historically disadvantaged through reasonable accommodation. At one level, inclusiveness is about increased minority presence through removal of discriminatory barriers and the introduction of proactive measures to create services that are available, accessible, and appropriate ("inclusion"). At another level, it's about redesigning institutional structures, values, and practices in ways reflective of, respectful of, and responsive to minority differences ("inclusivity").

Institutional power   The ability to influence others because patterns of power are ingrained

within the foundational principles of society and backed up by the coercive authority of the state.

Institutional racism   Those organizational policies, programs, and practices that openly deny or inadvertently exclude minorities from full and equal participation in society.

Instrumentalist explanation   In explaining the surge and popularity of ethnicity, the instrumentalist approach argues that people collectively mobilize under the banner of an ethnicity as a show of collective strength in a competitive world.

Insurgent ethnic identity   A politicized ethnic identity involving a strong identification with one's own group, often accompanied by an intense dislike of others, who are seen as inferior or a threat.

Integration   A model of race and ethnic relations as well as a policy framework for managing diversity that involves a set of policy ideals and practices opposing the principles of segregation or separation. As governance, integration involves a commitment to incorporate minorities into the mainstream as equals without sacrificing their distinctive identities. Integration can also refer to a process in which different cultures fuse as "paints in a bucket" to create a distinct cultural amalgam.

Integrative multiculturalism   Canada's official Multiculturalism is not about celebrating differences but about ensuring an inclusive Canada that integrates migrants and minorities into society through removal of prejudicial and discriminatory barriers.

Interactionism   A sociological perspective that envisions society as an ongoing human accomplishment involving a dynamic process whereby social reality is created and recreated by individuals who engage in meaningful interaction. Also called "symbolic interactionism."

Internal colonialism   A fundamentally exploitative relationship in which Indigenous peoples are forcibly incorporated into a system not of their own making with a corresponding loss of land, identity, and political voice.

Intersectional analysis   A theoretical approach to the study of inequality that incorporates the interplay of gender with race, ethnicity, and class in defining outcomes. Gender is superimposed on and intersects with race, ethnicity, and class to create interlocking patterns of domination that intensify the exclusion or exploitation.

Islamophobia   An irrational fear of Islam, ranging from stereotypes to acts of violence, whereby followers of Islam religion are racialized as a threat to security and Muslim-based cultures are demonized as barriers to integration.

Lived ethnic identity   A kind of ethnic identity that is performed on an everyday basis. Compare with "symbolic ethnic identity."

Marxism   A philosophy or ideology based on interpreting the work of Karl Marx. According to Marxism, both the dynamics of history and the organization of society can be understood as an ongoing and evolving clash between the ruling (capitalist) class and the working class in the competition for scarce resources.

Melting pot   A metaphor used to describe the preferred ideal in American race and ethnic relations. The concept of a melting pot suggests the fusion of minority differences to create a new and improved national culture. The ideal, however, does not match the reality for many racial minorities who, by choice or by circumstances, remain unmeltable. *See also* Mosaic, Integration.

Merit/Meritocracy   The act of rewarding a person on the basis of credentials or achievement. Three features make a judgment meritocratic: the measurement of achievement against a commonly accepted scale applied to all candidates; assurances that every candidate is measured impersonally on the basis of performance rather than personality; and the selection of examiners on the strength of their excellence and impartiality.

Micro-aggressions   refers to those covert and subtle expressions of racism (from slurs to slights) that superficially look innocuous enough but implicitly embed an affront or invalidation *identified as such* by the micro-aggressed.

Minority group   Any socially defined category of individuals who are perceived as different and inferior and treated accordingly by the majority. References to minorities are about power relations, not about numbers. *See also* Subdominant group, Visible minorities.

Misogyny   Hatred of women.

Modernity   A world view based on the legitimacy of scientific inquiry and rationality as the organizing principle for thought, action, and social life. Modernity is viewed as the triumph of the universal over the particular, citizenship over identity, individual rights over tribal rights, achievement over ascription, and reason over emotion. Additional features include a belief in (1) the attainment of absolute knowledge, given the existence of a knowable world out there that can be accessed through appropriate methodologies and methods, (2) an unfolding of history in the direction of progress, (3) universal categories of experience, (4) explanation through grand theory, and (5) the centrality of reason and science for solving problems and improving society.

Mosaic   A metaphor to describe the ideal arrangement of unity within diversity related to various racial and ethnic groups in Canada. The proposed image is that of a patterned entity comprising disparate and distinct elements arranged into a cohesive and recognizable whole. Proponents admire the positive images associated with the mosaic; detractors denounce it as a gross distortion that neither fits reality nor escapes the conceptual trap of freezing cultural diversity at a particular point in time and space.

Multicultural education   A philosophy of education based on the belief that schooling should not only reflect, reinforce, and advance cultural diversity within the classroom, but also improve students' appreciation for cultural differences. Four key models exist—enrichment, enlightenment, embracive, and empowerment—each of which can be contrasted to the other in terms of underlying assumptions, styles, and proposed outcomes.

Multicultural minorities   Those non-French and non-English immigrants and descendants of immigrants whose priorities and interests differ from the more politicized concerns of Aboriginal peoples. *See also* Racialized, Immigrant, Visible minorities.

Multiculturalism   A belief that a society of many cultures is possible as long as certain rules are in place as a basis for "living together with differences." Reference to multiculturalism may include four ideal-typical scenarios for managing differences: (1) differences are rejected, (2) differences are tolerated, (3) differences are taken into account, or (4) differences are taken seriously. Different levels of meaning can be discerned, including multicultural as a statement of empirical fact; a set of ideals; an official policy; a set of practices; and a critique. *See also* Official Multiculturalism.

Multiversal   Literally refers to the existence of multiple universes. Used sociologically, multiversal implies a complex and fluid world of diverse diversities and a commitment to differently accommodate a diversity-of-diversities.

Nation   A politicized community of "like-minded" people who share a common homeland, language, identity, set of grievances, and cultural and historical symbols. Unlike a *state*, which is essentially a political and administrative system, a *nation* consists of people who believe they are fundamentally different, express a political consciousness as a distinct people, insist on self-determination at social and cultural levels, propose political autonomy on those grounds, and claim to speak the language of nationhood. Both Québécois and Aboriginal peoples prefer to see themselves as "nations" within the framework of Canadian society.

Nationalism   A political/ideological expression of a community of people who, by virtue of shared destiny, common history, common ancestry, and homeland, have the right to call themselves a nation with an attendant right to

claim self-determining autonomy ("self-rule") up to and including independence. *See also* Ethnic nationalism, Civic nationalism.

Nations within   A term normally employed to describe Aboriginal ambitions for self-determination in Canada. The "nations within" concept acknowledges the relative autonomy of Aboriginal peoples but does not advocate outright secession or independence. *See also* Self-government.

Normative racism   Reflects a largely unconscious bias toward others because of prevailing cultural values, beliefs, and norms. *See also* Ideological Racism.

Official language minorities   French-speaking Canadians who live outside Quebec and English-speaking Canadians who reside in Quebec have certain rights that provide them with access to services in their language (where numbers warrant), in addition to rights to exercise control over institutions, such as education.

Official Languages Act   Passage of this Act in 1969/1986 established Canada as an officially bilingual society. The Act ensures bilingual services and workplaces within federal institutions across the country, while protecting the language rights of official-language minorities (French outside Quebec, English in Quebec).

Official Multiculturalism   The transformation of multicultural principles into official policy began with an all-political party agreement in 1971, followed by the entrenchment of multiculturalism in the *Canadian Charter of Rights and Freedoms* in 1982, and enshrinement with the passage of the *Multiculturalism Act* in 1988. As an aspirational blueprint, an official Multiculturalism embraces a commitment to an inclusive and cohesive Canada by integrating migrants and minorities into the existing social framework.

Patriarchy   The notion of society as designed by, for, and about men so that the constitutional order (in terms of core values, key institutions, and distribution of power) reflects, reinforces, and advances male privilege and power.

People of colour   *See* Visible minorities, Multicultural minorities, Racialized minorities.

Pluralism   The belief that culturally different groups can coexist in society and that such a condition is both attainable and socially beneficial. The principles of multiculturalism represent one variant of a pluralist society.

Polite racism   A dislike of others that is indirect because it is coded in euphemistic language.

Politicization   The process by which issues are pulled from the personal or private domain and drawn into the public domain in the competition for valued resources.

Postcolonial social contract   A proposed restructuring of Aboriginal peoples' relationship with Canada. The (neo)colonial assumptions of the past are rejected in favour of a new constitutional arrangement involving the inclusivity principles of partnership, power sharing, meaningful participation, property return, and a commitment to respect, recognition, and restoration.

Postcolonialism   The "post" in postcolonialism is not intended in the sense of "over" or "after." More accurately, it reflects a commitment to challenge the persistent neo-colonialism that governs the foundational principles of a society's constitutional order.

Postethnic   The concept of ethnicity is increasingly framed as dynamic, constructed, and contested ('doing ethnicity' or a kaleidoscope metaphor) rather than something that is stable, deterministic and uniform (a mosaic metaphor).

Postmodern ethnic identity   A kind of ethnic identity based on a dynamic integration of past with the present and the situational. A hybridic notion of "who am I" is constructed that is fluid, contextual, and multiple, without reflecting a sense of contradiction or confusion in the process. Also called "hybridic ethnic identity."

Postmodern(ism)   A discourse that rejects the modernist claim for a unified thought and organized way of thinking about the world from a fixed and objective point of view.

Postmodernism argues that there is no such thing as objective reality with a rational core of meaning in the centre, but only discourses about reality, whose truthfulness reflects social location and power relations. Postmodernism also espouses a mind-dependent world where there is no centre of authority, only different viewpoints where everything is relative and true because nothing is absolutely knowable, and where nothing is neutral or impartial because everything/everyone is located in time and space.

Power   In everyday language, the ability to make others do what they normally wouldn't want to do. Along more systemic lines, power should not be thought of as a thing out there, but as a process inherent to relationships and contexts. The relational nature of power shifts from context to context, suggesting that minorities can wield power in certain situations, although access to institutionalized power (power backed by the coercive authority of the state) remains elusive.

Prejudice   A set of biased and generalized prejudgments of others based on faulty, unfounded, and inflexible generalizations. Rather than being viewed as a purely psychological phenomenon involving an irrational mindset of the ignorant, prejudice should be interpreted in sociological terms, insofar as it originates when the dominant sector invokes negative ideas to justify and entrench its power and privilege.

Primordial explanation   A perspective that explains the staying power of ethnicity by reference to some deep biological yearning (or hard-wiring) that compels people to seek out their "own kind" as a basis for belonging, entitlement, and identity. *See also* Constructivist explanation.

Profiling   *See* Racial profiling.

Protected Persons   *See* Refugee.

Race   Currently defined as a biologically based social construct involving the classification of persons (typology) into hierarchical categories (taxonomy) on the basis of real or imagined characteristics. Race has neither empirical validity nor scientific value; nevertheless, people continue to believe it does and act accordingly with often negative effects, thus reinforcing the sociological axiom that phenomena do not have to be real to be real in their consequences.

Racial profiling Discriminatory actions based on stereotypes and prejudice that unfairly and disproportionately subject members of racialized groups to higher surveillance levels, ostensibly for reasons of security or safety.

Racial typologies Classifications whereby racial groups are evaluated and hierarchically arranged in ascending and descending orders of superiority or inferiority to justify patterns of privilege and power.

Racialization A socially constructed process whereby certain groups are negatively defined (or raced) as different or inferior and subject to differential and unequal treatment because of preconceived notions related to race.

Racialized inequality The embeddedness of race-based (dis)advantages within the institutional framework of society in a way that reflects, reinforces, and advances as normal and necessary the interests and agendas of those with the power to define or control it.

Racialized minorities This term is increasingly preferred over "visible minorities" or "people of colour." It acknowledges how attaching a race label to minorities reflects a socially constructed process rather than a description of reality based on alleged biological traits. Racialization also acknowledges that there is no such thing as race but only individuals who are labelled as such by those with the power to make such labels stick.

Racialized stratification A hierarchical ranking of racial and ethnic minorities in ascending/descending order of superiority/ inferiority based on the criteria of income, education, or social class. Think of Canada as "layered" into "strata" in terms of how different minorities fare in the competition for valued resources, with "whites" on top and groups such as Aboriginal peoples and racialized minorities near the bottom.

Racism Racism refers to a relatively organized set of ideas and ideals (ideology) that asserts or implies natural superiority of one group over another in terms of entitlements and privileges, together with the institutionalized power to put these beliefs into practice in a way that provides advantages for those in control but denies or excludes those who belong to a devalued category.

Reasonable accommodation Institutional adjustments (within limits and without undue hardship) that intend to improve the full and equal participation of those historically excluded.

Refugee Defined by the United Nations as a person who flees his or her country because of a well-grounded fear of persecution based on race, national origins, or religious background. Refugees consist of those whose application for asylum has been granted in-country or have arrived with formal refugee status.

Refugee claimants Unlike convention refugees who are privately sponsored or government selected from UN-defined camps, these asylum seekers arrive unannounced and invoke their right to claim refugee status. Also called "in-Canada refugees" or "inland claimants."

Resource mobilization theory Accounting for ethnicity by acknowledging how like-minded people will mobilize into action groups to improve their competitive edge in the competition for scarce resources.

Reversing discrimination In contrast to reverse discrimination, which argues that special rights for minorities are a kind of discrimination in reverse, reversing discrimination contends that special measures for minority women and men are intended to reverse (remove) the discrimination that historically has denied or excluded them.

Scientific racism The belief that racial capacities between populations (or races) could be measured and evaluated by intelligence tests, especially the IQ (Stanford-Binet) test.

Segregation The process and practice of separating groups on the basis of race or culture. This separation can occur voluntarily or involuntarily, can involve formal or informal measures, and may be interpreted as empowering or disempowering.

Self-determination   *See* Self-determining autonomy.

Self-determining autonomy   As fundamentally autonomous political communities that are sovereign and share sovereignty over the land, Aboriginal peoples claim to have inherent and collective rights to aboriginal models for controlling jurisdictions (or domains) of immediate concern related to land, identity, and political voice. Recourse to self-determining autonomy is not the same as independence; rather, it involves a commitment to restructure the foundational principles of a colonial constitutional order along the lines of a new (postcolonial) social contract.

Self-government   A term that is usually employed within the context of aboriginal demands for aboriginal models of self-determining autonomy. Aboriginal peoples claim that self-government provides the political expression of their demand for control over internal affairs. *See also* Aboriginal self-governance.

Separation   *See* Segregation.

Sexism   A belief in the superiority of men over women. *See also* Androcentrism, Patriarchy.

Situational ethnic identity   *See* Symbolic ethnic identity.

Social Contract   *See* Postcolonial social contract.

Social Darwinism   A doctrine of racial superiority that reworked Darwin's ideas on evolution and applied them to group relations. With its notion of a struggle for survival and survival of the fittest, the world under social Darwinism resembled an arena where populations were locked in competition for scarce resources. Those with the adaptive skills survive and prosper, according to social Darwinists; those without are doomed.

Society-building   The ongoing process by which contemporary societies use policies and programs to create political and moral communities of value and values in the face of internal demands and external pressures. The term "nation-building" may also be used because most states (or societies) are seeking to become more nation-like.

Sovereignty   The exercise of exclusive and final authority over land, peoples, rules, and all legal and political matters within a strictly bounded territory. For some, sovereignty is about borders; for others, especially Aboriginal peoples, it is about establishing a respectful, productive and meaningful relationship with society at large.

Specific treaty claims   The need for reparations involving Crown breaches of existing treaty provisions. *See also* Treaties, Comprehensive claims.

State   A political, legal, and administrative unit that claims to exercise final authority over a specific territory, monopolizes the legitimate use of force to enforce decisions and keep the peace, and is governed by authorities who purport to represent the inhabitants.

Stereotype   A shorthand way of classifying social reality into convenient categories on the basis of common properties. As a generalization, it provides an oversimplification or exaggerated version of the world, reflecting preconceived and unwarranted notions that apply to all members of the devalued group.

Subdominant group   Also called subordinate, subdominant groups stand in an unequal relationship to dominant groups because of differences in power, privilege, and wealth.

Subliminal racism   A subconscious racism involving deeply entrenched prejudices that individuals are unaware of although these biases influence their beliefs and behaviour. In unattended moments, this subconscious racism is masked by the use of principled arguments that endorse the principle of equality but reject the means to achieve it by justifying the inaction.

Substantive equality (equity)   Based on the idea that differences sometimes have to be taken into account for a real equality (i.e., an equality of outcomes). This colour-conscious approach to equality appears to be at variance with colour-blind notions whereby everyone is thought to be equally the same and treated accordingly. *See also* Equity.

Symbolic ethnic identity   (Also called "situational ethnic identity") A process in which an individual retains a cognitive or emotional affiliation with a cultural past while continuing to fully participate in the wider society.

Symbolic interactionism   *See* Interactionism.

Systematic racism   A direct attempt by institutions, employing explicit rules and deliberate practices, to prevent the full and equal participation of minorities.

Systemic discrimination   A biasing process that arises from treating everyone the same, despite a need to take into account their difference-based disadvantages. A systemic discrimination acknowledges how the even and equal application of one-size-fits-all rules or business-as-usual practices of an institution may inadvertently exert a negative effect on certain minorities through no fault of their own. The concept is based on the principle that bias and barriers may be built-in (inherent) and deeply embedded (institutionalized) within the normal functioning of an institutional system, yet appear neutral on the surface or beyond the awareness level of institutional actors.

Systemic racism   *See* Systemic discrimination.

Systemic White Supremacist Society   The concept is not used in the flagrant sense of a caste-like white apartheid system commandeered by right-wing political parties. The expression is employed in the structural sense; that is, it's about acknowledging Canada as structured around the principles and practices of a socially constructed and ideologically loaded system in which (a) founding assumptions and foundational principles embody a commitment to a Euro-white constitutional order (b) the system is designed, organized, and controlled by, for, and about whites; (c) the system reflects, reinforces and advances white

interests as normal, desirable, and acceptable in both overt (systematic) and covert (systemic) ways; and (d) white activities, perspectives, and characteristics are valued as the norm or superior, while other realities are dismissed as inferior, irrelevant or threatening.

Tolerance   A dislike of other practices, but a willingness to put up with these dislikes in the name of public peace or social justice. Tolerance is about a contrived indifference rather than acceptance.

Transnational ethnic identity   An ethnic identity reflecting the way in which globalization has changed the conventional notions of belonging that linked a person's identity with a particular place. Rather than treating homeland country as an either–or dichotomy, a transnational ethnic identity captures new notions of multiple attachments across diverse homelands.

Treaties   Transactions between the Crown and Aboriginal peoples involving an exchange of rights, duties, and obligations. Treaties of alliance and friendship exist; nevertheless, most treaties involve a transaction in which Aboriginal peoples surrender large swathes of land in exchange for goods, entitlements, and services in perpetuity, including rights of use of unoccupied or underutilized Crown land.

Universal citizenship   The idea that everyone in Canada belongs in the same way because everybody possesses identical rights, duties, and obligations.

Visible minorities   Used to designate those who are non-white, non-Aboriginal, non-Caucasian in origin or identity (regardless of place of birth), and those who are defined as such by the government or have agreed to this label for purposes of employment equity or census taking. This term is used interchangeably with "people of colour" or, increasingly, "racialized minorities."

White Paper   A bill tabled by the Liberal government in 1969 to abolish Aboriginal peoples as a distinct status group in Canada. An exercise in assimilation behind a smokescreen of integration, the bill proposed to repeal the *Indian Act*, dismantle the Department of Indian Affairs, and mothball the reserves by allocating land to Aboriginal peoples on an individual basis to do as they want. Aboriginal leaders strongly resisted the White Paper, a move that many see as the catalyst that mobilized Aboriginal peoples into action for redefining their relational status in Canada.

White Supremacist Society   A society that is designed, informed, and organized by, for, and about the belief that whites are superior and deserve preferential access to power and privilege. To be sure, there are those perceived as whites who face prejudice and discrimination because of their ethnicity or geographical origins (for example, southern Europeans). *See also* Systemic white supremacy society.

References

Abel, Allen. 2001. "P is for Prejudice." *Saturday Night*, June 23/30.

Abele, Frances. 2004. *Urgent Need, Serious Opportunity: Towards a New Social Model for Canada's Aboriginal Peoples*. CPRN Social Architecture Papers. Research Paper F/39. April.

Abele, Frances, Russell LaPointe, and Michael Prince. 2005. "Symbolism, Surfacing, Succession, and Substance: Martin's Aboriginal Policy Style." In *How Ottawa Spends*. B. Doern, ed., 99–121. Montreal/Kingston: McGill-Queen's University Press.

Abella, R. S. 1984. *Report of the Royal Commission on Equality in Employment*. Ottawa: Minister of Supply and Services.

Abella, Manolo. 2006. Policies and Best Practices for Management of Temporary Workers. International Symposium on International Migration and Development. United Nations. Turin, Italy. June.

Aboriginal Affairs and Northern Development Canada (AANDC). 2013a. Aboriginal Demographics. From the 2011 National Household Survey. May.

Aboriginal Affairs and Northern Development Canada (AANDC). 2013b. Report on Plans and Priorities: 2013–14 Estimates. Author.

Aboriginal Affairs and Northern Development Canada (AANDC). 2014. Urban Aboriginal Peoples. 1 December.

Aboriginal Affairs and Northern Development Canada (AANDC). 2015. Comprehensive Claims. Retrieved July 13, 2015 (www.aadnc-aandc. gc.ca/eng/1100100030577/1100100030578).

Aboriginal Institutes' Consortium. 2005. *Aboriginal Institutions of Higher Education: A Struggle for the Education of Aboriginal Students, Control of Indigenous Knowledge and Recognition of Aboriginal Institutions: An Examination of Government Policy*.

Toronto: Canadian Race Relations Foundation.

Abraham, M. E. S., Chow, L. Maratou-Alipranti, and E. Tastsoglou. 2010. *Contours of Citizenship: Women, Diversity, and the Practices of Citizenship*. Burlington, VT: Ashgate Publishing.

Abrams, Laura, and Jene Moio. 2009. Critical Race Theory and the Cultural Competence Dilemma in Social Work Education. *Journal of Social Work Education* 45(2):245–261.

Abu-Laban, Yasmeen. 1999. "The Politics of Race, Ethnicity, and Immigration," in *Canadian Politics*. J. Bickerton and A.-G. Gagnon, eds. Peterborough, ON: Broadview Press.

Abu-Laban, Yasmeen. 2015. Transforming Citizenship: Power, Policy, and Identity. *Canadian Ethnic Studies* 47(1):1–10.

Abu-Laban Y., and B. Abu-Laban. 2007. "Reasonable Accommodation in a Global Village." *Policy Options* (September), 28–33.

Abu-Laban, Y., T. Derwing, and M. Mulder. 2004. "Why Canada Should Accept Refugees." *Canadian Issues* (March), 33–36.

Abu-Laban, Yasmeen, and Christina Gabriel. 2002. *Selling Diversity: Immigration, Multiculturalism, Employment Equity, and Globalization*. Peterborough, ON: Broadview.

ACS/Environics. 2002. "Public Opinion Poll." *Canadian Issues* (February), 4–5.

ACS/Leger Marketing, 2015. History. Association for Canadian Studies Newsletter. October.

Adams, Howard. 1999. *Tortured People: The Politics of Colonization*. Penticton, BC: Theytus.

Adams, Michael. 1997. *Sex in the Snow: Canadian Social Values at the End of the Millennium*. Toronto: Penguin.

Adams, Michael. 2007. *Unlikely Utopia.* Toronto: Penguin.

Adelman, Howard. 2004. "Introduction." *Canadian Issues* (March), 3–4.

Adorno, T. S., E. Frenkel-Brunswick, D. J. Levinson, and R. N. Sanford. 1950. *The Authoritarian Personality.* New York: Harper and Row.

African Canadian Legal Clinic. 2006. *Bill C-27 and the Issue of Female Genital Mutilation.* Retrieved online.

Agnew, Vijay, ed. 2007. *Interrogating Race and Racism.* Toronto: University of Toronto Press.

Agocs, Carol, and Monica Boyd. 1993. "Ethnicity and Ethnic Inequality," in *Social Inequality in Canada* (2ⁿᵈ ed.). J. Curtis et al., eds., 330–352. Toronto: Prentice-Hall.

Agocs, Carol, and Harish Jain. 2010. Systemic Racism in Employment in Canada: Diagnosing Systemic Racism in Organizational Culture. *Directions (Canadian Race Relations Foundation)*, 5(2):149–158.

Agrell, Siri. 2010. The Face of Ethnic Media. *Globe and Mail*, 18 November.

Aguirre, Adalberto Jr., and Jonathan Turner. 1995. *American Ethnicity: The Dynamics and Consequences of Discrimination.* New York: McGraw Hill.

Akdenizli, Banu. 2008. *Democracy in the Age of New Media: A Report on the Media and the Immigration Debate.* Los Angeles: The Brookings Institute. University of Southern California, Norman Lear Centre.

Alaggia, Ramona, Cheryl Regehr, and Giselle Rishchynski. 2009. Intimate Partner Violence and Immigration Laws in Canada: How Far Have We Come? *International Journal of Law and Psychiatry* 32(6):335–341.

Alba, Richard, and Nancy Foner. 2015. Integration's Challenge and Opportunities in the Wealthy West. *Journal of Ethnic and Migration Studies.* Retrieved November 17, 2015 (www.tandfonline.com/doi/full/10.1080/1369183X.2015.1083770).

Alboim, Naomi. 2009. *Adjusting the Balance: Fixing Canada's Economic Immigration Policies.* Toronto: Maytree Foundation.

Alboim, Naomi, and Elizabeth McIsaac. 2007. "Making the Connections: Ottawa's Role in Immigrant Employment." Retrieved November 16, 2015 (http://irpp.org/research-studies/choices-vol13-no3/).

Alboim, Naomi, and Karen Cohl. 2012. "Shaping the Future: Canada's Rapidly Changing Immigration Policies." Maytree Foundation. October.

Alcantara, Christopher. 2013. Negotiating the Deal. Comprehensive Land Claims Agreements in Canada. University of Toronto Press.

Alcantara, Christopher, and Michael Morden. 2015. Aboriginal Title One Year After Tsilhqot'in. *Policy Options.* May.

Alcantara, Christopher, and Greg Whitfield. 2010. Aboriginal Self-Government through Constitutional Design: A Survey of Fourteen Aboriginal Constitutions. *Journal of Canadian Studies* 44(2):122–145.

Alcoba, Natalie. 2007. "Culture Not Behind Girl's Death, Brother." *National Post*, 13 December.

Alexander, Chris. 2014. "Message from the Minister of Citizenship and Immigration." *2014 Annual Report to Parliament on Immigration.* Ottawa: Government of Canada.

Alexander, Michelle. 2012. *The New Jim Crow: Mass Incarceration in the Age of Colorblindness.* New York: New Press.

Alfred, Taiaiake. 1999. *Peace, Power, and Righteousness: An Indigenous Manifesto.* Toronto: Oxford University Press.

Alfred, Taiaiake. 2001. "Mexico Laps Canada in Fight for Rights Recognition." *Windspeaker*, April.

Alfred, Taiaiake. 2005. *Wasase: Indigenous Pathways to Action and Freedom.* Peterborough, ON: Broadview.

Alfred, Taiaiake, 2009. "First Nation Perspectives on Political Identity." Published by the *First Nation Citizenship Research & Policy Series: Building Toward Change.* June.

Alfred, Taiaiake, 2011. Foreword, In *Unsettling the Settler Within: Indian Residential Schools, Truth Telling, and Reconciliation in Canada.* Paulette Regan. Vancouver: UBC Press.

Alfred, Taiaiake, and Jeff Corntassel. 2005. Being Indigenous: Resurgences Against Contemporary Colonialisms. *Government and Opposition* 40(4):597–614.

Alfred, Taiaiake, and Lana Lowe. 2005. "Warrior Societies in Contemporary Indigenous Communities". *Ipperwash Inquiry.*

Alfred, Taiaiake, and Lana Lowe. 2006. What are Warrior Societies? *New Socialist* 58:4–7.

Al-Krenawi, Alean, and John R Graham, eds. 2003. *Multicultural Social Work in Canada.* Toronto: Oxford University Press.

Alladin, Ibrahim. 1996. "Racism in Schools: Race, Ethnicity, and Schooling in Canada," in *Racism in Canadian Schools.* I. Alladin, ed., 4–21. Toronto: Harcourt Brace.

Allan, Mary, 2015. *Police-Reported Hate Crime in Canada*. Canadian Centre for Justice Statistics, Statistics Canada. 9 June.

Allan, B., and J. Smylie. 2015. *First Peoples, Second Class Treatment: The Role of Racism in the Health and Well-Being of Indigenous Peoples in Canada*. Toronto: The Wellesley Institute.

Allegritti, Inta. 2010. "Multiculturalism and Cultural Citizenship," in *Cultural Citizenhip and the Challenges of Globalization*. W. Ommundsen et al., eds. Cresskill, NJ: Hampton.

Allen, Robert. 1993. *His Majesty's Indian Allies: British Indian Policy in the Defence of Canada, 1774–1815*. Toronto: Dundurn Press.

Alliance of Civilizations. 2006. *Research Base for the High-Level Group Report: Analysis on Media*. New York: United Nations.

Allport, Gordon. 1954. *The Nature of Prejudice*. New York: Doubleday and Company.

Alston-O'Connor, Emily. 2010. The Sixties Scoop: Implications for Social Workers and Social Work Education. *Critical Social Work* 11(1): 53–61.

Alsultany, Evelyn. 2012. Arabs and Muslims in the Media: Race and Representation After *9/11*. New York: NY University Press.

Alumkal, Antony W. 2008. "Analyzing Race in Asian American Congregations." *Sociology of Religion* 69(2):151–168.

Alvarez, Alvin N., and Linda P. Juang. 2010. Filipino Americans and Racism: A Multi Mediation Model of Coping. *Journal of Counseling Psychology* 57(2):167–178.

Amarasingam, Amarnath. 2008. "Religion and Ethnicity among Sri Lankan Tamil Youth in Ontario." *Canadian Ethnic Studies* 40(2):149–169.

American Psychological Association (APA). 2009. "Q&A with Psychologists on Racial Attitudes—in Honor of Black History Month." 10 February.

Amnesty International. 2004. *Stolen Sisters: Discrimination and Violence Against Indigenous Women in Canada*. London, UK: Author.

Amnesty International. 2009. *Refugees in Canada: History of Refugees*. Available online at www.amnesty.ca.

Amnesty International. 2014. "Concerns Regarding the Proposed Changes to the Canadian Citizenship Act." Amnesty International Canada. 9 June.

Anand, Raj. 2014. Minority Rights Issue Shouldn't be Resolved by Polling, Outcries. *Toronto Star,* 19 January.

Anaya, James. 2013. Report to the Human Rights Council, 15 October.

Anaya, James. 2014. The Situation of of Indigenous Peoples in Canada. Report of the Special Rapporteur on the Rights of Indigenous Peoples. Human Rights Council. 27th Session. United Nations General Assembly.

Andersen, Chris. 2014. *Metis: Race, Recognition, and the Struggle for Indigenous Peoplehood*. Vancouver: UBC Press.

Andersen, Margaret L., and Patricia Hill Collins, eds. 2007. *Race, Class, and Gender: An Anthology* (6th ed.). Belmont, CA: Wadsworth.

Anderson, Kay. 2007. *Race and the Crisis of Humanism*. New York: Routledge.

Anderson, Kim. 2000. *A Recognition of Being: Reconstructing Native Womanhood*. Toronto: Sumac Press.

Anderson, Kim. 2009. "Leading by Action: Female Chiefs and the Political Landscape," in *Restoring the Balance*, G Valaskakis et al., eds., 99–124. Winnipeg: University of Manitoba Press.

Anderssen, Erin, and Michael Valpy. 2003. "Face the Nation: Canada Remade." *Globe and Mail*, 6 June.

Andrew, Caroline. 2004. "Introduction." *Our Diverse Cities* 1(1):8–11.

Ang, Ien. 2010. "Between the National and the Transnational: Multiculturalism in a Globalising World." Keynote address at the Biennial Malaysian Studies Conference. Penang. March

Ang, Ien. 2011. "Ethnicities and Our Precarious Future." Sage Journals, *Ethnicities* 11(1):37–41 (http://etn.sagepub.com).

Angus, Charlie. 2011. "Attawapiskat's Impact: Canada's Katrina Moment." 2 December Available online at www.huffingtonpost.ca.

Angus, Charlie. 2014. "Letter to Bernard Valcourt, Minister for Aboriginal Affairs." 2 June.

Angus, Charlie. 2015. *Children of the Broken Treaty*. Regina SA: University of Regina Press.

Angus, Ian. 2002. "Cultural Plurality and Democracy." *International Journal of Canadian Studies* 25.

Angus Reid Group Inc. 1991. *Multiculturalism and Canadians: Attitude Study, 1991*. National survey report submitted to the Department of Multiculturalism and Citizenship.

Angus Reid. 2010. "More Canadians Questioning the Benefits of Immigration. Survey Poll." 14 September.

Anisef, Paul, and Kenise Murphy Kilbride, eds. 2003. *Managing Two Worlds: The Experiences and Concerns of Immigrant Youth in Ontario.* Toronto: Canadian Scholars Press.

Ansley, Bruce. 2004. "Stealing a March." *Listener NZ*, 15 May.

Applebaum, Barbara. 2010. *Being White, Being Good.* Toronto: Lexington Books.

Arbatli, C. E., Q. H. Ashraf, and O. Galor. 2015. *The Nature of Conflict.* Working Paper 21079. Cambridge MA: National Bureau of Economic Research. April.

Asch, Michael. 1997. *Aboriginal and Treaty Rights in Canada: Essays on Law, Equality, and Respect for Differences.* Vancouver: UBC Press.

Ashini, Napes. 2002. "Niassinam: Cariboo and F16s," in *Nation to Nation.* J. Bird et al., eds., 74–81. Toronto: Irwin.

Assante, Molefi Kete. 2003. *Erasing Racism: The Survival of the American Nation.* Amherst, NY: Prometheus Books.

Atanackovic, Jelena, and Ivy Lyn Bourgeault. 2013. "The Economic and Social Integration of Immigrant Live-In Caregivers in Canada." Metropolis Conference, Ottawa, 14 March.

Auclair, Gregory, and Jeanne Batalova. 2013. "Green Card Holders and Legal Immigrants to the United States." Migration Policy Institute. 20 November.

Augoustinos, M., and K. J. Reynolds, eds. 2001. *Understanding Prejudice, Racism and Social Conflict.* Thousand Oaks CA: Sage.

Aulakh, Raveena. 2014. "Grassy Narrows Denied Assessment on Clear-Cutting." *Toronto Star*, 30 December.

Austin, Carly, and Harald Bauder. 2012. Jus Domicile: A Pathway to Citizenship for Temporary Foreign Workers. In *Immigration and Settlement.* H Bauder, ed., 21–36. Toronto: Canadian Scholars Press.

Avery, Donald H. 1995. *Reluctant Hosts: Canada's Response to Immigrant Workers, 1896–1994.* Toronto: McClelland & Stewart.

Aydemir, A., and M. Skuterud. 2004. "Explaining the Deteriorating Entry Earnings of Canada's Immigrant Cohorts: 1996–2000." Family and Labour Studies Division, Statistics Canada. 11F0019MIE. No. 225.

Ayers, Tom. 2015. "68 Years After Desmond's Stand, Racism 'Definitely Part' of Society." *Halifax Chronicle Herald*, 15 February.

Aylward, Carol A. 2009. Intersectionality: Crossing the Theoretical and Praxis Divide. *Journal of Critical Race Inquiry* 1(1):1–22.

Baber, Zaheer. 2010. Racism without Races: Reflections on Racialization and Racial Projects. *Sociology Compass* 4(4):241–248.

Back, Les. 2002. "The New Technologies of Racism," in *A Companion to Race and Ethnic Studies.* D. T. Goldberg and J. Solomos, eds., 365–378. Malden, MA: Blackwell.

Backhouse, Constance. 1999. *Colour-Coded: A Legal History of Racism in Canada: 1900–1950.* Toronto: University of Toronto Press.

Bakan, Abigail B., and Enakshi Dua, eds. 2014. *Theorizing Anti-Racism: Linkages in Marxism and Critical Race Theories.* University of Toronto Press.

Bakanic, Von. 2009. *Prejudice: Attitudes about Race, Class, and Gender.* Upper Saddle River, NJ: Pearson Prentice Hall.

Baker, Lauren, Michael Dove, Dana Graef, Alder Keleman, David Kneas, Sarah Osterhoudt, and Jeffrey Stoike. 2013. Whose Diversity Counts? The Politics and Paradoxes of Modern Diversity. *Sustainability* 5:2495–2518.

Baldwin, Andrew, Laura Cameron, and Audrey Kobayashi, eds. 2011. *Rethinking the Great White North: Race, Nature, and the Historical Geographies of Whiteness in Canada.* Vancouver: UBC Press

Banaji, Mahazir. 2003. "Colour Blind?" *This Magazine*, January/February.

Banaji, M., and A. G. Greenwald. 2013. *Blindspot: Hidden Biases of Good People.* Delacorte Press.

Bangash, Sabina Ahmed. 2012. "The Silent Voice of the Minority: Immigrant Women in American Media." Global Press Institute. 5 February.

Bannerji, Himani. 2000. *The Dark Side of the Nation.* Toronto: Canadian Scholars' Press.

Banting, Keith, Thomas J. Courchene, and Leslie Seidle, eds. 2007. *Belonging? Diversity, Recognition, and Shared Citizenship in Canada.* Montreal: Institute for Research on Public Policy.

Banton, Michael. 1987. *Racial Theories.* Cambridge: Cambridge University Press.

Banton, Michael. 2000. "Racism Today." *Ethnic and Racial Studies* 22(3):606–615.

Banton, Michael. 2005. "Historical and Contemporary Modes of Racialization," in *Racialization*. K. Murji and J. Solomos, eds. Oxford, UK: Oxford University Press.

Barbee, Evelyn L. 1993. Racism in U.S. Nursing. *Medical Anthropology Quarterly* 7(4):346–362.

Barelli, Mauro. 2012. Free, Prior, and Informed Consent in the Aftermath of the UN Declaration on the Rights of Indigenous Peoples: Developments and Challenges Ahead. *International Journal of Human Rights* 16(1):1–24.

Barker, Adam J. 2009. "The Contemporary Reality of Canadian Imperialism: Settler Colonialism and the Hybrid Colonial State." *American Indian Quarterly* 33(3):325–351.

Barker, Adam J. 2012. Already Occupied: Indigenous Peoples, Settler Colonialism, and the Occupy Movements in North America. *Social Movement Studies* 11(3-4):327–334.

Barker, Adam, J. 2015. A Direct Act of Resurgence, A Direct Act of Sovereignty: Reflections on Idle No More, Indigenous Activism, and Canadian Settler Colonialism. *Globalizations* 12(1):43–65.

Barker, M. 1981. *New Racism.* London: Junction Books.

Barkun, Michael. 1994. *Religion and the Racist Right: The Origins of the Christian Identity Movement.* Chapel Hill, NC: University of North Carolina Press.

Barlow, Andrew L. 2012. *Between Fear and Hope: Globalization and Race in the United States.* New York: Rowman & Littlefield, 2003.

Barnett, Laura, Julia Nicol, and Julian Walker. 2012. "An Examination of the Duty to Accommodate in the Canadian Human Rights Context." Background Paper, Publication No 2012-01-E. Library of Parliament, Ottawa, 10 January.

Barnsley, Paul. 1999. "Cree Chief Slams Gathering Strength." *Windspeaker.*

Barrett, Stanley R. 1987. *Is God a Racist? The Right Wing in Canada.* Toronto: University of Toronto Press.

Barrett, Stanley R. 2007. "The Role of Violence in the Far Right in Canada," in *Racial, Ethnic, and Homophobic Violence.* M. Prum et al., eds., 73–82. New York: Routledge-Cavendish.

Barth, Frederick. 1969. *Ethnic Groups and Boundaries.* Boston: Little, Brown.

Basok, Tanya, and Marshal Bastable. 2009. "Knock, Knock, Knockin' on Heaven's Door": Immigrants and the Guardians of Privilege in Canada. *Labour/Le Travail, 63,* 207–219.

Basok, Tanya, and Suzan Ilcan. 2013. *Issues in Social Justice: Citizenship and Transnational Struggles.* Toronto: Oxford University Press.

Bastia, Tanja. 2013. *Migration and Inequality.* New York: Routledge.

Baubock, Rainer. 2005. "If You Say Multiculturalism Is the Wrong Answer, Then What Was the Question You Asked?" *Canadian Diversity* 4(1):90–94.

Bauder, Harald. 2003. "Equality, Justice, and the Problem of International Borders: The Case of Canadian Immigration Regulation." *ACME* 2(2):167–182.

Bauder, Harald. 2008. "Dialectics of Humanitarian Immigration and National Identity in Canadian Public Discourse." *Refuge* 25(1):84–94.

Bauder, Harald. 2011. *Immigration Dialectic: Imagining Community, Economy, and Nation.* University of Toronto Press.

Bauder, Harald, ed. 2012. *Immigration and Settlement: Challenges, Experiences, and Opportunities.* Toronto: Canadian Scholars Press.

Bauder, Harald, and Christian Matthies. 2015. *Migration Policy and Practice: Intervention and Solutions.* New York, NY: Palgrave.

Bauder, Harald, and John Shields. 2015. *Immigrant Experiences in North America: Understanding Settlement and Integration.* Toronto: Canadian Scholars Press.

Bauer, William. 1994. "How the System Works." *The Globe and Mail*, 12 November.

Bauer, William. 2009. "Saving Canada's Dysfunctional Refugee System." *National Post*, 12 May.

Bauerlein, Mark. 2001. "Social Constructionism: Philosophy for the Academic Workplace." *Partisan Review* 68(2):228–241.

Bauman, Zygmunt. 2011. *Culture in a Liquid Modern World.* London: Polity.

BC News. 2014. "New Agreements Confirm Benefits of Nisga'a Self-Government." 31 July.

Beach, Charles M. 2008. Canada's Aging Workforce: Participation, Productivity and Living Standards. Bank of Canada. A Festschrift in Honour of David Dodge. November.

Beach, Charles, M. Alan, G. Green, and Jeffrey G. Reitz, eds. 2003. *Canadian Immigration Policy for the 21ˢᵗ Century.* Kingston, ON: John Deutsch Institute for the Study of Economic Policy, Queen's University.

Beardsley, Keith. 2011. "Put Attawapiskat's People First, and Politics Second." *Huff Post Politics.* Canada. December 8. Available online at www.huffingtonpost.ca.

Beare, Margaret. 2003. "Policing with a National Security Agenda." Commissioned by the Department of Canadian Heritage for the National Forum on Policing in a Multicultural Society.

Beaton, Danny. 2013. "Mohawk Community Advised to Boil Water For Over Five Years by Canadian Government." *First Nations Drum.* September.

Beaujot, Roderic P. 1999. "Immigration and Demographic Structures," in *Immigrant Canada.* S. Halli and L. Driedger, eds. Toronto: University of Toronto Press.

Behrens, G. 1994. "Love, Hate, and Nationalism." *Time,* 21 March.

Belanger, Yale, ed. 2008. *Aboriginal Self-Government in Canada* (3ʳᵈ ed.). Saskatoon: Purich.

Belkhodja, Chedly. 2014. Ethnic Identity Formation and Change in Canada. An Introduction. *Canadian Ethnic Studies* 46(2):1–3.

Belkhodja, Chedly, John Biles, Ian Donaldson, and Jennifer Hyndman. 2006. Introduction. Multicultural Futures: Challenges and Solutions? *Canadian Ethnic Studies* 38(3): ii–v.

Bell, Catherine. 1997. "Métis Constitutional Rights in Section 35(1)." *Alberta Law Review* 36(1):180–204.

Bell, Derrick A. 2006. "Foreword: The Perils of Racial Prophecy," in *Images of Color, Images of Crime: Readings* (3ʳᵈ ed.). Coramae R. Mann, Marjorie S. Zatz, and Nancy Rodriguez, eds. Cary, NC: Roxbury Publishing Company.

Bell-Fialkoff, Andrew. 1993. "Ethnic Conflict." *The World and I* (July), 465–477.

Bem, Sandra Lipsitz. 1994. "In a Male-Centered World, Female Differences Are Transformed into Female Disadvantages." *Chronicle of Higher Education,* 17 August, B1–2.

Benjamin, Akua, David Este, Carl James, Bethan Lloyd, Wanda Thomas Bernard and Tana Turner. 2010. *Race and Well-Being. The Lives, Hopes, and Activism of African Canadians.* Halifax: Fernwood.

Bern, John, and Susan Dodds. 2000. "On the Plurality of Interests: Aboriginal Self-Government and Land Rights," in *Political Theory and the Rights of Indigenous Peoples.* D. Ivison et al., eds., 163–182. Oakleigh, Australia: Cambridge University Press.

Berry, Brent and Eduardo Bonilla-Silva. 2007. 'They should hire the one with the best score.' White Sensitivity to Qualification Differences in Affirmative Action Hiring Decisions. *Ethnic and Racial Studies* 31:215–242.

Berry, John. 2006. "Mutual Attitudes among Immigrants and Ethnocultural Groups in Canada." *International Journal of Intercultural Relations* 30:719–734.

Berry, John. 2014. Multiculturalism: Psychological Perspectives. In *The Multiculturalism Question: Debating Identity in 21ˢᵗ-Century Canada.* Jack Jedwab, ed. 225–240. Queen's Policy Studies Series. School of Policy Studies, Queen's University. Montreal/Kingston: McGill-Queen's University Press.

Berry, John W., Rudolph Kalin, and Donald M. Taylor. 1977. *Multiculturalism and Ethnic Attitudes in Canada.* Ottawa: Ministry of Supply and Services in Canada.

Better, Shirley. 2007. Institutional Racism (2ⁿᵈ ed) Rowman & Littlefield.

Bevelander, Pieter, and Raymond Taras. 2012. The Twilight of Multiculturalism? Findings From Across Europe. In *Challenging Multiculturalism: European Models of Diversity.* R. Taras, ed., 3–21. Edinburgh University Press.

Bhabha, Homi K. 1998. The White Stuff. *Artforum International* 36(9).

Bharucha, R. 2000. *The Politics of Cultural Practice: Thinking through Theatre in an Age of Globalization.* Hanover, NH: University Press of New England.

Bhavnani, R., H. S. Mirza, and V. Meetoo. 2005. *Tackling the Roots of Racism: Lessons for Success.* Bristol, UK: Joseph Rountree Foundation and Polity Press.

Bibby, Reginald W. 1990. *Mosaic Madness: The Potential and Poverty of Canadian Life.* Toronto: Stoddart.

Bickerton, J., and A.-G. Gagnon, eds. 2004. *Canadian Politics.* Peterborough, ON: Broadview.

Biddiss, Michael D., ed. 1979. *Images of Race.* New York: Holmes and Meier.

Biles, John. 2002. "Everyone's a Critic." *Canadian Issues* (February), 35–38.

Biles, John, and Meyer Burstein. 2003. "Immigration: Economics and More." *Canadian Issues* (April), 13–15.

Biles, John, and Paul Spoonley. 2007. "Introduction: National Identity: What Can It Tell Us about Inclusion and Exclusion?" *National Identities* 9(3):191–195.

Biles, John, Erin Tolley, and Humera Ibrahim. 2005. "Does Canada Have a Multicultural Future?" *Canadian Diversity* 4(1):23–28.

Binder, Leonard, ed. 1999. *Ethnic Conflict and International Politics in the Middle East.* Florida: University Press of Florida.

Birch, Kean. 2015. Neoliberalism: The Whys and the Wherefores . . . and Future Directions. *Sociology Compass* 9(7):571–584.

Bird, John, Lorraine Land, and Murray Macadam. 2002. *Nation to Nation: Aboriginal Sovereignty and the Future of Canada* (2nd ed.). Toronto: Irwin.

Bishop, Anne. 2005. *Beyond Token Change: Breaking the Cycle of Oppression in Institutions.* Halifax: Fernwood.

Bissett, James. 2008. "Demography Is Destiny: Toward a Canada First Immigration Policy." Canadian Centre for Policy Studies. Retrieved November 16, 2015 (http://www.meigheninstitute. org/documents/Demography_is_Destiny.pdf).

Bissett, James. 2009. "The Current State of Canadian Immigration Policy," in *The Effects of Mass Immigration on Canadian Living Standards and Society.* Herbert Grubel, ed., 3–38. Calgary: Fraser Institute.

Bissett, James. 2010. *Abusing Canada's Generosity and Ignoring Genuine Refugees.* Frontier Centre for Public Policy. Policy Series No 96. October.

Bissoondath, Neil. 1993. "A Question of Belonging: Multiculturalism and Citizenship," in *Belonging: The Meaning and Future of Canadian Citizenship.* William Kaplan, ed. Montreal/Kingston/: McGill-Queen's University Press.

Bissoondath, Neil. 1994. *Selling Illusions: The Cult of Multiculturalism.* Toronto: Stoddart.

Black, Debra. 2012. Refugee Trend Called "Disturbing." *Toronto Star,* 2 November.

Black, Errol. 2011. Fast Facts: "Mean Streets" Society Coming. Canadian Centre for Policy Alternatives. 19 May.

Black, Mary, K. Basile, M. J. Breiding, S. G. Smith, M. L. Walters, M. T. Merrick, J. Chen, and M. R. Stevens. 2011. "National Intimate Partner and Sexual Violence Survey: Summary Report." Atlanta: National Center for Injury Prevention and Control, Centers for Disease Control and Prevention.

Blackwell, Tom. 2000. "Judge Rules Métis Don't Need License to Hunt in Ontario." *National Post,* 21 January.

Blackwell, Tom. 2004. "Ontario Cracks Down on Migrant Sponsors." *National Post,* 26 November.

Blank, Rebecca M., Marilyn Dabady, and Constance Citro, eds. 2004. *Measuring Racial Discrimination.* Washington, DC: National Academies Press.

Blaser, Mario, Ravi de Costa, Deborah McGregor, and William D. Coleman, eds. 2011. *Indigenous Peoples and Autonomy: Insights for a Global Age.* Vancouver: UBC Press.

Blatchford, Christie. 2011. *Helpless: Caledonia's Nightmare of Fear and Anarchy and How the Law Failed All of Us.* Toronto: Anchor Books.

Blauner, Rob. 1972. *Racial Oppression in America.* New York: HarperCollins.

Blauner, Rob. 1994. "Talking Past Each Other: Black and White Languages," in *Race and Ethnic Conflicts.* Fred L. Pincus and Howard J. Ehrlich, eds., 18–28. Boulder, CO: Westview Press.

Blaut, James M. 1992. "The Theory of Cultural Racism." *Antipode* 23:289–299.

Blee, Kathleen, and Kimberly Creasap. 2010. Conservative and Right Wing Movements. *Annual Review of Sociology* 36:269–286.

Block, Sheila. 2010. "How Do Race and Gender Factor into Income Inequality?" *Canadian Centre for Policy Alternatives,* 2 June.

Block, Sheila. 2013. "Rising Inequality, Declining Health: New Report." Wellesley Institute: Toronto.

Block, Sheila, and Grace-Edward Galabuzi. 2011. "Canada's Color-Coded Labour Market: The Gap for Racialized Workers." *Canadian Centre for Policy Alternatives,* March.

Blodorn, Alison and Laurie T. O'Brien. 2011. Perceptions of Racism in Hurricane Katrina-Related Events: Implications for Collective Guilt and Mental Health Among White Americans. *Analysis of Social Issues and Public Policy* 11(1):127–140.

Bloemraad, Irene. 2006. *Becoming a Citizen: Incorporating Refugees and Immigrants in the United States and Canada.* Berkeley, CA: University of California Press.

Bloemraad, Irene. 2007. "Citizenship and Pluralism: Multiculturalism in a World of Global Migration," in *Citizenship and Immigrant Incorporation.* G. Yurdakul and M. Bodemann, eds., 57–74. New York: Palgrave Macmillan.

Bloemraad, Irene. 2014. Commentary. In *Controlling Immigration: A Global Perspective* (3rd ed). J. Hollifield, P. L. Martin, and P. Orrenius, eds., 117–122. Stanford, CA: Stanford University Press.

Bloemraad, Irene. 2015. Theorizing and Analyzing Citizenship in Multicultural Societies. *The Sociological Quarterly* 56(4):591–606.

Blommaert, Jan. 2012. Citizenship, Language & Superdiversity: Towards Complexity. Urban Language & Literacies Paper No 95.

Bloomberg Business. 2014. "Germany Top Migration Land after U.S. in new OECD Ranking." By Alex Webb. 20 May.

Blumer, Herbert, and Troy Duster. 1980. "Theories of Race and Social Action," in *Sociological Theories: Race and Colonialism.* UNESCO ed. Paris. 211–238.

BMO Report. 2014. The Country's 6.7 Million New Canadians Face Unique Challenges—Financial and Cultural. Toronto. 1 October.

Bolaria, B. Singh, and Peter S. Li. 1988. *Racial Oppression in Canada* (2nd ed.). Toronto: Garamond.

Boldt, Edward. 1993. *Surviving as Indians: The Challenges of Self-Government.* Toronto: University of Toronto Press.

Bonilla-Silva, Eduardo. 1997. Rethinking Racism: Toward a Structural Interpretation. *American Sociological Review* 62(3):465–480.

Bonilla-Silva, Eduardo. 2015. More than Prejudice: Restatement, Reflections, and New Directions in Critical Race Theory. *Sociology of Race and Ethnicity* 1(1):75–89.

Bonnett, Alastair. 2000. *Anti-racism.* London: Routledge.

Borrows, John, and Leonard Rotman. 1997. "The Sui Generis Nature of Aboriginal Rights: Does It Make a Difference?" *Alberta Law Review* 36:9–45.

Bosniak, Linda. 2000. "Citizenship Denationalized." *Indiana Journal of Global Legal Studies* 7(2):447–509.

Boston, Jonathon. 2005. "The Policy Implications of Diversity." Paper presented to the NZ Diversity Forum, at Te Papa Museum, Wellington, August 23rd.

Bouchard, Gerard, and Charles Taylor. 2008. "Building the Future: A Time for Reconciliation." Abridged Report of the Commission for Reasonable Accommodation of Religious and Cultural Minorities. Quebec City: Government of Quebec.

Bourdieu, Pierre. 1991. *Language and Symbolic Power.* Harvard University Press.

Boyd, Monica. 2006. "Social Mobility or Social Inheritance. Unpacking Immigrant Offspring Success." Paper presented at the Annual Meetings of the Canadian Association of Sociology and Anthropology, York University. June 1–3.

Boyd, Monica. 2013. Changing Migration Management. *Diplomat Magazine,* September, 1–5.

Boyd, Monica, and Deanna Pikkov. 2008. "Finding a Place in Stratified Structures: Migrant Women in North America," in *New Perspectives on Gender and Migration.* N. Piper, ed., 19–58. New York: Routledge.

Boyd, Monica, and Michael Vickers. 2000. "100 Years of Immigration in Canada." *Canadian Social Trends* (Autumn), 2–12.

Brace, C. Loring. 2005. *"Race" Is a Four-Letter Word: The Genesis of the Concept.* New York: Oxford University Press.

Bramadat, Paul, and David Selijak, eds. 2005. *Religion and Ethnicity in Canada.* Toronto: Pearson Longman.

Bramadat, Paul, and David Seljak, eds. 2008. *Christianity and Ethnicity in Canada.* University of Toronto Press.

Brand, Dionne. 1994. *Bread Out of Stone: Recollections, Sex, Recognitions, Race, Dreaming, Politics.* Toronto: Coach House Press.

Brattain, Michelle. 2007. "Race, Racism, and Antiracism: UNESCO and the Politics of Presenting Science to the Postwar Public." *The American Historical Review* 112(5).

Braziel, Jana Evans, and Anita Mannur. 2003. "Nation, Migration, Globalization: Points of Contention in Diasporic Studies," in *Theorizing Diaspora: A Reader.* J. E. Braziel and A. Mannur, eds., 1–22. Oxford: Blackwell.

Breen, Richard, and David B. Rottman. 1995. *Class Stratification: A Comparative Perspective.* Harvester Wheatsheaf.

Brennan, Richard J. 2011. "Northern Ontario Reserve Begging for Evacuation." *Waterloo Region Record*, 21 November.

Breton, Eric. 2001. "Canadian Federalism, Multiculturalism, and the Twenty-First Century." *International Journal of Canadian Studies* 21(Spring): 160–175.

Breton, Raymond. 1989. "Canadian Ethnicity in the Year 2000," in *Multiculturalism and Intergroup Relations*. James Frideres, ed., 149–152. New York: Greenwood.

Breton, Raymond, Wsevolod W. Isajiw, Warren E. Kalbach, and Jeffrey G. Reitz. 1990. *Ethnic Identity and Equality: Varieties of Experience in a Canadian City*. Toronto: University of Toronto Press.

Bricker, Darryl, and John Ibbitson. 2013. *The Big Shift*. Toronto: HarperCollins.

Bristow, Peggy, Dionne Brand, Linda Carty, Afua A. Cooper, Sylvia Hamilton, and Adrienne Shadd. 1993. *We're Rooted Here and They Can't Pull Us Up: Essays in African Canadian Women's History*. Toronto: University of Toronto Press.

Brock, Kathy L. 1991. "The Politics of Aboriginal Self-Government: A Paradox." *Canadian Public Administration* 34(2):272–285.

Brodie, Janine. 2002. Citizenship and Solidarity: Reflections on the Canadian Way. *Citizenship Studies* 6(4):377–394.

Brooks, Stephen. 1998. *Public Policy in Canada: An Introduction*. Toronto: Oxford University Press.

Brooks, Stephen. 2004. "Political Culture in Canada: Issues and Directions," in *Canadian Politics* (4th ed.). J. Bickerton and A.-G. Gagnon, eds., 55–78. Peterborough, ON: Broadview.

Brosseau, Jonathan. 2013. Quebec Secularism, The Crucifix, and the Infamous Historical Argument. *McGill Daily*, 5 September.

Brown, David. 1989. "Ethnic Revival: Perspectives on State and Society." Third World Quarterly, 11(4):1–17.

Brown, Louise. 2005. "Amid Debate, Race-based School Thrives." *Toronto Star*, 15 September.

Brown, Maureen J. 2004. *In Their Own Voices: African-Canadians in the Greater Toronto Area Share Experiences of Police Profiling*. Commissioned by the African-Canadian Community Coalition on Racial Profiling.

Brown, Michael. 2005. *Whitewashing Race. Myth of a Color-Blind Society*. Berkeley, CA: University of California Press.

Brown, Rupert. 2010. *Prejudice: Its Social Psychology* (2nd ed.). Wiley-Blackwell.

Brown, Wendy. 2014. *Walled States, Waning Sovereignty*. Cambridge MA: MIT Press.

Brubaker, Rogers. 2002. Ethnicity Without Groups. *European Journal of Sociology* 43(2):163–189.

Brunon-Ernst, Anne, ed. 2012. *Beyond Foucault: New Perspectives on Bentham's Panopticon*. Farnham Surrey: Ashgate.

Byrd, W. Carson. 2011. Conflating Apples and Oranges: Understanding Modern Forms of Racism. *Sociology Compass* 5(11):1005–1017.

Bryd, W. C., and Matthew W. Hughey. 2015. "Born That Way? 'Scientific' Racism is Creeping Back Into Our Thinking. Here's What to Watch Out For." *Washington Post,* 28 September.

Buckley, Helen. 1992. *From Wooden Ploughs to Welfare: Why Indian Policy Failed in the Prairie Provinces*. Toronto: McMillian Collier.

Bunzl, Matti. 2005. "Between Anti-Semitism and Islamophobia: Some Thoughts on the New Europe." *American Ethnologist* 32(4):499–508.

Bureau of Public Affairs, US Department of State. 2010. Trafficking in Persons: Ten Years of Partnering to Combat Modern Slavery (Fact Sheet). Washington: US State Department. Retrieved November 16, 2015 (www.state.gov/r/pa/scp/fs/2010/143115.htm).

Burgess, Michael. 1996. "Ethnicity, Nationalism, and Identity in Canada–Quebec Relations: The Case of Quebec's Distinct Society." *Journal of Commonwealth and Comparative Politics* 34(2):46–64.

Burnet, Jean. 1981. "The Social and Historical Context of Ethnic Relations," in *A Canadian Social Psychology of Ethnic Relations*. Robert C. Gardiner and Rudolph Kalin, eds., 17–36. Toronto: Methuen.

Burnett, Jon. 2015. Anti-Racism: Totem and Taboo: A Review Article. *Race & Class* 57(1):78–87.

Burnett, Jon. 2015. "Youth, Welfare, and the Legacy of Structural Racism." Institute of Race Relations, www.irr.org.uk/news. 3 September.

Byrne, Bridget. 2010. *White Lives: The Interplay of "Race," Class, and Gender in Everyday Life*. New York: Routledge.

Cahill, D., G. Bouma, H. Dellal, and M. Leahy. 2006. *Religion, Cultural Diversity, and Safeguarding Australia*. Published by the Department of Immigration and Multicultural and Indigenous Affairs and Australian Multicultural Foundation.

Caines, Lisa. 2004. "The Deep Roots of Prejudice." *Research*, (Spring): 38.

Cairns, Alan. 2000. *Citizens Plus: Aboriginal Peoples and the Canadian State.* Vancouver: UBC Press.

Cairns, Alan. 2003. "Aboriginal Peoples in the Twenty-First Century: A Plea for Realism," in *A Canadian Social Psychology of Ethnic Relations.* Robert C. Gardiner and Rudolph Kalin, eds., 17–36. Toronto: Methuen.

Cairns, Alan C. 2005. *First Nations and the Canadian State: In Search of Coexistence.* Kingston: Queen's University Institute of Intergovernmental Relations.

Cairns, Alan. 2007. "Bouchard-Taylor and Nation-Building." *Inroads* 22:64–69.

Calder, Gideon, and Emaneula Ceva, eds. 2011. *Diversity in Europe: Dilemmas of Differential Treatment in Theory and Practice.* New York: Routledge.

Cameron, Elspeth, ed. 2004. *Multiculturalism and Immigration in Canada: An Introductory Reader.* Toronto: Canadian Scholars' Press.

Canadian Centre for Immigration Policy Reform. 2010. Policy Statement. Retrieved online.

Canadian Centre for Immigration Policy Reform. 2011. Immigration Overview. Retrieved online.

Canadian Council for Refugees. 2000. *Report on Systemic Racism and Discrimination in Canadian Refugee and Immigration Policies.* In preparation for the UN World Conference Against Racism, Racial Discrimination, Xenophobia and Related Intolerance. Montreal.

Canadian Council for Refugees. 2001. "Refugee Women Fleeing Gender-Based Persecution." Retrieved November 16, 2015 (http://ccrweb.ca/sites/ccrweb.ca/files/static-files/gendpers.html).

Canadian Council for Refugees. 2013. "New Refugee System—One Year On." 9 December. Available online at www.ccrweb.ca.

Canadian Feminist Alliance for International Action (CFAFIA). 2008. *Women's Inequality in Canada.* Submission of CAFAFIA to the UN Committee on the Elimination of Discrimination Against Women on the occasion of the Committee's Review of Canada's 6th and 7th Reports.

Canadian Heritage. 2001. *Canadian Diversity: Respecting Our Differences.* Ottawa.

Canadian Heritage. 2005/6. "Annual Report on the Operation of the Canadian *Multiculturalism Act.*" Retrieved online.

Canadian Islamic Congress. 2005. "Anti-Islam in the Media." Summary of the Sixth Annual Report for the Year 2003. 31 January. Retrieved online.

Canadian Issues. 2005. "Immigration and the Intersections of Diversity." Spring.

Canadian Labour Congress. 2008. "Equality, Once and For All." Retrieved online.

Canadian Press. 2007a. "Immigration Policies Need Changing, Flaherty Advised." *KW Record*, 1 September.

Canadian Race Relations Foundation (CRRF). 2003. *Facts about Racism and Policing.* Available online at www.crr.ca.

Canadian Race Relations Foundation (CRRF). 2008. *What Is Canadian Racism? A National Symposium.* Calgary, AB. 30 April to 2 May.

Canadian Race Relations Foundation (CRRF). 2014. Survey on Religion, Racism, and Intergroup Relations in Canada Shows Differences in Attitudes Among Anglophones, Francophones, and Other Groups. 2 May. Retrieved from www.newswire.ca.

Canadian Race Relations Foundation (CRRF). 2014. "Report on Canadian Values." 19 November.

Canadian Women's Foundation. 2012. The Facts About Violence Against Women. Retrieved from www.canadianwomen.org.

Cannon, Martin, J. 2012. Changing the Subject in Teacher Education: Centering Indigenous, Diasporic, and Settler Colonial Relations. *Cultural and Pedogogical Inquiry* 4(2):21–37.

Cannon, Martin J., and Lina Sunseri, eds. 2011. *Race, Colonialism and Indigeneity in Canada.* Toronto: Oxford University Press.

Caplan, Gerald. 2005. "The Genocide Problem: Never Again or All Over Again." *The Walrus*, 68–76.

Caplan, Gerald. 2007. "Talk but No Action on Genocide." Cited in Carol Goar. *Toronto Star*, 25 April.

Caplan, Gerald. 2010. "Honour Killings in Canada: Even Worse Than We Believe." *The Globe and Mail*, 23 July.

Caplan, Paul J., and Jordan C. Ford. 2014. The Voices of Diversity: What Students of Diverse Races/Ethnicities and Both Sexes Tell Us About Their College Experiences and Their Perceptions About Their Institutions' Progress Toward Diversity. *Aporia* 6(3).

Capps, Randy, and Kathleen Newland. 2015. "The Integration Outcomes of U.S. Refugees: Successes and Challenges." Migration Policy Institute. June

Cardinal, Harold. 1969. *The Unjust Society.* Edmonton: Hurtig.

Cardozo, Andrew. 2005. "Multiculturalism vs. Rights." *Toronto Star*, 15 September.

Cardozo, Andrew, and Luis Musto, eds. 1997. *Battle over Multiculturalism: Does It Help or Hinder Canadian Unity?* Ottawa: Pearson-Shoyama Institute.

Carletti, Fabiola, and Janet Davison. 2012. Who's Looking Out for Tim Hortons' Temporary Foreign Workers? *CBC News*. 12 December.

Carlson, Kathryn Blaze. 2011. "Attawapiskat: A 'Homeland' at the Crossroads." *National Post*, 3 December.

Carment, David. 2007. "Exploiting Ethnicity: Political Elites and Domestic Conflict." *Harvard International Review* 28(4).

Carruthers, Ashley. 2013. National Multiculturalism, Transnational Identities. *Journal of Intercultural Studies* 34(2):214–228.

Carter, Sarah. 1990. *Lost Harvests*. Montreal/Kingston: McGill-Queen's University Press.

Caselli, Francesco, and Wilbur John Coleman II. 2006/2010. *On the Theory of Ethnic Conflict*. Working Paper No. 12125 for National Bureau of Economic Research Cambridge, MA.

Cassin, A. M., T. Krawchenko, and M. VanderPlaat. 2007. *Racism and Discrimination in Canada. Laws, Policies, and Practices*. Atlantic Metropolis Centre. Multiculturalism and Human Rights Research Reports. No 3. Ottawa: Department of Canadian Heritage.

Castellano, Marlene Brant. 2009. "Heart of the Nations: Woman's Contribution to Community Healing," in *Restoring the Balance*. G. Valaskakis et al., eds., 203–236. Winnipeg: University of Manitoba Press.

Castellano M., L. Archibald, and M. Degagne, eds. 2008. *From Truth to Reconciliation: Transforming the Legacy of Residential Schools*. 183–203. Ottawa: Aboriginal Healing Foundation.

Castells, Manuel. 1997. *The Power of Identity*. Oxford: Blackwell.

Castles, Stephen. 2006. Guest Workers in Europe: A Resurrection? *International Migration Review* 40(4):741–766.

Castles, Stephen, Hein de Haas, and Mark Miller. 2013. *The Age of Migration. International Population Movements in the Modern World* (5th ed.). New York: Guilford.

Castles, Stephen, and Mark J. Miller. 2003. *The Age of Migration* (3rd ed.). New York: Guilford.

Castles, Stephen, and Mark J. Miller. 2009. *The Age of Migration: International Population Movements in the Modern World* (4th ed.). New York: Guilford.

Caulfield, Timothy, and Gerald Robertson. 1996. "Eugenics Policies in Alberta: From the Systematic to the Systemic." *Alberta Law Review* 35(1):59–81.

Caws, Peter. 1994. "Identities: Cultural, Transcultural, and Multicultural," in *Multiculturalism: A Critical Reader*. D. T. Goldberg, ed., 371–378. Oxford: Blackwell.

CBC News. 2010. "Rights Icon Desmond Gets N.S. Apology." 16 April. Retrieved November 16, 2015 (www.cbc.ca/news/canada/nova-scotia/rights-icon-desmond-gets-n-s-apology-1.892821).

Centre for Israel and Jewish Affairs. 2013. Backgrounder: Change to Canada's Immigration and Refugee System. 15 July. Retrieved from www.cija.ca.

Centre for Social Justice. 2010. *Aboriginal Issues*. Retrieved November 16, 2015 (www.socialjustice.org/index.php?page=aboriginal-issues).

Chan, Raymond. 2003/4. "A Message from the Minister of State (Multiculturalism)." *Annual Report on the Operation of the Canadian Multiculturalism Act*. Ottawa.

Chan, Wendy, and Kiran Mirchandani. 2002. "From Race and Crime to Racialization and Criminalization," in *Crimes of Colour: Racialization and the Criminal Justice System in Canada*. W. Chan and K. Mirchandani, eds., 9–23. Peterborough, ON: Broadview.

Chandler, J. J., and C. Lalonde. 1998. "Cultural Continuity as a Hedge Against Suicide in Canada's First Nations." *Transcultural Psychiatry* 35(2):191–219.

Charlesworth, Hilary and Emma Larking, eds. 2015. *Human Rights and the Universal Periodic Review: Rituals and Ritualism*. Cambridge University Press.

Chartrand, Paul. 1992. "Aboriginal Self-Government: The Two Sides of Legitimacy," in *How Ottawa Spends: A More Democratic Canada . . . ?* Susan D. Phillips, ed., 231–256. Ottawa: Carleton University Press.

Chartrand, Paul L., and Albert Peeling. 2004. "Sovereignty, Liberty, and the Legal Order of the 'Freemen' (Otipahemsu'uk): Towards a Constitutional Theory of Métis Self-Government." *Saskatchewan Law Review* 67(1):339.

Chazan, May, Lisa Helps, Anna Stanley, and Sonali Thakkar. 2011. Introduction. In *Home and Native Land: Unsettling Multiculturalism in Canada.* May Chazan et al., eds.,1–14. Toronto: Between the Lines.

Cheng, Hau Ling. 2005. "Constructing a Transnational, Multilocal Sense of Belonging: An Analysis of Ming Pao (West Canadian Edition)." *Journal of Communication Inquiry* 29(2):141–159.

Chesler, Mark, Amanda E. Lewis, and James E. Crowfoot. 2005. *Challenging Racism in Higher Education: Promoting Justice.* Lanham, MD: Rowman & Littlefield.

Chomsky, Aviva. 2007. *"They Take Our Jobs!" And 20 Other Myths about Immigration.* Boston: Beacon Press.

Choudhry, Sujit. 2007. "Does the World Need More Canada? The Politics of the Canadian Model in Constitutional Politics and Political Theory." *I-CON* 5(4):606–638.

Choudhury, Shakil. 2015. *Deep Diversity: Overcoming Us vs. Them.* Toronto: Between the Lines.

Christchurch Press. 2010. "Black Farmers Win $1.8b [NZ] Discrimination Case." 20 February.

Christiano, K. J. 2013. European Principles and Canadian Practices: Developing Secular Contexts for Religious Diversity. RECODE Working Paper Series No 15.

Christie, Gordon. 2002. *Challenges to Urban Aboriginal Governance.* Presented to the Institute for Intergovernmental Relations. Queens University. 1 November.

Christie, Gordon. 2005. "Aboriginal Resource and Subsistence Rights after Delgamuukw and Marshall." In *Advancing Aboriginal Claims: Visions, Strategies, Directions.* Kerry Wilkins, ed. Saskatoon: Purich.

Chung, Andrew. 2010. "Police Profiling 'Alarming' in Montreal." *Toronto Star*, 9 August.

Churchill, Ward. 1999. *Fantasies of the Master Race: Literature, Cinema, and the Colonization of North American Indians.* Winnipeg: Arbeiter Ring.

Churchill, Ward. 2002. *Perversions of Justice Indigenous Peoples and Angloamerican Law.* San Francisco: City Lights Publishers.

Churchill, Ward. 2004. *Kill the Indian, Save the Man: The Genocidal Impact of American Indian Residential Schools.* San Francisco: City Lights.

Citizenship and Immigration Canada (CIC). 2009. "Facts and Figures 2009—Immigration Overview: Permanent and Temporary Residents." Ottawa.

Citizenship and Immigration Canada (CIC). 2010. *The Current State of Multiculturalism in Canada and Research Themes on Canadian Multiculturalism.* Available online at www.cic.gc.ca.

Citizenship and Immigration Canada (CIC). 2011a. Annual Report on the Operation of the Canadian Multiculturalism Act. "Promoting Integration." Ottawa.

Citizenship and Immigration Canada (CIC). 2011b. Backgrounder: Stakeholder Consultations on Immigration Levels and Mix. Ottawa.

Citizenship and Immigration Canada (CIC). 2011c. Becoming Canadian: Combatting Immigration Fraud, 10 August.

Citizenship and Immigration Canada (CIC). 2012a. Annual Report to Parliament on Immigration. Ottawa.

Citizenship and Immigration Canada (CIC). 2012b. An Immigration System that Works for Canada. News Release. Ottawa, 19 December.

Citizenship and Immigration Canada (CIC). 2012c. Backgrounder: An Overview of Reforms to Canada's Refugee System. Ottawa, 16 February.

Citizenship and Immigration Canada (CIC). 2013. Canada Facts and Figures. Immigration Overview: Permanent and Temporary Residents 2012.

Citizenship and Immigration Canada (CIC). 2014. "Facts and Figures 2013: Immigrant Overviews: Permanent and Temporary Resident" (http://www.cic.gc.ca/english/resources/statistics/menu-fact.asp).

Citizenship and Immigration Canada (CIC). 2014. 2014 Annual Report to Parliament on Immigration. Ottawa: Government of Canada.

Citizenship and Immigration Canada (CIC) News. 2015. Potential Options to Remain in Canada for TFWs Facing Uncertain Futures. Retrieved from www.cicnesw.com. 24 March.

Clarfield, Geoffrey. 2007. "Where Tribe Is Everything." *National Post*, 15 December.

Clark, Bruce, 1990. *Native Liberty, Crown Sovereignty: The Existing Aboriginal Right of Self-Government in Canada.* Kingston, ON: McGill-Queen's University Press.

Clark-Avery, Kristen. 2007. "Introduction." *Souls: A Critical Journal of Black Politics, Culture, and Society* 9(1):1–3.

Clarke, D. E., A. Colantonio, A. E. Rhodes, and M. Escobar. 2008. Ethnicity and Mental Health: Conceptualization, Definition, and Operationalization of Ethnicity From a Canadian Context. *Chronic Diseases in Canada* 28(4):128–137.

Clarkson, Adrienne. 2014. *Belonging: The Paradox of Citizenship*. Anansi.

Clement, Wallace and Rick Helmes-Hayes. 2015. Foreword. In *The Vertical Mosaic: An Analysis of Social Class and Power in Canada. 50ᵗʰ Anniversary Edition*, John Porter, ed. Toronto: University of Toronto Press.

Cliplef, Juliana Helene. 2014. Is the Direction of Canadian Immigration Policy in Keeping With Our Commitment to Multiculturalism? *Windsor Review of Legal and Social Issues* 1(article 4). Digital Companion 48.

Closs, William J., and Paul F. McKenna. 2006. "Profiling a Problem in Canadian Police Leadership: The Kingston Police Data Collection Problem." *Canadian Public Administration* 49(2):143–160.

CMHC. 2007. "Fire Prevention in Aboriginal Communities: Research Highlight." Socio-economic Series 07-009. October.

Coates, Ken. 2013. "Canada Needs More Non-Aboriginal Engagement with First Nations People." Retrieved from the MacDonald-Laurier Institute. 17 January.

Coates, Ken. 2014. *#Idle No More, and the Remaking of Canada*. Regina: University of Regina Press.

Coates, Ken. 2015. "Sharing the Wealth: How resource revenue agreements can honour treaties, improve communities, and facilitate Canadian development Retrieved November 17, 2015 (www.macdonaldlaurier.ca/files/pdf/MLIresourcerevenuesharingweb.pdf).

Coates, Rodney D. 2008. "Covert Racism in the USA and Globally." *Sociology Compass* 2(1):208–231.

Coates, Ta-Nehisi. 2015. *Between the World and Me*. Spiegel & Grau.

Cobb, Chris. 1995. "Multiculturalism Policy May be Outdated, Says MPs." *Ottawa Citizen*, 4 July.

Coderre, Dennis. 2003. "Interview with the Minister of Immigration and Citizenship." *Canadian Issues* (April), 4–7.

Codrescu, Andrei. 1995. "Faux Chicken & Phony Furniture." *Utne Reader* (May/June), 47–48. Originally published in the *The Nation*, 12 December 1984.

Cohen, Lisa J. 2011. The Psychology of Prejudice and Racism. *Psychology Today*, 24 January.

Cohen, Randy. 1999. "Cut Rate Rationale." *NY Times Magazine*, 18 July.

Cohen, Tobi. 2012. "Skilled Migrant Program Returns." *National Post*, 20 December.

Cohen, Tobi. 2013. "Number of Asylum Claims Drop Dramatically After Ottawa Releases List of 'Safe' Countries." *Postmedia News/National Post,* 13 August.

Cohn, Martin Regg. 2015. "Smear and Goading: How Harper Lifted the Veil on Our Phobias." *Toronto Star*, 4 October.

Colaiavoco, Innessa. 2013. Not Just the Facts: Adjudicator Bias and Decisions of the Immigration and Refugee Board of Canada (2006–2011). *Journal of Migration and Human Security* 1(1):122-147.

Cole, Desmond. 2015. "The Skin I'm In." *Toronto Life*, April.

Collacott, Martin. 2006. "A Refugee System in Need of Overhaul." *National Post*, 9 March.

Collett, Elizabeth. 2010. "Europe: A New Continent of Immigration," in *Rethinking Immigration and Integration: A New Centre-Left Agenda. Olaf Cramme and Constance Motte, eds., 10–18. London, UK: Policy Network.

Collier, Paul. 2007. "Ethnic Civil Wars: Questioning the Received Wisdom." *Harvard International Review* 28(4).

Colombo, Enzo. 2015. Multiculturalisms: An Overview of Multicultural Debates in Western Societies. *Current Sociological Review* 63(6):800–824.

Colour of Poverty Campaign. 2007. "Understanding the Racialization of Poverty in Ontario: Fact Sheets." Retrieved online.

Conference Board of Canada. 2004. *The Voices of Visible Minorities: Speaking Out on Breaking Down Barriers*. September.

Conference Board of Canada. 2008. *Renewing Immigration: Toward a Convergence and Consolidation of Canada's Immigration Policies and Systems*. Ottawa: Author.

Conference Notes. 2013. "Transforming Citizenship: Ethnicity, Transnationalism, and Belonging in Canada." The Association of Canadian Studies and the Canadian Ethnic Studies Association 4ᵗʰ Annual Conference. October 24–26, Campus Saint-Jean, University of Alberta, Edmonton.

Connor, Walker. 2000. "National Self-Determination and Tomorrow's Political Map," in *Citizenship, Diversity, and Pluralism*. A. Cairns, J. C. Courtney, Peter MacKinnon, Hans J. Michelmann, and David E. Smith, eds., 163–176. Montreal/Kingston: McGill-Queen's University Press.

Cooke, Martin, and David Long. 2011. Moving Beyond the Politics of Aboriginal Well-Being, Health, and Healing. In *Visions of the Heart*. D. Long and O. P. Dickason, eds., 292–327. Toronto: Oxford.

Cooke, Martin, Francis Mitrou, David Lawrence, Eric Guimond, and Dan Beavon. 2007. "Indigenous Well-Being in Four Countries: An Application of the UNDP's Human Development Index to Indigenous Peoples in Australia, Canada, New Zealand and the United States." *BMC International Health and Human Rights*. 7(9). Available online at www.biomedcentral.com/1472-698X/7/9.

Cooke, Martin, and Jennifer McWhirter. 2010. "Public Policy and Aboriginal Peoples in Canada: Taking a Life Course Perspective." *Canadian Public Policy* 37:S15–S31.

Cooke, Martin, Francis Mitrou, David Lawrence, David Povah, Elina Mobilia, Eric Guimond, and Stephen Zubrik. 2014. "Gaps in Indigenous Disadvantage Not Closing: A Census Cohort Study of Social Determinants of Health in Australia, Canada, and New Zealand from 1981–2006." *BMC (BioMed Central) Public Health* 14:201–210.

Cooper, Afua. 2006. *The Hanging of Angelique*. Toronto: HarperCollins.

Cornell, Stephen, and Douglas Hartmann. 2007. *Ethnicity and Race. Making Identities in a Changing World*. Thousand Oaks, CA: Sage.

Cornell, Stephen, and Joseph P. Kalt. 2003. *Sovereignty and Nation-building: The Development Challenge in Indian Country Today*. Joint Occasional Papers on Native Affairs NO 2003-03. Originally published in the *American Indian Culture and Research Journal*, 1998.

Corntassel, Jeff. 2008. Toward Sustainable Self-Determination: Rethinking the Contemporary Indigenous-Rights Discourse. *Alternatives* 33:105–132.

Cose, Ellis. 1997. *Color-Blind: Seeing Beyond Race in a Race-Obsessed World*. New York: HarperCollins.

Cote-Meek, Sheila. 2014. *Colonized Classrooms: Racism, Trauma, and Resistance in Post-Secondary Education*. Halifax, NS: Fernwood.

Cotler, Irwin. 2007. "The New Antisemitism: An Assault on Human Rights," in *Antisemitism: The Generic Hatred*. M. Fineberg et al., eds., 15–33. Portland, OR: Vallentine Mitchell Publishers.

Coulthard, Glen. 2014. *Red Skins, White Masks. Rejecting the Colonial Politics of Recognition*. Minneapolis, University of Minnesota Press.

Council of Europe. 2008. "Living Together as Equals in Dignity": White Paper on Intercultural Dialogue. Strasbourg.

Council of the European Union. 2004. *Draft Conclusions of the Council and the Representatives of the Governments of the Member States on the establishment of Common Basic Principles for immigrant integration policy in the European Union*. Brussels, Belgium.

Courchene, Thomas. 2007. "Introduction and Overview." In *Canada: The State of the Federation: Annual Review*, 1–23. Queen's University, Kingston: Institute of Intergovernmental Relations.

Coyne, Andrew. 2015. "To Uncover or Not to Uncover: Why the Niqab Issue is Ridiculous." *National Post*, 30 September.

Craig, Gary. 2015. *Migration and Integration: A Local and Experiential Perspective*. Institute for Research in Superdiversity. Working Paper Series 7. University of Birmingham.

Crawford, Beverly. 2006. "The Causes of Cultural Conflict: An Institutional Approach." In *The Myth of "Ethnic Conflict:" Politics, Economics, and "Cultural" Violence*. B. Crawford and R. Lipschutz, eds. University of California, Berekley, 3–43.

Crawford, Beverly, and Ronnie D. Lipschutz, eds. 1999. *The Myth of "Ethnic Conflict": Politics, Economics, and "Cultural" Violence*. University of California International and Area Studies Digital Collection. Research Series #98.

Crepeau, Francois, and Kinga Janik. 2008. Submission to the United Nations Human Rights Council in relations to the Universal Periodic Review of Canada. Available online at www.cerium.ca.

Crepeau, Francois, and Delphine Nakache. 2006. "Controlling Irregular Migration in Canada:

Reconciling Security Concerns with Human Rights Protection." *IRPP Choices* 12(1).

Crompton, Rosemary. 2008. *Class and Stratification* (3rd ed.) Polity.

Cross, Pamela. 2007. "Violent Partners Create War Zone for Women." *Toronto Star*, 6 July.

Crouch, Carl. 2011. *The Strange Non-Death of Neo-Liberalism*. Polity.

Crowley, Brian Lee, and Ken Coates. 2012. "Aboriginal Prosperity Must be Earned." *Waterloo Region Record*, 29 December.

Crowley, Brian Lee, and Ken Coates. 2013. "The Way Out: Aboriginal Equity." *Globe and Mail*, 3 January.

Crowley, Brian Lee, and Ken Coates. 2015. Preface. *Sharing the Wealth: Aboriginal Canada and the Natural Resource Economy*. Series 6. A Macdonald-Laurier Institute Publication, January.

Cudmore, James. 2001. "Inuk Accuses Ottawa of Discrimination." *National Post*, 22 March.

Cummings, Joan Grant. 2007. "Foreword." In *Theorizing Empowerment*. N. Massaquoi and N. N. Wane, eds., xiii–xiv. Toronto: Inanna Publications.

Curran, Peggy. 2010. "Young Blacks More Apt to be Pulled Over by Police, Report." *Montreal Gazette*, 10 August.

Curry, Bill. 2008. "Native Band Sues for $550 Billion, Saying Mine Sites Belong to Them." *Globe and Mail*, 14 May.

Curry, Bill, and Tu Thanh Ha. 2013. "Who are the Métis and Non-status Indians?" *Globe and Mail*, 9 January.

Curtis, Christopher. 2015. "Canada Says It, Not Kahnawake, Gets to Decide on Band Membership Issues." *Montreal Gazette*, 6 July.

Curtis, Michael. 1997. "Review Essay. Antisemitism: Different Perspectives." *Sociological Forum* 12(2):321–327.

Da Costa, Kimberly McClain. 2007. *Making Multiracials: State, Family, and Market in the Redrawing of the Color Line*. California: Stanford University Press.

Dalmage, Heather M., ed. 2004. *The Politics of Multiculturalism: Challenging Racial Thinking*. Albany: State University of New York.

Daniel, Lauren, and Wendy Cukier. 2014. *Addressing the Discrimination Experience by Somali Canadians. The 360 Project—Addressing Racism in Toronto*. Published by Urban Alliance on Race Relations and Ryerson University's Diversity Institute.

Daschuk, James. 2013. *Clearing the Plains: Disease, Politics of Starvation, and the Loss of Aboriginal Life*. Regina SA.: University of Regina Press.

Das Gupta, Tania. 2009. *"Real" Nurses and Others: Racism in Nursing*. Halifax: Fernwood.

Das Gupta, Tania, Carl E. James, Roger Maaka, Grace Edward Galabuzi, and Chris Anderson, eds. 2007. *Race and Racialization: Essential Readings*. Toronto: Canadian Scholars' Press.

Dasko, Donna. 2005. "Public Attitudes toward Multiculturalism and Bilingualism." Canadian and French Perspectives on Diversity Conference, 16 October 2003. Ottawa: Canadian Heritage for the Minister of Supply and Public Works.

Dauvergne, Catherine. 2004. "Why Judy Sgro Is Just Plain Wrong—No One Is Illegal." *Globe and Mail*, 2 August.

Dauvergne, Catherine. 2013. "Refugee Rules the End of Canada's Humanitarian Tradition." *Globe and Mail*, 29 January.

Davin, Nicholas Flood. 1879. "Report on Industrial Schools for Indians and Half Breeds." Submission to the Minister of the Interior.

Davis, Angela. 1998. "Masked Racism: Reflections on the Prison Industrial Complex." *Colorlines*, Fall, 1–4. Retrieved November 16, 2015 (www.colorlines.com/articles/masked-racism-reflections-prison-industrial-complex).

Davis, Angela. 2012. Recognizing Racism in the Era of Neoliberalism. In *The Meaning of Freedom and Other Difficult Dialogues*. A. Davis, ed. San Francisco: City Lights Books.

Davis, Dana-Ain. 2007. Narrating the Mute: Racializing and Racism in the Neoliberal Moment. *Souls* 9(4):346–360.

Davis, Kingsley, and Wilbert E. Moore. 1945. "Some Principles of Stratification." *American Sociological Review* 5: 242–249.

Day, Richard. 2000. *Multiculturalism and the History of Canadian Diversity*. Toronto: University of Toronto Press.

Dean, Bartholomew, and Jerome M. Levi, eds. 2006. *At the Risk of Being Heard: Identity, Indigenous Rights, and Postcolonial States*. Ann Arbor: University of Michigan Press.

Deckha, Manisha. 2010. Gender, Culture, and Violence: Toward a Paradigm Shift? *Equity Matters.* Fedcan Blog. Retrieved November 16, 2015 (www.ideas-idees.ca/blog/gender-culture-and-violence-toward-paradigm-shift).

Dedi, Barb. 2015. *Canada: Anti-Muslim Bigotry on Rise.* Retrieved from http://muslimvillage.com.

Dei, George Sefa. 1996a. "Black/African-Canadian Students' Perspectives on School Racism," in *Racism in Canadian Schools*, I. Alladin, ed., 2–61. Toronto: Harcourt Brace.

Dei, George Sefa. 1996b. *Anti-racism Education: Theory and Practice.* Halifax: Fernwood.

Dei, George Sefa. 2000. "Contesting the Future: Anti-racism and Canadian Diversity," in *21ˢᵗ Century Canadian Diversity.* S. Nancoo, ed., 295–319. Toronto: Canadian Scholars' Press.

Dei, George Sefa. 2004. "Why I Back School Board Plan." *Toronto Star*, 26 November.

Dei, George Sefa. 2005. "Anti-racist Education—Moving Yet Standing Still. Editorial Commentary." *Directions* 3(1):6–9.

Dei, George Sefa. 2006. "On Race, Anti-racism, and Education." *Directions* 3(1):27–34.

Dei, George J. Sefa. 2007. "Speaking Race: Silence, Salience, and the Politics of Anti-racist Scholarship," in *Race and Racism in 21ˢᵗ Century Canada.* S. P. Hier and B. S. Bolaria, eds., 53–66. Peterborough, ON: Broadview.

Dei, George J. Sefa. 2010. Black Focused Schools: A Call For Re-Visioning. *Education Canada* 46(3):27–31.

Dei, George Sefa, Irma Marcia James, Leeno Luke Karumanchery, Sonia James Wilson, and Jasmin Zine. 2000. *Removing the Margins: The Challenges and Possibilities of Inclusive Schooling.* Toronto: Canadian Scholars' Press.

Delaney, Joan. 2008. "Fear of Extinction Leads to Francophone Multicultural Malaise." *Epoch Times*, 27 March–2 April.

Delanty, Gerard. 2000. *Citizenship in a Global Age: Society, Culture, Politics.* Philadelphia: Open University Press.

Delic, Senada, and Francis Abele. 2010. "The Recession and Aboriginal Workers," in *How Ottawa Spends 2010/2011*. G. B. Doern and C. Stoney, eds., 187–216. Montreal/Kingston: McGill-Queen's University Press.

Dempsey, Colleen, and Soojin Yu. 2004. "Refugees to Canada: Who Are They and How Are They Faring?" *Canadian Issues* (March), 5–10.

Dench, Janet. 2004. "Why Take Refugees?" *Canadian Issues* (March), 11–13.

Dench, Janet. 2007. "The Safe Country Dilemma: Why Offering Asylum Is an Obligation." *Globe and Mail*, 6 December.

Denis, Ann. 2008. "Intersectional Analysis: A Contribution of Feminism to Sociology." *International Sociology* 23(5):677–694.

Denis, Claude. 1996. "Aboriginal Rights in/and Canadian Society: A Syewen Case Study." *International Journal of Canadian Studies*, 14(Fall):13–34.

Denis, Claude. 1997. *We Are Not You: First Nations and Canadian Modernity.* Peterborough, ON: Broadview.

Department of Canadian Heritage. 2005. *Canada's Diversity: Respecting Our Differences.* Annual Report on the Operation of the Canadian *Multiculturalism Act 2000–2004*. Ottawa: Minister of Public Works and Government Services.

Department of Justice. 2009. *Family Violence. Overview Paper.* Retrieved online.

Department of Justice. 2012. Protecting Canada's Immigration System Act. Assented 28 June.

Department of Justice. 2012. Family Violence Initiatives. Retrieved from www.justice.gc.ca.

DePratto, Brian. 2015. Precarious Employment in Canada: Does the Evidence Square with the Anecdotes? *Special Report, TD Economics*, 26 March.

Desmond, Matthew, and Mustafa Emirbayer. 2009. *Racial Domination, Racial Progress.* New York: McGraw-Hill.

Deutsche, Welle. 2010. *Berlin Announces Plans to Promote Integration and Attract Skilled Workers.* Available online at www.dw-world.de.

Deveaux, Monique. 2006. *Gender and Justice in Multicultural Liberal States.* New York: Oxford University Press.

Devine, Fiona, Miles Savage, John Scott, and Rosemary Crompton. 2005. *Rethinking Class: Culture, Identities, and Lifestyle.* New York: Palgrave Macmillan.

Dhamoon, Rita. 2009. *Identity/Difference Politics: How Difference Is Produced and Why It Matters.* Vancouver: UBC Press.

Dijkstra, S., K. Geutjen, and A. De Ruijter. 2001. "Multiculturalism and Social Integration in Europe." *International Political Science Review* 22(1):55–84.

Diller, Jerry V. 2004. *Cultural Diversity: A Primer for the Human Services* (2nd ed.). Belmont, CA: Thompson–Brooks/Cole.

Dinovitzer, Ronit, John Hagan, and Ron Levi. 2009. "Immigration and Youthful Illegalities in a Global Edge City." *Social Forces* 88(1):337–372.

Dinsdale, Peter. 2009. "Urban Aboriginals: The Policy Void at the Centre of Canadian Politics." *Inroads: A Canadian Journal of Public Opinion*, 22 June.

Diocson, Cecilia. 2005. "Filipino Women in Canada's Live-in Caregiver Program." *Philippine Reporter* (March), 16–31.

Doane, Ashley. 2006. "What Is Racism?" Racial Discourse and Racial Politics. *Critical Sociology* 32(2–3):255–275.

Doane, Ashley. 2007. "The Changing Politics of Color-Blind Racism." *The New Black: Alternative Paradigms and Strategies for the 21st Century Research in Race and Ethnic Relations* 14:159–174.

Dobbin, Murray. 2013. "The Power of Idle No More's Resurgent Radicalism." *The Tyee,* 14 January.

Dodd, Douglas. 2013. "Growing Poverty Among Canadian Immigrants Could Explode: Study." *Vancouver Sun*, 28 June.

Dogan, Recep. 2011. Is Honor Killings a "Muslim Phenomenon"? Textual Interpretations and Cultural Representations. *Journal of Muslim Minority Affairs* 31(3).

Donaldson, Ian. 2004. "Identity, Intersections of Diversity, and the Multicultural Program." *Canadian Diversity* 3(1):14–16.

Donkin Karissa. 2013. "#idlenomore: Hashing Out an Online Movement." *Toronto Star,* 12 January.

Dosman, Edgar. 1972. *Indians: The Urban Dilemma.* Toronto: McClelland & Stewart.

Doucet, Isabeau. 2013. "Rising Anger of Canada's First Nations." *Guardian Weekly*, 4 January.

Douglas, Debbie. 2005. Cited in "Award Winner Battles for Immigration Workers," by Debra Black. *Toronto Star*, 9 March.

Douglas, Stacy and Suzanne Lenon. 2014. Introduction. *Canadian Journal of Law and Society* 29(2):141–143.

Dovidio, John, M. Hewstone, P. Glick, and V. M. Esses. 2010. "Prejudice, Stereotyping, and Discrimination: Theoretical and Empirical Overview" In *The Sage Handbook of Prejudice, Stereotyping, and Discrimination*. J. F. Dovidio et al., eds., 3–28. Thousand Oaks, CA: Sage.

Dovidio, John, Agata Gluszek, Melissa-Sue John, Ruth Ditlmann, and Paul Lagunes. 2010. "Understanding Bias toward Latinos: Discrimination, Dimensions of Difference, and Experiences of Exclusion." *Journal of Social Issues* 66(1):59–78.

Dovidio John F., Samuel L. Gaertner, and Kerry Kawakami. 2010. "Racism." In *The Sage Handbook of Prejudice, Stereotyping, and Discrimination*. J. F. Dovidio et al., eds. Thousand Oaks, CA: Sage.

Dow, Steve. 2003. "Racism Caught in the Net." Retrieved November 16, 2015 (www.smh.com.au/articles/2003/03/24/1048354541423.html).

Driedger, Leo. 1989. *The Ethnic Factor: Identity in Diversity.* Toronto: McGraw-Hill Ryerson.

Drohan, Madelaine. 2011. Canada as Colonial Power: Not Quite the Way We Like to Think of Ourselves. *Literary Review of Canada*, January, 1–9.

Drost, Herman, Brian Lee Crowley, and Richard Schwindt. 1995. *Marketing Solutions for Native Poverty.* Toronto: CD Howe.

Drummond, Don, and Francis Fong. 2010. "An Economics Perspective on Canadian Immigration." *Policy Options* (July/August).

Drummond, Lee. n.d. "Toward a Semiotic Analysis of Ethnicity in Quebec." Originally Prepared for Institut Quebecois de Recherche sur la Culture, and published in *Questions de Culture 2: Migrations et Communautes Culturelles.* Centre for Peripheral Studies.

Du Bois, W. E. B. 1940. *Dusk of Dawn.* New York: Harcourt, Brace, 96.

Duffy, Andrew. 1999. "Ex-Prostitute with AIDS Wins Deportation Delay." *Windsor Star*, 20 November.

Dufraiment, Lisa. 2002. "Continuity and Modification of Aboriginal Rights in the Nisga'a Treaty." *UBC Law Review* 35(2):455–477.

Duncan, Howard. 2005. Multiculturalism: Still a Viable Concept for Integration? *Canadian Diversity* 4(1):12–14.

Duncan, Howard. 2006. "Diasporas and Transnationalism." *Metropolis World Bulletin* 6:2.

Duncanson, John, Dale Ann Freed, and Chris Sorensen. 2003. "There's Racism All Over the Place." *Toronto Star*, 26 February.

Dungan, Peter, Tony Fang, and Morley Gunderson. 2012. Macroeconomic Impacts of Canadian Immigration: Results From a Macro Model. Discussion Paper No 6743. July, Bonn: IZA (Study of Labour).

Dunn, K. M., N. Klockerm, and T. Salabay. 2007. "Contemporary Racism and Islamophobia in Australia." *Ethnicities* 7(4):564–589.

Durie, Mason. 2005. "Race and Ethnicity in Public Policy: Does It Work?" *Social Policy Journal of New Zealand* 24, April.

Dustin, Donna. 2007. *The McDonaldization of Social Work.* Aldershot, UK: Ashgate.

Early, G. 1993. "American Education and the Postmodernist Impulse." *American Quarterly* 45(2):220–221.

Early, James. 2014. Obama and the "Post Racial Society": Reality Asserts Itself, Pt 2. *Real News Network*, 3 October.

Easteal, Patricia. 1996. *Shattered Dreams: Marital Violence Against Overseas-Born Women in Australia.* Canberra: Australia National University Press.

Economist. 2009. "The Price of Prejudice." 17 January.

Economist. 2010. "*Multikulturell Wir?*" 13 November.

Economist. 2015a. "Angela the Beleaguered." 10 October.

Economist. 2015b. "Merkel at Her Limit." 10 October.

Editorial. 2010a. "Racial Profiling Study Demands Action." *Montreal Gazette*, 10 August.

Editorial. 2010b. "Viola Desmond's Stand." *Toronto Star*, 19 April.

Editorial, International Working Group on Indigenous Affairs (IWGIA). 2015. The Indigenous World, 2015. Copenhagen.

Eisenkraft, Harriet. 2010. "Racism in the Academy." *University Affairs,* 12 October.

Eisenstein, Zillah. 1996. *Hatreds: Racialized and Sexualized Conflicts in the Twenty-first Century.* New York: Routledge.

Eisenstein, Zillah. 2004. *Against Empire: Feminism, Racism, and the West.* New York: Zed Books.

EKOS. 2004. *Fall 2003 Survey of First Nations People Living On-Reserve.* Integrated Final Report by EKOS Research Associates. March.

EKOS. 2013. "Attitudes Toward Immigration and Visible Minorities. A Historical Perspective." Retrieved from www.ekospolitics.ca. 26 February.

Elabor-Idemudia, Patience. 1999. "The Racialization of Gender in the Social Construction of Immigrant Women in Canada: A Case Study of African Women in a Prairie Province." *Canadian Woman Studies* 19(3):38–44.

Elgersma, Sandra. 2014. "Temporary Foreign Workers." Library of Parliament Research Publications. Background Paper No 2014-79-E. 1 December.

Elliott, Jean Leonard. 1983. *Two Nations, Many Cultures: Ethnic Groups in Canada.* Toronto, ON: Prentice-Hall.

ENAR. 2012. "Shadow Report 2011/12 on Racism in Europe: Key Findings on Muslim Communities and Islamophobia." Author.

Endelman, Todd M. 2005. "Anti-Semitism in Western Europe Today." In *Contemporary Anti-Semitism.* D. Penslar et al., eds., 64–79. Toronto: University of Toronto Press.

Ensemble and Association for Canadian Studies. 2013. "Probing Prejudice. A Ground-breaking Study on Place, Frequency, and Sources." Leger Marketing, 20 March.

Entman, Robert. 1993. "Framing: Toward a Clarification of a Fractured Paradigm." *Journal of Communication* 43(4):51–58.

Environics Institute. 2010a. "Urban Aboriginal Peoples Increasingly Significant Presence in Canadian Cities Today" [Press release]. 6 April.

Environics Institute. 2010b. *Urban Aboriginal Peoples Study.* Retrieved September 30, 2015 (www.uaps.ca/wp-content/uploads/2010/03/UAPS-Main-Report_Dec.pdf).

Environics Institute. 2015. Canadian Public Opinion about Immigration and Multiculturalism. Keith Newman and Michael Adams, Focus Canada, Spring 2015, 30 June.

Epilepsy Foundation. 2007. "Reasonable Accommodation (ADA Title 1)." Retrieved November 16, 2015 (http://old.epilepsyfoundation.org/living/wellness/employment/accommodation.cfm#.VknxuPmrTIU).

ERASE Racism. 2005. "What Is Institutional Racism?" Retrieved online.

Erasmus, G., and J. Sanders. 2002. "Canadian History: An Aboriginal Perspective." In *Nation to Nation: Aboriginal Sovereignty and the Future of Canada.* John Bird, Lorraine Land, and Murray MacAdam, eds. Toronto: Irwin.

Esposito, John L. 2012. Foreword. In *The Islamophobia Industry: How the Right Manufactures Fears of Muslims.* Nathan Lean, ed. Pluto Press.

Essed, Philomena. 1991. *Understanding Everyday Racism: An Interdisciplinary Study*. Newbury Park, CA: Sage.

Essed, Philomena. 2002. "Everyday Racism," in *A Companion to Race and Ethnic Studies*. D. T. Goldberg and J. Solomos, eds., 202–216. Malden, MA: Blackwell.

Este, David. 2008. Cited in "Immigrant Men Learn How to Broaden Paternal Role," by Andrea Gordon. *Toronto Star*, 17 May.

Etherington, Frank. 2005. "Newcomers Have Complex Needs." *KW Record*, 19 March.

Evans, M., R. Hole, L. D. Berg, P. Hutchinson, and D. Sookraj. 2009. "Common Insights, Different Methodologies: Toward an Infusion of Indigenous Methodologies, Participatory Action Research, and White Studies in an Urban Aboriginal Research Agenda." *Qualitative Inquiry* 15. Published originally online March 23, 2009.

Ewan, E., and S. Ewan. 2006. *Typecasting: On the Arts and Sciences of Human Inequality*. New York: Seven Stories Press.

Faraday, Fay. 2012. "Made in Canada: How the Law Constructs Migrant Workers' Insecurity." Summary Report for the Metcalfe Foundation. September.

Farley, John E. 2005. "Race, Not Class: Explaining Racial Housing Segregation in the St. Louis Metropolitan Area, 2000." *Sociological Focus* 38(2):133–150.

Feagin, Joe. 2006. *Systemic Racism: A Theory of Oppression*. New York: Routledge.

Feagin, Joe, and José Cobas. 2008. "Latinos/as and White Racial Frame: The Procrustean Bed of Assimilation." *Sociological Inquiry* 78(1):39–53.

Fekete, Liz. 2009. *A Suitable Enemy: Racism, Migration, and Islamophobia in Europe*. London, UK: Pluto Press.

Fekete, Liz, ed. 2010. *Alternative Voices on Integration*. Institute of Race Relations.

Feldman, Michelle E., and Allyson J. Weseley. 2013. Which Name Unlocks The Door? The Effect of Tenant Race/Ethnicity on Landlord Response. *Journal of Applied Social Psychology* 43:416–425.

Fenwick, Fred. 2005. *Supreme Court Confirms Duty to Consult with Aboriginal Peoples: Haida Nation v. British Columbia*. Retrieved November 16, 2015 (www.thefreelibrary.com/Supreme+Court+confirms+duty+to+consult+with+aboriginal+peoples%3A+Haida . . . -a0130568771).

Ferber, Abby L. 1998. *White Man Falling: Race, Gender, and White Supremacy*. Boston: Rowman & Littlefield.

Ferguson, Susan J. 2012. *Race, Gender, Sexuality, and Social Class: Dimensions of Inequality*. Thousand Oaks: Sage.

Fernando, Shanti. 2006. *Race and the City: Chinese-Canadian and Chinese-American Political Mobilization*. Vancouver: UBC Press.

Fine, Sean. 2014. "Historic Ruling Upholds Land Rights." *Globe and Mail*, 27 June.

Fine, Sean. 2015. "Court Backs Wearing Niqab in Citizenship Ceremony." *Globe and Mail*, 6 October.

Finnie, Ross, and Ronald Meng. 2002. "Are Immigrants' Human Capital Skills Discounted in Canada?" Ottawa: Statistics Canada, Business and Labour Market Analysis Division.

Fish, Stanley. 1997. "Boutique Multiculturalism, or Why Liberals Are Incapable of Thinking about Hate Speech." *Critical Inquiry* (Winter), 378–395.

Fishman, Mark. 1980. *Manufacturing News*. Austin, TX: University of Austin Press.

Fisk, Robert. 2015. "Niqab Row: Canada's Government Challenges Ruling Zunera Ishaq Can Wear Veil While Taking Oath of Citizenship." *The Independent*, 30 September.

Fiss, Tanis. 2004. *Apartheid: Canada's Ugly Secret*. Calgary: Centre for Aboriginal Policy Change.

Fiss, Tanis. 2005a. *Dividing Canada: The Pitfalls of Native Sovereignty*. Calgary: Centre for Aboriginal Policy Change.

Fiss, Tanis. 2005b. *Road to Prosperity: Five Steps to Change Aboriginal Policy*. Calgary: Centre for Aboriginal Policy Change.

Fitzgerald, Lindsay. 2015. "The New Racism: How to Deal with Everyday Microaggressions." *The Ryersonian*, 6 February.

Flanagan, Tom. 1999. *First Nations? Second Thoughts*. Montreal/Kingston: McGill-Queen's University Press.

Flanagan, Tom. 2001. "Property Rights on the Rez." *National Post*, 11 December.

Flanagan, Tom, Chistopher Alcantara, and Andre Le Dressay. 2010. *Beyond the* Indian Act: *Restoring Aboriginal Property Rights*. Montreal/Kingston: McGill-Queen's University Press.

Flanagan, Tom and Katrine Beauregard. 2013. "The Wealth of Nations: An Exploratory Study." Centre for Aboriginal Policy Studies. Fraser Institute. June.

Fleming, Crystal M., and Aldon Morris, 2015. "Theorizing Ethnic and Racial Movements in the Global Age: Lessons from the Civil Rights Movement." *Sociology of Race and Ethnicity* 1(1):105–126.

Fleras, Augie. 1993. "From Culture to Equality: Multiculturalism as Ideology and Policy," in *Social Inequality in Canada* (2nd ed.). James Curtis, Edward Grab, and Neil Guppy, eds., 330–352. Toronto: Prentice-Hall.

Fleras, Augie. 2000. "The Politics of Jurisdiction." In *Visions of the Heart: Canadian Aboriginal Issues* (2nd ed.). David Long and Olive Dickason, eds. Toronto: Harcourt.

Fleras, Augie. 2001. *Social Problems in Canada: Constructions, Conditions, and Challenges* (3rd ed.). Don Mills, ON: Pearson Education.

Fleras, Augie. 2002. *Engaging Diversity: Multiculturalism in Canada: Politics, Policies, and Practices*. Scarborough, ON: Nelson.

Fleras, Augie. 2005. "Institutionalizing Racism/ Racializing Institutions." Directions: Research and Policy on Eliminating Racism. Canadian Race Relations Foundations, 2(2), 18–24.

Fleras, Augie. 2006a. "Media and Minorities," in *Media and Migration: A Comparative Perspective*. R. Geissler and H Pottker, eds., 179–222. Berlin: Transcript Publishers.

Fleras, Augie. 2006b. *Towards a Cultural Empowerment Model for Mental Health Services*. Paper presented to the Mental Health Conference by Centre for Research on Health and Education Services, Wilfrid Laurier University, Waterloo, Ontario, December.

Fleras, Augie. 2007. *Newsmedia as Systemic Propaganda*. Paper presented to the "20 Years of Propaganda Model Conference." University of Windsor, 16 May.

Fleras, Augie. 2008. *The Politics of Re/Naming*. Paper Commissioned by the Department of Justice and Delivered at the Ninth National Metropolis Conference in Halifax, 6 April.

Fleras, Augie. 2009a. *The Politics of Multiculturalism: Cross National Perspectives in Multicultural Governance*. New York: Palgrave Macmillan.

Fleras, Augie. 2009b. "Towards an Indigenous Grounded Analysis Policymaking Framework" (with Roger Maaka). *International Indigenous Policy Journal* (online). Volume 1.

Fleras, Augie. 2010. *Customizing Immigration, Commodifying Migrant Labour*. Paper presented at the Conference on the 25 Years of Canadian Studies at the University of Augsburg, Germany, December 9.

Fleras, Augie. 2011a. *The Media Gaze: Representations of Diversity in Canada*. Vancouver: UBC Press.

Fleras, Augie. 2011b. *The Politics of Multicultural Governance in a Globalizing World: A Case for Multiversalism and Multiculturalism in Canada*. Paper presented at the Conference commemorating 15 Years of Canadian Studies at the University of Matanzas, Cuba, 24 February.

Fleras, Augie. 2012. Cooling Out Troublesome Constituents: The Politics of Managing "Isms" in the Antipodes. In *Managing Ethnic Diversity*. Reza Hasmath, ed. Farnham, Surrey: Ashgate.

Fleras, Augie. 2014a. *"Racisms in a Multicultural Canada: Paradoxes, Politics, and Resistance"*. Waterloo Ontario: Wilfrid Laurier Press.

Fleras, Augie. 2014b. *Immigration Canada*. Vancouver: UBC Press.

Fleras, Augie. 2014c. "Mainstream Media as White Ethnic Press." Paper Delivered to the Media and Minority Conference. Jewish Museum. Berlin. November.

Fleras, Augie. 2015a. Moving Positively Beyond Multiculturalism: Toward a Postmulticultural Governance in a Diversifying Canada. *Zeitschrift fur Kanada Studien* 35: February. Based on a paper delivered to the University of Augsburg, Germany, 22 April 2014.

Fleras, Augie. 2015b. Beyond Multiculturalism: Managing Complex Diversities in Postmulticultural Canada. In *Revisiting Multiculturalism in Canada*. S. Guo and L. Wong, eds., 297–321. Rotterdam: Sense Publishers.

Fleras, Augie. 2016 (in press). *Social Inequality in Canada*. Toronto: Oxford University Press.

Fleras, Augie, and Jean Leonard Elliott. 1992. *The Nations within: Aboriginal-State Relations in Canada, the United States, and New Zealand*. Toronto: Oxford University Press.

Fleras, Augie, and Vic Krahn. 1992. *From Community Development to Inherent Self-Government: Restructuring Aboriginal–State Relations in Canada*. Paper presented at the Annual Meeting of Learned Societies. Charlottetown. June.

Fleras, Augie, and Jean Lock Kunz. 2001. *Media and Minorities: Misrepresenting Minorities in a Multicultural Canada*. Toronto: TEP.

Fleras, Augie, and Roger Maaka. 2009. Mainstreaming Indigeneity, Indigenizing Policymaking. *Indigenous Policy Journal*, October.

Fleras, Augie, and Paul Spoonley. 1999. *Recalling Aotearoa: Indigenous Politics and Ethnic Dynamics in New Zealand.* Auckland: Oxford University Press.

Flynn, J. R. 1984. "The mean IQ of Americans: Massive Gains 1932 to 1978." *Psychological Bulletin* 95(1):29–51.

Folson, Rose Baaba. 2005. *Calculated Kindness: Global Restructuring, Immigration, and Settlement in Canada.* Halifax: Fernwood.

Fong-Bates, Judy. 2005. *Midnight at the Dragon Café.* Emblem.

Fong-Bates, Judy. 2010. *The Year of Finding Memory.* Vintage.

Fontaine, Phil. 1998. Cooperation Not Confrontation. *Saskatchewan Indian* 18(1):9.

Fontaine, Phil. 2003. "Native Status Not an Obstacle." Letter to the *National Post*, 3 November.

Fontaine, Phil, and Bernie Farber. 2013. "What Canada Committed Against First Nations Was Genocide: The UN Should Recognize It." *Globe and Mail*, 14 October.

Forbes, Hugh Donald. 2007. "Trudeau as the First Theorist of Canadian Multiculturalism," in *Multiculturalism and the Canadian Constitution.* S. Tierney, ed. Vancouver: UBC Press.

Ford, Caylan, and Joan Delaney. 2008. "Is Official Multiculturalism Failing in Its Own Heartland?" *Epoch Times*, 17 February.

Ford, Chandra, and Collins Airhihenbuwa. 2010. Critical Race Theory, Race Equity, and Public Health: Toward Anti-Racism Praxis. *American Journal of Public Health* 100 (Supple.1): S30–S35.

Forsythe, David P. 2006. *Human Rights in International Relations.* New York: Cambridge University Press.

Forum. 2009. "American Religion and 'Whiteness' Religion and American Culture." *Journal of Interpretation* 19(1):1–35.

Foster, Cecil. 2005. *Where Race Does Not Matter: The New Spirit of Modernity.* Toronto: Penguin.

Foster, Jason. 2012. Making Temporary Permanent: The Silent Transformation of the Temporary Foreign Worker Program. *Just Labour: A Canadian Journal of Work and Society* 19(autumn):22–33.

Foster, Lorne. 1998. *Turnstile Immigration: Multiculturalism, Social Order, and Social Justice in Canada.* Toronto: Thompson Education.

Foster, Lorne. 2011. The Foreign Credentials Gap in Canada. The Case of Targetted Universalism. *Directions* (Canadian Race Relations Foundation) 6(2):23–36.

Foucault, Michel. 1980. *Power/Knowledge: Selected Interviews and Other Writings, 1972–1977.* Vintage.

Fournier, Pierre. 1994. *A Meech Lake Post-mortem: Is Quebec Sovereignty Inevitable?* Montreal/Kingston: McGill-Queen's University Press.

Fournier, Suzanne. 2013. "Idle No More Energizers." *The Tyee*, 22 January.

Fox, Nick J., and Katie J. Ward. 2008. "What Governs Governance, and How Does It Evolve? The Sociology of Governance-in-Action." *British Journal of Sociology* 59(3):519–538.

Francis, Diane. 2002. *Immigration: The Economic Case.* Toronto: Key Porter.

Francis, Diane. 2005. "Immigration Issues Should Be Probed." *National Post*, 28 April.

Frankenberg, Ruth. 1993. *White Women, Race Matters: The Social Construction of Whiteness.* Minneapolis: University of Minnesota Press.

Frappier, Andre. 2013. "Debating Values in Quebec." *Canadian Dimension*, 13 November.

Fraser, Graham. 2004. "Premiers Reminded of Suicide Epidemic." *Toronto Star*, 26 September.

Fraser, Nancy. 1996. Social Justice in the Age of Identity Politics. Redistribution, Recognition, and Participation. The Tanner Lectures on Human Values. Stanford University. April 30–May 2.

Fraser, Nancy. 2008. *Adding Insult to Injury: Nancy Fraser Debates Her Critics.* Verso Publications.

Frederickson, G. M. 1999. "Mosaics and Melting Pots." *Dissent* (Summer), 36–43.

Frederickson, G. M. 2002. *Racism: A Short History.* Princeton, NJ: Princeton University Press.

Frederico, Christopher, and Samantha Luks. 2005. "The Political Psychology of Race." *International Journal of Political Psychology*, 26(6):661–674.

Freeland, Benjamin. 2010. "Gains in Native Entrepreneurship Impeded by Lack of Education." *Globe and Mail*, 1 September.

Freeze, Colin. 2008. "Heritage Department Takes Aim at Religious Radicals." *Globe and Mail*, 1 September.

Frelick, Bill. 2015. "Will Europe Make the Migration Crisis Worse?" Human Rights Watch. Reported on CNN, 21 April.

Frideres, James S. 2005. "Ethnogenesis: Immigrants to Ethnics and the Development of a Rainbow Class Structure." *Canadian Issues* (Spring), 58–60.

Frideres, James. 2006. "Cities and Immigrant Integration: The Future of Second and Third-Tier Cities." *Our Diverse Cities* 2:3–8.

Frideres, James. 2011. *First Nations in the Twenty-first Century*. Toronto: Oxford University Press.

Frideres, James S., and René R. Gadacz. 2012. *Aboriginal Peoples in Canada* (8th ed.). Scarborough: Pearson Education Canada.

Friends of the Simon Wiesenthal Center for Holocaust Studies. 2008. "Letter to the president of the University of Toronto." *National Post*, 5 February. (http://www.friendsofsimonwiesenthalcenter.com/downloads/news_020408.pdf)

Friesen, Joe. 2005. "Blame Canada (for Multiculturalism)." *Globe and Mail*, 20 August.

Friesen, Joe. 2015. "Tories Apply Specific Criteria for Refugees." *Globe and Mail*, 9 October.

Frith, Rosaline. 2003. "Integration." *Canadian Issues* (April), 35–36.

Fudge, Judy. 2011. "The Precarious Migrant Status and Precarious Employment: The Paradox of International Rights for Migrant Workers." Working Paper Series. Metropolis British Columbia.

Fudge, Judy and Fiona McPhail. 2009. The Temporary Foreign Worker Program in Canada: Low Skilled Workers as an Extreme Form of Flexible Labour. *Comparative Labour Law and Policy Journal* 31:101–139.

Fukawa, Masaka (with Stanley Fukawa). 2009. *Spirit of the Nikkei Fleet: BC's Japanese Canadian Fisherman*. Harbour Publishing.

Fukuyama, Frances. 1994. "The War of All against All." *New York Times Book Review*, 10 April.

Fulford, Robert. 2003. "From Russia, with Stories: David Bezmozgis Captures the Essence of Immigrant Life in His New Fiction." *National Post*, 27 May.

Gagnon, Alain-G., M. Guibernau, and F. Rocher. 2003. *The Conditions of Diversity in Multinational Democracies*. Montreal: Institute for Research on Public Policy.

Gagnon, Alain-G., and Raffaelle Iacovino. 2007. *Federalism, Citizenship, and Quebec: Debating Multinationalism*. Toronto: University of Toronto Press.

Galabuzi, Grace-Edward. 2006. *Canada's Economic Apartheid: The Social Exclusion of Racialized Groups in the New Century*. Toronto: Canadian Scholars' Press.

Galabuzi, Grace-Edward. 2011. Hegemonies, Continuities, and Discontinuities of Multiculturalism and the Anglo-Franco Conformity Order. In *Home and Native Land: Unsettling Multiculturalism in Canada*. May Chazan et al., eds., 58–84. Toronto: Between the Lines.

Gallagher, Bill. 2012. *Resource Rulers: Fortune and Folly on the Way to Canada's Road to Resources*. Author.

Gallagher, Charles A. 2007. *Rethinking the Color Line: Readings in Race and Ethnicity* (3rd ed.). New York: McGraw-Hill.

Gallagher, Charles A. 2009. "The End of Racism" as the New Doxa: New Strategies for Researching Race. In *White Logic, White Methods*. T. Zuberi and E. Bonilla-Silva, eds., 163–178. Lanham MD: Rowman & Littlefield.

Gallagher, Stephen. 2003. "Canada's Dysfunctional Refugee Determination System." Occasional Paper No. 78 of the Fraser Institute.

Gallagher, Stephen. 2004. "Canada and the Challenge of Asylum Migration." *Canadian Issues* (March), 43–44.

Gallagher, Stephen. 2008a. *Canada and Mass Immigration: The Creation of a Global Suburb and Its Impact on National Unity*. Available online at www.immigrationwatchcanada.org.

Gallagher, Stephen. 2008b. "Mass Migration in Canada." Paper presented to the Canadian Immigration Policy Conference. Sponsored by the Fraser Institute. Montreal, 4 June.

Galloway, Gloria. 2010. "Jason Kenney Trumpets Hard-Fought Immigration Reform." *Globe and Mail*, 1 July.

Galloway, Gloria. 2011. "Arguing the Agony of Attawapiskat." *Globe and Mail*, 1 December.

Garner, Steve. 2007. *Whiteness: An Introduction*. New York: Routledge.

Garvey, John, and Noel Ignatieff. 1996. *Race Traitor*. New York: Routledge.

Gay, G. 1997. "Educational Equality for Students of Color," in *Multicultural Education*. J. Banks and C. Banks, eds., 195–228. Toronto: Allyn and Bacon.

Gee, Ellen M., Karen M. Kobayashi, and Steven G. Prus. 2007. Ethnic Inequality in Canada: Economic and Health Dimensions. In *Dimensions of Inequality in Canada.* D. Green and J. Kesselman, eds. Vancouver: UBC Press.

George, Usha. 2006. "Immigration Integration: Simple Questions, Complex Answers." *Canadian Diversity* 5(1):3–6.

George, Usha, and Ferzana Chaze. 2014. Discrimination at Work: Comparing the Experiences of Foreign-Trained and Locally-Trained Engineers in Canada. *Canadian Ethnic Studies* 46(1):1–21.

Ghosh, Ratna. 2002. *Redefining Multicultural Education* (2nd ed.). Toronto: Nelson.

Ghosh, Ratna, and Ali A. Abdi. 2004. *Education and the Politics of Difference: Canadian Perspectives.* Toronto: Canadian Scholars' Press.

Ghosh, Ratna, and Mariusz Galczynski. 2014. *Redefining Multicultural Education: Inclusion and the Right to be Different* (3rd ed.). Toronto: Canadian Scholars Press.

Gibb, Heather. 2010. "Missing from Temporary Foreign Worker Programs: Gender Sensitive Approaches." *Canadian Issues* (Spring), 94–98.

Gibb, J. T., and L. Huang. 2003. *Children of Color: Psychological Intervention with Culturally Diverse Youth* (2nd ed.). San Francisco: Jossey-Bass.

Gibbins, Roger, and Guy Laforest, eds. 1998. *Beyond the Impasse: Toward Reconciliation.* Montreal: Institute of Research for Public Policy.

Gibson, Gordon. 1998. "Nisga'a Treaty: The Good, the Bad, and the Alternative." *The Globe and Mail*, 13 October.

Gibson, Gordon. 2005. "Canada's Apartheid World." *Globe and Mail*, 15 July.

Gibson, Gordon. 2009a. *A New Look At Canadian Indian Policy: Respect the Collective—Promote the Individual.* Calgary: Fraser Institute.

Gibson, Gordon. 2009b. "The Politics of Canadian Immigration Policy," in *The Effects of Mass Immigration on Canadian Living Standards and Society.* H Grubel, ed. Calgary: Fraser Institute.

Gillborn, David. 2006. "Rethinking White Supremacy: Who Counts in 'White World.'" *Ethnicities* 6(3):318–340.

Gillette, Aaron. 2007. *Eugenics and the Nature–Nurture Debate in the Twentieth Century.* New York: Palgrave Macmillan.

Gilmour, R. J., D. Bhandar, and J. Heer, eds. 2012. "Too Asian?" *Racism, Privilege, and Post-Secondary Education.* Toronto: Between the Lines.

Gilroy, Paul. 2004. *After Empire: Melancholia or Convivial Culture?* London: Routledge.

Giroux, H. A. 1994. "Insurgent Multiculturalism as the Promise of Pedagogy," in *Multiculturalism: A Critical Reader.* D. T. Goldberg, ed., 325–343. Oxford: Blackwell.

Giroux, H. 1999. "Rewriting the Discourse of Racial Identity: Towards a Pedagogy and Politics of Whiteness." *Harvard Educational Review* 67(2):285–320.

Giroux, Henry A. 2006. *America on Edge: Henry Giroux on Politics, Education, Culture.* New York: Palgrave Macmillan.

Giroux, Henry. 2008. *The Terror of Neoliberalism: Authoritarianism and the Eclipse of Democracy.* Boulder CO: Paradigm Press.

Glasser, Theodore L., Isabel Awad, and John W. Kim. 2009. "The Claims of Multiculturalism and the Journalists' Promise of Diversity." *Journal of Communication* 59:57–78.

Glazer, Nathan. 1997. *We Are All Multiculturalists Now.* Cambridge, MA: Harvard University Press.

Glazer, Nathan. 2010. Democracy and Deep Divides. *Journal of Democracy* 21(2).

Godlewska, Christina and Jeremy Webber. 2007. The Calder Decision: Aboriginal Title, Treaties, and the Nisga'a. In *Let Right Be Done.* H. Foster, H. Raven, and J. Webber, eds. 1–36. Vancouver: UBC Press.

Goldberg, David Theo. 1993. *Philosophy and the Politics of Meaning.* Oxford: Basil Blackwell.

Goldberg, David Theo. 1994a. "Introduction: Multicultural Conditions," in *Multiculturalism: A Critical Reader*, D. T. Goldberg, ed., 1–44. Malden, MA: Basil Blackwell.

Goldberg, David Theo., ed. 1994b. *Multiculturalism: A Critical Reader.* Malden, MA: Blackwell.

Goldberg, David Theo. 2002. "Racial States," in *A Companion to Racial and Ethnic Studies.* D. T. Goldberg and J. Solomos, eds., 233–258. Malden, MA: Blackwell.

Goldberg, David Theo. 2005. "Racial Americanization." In *Racialization.* K. Murji and J. Solomos, eds., 87–102. Oxford: Oxford University Press.

Goldberg, David Theo. 2007. "Raceless States." In *Race, Racialization, and Anti-racism in Canada and Beyond.* G. F. Johnson and R. Enomoto, eds., 206–232. University of Toronto Press.

Goldberg, David Theo, and John Solomos, eds. 2002. *A Companion to Racial and Ethnic Studies.* Malden, MA: Blackwell.

Goldberg, Jonah. 2006. "Racism by Any Other Name," *National Review Online*. Retrieved October 7, 2015 (www.nationalreview.com/article/219258/racism-any-other-name-jonah-goldberg).

Goldring, Luin, and Patricia Landolt. 2012. "The Impact of Precarious Legal Status on Immigrant Economic Outcomes." Institute for Research on Public Policy. April.

Goldring, Luin, and Patricia Landolt. 2013. *Producing and Negotiating Non Citizenship: Precarious Legal Status in Canada.* Toronto: University of Toronto Press.

Goldsborough, James. 2000. "Out of Control Immigration." *Foreign Affairs* (September/October), 89–101.

Goldstein, Eric L. 2006. *The Price of Whiteness.* Princeton University Press.

Gopalkrishnan, Narayan, and Hurriyet Babacan, eds. 2007. Introduction. In *Racisms in the New World Order: Realities of Cultures, Colours, and Identity.* Cambridge Scholars Publishing.

Gordon, Andrea. 2008. "Immigrant Men Learn to Broaden Paternal Role." *Toronto Star*, 17 May.

Goren, William D. 2007. "Concept of Undue Hardship and Reasonable Accommodation in the Employment Context." Retrieved November 16, 2015 (www.mediate.com/articles/gorenW2.cfm).

Gorski, Paul. 2004. "Language of Closet Racism: An Introduction. Race, Racism, and the Law. Speaking Truth to Power." Available online at http://academic.udayton.edu.

Gosine, Andil. 2003. "Myths of Diversity." *Alternatives Journal* 29(1):1–4.

Gottschalk, Peter, and Gabriel Greenberg. 2008. *Islamophobia: Making Muslims the Enemy.* Toronto: Rowman & Littlefield.

Goutor, David, and Chris Ramsaroop. 2010. "No Thanksgiving for Migrant Workers." *Toronto Star*, 8 October.

Government of Canada. 2005. "A Canada for All: Canada's Action Plan Against Racism." Retrieved November 16, 2015 (http://publications.gc.ca/collections/Collection/CH34-7-2005E.pdf).

Government of Canada. 2010. "Aboriginal People as Victims of Crime." Retrieved online.

Grabb, Edward. 2009. *Theories of Social Inequality* (5th ed.). Toronto, ON: Thompson.

Grabb, Edward, and Neil Guppy, eds. 2010. *Social Inequality in Canada. Patterns, Problems & Policies* (5th ed.). Toronto, ON: Pearson.

Graham, Katherine A. H. 2007. "Introduction." *Our Diverse Cities: Ontario, 4*(Fall), 3–6.

Granatstein, J. L. 2007. *Whose War Is It? How Canada Can Survive in the Post 9/11 World.* Toronto: HarperCollins.

Grant, Hugh M., and Ronald R. Oertel. 1999. "Diminishing Returns to Immigration? Interpreting the Economic Experience of Canadian Immigrants." *Canadian Ethnic Studies* 31(3):56–66.

Grant, Tavia. 2013. "Starting Up a New Native Economy." *Globe and Mail*, 19 February.

Graves, Frank. 2015. "The Ekos Poll: Are Canadians Getting More Racist?" *iPolitics*, 12 March

Gray, John. 1997. "AFN Rivals Embody Competing Visions." *Globe and Mail*, 28 July.

Green, David. A. and Jonathan R. Kesselman. 2006. *Dimensions of Inequality in Canada.* Vancouver: UBC Press.

Green, David, A., W. Craig Riddell, and France St. Hilaire. 2015. Income Inequality: The Canadian Story. Art of the State Series V. Institute for Research on Public Policy.

Green, Joyce. 2003. "Decolonizing in the Age of Globalization." *Canadian Dimension* (March/April), 3–5.

Green, Joyce, ed. 2007. *Making Space for Indigenous Feminism.* London: Zed Books.

Green, Joyce. 2008. "Aboriginal Rights in a Neo-Liberal World." *Canadian Dimension* (March/April), 22–25.

Green, Joyce, ed. 2014. *Indivisible: Indigenous Human Rights.* Halifax, NS: Fernwood.

Greenberg, Joshua. 2000. "Opinion Discourses and Canadian Newspapers: The Case of the Chinese 'Boat People.'" *Canadian Journal of Communication* 25(4).

Greenspon, Edward. 2001. "Building the New Canadian Identity." *Globe and Mail*, 10 November.

Gregg, Allan. 2006. "Identity Crisis: Multiculturalism: A Twentieth-Century Dream Becomes a Twenty-first-Century Conundrum." *The Walrus* (March), 28–38.

Grewal, San. 2015. "Blacks Three Times More Likely to be Carded by Peel Police Than Whites." *Toronto Star*, 24 September.

Grey, Julius. 2007. "The Paradoxes of Reasonable Accommodation." *Policy Options* (September), 34–40.

Grez, E. E. 2008. "Migrant Workers Reap Bitter Harvest in Ontario." *Toronto Star,* 28 October.

Griffith, Andrew. 2013. *Policy Arrogance or Innocent Bias: Resetting Citizenship and Immigration.* Ottawa: Anar Press.

Grillo, R. 2007. "An Excess of Alterity? Debating Difference in a Multicultural Society." *Ethnic and Racial Studies* 30(6):979–998.

Gross, Michael L. 1996. "Restructuring Ethnic Paradigms: From Premodern to Postmodern Perspectives." *Canadian Review of Studies in Nationalism* 23(1–2):51–65.

Grubel, Herbert. 2005. "Immigration and the Welfare State in Canada: Growing Conflicts, Constructive Solutions." *Public Policy Sources* 84. Retrieved November 16, 2015 (www.fraserinstitute.org/sites/default/files/ImmigrationandWelfareState.pdf).

Grubel, Herbert. 2009. *The Effects of Mass Immigration on Canadian Living Standards and Society.* Calgary: Fraser Institute.

Grubel, Herbert, and Patrick Grady. 2011. *Immigration and the Canadian Welfare State.* Calgary: Fraser Institute.

Guess, Teresa J. 2006. "The Social Construction of Whiteness: Racism by Intent, Racism by Consequence." *Critical Sociology* 32:649–673.

Guibernau, Montserrat. 2007. *The Identity of Nations.* Malden, MA: Polity Press.

Guimond, Eric, Don Kerr, and Roderic Beaujot. 2004. "Charting the Growth of Canada's Aboriginal Populations: Problems, Options, and Implications." *Canadian Studies in Population* 31(3):55–82.

Guinier, Lani, and Gerald Torres. 2002. The Miner's Canary: Enlisting Race, Resisting Power, Transforming Democracy. Harvard University Press.

Gunew, Sneja. 2004. *Haunted Nations: The Colonial Dimension of Multiculturalism.* New York: Routledge.

Gunter, Lorne. 2011a. "Nothing will Improve on Reserves until Aboriginal Politicians are Accountable." *National Post*, 4 March.

Gunter, Lorne. 2011b. "The Problem is the Indian Act." *National Post*, 7 December.

Guo, Shibao, and Yan Guo. 2015. Rethinking Multiculturalism in Canada: Tensions Between Immigration, Ethnicity and Minority Rights. In *Revisiting Multiculturalism in Canada.* S. Guo and L. Wong, eds., 109–126. Rotterdam: Sense Publishers.

Guo, Shibao & Lloyd Wong, (eds.), 2015. *Revisiting Multiculturalism in Canada. Theories, Policies, and Debates.* Rotterdam: Sense Publishers.

Gurr, Ted Robert. 2001. *Peoples vs States: Minorities at Risk in the New Century.* Washington, DC: United States Institute for Peace.

Guterres, Antonio. 2007. "People on the Move—Ideally, Out of Choice." *The Globe and Mail*, 3 December.

Gwyn, Richard. 1994. "The First Borderless State." *Toronto Star*, 26 November.

Gwyn, Richard. 1996. *Nationalism without Walls: The Unbearable Lightness of Being Canadian.* Toronto: McClelland & Stewart.

Gwyn, Richard. 2000. "A Visionary Challenges Our Policy on Immigration." *Toronto Star*, 12 March.

Gwyn, Richard. 2001a. "Old Canada Disappears." *Toronto Star*, 21 March.

Gwyn, Richard. 2001b. "Racism Must Be Addressed." *KW Record*, 5 September.

Ha, Tu Thanh. 2007. "Quebecker's Insecurities Said to Fuel Backlash Against Minorities." *The Globe and Mail*, 15 August.

Habacan, Alden E. 2007. "Beyond the Mosaic: Canada's Multiculturalism 2.0." Paper to the Annual Summer Conference. The Stranger Next Door: Making Diversity Work. Orillia ON: Couchiching Institute on Public Affairs, August 9–12.

Habacan, Alden E. 2012. A Renewal of Multiculturalism. *Culture West*, Winter:13–19.

Habyarimana, James, Macartan Humphreys, Daniel Posner, and Jeremy Weinstein. 2008. "Is Ethnic Conflict Inevitable?" *Foreign Affairs*, July/August.

Hage, G. 1998. *White Nation: Fantasies of White Supremacy in a Multicultural Society.* Sydney, Australia: Pluto Press.

Hage, Ghassan. 2006. "The Doubts Down Under." *Catalyst Magazine*, 17 May.

Hagey, Rebecca. 2004. "Implementing Accountability for Equity." *Directions* 2(1):59–77.

Hailey, Sarah E., and Kristina R. Olson, 2013. A Social Psychologist's Guide to the Development of Racial Attitudes. *Social and Personality Psychology Compass* 7(7):457–469.

Hall, Anthony J. 2000. "Racial Discrimination in Legislation, Litigation, Legend, and Lore." *Canadian Ethnic Studies* 32(2):119–137.

Hall, Stuart. 1996. "New Ethnicities," in *Stuart Hall in Critical Studies*, D. Marley and K. H. Chen, eds. London: Routledge.

Halli, Shiva S., and Leo Driedger, eds. 1999. *Immigrant Canada: Demographic, Economic, and Social Challenges*. Toronto: University of Toronto Press.

Halli-Vedanand, Shiva S. 2007. "The Problem of Second-Generation Decline: Perspectives on Integration in Canada." *International Migration and Integration* 8:277–287.

Halstead, Mark 1988. *Education, Justice, and Cultural Diversity: An Examination of the Honeyford Affair, 1984–85*. London: Falmer Press.

Hanamoto, Darrell. 1995. *Monitored Peril. Asian Americans and the Politics of Representation*. St. Paul, MN: University of Minnesota Press.

Handa, Amita. 2003. *Of Silk Saris and Mini-Skirts: South Asian Girls Walk the Tightrope of Culture*. Toronto: Women's Press.

Hanlon, Michael. 2014. "The Concept 'There is not Just a Universe, But a Multiverse,' Has Come into the Scientific Mainstream." The Telegraph, printed in *National Post*, 22 April.

Hannah, Daryl C. 2009. Can Racism Lead to Weight Gain? Available online at www.diversityinc.com.

Hansen, Randall. 2007. "Diversity, Integration, and the Turn from Multiculturalism in the United Kingdom," in *Belonging?* K. Banting et al., eds., 351–386. Montreal: Institute for Research on Public Policy.

Hansen, Randall. 2013. "Q&A with Randall Hansen: Major Debates and Challenges in Immigration—Canada and Europe." Interview by Loretta Ho and Harbi Natt. Munk School of Global Affairs. University of Toronto. 22 February.

Harada, M. Masanori Hanada, Masami Tajiri, Yukari Inoue, Nobuyuki Hotta, Tadashi Fujino, Shigeru Takaoka, and Keishi Ueda. 2011. "Mercury Pollution in First Nations Groups in Ontario, Canada: 35 Years of Minimata Disease in Canada." *Journal of Minimata Studies* 3:3–30.

Harding, Robert. 2010. "The Demonization of Aboriginal Child Welfare Authorities in the News." *Canadian Journal of Communication* 35(1):85–108.

Harding, Sandra. 2002. "Science, Race, Culture, Empire," in *Companion to Racial and Ethnic Studies*. D. T. Goldberg and J. Solomos, eds., 217–228. Malden, MA: Blackwell.

Harell, Allison, and Dietlind Stolle. 2010. "Diversity and Democratic Politics: An Introduction." *Canadian Journal of Political Science* 43(2):235–256.

Harmon, Bryan. n.d. "Inclusion/Integration? Is There a Difference?" Retrieved November 10, 2015 (www.cdss.ca/images/pdf/general_information/integration_vs_inclusion.pdf).

Harris, Fred. 1995. *Multiculturalism from the Margins*. Westport, CT: Bergin and Garvey.

Harris, Paul. 1997. *Black Rage Confronts the Law*. New York: New York University Press.

Harris, Scott. 2001. What Can Interactionism Contribute to the Study of Inequality? The Case of Marriage and Beyond. *Symbolic Interaction* 24:445–480.

Harris-Short, Sonia. 2007. "Self-Government in Canada: A Successful Model for the Decolonisation of Aboriginal Child Welfare," in *Accommodating Cultural Diversity*. S. Tierney, ed. Hampshire, UK: Ashgate.

Hartmann, Douglas. 2015. Reflections on Race, Diversity, and the Crossroads of Multiculturalism. *The Sociological Quarterly* 56(4):623–639.

Harty, Siobhan, and Michael Murphy. 2005. *In Defence of Multinational Citizenship*. Vancouver: UBC Press.

Harvey, Edward B., Bobby Siu, and Kathleen D. V. Reil. 1999. "Ethnocultural Groups, Period of Immigration and Socioeconomic Situation." *Canadian Ethnic Studies* 31(3):95–108.

Hassan, Farzana. 2008. "Muslim Feminist Perspectives on International Women's Day." *Montreal Gazette*, 8 March.

Hawkes, David. 2000. "Review of Citizens-Plus." *Isuma* (Autumn):141–142.

Hawkins, Freda. 1974. *Canada and Immigration*. Kingston: McGill/Queen's University Press.

Hawthorne, Lesleyanne. 2007. *Foreign Credential Recognition and Assessment: An Introduction*. Retrieved November 16, 2015 (http://canada.metropolis.net/pdfs/Hawthorne_intro_en.pdf).

Hawthorne, Lesleyanne. 2008. "The Impact of Economic Selection Policy on Labour Market Outcomes for Degree Qualified Migrants in Canada and Australia." *IRPP Choices* 14(5). May.

Health Canada. 2006. *First Nations, Inuit, and Aboriginal Health: Suicide Prevention*. Available online at Health Canada. 2013. *Drinking Water and Wastewater: First Nations and Inuit Health*. Retrieved from www.hc-sc.gc.ca.

Heath, A. F., and J. R. Tilley. 2005. "National Identity and Xenophobia in an Ethnically Divided Society." *International Journal on Multicultural Societies* 7(2):119–132.

Heath, Anthony, and Sin Yi Cheung. 2007. "The Comparative Study of Ethnic Minority Disadvantage," in *Unequal Chances: Ethnic Minorities in Western Labour Markets*. A. Heath and S. Y. Cheung, eds., 1–44. New York: Oxford University Press.

Heath, Joseph. 2014. "Misunderstanding Canadian Multiculturalism." *Global Brief*, 24 March.

Hebert, Yvonne M., and Alan Sears. 2004. *Citizenship Education*. Toronto: Canadian Education Association.

Hebert, Yvonne M., and Lori Wilkinson. 2002. "The Citizenship Debates: Conceptual, Policy, Experiential, and Educational Issues," in *Citizenship in Transformation in Canada*. Y. Hebert, ed., 3–36. Toronto: University of Toronto Press.

Hechter, Michael. 1975. *Internal Colonialism: The Celtic Fringe in British National Development*. Berkeley, CA: University of California Press.

Hedican, Edward J. 2013. *Ipperwash: The Tragic Failure of Canada's Aboriginal Policy*: University of Toronto Press.

Heer, Jeet. 2012. "Why Did *Hunger Games* Hit a Nerve: It's the Economy Stupid." *Globe and Mail*, 23 March.

Heider, Karl. 1988. The Rashomon Effect: When Ethnographers Disagree. *American Anthropologist* 90(1):73–81.

Helin, Calvin. 2006. *Dances with Dependency*. Vancouver: Orca Spirit Publishing.

Helly, Denise. 1993. "The Political Regulation of Cultural Plurality: Foundations and Principles." *Canadian Ethnic Studies* 25(2):15–31.

Helmes-Hayes, Rick, and James Curtis, eds. 1998. *The Vertical Mosaic Revisited*. Toronto, ON: University of Toronto Press.

Henderson, Jennifer, and Pauline Wakeham. 2013. *Reconciling Canada: Critical Perspectives on the Culture of Redress*. Toronto, ON: University of Toronto Press.

Hennebry, Jenna. 2010. Who Has Their Eye on the Ball? "Jurisdictional Futbol" and Canada's Temporary Foreign Worker Program. *Policy Options*, 63:62–68.

Hennebry, Jenna. 2012. Permanently Temporary? Agricultural Workers and their Integration in Canada. *Institute for Research in Public Policy*, Study No. 26.

Hennebry, Jenna L., and Janet McLaughlin. 2011. Key Issues and Recommendations for Canada's Temporary Foreign Worker Program: Reducing Vulnerabilities and Protecting Rights. Policy Points. International Migration Research Centre. Issue 11.

Hennebry, Jenna, and Bessma Momani. 2013. "Introduction: Arab Canadians as Targeted Transnationals." In *Targeted Transnationals: The State, the Media, and Arab Canadians*, Jenna Hennebry and Bessma Momani, eds., 1–14. Vancouver: UBC Press.

Hennebry, Jenna L., and Kerry Preibish. 2010. "A Model for Managed Migration? Re-Examining Best Practices in Canada's Seasonal Agricultural Worker Program. *International Migration* 50(s1), e19–e40.

Henry, Frances. 2006. A Response to Hier and Walby's article: Competing Analytical Paradigms in the Sociological Study of Racism in Canada. *Canadian Ethnic Studies* 38(2).

Henry, Frances, and Carol Tator. 1993. "The Show Boat Controversy." *Toronto Star*, 28 May.

Henry, Frances, and Carol Tator. 2002. *Discourses of Domination: Racial Bias in the Canadian English-Language Press*. Toronto: University of Toronto Press.

Henry, Frances, and Carol Tator. 2003. *Racial Profiling in Toronto: Discourses of Domination, Mediation, and Opposition*. Final Draft Submitted to the Canadian Race Relations Foundation.

Henry, Frances, and Carol Tator. 2006. *The Colour of Democracy: Racism in Canadian Society* (3rd ed.). Toronto: Harcourt Brace/Nelson.

Henry, Frances, and Carol Tator, eds. 2009. *Racism in the Canadian University: Demanding Social Justice, Inclusion, and Equity*. Toronto: University of Toronto Press.

Henry, Frances, and Carol Tator. 2010. *The Colour of Democracy. Racism in Canadian Society* (4th ed.). Toronto: Thomson Nelson.

Henshaw, Peter. 2007. "John Buchan and the British Imperial Origins of Canadian Multiculturalism," in *Canadas of the Mind*. N. Hillmer and A. Chapnick, eds. Montreal/Kingston: McGill-Queen's University Press.

Hesse, Barnor. 2004. "Discourses on Institutional Racism, The Geneology of a Concept," in *Institutional Racism in Higher Education*. I. Law et al., eds., 131–148. Sterling, VA: Trentham Books.

Hiebert, Dan. 2000. "Immigration and the Changing Canadian City." *Canadian Geographer* 44(1):25–43.

Hiebert, Dan. 2006. "Winning, Losing, and Still Playing the Game: The Political Economy of Immigration in Canada." *Journal of Economic and Social Geography* 97(1):38–48.

Hiebert, Dan. 2011. "Superdiversity in Canada: New Challenges of Integration." Presentation to the Cross Cultural Mental Health Conference. Vancouver, BC. 3–4 October.

Hiebert, Dan, Jock Collins, and Paul Spoonley. 2003. *Uneven Globalization: Neoliberal Regimes, Immigration, and Multiculturalism in Australia, Canada, and New Zealand*. Working Paper Series No. 03-05. Research on Immigration and Integration in the Metropolis.

Hiebert, Dan, and David Ley. 2006. "Introduction: The Political Economy of Immigration." *Journal of Economic and Social Geography* 97(1):3–6.

Hier, Sean, and B. Singh Bolaria. 2007. *Identity and Belonging: Rethinking Race and Ethnicity in Canadian Society*. Toronto: Canadian Scholars' Press.

Hier, Sean, and Joshua Greenberg. 2002. "News Discourses and the Problematization of Chinese Migration to Canada," in *Discourses of Domination*. F. Henry and C. Tator, eds., 138–162. Toronto: University of Toronto Press.

Hier, Sean, and Kevin Walby. 2006. "Competing Analytical Paradigms in the Sociological Study of Racism in Canada." *Canadian Ethnic Studies* 38(1).

Hill, Jane H. 2012. *The Everday Language of White Racism*. Wiley-Blackwell.

Hiller, Harry. 2000. *Canadian Society: A Macro Analysis* (4th ed.). Toronto: Prentice-Hall.

Hinton, M., E. Johnston, and D. Rigney. 1997. *Indigenous Australians and the Law*. Sydney: Cavendish Publishing.

Historica-Dominion Institute. 2010. *What the World Thinks of Canada: Canada and the World in 2010, Immigration & Diversity*. Available online at http://cms.juntos.ca/docs/Db-Historica Dominion/June_22_Canada_and_the_World_EN.pdf

Hitchens, Christopher. 2010. "The Good Intentions Paving Company." *National Post*, 25 June.

Hoberman, John M. 2007. Medical Racism and the Rhetoric of Exculpation: How Do Physicians Think About Race? *New Literary History* 38(3):505–525.

Hoberman, John M. 2012. *Black & Blue: The Origins and Consequences of Medical Racism*. University of California Press.

Hochschild, Jennifer. 2002. "Affirmative Action as Culture War," in *A Companion to Racial and Ethnic Studies*. D. T. Goldberg and J. Solomos, eds., 282–303. Malden, MA: Blackwell.

hooks, bell. 1992. *Black Looks: Race and Representation*. Boston: South End Press.

hooks, bell. 1994. *Outlaw Culture: Resisting Representations*. New York: Routledge.

hooks, bell. 1995. *Killing Rage*. Boston: South End Press.

hooks, bell. 2013. *Writing Beyond Race: Living Theory and Practice*. New York: Routledge.

Holdaway, Simon. 2003. Police Race Relations in England and Wales: Theory, Policy, and Practice. *Police and Society* 7:49–74.

Hollinger, David A. 2006. *Postethnic America: Beyond Multiculturalism*. New York, NY: Basic Books.

Hopper, Tristan. 2012. How the Idle No More Movement Started and Where It Might Go From Here. *National Post*, 26 December.

Hopper, Tristin. 2015. "Canada's Vaunted Refugee Acceptance Falls Short." *National Post*, 10 September.

Horizons. 2008. *Hope or Heartbreak: Aboriginal Youth and Canada's Future [entire issue]*. 2008. Policy Research Initiative 10(1).

Horton, James O., and Lois E. Horton. 2004. *Slavery and the Making of America*. New York, NY: Oxford University Press.

Hou, Feng, and Garnett Picot. 2014. Annual Levels of Immigration and Immigrant Entry Earnings in Canada. *Canadian Public Policy* 40(2):166–181.

Howard-Hassmann, Rhoda E. 1999. "Canadian" as an Ethnic Category: Implications for Multiculturalism and National Unity. *Canadian Public Policy* xxv(4):523–534.

Howe, Miles. 2015. *Debriefing Elsipogtog. The Anatomy of a Struggle*. Halifax: Fernwood.

Hoyos, Kathleen. 2014. Canadian Multiculturalism: Same as it ever was? *Coolabah* 13 (Australian Studies Centre, University of Barcelona).

Hrushetska, Maryna. 2013. "Beyond Multiculturalism." Opinion. Retrieved from www.aljazeera.com.

Hudson, Michael. 1987. "Multiculturalism, Government Policy, and Constitutional Entrenchment—A Comparative Study." In *Multiculturalism and the Charter: A Legal Perspective*. Canadian Human Rights Foundation, 59–122. Toronto: Carswell.

Hum, Derek, and Wayne Simpson. 2000. "Not All Visible Minorities Face Labour Market Discrimination." *Policy Options* (December), 45–51.

Hum, Derek, and Wayne Simpson. 2005. *Economic Assimilation of Canadian Immigrants: Cross Sectional and Panel Data Estimates*. Final Report Presented to the Prairie Centre for Excellence in Research on Immigration and Integration.

Hum, Derek, and Wayne Simpson. 2007. Revisiting Equity and Labour: Immigration, Gender, Minority Status and Income Differentials in Canada. In *Race and Racism in 21st Century Canada: Continuity, Complexity, and Change*. S. P. Hier and B. S. Bolaria, eds. Peterborough, ON: Broadview.

Human Resources and Skills Development Canada (HRSDC). 2011. Understanding Homelessness. Available online at www.hrsdc.gc.ca.

Human Rights Watch. 2013. *Those Who Take Us Away: Abusive Policing and Failures in Protection of Indigenous Women and Girls in Northern British Columbia*. New York.

Huntington, Samuel. 1993. *The Clash of Civilizations and the Remaking of World Order*. New York: Simon and Schuster.

Hurley, Mary C. 2009. *The Indian Act*. Parliamentary Information and Research Service. 23 November.

Hurst, Lynda. 2003. "A Critical Measure of Bias." *Toronto Star*, 12 April.

Hurst, Lynda. 2006. "Discontent in Eurabia." *Toronto Star*, 11 February.

Hurtado, Aida. 1996. *The Color of Privilege: Three Blasphemies on Race and Feminism*. Michigan: University of Michigan Press.

Hurwitz, Jon, and Mark Peffley. 2010. "And Justice for Some: Race, Crime, and Punishment in the US Criminal Justice System." *Canadian Journal of Political Science 43*(2):457–479.

Huston, Patricia. 1995. "Intellectual Racism?" *Canadian Medical Association Journal* 153:1219.

Hutchinson, John, and Anthony D. Smith, eds. 1996. *Ethnicity*. Oxford: Oxford University Press.

Hylton, John H, ed. 1994/1999. *Aboriginal Self-Government in Canada: Current Trends and Issues*. Saskatoon: Purich Publishing.

Hyman, Ilene. 2009. *Racism as a Determinant of Immigrant Health*. Policy brief commissioned by the Public Health Agency of Canada and supported by Metropolis. Submitted 30 March.

Hyndman, Jennifer. 1999. "Gender and Canadian Immigration Policy: A Current Snapshot." *Canadian Woman Studies* 19(3):6–10.

Ibbitson, John. 2005. *The Polite Revolution: Perfecting the Canadian Dream*. Toronto: McClelland & Stewart.

Ibbitson, John. 2014. *Bootstrap Immigrants: Assessing the Conservative Transformation of Canada's Immigration Program*. Policy Brief No 52. CIGI, Waterloo Ontario. December.

Ignace, M. B., and R. E. Ignace. 1998. "The Old Wolf in Sheep's Clothing: Canadian Aboriginal Peoples." In *Multiculturalism in a World of Leaking Boundaries*. D. Haselbach, ed., 101–132. New Brunswick, NJ: Transaction Publishers.

Ignatieff, Michael. 1994. *Blood and Belonging: Journeys into the New Nationalism*. Toronto: Viking.

Ignatieff, Michael. 1995. "Nationalism and the Narcissism of Minor Differences." *Queens Quarterly* 102(1):1–25.

Ignatieff, Michael. 2001. "Human Rights and the Rights of the State: Are They on a Collision Course?" Hagey Lecture. University of Waterloo, 24 January.

Ignatieff, Michael. 2005. "The Coming Constitutional Crisis." *Globe and Mail*, 16 April.

Ikuenobe, Polycarp. 2013. Conceptualizing and Theorizing About the Idea of a "Post Racial" Era. *Journal for the Theory of Social Behaviour* 43(4):446–468.

Imai, Shin. 2007. *The Structure of the Indian Act: Accountability in Governance*. Research Paper for the National Centre for First Nations Governance. July.

Immigration Watch Canada 2011. Canada – Immigration Intake, 1860 to 2013. Retrieved from www.immigrationwatchcanada.org.

Immigration Watch Canada. 2015. Canadian Immigration Policy: Heading for Disaster. Part 1. Peter Goodchild. Retrieved June 24, 2015 (www.immigrationwatchcanada.org).

INAC. 2004. *Sustainable Development Strategy 2004–2006: On the Right Path Together: A Sustainable Future for First Nations, Inuit, and Northern Communities.* Available online at www.nunavuteconomicforum.ca/public/files/library/POLITICA/INAC%20Sustainable%20Dev%20Strategy.pdf.

INCITE: Women of Color Against Violence. 2006. *Color of Violence: The INCITE Anthology.* Cambridge, MA: South End Press.

Indian and Northern Affairs Canada. 1995. *Inherent Right of Self-Government Policy.* Ottawa: Author.

Institute of Race Relations (IRR). 2010. *Racial Violence: The Buried Issue.* Retrieved November 16, 2015 (www.irr.org.uk/news/racial-violence-the-buried-issue/).

Institute for Survey Research. 2015. "Canadian Public Opinion about Immigration and Multiculturalism", *The Environics* (http://www.environicsinstitute.org/uploads/institute-projects/environics%20institute%20-%20focus%20canada%20spring%202015%20survey%20on%20immigration-multiculturalism%20-%20final%20report%20-%20june%2030-2015.pdf)

International Working Group on Indigenous Affairs (IWGIA). 2015. *The Indigenous World, 2015.* Copenhagen.

Isajiw, Wsevolod, ed. 1997. *Multiculturalism in North America and Europe: Comparative Perspectives on Interethnic Relations and Social Incorporation.* Toronto: Canadian Scholars' Press.

Isajiw, Wsevolod W. 1999. *Understanding Diversity: Ethnicity and Race in the Canadian Context.* Toronto: Thompson Education.

Isin, Engin. 1996. "Global City-Regions and Citizenship," in *Local Places in the Age of the Global City.* D. Bell, R. Keil, and G. Wekerle, eds. Montreal: Black Rose Books.

Itwaru, Arnold, ed. 2009. *The White Supremacist State.* Toronto: Other Eye Publishers.

Ivison, John. 2012. Native Fury Versus Western Oil. Comment. *National Post,* 5 December.

Jackson, Andrew. 2014. Canadian-born Visible Minority Youth Facing an Unfair Job Future. *Globe and Mail,* 29 May.

Jackson, Margaret A. 1999. Canadian Aboriginal Women and Their 'Criminality': The Cycle of Violence in the Context of Difference. *Australian and New Zealand Journal of Criminology* 32(2):197–208.

Jain, Harish C. 1988. "Affirmative Action/Employment Equity Programs and Visible Minorities in Canada." *Currents* 5(1):3–7.

Jain, Harish C., and Rick D. Hackett 1989. "Measuring Effectiveness of Employment Equity Programs in Canada: Public Policy and a Survey." *Canadian Public Policy* 15(2):189–204.

Jakubowicz, Andrew. 2005. "Multiculturalism in Australia: Apogee or Nadir?" *Canadian Diversity* 4(1):15–18.

Jakubowicz, Andrew. 2007. "Political Islam and the Future of Australian Multiculturalism." *National Identities* 9(3):265–280.

James, Carl. 1998. *Seeing Ourselves: Exploring Race, Ethnicity, and Culture* (2nd ed.). Toronto: Thompson Education.

James, Carl E. 2002. "Introduction: Encounters in Race, Ethnicity, and Language." In *Talking about Identity.* Carl James and Adrienne Shadd, eds., 1–8. Toronto: Between the Lines.

James, Carl, ed. 2005. *Possibilities and Limitations: Multicultural Policies and Programs in Canada.* Halifax: Fernwood.

James, Carl. 2008. "'It Will Happen without Putting in Place Special Measures': Racially Diversifying Universities," in *Racism in the Canadian University.* F. Henry and C. Tator, eds., 128–159. Toronto: University of Toronto Press.

James, Carl, David Este, and Wanda Thomas Bernard. 2010. *Race and Well-Being: The Lives, Hopes, and Activism of African Canadians.* Halifax: Fernwood

James, Carl, and Adrienne Shadd, eds. 1994. *Talking about Differences: Encounters in Culture, Language, and Identity.* Toronto: Between the Lines.

James, Carl, and Adrienne Shadd, eds. 2001. *Talking about Identity: Encounters in Race, Ethnicity, and Language.* Toronto: Between the Lines.

Jaret, Charles. 1995. *Contemporary Racial and Ethnic Relations.* Scarborough, ON: Harper Collins.

Jaworsky, John. 1979. *A Case Study of Canadian Federal Government's Multicultural Policies.* Unpublished MA Thesis. Political Science. Ottawa: Carleton.

Jedwab, Jack. 2002. "Melting Mosaic: Changing Realities in Cultural Diversity in Canada and the United States." *Canadian Issues* (February), 19–23.

Jedwab, Jack. 2004. "Notional Nations: The Myth of Canada as a Multinational Nation." *Canadian Diversity* 3(2):19–22.

Jedwab, Jack. 2005. "Neither Finding Nor Losing Our Way: The Debate over Canadian Multiculturalism." *Canadian Diversity* 4(1):95–102.

Jedwab, Jack. 2006. "Canadian Integration: The Elusive Quest for Models and Measures." *Canadian Diversity* 9(1):97–103.

Jedwab, Jack. 2007. "Canadian 'Separatists' Value Accommodation of Religious Minorities: Exploring the Relationship between Church–State Separation and Reasonable Accommodation." Montreal: Association for Canadian Studies.

Jedwab, Jack. 2011. "Multicultural vs Intercultural: A Superficial Exercise in Branding." *Montreal Gazette*, 7 March.

Jedwab, Jack. 2012. The Economic Integration of Immigrants in Canada and the Quebec Difference. In *Managing Diversity in Canada*, D. Rodriguez-Garcia, ed., 203–222. Kingston: School of Policy Studies, Queens University.

Jedwab, Jack. 2014. Debating Multiculturalism in 21st Century Canada. In *The Multiculturalism Question. Debating Identity in 21st-Century Canada*. Jack Jedwab, ed., 1–29. Queen's Policy Studies Series. School of Policy Studies, Queen's University. Montreal/Kingston: McGill-Queen's University Press.

Jedwab, Jack, and Vic Satzewich. 2015. Introductory Essay. In *The Vertical Mosaic: An Analysis of Social Class and Power in Canada*. 50th Anniversary Edition. John Porter, xvii–xxxvii. Toronto: University of Toronto Press.

Jensen, Robert. 2009. "In South Africa, Apartheid Is Dead, But White Supremacy Lingers On." Retrieved November 16, 2015 (www.counterpunch.org/2009/06/09/in-south-africa-apartheid-is-dead-but-white-supremacy-lingers-on/).

Jenson, Jane. 2002. *Citizenship: Its Relationship to the Canadian Diversity Model*. Paper for the Program and Policy Officers of the Department of Canadian Heritage. Ottawa.

Jenson, Jane, and Martin Papillon. 2001. "The Changing Boundaries of Citizenship: A Review and a Research Agenda." Available online at www.cprn.org/doc.cfm?l=en&doc=182.

Jhappan, Radha. 1995. "The Federal–Provincial Power Grid and Aboriginal Self-Government," in *New Trends in Canadian Federalism*. F. Rocher and M. Smith, eds.,15–186. Peterborough, ON: Broadview Press.

Jimenez, Marina. 2006. "When Multi Morphs into Plural." *Globe and Mail*, 8 December.

Jimenez, Marina. 2009. "Right Resume, Wrong Name." *Globe and Mail*, 21 May.

Jiwani, Yasmin. 2001. "Intersecting Inequalities: Immigrant Women of Colour, Violence, and Health Care." Retrieved November 16, 2015 (http://fredacentre.com/wp-content/uploads/2010/09/Jiwani-20011.pdf).

Jiwani, Yasmin. 2006. *Discourses of Denial: Mediations on Race, Gender, and Violence*. Vancouver: UBC Press.

Jiwani, Yasmin. 2010. "Erasing Race. The Story of Reena Virk," in *Reena Virk*, M. Rajiva and S. Batacharya, eds., 82–121. Toronto: Canadian Scholars' Press.

Johnson, Heather Beth. 2015. *The American Dream and the Power of Wealth* (2nd ed.). New York, NY: Routledge

Johnson, Genevieve Fuji, and R. Enomoto. 2007. "Preface." In *Race, Racialization, and Anti-racism in Canada and Beyond*. G.F. Johnson and R. Enomoto, eds. Toronto, ON: University of Toronto Press.

Johnson, Kerri L., Kristin Pauker, and Jonathan B. Freeman. 2012. Race is Gendered: How Covarying Phenotypes and Stereotype Bias Sex Categorization. *Journal of Personality and Social Psychology* 102(1):116–131.

Johnson, Lyndon B. 1965. "Commencement Address at Howard University: 'To Fulfill These Rights,'" June 4, 1965, in *Public Papers of the Presidents of the United States: Lyndon B. Johnson*. Vol. 2, 635–640. Washington, D.C.: Government Printing Office, 1966.

Johnson, Richard, Mike Faille, and Andrew Barr. 2013. "Aboriginal Canada." *National Post*, 13 May.

Jones, Martin, and France Houle. 2008. Building a Better Refugee Status Determination System. *Refuge* 25(2):3–8.

Joppke, Christian. 2007. "Beyond National Models: Civic Integration Policies for Immigrants in Western Europe." *West European Politics* 30(1):1–22.

Joseph, Janelle, Simon Darnell, and Yuka Nakamura. 2012. *Race and Sport in Canada: Intersecting Inequalities*. Toronto: Canadian Scholars Press.

Justice Canada. 2012. *An Estimation of the Economic Impact of Spousal Violence in Canada*. Ottawa, ON: Author.

Kalbach, M. A., and W. E. Kalbach. 1999. "Demographic Overview of Ethnic Origins: Groups in Canada," in *Race and Ethnic Relations in Canada* (2nd ed.), 3–20. Toronto: Oxford University Press.

Kamalipour, Y. R., and T. Carilli, eds. 1998. *Cultural Diversity and the U.S. Media.* New York: State University of New York Press.

Kapur, Devesh. 2005. *Give Us Your Best and Brightest.* Washington, DC: Center for Global Development.

Karim, Karim. 2002. *Islamic Peril: Media and Global Violence.* Montreal, QC: Black Rose Books.

Karim, Karim. 2006. "American Media's Coverage of Muslims: The Historical Roots of Contemporary Portrayals," in *Muslims and the News Media.* E. Poole and J.E. Richardson, eds., 116–127. New York: I.B. Taurus.

Karim, Karim. 2007. Nation and Diaspora: Rethinking Multiculturalism in a Transnational Context. *International Journal of Media and Cultural Studies* 2(3).

Karner, Christian. 2007. *Ethnicity and Everyday Life.* London: Routledge.

Kashima, Y., K. Fiedler, and P. Freytag, eds. 2008. *Stereotype Dynamics: Language-Based Approaches to the Formation, Maintenance, and Transformation of Stereotypes.* New York: Lawrence Erlbaum Associates.

Kauffmann, Sylvie. 2015. Refugee Tragedy Tests Europe's Solidarity. *Waterloo Region Record,* 23 June.

Kaushal, Asha, and Catherine Dauvergne. 2011. The Growing Culture of Exclusion: Growing Trends in Canadian Refugee Exclusions. Working Paper Series. Metropolis British Columbia.

Kawakami, Kerry, Elizabeth Dunn, Francine Karmali, and John Dovidio. 2009. "Mispredicting Affective and Behavioral Response to Response." *Science* 323(5911):276–278.

Kay, Jonathan. 2008. "Jonathan Kay Reads the Bouchard-Taylor Report on 'Reasonable Acommodation in Quebec.'" *National Post,* 24 May.

Kazemipur, A. 2014. *The Muslim Question in Canada: A Story of Segmented Integration.* Vancouver: UBC Press.

Kazemipur, A., and S. S. Halli. 2003. "Poverty Experiences of Immigrants: Some Reflections." *Canadian Issues* (April), 18–20.

Keevak, Michael. 2011. *Becoming Yellow: A Short History of Racial Thinking.* Princeton, NJ: Princeton University Press.

Kelley, Deidre M. 2006. "Frame Work: Helping Youth Counter Their Misrepresentations in Media." *Canadian Journal of Education* 29(1):27–48.

Kelley, Ninette, and Michael Trebilcock. 2010. *The Making of the Mosaic: A History of Canada's Immigration Program* (2nd ed.). University of Toronto Press.

Kelly, Jennifer. 1998. *Under the Gaze: Learning to be Black in White Society.* Halifax: Fernwood.

Kernerman, Gerald. 2005. *Multicultural Nationalism: Civilizing Difference, Constituting Community.* Vancouver: UBC Press.

Keung, Nicholas. 2004. "A Business Case for Diversity." *Toronto Star,* 6 May.

Keung, Nicholas. 2008. "Wait Time to Grow from 6 to 10 Years." *Toronto Star,* 26 May.

Keung, Nicholas. 2010. "Will a New Bill Solve the Refugee Mess?" *Toronto Star,* 4 April.

Keung, Nicholas. 2015. "One in Four Failed Refugees Win on Appeal, Study Finds." *Toronto Star,* 20 August.

Khan, Sheema. 2010. "The Blame of Honour Crimes." *The Globe and Mail,* 22 June.

Khan, Sheema. 2013. "Coming Together to Prevent Crimes of 'Honour.'" *Globe and Mail,* 30 January.

Khayatt, Didi. 1994. "The Boundaries of Identity at the Intersections of Race, Class, and Gender." *Canadian Woman Studies* 14(2):6–13.

Khoday, Amar. 2007. "'Honour Killings' Hide Racist Motives." *Toronto Star,* 8 March.

Khoo, S.-E., E. Ho, and C. Voigt-Graf. 2008. "Gendered Migration in Oceania: Trends, Policies, and Outcomes," in *New Perspectives in Gender and Migration.* N. Piper, ed., 101–136. New York: Routlege.

Kil, Sang Hea. 2010. "Review of Whiteness: An Introduction. By Steve Garner." *Journal of Ethnic and Migration Studies* 36(3):538–538.

Killian, Crawford. 2013. "Media Elders Failed Us by Sneering at Idle No More." *The Tyee,* 16 January.

Kim, Won. 2006. "Racial Discrimination Is Bad for Your Health—Literally." *DiversityInc.,* 31 October.

King, Joyce E. 1991. Dysconscious Racism: Ideology, Identity, and the Miseducation of Teachers. The Journal of Negro Education 60(2):133–146.

Kino-nda-niimi Collective. 2014. *The Winter We Danced. Voices from the Past, the Future, and the Idle No More Movement.* Arbeiter Ring Publishing.

Kinsella, Warren. 1994. *Web of Hate: The Far-Right Network in Canada.* Toronto: HarperCollins.

Kitaro, Harry. 1997. *Race Relations.* Englewood Cliffs, NJ: Prentice-Hall.

Kivel, Paul. 1996. *Uprooting Racism: How White People Can Work for Justice.* Philadelphia: New Society Publishers.

Kivisto, Peter. 2015. Introduction: The Puzzle of Incorporation and Solidarity. *The Sociological Quarterly* 56(4):581–590.

Kivisto, Peter, and Wendy Ng. 2005. *Americans All* (2nd ed.). Los Angeles: Roxbury.

Knafla, Louis A., and Haijo Westra. 2010. *Aboriginal Title and Indigenous Peoples. Canada, Australia, and New Zealand.* Vancouver: UBC Press.

Knowles, Valerie. 2007. *Strangers at Our Gates: Canadian Immigration and Immigration Policy: 1540–2006.* Toronto: Dundurn.

Kobayashi, Audrey. 1999. "Multiculturalism and Making Difference: Comments on the State of Multiculturalism Policy in Canada." *Australian-Canadian Studies* 17(2):33–39.

Kobayashi, Audrey. 2003. "Police Need Better Race Training, Expert: Accept Racism Exists Professor Urges." *Kingston Whig-Standard,* 13 June.

Kobayashi, Audrey. 2005. "Employment Equity in Canada: The Paradox of Tolerance and Denial," in *Possibilities and Limitations.* C. James, ed., 154–162. Halifax: Fernwood.

Kobayashi, Audrey. 2009. Now You See Them, How You See Them: Women of Colour in Canadian Academia. *Racism in the Canadian University,* F. Henry and C. Tator, eds., 60–75: University of Toronto Press.

Kobayashi, Audrey, and Genevieve Fuji Johnson. 2007. "Introduction," in *Race, Racialization, and Anti-racism in Canada and Beyond.* G. F. Johnson and R. Enomoto, eds., 3–16. Toronto: University of Toronto Press, 1.

Koenig, Matthias, and Paul de Guchteneire. 2007. *Democracy and Human Rights in Multicultural Societies.* Burlington, VT: Ashgate Publishing.

Koenigsberg, Richard. 2004. "Dying for One's Country: The Logic of War and Genocide." See www.academia.edu/593769/Dying_for_Ones_Country_The_Logic_of_War_and_Genocide.

Kogawa, Joy. 1994. *Itsuka.* New York: Doubleday.

Korteweg, Anna C., and G. Yurdakul. 2010. "Religion, Culture, and the Politicization of Honour-Related Violence." Gender and Development Programme Paper No 12. October. UN Research Institute for Social Development.

Kostash, Myrna. 2000. *The Next Canada: In Search of Our Future Nation.* Toronto: McClelland & Stewart.

Kraus, Peter. 2012. The Politics of Complex Diversity: A European Perspective. *Ethnicities* 12(1):3–25.

Kristof, Nicholas D. 2013. "Slavery Isn't a Thing of the Past." *New York Times,* 17 November.

Kruhlak, Orest. 2003. *Annual Shevchenko Lecture.* University of Alberta, Edmonton, 14 March.

Kulchyski, Peter, ed. 1994. *Unjust Relations: Aboriginal Rights in Canadian Courts.* Toronto: Oxford University Press.

Kulchyski, Peter. 2005. "Bush Life." *Canadian Dimensions Magazine,* May/June.

Kulchyski, Peter. 2013. *Aboriginal Rights are Not Human Rights: In Defence of Indigenous Struggles.* Arbeiter Ring.

Kumin, Judith. 2001. "Gender: Persecution in the Spotlight." *Refugee* 2(123):12–13.

Kumin, Judith. 2004. "Can This Marriage Be Saved? National Interest and Ethics in Asylum Policy." *Canadian Issues* (March), 14–17.

Kunz, Jean Lock. 2005. "Applying Life Course Lens to Immigration Integration." *Canadian Issues* (Spring), 41–43.

Kunz, Jean Lock, Anne Milan, and Sylvain Schetagne. 2001. *Unequal Access: A Canadian Profile of Racial Differences in Education, Employment, and Income.* Toronto: Canadian Race Relations Foundation.

Kunz, Jean, and Stuart Sykes. 2007. *From Mosaic to Harmony: Multiculturalism Canada in the 21st Century.* Ottawa: Policy Research Institute.

Kuokkanen, Rauna. 2007. *Reshaping the University: Responsibility, Indigenous Epistemes, and the Logic of the Gift.* Vancouver: UBC Press.

Kurien, Prema A. 2006. "Multiculturalism and American Religion: The Case of Hindu Indian Americans." *Social Forces* 85(2):723–741.

Kurlantzick, Joshua. 2012. *Democracy in Retreat.* New Haven, CT: Yale University Press.

Kurthen, Hermann. 1997. "The Canadian Experiences with Multiculturalism and Employment Equity: Lessons for Europe." *New Community* 23(2):249–270.

Kymlicka, Will. 1992. "The Rights of Minority Cultures: Reply to Kukathas." *Political Theory* 20:140–145.

Kymlicka, Will. 1995. "Misunderstanding Nationalism." *Dissent* (Winter), 131–137.

Kymlicka, Will. 1998a. *Finding Our Way: Rethinking Ethnocultural Relations in Canada.* Toronto: Oxford University Press.

Kymlicka, Will. 1998b. "Multinational Federalism in Canada: Rethinking the Relationship," in *Beyond the Impasse.* R. Gibbins and G. Laforest, eds., 15–50. Montreal: Institute for Research on Public Policy.

Kymlicka, Will. 2001. *Politics in the Vernacular: Nationalism, Multiculturalism, and Citizenship.* Toronto: Oxford University Press.

Kymlicka, Will. 2003. "Immigration, Citizenship, Multiculturalism: Exploring the Links." *The Political Quarterly,* 195–208.

Kymlicka, Will. 2004. *The Canadian Model of Diversity in a Comparative Perspective.* Eighth Standard Life Visiting Lecture. University of Edinburgh. 29 April.

Kymlicka, Will. 2005. "The Uncertain Futures of Multiculturalism." *Canadian Diversity* 4(1):82–85.

Kymlicka, Will. 2007. *Multicultural Odysseys: Navigating the New International Politics of Diversity.* Oxford, UK: Oxford University Press.

Kymlicka, Will. 2010. "Testing the Liberal Multiculturalist Hypothesis: Normative Theories and Social Science Evidence." *Canadian Journal of Political Science* 43:257–271.

Kymlicka, Will. 2011. "Multiculturalism in Normative Theory and Social Science." *Ethnicities* 11(1):5–31.

Kymlicka, Will. 2014. The Essentialist Critique of Multiculturalism: Theories, Policies, Ethos. EUI Working Paper RSCAS 2014/59. European University Institute. Budapest.

Kymlicka Will. 2015. The Three Lives of Multiculturalism. In *Revisiting Multiculturalism in Canada.* S. Guo and L. Wong, eds., 3–22. Rotterdam: Sense Publishers.

Kymlicka, Will, and Kathryn Walker, eds. 2012. *Rooted Cosmopolitanism.* Vancouver: UBC Press.

Labonte, Ronald, Abdullahi Hadi, and Xavier E. Kauffmann. 2011. "Indicators of Social Exclusion and Inclusion: A Critical and Comparative Analysis of the Literature." Globalization and Health Equity Research Unit, Institute of Population Health. University of Ottawa.

Lamoin, Amy, and Cassandra Dawes. 2010. "Racism in Australia: Is Denial Still Possible?" *Race/Ethnicity: Multidisciplinary Global Perspectives* 3(2).

Land, Lorraine, and Roger Townshend. 2002. "Land Claims: Stuck in Never-Never Land." In *Nation to Nation.* J. Bird, L. Land, and M. Macadam, eds., 53–62. Toronto: Public Justice Resource Centre.

LaSelva, Samuel V. 2004. "Understanding Canada: Federalism, Multiculturalism and the Will to Live Together," in *Canadian Politics.* J. Bickerton and A.-G. Gagnon, eds., 17–34. Peterborough, ON: Broadview.

Latham, Robert. 2007/08. What Are We? From a Multicultural to a Multiversal Canada. *International Journal* 63(1):23–42.

Latham, Robert. 2008. "Canadian Society is not Just Multicultural; It is Multiversal." *ResearchSnapShot.* York University, Toronto.

Latour, Sophie Guerard de, and Peter Balint. 2013. The Fair Terms of Integration: Liberal Multiculturalism Reconsidered. In *Liberal Multiculturalism and the Fair Terms of Integration,* P. Balint and S. Latour, eds., 1–16: New York: Palgrave.

Law, Ian. 2014. Mediterranean Racisms: *Connections and Complexities in the Racialization of the Mediterranean Region.* New York: Palgrave Macmillan.

Lean, Nathan. 2012. *The Islamophobia Industry: How the Right Manufactures Fears of Muslims.* London: Pluto Press.

Leblanc, Daniel. 2012. "Ottawa Targets Romanian Refugees." *Globe and Mail,* 7 November.

Lee, Jo-Anne, and John Lutz, eds. 2005. "Introduction: Towards a Critical Literacy of Racisms, Antiracisms? and Racialization 3." In *Situating "Race" and Racisms in Time, Space, and Theory: Critical Essays for Activists and Scholars.* J. Lee and J. Lutz, eds., 3–29: Montreal/Kingston: McGill-Queen's University Press.

Legal Strategy Coalition on Violence Against Indigenous Women (LSC). 2015. Review of Reports and Recommendations. Executive Summary. 26 February.

Legrain, Philippe. 2007. *Immigrants: Your Country Needs Them*. Princeton, NJ: Princeton University Press.

Le Guin, Ursula. 1975. "The Ones Who Walk Away from Omelas." In *The Wind's Twelve Quarters*. London: Orion Books.

Lehrman, Sally. 2003. Colorblind Racism. Posted September 18. Available online at www.alternet.org.

Lehrman, Sally. 2014. "Creating an Inclusive Public Commons: Values and Structures in Journalism that can Promote Change." Paper presented to the Media and Minorities Conference sponsored by the Academy of the Jewish Museum Berlin and Council of Migration, Berlin, 27 November.

Leigh, Darcy. 2009. Colonialism, Gender, and the Family in North America: For a Gendered Analysis of Indigenous Struggles. *Studies in Nationalism and Ethnicity* 9(1):70–88.

Lemieux, Tracy and Jean-Francois Nadeau. 2015. *Temporary Foreign Workers in Canada: A Look at Regions and Occupational Skill*. Published by the Office of the Parliamentary Budget Office, 3 March.

Lenard, Patti Tamara, and Christine Straehle, eds. 2012. *Legislated Inequality: Temporary Labour Migration in Canada*. Montreal/Kingston: McGill-Queen's University Press.

Lentin, Alana. 2004. "Racial States, Anti-racist Responses: Picking Holes in 'Culture' and 'Human Rights.'" *European Journal of Social Theory* 7(4):427–443.

Lentin, Alana. 2008. *Racism: A Beginner's Guide*. Oxford

Lentin, A. and R. Lentin. 2006. *Race and State*. Cambridge Scholars Publishing.

Leonardo, Zeus. 2004. "The Color of Supremacy: Beyond the Discourse of 'White Privilege.'" *Educational Philosophy and Theory* 36(2).

Leong, Melissa, and Glynnis Mapp. 2006. "Murders of Women Have South Asians Worried about Abuse." *National Post*, 7 November.

Lerner, Gerda. 1997. *Why History Matters: Life and Thought*. New York: Oxford University Press.

Leroux, Darryl. 2014. Entrenching Euro-Settlerism: Multiculturalism and the Politics of Nationalism in Quebec. *Canadian Ethnic Studies* 46(2):133–140.

Leung, Ho Hon. 2015. Canadian Multiculturalism in the 21st Century: Emerging Challenges and Debates. In *Revisiting Multiculturalism in*

Canada. S. Guo and L. Wong, eds., 93–107. Rotterdam: Sense Publishers.

Levitas, R., C. Pantazis, E. Fahmy, D. Gordon, E. Lloyd, and D. Patsios. 2007. Report: *The Multi-Dimensional Analysis of Social Exclusion*. University of Bristol. January.

Levitt, Cyril. 1997. "The Morality of Race in Canada." *Society* (July/August), 32–37.

Levitz, Stephanie. 2015. Federal Government to Take Niqab Case to Supreme Court. *Canadian Press*, 16 September.

Ley, David. 2005. *Post-Multiculturalism?* Working Paper No. 05-17. Research on Immigration and Integration in the Metropolis. Vancouver: Vancouver Centre of Excellence.

Ley, David. 2007. "Multiculturalism: A Canadian Defence." *Metropolis*.

Ley, David, and Daniel Hiebert. 2001. "Immigration Policy as Population Policy." *The Canadian Geographer* 45(1):120–125.

Li, Jinling, and Kasper Juffermans. 2011. Multilingual Europe 2.0: Dutch-Chinese Youth Identities in an Era of Superdiversity. Working Papers in Urban Language & Literacies. Paper no 71.

Li, Peter. 1995. "Racial Supremacism under Social Democracy." *Canadian Ethnic Studies* 27(1):1–17.

Li, Peter S. 1998. *The Chinese in Canada* (2nd ed.). Toronto: Oxford University Press.

Li, Peter S. 2003. *Destination Canada: Immigration Debates and Issues*. Toronto: Oxford University Press.

Li, Peter. 2007. "Contradictions of 'Racial' Discourse," in *Interrogating Race and Racism*. V. Agnew, ed., 37–54. Toronto: University of Toronto Press.

Lian, Jason Z., and Ralph David Matthews. 1998. "Does the Vertical Mosaic Still Exist? Ethnicity and Income in Canada, 1991." *Canadian Review of Sociology and Anthropology* 35(4):461–477.

Lieberman, Robert. 2006. "Shaping Race Policies: the United States in Comparative Perspective. Princeton University Press. Reviewed by Erik Bleich." *Ethics & International Affairs* 20(1):133.

Linden, W. 1994. *Swiss Democracy*. New York: St. Martin's Press.

Lippard, C. D. 2011. Racist Nativism in the 21st Century. *Sociology Compass* 5(7):591–606.

Lipsitz, George. 1995. The Possessive Investment in Whiteness: Racialized Social Democracy and the

"White" Problem in American Studies. *American Quarterly* 47(3):369–387.

Lister, Ruth. 1997. *Citizenship: Feminist Perspectives.* London: Macmillan, 66.

Little, Adrian, and Terry Macdonald. 2015. Introduction to Special Issue: Real-World Justice and International Migration. *European Journal of Political Theory* 14(4):381–390.

Little, Matthew. 2010. "Fake Refugees a Threat to Immigration: Kenney." *Epoch Times,* October 28–November 3.

Little Bear, Leroy. 2004. "Aboriginal Paradigms: Implications for Relationships to Land and Treaty Making," in *Advancing Aboriginal Claims.* Kerry Wilkins, ed., 26–38. Saskatoon: Purich Publishing.

Littlefield, Marci Bounds. 2008. The Media as a System of Racialization. *American Behavioral Scientist,* 51(5):675–685.

Littleton, James, ed. 1996. *Clash of Identities: Essays on Media, Manipulation, and Politics of the Self.* Toronto: Prentice Hall.

Liu, James H., Tim McCreanor, Tracey McIntosh, Teresia Teaiwa, eds. 2006. *New Zealand Identities.* Wellington, NZ: Victoria University Press.

Llewellyn, Jennifer. 2002. Dealing with the Legacy of Native Residential School Abuse in Canada. Subsequently published in revised form as The Relationship between Truth and Reconciliation: Bridging the Gap. In *From Truth to Reconciliation: Transforming the Legacy of Residential Schools,* M. Castellano, L. Archibald, and M. Degagne, eds., 183–203. Ottawa: Aboriginal Healing Foundation.

Loney, Martin. 1998. *The Pursuit of Division: Race, Gender, and Preferential Hiring in Canada.* Montreal/Kingston: McGill-Queen's University Press.

Long, David, and Olive Patricia Dickason. 2011. *Visions of the Heart* (3rd ed.). Toronto: Oxford University Press.

Lopes, Tina, and Barb Thomas. 2006. *Dancing on Live Embers: Challenging Racism in Organizations.* Toronto: Between the Lines.

Lopez, Ian Haney. 2015. *Dog Whistle Politics: How Coded Racial Appeals Have Reinvented Racism and Wrecked the Middle Class.* Reprint Edition. New York: Oxford University Press.

Loppie, Samantha, Charlotte Reading, and Sarah deLeeuw. 2015. "Aboriginal Experiences with Racism and its Impacts." National Colloborating Centre for Aboriginal Health.

Louie, Clarence and Dawn Matahbee. 2015. "Economic Development for Aboriginal People Still Not on Track." Op-Ed. *Ottawa Citizen,* 17 June.

Lowe, Sophia. 2008. *"Designer Immigrants": Eliminating Barriers.* Retrieved November 16, 2015 (http://triec.ca/designer-immigrants-elimi/).

Lowe, Sophia. 2010. "Rearranging the Deck Chairs? A Critical Examination of Canada's Shifting (Im)migration Policies." *Canadian Issues* (Spring), 25–28.

Lupa, Alan. 1999. "When Generations and Cultures Clash." *Boston Sunday Globe*, 8 August.

Lupul, Manoly R. 1988. "Ukrainians: The Fifth Cultural Wheel in Canada," in *Ethnicity in a Technological Age.* Ian H. Angus, ed., 177–192. Edmonton: Canadian Institute of Ukrainian Studies, University of Alberta.

Lupul, Manoly. 2005. *The Politics of Multiculturalism: A Ukrainian-Canadian Memoir.* Edmonton: Canadian Institute of Ukrainian Studies Press.

Lyons, Noel. 1997. "Feds Criticized." Windspeaker. International working group for indigenous affairs, 2015. *The indigenous world 2015.* Copenhagen. 3 November.

Maaka, Roger, and Chris Andersen, eds. 2007. *The Indigenous Experience.* Toronto: Canadian Scholars' Press.

Maaka, Roger, and Augie Fleras. 2005. *The Politics of Indigeneity: Challenging the State in Canada and Aotearoa New Zealand.* Dunedin, NZ: University of Otago Press.

Maaka, Roger, and Augie Fleras. 2008. Contesting Indigenous Peoples Governance: The Politics of Self-Determination versus Self-Determining Autonomy. In *Aboriginal Self-Government in Canada: Current Issues and Trends* (3rd ed.). Y. Belanger, ed. Saskatoon, SK: Purich.

Maaka, Roger, and Augie Fleras. 2009. Towards an Indigenous Grounded Analysis Policymaking Framework. International Indigenous Policy Journal (online). Volume 1.

Mac an Ghaill, Mairtin. 1999. *Contemporary Racisms and Ethnicities: Social and Cultural Transformations.* Philadelphia: Open University Press.

Maccharles, Tonda. 2004. "Canada, U.S. in Refugee Deal." *Toronto Star*, 15 October.

Maccharles, Tonda. 2005. "High Court Supports Native Rights." *Toronto Star*, 19 November.

Macdonald, David. 2014. "Outrageous Fortune. Documenting Canada's Wealth Gap." Canadian Centre for Policy Alternatives. April.

Macdonald, David, Michael Dan, and Bernie M. Farber. 2015. "John A. Macdonld Was a Near Genocidal Extremist Even for His Time." *National Post,* 11 January.

Macdonald, David, and Daniel Wilson. 2013. *Poverty or Prosperity: Indigenous Children in Canada.* Canadian Centre for Policy Alternatives and Save the Children Canada.

MacDonald, L. Ian. 2007. "SES—Policy Options Exclusive Poll: The Limits of Reasonable Accommodation." *Policy Options* (September), 1–5.

Macedo, Donaldo, and Panayota Gounari. 2006. "Globalization and the Unleashing of New Racism: An Introduction." In *The Globalization of Racism.* D. Macedo and P. Gounari, eds. Boulder, CO: Paradigm Publishers.

Mackey, Eva. 1998. *The House of Difference: Cultural Politics and National Identity in Canada.* London: Routledge.

Mackie, Richard. 2001. "Sovereignty Support Near Low, Poll Finds." *The Globe and Mail,* 26 October.

Macklem, Patrick. 2001. *Indigenous Difference and the Constitution in Canada*: University of Toronto Press.

Macklin, Audrey. 1999. "Women as Migrants in National and Global Communities." *Canadian Woman Studies* 19(3):24–32.

Macklin, Audrey. 2015. "Mentally Ill Migrants Don't Belong in Jail." *Toronto Star,* 22 June.

Macklin, Audrey, and Frances Crepeau. 2010. "Multiple Citizenship, Identity, and Entitlement in Canada." Retrieved November 16, 2015 (http://irpp.org/research-studies/study-no6/).

MacLaren, Barbara, and Luc Lapointe. 2010. "Employment Insurance: How Canada Can Remain Competitive And Be Fair to Migrant Workers." *Policy Options,* February.

Maclure, Jocelyn. 2004. "Between Nation and Dissemination: Revisiting the Tension Between National Identity and Diversity," in *The Conditions of Diversity in Multinational Democracies.* A.-G. Gagnon et al., eds. Montreal: Institute for Research on Public Policy.

MacQueen, Ken. 1994. "I Am a Canadian. Don't Let Me Screw Up." *Kitchener-Waterloo Record,* 23 April.

Magnet, Joseph Eliot. 2004. *Modern Constitutionalism: Identity, Equality, and Democracy.* Toronto: Butterworths.

Magsino, R.F. 2000. "The Canadian Multiculturalism Policy: A Pluralist Ideal Revisited," in *21st Century Canadian Diversity.* S. Nancoo, ed., 320–341. Toronto: Canadian Scholars' Press.

Mahoney, Jill. 2007. "Leaping Over Education Adversity." *The Globe and Mail*, 5 December.

Mahtani, Minelle. 2002. "Interrogating the Hyphen-Nation: Canadian Multicultural Policy and Mixed Race Identities." *Social Identities* 8(1).

Mahtani, Minelle. 2008. "How Are Immigrants Seen—And What Do They Want to See. Contemporary Research on the Representation of Immigrants in the Canadian Language Media." In *Immigration and Integration in Canada.* John Biles et al., eds., 231–252. Montreal/Kingston: McGill-Queens University Press.

Mahtani, Minelle. 2015. *Mixed Race Amnesia: Resisting the Romanticization of Multiraciality.* Vancouver: UBC Press.

Maioni, Antonia. 2003. "Canadian Health Care," in *Profiles of Canada.* K. Pryke and W. Soderland, eds., 307–326. Toronto: Canadian Scholars Press.

Majka, Christopher. 2015. *Niqab? Radical Feminism or Female Subjugation?* Retrieved September 30, 2015 (www.rabble.ca).

Malik, Kenan. 2012. "What Is Wrong with Multiculturalism [Milton K Wong Lecture]." 3 June.

Malik, Kenan. 2012. *Conflicting Credos But the Same Vision of the World.* Paper presented at the Criticise This: Rethinking the Question of Difference Seminar, Ulcinj, Montenegro. Retrieved November 17, 2015 (http://kenanmalik.wordpress.com/?s=Conflicting+Credos+).

Malik, Kenan. 2013. "In Defence of Diversity: The New Humanist." Winter, 18 December, www.eurozine.com.

Manfredi, Christopher. 2004. "Fear, Hope and Misunderstanding: Unintended Consequences and the Marshall Decision," in *Advancing Aboriginal Claims.* Kerry Wilkins. ed., 190–201. Saskatoon: Purich.

Manji, Irshad. 2005. "Not All Traditions Deserve Respect." *NY Times.* Reprinted in the *National Post,* 11 August.

Mann, Michelle M. 2005. *Aboriginal Women: An Issues Backgrounder.* Prepared for the Status of Women in Canada. Retrieved November 16, 2015 (www.publications.gc.ca/collections/Collection/SW21-146-2005E.pdf).

Manning, Peter. 2006. "Australians Imagining Islam," in *Muslims and the News Media.* E. Poole and J. E. Richardson, eds., 128–141. New York: I.B. Taurus.

Manning, Alex, Douglas Hartmann, and Joseph Gerteis. 2015. Colorblindness in Black and White: An Analysis of Core Tenets, Configurations, and Complexities. *Sociology of Race and Ethncity* 1(4):532–546.

Mansouri, Fethi, and Boulou Ebanda de B'beri. 2014. *Global Perspectives on the Politics of Multiculturalism in the 21ˢᵗ Century: A Case Study Analysis.* New York: Routledge.

Manuel, Art, and Ron Derrickson. 2015. *Unsettling Canada: A National Wake-up Call.* Toronto: Between the Lines.

Mansur, Salim. 2010. *The Muddle of Multiculturalism. A Liberal Critque.* Halifax: Atlantic Institute for Market Studies.

Mansur, Salim. 2011. *Delectable Lie: A Liberal Repudiation of Multiculturalism.* Mantua Books.

Mapedzahama, V., T. Rudge, S. West, and A. Perron. 2012. Black Nurse in White Space? Rethinking the In/Visibility of Race Within the Australian Nursing Workplace. *Nursing Inquiry* 19(2):153–164.

Maracle, Brian. 1996. "One More Whining Indian Tilting at Windmills," in *Clash of Identities.* J. Littleton, ed., 15–20. Toronto: Prentice-Hall.

Marchi, Sergio. 1994. "Sergio Marchi on Immigration." *OpenParliament.* Retrieved November 16, 2015 (https://openparliament.ca/debates/1994/2/14/sergio-marchi-2/only/).

Marger, Martin. 1997. *Race and Ethnic Relations: American and Global Perspectives* (4ᵗʰ ed.). Toronto: Nelson/Thomson Learning.

Marger, Martin. 2001. *Race and Ethnic Relations: American and Global Perspectives* (5ᵗʰ ed.). Toronto: Nelson Thomson.

Markus, H. R., and P. Moya, eds. 2010. *21 Essays for the 21ˢᵗ Century.* New York: W. W. Norton.

Marr, Bill. 2015. Migration and Climate Change. Review. *Canadian Studies in Population* 42(1–2):170–171.

Martin, James G., and Clyde W. Franklin. 1973. *Minority Group Relations.* Columbus, OH: Charles E. Merrill.

Martin, Philip, Manolo Abella, and Christiane Kuptsch. 2005. *Managing Labour Migration in the Twenty-First Century.* Princeton, NJ: Yale University Press.

Mas, Susana. 2014. "New Citizenship Rules Target Fraud, Foreign Terrorism." Retrieved November 6, 2015 (www.cbc.ca/m/touch/news/story/1.2525404).

Mascarenhas, Michael. 2012. *Where the Waters Divide: Neoliberalism, White Privilege, and Environmental Racism in Canada.* Toronto: Lexington Books.

Mason, Gary. 2010. "Give First Nations the Power to Help Themselves." *Globe and Mail,* 17 June.

Masood, Ehsan. 2008. "Muslims and Multiculturalism: Lesson from Canada." *Open Democracy.* Retrieved November 16, 2015 (www.opendemocracy.net/globalization/canada_muslims_4414.jsp).

Massey, Douglas S. 2009. "The Political Economy of Migration in an Era of Globalization," in *International Migration and Human Rights: the Global Repercussions of U.S. Policy.* S. Martinez, ed., 25–41. Berkeley, CA: University of California Press.

Matas, Robert, Erin Anderssen, and Sean Fine. 1997. "Natives Win on Land Rights." *The Globe and Mail,* 12 December.

Matsuoka, Atsuko, and John Sorenson. 1999. "Eritrean Women in Canada: Negotiating New Lives." *Canadian Woman Studies* 19(3):104–109.

Mawani, Ayesha. 2008. *Transnationalism: A Modern Day Challenge to Canadian Multiculturalism.* Paper presented at the Annual Meeting of the International Communication Association, Montreal, May 22. See http://research.allacademic.com/meta/p_mla_apa_research_citation/2/3/2/0/5/p232055_index.html.

Mawani, Nurjehan. 1997. "Is Refugee Determination Fair?" *The Globe and Mail,* 13 December.

May, Harvey. 2004. *Broadcast in Colour: Cultural Diversity and Television Programming in Four Countries.* Australian Film Commission.

May, S., ed. 1999. *Critical Multiculturalism.* Madison, WI: University of Wisconsin Press.

May, Stephen. 2002. "Multiculturalism," in *A Companion to Racial and Ethnic Studies.* D. T. Goldberg and J. Solomos, eds., 124–144. Malden, MA: Blackwell.

Maybury-Lewis, David, 2003. *The Politics of Ethnicity: Indigenous Peoples in Latin American States.* Harvard University Press.

McAndrew, Marie. 1992. "Combating Racism and Ethnocentrism in Educational Materials: Problems and Actions Taken in Quebec."

In *Racism and Education: Different Perspectives and Experiences*. Ontario Teachers Federation, ed., 49–60. Ottawa: Canadian Teachers' Federation.

McCardle, Elaine. 2008. Sociologists on the Colorblind Question. *Contexts* Winter:34–37.

McCaskill, Don. 2012. "Discrimination and Public Perceptions of Aboriginal People in Canadian Cities." *Urban Aboriginal Research Paper Series.* Ottawa: Urban Aboriginal Knowledge Network.

McCaskill, Tim. 1995. "Anti-racist Education and Practice in the Public School System." In *Beyond Political Correctness*. S. Richer and L. Weir, eds., 253–272: University of Toronto Press.

McCormack, Mike. 2015. "Accusations of Police Racism are Baseless." *Toronto Star*, 21 July.

McCue, Duncan. 2014. Racism Still an Uncomfortable Truth in Canada. Analysis. *CBC News*, 12 November.

McDougall, Gay. 2009. *Statement by the United Nations Independent Expert on Minority Issues on the Conclusion of Her Visit to Canada*. United Nations, Office of the High Commissioner on Human Rights, 23 October.

McDowell, Adam. 2010. "New Regime." *National Post,* 31 March.

McGauran, the Honourable Peter. 2005. "The Australian Government Minister for Citizenship and Multicultural Affairs." *Canadian Diversity* 4(1):6–8.

McGill University. 1994. *Anti-racism and Race Relations*. Prepared by Monique Shebbeare. McGill's Equity Office, July.

McGregor, Gail. 2002. "Book Review of *Removing the Margins: The Challenges and Possibilities of Inclusive Schooling* (George Sefa Dei et al., 2000)." Retrieved online.

McHugh, Paul. 1998. "Aboriginal Identity and Relations: Models of State Practice and Law in North America and Australasia," in *Living Relationships*. K. Coates and P. McHugh, eds. Institute of Public Policy. Wellington, NZ: Victoria University of Wellington.

McIntosh, Peggy. 1988. *White Privilege and Male Privilege: A Personal Account of Coming to See Correspondences through Work in Women Studies*. Working Paper No. 189. MA: Wellesley College, Centre for Research on Women.

McIntyre, Sheila. 1993. "Backlash against Equality: The 'Tyranny' of the 'Politically Correct.'" *McGill Law Journal/Revue de Droit de McGill* 38(1):3–63.

McIsaac, Elizabeth. 2003. *Nation Building through Cities: A New Deal for Immigrant Settlement in Canada*. Ottawa: Caledon Institute.

McInturff, Kate. 2013a. "Closing Canada's Gender Gap." Canadian Centre for Policy Alternatives. April.

McInturff, Kate. 2013b. "The Gap in the Gender Gap." Canadian Centre for Policy Alternatives. July.

McKay, Ian. 2008. *Reasoning Otherwise: Leftists and the People's Enlightenment in Canada:1890–1920*. Toronto: Between the Lines.

McKee, Craig. 1996. *Treaty Talks in British Columbia*. Vancouver: UBC Press.

McKenna, Ian. 1994. "Canada's Hate Propaganda Laws—A Critique." *British Journal of Canadian Studies* 15:42.

McLachlin, Beverley. 2015. "Reconciling Unity and Diversity in the Modern Era: Tolerance and Intolerance." Annual Lecture. Global Centre for Pluralism. 28 May.

McMahon, Tamsin. 2014. "Second Class Children." *Macleans* 16–21, 21 July.

McMullin, Julie. 2010. *Understanding Social Inequality in Canada. Intersections of Class, Age, Gender, Ethnicity and Race*. Toronto: Oxford University Press.

McMurtry, Alyssa. 2013. "Modern Day Slavery." *Canadian Dimension,* 3 April.

McNamee, Stephen J. 2014. *The Meritocracy Myth* (3rd ed.). Lanham, MD: Rowman & Littlefield.

McRoberts, Kenneth. 1996. "Introduction (Citizenship and Rights)." *International Journal of Canadian Studies* 14(Fall), 5–12.

McRoberts, Kenneth. 1997. *Misconceiving Canada: The Struggle for National Unity*. Toronto: Oxford University Press.

McRoberts, Kenneth. 2001. "Canada and the Multinational State." *Canadian Journal of Political Science* 24(4):683–713.

McRoberts, Kenneth. 2003. "Managing Cultural Differences in Multinational Democracies," in *The Conditions of Diversity in Multinational Democracies*. A.-G. Gagnon et al., eds., 1–14. Montreal: Institute for Research on Public Policy.

McRoberts, Kenneth. 2004. "The Future of the Nation State and Quebec–Canada Relations." In *The Fate of the Nation State*. M. Seymour, ed. Montreal/Kingston: McGill-Queen's University Press.

McVeigh, Robbie, and Ronit Lentin. 2006. "Situated Racisms: A Theoretical Introduction." In *Racism and Anti-racism in Ireland*. R. Lentin and

R. McVeigh, eds. Belfast, IE: Beyond the Pale Publications.

McWhorter, John. 2014. "Microaggression" is the New Racism on Campus. *TIME*, 21 March. Retrieved from http://time.com.

Mead, Walter Russell. 1993. "This Land Is My Land." *New York Times Book Review*, 7 November.

Medrano, J. D., and M. Koenig. 2005. "Nationalism, Citizenship, and Immigration in Social Science Research—Editorial Introduction." *International Journal on Multicultural Societies* 7(2):82–89.

Meer, Nasar and Anoop Nayak. 2013. Race Ends Where? Race, Racism, and Contemporary Sociology. Introduction to E-Special, Issue 2:1–18. Web.

Melchers, Ron. 2005. Cited in *Race Study Results under Fire*. See www.ottawamenscentre.com/news/20050607_fire.htm.

Melle, Tilden J. 2009. "Race in International Relations." *International Studies Perspectives 10*:77–83.

Mendelsohn, Matthew. 2003. "Birth of a New Ethnicity." In *The New Canadians*. E. Anderssen and M. Valpy, eds., 59–66. Toronto: McClelland & Stewart.

Mendelson, Michael. 2006. *Aboriginal Peoples and Postsecondary Education in Canada*. Ottawa: Caledon Institute of Social Policy.

Mercredi, Ovide, and Mary Ellen Turpel. 1993. *In the Rapids: Navigating the Future of First Nations*. Toronto: Penguin.

Metis Nation of Ontario. 2013. *Selected Demographics: Aboriginal and Metis Populations of Canada*. Ottawa: Author.

Metropolis Presents. 2004. *Conference Notes on Media, Immigration and Diversity: Informing Public Discourse or Fanning the Flames of Intolerance?* March 30. Ottawa: National Library.

Meyers, Eytan. 2002. "The Causes of Convergence in Western Immigration Control." *Review of International Studies* 28:123–141.

Michaelis, Arno, 2010. "My Life After Hate." Washington Post.

Midlarsky, Manus. 2005. *The Killing Trap: Genocide in the Twentieth Century*. Cambridge, UK: Cambridge University Press.

Migration Policy Institute. 2007. "Annual Immigration to the United States." Fact Sheet No. 16, May.

Miles, Robert. 1982. *Racism and Migrant Labour*. London: Routledge and Kegan Paul.

Miller, J. R. 1989. *Skyscrapers Hide the Heavens: A History of Indian–White Relations in Canada*. Toronto: University of Toronto Press.

Miller, J. R. 1999. *The State, the Church, and Residential Schools in Canada*. Paper presented at the Conference on Religion and Public Life: Historical and Comparative Themes, Queen's University, 13–15 May.

Miller, John. 2005. *Ipperwash and the Media: A Critical Analysis of How the Story Was Covered*. Paper prepared for the Aboriginal Legal Foundation in Toronto. Retrieved November 16, 2015 (www.attorneygeneral.jus.gov.on.ca/inquiries/ipperwash/policy_part/projects/pdf/ALST_Ipperwash_and_media.pdf).

Millman, Jennifer. 2007a. "Affirmative Action News: Why Race Counts in School Segregation." *DiversityInc*, 12 November.

Millman, Jennifer. 2007b. "Why Color-Blind Isn't the Answer." *DiversityInc*, 24 July.

Millman, Joel. 1997. *The Other Americans: How Immigrants Renew Our Country, Our Economy, and Our Values*. New York: Penguin.

Mills, Charles W. 1997. *Racial Contract*. Ithaca, NY: Cornell University Press.

Milloy, John. 2001. *A National Crime: The Canadian Government and the Residential School System, 1879–1996*. Winnipeg: University of Manitoba Press.

Minikel-Lacoque, Julie. 2013. Racism, College, and the Power of Words: Racial Microaggressions Reconsidered. *American Educational Research Journal* 50(3):432-465.

Minister of Indian Affairs and Northern Development. 1997. *Gathering Strength, Canada's Aboriginal Action Plan*. Ottawa: Minister of Public Works and Government Services Canada.

MIPEX (Migration Integration Policy Index). 2015. *Integration Policies: Who Benefits?* Author.

Mistry, Minal, and Javed Latoo. 2009. Uncovering the Face of Racism in the Workplace. *British Journal of Medical Practitioners* 2(2):20–24.

Mitchell, Brenda. 1993. "Color Me Multicultural." *Multi-Cultural Review* 1(4):15–17.

Mittler, P. 2000. *Working toward Inclusive Education: Social Contexts*. London: Fulton.

Modan, Gabriella Gahlia. 2007. *Turf Wars*. Discourse Diversity and the Politics of Place. Malden MA: Blackwell Publishing.

Modood, Tariq. 2003. "Muslims and the Politics of Difference" *The Political Quarterly* (Special Issue), 100–115.

Modood, Tariq. 2005. *Multicultural Politics: Racism, Ethnicity, and Muslims in Britain.* Minneapolis, MN: University of Minnesota Press.

Modood, Tariq. 2007. "Multiculturalism and Nation-Building Go Hand in Hand." *Guardian Unlimited,* 23 May.

Moens, Alexander, and Martin Collacott, eds. 2008. *Immigration Policy and the Terrorist Threat in Canada and the United States.* Calgary: Fraser Institute.

Montreuil, Annie, and Richard Y. Bourhis. 2004. "Acculturation Orientations of Competing Host Communities toward Valued and Devalued Immigrants." *International Journal of Intercultural Relations* 28(6):507–532.

Monture, Patricia. 2004. "The Rights of Inclusion: Aboriginal Rights and/or Aboriginal Women?" in *Advancing Aboriginal Claims.* Kerry Wilkins, ed., 39–66. Saskatoon: Purich.

Monture, Patricia A. 2011. The Need for Radical Change in the Criminal Justice System: Applying a Human Rights Framework. In *Visions of the Heart,* D. Long and O. P. Dickason, eds., 238–257. Toronto: Oxford University Press.

Monture-Angus, Patricia. 2002. *Journeying Forward: Dreaming First Nations' Independence.* Halifax, NS: Fernwood.

Mooney, Chris. 2014. "The Science of Why Cops Shoot Young Black Men." *Mother Jones,* 1 December.

Moore, Robert. 1992. *Racism in the English Language.* New York: The Racism and Sexism Resource Center for Educators.

Moosa, Zohra. 2007. "Minding the Multicultural Gap." *Catalyst,* 16 March.

Morphet, Janet. 2007. "Embracing Multiculturalism: The Case of London," in *Migration and Cultural Inclusion in the European City.* William J.V. Neill and Hanns-Uve Schwedler, eds., 167–183. New York: Palgrave.

Morris, Barry, and Gillian Cowlishaw, eds. 1997. *Race Matters: Indigenous Australians and "Our" Society.* Canberra, AU: Aboriginal Studies Press.

Morse, Bradford W., ed. 1985. *Aboriginal Peoples and the Law.* Ottawa: Carleton University Press.

Moseby, Ian. 2013. "Administering Colonial Science: Nutrition Research and Human Biomedical Experimentation in Aboriginal Communities and Residential Schools, 1942–1952." *Social History* 46(91):145–172.

Mothers United Against Racism. 2005. "The Police's Fight against Incivilities Encourages Racial Profiling and Harassment: Minority Mothers." Press release, 16 May.

Motomura, Hiroshi. 2006. *Americans in Waiting: The Lost Story of Immigration and Citizenship in the United States.* New York: Oxford University Press.

Muharrar, Mikal. 2005. Cited in "Ethnic Profiling and Gang and Gun Violence," Patricia Hylton. *Pride* (October), 12–18.

Muir, Rick, and Margaret Wetherell. 2010. *Identity, Politics, and Public Policy.* London, UK: Institute for Public Policy Research.

Mukherjee, Arun, Alok Mukherjee, and Barbara Godard, 2006. Translating Minoritized Cultures: Issues of Class, Caste, and Gender. *Postcolonial Text* 2(3).

Mukherjee, Bhahrati. 1989. *The Middleman and Other Stories.* Toronto: Penguin.

Munz, Rainer, and Rainer Ohliger, eds. 2003. *Diasporas and Ethnic Migrants: Germany, Israel and Post-Soviet Successor States in Comparative Perspective.* Portland, OR: Frank Cass.

Murphy, Michael. 2001. "Culture and Courts: A New Direction in Canadian Jurisprudence on Aboriginal Rights?" *Canadian Journal of Political Science* 34(1):109–129.

Murphy, Michael, ed. 2005. *Canada: The State of the Federation 2003: Reconfiguring Aboriginal–State Relations.* Published by the Institute of Intergovernmental Relations. School of Policy Studies. Kingston: Queen's University.

Murray, Catherine. 2009. "Designing Monitoring to Promote Cultural Divesification in TV." *Canadian Journal of Communication* 34(4):675–699.

Murray, Charles, and Richard J. Herrnstein. 1994. *The Bell Curve: Intelligence and Class Structure in American Life.* New York: The Free Press.

Nagel, Joane, and Susan Olzak. 1982. "Ethnic Mobilization in the New and Old States: An Extension of the Competition Model." *Social Problems* 30(2):127–142.

Nakache, Delphine. 2010. Temporary Workers: Permanent Rights? *Canadian Issues,* Spring, 45–49.

Nakache, Delphine, and Paula J. Kinoshita. 2010. "The Canadian Temporary Foreign Worker Program," Retrieved November 16, 2015 (http://irpp.org/research-studies/study-no5/).

Nakache, Delphine & Leanne Dixon-Perera, 2015 Temporary or Transitional? IRRP Study, No 55. October

Nakhaie, Reza M. 2007. "Ethnoracial Origins, Social Capital, and Earnings." *International Migration and Integration* 8:307–325.

Nakhaie, M. Reza, and A. Kazemipur. 2013. Social Capital, Employment and Occupational Status of the New Immigrants in Canada. *International Migration and Integration* 14:419–437.

Nancoo, Stephen. 2004. *Contemporary Issues in Community Policing.* Mississauga, ON: Canadian Education Press.

Nanos, Nik. 2008. "Nation-Building through Immigration: Workforce Skills Come Out on Top." *Policy Options* (June), 30–32.

Nanos, Nik. 2010. "Canadians Strongly Support Immigration, But Don't Want Current Levels Increased." *Policy Options* (July/August).

National Aboriginal Economic Development Board. 2015. *The Aboriginal Economic Progress Report.* Gatineau, June.

National Council of Welfare. 2011. "The Dollars and Sense of Solving Poverty." 28 September.

National Film Board of Canada. 2006. *Race Is a Four-Letter Word* [Film].

Native Women's Association of Canada. 2004. *Background Document on Aboriginal Women's Health.* Ottawa: Author.

NCFNG. 2010. "Rebuilding Our Nations." *National Newsletter of the National Centre for First Nations Governance.* Fall.

Neeganawedgin, Erica. 2012. Chattling the Indigenous Other: A Historical Examination of the Enslavement of Aboriginal Peoples in Canada. *AlterNative* 8(1).

Neill, William J. V., and Hanns-Uve Schwedler, eds. 2007. *Migration and Cultural Inclusion in the European City.* New York: Palgrave.

Nelson, Adie. 2009. *Gender in Canada* (4th ed.). Toronto: Pearson.

Nell, Sarah. 2012. Got Whiteness? Scholars Say You're Racist. *Sociology in Focus*, 9 January.

Nestel, Sheryl. 2012. *Colour Coded Health Care. The Impact of Race and Racism on Canadians' Health.* Wellesley Institute, Toronto. January.

Neu, Dean, and Richard Therrien. 2003. *Accounting for Genocide. Canada's Bureaucratic Assault on Aboriginal People* (193). Black Point, NS: Fernwood.

Neufeld-Rocheleau, Melody, and Judith Friesen. 1987. Isolation: A Reality for Immigrant Women in Canada. *Saskatchewan Multicultural Magazine* 6(2):12–13.

New Canadian Media. 2013. "The Third Opinion: Moving Beyond Multiculturalism." *New Canadian Media,* 28 January.

New Black Woman. 2011. "Study: Whites Believe They are the Victims of Racism More Often Than Blacks." *New Black Woman.* 24 May.

Newhouse, David and Yale Belanger. 2011. The Canada Problem in Aboriginal Politics. In *Visions of the Heart.* D. Long and O. P. Dickason, eds., 352–380. Toronto: Oxford University Press.

Newhouse, David, Kevin FitzMorris, Tricia McGuire-Adams, and Daniel Jette. 2012. *Well-Being in the Urban Aboriginal Community.* Toronto: Thompson.

Newhouse, David, and Evelyn Peters. 2003. *Not Strangers in These Parts. Urban Aboriginal Peoples.* Ottawa: Policy Research Initiative.

Newhouse, David, Cora Voyageur, and Dan Beavon, eds. 2007. *Hidden in Plain Sight. Contributions of Aboriginal Peoples to Canadian Identity and Culture.* Toronto: University of Toronto Press.

Newman, David M. 2012. *Identities and Inequalities: Exploring the Intersections of Race, Class, Gender, and Sexuality* (2nd ed.). Markham, ON: McGraw Hill.

Newport, Frank, David W. Moore, and Lydia Saad. 1999. "Long-Term Gallup Poll Trends: A Portrait of American Public Opinion Through the Century." 20 December. Retrieved from www.gallup.com.

Neyfakh, Leon. 2015. "How White Supremacist Groups Have Used the Deaths of Trayvon Martin and Other Black Men to Grow Their Ranks." *National Post*, 24 June.

Niemonen, Jack. 2007. Antiracist Education in Theory and Practice: A Critical Assessment. *American Sociologist* 38:159–177.

Niezen, Ronald. 2003. *The Origins of Indigenism: Human Rights and the Politics of Identity.* Berkeley: University of California Press.

Nopper, Tamara K. 2003. "The White Anti-Racist is an Oxymoron." *Race Traitor*, Fall.

Norton, Michael I., and Samuel R. Sommers. 2011. Whites See Racism as a Zero-Sum Game That They are Now Losing. *Association for Psychological Science* 6(3):215–218.

Novac, Sylvia. 1999. "Immigrant Enclaves and Residential Segregation: Voices of Racialized Refugees." *Canadian Woman Studies* 19(3):97–103.

NWAC. 2012. "Understanding Native Women's Association of Canada's Position on Prostitution." November.

Odartey-Wellington, Felix. 2011. Erasing Race in the Canadian Media: The Case of Suaad Hagi Mohamud. *Canadian Journal of Communication* 36:395–414.

O'Doherty, Kieran, and Martha Augoustinos. 2008. "Protecting the Nation: Nationalist Rhetoric on Asylum Seekers and the Tampa." *Journal of Community & Applied Social Psychology* 18:576–592.

Okin, Susan, ed. 1999. *Is Multiculturalism Bad for Women?* Princeton, NJ: Princeton University Press.

Olsen, Gregg M. 2011. *Power & Inequality: A Comparative Introduction.* Toronto: Oxford University Press.

Olson, Alexandra. 2013. "Canada Faces 'Crisis' over Aboriginal Issues," Anaya Tells the UN. *Globe and Mail,* 22 October.

Omi, M., and H. Winant. 1994. *Racial Formation in the United States* (2nd ed.). New York: Routledge.

Omidvar, Ratna. 2010. "Canada's Immigration Score: Recommendations for a Win-Win." *Policy Options* (July/August).

Omidvar, Ratna. 2013. "Temporary Immigrants, Temporary Loyalties." *Globe and Mail,* 20 May.

Ominayak, Bernard, and Ed Bianchi. 2002. "Lubicon Cree: Still No Settlement after All These Years," in *Nation to Nation.* J. Bird et al., eds., 163–174. Toronto: Irwin.

Ommundsen, Wenche, Michael Leach, and Andrew Vandenberg. 2010. "Multiculturalism and Cultural Citizenship." In *Cultural Citizenship and the Challenges of Globalization.* W. Ommundsen et al., eds. Cresskill, NJ: Hampton Press.

O'Neill, Peter. 2008. "Canada Sets Example in Diversity: Jean." *Canwest News Service,* 6 May.

Ontario Human Rights Commission. 2005a. "Fishing without Fear: Report on the Inquiry into Assaults on Asian-Canadian Anglers." Toronto: Author.

Ontario Human Rights Commission. 2005b. "Paying the Price: The Human Cost of Racial Profiling." Toronto: Author.

Oppal, Wally T. 2012. "Foresaken: The Report of the Missing Women Commission of Inquiry." Ministry of Justice. British Columbia.

O'Regan, Tipene. 1994. *Indigenous Governance: Country Study—New Zealand.* Study prepared for the Royal Commission on Aboriginal Peoples. Ottawa.

Oreopoulos, Philip, 2009. Why Do Skilled Immigrants Struggle in the Labour Market? Working Paper Series No 09-03. Metropolis British Columbia, Vancouver B.C.

Ornstein, Michael. 2006. *Ethno-Racial Groups in Toronto, 1971–2001: A Demographic and Socio-Economic Profile.* Toronto: Institute for Social Research.

Orwin, Clifford. 2010. "No Room at the Inn for Veiled Women? Get Real, Canada." *Globe and Mail,* 30 March.

Ossewaarde, Marinus. 2014. The National Identities of the "Death of Multiculturalism" Discourse in Western Europe. *Journal of Multicultural Discourses* 9(3):173–189.

Our Diverse Cities. 2004. Volume 1, Number 1.

Our Diverse Cities. 2006. No 2. Summer.

Our Diverse Cities. 2007. No 4. Fall.

Pager, Devah 2007. Marked. Race, Crime, and Finding Work in an Era of Mass Incarceration. University of Chicago Press.

Paikin, Steve. 2010. "Racism, Then and Now." *The Agenda.* Aired on TVOntario, 10 April.

Palmater, Pam. 2013. Why Idle No More Matters To Us All. *Now Magazine,* 10 January.

Palmater, Pam. 2014. Why We Are Idle No More. In Kino-nda-niimi Collective, ed., *The Winter We Danced,* 37–40. Winnipeg: Arbeiter Ring.

Palmater, Pam, 2015. *Indigenous Nationhood. Empowering Grassroots Citizens.* Halifax: Fernwood.

Palmer, Douglas L. 1996. "Determinants of Canadian Attitudes toward Immigration: More Than Just Racism?" *Canadian Journal of Behavioural Science* 28(3):180–192.

Palmer, Howard, ed. 1975. *Immigration and the Rise of Multiculturalism.* Toronto: Copp Clark.

Paolucci, Paul. 2006. "Race and Racism in Marx's Camera Obscura." *Critical Sociology* 32(4).

Papademetriou, Demetrios G. 2003. "Managing Rapid and Deep Change in the Newest Age of Migration." *The Political Quarterly* (Special Issue), 39–58.

Papillon, Martin. 2002. *Immigration, Diversity and Social Inclusion in Canada's Cities.* Discussion Paper F/27. Canadian Policy Research Network.

Papp, Aruna. 2010. *Culturally Driven Violence against Women: A Growing Problem in*

Canada's Immigration Communities. Winnipeg: Frontier Centre for Public Policy.

Paquet, Gilles. 2008. *Canada's Deep Diversity: A Governance Challenge*. Ottawa: University of Ottawa Press.

Paquet, Gilles. 2011. "About Dumbfounding Aspects of Canadian Immigration Policy." 2011 Paper Presented to the Roundtable Organized for the 45th Annual Meeting of the Canadian Economics Association. June.

Paquet, Mireille. 2015. Bureaucrats as Immigration Policy Makers: The Case of Subnational Immigration Activism in Canada, 1990–2010. *Journal of Ethnic and Migration Studies* 41(11):1815–1835.

Paradies, Yin C. 2006. "Beyond Black and White: Essentialism, Hybridity, and Indigeneity." *Journal of Sociology* 42(4):355–367.

Paradkar, Bageshree. 2000. "Suffering in Silence." *Toronto Star*, 24 June.

Parekh, Bhikhu. 1997. "Foreward," in *Ethnic Minorities in Britain*. T. Modood and R. Berthoud, eds. London: Policy Studies Institute.

Parekh, Bhikhu. 2000. "Preface," in *The Future of Multi-Ethnic Britain—Report of the Commission on the Future of Multi-Ethnic Britain*. Bhikku Parekh (chair). London: Profile Books.

Park, Augustine S. J. 2013. Introduction: The Labour of Race. *Canadian Journal of Sociology* 38(4):453–466.

Parkin, Andrew. 2001. "Introduction," in *What Will Hold Us Together?* Centre for Policy Research in Canada.

Parkin, Andrew. 2015. International Report Card on Public Education: Key Facts on Canadian Achievement and Equity. Final Report for the Environics Institute. June.

Parkin, Andrew. 2003. *A Changing People: Being Canadian in a New Century*. CRIC Paper No. 9. Montreal: Centre for Research and Information on Canada.

Pascal, Julia. 2006. "What's in a Name?" *Catalyst*, 20 November.

Pascale, Celine-Marie. 2007. *Making Sense of Race, Class, and Gender: Common Sense, Power, and Privilege in the United States*. New York: Routledge.

Pateman, Carole. 1988. *Sexual Contract*. Cambridge, MA: Polity Press.

Patriquin, Martin. 2007. "The End of Separatism?" *Maclean's*, 13 August.

Patriquin, Martin. 2012. "Canada, Home to the Suicide Capital of the World." *Maclean's*, 30 March.

Pauktuutit. 2006. *National Strategy to Prevent Abuse in Inuit Communities and Sharing Knowledge, Sharing Wisdom*. Iqaluit, NU: Pauttutit Inuit Women of Canada.

Paul, Daniel. 2012. "We Were Not the Savages." In *Power and Resistance: Critical Thinking About Canadian Social Issues* (5th ed.) L. Samuelson and W. Antony, eds., 146–166. Halifax: Fernwood.

Peach, Ian. 2005. "The Politics of Self-Government." *SIPP News* (Spring), 4–6.

Pearson, David 1994. *Canada Compared: Multiculturalism and Biculturalism in Settler Societies*. St. John's: Institute of Social and Economic Research, Memorial University.

Pearson, David. 2001. *The Politics of Ethnicity in Settler Societies*. London: Palgrave Macmillan.

Pearson, Noel. 2014. "A Rightful Place: Race, Recognition, and a More Complete Commonwealth." *Quarterly Essay* 55:September.

Pecoskie, Teri. 2013. "Standing Still: Running Water Remains a Dream for Most on Six Nations." *Hamilton Spectator*, 13 April.

Pecoud, Antoine, and Paul de Guchteneire. 2005. *Global Migration Perspectives*. No 27. Switzerland: Global Commission on International Migration.

Pecoud, Antoine, and Martin Geiger, eds. 2010. *The New Politics of Migration Management. Actors, Discourses, and Practices*. New York: Springer.

Peeples, Jennifer Ann. 2006. Review of the New Politics of Race: Globalism, Difference, Justice. *Rhetoric and Public Affairs* 9(4):718–720.

Pendakur, Krishna. 2005. *Visible Minorities in Canada's Workplaces: A Perspective on the 2017 Projection*. Vancouver: Metropolis Project.

Pendakur, Krishna, and Ravi Pendakur. 2004. *Colour My World: Has the Majority–Minority Earnings Gap Changed over Time?* Working Paper No. 04-11. Research on immigration and integration in the metropolis. Vancouver: Vancouver Centre of Excellence.

Pendakur, Krishna, and Ravi Pendakur. 2011a. Color by Numbers: Minority Earnings in Canada 1995–2005. *Journal of International Migration and Integration* 12(3):305–329.

Pendakur, Krishna, and Ravi Pendakur. 2011b. Aboriginal Income Disparity in Canada. *Canadian Public Policy* 37(1):61–83.

Pendakur, Ravi. 2000. *Immigrants and the Labour Force: Policy, Regulation, and Impact*. Montreal/Kingston: McGill-Queen's University Press.

Penner, A. M., and A. Saperstein. 2013. Engendering Racial Perceptions. *Gender and Society* 27(3):319–344.

Penslar, Derek J. 2005. "Introduction," in *Contemporary Antisemitism: Canada and the World*. D. J. Penslar, ed. Toronto: University of Toronto Press.

Perreault, Samuel. 2011. "Violent Victimization of Aboriginal People in the Canadian Provinces, 2009." Statistics Canada. Publication 85–002-x.

Perreaux, Les. 2010. "The Face of Quebec Revealed in Niqab Debate." *Globe and Mail*, 20 March.

Perry, Barbara. 2015. Disrupting the Mantra of Multiculturalism: Hate Crime in Canada. *American Behavioral Scientist* 59(13):1637–1654.

Peter, K. 1978. "Multi-cultural Politics, Money, and the Conduct of Canadian Ethnic Studies." *Canadian Ethnic Studies Association Bulletin* 5:2–3.

Peters, Evelyn. 2001. "Geographies of Aboriginal People in Canada." *Canadian Geographer* 45(1):138–144.

Peters, Evelyn, 2004. *Three Myths about Aboriginals in Cities. Breakfast on the Hill Seminar Series (25 March)*. Ottawa: Canadian Federation for the Humanities and Social Sciences.

Petrou, Michael, and Luiza Ch. Savage. 2006. "Genocide in Slow Motion." *Maclean's*, 11 December.

Pettinicchio, David. 2012. Migration and Ethnic Nationalism: Anglophone Exit and the "Decolonisation" of Quebec. *Nations and Nationalism* 18(4):719–743.

Pettigrew, Todd. 2014. "McGill Students Apologize for Forcing Farnan to Say Sorry." *Maclean's*, 10 March.

Pew Research Center. 2014. *5 Facts About Illegal Immigration in the United States*. 18 November.

Pew Forum on Religion and Public Life. 2008. *U.S. Religious Landscape Survey: Report 1: Religious Affiliation*. Retrieved November 16, 2015 (www.pewforum.org/files/2013/05/report-religious-landscape-study-full.pdf).

Philip, M. Nourbese. 1996. "How White Is Your White?" *Borderlines* 37:19–24.

Phillips, Anne. 2007. *Multiculturalism without Culture*. Princeton, NJ: Princeton University Press.

Phillips, A., and S. Saharso. 2008. Introduction to "The Rights of Women and the Crisis in Multiculturalism." *Ethnicities* 8(3):291–301.

Picard, Andre. 2012. "Tories 'Want Out of the Aboriginal Business.'" *Globe and Mail*, 10 April.

Picca, Leslie Houts, and Joe Feagin. 2007. *Two-Faced Racism: Whites in the Backstage and the Frontstage*. New York: Routledge.

Piche Victor. 2010. *Global Migration Management or the Emergence of a New Restrictive and Repressive Migration World Order*. International Workshop—Institute for Migration and Intercultural Studies. University of Osnabruck, Germany, 13 November.

Piche, Victor. 2011. In and Out the Back Door: Canada's Temporary Worker Programs in a Global Perspective. In *The Politics of International Migration Management: Migration Management and its Discontents*. Proceedings of a Conference at the University of Osnabruck, Institute for Migration Research and Intercultural Studies. November.

Pickering, Michael. 2001. *Stereotypes: The Politics of Representation*. New York: Palgrave.

Picot, G., F. Hou, and S. Coulombe. 2007. *Chronic Low Income and Low-Income Dynamics among Recent Immigrants*. Analytical Studies Branch Research Paper Series 2007(294). Ottawa: Statistics Canada.

Pierce, Chester. 1974. Psychiatry Problems of the Black Minority. In *American Handbook of Psychiatry*, S. Arieta, ed., 512–523. New York: Basic Books.

Pieterse, Jan Nederveen. 2007. *Ethnicities and Global Multiculture*. Lantham, MD: Rowman & Littlefield.

Pilkington, Andrew. 2011. *Institutional Racism in the Academy: A Case Study*. Stoke-on-Trent, UK: Trentham.

Pinder, Sherrow O. 2010. *The Politics of Race and Ethnicity in the United States*. New York: Palgrave Macmillan.

Pinder, Sherrow O. 2013. Introduction: The Concept and Definition of American Multicultural Studies. In *American Multicultural Studies: A Diversity of Race, Ethnicity, Gender, and Sexuality*. S. O. Pinder, ed., ix–xxii. Thousand Oaks: Sage.

Pinker, Susan. 2008. *The Sexual Paradox: Extreme Men, Gifted Women and the Real Gender Gap*. Toronto: Random House.

Piper, Nicola. 2008. "International Migration and Gendered Axes of Stratification: Introduction," in *New Perspectives on Gender and Migration.* N. Piper, ed., 1–18. New York: Routledge.

Piper, Nicola. 2010. "Temporary Economic Migration and Rights Activism: An Organizational Perspective." *Ethnic and Racial Studies,* 33:108–125.

Pirkle, Catherine M. 2014 Food Insecurity and Nutritional Biomarkers in Relation to Stature in Inuit Children in Nunavik. *Journal of the Canadian Public Health Association* 105(4):213–218.

Pitcher, Ben. 2009. *The Politics of Multiculturalism: Race and Racism in Contemporary Britain.* New York: Palgrave Macmillan.

Pitsula, James M. 2013. Keeping Canada British: The Ku Klux Klan in 1920s Saskatchewan. Vancouver: UBC Press.

Plaut, Rabbi W. Gunther. 1989. "Unwanted Intruders or People in Flight." *Perception* 13(2):45–46.

Ponting, J. Rick. 1986. *Arduous Journey: Canadian Indians and Decolonization.* Toronto: McClelland & Stewart.

Ponting, J. Rick. 1997. *First Nations in Canada: Perspectives on Opportunities, Empowerment, and Self-Determination.* Toronto: McGraw-Hill Ryerson.

Ponting, J. Rick, and Roger Gibbins. 1980. *Out of Irrelevance: A Socio-Political Introduction to Indian Affairs in Canada.* Toronto: Butterworths.

Poole, Deborah. 2008. *The Minga of Resistance: Policy-Making from Below.* NACLA Report on the America's.

Porter, Henry. 2005. "It's Great Up North." *Guardian Weekly,* 2–8 December.

Porter, John. 1965. *The Vertical Mosaic.* Toronto: University of Toronto Press.

Porter, Robert Odawi. 2005. *Sovereignty, Colonialism and the Indigenous Nations: A Reader.* Durham, NC: Carolina Academic Press.

Possner, Michael. 1997. "A Battlefield Primer on Multiculturalism." *A Review,* 12 July.

Powell, Adam, A., Nyla R. Branscombe, and Michael T. Schmitt. 2005. "Inequality as Ingroup Privilege or Outgroup Disadvantage: The Impact of Group Focus on Collective Guilt or Interracial Attitudes." *Society for Personality and Social Psychology Bulletin* 31(4):508–522.

Preibisch, Kerry. 2010. Pick Your Own Labour: Migrant Workers and Flexibility in Canadian Agriculture. *International Migration Review* 44(2):404–441.

Price, Richard. 1991. *Legacy: Indian Treaty Relationships.* Edmonton: School of Native Studies, University of Alberta.

Proudfoot, Shannon. 2010. "Diversity Can Be Good for Big Cities." *Vancouver Sun,* 13 April.

Prus, Robert. 1999. *Beyond the Power Mystique: Power as Intersubjective Accomplishment.* Albany: State University of New York.

Public Safety Canada. 2007. *Aboriginal Policing Update* 1(2).

Public Service Alliance of Canada. 2010. *A Critical Analysis of the Annual Report on Employment Equity in the Federal Public Sector Service 2008–09.* Retrieved online.

Purich, Donald. 1986. *Our Land: Native Peoples in Canada.* Toronto: James Lorimer and Sons.

Purvis, Andrew. 1999. "Whose Home and Native Land?" *Time,* 15 February: 16–26.

Putnam, Robert. 2007. "*E Pluribus Unum*: Diversity and Community in the Twenty-First Century." *Scandinavian Political Studies* 30(2).

Qadeer, Mohammad A. 2007. "The Charter and Multiculturalism." *Policy Options* (February), 89–97.

Qadeer, Mohammad A., and Sandeep Agrawal. 2009. "Ethnic Enclaves Bloom Amid City Landscape." *Toronto Star,* 5 July.

Qadeer, Mohammad A., Sandeep Agrawal, and A. Lovell. 2009. *Evolution of Ethnic Enclaves in the Toronto Metropolitan Area 2001–06.* [PowerPoint presentation].

Quan, Douglas. 2015. "Canada Now Sheltering More Hungarian Roma Refugees." *National Post,* 25 August.

Quebec Human Rights Commission. 2011. *Racial Profiling and Its Consequences.* Quebec City: Author.

Quesnel, Joseph. 2012. A Decade of Nisga'a Self-Government. *Inroads* 31:47–57.

Quesnel, Joseph and Conrad Winn. 2011. The Nisga'a Treaty: Self Government and Good Governance: The Jury is Still Out. Frontier Centre for Public Policy.

Race Traitor. n.d. "Abolish the White Race—By Any Means Necessary." (http://racetraitor.org/abolish.html).

Rajagopal, Indhu. 2006. *Hidden Academics: Contract Faculty in Canadian Universities.* Toronto: University of Toronto Press.

Rajiva, Mythili. 2005. *Bridging the Generation Gap.* Available online at http://canada.metropolis.net/pdfs/ Rajiva_e.pdf.

Rajiva, Mythili, and Sheila Batacharya, eds. 2010. *Reena Virk: Critical Perspectives on a Canadian Murder*. Toronto: Canadian Scholars Press.

Ralston, Helen. 1999. "Canadian Immigration Policy in the Twentieth Century: Its Impact on South Asian Women." *Canadian Woman Studies* 19(3):33–37.

Ramirez, Judith. 2001. "Canada at Forefront in Gender Guidelines for Refugee Status." *Toronto Star*, 4 May.

Rand, David. 2014. The Charter, The Turban and the Monarchy. *Humanist Perspective* 187:1–3.

Rao, Govind. 2007. "Multiculturalism in Canada and Austria: Paradoxes of Assimilation and Integration." A Presentation to the Austrian-Canadian Society. Vienna. 17 April.

Rao, Govind. 2010. In Praise of Canadian Contradictions: Making Our Way in a Globalized World. *Education Canada* 44(2). Retrieved from www.cea-ace.ca.

Ratcliffe, Peter. 2004. *"Race," Ethnicity, and Difference: Imagining the Inclusive Society*. New York: Open University Press.

Razack, Sherene. 1994. "What Is to Be Gained by Looking White People in the Eye? Culture, Race, and Gender in Cases of Sexual Violence." *Signs* (Summer), 894–922.

Razack, Sherene, ed. 2002. *Race, Space, and the Law: Unmapping a White Settler Society*. Toronto: Between the Lines.

Razack, Sherene. 2004. *Dark Threats and White Knights: The Somalia Affair, Peacekeeping, and the New Imperialism*. Toronto: University of Toronto Press.

Razack, Sherene. 2008. *Casting Out: The Eviction of Muslims from Western Law and Politics*. University of Toronto Press.

Razack, Sherene, Malinda Smith, and Sunera Thobani. 2010. Introduction: States of Race: Critical Race Feminisms for the 21st Century. In *States of Race: Critical Race Feminisms for the 21st Century*. S. Thobani, S. Razack, and M. Smith, eds., 1–22. Toronto: Between the Lines.

RCMP. 2014. "Murdered and Missing Aboriginal Women: A National Operational Overview." Ottawa: Author.

Rebick, Judy. 2013. Idle No More: A Profound Social Movement That is Already Succeeding. *Canadian Dimension* (blog), 12 January.

Rebick, Judy. 2014. "A Reminder to Uproot Our Culture of Misogyny." 5 December, www.rabble.ca.

Redhead, Mark. 2003. "Charles Taylor's Deeply Diverse Response to Canada's Fragmentation: A Project Often Commented on but Seldom Explored." *Canadian Journal of Political Science* 36(1):61–83.

Refugees. 2007. "Refugee or Migrant?" Published by UNHCR #148 (2).

Regan, Paulette. 2011 *Unsettling the Settler Within: Indian Residential Schools, Truth Telling, and Reconciliation in Canada*. Vancouver: UBC Press.

Rehaag, Sean. 2013. Judicial Review of Refugee Determination: The Luck of the Draw? *Queen's Law Journal* 38(1).

Rehaag, Sean. 2015. Unappealing: An Assessment of Limits on Appeal Rights in Canada's New Refugee Determination System. Osgoode Legal Society Research Paper No 42/2015.

Reicher, Stephen. 2007. Rethinking the Paradigm of Prejudice. *South African Journal of Psychology* 37(4):820–834.

Reid, Scott. 1993. *Lament for a Notion: The Life and Death of Canada's Bilingual Dream*. Vancouver: Arsenal Pulp Press.

Reinhart, Anthony. 2007. "A Nation of Newcomers." *Globe and Mail*, 5 December.

Reinhart, Anthony, and James Rusk. 2006. "Immigrants Suffer in Silence within Walls of Suburbs." *Globe and Mail*, 11 March.

Reitman, Oonagh. 2005. "Multiculturalism and Feminism: Incompatibility, Compatibility, and Synonymity?" *Ethnicities* 5(2):216–247.

Reitz, Jeffrey. 1998. *Warmth of the Welcome: The Social Causes of Economic Success for Immigrants in Different Nations and Cities*. Boulder, CO: Westview Press.

Reitz, Jeffrey. 2005. "Tapping Immigrants' Skills: New Directions for Canadian Immigration Policy in the Knowledge Economy." *IRRP Choices* 11(1). Retrieved November 16, 2015 (http://irpp.org/research-studies/choices-vol11-no1/).

Reitz, Jeffrey. 2009. "Assessing Multiculturalism as a Behavioural Theory," in Multiculturalism and Social Cohesion. J. Reitz et al., eds., 1–43. New York: Springer Science+Business Media.

Reitz, Jeffrey. 2010. "Selecting Immigrants for the Short Term: Is it Smart in the Long Run?" *Policy Options* (July/August).

Reitz, Jeffrey. 2014a. Multicultural Policies and Popular Multiculturalism in the Development of Canadian Immigration. In *The Multiculturalism Question:*

Debating Identity in 21ˢᵗ-Century Canada, Jack Jedwab, ed. Queen's Policy Studies Series. School of Policy Studies, Queen's University. Montreal/Kingston: McGill-Queen's University Press.

Reitz, Jeffrey. 2014b. Canada: New Initiatives and Approaches to Immigration and Nation-Building. In *Controlling Immigration: A Global Perspective*, (3ʳᵈ ed.) J. Hollifield, P. L. Martin, and P. Orrenius, eds., 88–116. Stanford, CA: Stanford University Press.

Reitz, Jeffrey, and Rupa Banerjee. 2007. "Racial Inequality, Social Cohesion, and Policy Issues," in *Belonging?* K. Banting et al., eds., 489–546. Montreal: Institute for Research on Public Policy.

Reitz, Jeffrey, and Raymond Breton. 1994. *The Illusion of Difference: Realities of Ethnicity in Canada and the United States*. Toronto: CD Howe Institute.

Reitz, Jeffrey, Mai. B. Phan, and Rupa Banerjee. 2015. Gender Equity in Canada's Newly Growing Religious Minorities. *Ethnic and Racial Studies* 38(5):681–699.

Report of the Commission of Inquiry into Systemic Racism in Ontario's Criminal Justice System. 1995. Toronto: Queen's Printer of Ontario.

Report. 2014a. "Gap Between Rich and Poor." Toronto Vital Signs Report.

Report. 2014b. "Murdered and Missing Aboriginal Women in British Columbia Canada." Inter-American Commission on Human Rights. Washington, DC. 21 December.

Reputation Institute. 2015. The World's Most Reputable Countries. New York. July

Resnick, Philip. 2000. "Civic and Ethnic Nationalism: A Canadian Perspective," in *Canadian Political Thought*. Ron Beiner and Wayne Norman, eds. Toronto: Oxford University Press.

Resnick, Philip. 2001. *The Politics of Resentment: British Columbia Regionalism and Canadian Unity*. Vancouver: UBC Press.

Rex, John. 2004. "Multiculturalism and Political Integration in the Modern Nation State." Documentos CIDOB, *Dinamicas Interculturales*. Numero Uno.

Rex, John, and Gurharpal Singh. 2004. *Governance in Multicultural Societies*. London, UK: Ashgate.

Reyna, Christine, A. Tucker, W. Korfmacher, and P. J. Henry. 2005. "Searching for Common Ground Between Supporters and Opponents of Affirmative Action." *Political Psychology* 26(5):667–681.

Ricard, Danielle, and Rima Wilkes. 2008. *Newspaper Framing of Protest by Indigenous Peoples and the Construction of National Identity*. Retrieved November 16, 2015 (http://research.allacademic.com).

Richards, John. 2014. "Are We Making Progress?" New Evidence on Aboriginal Education Outcomes in Provincial and Reserve Schools. Commentary No 408. C.D. Howe Institute, Toronto, April.

Richards, John, and M. Scott. 2009. *Aboriginal Education: Strengthening the Foundations*. Ottawa: Canadian Policy Research Networks.

Richmond, Ted, and Anver Saloojee. 2005. Social Inclusion: Canadian Perspectives. Halifax: Fernwood.

Richomme, Olivier. 2012. The Post-Racial Illusion: Racial Politics and Inequality in the Age of Obama. Revue de Recherche en Civilisaton Americaine. 3.

Roberts, David J., and Minelle Mahtani, 2010. Neoliberalizing Race, Racing Neoliberalism: Placing "Race" in Neoliberal Discourse. *Antipode* 42(2):248–257.

Roberts, Dorothy. 2011. *Fatal Intervention: How Science, Politics, and Big Business Recreate Race in the Twenty-First Century*. New York: The New Press.

Roberts, Julian V., and Ronald Melchers. 2003. "The Incarceration of Aboriginal Offenders: Trends from 1978 to 2001." *Canadian Journal of Criminology and Criminal Justice* 45(2):1–18.

Roberts, Lance W., and Rodney A. Clifton. 1990. "Multiculturalism in Canada: A Sociological Perspective," in *Race and Ethnic Relations in Canada*, Peter S. Li, ed., 20–147. Toronto: Oxford University Press.

Robson, Karen L. 2013. *Sociology of Education in Canada*. Toronto: Pearson

Rodriguez, Ilia. 2009. "'Diversity Writing' and the Liberal Discourse on Multiculturalism in Mainstream Papers." *The Howard Journal of Communication* 20:167–188.

Rodriguez-Garcia, Dan. 2010. "Beyond Assimilation and Multiculturalism: A Critical Review of the Debate on Managing Diversity." *International Migration and Integration* 11:251–272.

Rodriguez-Garcia, Dan. 2012. "Introduction: Managing Migration and Diversity in the New Age of Migration: A Transatlantic Dialogues."

In *Managing Immigration and Diversity in Canada*. D. Rodriguez-Garcia, ed., 1–60. Montreal/Kingston: McGill-Queen's University Press.

Rolfsen, Catherine. 2008. "After the Apology." *This Magazine*, September/October.

Romero, A., C. Wiggs, C. Valencia, and S. Bauman. 2013. Latina Teen Suicide and Bullying. *Hispanic Journal of Behavioral Science* 35(2):159–173.

Rooney, Frances. 2008. "Viola Desmond, Unintentional Revolutionary." 29 January. Retrieved November 16, 2015 (http://section15.ca/features/people/2008/01/29/viola_desmond/).

Root, J., E. Gates-Gasse, J. Shields, and H. Bauder. 2014. "Discounting Immigrant Families: Neoliberalism and the Framing of Canadian Immigration Policy Change: A Literature Review." Working Paper No 2014/7. Toronto: Ryerson Centre for Immigration and Settlement.

Roscigno, Vincent, J. L. Garcia, S. Mong, and R. Byron. 2007. "Racial Discrimination at Work: Its Occurrence, Dimensions, and Consequences. The New Black, Alternative Paradigms and Strategies for the 21st Century." *Research in Race and Ethnic Relations* 14:111–135.

Rosin, Hanna. 2012. *The End of Men: And the Rise of Women*. Riverhead Books.

Roth, Lorna. 1998. "Television Broadcasting North of 60," in *Images of Canadianess*. L. d'Haenens, ed., 147–166. Ottawa: University of Ottawa Press.

Rothenberg, Paula S., ed. 2001. *Race, Class, and Gender in the United States* (5th ed.). New York: Worth Publishers.

Rotman, Leonard Ian. 1996. *Parallel Paths: Fiduciary Doctrine and the Crown–Native Relationship in Canada*. Toronto: University of Toronto Press.

Rotman, Leonard. 2004. "Let Us Face It, We Are All Here to Stay. But Do We Negotiate or Litigate?" in *Advancing Aboriginal Claims*. Kerry Wilkins, ed., 202–240. Saskatoon: Purich.

Royal Commission on Aboriginal Peoples. 1992. *Framing the Issues: Discussion Paper No 1*. Ottawa: Royal Commission on Aboriginal Peoples.

Royal Commission on Aboriginal Peoples. 1996a. *Final Report*. Volume One, Chapter 13, "Conclusions" section 1. Primary source: DCS 1920 HC Special Committee.

Royal Commission on Aboriginal Peoples. 1996b. *People to People, Nation to Nation: Highlights from the Report on the Royal Commission on Aboriginal Peoples*. Ottawa: Minister of Supply and Services Canada.

Ruddick, E. 2003. "Immigrant Economic Performance." *Canadian Issues* 5:16–17.

Rumbaut, Rubén G. 2009. "Pigments of Our Imagination: On the Racialization and Racial Identities of 'Hispanics' and 'Latinos'." In *How the U.S. Racializes Latinos: White Hegemony and Its Consequences*. José A. Cobas, Jorge Duany and Joe R. Feagin, eds. Boulder, CO: Paradigm Publishers.

Rumbaut, Rubén. 2011. *Pigments of Our Imagination: The Racialization of the Hispanic-Latino Category*. Migration Policy Institute. 27 April.

Rummel, R. J. 2005. *Genocide: Meaning and Definition*. Retrieved online.

Runnymede Trust. 2000. *The Future of Multi-Ethnic Britain: Report of the Commission on the Future of Multi-Ethnic Britain*. London, UK: Profile Books.

Ruparelia, Rakhi. 2012. "The Currency of Racism in Canada." *Toronto Star*, 22 August.

Rushowy, Kristin. 2001. "Native Students Return to Roots at School in the Heart of the City." *Toronto Star*, 15 October.

Rushton, J. P., and A. R. Jensen. 2005. "Thirty Years of Research on Race Differences in Cognitive Ability." *Psychology, Public Policy, and Law, 11*, 235–294.

Rushton, Philippe. 1994. *Race, Evolution, and Behavior: A Life History Perspective*. Retrieved November 17, 2015 (www.udel.edu/educ/gottfredson/reprints/1996reviewRushton.pdf).

Rushton, Philippe. 1995. *Race, Evolution, and Behavior: A Life History Perspective*. New Brunswick, NJ: Transaction.

Rusk, James. 2005. "Conditions on Reserve 'Atrocious' Doctor Says." *Globe and Mail*, 24 October.

Russell, Peter. 2005. *Recognizing Aboriginal Title: The Mabo Case and Indigenous Resistance to English-Settler Colonialism*: University of Toronto Press.

RVH (Racism, Violence, and Health) Project. 2002/3. *Racism Makes You Sick—It's a Deadly Disease*. Halifax: Dalhousie University, 14.

Ryan, Phil. 2010. *Multicultiphobia*. Toronto: University of Toronto Press.

Sajoo, Amyn B. 1994. "New Dances with Diversity." *Policy Options* (December), 14–19.

Salee, Daniel. 2003. "Transformative Politics: The State and the Politics of Social Change in

Quebec," in *Changing Canada: Political Economy as Transformation.* Wallace Clement and Leah Vosko, eds., 25–50. Montreal/Kingston: McGill-Queen's University Press.

Salee, Daniel, and William Coleman. 1997. "The Challenges of the Quebec Question: Paradigm, Counter-Paradigm, and the Nation-State," in *Understanding Canada.* W. Clement, ed. Montreal/Kingston: McGill-Queen's University Press.

Saloojee, Anver. 2003. "Social inclusion, anti-racism and democratic citizenship." Perspectives on Social Inclusion. Laidlaw Foundation Working Paper Series. January.

Saloojee, Anver. 2005. Social Inclusion, Anti-racism, and Democratic Citizenship. *Policy Matters* 14 (January):1–4. A report of CERIS–The Ontario Metropolis Centre.

Sammel, Ali. 2009. "Turning the Focus from 'Other' to Science Education. Exploring the Invisibility of Whiteness." *Cultural Studies of Science Education* 4(3):649–656.

Samson, Colin. 2003. *A Way of Life That Does Not Exist: Canada and the Extinguishment of the Innu.* St. John's: ISER Books.

Samuel, Edith. 2006. *Integrative Antiracism: South Asians in Canadian Academe.* Toronto: University of Toronto Press.

Samuel, Edith, and Shehla Burney. 2003. "Racism, Eh? Interactions of South Asian Students with Mainstream Faculty in a Predominantly White Canadian University." *The Canadian Journal of Higher Education 33*(2):81–103.

Samuelson, Les. 2012. Crime as a Social Problem. From Definition to Reality. In *Power and Resistance: Critical Thinking About Canadian Social Issues,* (5th ed.). L. Samuelson and W Antony, eds., 373–404. Halifax: Fernwood

Sandercock, Leonie. 2003. *Rethinking Multiculturalism for the 21st Century.* Working Paper No. 03-14. Research on Immigration and Integration in the Metropolis. Vancouver: Vancouver Centre of Excellence.

Sandercock, Leonie. 2006. *Mongrel Cities of the 21st Century: In Defense of Multiculturalism.* UBC Laurier Lecture.

Sapers, Howard. 2013. "Spirit Matters: Aboriginal People and the Corrections and Conditional Release Act." Report Office of the Correctional Investigator.

Sargut, Gokce, and Rita Gunther McGrath. 2011. Learning to Live with Complexity. *Harvard Business Review.* September.

Sarich, Vincent, and Frank Miele. 2004. *Race: The Reality of Human Differences.* Boulder, CO: Westview Press.

Sarick, Lila. 1999. "Serbian Community Feeling Betrayed." *Globe and Mail,* 8 May.

Sarlo, Christopher. 2013. Poverty: Where Do We Draw the Line? Fraser Institute. November.

Satzewich, Vic, ed. 1998. *Racism and Social Inequality in Canada.* Toronto: Thompson Education.

Satzewich, Vic. 2000. "Whiteness Limited: Racialization and the Social Construction of 'Peripheral Europeans.'" *Histoire sociale/Social History* 23:271–290.

Satzewich, Vic. 2004. "Racism in Canada: Change and Continuity." *Canadian Dimensions* (January/February), 20.

Satzewich, Vic. 2007. "Whiteness Studies: Race, Diversity, and the New Essentialism." In *Race and Racism in 21st Century Canada.* S. P. Hier and B. S. Bolaria, eds., 67–84. Peterborough, ON: Broadview.

Satzewich, Vic. 2011. *Racism in Canada.* Toronto: Oxford University Press.

Satzewich, Vic, and Nikolaos Liodakis. 2013. *"Race" and Ethnicity in Canada: A Critical Introduction* (3rd ed.). Toronto: Oxford University Press.

Satzewich, Vic, and William Shaffir. 2009. Racism versus Professionalism: Claims and Counterclaims about Racial Profiling. *Canadian Journal of Criminology and Criminal Justice* 53(1):65–74.

Satzewich, Vic, and Lloyd Wong, eds. 2006. *Transnational Identities and Practices in Canada.* Vancouver: University of British Columbia Press.

Saul, John Ralston. 1998. *Reflections of a Siamese Twin: Canada at the End of the Twentieth Century.* Toronto: Penguin.

Saul, John Ralston. 2014. *The Comeback: How Aboriginals are Reclaiming Power and Influence.* Toronto: Viking.

Saunders, Barbara, and David Haljan, eds. 2003. *Wither Multiculturalism? A Politics of Dissensus.* Leuven, BE: Leuven University Press.

Sauvageau, Florian, David Schneiderman, and David Taras. 2006. *The Last Word. Media Coverage of the Supreme Court of Canada.* Vancouver: UBC Press.

Savard, P., and B. Vignezzi. 1999. *Multiculturalism and the History of International Relations from the 18th Century Up to the Present.* Ottawa: Carleton University Press.

Sawchuk, Joe. 1998. *The Dynamics of Native Politics: The Alberta Métis Perspective.* Saskatoon: SK Publishing.

SBS (Special Broadcasting Service). 2008. "Multicultural Australia: A Nation of Paradoxes—Study Finds." [Press release].

Schachar, Ayelet. 2005. "Religion, State, and the Problem of Gender: Re-Imagining Citizenship and Governance in Diverse Societies." *McGill Law Journal* 50: 49–88.

Schellenberg, Grant, and Feng Hou. 2005. "The Economic Well-Being of Recent Immigrants to Canada." *Canadian Issues* (Spring), 49–52.

Schellenberg, Grant, and Helene Maheux. 2007. "Immigrants' Perspectives on Their First Four Years in Canada." *Canadian Social Trends,* Catalogue no. 11-008. Ottawa: Statistics Canada.

Schertow, John Ahni. 2008. *Anishinabek Outlaw Term "Aboriginal."* 30 June. Retrieved November 16, 2015 (https://intercontinentalcry.org/anishinabek-outlaw-term-aboriginal/).

Scheurich, J. J., and M. D. Young. 2002. "White Racism among White Faculty." In *The Racial Crisis in American Higher Education,* W. A. Smith, P. G. Altbach, and K. Lomotey, eds., 221–239. Albany, NY: State University of New York.

Schick, Carol. 2008. "Keeping the Ivory Tower White: Discourses of Racial Domination," in *Rethinking Society in the 21st Century: Critical Readings in Sociology.* Michelle Webber, ed. Markham, ON: IPP.

Schick, Carol, and Verna St. Denis. 2005. "Troubling National Discourses in Anti-racist Curriculum Planning." *Canadian Journal of Education* 28(3): 295–317.

Schlesinger, Arthur M., Jr. 1992. *The Disuniting of America: Reflections on a Multicultural Society.* New York: W.W. Norton.

Schliesman, Paul. 2012. *Honour on Trial: The Shafia Murders and the Culture of Honour Killing.* Fitzhenry and Whiteside.

Schoenfeld, Gabriel. 2004. *The Return of Anti-Semitism.* San Francisco: Encounter Books.

Schouls, Tim. 1997. "Aboriginal Peoples and Electoral Reform in Canada: Differentiated Representation versus Voter Equality." *Canadian Journal of Political Science* 24(4):729–749.

Scoffield, Heather. 2010. "Moving Target: Migrants and the Law." *Globe and Mail,* 15 October.

Scott, Craig. 1996. "Indigenous Self-Determination and the Decolonization of the International Imagination." *Human Rights Quarterly* 18: 815–820.

Scott, Duncan Campbell. Quoted in John Leslie, 1978, *The Historical Development of the Indian Act* (2nd ed.). Ottawa: Department of Indian Affairs and Northern Development, Treaties and Historical Research Branch:114.

Scott, James C. 1998. *Seeing Like a State.* Princeton, NJ: Yale University Press.

See, Katherine, and William J. Wilson. 1988. "Race and Ethnicity," in *Handbook of Sociology,* Neil J. Smelzer, ed., 223–242. Newbury Park: Sage.

Segal, Uma A., Doreen Elliott, and Nazneen S. Mayadas, eds. 2009. *Immigration Worldwide: Policies, Practices, and Trends.* New York: Oxford University Press.

Seidle, F. Leslie. 2007a. "Citizenship Rule and Naturalization Rates." Paper prepared for the Bouchard-Taylor Commission on Reasonable Accommodation. 15 June.

Seidle, Leslie. 2007b. *Diversity, Recognition, and Shared Citizenship in Canada.* Paper presented to the Roundtable: The Future of Multiculturalism—A German-Canadian Debate. Berlin. 29 March.

Seiler, Tamara Palmer. 2002. "Thirty Years Later: Reflections on the Evolution and Future Prospects of Multiculturalism." *Canadian Issues* (February), 6–8.

Seljak, David. 2009. *Dialogue among the Religions in Canada.* Ottawa: Policy Research Initiative, Government of Canada.

Sellers, Frances Stead. 2005. "Multiculturalism." *Kitchener-Waterloo Record,* 25 August.

Selley, Chris. 2015. "On Niqabs and 'Canadian Values.'" *National Post,* 1 October.

Semyonov, M., R. Raijman, and A. Gorodzeisky. 2008. "Foreigners' Impact on European Societies: Public Views and Perceptions in a Cross-National Comparative Perspective." *International Journal of Comparative Sociology* 49(1):5–29.

Sen, Amartya. 2006. *Identity and Violence: The Illusion of Destiny.* New York: W.W. Norton.

Senate. 2013. "Reducing Barriers to Social Inclusion and Social Cohesion." Report of the Standing Senate Committee on Social Affairs, Science and Technology. K. K. Ogilvie and A. Eggleton. June.

Seshia, Maya. 2012. From Foreign to Canadian: The Case of Air India and the Denial of Racism. *Topia* 27:215–228.

Shaheen, Jack. 2009. *Reel Bad Arabs: How Hollywood Vilifies a People*. Olive Branch Press.

Shakir, Uzma. 2010. *Canada's Immigration Fall from Grace*. Toronto: Atkinson Charitable Foundation.

Shapiro, Thomas M. 2004. *Racial Inequality: The Hidden Cost of Being African-American*. New York: Oxford University Press.

Sharma, Nandita. 2006. *Home Economics: Nationalism and the Making of "Migrant Workers" in Canada*. University of Toronto Press.

Shaykhutdinov, Renat and Belinda Bragg. 2011. Do Grievances Matter in Ethnic Conflict? An Experimental Approach. *Analysis of Social Issues and Public Policy* 11(1):141–143.

Sheehy, Elizabeth. 2010. "Misogyny Is Deadly: Inequality Makes Women More Vulnerable to Being Killed." *Canadian Centre for Policy Alternatives Newsletter* (July/August).

Shipler, David K. 2001. "A Conflict's Bedrock Is Laid Bare." *New York Times*, 27 May.

Shkilnyk, Anastasia M. 1985. *A Poison Stronger Than Love*. New Haven, CT: Yale University Press.

Shoemaker, Pamela J., and Akiba A. Cohen. 2006. *News around the World*. New York: Routledge.

Shohat, Ella, and Robert Stam. 1994. *Unthinking Eurocentrism: Multiculturalism and the Media*. New York: Routledge.

Showler, Peter. 2005. "Refugee Laws Are Not the Problem." *The Globe and Mail*, 29 April.

Showler, Peter. 2006. *Refugee Sandwich: Stories of Exile and Asylum*. Montreal/Kingston: McGill-Queen's University Press.

Showler, Peter. 2009. "Fast, Fair, and Final: Reforming Canada's Refugee Sysytem." Toronto: Maytree Foundation.

Showler, Peter (with Maytree Foundation). n.d. "Fast, Fair, and Final: Reforming Canada's Refugee System. Questions and Answers for Media." Available online at www.maytree.com.

Siddiqui, Haroon. 2007. "Don't Scapegoat Multiculturalism." *Toronto Star*, 10 June.

Siddiqui, Haroon. 2008. "In Quebec, Equality for Minorities Just Talk." *Toronto Star*, 25 May.

Siemiatycki, Myer. 2005. "Introduction." *Canadian Issues* (Spring), 3–4.

Siemiatycki, Myer. 2007. Invisible City: Immigrants without Voting Rights in Urban Ontario. *Our Diverse Cities* 4 (Fall):166–168.

Siemiatycki, Myer. 2010. Marginalizing Migrants: Canada's Rising Reliance on Temporary Foreign Workers. *Canadian Issues* (Spring), 60–63.

Siemiatycki, Myer. 2012. The Place of Immigrants: Citizenship, Settlement, and Socio-Cultural Integration in Canada. In *Managing Immigration and Diversity in Canada*. D. Rodriguez-Garcia, ed., 223–248. Montreal/Kingston: McGill-Queen's University Press.

Siemiatycki, Myer, 2015. Continuity and Change in Canadian Immigration Policy. In *Immigration Experiences in North America: Understanding Settlement and Integration*. H. Bauder and J. Shields, eds., 93–117. Toronto: Canadian Scholars Press.

Signs. 2013. Intersectionality: Theorizing Power, Empowering Theory. 38(4).

Simeon, Richard, and Ian Robinson. 2004. "The Dynamics of Canadian Federalism," in *Canadian Politics*. J. Bickerton and A.-G. Gagnon, eds. Peterborough, ON: Broadview.

Simmons, Alan. 2010. *Immigration and Canada. Global and Transnational Perspectives*. Toronto: Canadian Scholars' Press.

Simon, Patrick, and Victor Piche. 2011. Accounting for Racial and Ethnic Diversity: The Challenge of Enumeration. *Racial and Ethnic Studies* 35(8):1357–1365.

Simon-Kumar, Rachel. 2012. Difference and Diversity in Aotearoa/New Zealand: Post-neoliberal Constructions of the Ideal Ethnic Citizen. *Ethnicities* 14(1):136–159.

Simon-Kumar, Rachel. 2015. Neoliberalism and the New Race Politics of Migration Policy: Changing Profiles of the Desirable Migrant in New Zealand. *Journal of Ethnic and Migration Studies* 41(7):1172–1191.

Simpson, Leanne. 2013. "Another Story from Elsipogtog." *The Tyee,* 21 October.

Singh, Rashmee. 2014. Stephen Harper is Wrong: Crime and Sociology are the Same Thing. *Globe and Mail*, 4 September.

Singh, Renu. 2012. "The Reality of Honour Killings in Canada." *Darpan Magazine*. March. Retrieved from http://www.darpanmagazine.com.

Sinha, Maire. 2013. Measuring Violence Against Women: Statistical Trends. Juristat article. Component of Statistics Canada catalogue no 85-002-x. 25 February.

Sinha, Shalini. 2006. "Generating Awareness for the Experiences of Women of Colour in Ireland," in *Racism and Anti-racism in Ireland*. R. Lentin and R. McVeigh, eds. Belfast, IE: Beyond the Pale Publications.

Sinha, V., and A. Blumenthal. 2014. From the House of Commons Resolution to Pictou Landing Band Council and Maurina Beadle v. Canada: An Update on the Implementation of Jordan's Principle. *First Peoples Child and Family Review* 9(1).

Sirin, S. R., and L. Rogers-Sirin. 2015. "The Educational and Mental Health of Syrian Refugee Children." Migration Policy Institute Report, October.

Sirna, Tony. 1996. "Creating a 'Society of Communities.'" *Communities Journal for Cooperative Living*, 50–53.

Sissons, Jeffrey. 2005. *First Peoples: Indigenous Cultures and Their Futures*. London: Reaktion Books.

Sivanandan, A. 2007. "Foreword," in *The End of Tolerance*. A. Kundnani, ed. London, UK: Pluto Press.

Sivanandan, A. 2009. "Foreword," In *A Suitable Enemy*. L. Fekete, ed., viii–xiv. London, UK: Pluto Press.

Skaggs, Sheryl, and Jennifer Bridges. 2013. Race and Sex Discrimination in the Employment Process. *Sociology Compass* 7(5):404–415.

Skidelsky, Robert. 2004. "The Killing Fields." *New Statesman*, 26 January.

Slattery, Brian. 1997. "Recollection of Historical Practice," in *Justice for Natives: Search for a Common Ground*. Andrea P. Morrison, ed. 76–82. Montreal/Kingston: McGill-Queen's University Press.

Small, Stephen. 2002. "Racisms and Racialized Hostility at the Start of the New Millenium," in *A Companion to Racial and Ethnic Studies*. D. T. Goldberg and J. Solomos, eds., 259–281. Malden, MA: Blackwell.

Smith, Anthony D. 1993. "The Problem of Nationalist Identity: Ancient, Medieval, or Modern." *Ethnic and Race Relations*.

Smith, Anthony D. 1996. "LSE Centennial Lecture: The Resurgence of Nationalism? Myth and Memory in the Renewal of Nations." *British Journal of Sociology* 47(4):1–16.

Smith, Charles C., ed. 2010. "Anti-Racism in Education: Missing in Action." Canadian Centre for Policy Alternatives.

Smith, D. E. 1999. *Writing the Social: Critique, Theory, and Investigations*. Toronto: University of Toronto Press.

Smith, Ekuwa. 2004. *Nowhere to Turn? Responding to Partner Violence against Immigrant and Visible Minority Women*. Ottawa: Canadian Council of Social Development.

Smith, Joanna, and Bruce Campion-Smith. 2013. "Chiefs Threaten to Pull Cord." *Toronto Star*, 11 January.

Smolash, Wendy Naava. 2009. "Mark of Cain(ada). Racialized Security Discourse in Canada's National Papers." *University of Toronto Quarterly* 78(2):1–15.

Snyder, Jack L. 2000. *From Voting to Violence: Democratization and Nationalist Conflict*. New York: W.W. Norton.

Sobel, Nora. 2015. A Typology of the Changing Narratives of Canadian Citizens Through Time. *Canadian Ethnic Studies* 47(1):11–39.

Social Progress Index. 2015. "Social Progress Index 2015 Report." Social Progress Imperative. 8 April.

Soennecken, Dagmar. 2014. Germany and the Janus Face of Immigration Federalism: Devolution vs. Centralization. In *Immigration Regulation in Federal States: Challenges and Responses in Comparative Perspective*. S. Baglay and D. Nakache, eds. New York: Springer.

Solomos, John, and Les Back. 1996. *Racism and Society*. London: Macmillan.

Solomos, John, and Martin Bulmer. 2005. *Researching Race and Racism*. New York: Routledge.

Soroka, Stuart, Richard Johnston, and Keith Banting. 2006. *Ties that Bind? Social Cohesion and Diversity in Canada*. Montreal: Institute for Research on Public Policy.

Soroka, Stuart, and Sarah Roberton. 2010. "A Literature Review of Public Opinion Research on Canadian Attitudes Toward Multiculturalism and Immigration." Citizenship and Immigration Canada. March.

Southey, Tabatha. 2015. "Inspired by the Veiled Threat: Give Up a Right Day." *Globe and Mail*, 19 September.

Sowell, Thomas. 2004. *Affirmative Action around the World: An Empirical Study*. New Haven, CT: Yale University Press.

Spencer, Sarah. 2003. "Introduction." *The Political Quarterly* (Special Issue), 1–24.

Speri, Alice. 2014. "Half of America Thinks We Live in a Post-Racial Society, the Other Half, Not So Much." *Vice News*, 9 December.

Spoonley, Paul. 1993. *Racism and Ethnicity in New Zealand*. Auckland, NZ: Oxford University Press.

Spoonley, Paul. 2005. "Multicultural Challenges in a Bicultural New Zealand." *Canadian Diversity* 4(1):19–22

Spoonley, Paul. 2010. "Rethinking Immigration." Wellington: Asia New Zealand Foundation.

Spoonley, Paul, and Andrew Butcher. 2009. "Reporting Superdiversity: The Mass Media and Immigration in New Zealand." *Journal of Intercultural Studies* 30(4):355–372.

Spoonley, Paul, and Richard Bedford. 2012. *Welcome to Our World? Immigration and the Reshaping of New Zealand.* Palmerston North, NZ: Dunmore Press.

Squires, Judith. 2007a. "Negotiating Equality and Diversity in Britain: Towards a Differentiated Citizenship." *Critical Review of International Social and Political Philosophy* 10(4):531–559.

Squires, Judith. 2007b. *The New Politics of Gender Equality.* New York: Palgrave Macmillan.

Stadelmann-Elder Markus. 2011. "A Fast and Fair Refugee System: A Slogan or a Reality?" *Maytree Conversations.* 1 May.

Standing Senate Committee on Human Rights. 2010. *Reflecting the Changing Face of Canada. Employment Equity in the Federal Public Service.* Author.

Stanley, Timothy J. 2011. *Contesting White Supremacy: School Segregation, Anti-Racism and the Making of Chinese Canadians.* Vancouver: UBC Press.

Stanley, Timothy J. 2012. Analyzing Racisms in the Workplace. *Canadian Diversity* 9(1):53–57.

Stasiulis, Daiva K. 1990. "Theorizing Connections: Gender, Race, Ethnicity, and Class," in *Race and Ethnic Relations in Canada.* Peter S. Li, ed., 69–305. Toronto: Oxford University Press.

Stasiulis, Daiva K. 1999. "Feminist Intersectional Theorizing" in *Race and Ethnic Relations in Canada* (2nd ed.). Peter Li, ed., 347–397. Toronto: Oxford University Press.

Stasiulis, Daiva K., and Abigail B. Bakan. 1997. "Negotiating Citizenship: The Case of Foreign Domestic Workers in Canada." *Feminist Review*, 57:112–139.

Statistical Analysis Unit. 2010. *Impact of the Employment Equity Act and the CHRC Employment Equity Program over the Years.* March.

Statistics Canada. 2002. *Ethnic Diversity Study.* Retrieved November 16, 2015 (www23.statcan.gc.ca/imdb/p2SV.pl?Function=getSurvey&SDDS=4508).

Statistics Canada. 2003. "Low-Income Rates among Immigrants: 1980–2000." *The Daily*, 19 June. Retrieved November 16, 2015 (www.statcan.gc.ca/daily-quotidien/030619/dq030619a-eng.htm).

Statistics Canada. 2005a. "Women in Canada: A Gender-Based Statistical Report." Catalogue No. 89–503 XIE.

Statistics Canada. 2006a. "Immigration in Canada: A Portrait of the Foreign-born Population, 2006 Census: Findings." Retrieved November 16, 2015 (www12.statcan.ca/census-recensement/2006/as-sa/97-557/index-eng.cfm).

Statistics Canada. 2006b. "Measuring Violence against Women: Statistical Trends." Catalogue No. 85-570.

Statistics Canada. 2007. "Study: Low-Income Rates among Immigrants Entering Canada." *The Daily*, 30 January.

Statistics Canada. 2008. "Aboriginal Peoples in Canada in 2006: Inuit, Métis, and First Nations, 2006 Census." Retrieved November 16, 2015 (www12.statcan.ca/census-recensement/2006/as-sa/97-558/pdf/97-558-XIE2006001.pdf).

Statistics Canada. 2009. "Earning Differences Between Immigrants and The Canadian-born: The Role of Literacy Skills." Publication no 81-004, p.x. Ottawa, Government of Canada.

Statistics Canada. 2013. Study: Select Health Indicators of First Nations People Living Off Reserve, Metis, and Inuit. 2007–2010. In *Health At a Glance*, catalogue No 82–221–x. Statistics Canada. 29 January.

Statistics Canada. 2013. *National Household Survey: Aboriginal Peoples in Canada: First Nations People, Metis, and Inuit.* Author. 8 May.

Statistics Canada. 2015a. Police Reported Hate Crimes. The Daily. 9 June.

Statistics Canada. 2015b. Sense of Belonging to Canada, the Province of Residence, and the Local Community. Publications 89-652-x. Government of Canada, 29 June.

Status of Women Canada. 2007. *Gendering Canada's Refugee Process.* Retrieved online.

Steele, Shelby. 2006. *White Guilt.* New York: HarperCollins.

Stein, Janice Gross. 2007. "Religion versus the Charter." *University of Toronto Magazine* (Winter). Retrieved November 16, 2015 (http://magazine.utoronto.ca/winter-2007/religion-in-canada-charter-of-rights-and-freedoms-and-multiculturalism/).

Stein, Janice, David Robertson Cameron, John Ibbitson, Will Kymlicka, John Meisel, Haroon Siddiqui, and Michael Valpy. 2007. *Uneasy Partners, Multiculturalism and Rights in Canada*. Waterloo, ON: Wilfrid Laurier Press.

Steinberg, Stephan. 1989. *The Ethnic Myth: Race, Ethnicity, and Class in America* (2nd ed.). New York: Athenium.

Stepan, Nancy. 1982. *The Idea of Race in Science: Great Britain, 1800–1960*. London: Macmillan Press.

Sternberg, Robert J., and Elena Grigorenko. 1997. *Intelligence, Heredity, and Environment*. New York: Columbia University Press.

Steyn, Mark. 2006. "Keepin' It Real Is Real Stupid." *Maclean's*, 2 October: 58–59.

Stocking, George. 1968. *History of Anthropological Theory*. New York: Free Press.

Stoffman, Daniel. 1997. "Making Room for Real Refugees." *International Journal* (Autumn), 575–581.

Stoffman, Daniel. 2002. *Who Gets In: What's Wrong with Canada's Immigration Program—and How to Fix It*. Toronto: McClelland & Stewart.

Stoffman, Daniel. 2003. "The Mystery of Canada's High Immigration Levels." *Canadian Issues* (April), 23–24.

Stoffman, Daniel. 2008. "Truths and Myths about Immigration," in *Immigration Policy and the Terrorist Threat in Canada and the United States*. A. Moens and M. Collacott, eds., 3–21. Calgary: Fraser Institute.

Stoffman, Daniel. 2009. "Are We Safe Yet?" *The Walrus*. May.

Stokes, J., I. Peach, and R. Blake. 2004. *Rethinking the Jurisdictional Divide: The Marginalization of Urban Aboriginal Communities and Federal Policy Responses*. Public Policy Paper 28. Regina: Saskatchewan Institute of Public Policy.

Stote, Karen. 2015. *An Act of Genocide: Colonialism and the Sterilization of Aboriginal Women*. Halifax: Fernwood.

Strategic Council. 2008. "A Report to *The Globe and Mail* and CTV: Attitudes Towards Canada's Growing Visible Minority Population." Toronto: Strategic Council.

Strauss, Julian. 2006. "Is the Canadian Model for Relations with Aboriginals Beyond Repair?" *Globe and Mail*, 16 January.

Strmic-Pawl, H. V. 2015. More Than a Knapsack: The White Supremacy Flower as a New Model for Teaching Racism. *Sociology of Race and Ethnicity* 1(1):192–197.

Suarez-Orozco, Carola, and Marcelo M. Suarez-Orozco. 2001. *Children of Immigration*. Cambridge, MA: Harvard University Press.

Sue, Derald Wing. 2003. *Overcoming Racism: The Journey to Liberation*. San Francisco: John Wiley and Sons.

Sue, Derald Wing. 2010. *Microaggressions in Everyday Life: Race, Gender, and Sexual Orientation*. Hoboken NJ: Wiley.

Sue, Derald Wing. 2011. *Microaggressions and Marginality: Manifestations, Dynamics, and Impact*. Hoboken NJ: Wiley

Sue, Derald Wing, Capodilupo, Christina M., Torino, Gina C., Bucceri, Jennifer M., Holder, Aisha M. B., Nadal, Kevin L., and Marta Esquilin. 2007. "Racial Microaggressions in Everyday Life, Implications for Clinical Practice." Teachers College, Columbia University. American Psychologist, May-June.

Sun Media. 2007. "Racial Tolerance Report." Leger Marketing. January.

Surette, Ray. 2007. *Media Crimes and Criminal Justice: Images and Realities* (2nd ed.). Toronto: Wadsworth.

Suro, Roberto. 2008. *The Triumph of No: How the Media Influence the Immigration Debate*. A report by Governance Studies at the Brookings Institution and the Norman Lear Center at USC-Annenberg, 2008, Washington, DC.

Suro, Roberto. 2009. *Promoting Misconceptions. News Media Coverage of Immigration*. Los Angeles, CA: Centre for the Study of Immigrant Integration, University of Southern California.

Swain, Carole. 2002. *The New White Nationalism in America*. Cambridge: Cambridge University Press.

Swain, Carole, ed. 2007. *Debating Immigration*. New York: Cambridge University Press.

Swaine, J., O.Laughland, and J. Lartey. 2015. "Unarmed Black People Twice as Likely to be Killed by Cops as White People, Says Report." *The Guardian*, 1 June.

Swan, Michael. 2011. "Ethnic Vote Takes Harper to the Promised Land." *Catholic Register*, 3 May.

Sweetman, Arthur, and Casey Warman. 2010. "Canada's Temporary Foreign Worker's Program." *Canadian Issues.* (Spring): 19–24.

Switzer, Maurice. 1997. "The Canadian Media Have Declared Open Season on Indians." *Aboriginal Voices* (December): 8.

Sykes, Stuart. 2008. *A Story of Reefs and Oceans: A Framework for the Analysis of the "New" Second Generation in Canada.* Discussion Paper. Ottawa: Policy Research Initiative.

Taibbi, Matt. 2015. "Why Baltimore Blew Up." *Rolling Stone*1236:40–47. 4 June.

Tal, Benjamin. 2012. The Haves and the Have-Nots in Canada's Labour Market: In Focus. *CIBC Economics*, 3 December.

Tanovich, David M. 2006. *The Colour of Justice: Policing Race in Canada.* Toronto: Irwin Law.

Taras, Raymond C., and Rajat Ganguly. 2002. *Understanding Ethnic Conflict: The International Dimension* (3rd ed.). Montreal: Longman.

Taras, Raymond C., and Rajat Ganguly. 2009. *Understanding Ethnic Conflict: The International Dimension* (4th ed.). Montreal: Longman.

Taras, Raymond. 2012a. *Xenophobia and Islamophobia in Europe.* Edinburgh University Press.

Taras, Raymond, ed. 2012b. *Challenging Multiculturalism: European Models of Diversity.* Edinburgh University Press.

Tastsoglou, E., and V. Preston. 2006. "Gender, Immigration, and the Labour Market: Where We Are and What We Still Need to Know." *Ceris Policy Matters* 18.

Tastsoglou, E., B. Ray, and V. Preston. 2005. "Gender and Migration Intersections in a Canadian Context." *Canadian Issues* (Spring), 91–93.

Tator, Carol, and Francis Henry. 2006. *Racial Profiling in Canada: Challenging the Myth of a Few Bad Apples.* Toronto: University of Toronto Press.

Tatum, Dale C. 2010. *Genocide at the Dawn of the 21st Century.* New York: Palgrave Macmillan.

Taylor, Alison, and Jason Foster. 2014. "Migrant Workers and the Problem of Social Cohesion." *International Migration & Integration.* Published online, 15 March.

Taylor, Charles. 1993. "The Deep Challenge of Dualism," in *Quebec: State and Society* (2nd ed.). A.-G. Gagnon, ed., 82–95. Toronto: Nelson.

Taylor, Jillian. 2015. "Shamattawa Suicides Shake Northern Manitoba Reserve." *CBC News,* 26 March.

Taylor, Leanne, Carl James, and Roger Saul. 2007. "Who Belongs? Exploring Race and Racialization in Canada." In *Race, Racialization, and Anti-racism in Canada and Beyond.* G. F. Johnson and R. Enomoto, eds., 151–178. Toronto: University of Toronto Press, 1.

Taylor, Lesley Ciarula. 2009. "Best Immigrants Not a Priority." *Toronto Star,* 22 July.

Taylor, Peter Shawn. 2005. "Help Wanted." *Canadian Business* (March 14–27), 29–34.

Teelucksingh, Cheryl, ed. 2006. *Claiming Space: Racialization in Canadian Cities.* Waterloo, ON: Wilfrid Laurier Press.

Teelucksingh, Cheryl, and Grace-Edward Galabuzi. 2005. *Working Precariously: The Impact of Race and Immigrant Status on Employment Opportunities and Outcomes in Canada.* Toronto: Canadian Race Relations Foundation.

Teelucksingh, Cheryl, and Grace-Edward Galabuzi. 2010. "Social Cohesion, Social Exclusion, Social Capital." Region of Peel Immigration Discussion Paper. February. Region of Peel Human Services.

Temelini, Michael. 2007. "Multicultural Rights, Multicultural Virtues: A History of Multiculturalism in Canada," in *Multiculturalism and the Canadian Constitution.* S. Tierney, ed. Vancouver: UBC Press.

Tepper, Elliot L. 1988. *Changing Canada: The Institutional Response to Polyethnicity: The Review of Demography and Its Implications for Economic and Social Policy.* Ottawa: Carleton University.

Tepperman, Lorne. 2012. Habits of Inequality. A New Approach to Sociology's Oldest Problem. Presentation at the James E. Curtis Memorial Lecture, University of Waterloo, 27 February.

ter Wal, Jessika, Leen d' Haenans, and Joyce Koeman. 2005. "(Re)presentation of Ethnicity in EU and Dutch Domestic Views: A Quantitive Analysis." *Media, Culture, and Society,* 27(6):937–950.

The Dominion Institute, 2008. *Becoming Canadian: A Generational Journey.* An Ipsos-Reid Survey commissioned by The Author, March.

Therborn, Goran. 2013. *The Killing Fields of Inequality.* Thousand Oaks: Sage.

Thielen-Wilson, Leslie. 2014. Troubling the Path to Decolonization: Indian Residential School Case Law, Genocide, and Settler Illegitimacy. *Canadian Journal of Law and Society* 29(2):181–199.

Thobani, Sunera. 1995. "Multiculturalism: The Politics of Containment," in *Social Problems in Canada Reader*. E. Nelson and A. Fleras, eds., 213–216. Toronto: Prentice-Hall.

Thobani, Sunera. 2000a. "Closing Ranks: Racism and Sexism in Canada's Immigration Policy." *Race & Class* 42(1):35–55.

Thobani, Sunera. 2000b. "Closing the Nation's Doors to Immigrant Women: The Restructuring of Canadian Immigration Policy." *Atlantis* 24(2):16–29.

Thobani, Sunera. 2007. *Exalted Subjects: Studies in the Making of Race and Nation in Canada*. Toronto: University of Toronto Press.

Thobani, Sunera, Malinda Smith, and Sherene Razack. 2010. Preface: A Decade of Critical Race Studies. In *States of Race: Critical Race Feminisms for the 21st Century*. S. Thobani, S. Razack, and M. Smith, eds., ix–xxi. Toronto: Between the Lines.

Thomas, Derrick. 2001. "Evolving Family Arrangements of Canada's Immigrants." *Canadian Social Trends* (Summer), 16–19.

Thomas, Derrick. 2010. *Foreign Nationals Working Temporarily in Canada*. Ottawa: Statistics Canada.

Thomas, James M. 2007. "Re-Upping the Contract with Sociology: Charles Mill's Racial Contract Revisited a Decade Later." *Sociology Compass* 1(1):255–264.

Thomas, Robyn, Albert J. Mills, and Jean Helms Mills. 2004. *Identity Politics at Work: Resisting Gender, Gendering Resistance*. New York: Routledge.

Thompson, Allan. 2005. "Immigration in Dire Need of Overhaul." *Toronto Star*, 22 January.

Thompson, Allan. 2006. "Time to Take a Look at Selection Process Flaws." *Toronto Star*, 11 March.

Thompson, Allan, John Herd, and Morton Weinfeld. 1995. "Entry and Exit: Canadian Immigration Policy in Context." *Annals of the American Academy AAPSS* 538 (March), 185–198.

Thompson, Elizabeth. 2006. "Harper Wins the Vote—But Loses a Cabinet Minister." *Montreal Gazette*, 28 November.

Tierney, Stephen, ed. 2007. *Multiculturalism and the Canadian Constitution*. Vancouver: UBC Press.

Tinkler, Justine E. 2012. Controversies in Implicit Race Bias Research. *Sociology Compass* 6(12):987–997.

Tishkov, Valery. 2004. *Chechnya: Life in a War Torn Society*. Berkeley: University of California Press.

Tolley, Erin. 2015. Racial Mediation in the Coverage of Candidates' Political Viability: A Comparison of Approaches. *Journal of Ethnic and Migration Studies* 41(6):963–984.

Tomsons, Sandra, and Lorraine Mayer. 2013. General Introduction. In *Philosophy and Aboriginal Rights: Critical Dialogues*. S. Tomsons and L. Mayer, eds. Toronto: Oxford University Press.

Toronto Board of Trade. 2010. *Lifting All Boats. Promoting Social Cohesion and Economic Inclusion in the Toronto Region*. Toronto: Author.

Tran, Kelly, Stan Kustec, and Tina Chui. 2005. "Becoming Canadian: Intent, Process, and Outcome." *Canadian Social Trends* (Spring), 8–10.

Transatlantic Trends. 2010. *Immigration 2010: Key Findings*. Washington, DC: Author.

Treasury Board of Canada Secretariat. 2010. *Employment Equity in the Public Service of Canada, 2008–09*. Retrieved November 16, 2015 (www.tbs-sct.gc.ca/reports-rapports/ee/2009-2010/ee05-eng.asp).

Trepagnier, Barbara. 2007. *Silent Racism*. Boulder, CO: Paradigm.

Trovato, Frank, and Anatole Romaniuk. 2014. Introduction. In *Aboriginal Populations: Social, Demographic, and Epidemiological Perspectives*. F. Trovato and A. Romaniuk eds., xiii–xxix. Edmonton: University of Alberta Press.

Truth and Reconciliation Commission Report. 2015. *Honouring the Truth, Reconciling for the Future*. Summary of the Final Report. Ottawa.

Trudel, Marcel. 2014. *Canada's Forgotten Slaves: Two Hundred Years of Bondage*. Vehicular Press.

True, Jacqui. 2012. *The Political Economy of Violence Against Women*. Toronto: Oxford University Press.

Tully, James. 1995. *Strange Multiplicity: Constitutionalism in an Age of Diversity*. Cambridge: Cambridge University Press.

Tunis, D. 2010. "Fostering An Integrated Society." Talk Delivered to the University of Western Ontario, London, ON. 19 October.

Turner, Bryan S. 2006. "Citizenship and the Crisis of Multiculturalism: Review Article." *Citizenship Studies* 10(5):607–618.

Turner, Dale. 2006. *This Is Not a Peace Pipe*: University of Toronto Press.

Turpel-Lafond, Mary Ellen. 2014. "Put Native Women on the Agenda." *Globe and Mail*, 21 August.

Turton, Anthony R. 2007. *Governance as a Trialogue: Government-Society-Science in Transition*. New York: Springer.

Tushnet, Mark. 2003. *The New Constitutional Order*. Princeton, NJ: Princeton University Press.

Tyyska, Vappu. 2008. *Youth and Society. The Long and Winding Road* (2nd ed.). Toronto: Canadian Scholars' Press.

Ucarer, Emek M. 1997. "Introduction: The Coming of an Era of Human Uprootedness: A Global Challenge," in *Immigration into Western Societies: Problems and Policies*. E. M. Ucarer and D. J. Puchala, eds., 1–16. London: Cassells.

Uitermark, J., U. Rossi, and H. van Houtum. 2005. "Multiculturalism, Urbanization, and Citizenship: Negotiation of Ethnic Diversity in Amsterdam." *International Journal of Urban and Regional Research* 29(3):622–640.

Ujimoto, K. Victor. 2000. "Multiculturalism, Ethnic Identity, and Inequality," in *Social Issues and Contradictions in Canadian Society*. B. Singh Bolaria, ed., 228–247. Toronto: Harcourt Brace.

United Nations. 2007. *Concluding Observations of the Committee on the Elimination of Racial Discrimination: Canada*. CERD. Convention for the Elimination of all Forms of Racial Discrimination.

United Nations. 2010. *15 Years of the United Nations Special Rapporteur on Violence Against Women (1994–2009). A Critical Review*. Retrieved November 16, 2015 (www2.ohchr.org/english/issues/women/rapporteur/docs/15YearReviewofVAWMandate.pdf).

United Nations High Commission for Refugees. 2015. *2014 Global Trends*. Paris: Author.

United Nations Office on Drugs and Crime (UNODC). 2012. *Global Report on Trafficking in Persons*. Vienna.

UNWomen. 2015. "Progress of the World's Women 2015–2016: Transforming Economies, Realizing Rights." United Nations. 27 April.

US Department of State. 2014. *2014 Trafficking in Persons Report*. Washington, June.

Valaskakis, Gail, Madeleine Dion Stout, and Eric Guimond, eds. 2009. *Restoring the Balance: First Nations Women, Community and Culture*. University of Manitoba Press.

Valpy, Michael. 2007. "Diversity Heading Down a Rough Road, Conference Told." *Globe and Mail*, 13 August.

van den Berghe, Pierre. 1967. *Race and Racism*. New York: John Wiley & Sons.

van den Berghe, Pierre. 1981. *The Ethnic Phenomenon*. New York: Elsevier.

van Dijk Teun. 1991. *Racism and the Press*. New York: Routledge.

van Dijk, Teun. 1998. *Ideology: A Multidisciplinary Approach*. London, UK: Sage.

van Kerckhove, Carmen. 2009. *How to Respond to a Racist Joke*. Retrieved November 16, 2015 (https://allisonfarnum.wordpress.com/2009/05/12/how-to-respond-to-a-racist-joke-by-carmen-van-kerckhove/).

Vasta, Ellie, and Stephen Castles. 1996. *The Teeth Are Smiling: The Persistence of Racism in a Multicultural Australia*. Sydney: Allen & Unwin.

Velez, William, ed. 1998. *Race and Ethnicity in the United States: An Institutional Approach*. Dix Hills, NY: General Hall.

Venne, Sharon. 1998. "Analysis of Delgamuukw." *Distributed by Gatt Watchdog*. 20 February. Retrieved from http://sisis.nativeweb.org.

Vega, Tanzina. 2014. "Colorblind Notions Aside, Colleges Grapple with Racial Tensions." *New York Times*, 24 February.

Vega, Tanzina. 2014. "Students See Many Slights as Racial 'Microaggressions'". *New York Times*, March 21.

Verkuyten, Maykel. 2007. "Social Psychology and Multiculturalism." *Social and Personality Psychology Compass* 1(1):280–297.

Vertovec, Steven. 2006. "Diasporas Good? Diasporas Bad?" *Metropolis World Bulletin* 6:5–8.

Vertovec, Steven. 2012. "Diversity" and the Social Imaginary. *European Journal of Sociology* 53(3):287–312.

Vertovec. Steven, and Wessendorf, Susanne. 2004. *Migration and Cultural, Religious, and Linguistic Diversity in Europe: An Overview of Issues and Trends*. COMPAS. University of Oxford.

Vickers, Jill. 2002. *The Politics of "Race": Canada, Australia, the United States*. Ottawa: The Golden Dog Press.

Vickers, Jill, and Micheline de Seve. 2000. "Introduction." *Journal of Canadian Studies*. [Special edition devoted to nationalism and gender.]

Vincent, Donovan. 2015. "Niqab Issue Bolsters Tory Support." *Toronto Star*, October 1.

Volpe, Joe. 2005. "Canada Needs More Skilled Immigrants, Minister Says." See www.workpermit.com, 29 April.

Voyageur, Cora. 2011. First Nations Women in Canada. In *Visions of the Heart*. D. Long and O. P. Dickason, eds., 213–237. Toronto: Oxford University Press.

Vucetic, Srdjan. 2014. Against Race Taboos. In *Race and Racism in International Relations: Confronting the Global Colour Line*. A. Anievas, N. Manchanda, and R. Shilliam, eds. London: Routledge.

Vukow, Tamara. 2003. "Imagining Communities through Immigration Policies. Government Regulation, Media Spectacles, and the Affective Politics of National Borders." *International Journal of Cultural Studies* 6(3):335–353.

Wade, Nicholas. 2014. *A Troublesome Inheritance. Genes, Race, and Human History*. Penguin.

Waggamese, Richard. 2011. "The Real Shame of Attawapiskat." *Globe and Mail,* 2 December.

Waldie, Paul. 1998. "More Refugees Sheltered in Canada by New Rules." *Globe and Mail,* 14 November.

Waldron, Jeremy. 2002. *Indigeneity? First Peoples and Last Occupancy?* Paper presented to the Quentin-Baxter Memorial Lecture. Victoria University of Wellington NZ, 5 December.

Walia, Harsha. 2010. Race and Imperialism: Migration and Border Control in a Canadian State. In *Racism and Borders*, Jeff Shantz, ed., 73–94. New York: Algora Publishing.

Walia, Harsha. 2010. "Transient Servitude: Migrant Labour in Canada and the Apartheid of Citizenship." Race Class 52:71–84.

Walker, James W. St. G. 1997. *"Race," Rights and the Law in the Supreme Court of Canada*. Waterloo, ON: Wilfred Laurier Press.

Walker, James. W. St. G. 2001a. "'Race' and Resistance in Nova Scotia, 1945–1970," in *Canada: Confederation to the Present*. R. Hesketh et al., eds. Edmonton: Chinook Multimedia.

Walker, James W. St. G. 2001b. *Routes of Diversity: Strategies for Change, 1945–1970*. A background paper prepared for the Multiculturalism Program, Department of Canadian Heritage.

Walkom, Thomas. 1998. "The Big Power Shift." *Toronto Star*, 5 December.

Wallace-Wells, Benjamin. 2014. "The Summer of 2014 and the Return of the Politics of Racism." *New York Magazine*, 19 August.

Wallis, Maria, and Augie Fleras. 2008. *The Politics of Race in Canada*. Toronto: Oxford University Press.

Wallis, Maria, and Siu-Ming Kwok. 2008. *Daily Struggles: The Deepening Racialization and Feminization of Poverty in Canada*. Toronto: Canadian Scholars' Press.

Walters, David, Kelli Phythian, and Paul Anisef. 2006. *Understanding the Economic Integration of Immigrants: A Wage Decomposition of the Earnings Disparities between Native-born Canadians and Immigrants of Recent Cohorts*. CERIS Working Paper No. 42. Toronto: Joint Centre of Excellence for Research and Immigration and Settlement.

Walton-Roberts, Margaret W. 2011. "Immigration, the University, and the Welcoming Second Tier City." *Journal of International Migration & Integration* (19 April).

Warry, Wayne. 2007. *Ending Denial: Understanding Aboriginal Issues*. Peterborough, ON: Broadview.

Warry, Wayne. 2009. *Ending Denial: Understanding Aboriginal Issues*. Toronto: University of Toronto Press.

Wayland, Sarah V. 2006. *Unsettled: Legal and Policy Barriers for Newcomers to Canada: Literature Review*. Ottawa: Law Commission of Canada/Community Foundations of Canada, 77.

Weaver, Sally M. 1981. *Making Canadian Indian Policy: The Hidden Agenda, 1968–1970*. Toronto: University of Toronto Press.

Weaver, Sally M. 1984. "Struggles of the Nation-State to Define Aboriginal Ethnicity: Canada and Australia," in *Minorities & Mother Country Imagery*. G. Gold, ed., 182–210. Institute of Social and Economic Research No. 13. St. John's: Memorial University Press.

Weaver, Sally M. 1993a. "First Nations Women and Government Policy 1970–1992: Discrimination and Conflict," in *Changing Patterns: Women in Canada* (2nd ed.). Sandra Burt et al., eds. Toronto: McClelland & Stewart.

Weaver, Sally M. 1993b. "Self-Determination, National Pressure Groups, and Australian Aborigines: The National Aboriginal Conference 1983–1985," in *Ethnicity and Aboriginality: Case Studies in Ethnonationalism*. Michael D. Levin, ed., 3–74: University of Toronto Press.

Webb, Alex. 2014. Germany Top Migration Land after U. S. in new OECD Ranking. *Bloomberg Business*, 20 May.

Webb, Jim. 2010. "Diversity and the Myth of White Privilege." *Wall Street Journal*, 22 July.

Webber, Jeremy. 1994. *Reimaging Canada: Language, Culture, Community, and the*

Canadian Constitution. Montreal/Kingston: McGill-Queen's University Press.

Weber, T. 2005. "Ottawa Targets Immigration." *Globe and Mail*, 18 April.

Weinfeld, Morton. 2001. *Like Everyone Else but Different: The Paradoxical Success of Canadian Jews.* Toronto: McClelland & Stewart.

Weinfeld, Morton. 2005. "The Changing Dimensions of Contemporary Canadian Antisemitism," in *Contemporary Antisemitism: Canada and the World.* D. J. Penslar, ed. Toronto: University of Toronto Press.

Weinfeld, Morton, and Lori A. Wilkinson. 1999. "Immigration, Diversity, and Minority Communities," in *Race and Ethnic Relations in Canada* (2nd ed.). Peter Li, ed., 55–87. Toronto: Oxford University Press.

Weisberger, Bernard A. 1999. "Natives and Other Americans." *American Heritage* (May/June), 14–19.

Wellman, David. 1993. *Portraits of White Racism.* New York, NY: Cambridge MA: Cambridge University Press.

Welsh, C. 2006. "Finding Dawn." National Film Board of Canada. Retrieved September 25, 2015 (www.nfb.ca/film/finding_dawn).

Wente, Margaret. 2015. "Why the Niqab Matters, Now and In Future." *Globe and Mail*, 29 September.

Wesley, Dana, and Shauna Shiels. 2007. Everyday Racism Is No Less Violent. *The Journal.* Queen's University, Kingston, ON. 26 October.

Wesley-Esquimaux, C., 2009. "Trauma to Resilience: Notes on Decolonization," in *Restoring the Balance.* G. Valaskakis et al., eds., 13–34. Winnipeg: University of Manitoba Press.

Weston, Mary Ann. 2003. *Journalists and Indians: The Clash of Cultures.* Keynote speech on Symposium on American Indian Issues in the California Press, 21 February. Retrieved November 16, 2015 (www.bluecorncomics.com/weston.htm).

Wetherell, M., and J. Potter. 1993. *Mapping the Language of Racism: Discourse and the Legitimation of Exploitation.* New York: Columbia University Press.

Whitaker, Reginald A. 1991. *Double Standard: The Secret Story of Canadian Immigration.* Toronto: Lester and Orpen Dennys.

White, Ismail K. 2007. "When Race Matters and When It Doesn't: Racial Group Differences in Response to Racial Cues." *American Political Science Review* 101(2):339–350.

White, N. J. 1999. "Beyond 2000: Home to the World." *Toronto Star*, 23 April.

Whittington, Les. 1998. "Canada Hailed as a Model for the 21st Century." *Toronto Star*, 10 August, A7.

Whyte, John D. 2007. "Multiculturalism Meets 'Reasonable Accommodation.'" *SIPP Policy Dialogue* (Fall), 4–5.

Widdowson, Frances. 2003. *Separate but Unequal: The Political Economy of Aboriginal Dependency.* Paper presented to the Annual Conference of the Canadian Political Sciences Association (unpublished).

Widdowson, Frances, and Albert Howard. 2002. "The Aboriginal Industry's New Clothes." *Policy Options* (March), 30–35.

Widdowson, Frances, and Albert Howard. 2008. *Disrobing the Aboriginal Industry.* Montreal/Kingston: McGill-Queen's University Press.

Wilk, Piotr, and Martin Cooke. 2015. Collaborative Public Health System Interventions for Chronic Disease Prevention Among Urban Aboriginal Peoples. *The International Indigenous Policy Journal* 6(4).

Wilkins, Kerry, ed. 2004. *Advancing Aboriginal Claims: Visions, Strategies, Directions.* Saskatoon: Purich.

Wilkinson, Lori. 2005. On the Intersectionality of Transnationalism and Citizenship. *Canadian International Education* 34(1) Article 9.

Wilkinson, Richard G. 2005. *The Impact of Inequality—How to Make Sick Societies Healthier.* London: Routledge.

Wilkinson, Richard, and Kate Pickett. 2009. *The Spirit Level: Why Equality is Better for Everyone.* Equality Trust London.

Willett, Cynthia. 1998. *Theorizing Multiculturalism: A Guide to the Current Debate.* Malden, MA: Blackwell.

Williams, Rhys. 2015. Religion and Multiculturalism: A Web of Legal, Institutional, and Cultural Connections. *Sociological Quarterly* 56(4):607–622.

Willis, Katie, and Brenda Yeoh, eds. 2000. *Gender and Migration.* Northampton, MA: Edward Elgar Publishing.

Willow, Anna, J. 2012. *Strong Hearts, Native Lands: Anti-Clearcutting Activism at Grassy Narrows First Nation.* Winnipeg: University of Manitoba Press.

Wilson, Clint C., Felix Gutierrez, and Lena M. Chao. 2003. *Racism, Sexism, and the Media. The Rise of Class Communication in Multicultural America* (3rd ed.). Thousand Oaks, CA: Sage.

Wilson, Daniel, and David Macdonald. 2010. *The Income Gap between Aboriginal Peoples and the Rest of Canada.* Ottawa: Canadian Centre for Policy Alternatives.

Wilson, Gary N. 2008. "Nested Federalism in Arctic Quebec: A Comparative Perspective." *Canadian Journal of Political Science* 41(1):71–92.

Wilson, William Julius. 1996. A Look at the Truly Disadvantaged. Online Forum. Available online at http://www.pbs.org.

Wimmer, Andreas. 2015. Race-Centrism: A Critique and a Research Agenda. *Ethnic and Racial Studies* 38(13):2186–2205.

Winant, Howard. 1998. "Racism Today: Continuity and Change in the Post–Civil Rights Era." *Ethnic and Racial Studies* 21(4):89–97.

Winant, Howard. 2004. *The New Politics of Race: Globalism, Difference, Justice.* University of Minnesota Press.

Winlow, Simon, and Steve Hall. 2013. *Rethinking Social Exclusion: The End of the Social?* Thousand Oaks, CA: Sage.

Winsor, Hugh. 2001. "The Medicine Man at Indian Affairs." *Globe and Mail*, 27 August.

Winter, Elke. 2001. "National Unity versus Multiculturalism? Rethinking the Logic of Inclusion in Germany and Canada." *International Journal of Canadian Studies* 24:169–182.

Winter, Elke. 2007. "How Does the Nation Become Pluralist?" *Ethnicities* 7(4):483–518.

Winter, Elke. 2009. "The Dialectics of Multicultural Identity." *World Political Science Review* 5(1).

Winter, Elke. 2015. "Rethinking Multiculturalism After Its 'Retreat': Lessons from Canada." *American Behavioral Scientist* 59(6):637–657.

Wise, Amanda, and S. Velayutham, eds. 2009. *Everyday Multiculturalism.* London, UK: Palgrave.

Wise, Tim. 1999. "Exploring the Depths of Racist Socialization." *Z Magazine* (July/August), 17–18.

Wise, Tim. 2005. "Race to Our Credit: Denial, Privilege and Life as a Majority." Retrieved November 16, 2015(www.timwise.org/2005/01/race-to-our-credit-denial-privilege-and-life-as-a-majority/).

Wise, Tim. 2008. *Explaining White Privilege to the Deniers and Haters.* Available online.

Wise, Tim. 2009. "Racism and Implicit Bias in Cambridge." *Racism Review.* Retrieved November 16, 2015 (www.racismreview.com/blog/2009/07/27/racism-and-implicit-bias-in-cambridge/).

Wise, Tim. 2010. *Color-Blind. The Rise of Post-Racial Politics and the Retreat from Racial Equity.* San Francisco, CA: City Lights Publishing.

Witt, Shirley Hill. 1984. "Native Women Today: Sexism and the Indian Woman," in *Feminist Frameworks.* A. Jaggar and P. Rothenberg, eds., 23–31. Toronto: McGraw-Hill.

Wong, Lloyd. 2008. "Multiculturalism and Ethnic Pluralism in Sociology. An Analysis of the Fragmentation Position Discourse." *Canadian Ethnic Studies* (Spring).

Wong, Lloyd. 2015. "Multiculturalism and Ethnic Pluralism in Sociology: An Analysis of the Fragmentation Position Discourse." In *Revisiting Multiculturalism in Canada.* S. Guo and L. Wong, eds., 55–75. Rotterdam: Sense Publishers.

Wong, Lloyd, L., and Annette Tezli. 2013. Measuring Social, Cultural, and Civic Integration in Canada: The Creation of an Index and Some Applications. *Canadian Ethnic Studies* 45(3):9–37.

Wood, Patricia, and Liette Gilbert. 2005. "Multiculturalism in Canada: Accidental Discourse, Alternative Vision, Urban Practice." *International Journal of Urban and Regional Research* 29(3):679–691.

Woons, Marc. 2015. Reconciling Canada: Critical Perspectives on the Culture of Redress. *Settler Colonial Studies* 5(4):400–406.

World Health Organization (WHO). 2012. "Violence Against Women." Fact Sheet #239. November.

World Health Organization (WHO). 2013. *Global and Regional Estimates of Violence Against Women: Prevalence and Health Effects of Intimate Partner Violence and Non-Partner Sexual Violence.* WHO reference number: 978 92 4 156462 5.

Worswick, Christopher. 2010. "Temporary Foreign Workers: An Introduction." *Canadian Issues.* Spring: 3–5.

Wortley, Scot. 2005. *Bias-free Policing: The Kingston Data Collection Project: Preliminary Results.* Toronto: University of Toronto and the Centre for Excellence for Research on Immigration and Settlement.

Wortley, Scot, and Julian Tanner. 2003. "Data, Denials, and Confusion: the Racial Profiling Debate in Toronto." *Canadian Journal of Criminology and Criminal Justice* 45(3):367–389.

Wotherspoon, Terry, and John Hansen. 2013. The "Idle No More" Movement: Paradoxes of First Nations Inclusion in the Canadian Context. *Social Inclusion* 1(1):21–36.

Wrench, John. 2007. *Diversity Management and Discrimination: Immigrants and Ethnic Minorities in the EU*. Burlington, VT: Ashgate.

Wright, Bruce. 2015. "Police Shooting Video: 6 Times Unarmed Black Men Were Killed by Police Officers and What This Means for Social Justice." *International Business Times*, 9 April.

Wright, Pike. 2007. "Essay of Borat and Sarah Silverman for Make Benefit of Cultural Learnings About Racism." *This Magazine* (January/February), 42–43.

Wrzesnewskyj, Borys. 2005. "Hell Is Still Darfur." *Globe and Mail*, 31 October.

Wynne, Ashley, and Cheryl L. Currie. 2011. Social Exclusion as an Underlying Determinant of Sexually Transmitted Infections Among Canadian Aboriginals. *Pimatisiwin: A Journal of Aboriginal and Indigenous Community Health* 9(1):113–129.

Xu, Kathy. 2009. "Public Service Remains Short on Visible Minorities' Proportional Representation." *Epoch Times*, 16 September.

Yalnizyan, Armine. 2012. "Why We're Seeing the Ugly New Face of Capitalism." *Globe and Mail*, 14 February.

Yamato, Gloria. 2001. "Racism: Something about the Subject That Makes It Hard to Name," in *Race, Class, and Gender: An Anthology.* Margaret L. Andersen and Patricia Hill Collins, eds., 150–158. Scarborough, ON: Wadsworth/ Nelson.

Yelaja, Prithi, and Nicholas Keung. 2005. "Living Is Where It's Like Home." *Toronto Star*, June.

Yinger, J. Milton. 1994. *Ethnicity: Source of Strength? Source of Conflict?* Albany, NY: SUNY Press.

Young, Iris Marion. 1990. *Justice and the Politics of Difference.* Princeton: Princeton University Press.

Young, Iris Marion. 2005. "Self-Determination as Non-Domination." *Ethnicities* 5(2):139–159.

Yu, Henry. 2012. The Allegory that Blows 'Too Asian' Apart. In Gilmour, R. J., D. Bhandar, and J. Heer, eds. *"Too Asian?" Racism, Privilege, and Post-Secondary Education*. Toronto: Between the Lines.

Yu, Soojin, and Anthony Heath. 2007. "Inclusion for All but Aboriginals in Canada," in *Unequal Chances: Ethnic Minorities in Western Labour Markets*. A. Heath and S. Y. Cheung, eds., 181–220. New York: Oxford University Press.

Yuval-Davis, Nira. 2007. "Intersectionality, Citizenship and Contemporary Politics of Belonging." *Critical Review of International Social and Political Philosophy* 10(4):561–574.

Zachariah, Mathew, Allan Sheppard, and Leona Barrett, eds. 2004. *Canadian Multiculturalism: Dreams, Realities, and Expectations.* Edmonton: Canadian Multicultural Education Foundation.

Zaman, Habiba. 2006. *Breaking the Iron Wall: Decommodification and Immigrant Women's Labor in Canada*. Lanham, MD: Lexington Books.

Zaman, Habiba. 2007. "Neo-Liberal Policies and Immigrant Women in Canada." *Neo-Liberalism, State Power, and Global Governance* 3:145–153.

Zaman, Habiba. 2010. "Asian Immigrants' Vision of an Alternative Society in Australia and Canada: Impossibly Utopian or Simply Social Justice?" *Journal of Identity and Migration Studies* 4(1):2–23.

Zawilski, Valerie, ed. 2010. *Social Inequality in Canada: A Reader on the Intersections of Gender, Race, and Class.* Toronto: Oxford University Press.

Zhou, Min. 1997. "Segmented Assimilation: Issues, Controversies, and Recent Research on the New Second Generation." *International Migration Review* 31(4):975–1008.

Zick, A., T. F. Pettigrew, and U. Wagner. 2008. "Ethnic Prejudice and Discrimination in Europe." *Journal of Social Issues* 64(2):233–251.

Zine, Jasmin. 2002. "Inclusive Schooling in a Pluralistic Society." *Education Canada* 42(3).

Zinn, Maxine Baca, Pierette Hondagneu-Sotelo, and Michael A. Messner, eds. 2011. *Gender through the Prism of Difference*. New York: Oxford University Press.

Zong, Jie, and Jeanne Batalova. 2015. "Frequently Requested Statistics on Immigrants and Immigration in the United States." MPI (Migration Policy Institute). Migration Information Source. 26 February.

Index